AFRICA
BIBLIOGRAPHY

AFRICA BIBLIOGRAPHY 1993

works published on Africa in 1993

compiled by
Christopher H. Allen
University of Edinburgh

with assistance from Katherine Allen

in association with the
International African Institute
London

EDINBURGH UNIVERSITY PRESS

Edinburgh University Press Ltd
22 George Square, Edinburgh

Typeset in Lasercomp Plantin by ROM-Data, Falmouth, Cornwall, and printed in Great Britain by Page Bros, Norwich.

A CIP record for this book is available from the British Library.

ISSN 0266–6731
ISBN 0 7486 0532 0

CONTENTS

FOREWORD

Publishing and Library Support for Africa: an Update[1]

Carol Priestley

Assistance to book and library development in African countries can take many forms. It ranges over a scale from support to local publishing ventures through loans for textbook procurement to donation of specialist journals and books to libraries. Today, assistance for indigenous publishing is being given higher priority chiefly because of the recognition that an appropriate and sustainable supply of books within Africa can only be provided by a viable African publishing industry. This is particularly true where publishing in local languages is concerned, but it is becoming increasingly clear that the needs of African readers for books in English, French and other international languages can be most effectively met by African publishers. Procurement from external sources is neither sustainable nor affordable in the long-term even if this were a desirable method of supplying books and journals to these markets. However, there is also a recognition that specialist and university libraries must remain part of the international world of scholarship and that assistance via purchase, exchange or donation of material remains important.

Publishing

Over the years the pattern of support to the supply of books has swung from large capital investments which are used to provide African countries with the textbooks they require to initiatives to help publishers in African countries to produce materials locally.

It is difficult to support publishing in African countries without running into the problems of the high costs of production and the lack of purchasing power of either governments or individuals. Though labour may be cheaper in developing countries, most equipment and materials for production have to be imported. Twenty to thirty years ago, with expansion then taking place in most educational systems in Africa, new textbooks were needed in large numbers. Textbooks dominated publishing and were a lucrative business (Per Gedin, 1991) attractive to private enterprise; indeed in anglophone countries in Africa textbooks accounted for 80–95 per cent of the total book market. Multinational publishing houses realised the potential of the market and many set up offices in African countries specifically to supply the textbook needs of each country, so squeezing out many indigenous publishers. With the recession, and profits on this scale no longer obtainable, the multinationals have closed or indigenised their local offices. For a few more years textbooks no longer needed in the North, particularly where changes of curriculum and GCSE examinations had rendered some of them out-of-date, were sold or even occasionally given free to various African countries, though their relevance to the recipients' school curricula was always doubtful. This has added to the pressure to create a viable publishing industry within these countries, and several agencies have been keen to support this development.

Early initiatives to support local publishing were often sporadic and uncoordinated: some focused on donation of paper or equipment (the latter sometimes without adequate provision for spare parts or maintenance), others on training potential writers or publishing staff in editing, marketing, etc. through workshops and seminars held in various African locations. From the 60s to the late 80s there were few examples of collaboration among donors. Some donors supported curriculum design, others production, others distribution. Some supported different aspects of publishing in different countries with no apparent logic behind the components of their programmes. Since then, the World Bank and bilateral donors, including the UK's Overseas Development Administration (ODA), have been seeking a comprehensive approach which would lead to the establishment of a well-functioning book provision system. A recent study of book and publishing assistance programmes (Priestley, 1992) approached 133 organisations – government, private, commercial – and identified fifty-nine, ranging from small charities to the World Bank and UNESCO, which are active in Africa. The conclusion from the information provided is that:

> however much individual merit one-off projects may claim, their impact is short-lived and very local; and the need for a policy and planning framework is not yet well understood. This has been recognised by some donors and recipients in the past 5–7 years, but systematic definition and monitoring of the components of the publishing process in each African country have still to be explored.

To publish locally and successfully in Africa, three areas might be highlighted, all interdependent:

- capital
- publishing skills
    - for editors
    - for production personnel
    - for marketing and distribution
    - for rights, co-publication and translation personnel
    - for senior managers
- equipment and technical support

Examples of initiatives aimed at alleviating the problems in these areas can be found:

1 capital

Publishing is perceived to be a high-risk, low profit business and many would-be developing country publishers find it difficult if not impossible to raise the necessary capital to launch their business. Finance is of course particularly acute for the small publishers whose capital is locked up in projects and for whom a book may take up to two years from the time of commissioning to the finalised copy, and then takes an even longer time to sell.

The lack of capital outlay generally discourages the growth and development of the publishing industry, restricts the number of titles that can be published in any period and renders small scale publishing a very expensive business.

The devaluation of currencies has badly affected an already ailing industry which relies heavily on import of paper, ink, and printing machines. The problems are compounded by high import duties and taxes.

An alternative concept has been developed by the Dag Hammarskjold Foundation, Uppsala. The basic element of the programme is to provide guarantee of repayment to banks and lending agencies so that African publishers can borrow the funds they need. The Foundation offers professional advice if needed but instead of funding specific requirements they guarantee loans which are taken in commercial banks in a normal way. Kenya was chosen as a pilot country as it had a fairly well developed book market, though dominated by multinational publishers.

To guarantee the loans, a certain capital was needed to cover losses and bank expenses. A sum of US$300,000 was deemed to be sufficient and the Dag Hammarskjold Foundation was successful in obtaining these funds from the Ford Foundation. The Hammarskjold Foundation wanted to create a normal situation between the bank and the publisher and wanted to emphasise that there was no donor dependency. They also wanted to show that the publisher was as reliable as any other business and that with adequate finance publishing could be a profitable industry.

2 publishing skills

Many of the failings of African publishing can be traced to a lack of appreciation of the importance of publishing skills. A 1985 report on textbooks prepared for the World Bank by Barbara Searle highlighted shortcomings – slow production schedules, inadequate paper procurement, teacher training out of phase with book publication, no coordination between curriculum and manuscript development and, above all, a failure to establish institutions that could continue to provide good quality books after project completion. The Bank has now realised that book publishing development cannot take place in isolation. The unknown factor in all aspects of training is of course the probable increase in the use of desk top publishing which will undoubtedly alter the future training needs of all the participants within the publishing field.

a) for editors

Examples of assistance to editorial teams are few and far between. But within the Faculty of Information Sciences at Moi University in Kenya a series of courses have been run with ODA support, aimed at covering all aspects of publishing, and including senior editorial managers. With the advent of desk top publishing, which will surely follow the pattern in the North where its use is more and more prevalent, the role of editors will change and become more powerful.

b) for production personnel

Again very few examples of training assistance for production personnel are to be found. Some of the help has come from UNESCO, the DSE and the IDRC. The DSE has supplied funds for two- or three-week workshops since 1980, using both expatriate and national teachers. These have been evaluated very highly, as have short courses supported by the UK's ODA.

c) for marketing and distribution

Often the weakest links in the chain in African publishing, most small indigenous publishers cannot afford publicity for their books and, until recently, joint lists or catalogues were an anathema. Even today, many publishers do not take advantage of existing opportunities for free international promotion of their books through such publications as *African Book Publishing Record* and the cumulative *African Books in Print* (both published by Hans Zell Publishers, Oxford). The book trade is undeveloped, as are attitudes to books and reading. One successful initiative is the Zimbabwe Book Marketing Scheme (ZBMS) which has three aims:

to encourage not only the book reading habit but also the habit of buying and owning books

to support indigenous publishers

to accelerate the emergence of a regional book market in southern Africa and develop pan-African book trading.

To date, ZBMS has attracted support from the Swedish International Development Authority (SIDA), the Zimbabwe Trust and CODE (the Canadian Organization for Development through Education). The scheme is now 63% self-sufficient. ZBMS is now exporting books from Zimbabwe to twenty countries, with substantial benefits to Zimbabwean publishers.

The main initiative for international distribution of African books has been the African Books Collective (ABC)[2] (see Jay, 1993), started in Oxford, UK under the aegis of Hans Zell, as a cooperative by eleven African publishers in 1985. ABC now serves forty-two African publishers, holds over 1200 titles in stock and sells throughout Europe and North America. For many of the publishers ABC has offered the first opportunity for them to have access to markets outside Africa and therefore to earn foreign exchange. Funding for the initial years of ABC's trading has been provided by Ford and Rockefeller Foundations, the Norwegian Agency for Development Cooperation (NORAD), SIDA, UNESCO and the Swedish Agency for Research Co-operation with Developing Countries (SAREC). Although ABC has made dramatic progress (from sales of £84,000 in 1991 to an estimated total income of £184,000 in 1994), it could not have taken off without financial support from donors.

d) for rights, co-publication, etc

Publishing skills are not acquired overnight and the consistent lack of a secure financial base has often destroyed whatever skill was available or prevented its development. The role of licensing or sub-licensing, i.e. acquiring rights to reproduce titles published elsewhere under a royalty agreement, offers a short to medium term solution. Indigenous publishers often need help to seize a potential opportunity to co-publish a book important to their own area, but which they have not managed to secure for the international market as the originating publisher. Such arrangements often depend, however, on mutual collaboration with the publishers from the North as few indigenous publishers have access to hard currency to enable them to pay the originating publisher. However, recent initiatives such as the APNET (African Publishers Network) workshop on African rights (see below) are working towards a better understanding of the possibilities.

e) for senior managers

Publishing is by its very nature an entrepreneurial activity and it has to be recognised that the context within which publishers work varies between and within countries and regions. The investment required for publishing is quite substantial and capital outlay is only recouped over a long period. Financial management and business planning are skill areas which have received less attention than they deserve.

3 equipment and technical support

a) desk top publishing (DTP)

If there is to be development of desk top publishing (DTP), following the pattern of the increasing use of computer-based book production in the North with the consequence of greater use of camera ready copy (CRC), then there will be new and different requirements for training and equipment for the new technology. Many of the techniques and equipment donated and passed on to African countries in the 1980s and earlier will become redundant. The potential for DTP in some sectors is significant, not least the possibility of transmitting text by E-mail and thus generating CRC from text produced elsewhere.

b) paper

Shortage of paper is one of the most frequent problems encountered in publishing in Africa. Canada and Sweden have been the principal sources of paper support programmes – the former through CODE and the latter through SIDA. CODE estimates that about 450 tonnes of paper, costing in excess of US$2m have been shipped to Africa since 1988. Finland and the former Soviet Union have also made paper available for specific publishing support projects.

Experience with the donation of paper has highlighted two pitfalls. The first is the difficulty of monitoring and controlling the allocation. Widespread misappropriation is not unknown. The second is that donation of paper to one publisher places others at a disadvantage. Subsidised publishers become dependent on free paper and when the donation comes to an end, so does the publishing programme.

To counteract the second of these problems, publishers are increasingly being asked to treat paper as a form of capital, tied to performance objectives. It has also been suggested that there should be a sliding scale of payment, according to the degree of need. In a struggling industry such as that of Burkina Faso, a local publisher might be asked to pay 10% of the value of the paper, while a Kenyan publisher might be asked to pay 75%. These funds would be used for purchasing the books consequent on the subsidy and distributing them to local libraries. CODE's practice is to recommend distribution of these books in rural areas, so that the publishers' commercial market in the cities is not undermined.

As stated earlier some donors have provided printing and binding equipment, or even the machinery for manufacturing paper. But without sufficient technical support and help with obtaining spare parts, problems can rapidly develop.

Each of the donor agencies involved in supporting local publishing has its own agenda. Although much has been written about donor coordination and cooperation, it is not easy to implement. Over the past few years, meetings among donors, notably the Bellagio Group (see below), have led to some joint funding and the sharing of information. Sometimes donors have met at the invitation of the potential recipient, but most donor/recipient dialogue takes place on a bilateral basis.

The long-term goal is self-sustainable indigenous publishing. A book market with a functioning infrastructure from writer to publisher to distributor to reader will not be created by a flood of donated material or by multinational publishers. Practitioners (writers, publishers, booksellers and librarians) must work together with development agencies and donors. There is no single solution, but rather many component solutions within a coordinated strategy. This makes it difficult to construct a list of priorities for donors, most of whom, within their terms of reference, have to opt for a particular facet of support. When there is an adequate market, publishing and publishing skills develop naturally. If money is made available for book purchase, books will flow. One of the central roles for donor agencies should therefore be to assist books to flow from indigenous publishers.

On this criterion, the Africa Books Collective (ABC) and the Zimbabwe Book

Marketing Scheme are two initiatives which can claim to maximise the effectiveness of donor support. Both of them could benefit from more regional funding.

One of the urgent needs is for bookbuyers in Africa to know what is available from other African countries. Many orders for African-produced books from other African countries pass through ABC in Oxford. Although a very large proportion of African publishers fail to use the available promotional services, still fewer librarians receive whatever book lists and publishers' catalogues are available. The importance of intra-African trade cannot be underestimated. The International African Institute (IAI) has received funding to establish an African Journals Distribution Programme (AJDP)[3] A pilot phase is providing current subscriptions to eighteen academic journals from eleven African countries to twenty university libraries in ten countries. The **Intra-African Book Support Scheme (IABSS)**[4], launched in 1991 was set up to ensure that books from the 42 publishers within the African Books Collective could reach the shelves of twelve major academic libraries in Africa.

Information sharing on the book and publishing industry

Many of the programmes presently available in support of indigenous publishing and library development are not achieving full potential. From the recipient's perspective it has not been easy to find out how professional partnerships and information exchange can be initiated, from the donor's point of view it has been difficult to keep informed of new initiatives. There is, however, a considerable amount of information available about library and book development on a local, regional and country/national basis, and there is even more information on bilateral, multilateral and NGO support and the potential for increasing such information sharing through the use of E-mail and other forms of networking is limitless. Recently, four networks have emerged to facilitate better sharing of information.

Firstly, the **African Publishers Network (APNET)**[5] is a pan-African network of publishers and national publishers' associations which works to support and promote indigenous publishing throughout Africa. Established in February 1992, APNET's founder members resolved that publishing in Africa would develop substantially through intra-African cooperation. Its objectives are based on the need to work across national and linguistic boundaries; the coordination and maximum utilisation of existing African training resources; and intra-African trade and collaboration between publishers and international agencies. APNET has evolved through a series of practical tasks – the first being a survey of publishing training in Africa which both gave a broad survey of existing possibilities and laid the foundation for future investment. There are now two APNET training coordinators in place: one for East Africa based in Nairobi and one for West Africa based in Togo. APNET is organising or supporting national and regional workshops to strengthen and update publishing skills throughout the continent. Further it has a bi-monthly journal the *African Publishing Review* which is distributed to over 1200 African publishers and interested organisations. This has become an invaluable medium for news, debate and information sharing. Trade in books, printing and licensing agreements are promoted through a multi-faceted programme, including publication annually of *African Rights*. In August 1994, APNET jointly organised a workshop with the Zimbabwe International Book Fair as a trade promotion and training exercise in rights. APNET also undertakes research and policy studies in key areas of publishing and book development.

Secondly, the **Bellagio Publishing Network**[6] is an informal association of organisations dedicated to the strengthening of African publishing. The group includes donor organisations and NGOs concerned with publishing and book development, and has provided a useful forum for discussion. The network maintains a Secretariat in Oxford which holds responsibility for organising meetings of the group and maintaining communications between donors and potential participants and a Research and Information Centre in Boston, which holds responsibility for the quarterly publication of the network newsletter, development of a research agenda focusing on problems of publishing in the Third World and commissioning and publishing research reports on specific issues.

Thirdly the **Donors to African Education (DAE)**[7], a consortium of multilateral, bilateral and non-governmental donors and African ministries of education and development bodies, has specific working groups on textbooks and libraries and on higher education. Although the early work of the 'Books' Working Group focused on the preparation and discussion of book sector studies, the group is now working closely with APNET to involve and support African educational publishers to enable them to take a central role in book provision.

The International Network for the Availability of Scientific Publications (INASP)[8], is a cooperative network of interested organisations and libraries from the North and the South. It has three immediate objectives, namely to support and strengthen existing programmes involved in the publication, distribution, exchange and donation of books, journals and related materials; to encourage new initiatives that will increase the availability of quality scientific literature; and to identify methods that will permit the ongoing and sustainable publication, exchange and distribution of scientific publications. The Network has created several computerised databases, including one which provides current information on existing programmes of support and activity in the provision of scientific material and another which provides inventories and profiles of institutions and libraries in the South. The Network also offers a clearinghouse and advisory service and assists in the development and establishment of new programmes or activities in the field. It can match donors to appropriate counterparts in developing countries and vice versa. Inter-regional projects to address the issues are being supported, for instance a health information network is being planned: in Africa this will bring together members of the Association for Health Information and Libraries in Africa (AHILA) with the funding and health information supporting organisations.

Library Support

In the international world of scholarship and research, it is essential that academics in institutions in Africa are enabled to write and continue with their research with the books and journals they need available in their own institution libraries. Here the role of donors and donor agencies is somewhat different, though it may overlap in some instances with support for indigenous publishing as in the case of the **African Journals Distribution Programme (AJDP)** mentioned above.

The task of building strong academic centres and postgraduate and research programmes in particular cannot be accomplished without strengthening information services and the provision of teaching and learning materials. The ability of many university libraries to support teaching and research in their institutions is now highly questionable. In general, universities have not been able to allocate financial resources for the procurement of new books, to continue journal subscriptions, to modernise information management procedures through the utilisation of new technologies or to provide more reading space for increasing student numbers.

Libraries, however, are one of the university facilities that are most resource-dependent and the deteriorating state of book and journal collections is a very evident result of dwindling university funds. What has kept African university libraries alive (if only barely) over the past five years is donor support. Donor programmes have stepped in to fill the gap in government funds. Without this, most might have collapsed completely. Support has been given in three main areas: materials (books and journals) purchase and donation; training, both long and short term; and acquisition of information technology (IT). A number of donors, international and bilateral, are involved; some concentrating on particular libraries or countries, others assisting throughout Africa. Support to university libraries appears to be popular with donors, perhaps because it can be easily specified, delivered and accounted for, for example the donation of a number of journal subscriptions.

It is now not unusual to find that, apart from the staff salaries, all inputs to a university library are provided by donors. However, coordination or even information sharing between donors is rare; for example, three or more donors may provide subscriptions to Western-published journals to the same university. Depending on which country is 'fashionable', aid may pour into one library, while another in a neighbouring country gets nothing.

All donor agencies now place much emphasis on aid leading to future sustainability. The relatively large amounts of support recently given to university libraries are aimed as a stop-gap measure to prevent further decline in collections and services during the period when university finances are put in order and plans for institutional effectiveness and efficiency are implemented. However, from the information available, the aid given to university libraries does not seem to be resulting in self-supporting libraries. There are many examples of the total cancellation of journal subscriptions once the outside funding ceases, of knowledge gained during training never being implemented, of IT systems proving too expensive to use and maintain, of plans for resource sharing being aborted before birth. And, of course, there is also a problem of security when resources are so scarce.

The recent profile of research libraries in sub-Saharan Africa undertaken by the American Association for the Advancement of Science (AAAS) (see Levey, 1993) gives details of thirty-one (mainly university) libraries. Of these, eight do not subscribe to any foreign periodicals with their own funds, and only twelve subscribe to over 100 journals. The University of Zimbabwe is shown to be the best endowed library and, although in receipt of donor assistance, most journal subscriptions (1578 out of 2699) are paid for with university funds. This is doubtless because the deans of relevant faculties have placed library needs first in allocating the university's foreign currency allowance. At the other end of the scale, the University of Nigeria, Nsukka, lacks both an acquisitions budget and donor support.

Some libraries have access to local currency which they can use to purchase UNESCO coupons, and in turn they can be used for the purchase of books, journals and other educational materials. The British Council and the World Health Organisation (WHO) also have programmes which utilise local currency payments. However, countries where such schemes operate are limited at present.

Of the book and journal donation programmes, those of SAREC and the AAAS are probably the most significant. The AAAS supplies up to 191 journal titles to 250 university and research libraries in 38 countries and is also now supplementing print journals with a small number of bibliographical and full text databases on compact disc. SAREC has substantial library support programmes in Eritrea, Ethiopia, Tanzania, Mozambique and Zimbabwe and for several years their programme has had three main components: supply of current journal subscriptions, library training and purchase of equipment. Each country is given an annual notional allocation, ranging from $150,000 to $450,000, and within this the libraries involved meet together to decide on their own priorities. The funds can be held within the country concerned, and local management and procurement is encouraged. Over the past 6 months discussions have been held with each participating partner, and possibilities for inter-library networking, alternative forms of document provision with the use of new technologies and electronic communication are being explored. Complementary to the provision of international scientific literature, SAREC have for some years also funded a small number of projects in support of indigenous publishing of scholarly journals.

The **International Campus Book Link (ICBL)**[9] is a modest targeted programme aiming to provide a coordinated scheme of book and periodical donations from British universities, colleges and individuals to university libraries and departments in Africa. It is hoped that the system of linking universities in the UK to counterparts in Africa will provide not only materials but also a communications link between faculties and academics which in turn can be the start of sustainable longer-term cooperation.

The application of new information technologies offers many opportunities and challenges to African university libraries. Twenty-one libraries are known to have CD-ROM capability and despite problems in installing and maintaining their systems there are some interesting success stories. The Medical Library at the University of Zimbabwe actively promotes its CD-ROM services to health and medical workers throughout the country. This has resulted in a dramatic growth in demand for CD-ROM literature searches – some 400 searches, for example, being undertaken in March 1993 alone. The Cheikh Anta Diop University, Dakar, Senegal, is a regional resource centre for seven francophone libraries and conducts literature searches for researchers in Côte d'Ivoire, Togo and Mali. The INFO-MED project at the Medical Library of the University of Zambia illustrates innovative use of new technologies. INFO-MED combines CD-ROM with electronic networking for lecturers, researchers and students in Lusaka as well as for practitioners and researchers throughout Zambia. Requests from outside Lusaka utilise the terrestrial telephone-based FIDONET E-mail network. Requests for full text literature are sent to the University of Florida Medical Library which has been twinned by SatelLife via a low earth orbit satellite. The University of Florida sends the documents on a monthly basis by mail.

Thus although for many African university libraries the current situation with regard to provision of information services remains bleak, it has been shown that where policy and decision makers have placed library services near the top of their list of priorities significant advances have been made. CD-ROM technology has provided improved access to information and current awareness. This in itself has increased the demand for information. Electronic networking and the use of electronic communications to access information held in the 'North' also hold immense potential.

Conclusion

Publishing has rarely received the attention it deserves, nor has there been a sufficient understanding that publishing is not just about production but also about consumption. Within the industry much may be possible, but unless the market develops, little will be achieved. Local publishers may encourage local authorship, original texts and much original thought, but the importance of a full understanding of market needs is important to ensure that resulting publications are viable. In many African countries an autonomous publishing industry has been thwarted from emergence. Too often and regrettably, book aid schemes have exacerbated the situation by flooding the market with free or very cheap books. The greatest challenge for the future will be to harness available donor funding and support in a way that will at the same time encourage new national and regional initiatives at a realistic and practical level. Resource sharing, sustainable collection development and new technology applications are high on the agenda of libraries and publishers throughout the world. The strengthening of publishing and libraries in Africa is essential for future development.

International African Institute
London

References

Gedin, Per. 1991. 'British publishers' contribution to African literature', *Logos, the professional journal of the book world*, 2(3).

—1992. 'Cultural pride: the necessity of indigenous publishing', in Philip Altbach (ed.), *Publishing and Development in the Third World.* Oxford: Hans Zell, pp. 43–53.

Jay, Mary. 1993. 'The African Books Collective' Foreword in CH Allen (ed.) *Africa Bibliography 1992*, Edinburgh: Edinburgh University Press for the International African Institute, pp.vi–xviii

Levey, Lisbeth A. 1993. *A Profile of Research Libraries in Sub-Saharan Africa: acquisition, outreach and infrastructure.* Washington DC: American Association for the Advancement of Science.

Priestley, Carol. 1992. *Book and Publishing Assistance Programs: a review and inventory.* Boston, MA: Bellagio Network Research and Information Center.

—1993a. 'Learning Resources in Higher Education in Developing Countries: the present position of libraries and book development', paper presented to the EADI information and Documentation Working Group meeting in Berlin.

—1993b. 'The difficult art of book aid: an African survey', *Logos, the professional journal of the book world* 4(4): 215–21.

—1994. 'Availability of publications in Africa: exchange of experience and future prospects', *FID Bulletin*, June 1994.

Notes

1. Much of this foreword updates and reconsiders material published earlier, see Priestley 1992, 1993a, 1993b and 1994
2. ABC, African Books Collective, The Jam Factory, 27 Park End Street, Oxford OX1 1HU.
3. AJDP, International African Institute, SOAS, Thornhaugh Street, Russell Square, London WC1H 0XG.
4. IABSS, African Books Collective, The Jam Factory, 27 Park End Street, Oxford OX1 1HU.
5. APNET, 78 Kaguvi Street, Harare, Zimbabwe.
6. Bellagio Publishing Network, Oxford Secretariat, 27 Park End Street, Oxford OX1 1HU. Research and Information Center, c/o School of Education, Campion Hall, 226 Boston College, Chestnut Hill, MA 02167.
7. DAE Working Group on Textbooks and Libraries, c/o Carol Priestley,

International African Institute, SOAS, Thornhaugh Street, Russell Square, London WC1H 0XG.
DAE Working Group on Higher Education, c/o William Saint, The World Bank, 1818 H Street NW, Washington, DC 20433.

8. INASP, PO Box 2564, London W5 1ZD.
9. ICBL is managed by Book Aid International, 39-41 Coldharbour Lane, Camberwell, London SE5 9NR.

INTRODUCTION

Scope and coverage

This bibliography records publications on Africa of interest to students of Africa, principally in the social and environmental sciences, humanities and arts. Some items from the medical, biological and natural sciences are included, and some more technical material from the major categories is excluded; in each case the criterion used is potential relevance to a reader from a social science/arts background. Thus material on AIDS (incidence, impact, and control) is included, but not that on a number of other diseases; and material on meteorology is normally excluded, but not that on climatic history or rainfall. The whole continent and associated islands are covered, but not the African diaspora. The 1993 edition aims to include material published in 1993, together with items from 1992, 1991 and 1990 not previously listed. The editor is always very glad to hear of any items omitted so that they may be included in subsequent editions. African government publications, and works of creative literature are not listed.

The principal sources of data for this issue are the book acquisitions and periodicals of Edinburgh University Library and the National Library of Scotland; use has also been made of other university libraries, notably that of the School of Oriental and African Studies and Northwestern University, and of material received by the International African Institute. Wherever possible, the periodicals listed in the next section have been scanned for the whole of the relevant period; only those issues yielding entries are however listed, and other periodicals will have been scanned without being listed (a list of journals not carrying Africanist material would, after all, be rather long).

Arrangement

The arrangement of the bibliography is by region and country, with a preliminary section for the continent as a whole. Within each section items are arranged by subject, in the order listed below; where an item might appear under more than one heading, this is indicated by cross-reference (see the 'see also' list immediately under each subject heading), or the subject index will guide users to it.

The subject fields are the same as last year, and explanations of changes made in that year can be found in the introduction to the 1992 volume. As no classification system is perfect, and as it will not be intuitively obvious where certain subcategories of material are placed, I list below some of the main subcategories included in the fields unchanged since 1991:

- *Demography* includes material on fertility and mortality;
- *Economic and Social History* includes demographic history but not religious or mission history;
- *Environmental* includes conservation, but not accounts of the environment (see Natural Resources);
- *Food* includes famine (and aspects

of drought), food (in)security, (mal)nutrition, and domestic food production, but not food preparation (see Sociology, and Anthropology);
• *Geography, human* is something of a residual category; where material by geographers is no less appropriately placed under another discipline, that is normally what is done;
• *Health and Welfare Services* focuses largely on health services and personal social services (see also Social Welfare);
• *Industry and Trade* includes materials on the informal sector, transport, and petty trade, except where these are better placed under Rural Economy;
• *Labour and Manpower* includes management;
• *Law* includes constitutional matters, the legal system and the judiciary, but not criminology (see Sociology);
• *Library-Documentation* includes information sciences, and some aspects of the use of information technology;
• *Natural Resources* includes energy (but not energy industries);
• *Social Welfare* includes community development;
• *Urban Studies* includes housing.

Entry types

The bibliography contains three types of entry: periodical articles, books and pamphlets, and chapters. Periodical entries give the conventional bibliographic information. Book entries give author, title, place, publisher, and pagination (but not ISBN numbers, or price). Entries for chapters in books largely not on African topics give full bibliographic information for the volume concerned. Where, however, a book contains many relevant chapters it is listed separately, and the chapter entry includes only a short version of the title, the name(s) of the editor(s), and the entry number of the book itself.

Indexes

The bibliography has author and subject indexes, which use the entry number to identify the relevant items. Since multiple authors are listed separately only when there are two of them (otherwise the first author is listed, followed by 'et al'), not every author of a given piece will appear in the author index.

The detailed subject index should be seen as supplementing the arrangement by subject fields. Where an item is sufficiently described by the subject heading, it will not appear in the subject index. The index is basically of the key-word type, and will often reflect the vocabulary of the original entry, modified to group together similar items. Most items have a country designation, for ease of use, except for entries of general interest. Since indexing will always reflect to some degree the idiosyncracies of the indexer, readers are urged to scan broadly, and particularly to check headings in the vicinity of that deemed most relevant.

Subject headings

Agriculture, scientific
Anthropology
Architecture
Arts
Current Affairs
Demography
Economic and Social History
Economy – Development
Education
Environment
Finance
Food
Gender
Geography, human
Geography, physical
Health and Welfare Services
History, general
History, early
History, C6–18th

History, C19th
History, C20th
Industry and Trade
International Economic Relations
International Relations
Labour and Manpower
Language
Law
Library – Documentation
Literature
Media
Medical
Natural Resources
Planning
Politics
Religion, Philosophy
Rural Economy
Science and Technology
Sociology
Social Welfare
Urban Studies

PERIODICALS LIST

Accident analysis and prevention
1993 25, 4

Accountant
1991 44, 1

Acta tropica
1993 55, 3

Africa
1993 63, 1-4

Africa (Rome)
1992 47, 3,4
1993 48, 1-3

Africa bibliography 1992

Africa development
1992 17, 1-4
1993 18, 2-4

Africa forum
1991 1, 2-4
1992 2, 1-4

Africa insight
1992 22, 3,4
1993 23, 1-4

Africa Marburgensia
1991 24, 1

Africa media review
1993 7, 1-3

Africa quarterly
1992/93 33, 1-4

Africa recovery
1993 7, 1,2

Africa today
1993 40, 2

African administrative studies
1992 38,39

African affairs
1993 92, 366-9

African archaeological review
1992 10
1993 11

African book publishing record
1993 19, 1-4

African christian studies
1992 8, 3

African communist
1993 132-5

African currents
1991 11-14

African development review
1992 4, 1,2
1993 5, 1

African environment
1990 7, 25-28

African farmer
1993 Nov.

African journal of international and comparative law

1992 4, 1-4
1993 5, 1

African journal of science and technology. Series C, General
1991 2, 2

African languages and cultures
1992 5, 1,2
1993 6, 1

African livestock research
1992 1, 2

African management development forum
1991 2, 1,2

African research and documentation
1991 57
1992 58-60
1993 61-63

African review
1991 18, 1/2

African studies
1993 52, 1,2

African studies review
1992 35, 2,3
1993 36, 1-3

African study monographs
1992 13, 1-4

African study monographs (supplementary issue)
1992 18,19

African urban quarterly
1990 5, 1/2

Africana bulletin
1992 40

Africana Gandensia
1992 7

Africana notes and news
1992/3 30, 4,5

Africanus
1992 22, 1/2

Afriche
1993 17,19

Afrika focus
1992 8, 1, 3/4

Afrika Jahrbuch 1990

Afrika Jahrbuch 1992

Afrika spektrum
1992 27, 3
1993 28, 1

Afrika Zamani
1993 NS 1

Afrique 2000
1993 12-15

Afrique contemporaine
1993 165-7

Afro-Asia
1992 15

Agricultural systems
1993 42, 1

Ahfad journal
1992 9, 2

AIDS care
1992 4, 4
1993 5, 1-3

AIDS education and prevention
1992 4, 4
1993 5, 3

AIDS
1991 5, 1
1992 6, 12
1993 7, 1-12

Al Qantara
1991 12, 1,2

ALA bulletin
1992 18, 4
1993 19, 1

Alternatives
1993 18, 1,2

Ambio
1993 22, 2-3

American anthropologist
1993 95, 1-4

American economic review
1992 82, 2

American ethnologist
1992 19, 2,3
1993 20, 2,4

American journal of agricultural economics
1992 74, 3
1993 75, 1

American journal of economics and sociology
1993 52, 1,2

American journal of physical anthropology
1992 89, 2
1993 92, 3

American journal of preventive medicine
1993 9, 1

American journal of public health
1993 83, 5-11

American journal of semiotics
1993 13, 3

American journal of sociology
1993 99, 1

American sociological review
1992 57, 6

Annales aequatoria
1992 13

Annales de la Faculté des lettres et sciences humaines (Dakar)
1991 21

Annales de la Société belge de médecine tropical
1993 73, 3

Annals of Borno
1989/1990 6/7

Annals of the Association of American Geographers
1993 83, 2

Anné africaine 1992/93

Annuaire de l'Afrique du nord
1990 28

Annuaire de l'Océan indien
1990/91 12

Annual conference (African Society of Comparative and International Law)
1991 3
1992 4

Annual review of anthropology
1993 22

Anthropologie
1993 97, 1

Anthropology and humanism quarterly
1992 17, 2

Anthropology today
1992 8, 5
1993 9, 4

Anthropos
1993 88, 1/2-3/4

Antipode
1992 24, 3
1993 25, 1

Antiquités africaines
1990 26

Antiquity
1993 67, 255,256

Antropologische Verkenningen
1992 11, 4

Applied economics
1993 25, 4,10

Applied geography and development
1992 40

Applied geography
1993 13, 3,4

Aproma
1992 27-29

Arab historical review for Ottoman studies
1990 1/2

Arbres, forêts et communautés rurales
1993 5

Archaeology
1993 46, 1

Archiv orientalni
1992 60, 2,4

Archives des sciences sociales des réligions
1992 79

Area
1993 25, 2

Ariel
1992 23, 4

Armed forces and society
1991 17, 2
1993 19, 2,3
1993 20, 1

Arts d'Afrique noire
1991 78
1992 84

Asian and African Studies (Haifa)
1991 25, 1

Au coeur de l'Afrique
1992 60, 1

Aussenpolitik
1993 44, 1,4

Australian journal of anthropology
1990 1, 2/3

Australian journal of politics and history
1993 39, 1,2

Behavioural medicine
1993 19, 3

Biblical archaeologist
1993 56, 2

Bioethics
1993 7, 2-3

Boletin de la Asociacion Espagñola de Orientalistas
1991 27

Botswana journal of technology
1992 1, 1

British journal of educational studies
1993 41, 3

British journal of industrial relations
1993 31, 1

British journal of medical psychology
1993 66, Sept.

British journal of psychiatry
1993 163, Nov.

British medical journal
1993 307, 6895

Bulletin des études africaines de l'INALCO
1992 9, 17/18

Bulletin des séances
1991 37, 1,3,4

Bulletin liaison CNDT
1991 no. spécial

Bulletin of francophone Africa
1993 2-4

Bulletin of mathematical biology
1993 55, 4

Bulletin of SOAS
1993 56, 1

Bulletin of the American Schools of Oriental Research
1992 288, 290-1

Bulletin of the atomic scientists
1993 49, 3

Bulletin of the John Rylands University Library of Manchester
1991 73, 3

Bulletin of the World Health Organisation
1993 71, 1,3/4

Business archives
1991 61,62

Business management review
1991 2, 2

Cahiers d'études africaines
1992 32, 126-129

Cahiers d'outre-mer
1992 45, 179/80
1993 46, 181, 183

Cahiers de géographie de Québec
1993 37, 100

Cahiers de l'IPAG
1990 10

Cahiers de l'URBAMA
1990 4,6

Cahiers de musiques traditionnelles
1992 5

Cahiers de sociologie économique et culturelle
1992 17,18

Cahiers des sciences humaines
1993 29, 1-3

Cahiers du CEDAF
1992 3-6

Cahiers du communisme
1993 69, 1,3

Cambridge anthropology
1992 16, 1,2

Cambridge law journal
1992 51, 2

Canadian journal of African studies
1992 26, 1-3
1993 27, 1-3

Canadian journal of development studies
1993 14, 2

Capital and class
1993 50

Economic history review
1993 46, 2

Economic journal
1993 103, 417

Economic review (Central Bank of Egypt)
1989/1990 30, 1

Economics
1991 43

Economics letters
1993 42, 2

Economie de la Réunion
1991 56
1992 57-62

Economist
1992 140, 4

Education for information
1993 11, 1,2

Educational review
1993 45, 2

Educational studies
1993 19, 2

Eire-Ireland
1992 27, 4

Energy policy
1993 21, 1-5

English Academy review
1992 9

English in Africa
1993 20, 1

Enquêtes et documents d'histoire africaine
1992 10

Enviromental management
1993 17, 3

Environment and planning, Series A
1993 25, 3,7

Environment and urbanisation
1992 4, 2
1993 5, 1,2

Epidemiology
1993 4, 1

Estudios africanos
1991/92 6, 10/11

Estudios Moçambicanos
1991 9

Ethiopian journal of development research
1990 12, 1
1991 13, 1

Ethiopian journal of education
1991 12, 1,2

Ethiopian journal of health development
1990 4, 1

Ethiopian medical journal
1992 30, 1
1993 31, 2

Ethiopiques
1991 7, 2
1992 56

Ethnologie française
1993 23, 2

Ethnology
1993 32, 1-3

Ethnos
1993 58, 3-4

Ethos
1993 21, 1

Etudes et documents berbères
1991 8

Etudes et statistiques (BEAC)
1992 195,196
1993 201

Etudes internationales
1993 24, 4

Etudes irlandaises
1992 17

Etudes maliennes
1992 46

Etudes rurales
1990 120

European economic review
1993 37, 2/3

European history quarterly
1993 23, 4

European journal of development research
1993 5, 1,2

European journal of epidemiology
1992 9, 5

European journal of operational research
1993 68, 2

European journal of operational research
1993 70, 2

European review of agricultural economics
1993 20, 4

Evaluation and program planning
1993 16, 3

Exchange
1992 21, 3

Executive
Nov. 1992
Dec. 1992-Jan. 1993

Famille, santé, développement
1992 24

Feminist review
1993 43

Finance
31.7.92;15.11.92;30.12.92
31.1.93

Fletcher forum of world affairs
1993 17, 2

Focus on Africa
1993 4, 1-4

Food policy
1992 17, 6
1993 18, 4-6

Food, nutrition and agriculture
1992 2, 4

Foreign affairs
1993 72, 1-5

Foreign policy
1993 91

Forensic science international
1993 59, 2

Forest ecology and management
1993 57, 1-4
1993 58, 3/4

Forum for development studies
1993 2

Forum for utviklungstudier
1990 1,2

Frankfurter afrikanistische Blätter
1992 4

French politics and society
1993 11, 2

Futures
1993 25, 4

General hospital psychiatry
1993 15, 2

Geoforum
1992 23, 4
1993 24, 1-4

Geographical education magazine
1992 15, 1,2

Geographical journal
1993 159, 1

Geographical journal of Zimbabwe
1991 22

Geographical review
1991 81, 4
1992 82, 4

Geographical review of India
1990 52, 3

Geographical review of Japan (series B)
1991 64, 2

Geographische Zeitschrift
1992 80, 3

Geography
1993 78, 341

Géopolitique africaine
1992 15, 2

Government information quarterly
1993 10, 3

Government publications review
1993 20, 3,5

Grands lacs
1991

Habitat international
1993 17, 2,3

Hague yearbook of international law
1991 4

Hamdard islamicus
1991 14, 4
1992 15, 3

Harvard civil rights-civil liberties law review
1993 28, 2

Health education research
1993 8, 4

Health policy and planning
1992 7, 1-4
1993 8, 1-3

Health policy
1993 24, 2
1993 25, 3

Health transition review
1993 3

Heritage of Zimbabwe
1990 9
1992 11

Higher education
1992 24, 4
1993 25, 2,4

Higher education quarterly
1991 45, 3

Historical journal
1993 36, 4

History in Africa
1993 20

History of education
1991 20, 3

History of the human sciences
1993 6, 2

History today
1993 43, July

History Workshop journal
1992 33,36

Horn of Africa
1990/1991 13/14, 1-4

Human biology
1993 65, 1,2

Human ecology
1992 20, 1-4
1993 21, 1-3

Human rights quarterly
1993 15, 3,4

Humor
1991 4, 2
1993 6, 2

IBLA
1992 169

IDS bulletin
1993 24, 1-4

IFLA journal
1993 19, 1

IFM journal of finance management
1992 1, 1

Immigrants and minorities
1992 11, 2

Ind-Africana
1991 4, 2

Index on censorship
1993 22, 1-10

Indian geographical journal
1991 66, 2

Indian journal of African studies
1992 5, 1

Indian journal of economics
1992 72, 286

Indian journal of industrial relations
1993 28, 3

Indian journal of political science
1991 52, 2

Industrial and labor relations review
1993 46, 2

Information trends
1992 5, 3

Informations et commentaires
1992 78

Intelligence
1993 17, 2

Interchange
1993 241/2

International affairs
1993 69, 1,2

International and comparative law quarterly review
1993 42, 1-4

International classification
1992 19, 4

International fiction review
1993 20, 1

International history review
1993 15, 3

International information and library review
1992 24, 4
1993 25, 1,2

International interactions
1992 18, 1

International journal
1993 48, 2

International journal of African historical studies
1993 26, 2,3

International journal of behavioural development
1993 16, 3

International journal of cancer
1993 54, 1

International journal of comparative sociology
1992 33, 1/2

International journal of educational development
1993 13, 1-4

International journal of environmental health research
1992 2, 4

International journal of epidemiology
1993 22, 1

International journal of forecasting
1992 8, 3

International journal of geriatric psychiatry
1993 8, 6

International journal of gynecology and obstetrics
1993 41, 2

International journal of health services
1993 23, 4

International journal of intercultural relations
1993 17, 1,3

International journal of mental health
1993 21, 4

International journal of offender therapy and comparative criminology
1993 37, 2

International journal of politics, culture and society
1993 6, 4

International journal of public administration
1993 16, 3,11

International journal of public opinion research
1993 5, 2

International journal of science education
1993 15, 3,6

International journal of STD & AIDS
1993 4, 4,5

International journal of the sociology of language
1993 100-104

International journal of the sociology of law
1993 21, 1

International journal of urban and regional research
1993 17, 2

International labour review
1992 131, 1-6

International migration
1992 30, 3-4

International migration review
1992 26, 4
1993 27, 3

International philosophical quarterly
1993 33, 1

International political science review
1993 14, 3

International regional science review
1992 15, 1

International review of education
1993 39, 1-4

International review of mission
1992 81, 323

International review of social history
1993 37, 3

International social science journal
1993 45, 135-137

International sociology
1991 6, 1,2
1992 7, 1,2
1993 8, 2

International studies
1991 28, 4
1992 29, 2

International studies quarterly
1993 37, 2

Internationale spectator
1992 46, 10,12
1993 47, 2,9

Internationales Afrikaforum
1992 28, 4

Irish historical studies
1992 28, 110

Islam et sociétés au Sud du Sahara
1992 6

Islamic and comparative law quarterly
1990/91 10/11

Issue
1993 21, 1/2

Itinerario
1992 16, 1

Jana na leo
1991 25

Jewish journal of sociology
1992 34, 2

Journal des africanistes
1992 62, 1,2
1993 63, 1-2

Journal of African economics
1992 1, 2,3
1993 2, 1-3

Journal of African history
1993 34, 1-3

Journal of African law
1991 35, 1/2

Journal of agricultural economics
1993 44, 1

Journal of AIDS
1993 6, 6,8

Journal of the American Medical Association
1993 270, 17

Journal of arid environments
1992 23, 1,3
1993 24, 1
1993 25, 1,4

Journal of Asian and African affairs
1993 4, 2

Journal of Asian and African studies
1992 27, 3/4
1993 28, 1-4

Journal of Asian and African studies (Tokyo)
1993 43,44

Journal of biosocial science
1993 25, 1-4

Journal of Black studies
1992 22, 3; 23, 1-3
1993 24, 1

Journal of business ethics
1992 12, 1

Journal of business research
1993 28, 3

Journal of business venturing
1993 8, 2

Journal of church and state
1992 34, 4

Journal of common market studies
1993 31, 3

Journal of Commonwealth and comparative politics
1993 31, 1-3

Journal of Commonwealth literature
1993 28, 1

Journal of comparative family studies
1993 24, 3

Journal of conflict resolution
1993 37, 2

Journal of contemporary African studies
1992 11, 1

Journal of contemporary history
1992 17, 1,2

Journal of criminal justice
1993 21, 2

Journal of cross-cultural psychology
1993 24, 1

Journal of democracy
1993 4, 2

Journal of developing areas
1993 27, 4

Journal of developing societies
1992 8, 2

Journal of development economics
1993 40, 2; 41, 2; 42, 1

Journal of development studies
1993 29, 4; 30, 1

Journal of eastern African research and development
1992 22

Journal of economic issues
1993 27, 2

Journal of education for library and information science
1992 33, 3

Journal of Egyptian archaeology
1992 78

Journal of environmental management
1992 36, 1
1993 37, 1; 38, 3,4

Journal of Ethiopian studies
1993 26, 1

Journal of field archaeology
1993 20, 4

Journal of folklore research
1992 29, 1

Journal of further and higher education
1991 15, 2

Journal of human resources
1993 28, 4

Journal of humanities
1991 5
1992 6

Journal of imperial and Commonwealth history
1993 21, 3

Journal of infectious diseases
1993 167, 1,3

Journal of information science
1992 18, 6
1993 19, 3-5

Journal of international development
1992 4, 6
1993 5, 1-3

Journal of international food and agribusiness marketing
1992 4, 2,4
1993 5, 1

Journal of legal pluralism and unofficial law
1992 32

Journal of librarianship and information science
1993 25, 2,4

Journal of Mauritian studies
1992 4, 1

Journal of modern African studies
1993 31, 1-4

Journal of multilingual and multicultural development
1993 13, 6

Journal of near eastern studies
1993 52, 2,3

Journal of Negro education
1993 62, 1

Journal of peace research
1993 30, 1-4

Journal of peasant studies
1992 20, 1
1993 20, 3,4

Journal of policy modelling
1993 15, 3,4

Journal of pragmatics
1992 18

Journal of psychology
1993 127, 4

Journal of reading
1993 37, 2

Journal of religion in Africa
1991 21, 4
1993 23, 1-4

Journal of research
1992 2

Journal of Roman studies
1992 82

Journal of rural development
1992 11, 6
1993 12, 3,4

Journal of rural development and administration
1992 24, 3

Journal of rural studies
1993 9, 2

Journal of social development in Africa
1993 8, 1,2

Journal of social psychology
1992 132, 6
1993 133, 1-4

Journal of social, political and economic studies
1992 17, 3/4

Journal of southern African studies
1993 19, 1-3

Journal of special education
1993 27, 1,3

Journal of the African Association for Literacy and Adult Education
1992 6, 1

Journal of the Anthropological Society of Oxford
1993 24, 1,2

Journal of the Network of African Countries on Local Building Materials and Technologies
1991 1, 4

Journal of the Royal Society of Health
1993 113, 1,3

Journal of theoretical politics
1993 5, 2

Journal of tropical ecology
1992 8, 3,4
1993 9, 2,3

Journal of tropical medicine and hygiene
1993 96, 2

Journal of tropical pediatrics
1993 39, 1,2

Journal of water resources planning and management
1993 119, 3

Journal of women's history
1990 2, 1
1991 3, 1
1993 4, 1-3

Journal of world prehistory
1993 7, 3,4

Journal of world trade
1992 26, 4

Journalism quarterly
1993 70, 1

Jusur
1992 8

Kenya journal of education
1991 5, 1

Kenya jurist
Jan 1992

L'ethnographie
1993 89, 2

Labour, capital and society
1992 25, 1

Land degradation and rehabilitation
1990 2, 2
1993 4, 2

Land use policy
1993 10, 1,3

Landscape and urban planning
1993 25, 1

Language in society
1993 22, 1

Lawyers' journal
1990 1, 2
1991 2, 1

Legal forum
1992 4, 1,2

Les langues modernes
1992 86, 4

Lesotho law journal
1990 6, 1
1991 7, 1

Liberian studies journal
1993 18, 1

Library quarterly
1993 63, 4

Libri
1993 43, 2

Libyan studies
1993 24

Logos
1990 1, 1-4
1991 2, 1-4
1992 3, 1-4
1993 4, 1-4

Magreb Machrek (Monde arabe)
1993 138,139,141

Makerere historical journal
1990/91 5, 1/2

Malawian geographer
1991 29

Man
1992 27, 4
1993 28, 1-4

Man and world
1993 26, 2

Mankind quarterly
1993 33, 3

Marine policy
1993 17, 1,4

Marriage and family review
1993 19, 1-2

Maseno journal of education, arts and science
1992 1, 1

Matatu
1993 10

Materials and society
1991 15, 4

Media, culture and society
1993 15, 3

Medische antropologie
1991 3, 2

Meta
1993 38, 3

Middle East journal
1993 47, 1,2

Middle East policy
1992 1, 2

Middle Eastern studies
1992 28, 3,4
1993 29, 1-3

Middle East Studies Association bulletin
1992 26, 2

Millenium
1993 22, 1

Mimar
1991 41
1992 43

Mining survey
1991 1,2

Missiology
1992 20, 3

Modern language notes
1992 107, 5

Modern language studies
1992 22, 4
1993 23, 3

Mondes en développement
1992 20, 77/78

Mondes et cultures
1990 50, 2-4

Monthly review
1993 45, 2

Museum
1992 44, 4

Muslim world
1992 82, 1

Psychopathologie africaine
1992 24, 2,3

Public administration
1993 71, 3

Public administration and development
1993 13, 1-5

Public culture
1993 5, 3

Public enterprise
1992 12, 3-4

Quarterly journal of administration
1991 25, 3/4

Quest
1992 6, 2
1993 7, 1,2

Race and class
1993 34, 2,3
1993 35, 2

Refugees
1993 93

Regional politics and policy
1993 3, 1

Research in African literatures
1993 24, 1-4

Research review (Legon)
1990 6, 1

Review of African political affairs
1990 4, 1/2
1991 5, 1/2
1992 6, 1/2

Review of African political economy
1993 56-58

Review of rural and urban planning in southern and eastern Africa
1992 1

Revista de Africa y Medio Oriente
1992 4, 1

Revista internacional de estudos africanos
1991 14/15

Revue africaine de théologie
1991 15, 30

Revue agricole et sucrière de l'ile Mauritius
1991 70, 1/2

Revue burkinabè de droit
1992 22,23

Revue congolaise de droit
1991 10

Revue de l'Institut de sociologie
1990/91

Revue de l'ISERT
1991 6/7

Revue de littérature comparée
1993 67, 1

Revue du droit public
1993 jan-feb

Revue du monde musulman et de la Méditerranée
1992 63/64,65

Revue française d'histoire d'outre-mer
1992 79, 297
1993 80, 298,300

Revue juridique et politique
1993 47, 1

Revue Madagascar, océan Indien
1991 6,7/8

Revue nouvelle
1993 Jan-Feb

Revue scientifique du Tchad
1993 3, 1

Revue tunisien de géographie
1992 21/22

Round table
1993 82, 325-328

Rural progress
1992 11, 1,2
1993 12, 1

Saeculum
1992 43, 4

Southern African political and economic monthly
1991 4, 6-12
1992 5, 7-12
1993 7, 2

Savings and development
1993 17, 1

Scandanavian journal of development alternatives
1993 12, 1

Scholarly publishing
1993 24, 3
1993 25, 1

Science, technology and development
1993 11, 1,2

Scopus
1992 15, 2

Security dialogue
1993 24, 1-4

Semeia
1992 59

Semiotica
1993 95, 1-2

Senri ethnological studies
1993 35,36

Signs
1993 18, 2

Sinet
1990 13, 1

Singapore journal of tropical geography
1993 14, 1

Slavery and abolition
1993 14, 1-3

Sloan management review
1993 34, 3

Social analysis
1993 33

Social anthropology
1992 1, 1A
1993 1, 3

Social justice
1992 18, 3

Social science and medicine
1992 35, 1-12
1993 36, 1-12; 37, 1-12

Social security documentation - African series
1991 12

Social work with groups
1993 16, 3

Socialist register 1993

Society
1992 2, 13-18

Society of Malawi journal
1993 46, 1

Sociologica ruralis
1993 33, 1

Sociological focus
1992 25, 4

Sociological perspectives
1993 36, 3

Sociologus
1992 42, 1,2
1993 43, 1

Sociology ethnology bulletin
1992 1, 2

Soil and tillage research
1993 27, 1-4

South Africa international
1992/1993 23, 2-4

South African geographical journal
1991 73, 2
1992 74, 2

South African journal of economics
1993 61, 1-3

South African journal of ethnology
1992 15, 4
1993 16, 1

South African journal of philosophy
1993 12, 3

South African journal of science
1993 89, 3,5

South African journal of sociology
1992 23, 4
1993 24, 1,2

South African journal on human rights
1992 8, 3,4
1993 9, 1

South African law journal
1992 109, 2-4

South African medical journal
1993 83, 1-11

South African yearbook of international law
1991/92 17

Southern African review of books
1993 5, 1-6

Special libraries
1993 84, 1

Stanford journal of international law
1992 29, 1

Storia urbana
1993 17, 63

Strategic management journal
1993 14, 4

Studia islamica
1990 71

Studies in comparative international development
1993 28, 1

Studies in family planning
1992 23, 5,6
1993 24, 1-5

Sub-Stance
1992 69

Sudanic Africa
1992 3

Survival
1993 35, 3

System dynamics
1993 9, 1

Systèmes de pensée en Afrique noire
1993 12

Systems practice
1993 6, 5

Taamuli
1990 1, 1/2

Tanzania economic trends
1992 4, 3/4
1992/93 5, 3/4

Technological forecasting and social change
1993 43, 3/4

Technology and culture
1993 34, 2

Technology and development
1993 6

Telecommunication policy
1993 17, 7

Tesol quarterly
1993 27, 3

Text
1993 13, 1

Theatre survey
1992 33, 2

Theoria
1993 81/2

Third world quarterly
1993 14, 1-4

Tidschrift voor economische en sociale geografie
1992 83, 1

Tiers Monde
1993 33, 133-136

Tizame
1992 3

Tourism research
1993 20, 1

Transactions of the American Philosophical Society
1992 82, P4

Transactions of the Royal Society of Tropical Medicine and Hygiene
1993 87, 1,4

Transafrican journal of history
1992 21

Transport reviews
1993 13, 2

Tropical and geographical medicine
1993 45, 2

Tulane drama review
1992 36, 4

Tulsa studies on women's literature
1992 11, 1

Ufahamu
1990/91 19, 2/3
1991/92 20, 1

Unesco courier

March 1993

UNESCO-Africa
1993 6

UNISWA research journal
1992 6, 1

Université, recherche et développement
1993 1

University of Louisville journal of family law
1993 31, 2

Urban forum
1992 3, 1,2
1993 4, 1

Urban geography
1992 13, 6

Urban League review
1992 15, 2

Urban studies
1993 30, 3

Verfassung und Recht in Ubersee
1992 25, 3,4

Veterinary quarterly
1993 15, 2

Vocational aspects of education
1993 45, 3

Wajibu
1992 7, 3,4

WAMP bulletin
1993 4

Water resources research
1993 29, 6

Water
1993 19, 3

West African journal of archaeology
1993 23

Whydah
1993 3, 3

Wisssenschaftliche Beiträge
1990 25, 4

Women and health
1993 20, 3

Women's studies international forum
1993 16, 5

Work in progress
1993 87-93

World archaeology
1993 25, 2

World Bank economic review
1993 7, 1

World development
1993 21, 1-12

World economy
1993 16, 5

World literature written in English
1991 31, 2

World politics
1993 46, 1

Wuqûf
1992 6

Ya Mkobe
1990 4

Yale French studies
1993 82

Yale journal of criticism
1991 5, 1

Yale law journal
1993 102, 4

Yearbook of cooperative enterprise
1993

Youth and society
1993 24, 4

Zaire Afrique
1992 269,270
1993 271-77

Zambia Library Assocation journal
1992 20

Zambian journal of agricultural science
1992 2, 1

Zeitschrift der deutschen morgenländischen Gesellschaft
1991 141, 2

Zeitschrift fur Ethnologie
1992 117

Zimbabwe engineer
1992 57, 7

Zimbabwe journal of educational research
1993 5, 1,2

Zimbabwe law review
1989/90 7/8

Zimbabwe science news
1992 26, 1/3

AFRICA

General

1 **Assogba**, Y, L'Afrique entre les rêves et l'histoire, *Afrique 2000,* 15 (1993) 83–94

2 **Ayittey, G B N**, *Indigeneous African institutions.* Ardsley on Hudson: Transnational, 1991, 547pp

3 **Bates, R H, et al** (eds), *Africa and the disciplines.* Chicago: University of Chicago Press, 1993, 245pp

4 **Bischoff, P,** African reference works: an annotated list of 1992 titles, *African book publishing record,* **19,** 2 (1993) 79–91

5 **Campbell, B K,** Research for whom, cooperation for what? The role of African studies in the 1990s, *Canadian journal of African studies,* **26,** 3 (1992) 586–600 (in French, 566–82)

6 **Centre d'études egyptologiques Cheikh Anta Diop**, *Cheikh Anta Diop et la signification de son oeuvre.* Kinshasa: Kaloma Diyoka, 1993, 47pp

7 **Elmahad, K,** Les droits de la femme dans la Charte africaine des droits de l'homme et des peuples, *Afrique 2000,* 14 (1993) 21–37

8 **Gann, L H,** Ex Africa: an Africanist's intellectual biography, *Journal of modern African studies,* **31,** 3 (1993) 477–98

9 **Gibbon, P,** Introduction: economic reform and social change in Africa, in Gibbon, P (ed), *Social change and economic reform (item 1880)*, 11–25

10 **Grandqvist, R** (ed), *Culture in Africa: an appeal for pluralism.* Uppsala: Scandinavian Institute of African Studies, 1993, 204pp

11 **Khadiagala, G M,** Notes on teaching interdisciplinary African studies courses, *Current bibliography on African affairs,* **24,** 4 (1993) 343–62

12 **Mkandawire, T,** Problems and prospects of social sciences in Africa, *International social science journal,* **45,** 135 (1993) 129–40

13 **Obasanjo, O,** Africa in the 21st century, *Security dialogue,* **24,** 2 (1993) 197–206

14 **Sanders, R,** The last decade: a content analysis of the *African studies review* 1982–1991, *African studies review,* **36,** 1 (1993) 115–26

15 **Siddiqui, R A** (ed), *Subsaharan Africa: a subcontinent in transition.* Aldershot: Avebury, 1993, 352pp

16 **Simons, E,** *Inventaire des études africaines en Belgique.* Brussels: CEDAF, 1993, 341pp

17 **Turco, A** (ed), *Terra d'Africa: anno 1992.* Milan: Unicopli, 1992, 304pp

18 **van Binsbergen, W** (ed), *De maatschappelijke betekenis van Nederlands Afrika-onderzoek in deze tijd: een symposium.* Leiden: Werkgemeenschap Afrika, 1993, 108pp

Agriculture, scientific

19 **Ashley, J,** Drought and crop adaptation, in Rowland, J R J (ed), *Dryland farming (Item 1078)*, 46–67

20 **Cromwell, E, et al,** *Sowing beyond the state: NGOs and seed supply in developing countries.* London: Overseas Development Institute, 1993, 143pp

21 **Dargie, J D, et al,** The FAO-IAEA-DGIS coordinated research programs on tryponosomiasis diagnosis and animal production in Africa, *Veterinary quarterly,* **15,** 2 (1993) 75–78

22 **Friis-Hansen, E,** *The failure of formal plant breeding to meet the needs of resource-poor peasants in African arid lands.* Uppsala: Scandinavian Institute of African Studies, 1992, 12pp

23 **Itty, P,** *Economics of village cattle production in tsetse affected areas of Africa: a study of trypanosomiasis control using trypano-tolerant cattle and chemotherapy in Ethiopia, Kenya, Côte d'Ivoire, the Gambia, Zaire and Togo.* Konstanz: Hartung Gorre, 1992, 316 + 44pp

24 **Paling, R W, Dwinger, R H,** Potential of trypanotolerance as a contribution to sustainable livestock production in tstese-affected Africa, *Veterinary quarterly,* **15,** 2 (1993) 60–67

25 **Reid, W,** *Genetic resources and sustainable agriculture: creating incentives for local innovation and adaptation.* Nairobi: ACTS, 1992, 31pp

26 **Smith, P,** Soil and water conservation, in Rowland, J R J (ed), *Dryland farming (Item 1078)*, 142–71

27 **Stroud, A,** Control of weeds, in Rowland, J R J (ed), *Dryland farming (Item 1078)*, 172–87

28 **Tsedeke Abate,** Control of other pests and diseases, in Rowland, J R J (ed), *Dryland farming (Item 1078)*, 188–204

29 **Zegeye Hailu, Runge-Metzger, A,** *Sustainability of landuse systems: the potential of indigenous measures for the maintenance of soil productivity in subsaharan Africa.* Weikersheim: Margraf, 1993, 168pp

Anthropology

See also: 311, 369, 403, 837, 977, 989, 1017

30 **Ardener, E,** The 'personal enemy' in African politics, *Journal of the Anthropological Society of Oxford,* **24,** 2 (1993) 105–110

31 **Baxter, P T W,** From anthropological texts to popular writings, *Bulletin of the John Rylands University Library of Manchester,* **73,** 3 (1991) 105–23

32 **Bernardi, B,** Africanistica e antropologia: dalla costruzione moderna alla deconstruzione postmoderna, *Africa (Rome),* **48,** 1 (1993) 1–20

33 **Bourdillon, M F C,** Anthropological approaches to the study of African religions, *Numen,* **40,** 3 (1993) 217–39

34 **Bouvier, P,** Aux sources du pouvoir africain, *Bulletin des séances,* **37,** 4 (1991) 529–41

35 **Burton, J W,** Representing Africa: colonial anthropology revisited, *Journal of Asian and African studies,* **27,** 3/4 (1992) 181–201

36 **Calderoli, L,** Marquages permanentes du corps en Afrique subsaharienne: le processus technique comme signifiant, *L'ethnographie,* **89,** 2 (1993) 105–30

37 **Fuchs, P, Krüger, G** (eds), *Verzeichnis der Völkerkundlichen*

Sammlung des Instituts für Völkerkunde des Georg-August Universität zu Göttingen. Teil IV: Afrika. Göttingen: Georg-August Universität, 1993, 347pp

38 **Görög-Karady, V** (ed), *D'un conte ... à l'autre: la variabilité dans la littérature orale.* Paris: CNRS, 1990, 603pp

39 **Herbert, E W,** *Iron, gender and power: rituals of transformation in African society.* Bloomington: Indiana University Press, 1993, 277pp

40 **Jacobson-Widding, A** (ed), *Body and space: symbolic models of unity and division in African cosmology and experience.* Uppsala: University of Uppsala/Almqvist and Wiksell, 1991, 348pp

41 **Janzen, J M,** Doing 'ngoma': a dominant trope in African religion and healing, *Journal of religion in Africa,* **21,** 4 (1991) 290–308

42 **Lagercrantz, S,** Notes on African trigger-systems, *Paideuma,* **38,** (1992) 31–107

43 **Lallemand, S,** *La circulation des enfants en société traditionelle: prêt, don, échange.* Paris: Harmattan, 1993, 220pp

44 **Maw, J, Picton, J** (eds), *Concepts of the body/self in Africa.* Vienna: Afro-Pub, 1992, 166pp

45 **Moore, S F,** Changing perspectives on a changing Africa: the work of anthropology, in Bates R H et al (eds), *Africa and the disciplines (item 3)*, 3–57

46 **Ogungbemi, S,** A philosophical view of witchcraft in Africa, *Journal of humanities,* 6 (1992) 1–16

47 **Oppong, C,** Traditional family systems in rural settings in Africa, in Berquo, E & Xenos, P (eds), *Family systems and cultural change* (Oxford: Clarendon, 1992), 69–86

48 **Schoffeleers, M,** Twins and unilateral figures in central and southern Africa: symmetry and asymmetry in the symbolisation of the sacred, *Journal of religion in Africa,* **21,** 4 (1991) 345–72

49 **Tardits, C,** Le roi et ses ancêtres, in Blondeau, A M & Schipper, K (eds), *Essais sur le rituel, Tome II* (Louvain: Peeters, 1990), 107–26

50 **Uka, E M** (ed), *Readings in African traditional religion.* Frankfurt: Lang, 1991, 391pp

51 **van der Geest, S, Kirby, J P,** The absence of the missionary in African ethnography, 1930–65, *African studies review,* **35,** 3 (1992) 59–103

Architecture

52 **Adahl, K,** The islamic architecture and art in subsaharan Africa: a problem of identity, in Granqvist, R (ed), *Culture in Africa (item 10)*, 131–43

Arts

See also: 699

53 **Agovi, K E,** Towards an authentic African theatre, *Ufahamu,* **19,** 2/3 (1990/1991) 67–79

54 **Binet, J,** Les vieillards dans l'art africain, *Afrique contemporaine,* 166 (1993) 39–44

55 **Blier, S P,** Truth and seeing: magic, custom and fetish in art history, in Bates R H et al (eds), *Africa and the disciplines (item 3)*, 139–66

56 **Gaudibert, P,** *L'art africain contemporain.* Paris: Cercle d'art, 1991, 175pp

57 **Gerdes, P,** *L'ethnomathématique comme nouveau domaine de recherche en Afrique.* Maputo: Higher Pedagogical Institute, 1993, 85pp

59 **Graham, R,** *The world of African music: Stern's guide to contemporary African music. Vol. 2.* London: Pluto, 1992, 235pp

60 **Kennedy, J**, *New currents, ancient rivers: contemporary African artists in a generation of change.* Blue Ridge Summit: Smithsonian Institution Press, 1992, 204pp

61 **Kerchache, J, et al,** *The art of Africa.* New York: Abrams, 1993, 619pp

62 **Laburthe-Tolba, P,** Afrique: du respect de son art comme chiffre absolue, *Journal des Africanistes,* **62,** 1 (1992) 127–34

63 **Lonoh Malangi Bokelenge,** *Négritude, Africanité et musique africaine.* Kinshasa: Centre des recherches pédagogiques, 1990, 78pp

64 **Ngakane, L,** Africa in the pictures, *Africa forum,* **1,** 3 (1991) 37–41

65 **Nketia, J H K,** Music and cultural policy in contemporary Africa, in Bauman, M P (ed), *Music in the dialogue of cultures* (Wilmenshaven: Noetzel, 1991), 77–94

66 **Scherer, J,** *Le théâtre en Afrique noire francophone.* Paris: PUF, 1992, 128pp

67 **Schmidt, N J,** Recent films by subsaharan African film makers (6), *ALA bulletin,* **19,** 1 (1993) 10–14

68 **Scruggs, L A,** The political economy of the illicit trade in African artifacts, *African review,* **18,** 1/2 (1991) 29–38

69 **Some, R,** Autour de l'esthétique africaine, *Journal des Africanistes,* **62,** 1 (1992) 113–26

70 **Ströter-Bender, J,** *Zeitgenösssische Kunst der 'Dritten Welt': Athiopien, … Kenia, Nigeria, Senegal und Tanzania.* Cologne: DuMont, 1991, 244pp

71 **Szalay, M** (ed), *Der Sinn des Schonen: Asthetik, Soziologie und Geschichte der afrikanischen Kunste.* Munich: Trickster, 1990, 191pp

Demography

See also: 312, 735, 743, 754, 1120, 1127

72 **Acsadi, G T F, et al** (eds), *Population growth and reproduction in subsaharan Africa: technical analyses of fertility and its consequences.* Washington: World Bank, 1990, 249pp

73 **Bos, E, Bulatao, R A,** The demographic impact of AIDS in subsaharan Africa: short-term and long-term projections, *International journal of forecasting,* **8,** 3 (1992) 367–84

74 **Caldwell, J C, et al,** Fertility decline in Africa: a new type of transition?, *Population and development review,* **18,** 2 (1992) 211–42

75 **Chimere-Dan, O,** *In search of explanations for fertility and reproductive behaviour in Africa.* Johannesburg: University of Witwatersrand, African Studies Institute, 1993, 24pp

76 **Cordell, D C, et al** (eds), *Population, reproduction, sociétés: perspectives et enjeux de démographie sociale.* Montreal: Presses de l'Université de Montréal, 1993, 450pp

77 **Engman, E VT,** *Population growth in Africa: the road beyond family planning in the shadows of Malthus.* Maiduguri: University of Maiduguri Press, 1991, 30pp

78 **Gendreau, F,** *La population de l'Afrique: manuel de démographie.* Paris: Karthala, 1993, 461pp

79 **Iyun, B F,** The geographical inequalities in mortality in Africa, *Social science and medicine,* **36,** 10 (1993) 1243–45

80 **Kamuzora, C L,** Defining the issues for realistic population-development policies in Africa, *African review,* **18,** 1/2 (1991) 71–86

81 **Ohadike, P O,** Population, policy development and implementation in subsaharan Africa, *African development review,* **4,** 2 (1992) 273–97

82 **Paul, B K,** Maternal mortality in Africa 1980–87, *Social science and medicine,* **37,** 6 (1993) 745–52

83 **Stengers, J,** Sur la critique des données démographiques en Afrique, *Civilisations,* **40,** 2 (1992) 25–40

84 **Vaidyanathan, K E,** Population trends, issues and implications, *African development review,* **4,** 2 (1992) 1–32

85 **van de Walle, E, Meekers, D,** The sociocultural context of family and fertility in subsaharan Africa, *African development review,* **4,** 2 (1992) 33–62

86 **Westhoff, C F,** *Age at marriage, age at first birth, and fertility in Africa.* Washington: World Bank, 1992, 22 +35pp

Economic and social history

See also: 2, 76, 352, 530

87 **Chandler, T, Tarver, J D,** Urbanisation in colonial Africa, *Africa insight,* **23,** 4 (1993) 250–54

88 **Cooper, F,** *Confronting historical paradigms: peasants, labour and the capitalist world system in Africa and Latin America.* Madison: University of Wisconsin Press, 1993, 422pp

89 **Coquery-Vidrovitch, C,** *Histoire des villes d'Afrique noire, des origines à la colonisation.* Paris: Albin Michel, 1993, 412pp

90 **Curto, J C,** Demografia historica e os efeitos do trafico de escravos em Africa: una analise des principais estudos quantitativos, *Revista internacional de estudos Africanos,* 14/15 (1991) 243–77

91 **Fetter, B,** Pease porridge in a pot: The social basis of health and healing in Africa, *History in Africa,* **20,** (1993) 43–51

92 **Gardinier, D,** O impacto frances na educação em Africa, 1817–1960, *Afro-Asia,* 15 (1992) 86–99

93 **Gervais, R R, Marcoux, R,** Saving Francophone Africa's statistical past, *History in Africa,* **20,** (1993) 385–90

94 **Hazemann, Y,** Crisis(es): Africa maltreated by history, *African environment,* 7, 25–28 (1990) 287–99

95 **Inikori, J E,** Slavery and Atlantic commerce, 1650–1800, *American economic review,* **82,** 2 (1992) 151–57

96 **Krozewski, G,** Sterling, the minor territories, and the end of formal empire, 1939–1958, *Economic history review,* **46,** 2 (1993) 239–65

97 **McCulloch, J,** The emperor's new clothes: ethnopsychiatry in colonial Africa, *History of the human sciences,* **6,** 2 (1993) 35–62

98 **Milner-Gulland, E J, Beddington, J R,** The exploitation of elephants for the ivory trade: an historical perspective, *Proceedings of the Royal Society of London; Series B: biological sciences,* **252,** 1333 (1993) 29–37

99 **Phillips, J E,** Some recent thinking on slavery in Islamic Africa and the Middle East, *Middle East Studies Association bulletin,* **26,** 2 (1992) 157–62

100 **Thiam, I D,** *Histoire du mouvement syndical africain, 1790–1929.* Paris: Harmattan, 1993, 287pp

101 **Zeleza, P T,** *A modern economic history of Africa. Vol 1: the nineteenth century.* Dakar: Codesria, 1993, 501pp

Economy - Development

See also: 9, 258, 346, 373, 739, 817, 865, 876, 902, 922, 947, 950, 951, 959, 1062, 4784

102 **Abbott, G,** *Debt relief and*

sustainable development in subsaharan Africa. Aldershot: Edward Elgar, 1993, 189pp
103 **Aboagye, A, et al,** Subsaharan Africa, *African environment,* 7, 25–28 (1990) 53–80
104 **Adedeji, A,** *Africa in the nineteen-nineties.* Lagos: NIIA, 1991, 40pp
105 **Adedeji, A,** The case for remaking Africa, in Rimmer, D (ed), *Action in Africa (Item 525),* 43–57
106 **Adedeji, A,** For Africa's sake (interview), *Africa forum,* **2,** 3/4 (1992) 6–13
107 **Ahene, R A, Katz, B S** (eds), *Privatisation and investment in subsaharan Africa.* New York: Praeger, 1992, 244pp
108 **Anya, A O,** Science, education and underdevelopment: the socio-political, economic and ecological dimensions of the African crisis, *Discovery and innovation,* **4,** 4 (1992) 4–11
109 **Asmerom, H K, et al** (eds), *Bureaucracy and developmental policies in the Third World.* Amsterdam: Free University of Amsterdam Press, 1992, 334pp
110 **Asombang, W W,** Funding sustainable development in subsaharan Africa, in Onimode, B (ed), *The African response (Item 186),* 37–44
111 **Assogba, Y,** Entre la rationalité des intervenants et la rationalité des populations bénéficaires: l'échec des projects en Afrique noire, *Cahiers de géographie de Québec,* **37,** 100 (1993) 49–66
112 **Barnett, A, Blaikie, P,** Simple methods for monitoring the socio-economic impact of AIDS: lessons from subsaharan Africa, in Cross, S & Whiteside, A (eds), *Facing up to AIDS (item 4753),* 261–92
113 **Barro-Chambrier, H A,** Quelques réflexions sur le traitement de la dette des pays d'Afrique sub-saharienne, *Mondes en développement,* **20,** 77/78 (1992) 119–30
114 **Bates, R H,** The politics of economic policy reform: a review article, *Journal of African economics,* **2,** 3 (1993) 417–33
115 **Bates, R H,** A reply, *World development,* **21,** 6 (1993) 1077–81
116 **Ben Abdallah, T, Mamaty, I,** Africa's debt crisis: events and proposals since 1980, *African environment,* 7, 25–28 (1990) 25–50
117 **Bigo, D,** Is there hope for subsaharan Africa?, *Contention,* **1,** 3 (1992) 171–88
118 **Blokland, A, et al** (ed), *Sustainable development in semi-arid subsaharan Africa.* The Hague: Ministry of Foreign Affairs, Development Cooperation Information Department, 1992, 100pp
119 **Blomström, M, Lundahl, M** (eds), *Economic crisis in Africa: perspectives on policy responses.* London: Routledge, 1993, 353pp
120 **Blomström, M, Lundahl, M,** Introduction, in Blomström, M & Lundahl, M (eds), *Economic crisis (Item 119),* 1–18
121 **Böhmer, J,** Die Auslandsverschuldung Subsahara-Afrikas: Entwicklung, neuere Initiativen der Gläubiger und Anzatspunkte für eine Problembewältigung, *Afrika spektrum,* 1 (1993) 5–35
122 **Bourenane, N,** What is the future of Africa?: an alternative approach to the dominant Afro-pessimism, *Southern Africa political & economic monthly,* **4,** 9 (1991) 9–15
123 **Boutros-Ghali, B,** *Mobilising support for Africa.* New York: UN, 1993, 8pp
124 **Brown, R P C,** The IMF and Paris Club rescheduling: a

conflicting role?, *Journal of international development,* **4,** 3 (1992) 292–313

125 Browne, R S, Alternative policy frameworks for African development in the 1990s, in Nyang'oro, J E & Shaw, T M (eds), *Beyond structural adjustment (Item 179),* 71–82

126 Cardoso, F G, Estado e integração económica na Africa dos anos 90, *Economia,* 7 (1991) 9–14

127 Cleary, S, Structural adjustment in Africa, *African environment,* **7,** 25–28 (1990) 353–71

128 Coetzee, S, Structural adjustment: a review of the state of the art, *Africa insight,* **23,** 2 (1993) 79–84

129 Collier, P, Africa and the study of economics, in Bates R H et al (eds), *Africa and the disciplines (item 3),* 58–82

130 Comeliau, C, Structural adjustment: what kinds of research?, *African environment,* **7,** 25–28 (1990) 301–306

131 Conway, P, Greene, J, Is Africa different?, *World development,* **21,** 12 (1993) 2017–28

132 Coquery-Vidrovitch, C, *Afrique noire: permanence et rupture.* Paris: Harmattan, 1993, 450pp

133 Cracknell, B, Project rehabilitation: lessons from evaluation findings, in Kirkpatrick, C (ed), *Project rehabilitation (Item 164),* 39–53

134 Cummings, R J, A historical perspective on the Lagos Plan of Action, in Nyang'oro, J E & Shaw, T M (eds), *Beyond structural adjustment (Item 179),* 29–47

135 de Lusignan, G, EDI and the management of change, in Kirkpatrick, C (ed), *Project rehabilitation (Item 164),* 3–19

136 Dei, G J S, Sustainable development in the African context: revisiting some theoretical and metholodological issues, *Africa development,* **18,** 2 (1993) 97–110

137 Development Cooperation Information Department, *Global coalition for Africa: documents on development, democracy and debt.* The Hague: Ministry of Foreign Affairs, 1992, 304pp

138 Engelhard, P, The paradigm of the World Bank and its critics: an epistemological curiosity, *African environment,* **7,** 25–28 (1990) 267–86

139 Engelhard, P, Ben Abdallah, T, Beyond adjustment: the IMF, the World Bank and structural adjustment, *African environment,* **7,** 25–28 (1990) 11–24

140 Fares, Z, *Afrique et démocratie: espoirs et illusions.* Paris: Harmattan, 1993, 186pp

141 Fundanga, C M, Debt and structural adjustment, *Southern Africa political & economic monthly,* **4,** 12 (1991) 14–18

142 Giovannetti, G, et al, Growth, capital flows and enforcement constraints - the case of Africa, *European economic review,* **37,** 2/3 (1993) 418–25

143 Giri, J, Rompre avec un demi-siècle d'antidéveloppement, *Politique africaine,* 49 (1993) 93–125

144 Godsell, B, Six strategies for African development, in Rimmer, D (ed), *Action in Africa (Item 525),* 29–33

145 Gooneratne, W, Mbilinyi, M J (eds), *Reviving local self-reliance: people's responses to the economic crisis in eastern and southern Africa.* Nagoya, Japan: United Nations Centre for Regional Development, 1992, 274pp

146 Grey-Johnson, C, The African informal sector at the crossroads: emerging policy options, *Africa development,* **17,** 1 (1992) 65–91

147 Gye-Wado, O, The African

debt crisis and a new legal initiative, *Annual conference (African Society of International and Comparative Law)*, **4,** (1992) 240–254

148 **Harsch, E,** Africa's grass troots on the cutting edge, *African farmer,* Nov. 1993 8, 26–29

149 **Herbst, J,** The transition to a post-apartheid economy: lessons from independent Africa, in Schrire, R (ed), *Wealth or poverty? (Item 4779)*, 77–88

150 **Hugon, P,** L'Afrique entre la marginalisation économique et la reprise économique, *Afrique 2000,* 15 (1993) 55–63

151 **Hugon, P,** *L'économie de l'Afrique.* Paris: La Decouverte, 1993, 123pp

152 **Husain, I, Helleiner, G K,** A comment on 'The IMF, the World Bank and Africa's adjustment and external debt problems: an unofficial view' (and reply), *World development,* **21,** 12 (1993) 2055–63

153 **Hussain, M N,** Between legitimacy and dominance: the AAF-SAP versus the IMF system, in Onimode, B (ed), *The African response (Item 186)*, 90–102

154 **Ihonvbere, J O,** Economic crisis in subsaharan Africa: issues, responses and prospects for recovery, *Pakistan horizon,* **44,** 4 (1991) 41–56

155 **Jalloh, S B,** Subsahara-Afrika - zwischen Reform und Untergang, *Internationales Afrikaforum,* **28,** 4 (1992) 351–373

156 **Juma, C, Ojwang, J B,** *Technology transfer and sustainable development: international policy issues.* Nairobi: ACTS, 1992, 40pp

157 **Kabou, A,** *Weder arm noch ohnmächtig: eine Sreitschrift gegen schwarze Eliten und wiesse Helfer.* Basle: Lenos, 1993, 260pp

158 **Kassé, M,** *Le développement par l'integration.* Dakar: Nouvelles editions africaines, 1991, 249pp

159 **Kay, G,** Whither Africa and development studies, *Area,* **25,** 2 (1993) 137–41

160 **Killick, T,** *Economic inflexibility in Africa: evidence and causes.* London: Overseas Development Institute, 1993, 52pp

161 **Killick, T,** The essence of Africa's development experience, *Africa forum,* **2,** 2 (1992) 32–36

162 **Kimmerle, H,** Art and philosophy in the development of subsaharan Africa, *International sociology,* **7,** 2 (1992) 173–86

163 **Kiplagat, P K,** Into the twilight zone: a comparative analysis of legal aspects of political and economic reforms in Eastern Europe and Africa, *African journal of international and comparative law,* **4,** 4 (1992) 927–960

164 **Kirkpatrick, C** (ed), *Project rehabilitation in developing countries.* London: Routledge, 1991, 271pp

165 **Kockläuner, G,** Positioning African low income countries, *East African economic review,* **8,** 2 (1992) 114–22

166 **Lalèyê, L P,** Temps et développement, *Quest,* **6,** 2 (1992) 44–61

167 **Logan, I B, Mengisteab, K,** IMF-World Bank adjustment and structural transformation in subsaharan Africa, *Economic geography,* **69,** 1 (1993) 1–24

168 **Loxley, J,** The African debt: doubts and problems, *Canadian journal of African studies,* **26,** 2 (1992) 330–36 (review article)

169 **Lussier, M,** Impacts of exports on economic performance: a comparative study, *Journal of African economics,* **2,** 1 (1993) 106–27

170 **Mhone, G,** Behind and beyond

the World Bank strategy, *Southern Africa political and economic monthly,* **4,** 12 (1991) 3–14

171 **Mohammed, N A L,** Economic growth and defence spending in subsaharan Africa: Benoit and Joerding revisited, *Journal of African economics,* **2,** 2 (1993) 145–56

172 **Mosley, P, Weeks, J,** Has recovery begun? 'Africa's adjustment in the 1980s' revisited, *World development,* **21,** 10 (1993) 1583–1606

173 **Muheme, B B G,** Les aspects productifs de l'économie informelle: recherche des indicateurs pour une réponse au développement en Afrique, *Afrika focus,* **8,** 1 (1992) 5–31

174 **Mukoko, B,** Exportations et cycle de croissance dans les pays africains à revenu intermédiare, *Tiers Monde,* **34,** 133 (1993) 69–88

175 **Mwamula-Lubandi, E D,** *Clan theory in African development studies analysis: reconsidering African development promotive bases.* Lanham: University Press of America, 1992, 233pp

176 **Mwanza, A,** Subsaharan Africa in crisis, *Southern Africa political and economic monthly,* **4,** 11 (1991) 22–25

177 **Nafziger, E W,** Debt, adjustment and economic liberalisation in Africa, *Journal of economic issues,* **27,** 2 (1993) 429–39

178 **Nafziger, E W,** *The debt crisis in Africa.* Baltimore: Johns Hopkins University Press, 1993, 287pp

179 **Nyang'oro, J O, Shaw, T M** (eds), *Beyond structural adjustment in Africa: the political economy of sustainable and democratic development.* Westport: Praeger, 1992, 190pp

180 **Nzomo, M,** Beyond structural adjustment programs: democracy, gender, equity, and development in Africa, with special reference to Kenya, in Nyang'oro, J E & Shaw, T M (eds), *Beyond structural adjustment (Item 179)*, 99–117

181 **Nzongola-Ntalaja,** *The African crisis: the way out.* Harare: Sapes books, 1992, 17pp

182 **O'Brien, S,** Structural adjustment and structural transformation in subsaharan Africa, in Gladwin, C H (ed), *Structural adjustment and African women farmers (Item 315)*, 25–45

183 **Odedokun, M O,** Factors responsible for the poor performance of Africa in the 1970s and 1980s: cross-sectional evidence from 42 countries, *African development review,* **5,** 1 (1993) 32–61

184 **Oiro, S,** Forgotten issues of LTPS, in Onimode, B (ed), *The African response (Item 186)*, 85–90

185 **Okigbo, P,** *Studies in the political economy of Africa.* Enugu: Fourth Dimension, 1993, 395pp

186 **Onimode, B** (ed), *The African response: adjustment or transformation.* London: IFAA, 1992, 164pp

187 **Onimode, B,** The objectives of the workshop, in Onimode, B (ed), *The African response (Item 186)*, 13–19

188 **Onimode, B,** The World Bank's LTPS and Africa's transformation, in Onimode, B (ed), *The African response (Item 186)*, 64–75

189 **Osagie, E,** Continental goals, *Africa forum,* **2,** 1 (1992) 40–48

190 **Othman, H,** *Towards an IMF state in Africa?: research notes.* Bergen: Chr. Michelsen Institute, 1993, 13pp

191 **Parfitt, T W,** Which African agenda for the 'nineties'? The ECA/World Bank alternatives, *Journal of international development,* **5,** 1 (1993) 93–106

192 **Peters, P E,** Is 'rational choice'

the best choice for Robert Bates? An anthropologist's reading of Bates' work, *World development,* **21,** 6 (1993) 1063–76

193 Platteau, J P, *Formalisation and privatisation of land rights in subsaharan Africa; a critique of current orthodoxies and structural adjustment programmes.* London: London School of Economics, Development Economics Research Programme, 1992, 70pp

194 Ramchandani, R R, A strategy of development: breaking the bonds of dependence, *African currents,* 11 (1991) 5–23

195 Salim, S A, Opening address, in Onimode, B (ed), *The African response (Item 186)*, 7–12

196 Schmale, M, *The role of local organisations in development: Tanzania, Zimbabwe and Ethiopia.* Aldershot: Avebury, 1993, 258pp

197 Shaw, T M, Revisionism in African political economy in the 1990s, in Nyang'oro, J E & Shaw, T M (eds), *Beyond structural adjustment (Item 179)*, 49–70

198 Singh, H, *The economy of Africa.* Delhi: Kalinga, 1990, 224pp

199 Spooner, N J, Smith, L D, *Structural adjustment policy sequencing in subsaharan Africa.* Rome: FAO, 1991, 129pp

200 Stein, H, Wilson, E J, The political economy of Robert Bates: a critical reading of rational choice in Africa, *World development,* **21,** 6 (1993) 1035–53

201 Stirrat, R L, Developing Africa?, *African affairs,* **92,** 367 (1993) 294–300 (review article)

202 Stymne, J, Reducing the debt burden of subsaharan Africa, in Blomström, M & Lundahl, M (eds), *Economic crisis (Item 119)*, 75–98

203 Susungi, S S, The origins of the development crisis and its aftermath in Africa, in Rimmer, D (ed), *Action in Africa (Item 525)*, 107–114

204 Taiwo, I O, Commodity prices and debt crisis in subsaharan Africa, *Eastern Africa economic review,* **7,** 2 (1991) 39–50

205 Tarp, F, *Stabilisation and structural adjustment: macroeconomic frameworks for analysing the economic crisis in subsaharan Africa.* London: Routledge, 1993, 212pp

206 Thioub, I, Axelle Kabou: *Et si l'Afrique refusait le développment?*; notes critiques, *Université, recherche et développement,* 1 (1993) 49–62

207 Tiyambe Zeleza, The development of African capitalism, *Africa development,* **17,** 1 (1992) 129–36 (review article)

208 UNECA, Reassessing participatory development: conceptual and methodological understanding of the preliminary issues in design elements, *Rural progress,* **11,** 2 (1992) 31–50

209 UNDP (Structural adjustment advisory teams for Africa), *Stabilization and adjustment.* New York: United Nations, 1991, 164pp

210 Zoukpo, R Z, African debt and the need to borrow more, in Rimmer, D (ed), *Action in Africa (Item 525)*, 115–118

Education

See also: 268, 331, 431, 716, 736, 959, 1099, 1100

211 Ajeyalemi, D (ed), *Science and technology education in Africa.* Lagos: University of Lagos Press, 1992, 194pp

212 Bergman, H, Primary school agriculture in subsaharan Africa: main features and structural elements, in Mades, G G (ed), *Primary school agriculture (item 222)*, 53–78

213 Colclough, C, Lewin, K M,

Educating all the children: strategies for primary schooling in the South. Oxford: Clarendon, 1993, 332pp

214 **Davies, L,** Teachers as implementers or subversives, *International journal of educational development,* **13,** 2 (1993) 161–70

215 **Harber, C, Dadey, A,** The job of head teacher in Africa: research and reality, *International journal of educational development,* **13,** 2 (1993) 147–60

216 **Hyde, K A L,** Subsaharan Africa, in King, E M & Hill, M A (eds), *Women's education in developing countries* (Baltimore: Johns Hopkins University Press, 1993), 100–135

217 **Jarousse, J P, Mingat, A,** *L'école primaire en Afrique: analyse pédagogique et économique.* Paris: Harmattan, 1993, 319pp

218 **Johnston, T,** Population, education and sustainable development, *African development review,* **4,** 2 (1992) 201–35

219 **Kellaghan, T, Greaney, T,** *Using examinations to improve education.* Washington: World Bank, 1992, 81pp

220 **Koso-Thomas, K,** Engineering education for the labour market in Africa, in Zymelman, M (ed), *Assessing engineering education in subsaharan Africa* (New York: World Bank, 1993), 43–50

221 **Koul, B N** (ed), *Distance education: a spectrum of case studies.* London: Kogan Page, 1990, 253pp

222 **Mades, G G** (ed), *Primary school agriculture in subsaharan Africa.* Eschborn: Deutsche Gesellschaft für technische Zusammenarbeit, 1992, 290pp

223 **Makany, R A,** Analyse prospective de l'université African, *Afrique 2000,* 12 (1993) 99–109

224 **Mamdani, M,** University crisis and reform: a reflection on the African experience, *Review of African political economy,* 58 (1993) 7–19

225 **Mamdani, M,** University crisis and university reform: a reflection on the African experience, *Codesria bulletin,* 3 (1993) 12–16

226 **Muito, G,** Initiatives and resistances in English-speaking African countries, *International review of education,* **39,** 1 (1993) 97–102

227 **Omolewa, M,** Trends in the study of education in Africa, in Falola, T (ed), *African historiography (Item 385)*, 132–44

228 **Riedmiller, S,** Analysis of the situation of primary school agriculture in subsaharan Africa: policies and practices (summary), in Mades, G G (ed), *Primary school agriculture (item 222)*, 39–43

229 **Saint, W S,** Initiating university reform: experience from subsaharan Africa, *Zimbabwe journal of educational research,* **5,** 1 (1993) 1–20

230 **Samoff, J,** The reconstruction of schooling in Africa, *Comparative education review,* **37,** 2 (1993) 181–222 (review article)

231 **Serpell, R,** *The significance of schooling: life-journeys in an African society.* Cambridge: CUP, 1993, 345pp

232 **Sokona, Y,** Training and human resource development for the energy sector, in Karekezi, S & Mackenzie, G A (eds), *Energy options (Item 796)*, 39–50

233 **Tapsoba, S J M,** Université et développement en Afrique subsaharienne: dilemme des années 90, *Université, recherche et développement,* 1 (1993) 1–24

234 **Toyoda, T,** Aid toward basic education with particular reference to educational development in Africa, *Technology and development,* 6 (1993) 41–56

235 **Zymelman, M** (ed), *Assessing engineering education in subsaharan Africa.* Washington: World Bank, 1993, 167pp

Environment

See also: 317, 358, 728, 796, 1029, 1040, 1047

236 **Barbier, E B, et al,** *Elephants, economics and ivory.* London: Earthscan, 1990, 154pp

237 **Bosquet, B,** Deforestation in subsaharan Africa: logging industry and the African governments, *Africa quarterly,* **33,** (1993) 107–50

238 **Darkoh, M B K,** Land degradation and soil conservation in eastern and southern Africa: a research agenda, *Desertification control bulletin,* 22 (1993) 60–68

239 **Davidson, O R,** Energy and carbon emissions: subsaharan African perspective, *Energy policy,* **21,** 1 (1993) 35–42

240 **Drijver, C A,** People's participation in environmental projects, in Croll, E & Parkin, D (eds), *Bush base, forest farm* (London: Routledge, 1992), 131–45

241 **Erikson, J, et al,** *Save our soils: evaluation of support to soil conservation in Africa.* Stockholm: SIDA, 1993, 80pp

242 **Ghaouti, M,** Endettement et environment in Afrique, *Annual conference (African Society of Comparative and International Law),* **3,** (1991) 189–97

243 **Hansen, S,** Population and the environment, *African development review,* **4,** 2 (1992) 118–64

244 **Hopp, J, Schwiebert, P** (eds), *Wüstenwind und Tropenregen.* Berlin: Reimer, 1993, 332pp

245 **Hudson, N, Cheatle, R J** (eds), *Working with farmers.* London: Intermediate Technology Publications, 1993, 272pp

246 **Korvenoja, T,** The environmental problems and politics of power: review of the African elite, *Nordic journal of African studies,* **2,** 1 (1993) 140–54

247 **Mercier, R,** *La déforestation en Afrique: situation et perspectives.* Aix en Provence: Edisud, 1991, 178pp

248 **Ndiaye, R,** Sciences, techniques et environnement: éléments de réflexion à travers quelques aspects de l'experience ENDA, in Mappa, S (ed), *Ambitions et illusions de la coopération Nord-Sud: Lomé IV* (Paris: Harmattan, 1990), 296–308

249 **Okidi, C O,** *Environment and development in Africa: policy initiatives.* Nairobi: ACTS, 1993, 42pp

250 **Roussel, B,** Les plantes américaines en Afrique tropicale, *Cahiers d'outre-mer,* **45,** 179/180 (1992) 373–386

251 **Savenjie, H, Huijsman, A** (eds), *Making haste slowly: strengthening local environmental management in agricultural development.* Amsterdam: KIT, 1991, 239pp

252 **Talbot, L M, Falloux, F,** *Crisis and opportunity: environment and development in Africa.* London: Earthscan, 1993, 358pp

253 **Thomas, D S G, Middleton, N J,** Salinisation: new perspectives on a major desertification issue, *Journal of arid environments,* **24,** 1 (1993) 95–105

254 **Touré, S M,** Nomadism and pastoralism and the protection of natural resources, in Dellière, R & Symoens, J J (eds), *Agricultural intensification and environment in the tropical areas* (Brussels: Académie royale des sciences d'outre-mer, 1991), 49–71

Finance

See also: 495, 516, 800

255 **Chybire, G K,** Financial control

for the public sector, *African management development forum,* **2,** 1 (1991) 52–56

256 **Essombe-Edimo, J R,** Contribution à l'analyse essentielle de la tontine africaine, *Africa development,* **18,** 2 (1993) 111–22

257 **Gentil, D, Fournier, Y,** *Les paysans peuvent-ils devenirs banquiers? Epargne-crédit en Afrique.* Paris: Syros, 1993, 276pp

258 **Ghura, D, Grennes, T J,** The real exchange rate and macroeconomic performance in subsaharan Africa, *Journal of development economics,* **42,** 1 (1993) 155–74

259 **Honoran, P,** Financial sector failures in Africa, *Journal of modern African studies,* **31,** 1 (1993) 49–65

260 **Ikhide, S I,** *The mobilisation of private savings in Africa: a case study of the role of banking systems in Africa.* Addis Ababa: Economic Commission for Africa, 1992, 29pp

261 **Ikhide, S I,** Positive interest rates, financial deepening and the mobilisation of savings in Africa, *Development policy review,* **11,** 4 (1993) 367–82

262 **Mamaty, I,** Devaluation experiments in subsaharan Africa, *African environment,* **7,** 25–28 (1990) 165–82

263 **Mathis, J,** *Monnaie et banques en Afrique francophone.* Paris: Edicef, 1992, 272pp

264 **Ojo, O O,** *An empirical investigation of capital flight in selected African countries.* Yaounde: African Development Bank, 1993, 34pp

265 **Pelletier, G,** La reconstruction des systèmes bancaires, *Afrique contemporaine,* 166 (1993) 51–56

266 **Plane, P,** *Exchange rate policies in Africa and requirements of stabilisation and structural adjustment.* East Lansing: University of Michigan Centre for Research on Economic Development, 1990, 24pp

267 **Seck, D, El Nii, Y N,** Financial liberalisation in Africa, *World development,* **21,** 11 (1993) 1867–81

Food

See also: 323, 439, 613, 1042, 1071

268 **Abe, L O,** Solving the African food crisis: the role of research training and educational institutions, in Chole, E (ed), *Food crisis (Item 275),* 225–44

269 **Anon,** Hunger in Africa: entitlement approach to food problem analysis, *Rural progress,* **12,** 1 (1993) 24–45

270 **Anon,** Operational approach efficiency of marketing systems as a pre-condition for increased food production at the small farmers' level, *Rural progress,* **12,** 1 (1993) 45–57

271 **Azoulay, G, Dillon, J C,** *La sécurité alimentaire en Afrique: manuel d'analyse et d'élaboration des stratégies.* Paris: Karthala, 1993, 295pp

272 **Bothomani, I B,** Analysis of agricultural policies and causes of the food crisis in Africa: a success case study, in Chole, E (ed), *Food crisis (Item 275),* 98–107

273 **Brandt, H,** Food security aspects in price and market policies for grain-based food systems of subsaharan Africa, in Chole, E (ed), *Food crisis (Item 275),* 137–52

274 **Brown, F, Shiva, V,** Can Africa afford a green revolution?, *Choices,* **2,** 2 (1993) 24–27

275 **Chole, E** (ed), *Food crisis in Africa.* New Delhi: Vikas, 1990, 270pp

276 **de Garine, I** (ed), *Les changements des habitudes et des politiques alimentaires en Afrique: aspects des sciences humaines, naturelles et sociales.* Paris: Publisud, 1991, 278pp

277 **de Waal, A,** War and famine in Africa, *IDS bulletin,* **24,** 4 (1993) 33–40

278 **Desai, M,** Population and poverty in Africa, *African development review,* **4,** 2 (1992) 62–78

279 **Efange, P, Balogun, M J,** The managerial dimension of Africa's food and agricultural crisis, in Chole, E (ed), *Food crisis (Item 275),* 129–36

280 **Ford, D R,** Comparative analysis of specific government policies and examination of critical factors for improved food situation, in Chole, E (ed), *Food crisis (Item 275),* 55–75

281 **Griffon, J, et al,** *Les politiques agricoles et alimentaires in Afrique: méthodes et outils d'analyse et d'aide à la décision.* Paris: Ministère de la coopération, 1991, 186pp

282 **Mukherjee, R,** African food crisis: a solution in sight?, *African currents,* 14 (1991) 18–31

283 **Operations Review Unit,** *Food aid and development: evaluation of Dutch food aid with special reference to subsaharan Africa.* The Hague: Ministry of Foreign Affairs, 1991, 117pp

284 **Orev, Y,** By the bootstraps: a contribution to the problem of enhanced food production in the Sudano-Sahel, *Desertification control bulletin,* 19 (1991) 26–28

285 **Ouedraogo, H, Oben, D,** The formulation, administration and management of price as an incentive to increase food production, in Chole, E (ed), *Food crisis (Item 275),* 111–28

286 **Perez-Escamilla, R,** Update on the breast-feeding situation in Africa, *Nutrition research,* **13,** 5 (1993) 597–609

287 **Quaye, R K,** The political economy of food and hunger: the dialectics of reproduction and production: the African experience, *Scandanavian journal of development alternatives,* **12,** 1 (1993) 5–14

288 **Richards, P,** Famine (and war) in Africa: what do anthropologists have to say?, *Anthropology today,* **8,** 5 (1992) 3–5

289 **Russell, N, Dowswell, C,** Green revolution, *Africa forum,* **2,** 3/4 (1992) 28–31

290 **Sahn, D E,** Implications of structural adjustment for household food security in Africa, *Food, nutrition and agriculture,* **2,** 4 (1992) 18–24

291 **Seaman, J,** Famine mortality in Africa, *IDS bulletin,* **24,** 4 (1993) 27–32

292 **Stephens, T W,** The link between food policy and management in Africa's food crisis, in Chole, E (ed), *Food crisis (Item 275),* 42–51

293 **Tandon, Y,** Policy issues and managment in the African food crisis, in Chole, E (ed), *Food crisis (Item 275),* 27–41

294 **Tekollo, Y,** The African food crisis, in Chole, E (ed), *Food crisis (Item 275),* 3–26

295 **Temu, P E,** Food and agriculture in Africa, in Nyang'oro, J E & Shaw, T M (eds), *Beyond structural adjustment (Item 179),* 83–98

296 **UNECA,** Sustainable development orientation for Africa's increased self-relience in food security: framework for strategic planning and management of the interventions, *Rural progress,* **11,** 2 (1992) 1–30

297 **van Braun, J, et al,** Labour intensive public works for food security in Africa: past experience and future potential, *International labour review,* **131,** 1 (1992) 19–33

298 **Von Braun, J, et al,** *Labor-intensive public works for food security: experience in Africa.* Washington: IFPRI, 1991, 141pp

299 **Wulf, W,** The effects of joint European policy on food self-sufficiency in subsaharan Africa, in Nett, B et al (eds), *Agricultural transformation (Item 1069)*, 223–38

300 **Yeboah, D,** Intra-African food trade: an empirical investigation, *Developing economies,* **31,** 1 (1993) 54–101

Gender

See also: 39, 82, 216, 674, 675, 708, 751, 767, 776, 930, 1062, 1117, 1126

301 **AAWORD,** *Women and reproduction in Africa/Femmes et reproduction en Afrique.* Dakar: Association of African Women for Research and Development, 1992, 150pp

302 **Afrik, T,** Non-literate women in extreme poverty, *UNESCO-Africa,* 6 (1993) 12–20

303 **A'Haleem, A M,** Claiming our bodies and our rights: exploring female circumcision as an act of violence in Africa, in Schuler, M (ed), *Freedom from violence: women's strategies from around the world* (New York: UN Development Fund for Women, 1992), 141–56

304 **Baylies, C, Bujra, J,** Challenging gender inequalities in Africa, *Review of African political economy,* 56 (1993) 3–10

305 **Brokerhoff, M, Eu, H S,** Demographic and socioeconomic determinants of female rural to urban migration in subsaharan Africa, *International migration review,* **27,** 3 (1993) 557–77

306 **Bryceson, D F, Howe, J,** Rural household transport in Africa: reducing the burden on women?, *World development,* **21,** 11 (1993) 1715–28

307 **Bryceson, D, Howe, J,** *Rural household transport in Africa: reducing the burden on women?* Leiden: African Studies Centre, 1993, 38pp

308 **CIADFOR,** *Femmes et développement en Afrique: bibliographie.* Abidjan: Centre interafricain pour le développement de la formation professionelle, 1992, 35pp

309 **Decosas, J, Pedneault, V,** Women and AIDS in Africa: demographic implications for health promotion, *Health policy and planning,* **7,** 3 (1992) 227–33

310 **Edemikpong, N B,** Women and AIDS, in Rothblum, E D & Cole, E (eds), *Women's mental health (item 338)*, 25–34

311 **Ekong, J M,** *Bridewealth, women and reproduction in subsaharan Africa: a theoretical overview.* Bonn: Holos, 1992, 274pp

312 **Eshete, A,** Population and women in development: gender issues in the context of population and development, *African development review,* **4,** 2 (1992) 79–11

313 **Forster, A,** Development and women's political leadership: the missing link in subsaharan Africa, *Fletcher forum of world affairs,* **17,** 2 (1993) 101–116

314 **Geiger, S,** Women and African nationalism, *Journal of women's history,* **2,** 1 (1990) 227–44 (review article)

315 **Gladwin, C H** (ed), *Structural adjustment and African women farmers.* Gainesville: University of Florida Press, 1991, 413pp

316 **Hoppe, K,** Whose life is it anyway? Issues of representation in life narrative texts of African women, *International journal of African historical studies,* **26,** 3 (1993) 623–36

317 **Jackson, C,** Environmentalism and gender interests in the Third World, *Development and change,* **24,** 4 (1993) 649–77

318 Kemp, J, *Women and sexually transmitted diseases in Africa: a discussion of the determinants of risk.* Norwich: Overseas Development Group, University of East Anglia, 1993, 75pp

319 Kerenge, A, *Women in development - training in subsaharan Africa.* Dakar: AAWORD, 1992, 102pp

320 Kettel, B, Gender distortions and development disasters: women and milk in African herding systems, *NWSA journal,* **4,** 1 (1992) 23–41

321 Kisekka, M N, Gender and mental health in Africa, in Rothblum, E D & Cole, E (eds), *Women's mental health (item 338),* 1–13

322 Konde, E, *Reconstructing the political roles of African women: a postrevisionist paradigm.* Boston: African Studies Center, Boston University, 1992, 27pp

323 Koopman, J, The hidden roots of the African food problem: looking within the rural household, in Folbre, N, et al (eds), *Women's work in the world economy* (Basingstoke: Macmillan, 1992), 82–103

324 Lachenmann, G, Frauen und gesellschaftliche Kraft in sozialen Wandel in Afrika, *Peripherie,* **12,** 47/48 (1992) 74–93

325 Ludwar-Ene, G, Reh, M (eds), *Gros-plan sur les femmes africaines.* Bayreuth: Breitinger, 1993, 204pp

326 Maurer, M, et al, *Leben und Arbeit von Frauen, Frauenforschuing und Frauenbewegung in Afrika.* Vienna: Fischer, 1993, 523pp

327 Mazrui, A A, The Black woman and the problem of gender: an African perspective, *Research in African literatures,* **24,** 1 (1993) 87–104

328 McFadden, P, Epistemological issues in conceptualising gender in Africa, *Southern Africa political and economic monthly,* **7,** 2 (1993) 68–72

329 McFadden, P, Sex, sexuality and the problem of AIDS in Africa, in Meena, R (ed), *Gender in southern Africa (item 4399),* 157–95

330 Meena, R, Women and sustainable development, *Southern Africa political and economic monthly,* **5,** 10 (1992) 38–41

331 Milimo, M C, Integrating gender issues into university curricula, *Southern Africa political and economic monthly,* **4,** 11 (1991) 41–44

332 Momsen, J H, Kinnaird, Y (eds), *Different places, different voices: gender and development in Africa, Asia and Latin America.* London: Routledge, 1992, 322pp

333 Mukabi-Kabira, W, et al, *Democratic change in Africa: a women's perspective.* Nairobi: ACTS, 1993, 147pp

334 Nindi, B C, Gender, exploitation development and agricultural transformation in subsaharan Africa, *East African economic review,* **8,** 2 (1992) 123–34

335 Ogundipe-Leslie, M, Beyond hearsay and academic journalism: the Black woman and Mazrui, *Research in African literatures,* **24,** 1 (1993) 105–112

336 Parpart, J, Listening to women's voices: the retrieval and construction of African women's history, *Journal of women's history,* **4,** 2 (1992) 171–79 (review article)

337 Prah, K K (ed), *Culture, gender, science and technology in Africa.* Windhoek: Harp, 1991, 150pp

338 Rothblum, E D, Cole, E (eds), *Women's mental health in Africa.* New York: Haworth, 1990, 98pp

339 Savanne, M A, Women on the march, *Africa forum,* **1,** 2 (1991) 18–22

340 Seidel, G, Women at risk: gender and AIDS in Africa, *Disasters,* **17,** 2 (1993) 133–42

341 Spring, A, Wilde, V, Women farmers, structural adjustment, and FAO's plan of action for integration of women in development, in Gladwin, C H (ed), *Structural adjustment and African women farmers (Item 315),* 387–408

342 Tienda, M, Booth, K, Gender, migration and social chage, *International sociology,* **6,** 1 (1991) 51–72

343 Turshen, M (ed), *Women and health in Africa.* Trenton: Africa World Press, 1992, 250pp

344 Turshen, M, Gender and health in Africa, in Turshen, M (ed), *Women and health (Item 343),* 107–29

345 Turshen, M, Taking women seriously: towards democratic health care in Africa, in Turshen, M (ed), *Women and health (Item 343),* 205–20

346 Weil, G, Caught in the crisis: women in the economies of subsaharan Africa, in Kahne, H & Giele, J Z (eds), *Women's work and women's lives* (Boulder: Westview, 1992), 47–68

347 Welch, C E, Human rights and African women: a comparison of protection under two major treaties, *Human rights quarterly,* **15,** 3 (1993) 549–74

348 Whitehead, A, *Wives and mothers: female farmers in Africa.* Geneva: ILO, 1990, 34pp

349 Young, K, Women and agriculture: the case of subsaharan Africa, in Young, K (ed), *Planning development with women* (London, Macmillan, 1993), 45–65

Geography, human

See also: 742

350 Carter, S E, Jones, P G, A model of the distribution of cassava in Africa, *Applied geography,* **13,** 4 (1993) 353–71

351 Casti Moreschi, E, Nomi et segni per l'Africa italiana: la carta geographica nel progetto coloniale, in Turco, A (ed), *Anno d'Africa (Item 17),* 13–60

352 Casti Moreschi, E, Gaffuri, L, Le 'carte de navigar' e la territorializzione mercantile in Africa, in Turco, A (ed), *Anno d'Africa (Item 17),* 283–301

353 Darkoh, M B K, Geography, research and development in eastern and southern Africa, the challenge, *Journal of eastern African research and development,* **22,** (1992) 1–10

354 Gaffuri, L, Ideologia et geographia: l'Africa coloniale nel contributo dei geographi italiani ai congressi specializzati (1871–1898), in Turco, A (ed), *Anno d'Africa (Item 17),* 61–109

355 Sierig, J (ed), *Staudammbau in Afrika.* Stuttgart: Informationszentrum Raum und Bau, 1990, 54pp

356 Warren, A, Khogali, M, *Assessment of desertification and drought in the Sudano-Sahelian region 1985–1991.* New York: United Nations Sudano-Sahelian Office, 1992, 102pp

357 Young, F W, Regional structure in subsaharan Africa, *Journal of Asian and African studies,* **28,** 1/2 (1993) 30–41

Geography, physical

358 Glantz, M H, *Global warming and regional environmental change: winners and losers in Africa.* Boston: African Studies Center, Boston University, 1992, 30pp

359 Kadzombe, E D, Desertification in Africa, *Malawian geographer,* 29 (1991) 6–13

360 **Waters, H,** Project management of mapping projects in developing countries in Africa, *Cartographic journal,* **340,** 1 (1993) 52–56

Health & welfare services

See also: 309, 343–45, 1139

361 **Beghin, D, Severyns, P,** Population et santé, *African development review,* **4,** 2 (1992) 165–200

362 **Beltrami, V,** Il problema della chirurgia in paese Africano, *Africa (Rome),* **48,** 1 (1993) 124–30

363 **Cabral, A J R,** AIDS in Africa: can the hospitals cope?, *Health policy and planning,* **8,** 2 (1993) 157–60

364 **Carrin, G, Vereecke, M,** *Strategies for health care finance in developing countries, with a focus on community financing in subsaharan Africa.* Basingstoke: Macmillan, 1992, 192pp

365 **Chirac, P, et al,** Drug marketing in French-speaking African countries, *Social science and medicine,* **36,** 12 (1993) 1541–43

366 **de la Moussaye, E, Jacquemot, P,** Politique de santé: les trois options stratégiques, *Afrique contemporaine,* 166 (1993) 15–26

367 **Feierman, S, Janzen, J M** (eds), *The social basis of health and healing in Africa.* Berkeley: University of California Press, 1992, 487pp

368 **Gbesemete, K P,** Preventive measures in the eradication of infectious diseases: what can the African countries learn from the British experience?, *Scandanavian journal of development alternatives,* **12,** 1 (1993) 32–48

369 **Gumede, M V,** *Traditional healers: a medical practitioner's perspective.* Braamfontein: Skotaville, 1990, 237pp

370 **Gwede, C, McDermott, R J,** AIDS In subsaharan Africa: implications for health education, *AIDS education and prevention,* **4,** 4 (1992) 350–61

371 **Jarrett, S W, Ofusu-Amaah, S,** Strengthening health services for MCH in Africa: the first four years of the 'Bamako Initiative', *Health policy and planning,* **7,** 2 (1992) 164–76

372 **Loewenson, R,** Structural adjustment and health policy in Africa, *International journal of health services,* **23,** 4 (1993) 717–30

373 **Logie, D E, Woodroffe, J,** Structural adjustment: the wrong medicine for Africa, *British medical journal,* **307,** 6895 (1993) 41–44

374 **McPake, B, et al,** Community financing of health care in Africa: an evaluation of the Bamako Initiative, *Social science and medicine,* **36,** 11 (1993) 1383–95

375 **McPake, B, et al,** *Implementing the Bamako Initiative in Africa: a review and five case studies.* London: School of Hygiene and Tropical Medecine, 1992, 114pp

376 **Monekosso, G L,** Achieving health for all: a proposal from the African Region of WHO, *Health policy and planning,* **7,** 4 (1992) 364–74

377 **Ochola, P, Kisubi, W,** *Primary health care: experiences in eastern and southern Africa.* Nairobi: African Medical and Research Foundation, 1992, 153pp

378 **Robertson, B M,** *Angels in Africa.* London: Radcliffe Press, 1993, 144pp

379 **Tarimo, E, Creese, A** (eds), *Achieving health for all by the year 2000: midway reports of country experiences.* Geneva: WHO, 1990, 262pp

History, general

See also: 336

380 Alagoa, E J, Oral tradition and oral history, in Falola, T (ed), *African historiography (Item 385)*, 4–13

381 Anignikin, S, Le concept d'histoire nationale: dimensions théorique et fonctions pratiques, *Afrika zamani,* NS 1 (1993) 9–21

382 Austen, M, 'Africanist' historiography and its critics: can there be an autonomous African history?, in Falola, T (ed), *African historiography (Item 385)*, 203–17

383 Barkindo, B, et al, *History of Africa and the wider world.* Ikeja: Longman-Nigeria, 1992, 192pp

384 Fage, J D, Reflections on the genesis of Anglophone African history after World War II, *History in Africa,* **20,** (1993) 15–26

385 Falola, T (ed), *African historiography.* London: Longman, 1993, 244pp

386 Feierman, S, African histories and the dissolution of world history, in Bates R H et al (eds), *Africa and the disciplines (item 3)*, 167–212

387 Jewsiewicki, B, African studies in the 1980s: epistemology and new approaches, in Falola, T (ed), *African historiography (Item 385)*, 218–27

388 Lovejoy, P E, The Ibadan school of history and its critics, in Falola, T (ed), *African historiography (Item 385)*, 195–202

389 McCracken, J, African history in British universities: past, present and future, *African affairs,* **92,** 367 (1993) 239–53

390 McLynn, F, *Hearts of darkness: the European exploration of Africa.* London: Hutchinson, 1992, 390pp

391 Moffa, C, La 'crisi' della storiografia Africanistica orale fra aspetti metodologica e dimensione storio-politica, *Africa (Rome)*, **48,** 3 (1993) 430–46.

392 Perrot, C H (ed), *Le passé de l'Afrique par l'oralité.* Paris: Documentation Française, 1993, 304pp

393 Perrot, C H (ed), *Sources orales de l'histoire de l'Afrique.* Paris: CNRS, 1993, 225pp

394 Tymowski, M, Sociétés sans état et sociétés à organisation étatique en Afrique noire precoloniale, *Africana bulletin,* 40 (1992) 7–52

395 Vansina, J, Some perceptions on the writing of African history: 1948–1992, *Itinerario,* **16,** 1 (1992) 77–91

396 Vansina, J, Unesco and African history, *History in Africa,* **20,** (1993) 337–52

History, early

See also: 2533

397 Aiello, L C, The fossil evidence for modern human origins in Africa: a revised view, *American anthropologist,* **95,** 1 (1993) 73–96

398 Andah, B W, et al, Archaeological investigations on the campus of the University of Ibadan (an unusual salvage experiment), in Andah, B W, et al (eds), *Imprints of West Africa's past (Item 2534)*, 98–108

399 Childs, S T, Killick, D, Indigenous African metallurgy: nature and culture, *Annual review of anthropology,* **22,** (1993) 317–37

400 Gordon, R M, Killick, D J, Adaptation of technology to culture and environment: bloomery iron-smelting in America and Africa, *Technology and culture,* **34,** 2 (1993) 243–70

401 McIntosh, S K, Archaeological heritage management and site inventory systems in Africa, *Journal of field archaeology,* **20,** 4 (1993) 500–504

402 Ridinger, R B M, *African archaeology: a selected bibliography.* New York: Hall, 1993, 311pp

403 Shott, M J, On recent trends in the anthropology of foragers - Kalahari revisionism and its archaeological implications, *Man,* **27,** 4 (1992) 848–71

404 Willoughby, P R, The Middle Stone Age in Africa and modern human origins, *African archaeological review,* **11,** (1993) 3–20

History, C18th

405 Bisseck, R E, Contribution de la Révolution de 1789 à l'émanicipation des peuples d'Afrique, in Kom, A & Ngoué, L (eds), *Le Code noir (Item 409)*, 111–119

406 Bley, H, et al (ed), *Sklaverei in Afrika: afrikanische Gesellschaften im Zusammenhang von europäischer und interner Sklaverei und Sklavenhandel.* Pfaffenweiler: Centaurus, 1991, 183pp

407 Brauer, R W, Can one glean contributions from the writings of the Arabic geographers towards the establishment of chronologies of events in pre-literate Africa in the Middle Ages?, in Harrak, A (ed), *Contacts between cultures (Item 1181)*, 45–51

408 dos Santos Lopes, M, *Afrika: eine neue Welt in deutschen Schriften des 16 und 17 Jahrhunderts.* Stuttgart: Steiner, 1992, 285pp

409 Kom, A, Ngoué, L (eds), *Le Code noir et l'Afrique.* Ivry: Nouvelles du Sud, 1991, 309pp

410 Lo, I, Les mines de sel de Taghazza dans les rivalités entre le Maroc et l'empire Songhay au 16è siècle, in Harrak, A (ed), *Contacts between cultures (Item 1181)*, 19–26

411 Russell-Wood, A J R, *A world on the move: the Portuguese in Africa, Asia and America, 1415–1808.* Manchester: Carcanet, 1992, 289pp

History, C19th

412 Hangula, L, *Die Grenzziehungen in den afrikanischen Kolonien Englands, Deutchlands und Portugals im Zeitalter des Imperialismus 1880–1914.* Frankfurt: Lang, 1991, 266pp

413 Hopkins, A G, 'Blundering and plundering': the scramble for Africa relived, *Journal of African history,* **34,** 3 (1993) 489–94 (review article)

414 Institut d'histoire des pays d'outre-mer (ed), *Histoire d'outre-mer: mélanges en l'honneur de Jean-Louis Miège.* Aix-en-Provence: Publications de l'Université de Provence, 1992, 2 vols, 714pp

415 Klein, M A (ed), *Breaking the chains: slavery, bondage and emancipation in Africa and Asia.* Madison: University of Wisconsin Press, 1993, 222pp

416 Koponen, J, The partition of Africa: a scramble or a mirage?, *Nordic journal of African studies,* **2,** 1 (1993) 117–39

417 Smitek, Z, et al, Notes sur les voyageurs slovènes, croates et serves en Afrique avant 1918 et sur les collections, *Revue française d'histoire d'outre-mer,* **80,** 300 (1993) 389–408

418 Stacher, I, Frühe Formen des antikolonialen Widerstandes in Afrika, in Feldbauer, P & Puhle, H J (eds), *Bauern in Widerstand* Vienna: Bohlau, 1992, 153–73

History, C20th

See also: 412, 414

419 Afigbo, A E, Colonial historiography, in Falola, T (ed), *African historiography (Item 385)*, 39–51

420 Antunes, J F, *O factor Africano 1890–1990.* Venda Nova: Bertrand, 1990, 149pp

421 **Bammann, H,** *Koinonia in Afrika: Koinonia bei Bruno Gutman (Tansania) und bei den Hermannsburger Missionaren im südlichen Afrika.* Bad Liebenzell: Liebenzeller Mission, 1990, 127pp
422 **Ekechi, F K,** Studies on missions in Africa, in Falola, T (ed), *African historiography (Item 385)*, 145–65
423 **Hargreaves, J D,** The Comintern and anticolonialism: new research opportunities, *African affairs,* **92,** 367 (1993) 255–61
424 **Kinda, N,** Les États-Unis et le nationalisme en Afrique noire à l'épreuve de la décolonisation, *Revue française d'histoire d'outre-mer,* **79,** 297 (1992) 533–555
425 **Lazarus, N,** Disavowing decolonisation: Fanon, nationalism, and the problematic of representation in current theories of colonial discourse, *Research in African literatures,* **24,** 4 (1993) 69–98
426 **Manchuelle, F,** Le rôle des Antillais dans l'apparition du nationalisme culturel en Afrique noire francophone, *Cahiers d'études africains,* **32,** 127 (1992) 375–408
427 **McClellan, W,** Africans and Black Americans in the Comintern schools, 1925–1934, *International journal of African historical studies,* **26,** 2 (1993) 371–90
428 **Ndege, P O,** Forces of history and the quest for freedom: a comparative analysis of the 1789 French revolution and African nationalism, *Makerere history journal,* **5,** 1/2 (1990-/91) 1–24
429 **Nwaubani, E,** The British Labour Party, the 'dual mandate' and Africa, 1945–51, *Transafrican journal of history,* 21 (1992) 93–110
430 **Nwaubani, E,** Getting behind a myth: the British Labour Party and decolonisation in Africa, 1945–51, *Australian journal of politics and history,* **39,** 2 (1993) 197–216
431 **Seck, P I,** *La stratégie culturelle de la France en Afrique: l'enseignement coloniale (1817–1960).* Paris: Harmattan, 1993, 240pp
432 **Skinner, E P,** *African Americans and US policy toward Africa 1850–1924: in defence of black nationality.* Washington: Howard University Press, 1992, 555pp
433 **Soyinka, W,** *The Blackman and the veil.* Accra: Sedco, 1993, 80pp
434 **Vaughan, M,** Madness and colonialism, colonialism as madness: re-reading Fanon - colonial discourse and the psychopathology of colonialism, *Paideuma,* **39,** (1993) 45–55
435 **Wedi-Pascha, B,** *Die deutsche Mittel-Afrika Politik.* Pfaffenweiler: Centaurus, 1992, 352pp

Industry & trade

See also: 174, 237, 306, 307, 479, 517, 1072, 1145

436 **Adebulugbe, A O,** Energy and efficiency in industry: a regional perspective, in Karekezi, S & Mackenzie, G A (eds), *Energy options (Item 796)*, 95–105
437 **Adeyemo, D O,** The political economy of public enterprises: an epitome of contradictions, *Review of African political affairs,* **6,** 1/2 (1992) 56–70
438 **Assaf, D,** UNIDO studies on industrial rehabilitation in Africa, in Kirkpatrick, C (ed), *Project rehabilitation (Item 164)*, 103–20
439 **Beynon, J, et al,** Market reform and private trade in eastern and southern Africa, *Food policy,* **17,** 6 (1992) 399–408
440 **Blunt, P, Jones, M L,** *Managing organisations in Africa.* Berlin: De Gruyter, 1992, 356pp
441 **Boehm, U, Kappel, R** (eds), *Kleintriebe des informellen Sektoren*

und Ausbildung im subsaharaischen Afrika. Hamburg: Institut für Afrika-Kunde, 1990, 231pp

442 **Davidson, O R,** Opportunities for energy efficiency in the transport sector, in Karekezi, S & Mackenzie, G A (eds), *Energy options (Item 796)*, 106–27

443 **de Villers, G,** Le pauvre, le hors-la-loi, le métis: la question de 'l'économie informelle' en Afrique, *Cahiers du CEDAF,* 6 (1992) 1–88

444 **Drum, B,** Privatisation in Africa, *Columbia journal of world business,* **28,** 1 (1993) 144–49

445 **Duquesne, B, Musyck, B,** The informal sector in Africa: a theoretical approach and case-study - the 'borom-sarets' of Zinguinchor, *African environment,* **7,** 25–28 (1990) 411–26

446 **Fauré, Y A,** *Entrepreneurs et entreprises d'Afrique subsaharienne: sélection bibliographique.* Talence: CEAN, Bordeaux University, 1993, 26pp

447 **Feldmann, P, et al** (eds), *Was boomt in informellen Sektor? Berufsbilding in informellen Sektor: Beispiele aus Afrika, Asien und Latinamerika.* Saarbrucken: Breitenbach, 1992, 238pp

448 **Gendarme, R,** L'industrialisation en Afrique sub-saharienne: deaux voies de recherche inexplorées, *Mondes en développement,* **20,** 77/78 (1992) 15–23

449 **Gordham, K,** Industrial development strategies, in Onimode, B (ed), *The African response (Item 186)*, 23–31

450 **Henry, A,** Les entreprises en Afrique: des progrès méconnus, *Afrique 2000,* 14 (1993) 83–92

451 **Henry, A,** Les privatisations, nouvelle "sorcellerie" des blancs?, *Afrique contemporaine,* 165 (1993) 10–18

452 **Huybrechts, A,** Le développement des petits et moyennes entreprises dans les pays en voie de développement et en Afrique noire en particulier, *Bulletin des séances,* **37,** 1 (1991) 133–42

453 **Jerome, A,** African countries and the prospects for export oriented industrialisation in the 1990s and beyond, *Scandanavian journal of development alternatives,* **12,** 1 (1993) 89–96

454 **Khennas, S** (ed), *Industrialisation, mineral resources and energy in Africa.* Dakar: Codesria, 1992, 340pp

455 **Lall, S,** Trade policies for development: a policy prescription for Africa, *Development policy review,* **11,** 1 (1993) 47–65

456 **Le Brun, O,** L'éléphant et les fourmis. L'état et les petites activités marchandes: problématique des politiques de développement du secteur informel en Afrique, *Cahiers du CEDAF,* 3/4 (1992) 249–62

457 **Mayor Gaalba, E,** Rationalisation of imports, refineries and distribution of petroleum in subsaharan Africa, *Natural resources forum,* **17,** 2 (1993) 109–116

458 **Pack, H,** Productivity and industrial development in subsaharan Africa, *World development,* **21,** 1 (1993) 1–16

459 **Rizet, C, Hine, J L,** A comparison of the costs and productivity of road freight transport in Africa and Pakistan, *Transport reviews,* **13,** 2 (1993) 151–65

460 **Scott, C V,** International capital and the oil-producing states in Africa: an analysis of Angola, Nigeria and Algeria, *Journal of developing societies,* **8,** 2 (1992) 179–93

461 Selassie, H G, Hill, R W, Factors determining joint venture formation in the agribusiness sector of subsaharan African countries, *Journal of international food and agribusiness marketing,* **5,** 1 (1993) 73–93

462 Takyi-Asiedu, S, Some sociocultural factors retarding entrepreneurial activity in subsaharan Africa, *Journal of business venturing,* **8,** 2 (1993) 91–98

463 van der Laan, H L, In defence of export marketing boards, *Aproma,* 27–29 (1992) 34–40

464 Villers, G, Petite économie marchange et phénomènes informels en Afrique, *Cahiers du CEDAF,* 3/4 (1992) 1–15

465 Weiss, J, Rehabilitation of manufacturing in subsaharan Africa: some macroeconomic issues, in Kirkpatrick, C (ed), *Project rehabilitation (Item 164)*, 175–95

International economic relations

See also: 121, 142, 178, 186, 234, 283, 299, 300, 584, 609, 642, 848, 872, 957, 1032, 1050, 1084, 4965

466 Adotevi, S S, Les fondations culturelles de l'intégration économique régionale en Afrique, *Afrique 2000,* 13 (1993) 89–96

467 Aghrout, A, Africa's experiences with regional co-operation and integration: assessing some groupings, *Africa (Rome),* **47,** 4 (1992) 563–586

468 Agyemang, A A, Protecting natural resource contracts from national measures in Africa: some comparisons with the Australian experience, *Comparative and international law journal of southern Africa,* **25,** 3 (1992) 273–92

469 Amale, S A, Ojo, S, Unequal global interdependence, the debt problem and the crisis of African political economy, *Quarterly journal of administration,* **25,** 3/4 (1991) 273–90

470 Arnould, D, Les options OTM à long terme sur marchandise: une innovation financière pour les pays endettés d'Afrique sub-saharienne, *Mondes en développement,* **20,** 77/78 (1992) 75–99

471 Asiwaju, A I, Borders and borderlands as lynchpins for regional integration in Africa: lessons of the European experience, *Africa development,* **17,** 1 (1992) 45–63

472 Bach, D, Europe-Afrique: le régionalisme sans co-prospérité, *Politique africaine,* 49 (1993) 31–46

473 Bach, D, Un ancrage à la dérive: la Convention de Lomé, *Tiers Monde,* **33,** 136 (1993) 748–58

474 Baofo-Arthur, K, Europe 1992: a challenge to subsaharan African development, *Africa development,* **17,** 2 (1992) 27–43

475 Barya, J J B, The new political conditionaltity of aid: an independent view from Africa, *IDS bulletin,* **24,** 1 (1993) 16–232

476 Berg, E (ed), *Rethinking technical cooperation: reforms for capacity building in Africa.* New York: UNDP, 1993, 336pp

477 Berg, E, Reappraising export prospects: regional trade arrangements, in Rimmer, D (ed), *Action in Africa (Item 525)*, 58–71

478 Brunel, S, *Le gaspillage de l'aide publique.* Paris: Seuil, 1993, 185pp

479 Burisch, M, *Foreign trade liberalization and the development for small-scale enterprise: an African case.* Copenhagen: Institut for International konomi og Virksomhedsledelse, 1993, 35pp

480 Bylka, T, Official and unofficial aid for subsaharan Africa, *Africana bulletin,* 40 (1992) 93–104

481 **Chikeka, C O,** *Africa and the European Economic Community, 1957–1992.* Lewiston: Mellen, 1993, 224pp

482 **Coleman, J R, Thigpen, E,** *Should subsaharan Africa expand cotton exports?* Washington: World Bank, 1993, 40pp

483 **Cook, A,** CDC in francophone Africa, *Bulletin of francophone Africa,* 2 (1993) 43–55

484 **Coquet, B, et al,** L'Europe et l'Afrique: flux et reflux, *Politique africaine,* 49 (1993) 6–30

485 **Derrick, J,** En route to integration, *Africa forum,* **1,** 4 (1991) 39–42

486 **Dirar, A A,** The Fraser Report and the OAU's position, in Onimode, B (ed), *The African response (Item 186),* 149–53

487 **Duncan, R C,** Agricultural export prospects for subsaharan Africa, *Development policy review,* **11,** 1 (1993) 31–45

488 **Ekanza, S-P,** La Communauté européenne et ses rapports avec l'Afrique noire depuis 1957, *Civilisations,* **40,** 2 (1992) 222–231

489 **Engelhard, P, et al,** The African debt, Third World debt, and world economic growth, *African environment,* **7,** 25–28 (1990) 309–34

490 **Estur, G,** African cotton: how to protect its market position, *Aproma,* 27–29 (1992) 21–25

491 **Fayolle, R** (ed), *Avec l'Afrique: les relations entre la France et l'Afrique subsaharienne francophone.* Paris: Cercle Condorcet, 1991, 64pp

492 **Fogui, J P,** L'ambiguité du discours française sur la coopération (1958–1981), *Afrique 2000,* 12 (1993) 53–56

493 **Foroutan, F, Pritchett, L,** Intra-subsaharan African trade: is it too little?, *Journal of African economics,* **2,** 1 (1993) 94–105

494 **Gastinne, J,** *La coopération française en direction de l'Afrique, des differentes formes, recherches de complémentarités.* Paris: Direction des journaux officiels, 1991, 135pp

495 **Géradin, H,** Intégration en Afrique, intégration en Europe: crise économique ou crise d'adaptation dans la Zone franc?, *Mondes en développement,* **20,** 77/78 (1992) 25–57

496 **Henry, C M,** A statistical portrait of the balance of trade of subsaharan Africa, *East African economic review,* **8,** 1 (1992) 26–40

497 **Herbst, J,** *US economic policy towards Africa.* New York: Council on Foreign Relations, 1993, 81pp

498 **Hermes, N, Lensink, R,** The magnitude and determinants of capital flight: the case for six subsaharan African countries, *Economist,* **140,** 4 (1992) 515–30

499 **Hickman, J,** Cue taking and distribution of Japanese ODA among African countries, *African development review,* **5,** 1 (1993) 62–69

500 **Husain, I,** Trade, aid and investment in subsaharan Africa, in Rimmer, D (ed), *Action in Africa (Item 525),* 75–106

501 **Ihonvbere, J O,** The dynamics of change in eastern Europe and their implications for Africa's international economic relations, *Nigerian journal of international affairs,* **16,** 2 (1990) 24–41

502 **Jakobeit, C,** Die CFA-Franczone vor dem Ende?: Wirtschafts-, Wahrungs-, Liquiditäts- und Bankenkrise im frankophonen Afrika, *Afrika Jahrbuch 1990,* 71–78

503 **Kanpur, R,** EC-Africa relations: a review article, *Journal of African economics,* **2,** 3 (1993) 434–46

504 **Kühne, W, Mair, S,** *European-African relations: challenges in the 1990s.* Ebenhausen: Eggenberg, 1992, 65pp

505 **Kwarteng, C O,** Africa and the European challenge after 1992, *International social science journal,* **45,** 137 (1993) 405–414

506 **Lelart, M,** La zone franc face à Maastricht, *Tiers Monde,* **33,** 136 (1993) 881–901

507 **Lele, U, Nabi, I** (eds), *Transitions in development: the role of aid and commercial flows.* San Francisco: ICS Press, 1991, 535pp

508 **Mehta, S C,** Indian joint ventures in Africa, *Ind-Africana,* **4,** 2 (1991) 52–68

509 **Mulikita, M N,** *The PTA and subregional integration in eastern and southern Africa: a comparative evaluation.* Konstanz: Hartung-Gorre, 1992, 439pp

510 **Muzan, A O,** The feasibility of economic integration in Africa by the year 2000, *African administrative studies,* 39 (1992) 59–76

511 **Ndulo, M,** Harmonisation of trade laws in the African economic community, *International and comparative law quarterly,* **42,** 1 (1993) 101–118

512 **Ngoy, B S,** Les nouvelles relations Est-Ouest et leurs incidences sur la coopération EEC-ACP, *Africa development,* **18,** 3 (1993) 21–36

513 **Ntahuminga, S,** *L'état juridique et l'activité de la Communauté économique des pays des Grands Lacs (CEPGL) dans l'ordre socialement africain.* Rome: Pontifica Universita Lateranese, 1992, 199pp

514 **Odock, C,** France, Africa and the EEC: the Lomé Conventions and the growth of French influence in Africa, in Jacob, H J & Omar, M (eds), *France and Nigeria (Item 3395),* 35–52

515 **Onah, F E** (ed), *The challenges of African economic integration.* Ibadan: Nigerian Economic Society, 1992, 172pp

516 **Ondo Ossa, A,** Taux de change du franc CFA et construction européenne, *Mondes en développement,* **20,** 77/78 (1992) 59–74

517 **O'Neill, D,** Mining investment in Africa: an Australian perspective, *Natural resources forum,* **17,** 4 (1993) 262–72

518 **Onimode, B,** Comments on the Fraser Report, in Onimode, B (ed), *The African response (Item 186),* 154–61

519 **Oyewumi, A,** The plan of plans, *Africa forum,* **1,** 4 (1991) 45–48

520 **Philippe, B,** Quelques pistes pour un réexamen de la politique commerciale de la Communauté européenne dans le cadre de la Convention de Lomé, *Mondes en développement,* **20,** 77/78 (1992) 169–76

521 **Pijls, N,** Die mid-term review van het Lomé IV-verdrag: financiele facelift of werkelijke verbetering?, *Internationale spectator,* **47,** 9 (1993) 515–20

522 **Prouvez, N,** La coopération commerciale ACP-CE: cadre, facteurs déterminants et perspectives d'avenir, *Annual conference (African Society of Comparative and International Law),* **3,** (1991) 155–69

523 **Quelch, J A, Austin, J E,** Should multinationals invest in Africa?, *Sloan management review,* **34,** 3 (1993) 107–119

524 **Rattse, J,** The asymmetric relationship between subsaharan Africa and the rest of the world: a theoretical analysis of the role of imports compression, *East African economic review,* **8,** 1 (1992) 1–11

525 **Rimmer, D** (ed), *Action in Africa.* London: Currey, 1993, 179pp

526 **Rimmer, D,** Introduction: the agenda of reform, in Rimmer, D (ed), *Action in Africa (Item 525)*, 1–19

527 **Robinson, M,** Aid, democracy and political conditionality in subsaharan Africa, *European journal of development research,* **5,** 1 (1993) 85–99

528 **Robson, P,** The new regionalism and developing countries, *Journal of common market studies,* **31,** 3 (1993) 329–48

529 **Rugiireheh-Runaku, J S M N,** The dilemma of the African Economic Community by AD 2025, *Ufahamu,* **19,** 2/3 (1990/1991) 3–21

530 **Schreurs, R,** L'Eurafrique dans les negotiations du Traité de Rome, 1956–1957, *Politique africaine,* 49 (1993) 82–92

531 **Sincere, R,** *Sowing the seeds of free enterprise: the politics of US economic aid in Africa.* Washington: International Freedom Foundation, 1990, 153pp

532 **Sommers, L M, Assefa Mehretu,** Trade patterns and trends in the African-European trading area: lessons for subsaharan Africa from the era of the Lomé accords 1975–1988, *Africa development,* **17,** 2 (1992) 5–26

533 **Sono, T,** *Japan and Africa.* Pretoria: HSRC, 1993, 435pp

534 **Spranger, C D,** Development cooperation with Africa, *Aussenpolitik,* **44,** 1 (1993) 3–12

535 **Stevens, C,** Le vent du changement pour l'Afrique: la CE et le développement, *Politique africaine,* 49 (1993) 63–81

536 **Svedberg, P,** Trade compression and economic decline in subsaharan Africa, in Blomström, M & Lundahl, M (eds), *Economic crisis (Item 119)*, 21–40

537 **Takirambudde, P N,** Rethinking regional integration structures and strategies in eastern and southern Africa, *Africa insight,* **23,** 3 (1993) 149–58

538 **Tomori, S,** Towards a solution to Africa's commodity problems, in Onimode, B (ed), *The African response (Item 186)*, 145–48

539 **van der Laan, H L,** Boosting agricultural exports? A 'marketing channel' perspective on an African dilemma, *African affairs,* **92,** 367 (1993) 173–201

540 **van Walraven, K,** Some aspects of regional economic integration in Africa, *Hague yearbook of international law,* **4,** (1991) 106–26

541 **Wilson, E J,** French support for structural adjustment programmes in Africa, *World development,* **21,** 3 (1993) 331–47

International relations

See also: 424, 491, 514, 533, 843, 874, 904, 939, 5005

542 **Adade, C Q,** Russia, after the Cold War: the ex-Soviet media and Africa, *Race and class,* **35,** 2 (1993) 86–95

543 **Adedeji, A,** Stable foundations, *Africa forum,* **1,** 3 (1991) 52–55

544 **Ajayi, J F A,** The search for a new world order: an African perspective, in Lundestad, G & Westad, O A (eds), *Beyond the cold war: new dimensions in international relations* (Oslo: Scandinavian University Press, 1993), 71–84

545 **Ake, C,** *The new world order: a view from the South.* Lagos: Malthouse, 1992, 62pp

546 **Amate, C O C,** The OAU and the conflicts in Africa, *Africa quarterly,* **33,** (1993) 59–75

547 **Amoo, S G,** Role of the OAU: past, present and future, in Smock, D R (ed), *Making war and waging peace (Item 600)*, 239–61

548 **Ate, B E,** Before perestroika: African and American perceptions of regional security in Africa, *Nigerian journal of international affairs,* **18,** 1 (1992) 120–30
549 **Bangoura, D,** A la recherche d'une stratégie-espace, facteur de la paix en Afrique, *Afrique 2000,* 15 (1993) 102–32
550 **Bangoura, D,** Le role juridique, politique et militaire de l'OUA en matière de defence, *Cahiers de l'IPAG,* 10 (1990) 26–73
551 **Bayart, J F,** La politique africaine de la France: de Charybe à Scylla?, *Politique africaine,* 49 (1993) 133–36
552 **Biad, A,** La résolution des conflits en Afrique: bilan et perspectives, *Annual conference (African Society of International and Comparative Law),* **4,** (1992) 255–264
553 **Boutros- Ghali, B,** Les Nations Unies et l'Afrique, *Afrique 2000,* 14 (1993) 5–17
554 **Campbell, H,** The Gulf War, Africans, and the new world disorder, *Southern Africa political and economic monthly,* **4,** 9 (1991) 25–30
555 **Chalker, L,** The proper role of government, in Rimmer, D (ed), *Action in Africa (Item 525),* 23–28
556 **Clark, E,** *African international relations: the post-cold war era.* Vienna: Lagos, 1991, 212pp
557 **Danfulani, S A,** Confidence building and regional security diplomacy in South Africa, *International social science journal,* **45,** 135 (1993) 83–90
559 **Domergue-Cloarec, D,** Sécurité internationale et coopération: l'Afrique subsaharienne, *Civilisations,* **40,** 2 (1992) 253–266
560 **Doza, B,** *Liberté confisquée: le complot franco-africain.* Paris: BibliEurope, 1991, 334pp
561 **Eribo, F,** Coverage of Africa South of the Sahara by *Pravda, Isvestia, Trud* and *Selskaya Zhizn,* 1979–1987: a content analysis, *Journalism quarterly,* **70,** 1 (1993) 51–57
562 **Fawole, W A,** The Soviet Union and subsaharan Africa in retrospect, *Journal of Asian and African affairs,* **4,** 2 (1993) 33–51
563 **Gambari, U,** Africa and the United Nations, *Africa forum,* **1,** 2 (1991) 62–66
564 **Gonidec, P F,** *L'OUA trente ans après.* Paris: Karthala, 1993, 160pp
565 **Herskovitz, J,** USA and Africa: time to look again, *Africa forum,* **2,** 3/4 (1992) 16–19
566 **Hufmeier, R,** Deutsche-Afrika Beziehungen 1992, *Afrika Jahrbuch 1992,* 14–21
567 **Ibrahim, I,** Towards a Nigerian perspective on the French problematic in Africa, in Jacob, H J & Omar, M (eds), *France and Nigeria (Item 3395),* 11–34
568 **Ihonvbere, J O, Turner, T,** Africa in the post-containment era: constraints, pressures and prospects for the 21st century, *Africa quarterly,* **33,** (1993) 33–58
569 **Ihonvbere, J O, Turner, T,** Africa in the post-containment era: constraints, pressures and prospects for the 21st century, *Round table,* **82,** 328 (1993) 443–60
570 **Imobighe, T O,** Security in subsaharan Africa, in Singh, J, Bernauer T (eds), *Security of Third World countries* (Aldershot: Dartmount, 1993), 83–108
571 **Jackson, R H,** The security dilemma in Africa, in Job, B L (ed), *The insecurity dilemma* (Boulder: Lynne Reiner, 1992), 81–94
572 **Jinadu, L A,** Regional integration in Africa, theoretical

perspectives and their implications, *Southern Africa political and economic monthly,* **5,** 9 (1992) 8–11

573 **Kamgang, H,** *Au-delà de la conférence nationale: pour les Etats-Unis d'Afrique.* Paris: Harmattan, 1993, 252pp

574 **Karangwa, E,** L'indispensable utopie de l'unité africaine, *Dialogue,* 160 (1992) 3–18

575 **Keller, E J,** Towards a new African order?, *Africa insight,* **23,** 3 (1993) 124–28

576 **Keller, E J,** Towards a new African order? Presidential address to the 1992 annual meeting of the ASA, *African studies review,* **36,** 2 (1993) 1–10

577 **Kum'a Ndumbe,** *Was will Bonn in Afrika?: zur Afrikapolitik der Bundesrepublik Deutschland.* Pfaffenweiler: Centaurus, 1992, 416pp

578 **Lancaster, C,** *United States and Africa: into the twenty-first century.* Washington: Overseas Development Council, 1993, 62pp

579 **Makolo Muswaswa,** Francophonie, démocratie et développement: co-responsabilité ou miroir aux alouettes?, *Zaire-Afrique,* **33,** 274 (1993) 211–23

580 **McKesson, J A,** France and Africa: the evolving saga, *French politics and society,* **11,** 2 (1993) 55–69

581 **Michaels, M,** Retreat from Africa, *Foreign affairs,* **72,** 1 (1993) 93–108

582 **Michailof, S** (ed), *La France et l'Afrique.* Paris: Karthala, 1993, 512pp

583 **Mosha, F G N,** One step forward, *Africa forum,* **1,** 3 (1991) 45–48

584 **Neugebauer, M T,** *Die österreichisch-afrikanischen Beziehungen seit 1955.* Vienna: Bohlau, 1992, 529pp

585 **Ofiemun, O,** Nkrumah of Africa, *Africa forum,* **2,** 2 (1992) 18–21

586 **Ofiemun, O,** Nkrumah: l'africain, *Afrique 2000,* 13 (1993) 115–22

587 **Otobo, E E,** The Gulf crisis: impact, implications and lessons for Africa, *African review,* **18,** 1/2 (1991) 57–70

588 **Otobo, E E,** When the elephants..., *Africa forum,* **2,** 2 (1992) 44–48

589 **Owoeye, J,** *Japan's policy in Africa.* Lewiston: Mellen, 1992, 186pp

590 **Pondi, J E,** *Relations internationales africaines: bibliographie annotée de vingt ans de recherche à l'Institut de relations internationales du Cameroun.* Berne: Lang, 1993, 225pp

591 **Rhee, S H,** *La Corée du Sud et l'Afrique.* Talence: CEAN, Université de Bordeaux, 1993, 23pp

592 **Rotberg, R I,** The Clinton administration and Africa, *Current history,* **92,** 574 (1993) 193–97

593 **Rouvez, A,** French, British and Belgian military involvement, in Smock, D R (ed), *Making war and waging peace (Item 600)*, 27–51

594 **Rwomire, A,** The role of the university in regional integration and cooperation, an African perspective, *Eastern African social science research review,* **6,** 1 (1990) 61–72

595 **Sawant, A B,** The Gulf crisis and subsaharan Africa: attitudes, responses and impact, *African currents,* 13 (1991) 5–17

596 **Schleicher, H G,** Die Afrikapolitik der DDR: Versuch einer Nachbetrachtung, *Afrika Jahrbuch 1990,* 32–45

597 **Schraeder, P J,** Reviewing the study of US policy towards Africa, *Third world quarterly,* **14,** 4 (1993) 775–86

598 Semilinko, S, Francophone summit: question of identity, *Africa forum,* **2,** 3/4 (1992) 20–23

599 Sil, N P, An African image of India, *Africa quarterly,* **33,** (1993) 25–33

600 Smock, D R (ed), *Making war and waging peace: foreign intervention in Africa.* Washington: United States Institute of Peace Press, 1993, 290pp

601 Smock, D R, Gregorian, H, Introduction, in Smock, D R (ed), *Making war and waging peace (Item 409)*, 1–26

602 Tesfatsion Medhanie (ed), *The shrinking deadlock? Developments in East/West relations and Africa.* Frankfurt: Interkulturelle Kommunikation, 1992, 101pp

603 Venter, D, *South Africa and the African comity of nations.* Pretoria: Africa Institute, 1993, 72pp

604 Volman, D, Africa and the new world order, *Journal of modern African studies,* **31,** 1 (1993) 1–30

605 Weil, R, Somalia in perspective: when the saints come marching in, *Review of African political economy,* 57 (1993) 103–109

606 Zartman, I W (ed), *Europe and Africa: the new phase.* Boulder: Lynne Reiner, 1993, 211pp

Labour & manpower

See also: 1140, 1142

607 Bonnet, M, Child labour in Africa, *International labour review,* **132,** 3 (1993) 371–89

608 Jamal, V, Weeks, J, *Africa misunderstood: or whatever happened to the rural-urban gap?* Basingstoke: Macmillan, 1993, 180pp

609 Kaijage, F J (ed), *Management consulting in Africa: utilising local experiences.* West Hartford: Kumarian, 1993, 213pp

610 Logan, J B, The brain-drain of professional, technical and kindred workers from developing countries - some lessons from the Africa-United States flow of professions (1980–1989), *International migration,* **30,** 3–4 (1992) 289–312

611 Sunmuno, H, Towards human centred development, in Onimode, B (ed), *The African response (Item 186)*, 103–107

612 Vandemoortele, J, *Employment issues in subsaharan Africa.* Nairobi: Initiatives, 1991, 41pp

613 von Braun, J, et al, Labor-intensive public works for food security in Africa: past experience and future potential, *International labour review,* **131,** 1 (1992) 9–34

Language

See also: 691

614 Andah, B W, Cultural literacy in Africa: an anthropological perspective, in Andah, B W, et al (eds), *Imprints of West Africa's past (Item 2534)*, 48–70

615 Chimhundu, H, The vernacularisation of African languages after independence, *Diogenes,* 161 (1993) 35–42

616 Dirven, R, The use of languages and language policy in Africa: goals of the LICCA program, *International journal of the sociology of language,* 100–101 (1993) 179–89

617 Djite, P G, Language and development in Africa, *International journal of the sociology of language,* 100–101 (1993) 149–66

618 Goke-Pariola, A, *The role of language in the struggle for power and legitimacy in Africa.* Lewiston: Mellen, 1993, 201pp

619 Lodhi, A Y, The language situation in Africa today, *Nordic journal of African studies,* **2,** 1 (1993) 79–86

620 **Massamba, D P B,** Language as a portrayal of culture, *Journal of Asian and African studies* (Tokyo), 43 (1992) 95–107

621 **Mazrui, A,** Language and the quest for liberation in Africa: the legacy of Frantz Fanon, *Third world quarterly,* **14,** 2 (1993) 351–63

622 **Mukama, R G,** Why the African national languages can never break through, *Journal of Asian and African studies* (Tokyo), 43 (1992) 45–62

623 **Myers-Scotton, C,** Elite closure as a powerful language strategy: the African case, *International journal of the sociology of language,* 103 (1993) 149–63

624 **Myers-Scotton, C,** *Social motivations for code-switching: evidence from Africa.* Oxford: Clarendon, 1993, 177pp

625 **Nama, C A,** Historical, theoretical and terminological perspectives of translation in Africa, *Meta,* **38,** 3 (1993) 414–25

626 **Schmeid, J** (ed), *English in East and Central Africa. Vol. 2.* Bayreuth: Bayreuth University, 1992, 113pp

627 **Swilla, I N,** The relation of local and foreign languages to national needs in Africa, *Journal of multilingual and multicultural development,* **13,** 6 (1993) 505–14

Law

See also: 347, 468, 511, 825

628 **Ailola, D A,** Remedies for human rights violations in the African Charter on Human and Peoples' Rights, *Journal of research,* 2 (1992) 49–82

629 **Akele Adua, P,** Prison, démocratie et sous-développement, *Zaire-Afrique,* **33,** 277 (1993) 433–40

630 **Amnesty International (Sektion des Bundesrepublik Deutschland),** *Afrika: auf dem Weg zur Abschaffung der Todesstraffe.* Bonn: Amnesty International, 1991, 79pp

631 **Arts, K C,** The international protection of children's rights in Africa: the 1990 OAU Charter on the Rights and Welfare of the Child, *African journal of international and comparative law,* **5,** 1 (1993) 139–62

632 **Auret, M,** Justice and peace, social problems and human rights, *Southern Africa political and economic monthly,* **4,** 11 (1991) 15–18

633 **Davidson, S,** The African system for protecting human and peoples' rights, in his *Human rights* (Buckingham: Open University Press, 1993), 152–62

634 **Dedo, K A,** Essai de réflexion sur la génèse, l'évolution et l'état actuel du droit des peuples à disposer d'eux-mêmes et sa signification actuelle dans le contexte africain, *Annual conference (African Society of International and Comparative Law),* **4,** (1992) 49–63

635 **Esu, L A,** Law and language: the African perspective, *Lawyers' journal,* **2,** 1 (1991) 45–51

636 **Gabou, A,** Principes et mécanismes de protection des droits de l'homme et des peuples : la Charte de Banjul, *Revue congolaise de droit,* 10 (1991) 98–122

637 **Ghai, Y,** Constitutions and governance in Africa: a prologomenon, in Adelman, S & Paliwala, A (eds), *Law and crisis in the Third World* (London: Zell, 1993), 51–75

638 **Ghai, Y,** The role of law in the transition of societies: the African experience, *Journal of African law,* **35,** 1/2 (1991) 8–20

639 **Higgins, R,** Africa and the Covenant on Civil and Political Rights during the first five years of

the 'Journal': some facts and some thoughts, *African journal of international and comparative law,* **5,** 1 (1993) 55–66

640 Kibwana, K, Development of democratic culture and civil society in Africa: an analysis of relevant constitutional initiatives and models, *Lesotho law journal,* **6,** 1 (1990) 13–56

641 Kufuor, K O, Sageguarding human rights: a critique of the African Commission on Human and Peoples' Rights, *Africa development,* **18,** 2 (1993) 65–77

642 Kwiatkowska, B, Ocean affairs and the law of the sea in Africa - towards the 21st century, *Marine policy,* **17,** 1 (1993) 11–43

643 Ladan, A M, The delimitation of the Exclusive Economic Zone in the practice of African states, *South African yearbook of international law,* **17,** (1991/92) 39–70

644 Maluwa, T, Succession to treaties in post-independence Africa: a retrospective consideration of some theoretical and practical issues with special reference to Malawi, *African journal of international and comparative law,* **4,** 4 (1992) 791–815

645 Mbaye, K, *Les droits de l'homme en Afrique.* Paris: Pedone, 1992, 312pp

646 Odinkalu, A C, Proposals for review of the rules of procedure of the African Commission of Human and People's Rights, *Human rights quarterly,* **15,** 3 (1993) 533–48

647 Ojwang, J B, Constitutionalism - in classical terms and in African nationhood, *Lesotho law journal,* **6,** 1 (1990) 57–74

648 Ojwang, J B, Liberal values in African constitutional development; some reflections, *Annual conference (African Society of Comparative and International Law),* **3,** (1991) 19–31

649 Okupa, E, Ethno-legal philosophy of customary law marriage, *Annual conference (African society of international and comparative law),* **4,** (1992) 278–292

650 Ouguergouz, F, *La Charte africaine des droits de l'homme et des peuples: un approche juridique des droits de l'homme entre tradition at modernité.* Geneva: IUHEI, 1993, 479pp

651 Paliwala, A, Family transformation and family law: some African developments in financial support on relationship breakdown, in Adelman, S & Paliwala, A (eds), *Law and crisis in the Third World* (London: Zell, 1993), 270–300

652 Selassie, A G, Ethnic identity and constitutional design for Africa, *Stanford journal of international law,* **29,** 1 (1992) 1–56

653 Slinn, P, A fresh start for Africa? New African constitutional perspectives for the 1990s, *Journal of African law,* **35,** 1/2 (1991) 1–7

Library - documentation

654 Afolabi, M, Spiritual matters: provision for independent African churches in general classification schemes, *International classification,* **19,** 4 (1992) 210–213

655 Aina, L O, The challenges of the emerging market and the education and training of information professionals in Africa, *Journal of librarianship and information science,* **25,** 4 (1993) 197–201

656 Aina, L O, *Who's who in library and information science training institutions in Africa 1990/1991.* Ibadan: Archlib, 1991, 56pp

657 Alegbeyele, G O, Reflections on information issues and information professionals in Africa,

Journal of information science, **19,** 4 (1993) 309–316

658 Alemna, A A, African library science journals: the missing link, *Scholarly publishing,* **25,** 1 (1993) 48–52

659 French, T (ed), *The SCOLMA directory of libraries and special collections on Africa in the United Kingdom and in Europe.* London: Zell, 1993, 355pp

660 Kahamba, J M, Resource sharing among libraries in southern Africa: some reflections, *African research and documentation,* 59/60 (1992) 17–20

661 Levey, L A, *Computer and CD-ROM capability in subsaharan African university and research libraries.* Washington: American Association for the Advancement of Science, 1990, 45pp

662 McIlwaine, J H, Writings on African archives, *African research and documentation,* 62 (1993) 25–37; and 63 (1993) 13–47

663 Nwafor, B U, University library buildings in subsaharan Africa, in Wise, M & Olden, A (eds), *Information and libraries (item 672),* 1–24

664 Otchere, F E, *African studies thesaurus: subject headings for library users.* New York: Greenwood, 1992, 435pp

665 Prichard, R J, African librarianship periodicals, in Wise, M & Olden, A (eds), *Information and libraries (item 672),* 182–200

666 Priestley, C, The difficult art of book aid: an African survey, *Logos,* **4,** 4 (1993) 215–21

667 Raseroka, H K, The role and purpose of the university library in a rapidly changing information environment with reference to the eastern and southern African region, *IFLA journal,* **19,** 1 (1993) 50–58

668 Roberts, W, IFLA activities in support of librianship in Africa, *African research and documentation,* 61 (1993) 1–11

669 Sene, H, Bibliographic organisation and exchange of information in the French-language African countries, in Wise, M & Olden, A (eds), *Information and libraries (item 672),* 47–58

670 Uganda Library Association, *Bibliographic control in the 1990s and beyond (Ninth standing conference of eastern, central and southern African librarians).* Kampala: the Association, 1990, 211pp

671 van Doorn, H C A, African documentation in the Netherlands, and possibilities for European cooperation, *African research and documentation,* 59/60 (1992) 9–16

672 Wise, M, Olden, A (eds), *Information and libraries in the developing world.* London: Library Association, 1990, 207pp

673 Zulu, S F C, Towards achieving bibliographic control of unpublished reports in Africa, *Libri,* **43,** 2 (1993) 123–33

Literature

674 Adams, A, Claiming her authority from life: twenty years of African women's literary criticism, *Matatu,* 10 (1993) 155–72

675 Ajayi, O, From his symbol to her icon: an analysis of the presentation of women in African contemporary literary works, *American journal of semiotics,* **13,** 3 (1993) 31–52

676 Ambadiango Mengele, T, Literary theory and cultural conflicts: about the determination of what is modern African literature, *Neohelicon,* **19,** 2 (1992) 173–93

677 Awuyah, C K, The concept of national literature in Africa and the

polysystem theory, *Neohelicon,* **20,** 1 (1993) 267–88
678 Dieke, I, *The primordial image: African, Afro-American and Caribbean mythopoetic text.* New York: Lang, 1993, 434pp
679 Galle, E, The probable young African hero, *Commonwealth: essays and studies,* **15,** 1 (1992) 29–35
680 Granqvist, R (ed), *Signs and signals: popular culture in Africa.* Stockholm: Almqvist & Wiksell, 1990, 242pp
681 Grobler, G M M, Briers, E W, *African literature: pilot bibliography of research in South Africa, 1908–1991.* Pretoria: University of South Africa, 1993, 152pp
682 Gunner, L, New African oral literatures, *Revue de littérature comparée,* **67,** 1 (1993) 91–99
683 Heinrichs, H J, *'Sprich deine eigene Sprache, Afrika!': von der negritude zur afrikanischer Literatur der Gegenwart.* Berlin: Reimer, 1992, 214pp
684 Hill, A, British publishers' constructive contribution to African literature, *Logos,* **3,** 1 (1992) 45–52
685 Huannou, A, *La critique et l'enseignement de la littérature africaine aux Etats-Unis.* Paris: Harmattan, 1993, 222pp
686 Innes, C L, *The devil's own mirror: the Irishman and the African in modern literature.* Washington: Three Continents Press, 1990, 113pp
687 Irele, A, African letters: the making of a tradition, *Yale journal of criticism,* **5,** 1 (1991) 69–100
688 Jendryschik, H, *Afrikanische Bauformen des Erzählens: spezifische Eigenarten des frankophonen Romans Schwarzafrikas.* Frankfurt: Lang, 1991, 321pp
689 Kane, M, Sur l'histoire littéraire africaine, *Annales de la Faculté des lettres et sciences humaines (Dakar),* 21 (1991) 95–115
690 Kane, M, Sur l'histoire littéraire africaine, *Bulletin des séances,* **37,** 3 (1991) 349–70
691 Kesteloot, L, L'influences des langues africaines sur la littérature africaine d'expression française, *Revue de l'Institut de sociologie,* 1990/91 155–63
692 Lordereau, P, Ntambwe, L L, *Littératures africaines à la Bibliothèque nationale: catalogue des ouvrages d'écrivains africains et de la littérature critique s'y rapportant entrés à la Bibliothèque nationale.* Paris: Bibliotheque nationale, 1991, 235pp
693 Lorenz, D, Pansch, M, L'Afrique 'francophone' se raconte: une decennie d'expression africaine, *Matatu,* 10 (1993) 39–59
694 Miller, C L, Literary studies and African literature: the challenge of intercultural identity, in Bates R H et al (eds), *Africa and the disciplines (item 3),* 213–31
695 Miller, C L, Nationalism as resistance and resistance to nationalism in the literature of francophone Africa, *Yale French studies,* 82 (1993) 62–100
696 Mugo, M M G, *African orature and human rights.* Roma: Institute of Southern African Studies, 1991, 44pp
697 Nazombe, A, Myth and literature in Africa, the theoretical issues, *Tizame,* 3 (1993) 28–36
698 Ngandu Nkashama, P, *Les années littéraraires en Afrique (1912–1987).* Paris: Harmattan, 1993, 455pp
699 Ngugi wa Thiong'o, *Moving the centre: the struggle for cultural freedom.* London: Currey, 1993, 176pp
700 Obiechina, E, Narrative proverbs in the African novel, *Oral tradition,* **7,** 2 (1992) 197–230

701 **Obiechina, E,** Narrative proverbs in the African novel, *Research in African literatures,* **24,** 4 (1993) 123–140
702 **Ofiemun, O,** The destiny of African writing, *Africa forum,* **1,** 2 (1991) 57–61
703 **Ogede, O J,** Negritude and Africa: Armah's account, *Third world quarterly,* **14,** 4 (1993) 792–801
704 **Ojaide, T,** Modern African literature and cultural identity, *African studies review,* **35,** 3 (1992) 43–57
705 **Okomba, O, Nandwa, J** (eds), *Reflections on theories and methods in oral literature.* Nairobi: Kenya Oral Literature Association, 1992, 167pp
706 **Okpewho, I,** *African oral literature: background, character and continuity.* Bloomington: Indiana University Press, 1993, 392pp
707 **Orisawayi, D** (ed), *Literature and Black aesthetics.* Ibadan: Heinemann, 1990, 339pp
708 **Ormerod, B, Volet, J M,** Francophone women writers from subsaharan Africa: an annotated bibliography, *ALA bulletin,* **18,** 4 (1992) 15–22
709 **Owomoleya, O,** *Visions and revisions: essays on African literature and criticism.* New York: Lang, 1991, 239pp
710 **Schulte-Engler, F,** Discourses of arrested modernisation: African literary theory in the 1980s, *Matatu,* 10 (1993) 9–26
711 **Skattum, I,** Pour une lecture ethnolinguistique de la littérature africaine moderne, *Revue de l'Institut de sociologie,* 1990/91 165–79
712 **Sougou, O,** The issue of literatures in African languages, *Université, recherche et développement,* 1 (1993) 63–78
713 **Trojanow, I, Ripken, P** (eds), *Afrikanissimo: ein heiter-sinnliches Leserbuch.* Wuppertal: Peter Hammer, 1991, 216pp
714 **Unwin, V, Currey, J,** The African Writers Series celebrates thirty years, *Southern African review of books,* **5,** 2 (1993) 3–6
715 **Wauthier, C, et al,** *Littératures africaines et histoire.* n.p.: Nouvelles de Sud, 1991, 145pp
716 **Wufela, A y'O,** Indépendances africaines et déscolarisation de la jeunesse: l'école occidentale dans la littérature africaine d'avant et d'après l'indépendance, *Journal of Asian and African studies (Tokyo),* 44 (1993) 145–66
717 **Yoder, C,** *White shadows: a dialectical view of the French African novel.* Washington: Three Continents Press, 1991, 237pp
718 **Zabus, C,** Criticism of African literatures in English: towards a horizon of expectation, *Revue de littérature comparée,* **67,** 1 (1993) 129–47

Media

See also: 560, 561, 684
719 **Blake, C,** Traditional African values and the right to communicate, *Africa media review,* **7,** 3 (1993) 1–17
720 **Gedin, P I,** Private enterprise publishing in Africa, *Logos,* **2,** 3 (1991) 133–39
721 **Hachten, W A,** *The growth of media in the Third World: African failures, Asian successes.* Amred: Iowa State University Press, 1993, 129pp
722 **Hoffman, V,** *Bildgestütze Kommunkation in Schwarz-Afrika: Grundlagen, Beispiele und Empfehlungen zu angepassen Kommunikationsverfahren in Ländlichen Entwicklungsprogrammen.* Weikersheim: Margraf, 1991, 331pp

723 **Irele, A,** The problems of African publishing, *Revue de littérature comparée,* **67,** 1 (1993) 115–119

724 **Jay, M,** African Books Collective, *Africa bibliography 1992,* vi-xviii (short version in *Yearbook of cooperative enterprise* 1993, 119–23)

725 **Karikari, K,** Africa; the press and democracy, *Race and class,* **34,** 3 (1993) 55–66

726 **Karikari, K,** Radio pluralism and manpower needs, *Africa media review,* **7,** 3 (1993) 105–110

727 **Kizito, R N,** *Communication and human rights in Africa: implications for development.* Nairobi: World Association for Christian Communication, 1992, 163pp

728 **Kwame Boafo, S T** (ed), *Media and environment in Africa: challenges for the future.* Nairobi: African Council on Communication Education, 1993, 111pp

729 **Lindfors, B,** Desert gold. Irrigation schemes for ending the book drought, *Matatu,* 10 (1993) 27–38

730 **Mbanga, T,** The Zimbabwe International Book Fair - Africa's publishing showcase, *African book publishing record,* **19,** 4 (1993) 223–28

731 **Membrey, D,** A resource package for African publishers, *Scholarly publishing,* **24,** 3 (1993) 166–70

732 **Meyer, R,** Die Rolle des Medien für Demokratie und Entwicklung in Afrika, *Afrika Jahrbuch 1992,* 57–64

733 **Nyahodu, P,** Africa and the New World Information Order: monopolisation of information and implications for finance capital, *African research and documentation,* 59/60 (1992) 25–32

734 **Ochieng, P,** *I accuse the press: an insider's view of the media and politics in Africa.* Nairobi: ACTS, 1992, 210pp

735 **POPIN-Africa,** *The press on African population issues.* Addis Ababa: UNECA, Population Information Network for Africa, 1992, 65pp

736 **Tedga, J P** (ed), *Presse africaine et enseignement.* Paris: ACCT, 1993, 159pp

737 **Vilasco, G, Zidouemba, D** (eds), *L'édition scientifique en Afrique francophone (actes de la Table ronde).* Dakar: Association des rédacteurs et éditeurs scientifiques d'Afrique francophone, 1990, 134pp

738 **Walsh, G,** *Publishing in Africa: a neglected component of development.* Boston: African Studies Center, Boston University, 1991, 33pp

739 **West, H G, Fair, J E,** Development communication and popular resistance in Africa: an examination of the struggle over tradition and modernity through media, *African studies review,* **36,** 1 (1993) 91–114

740 **Zell, H,** Africa: the neglected continent, *Logos,* **1,** 2 (1990) 19–27

741 **Ziegler, D, Asante, M K,** *Thunder and silence: the mass media in Africa.* Trenton: Africa World Press, 1992, 205pp

Medical

See also: 310, 318, 321, 329, 340, 1110, 1113, 1118, 5119

742 **Amat-Roze, J M,** Les inégalités géographiques et l'infection VIH et du SIDA en Afrique subsaharienne, *Social science and medicine,* **36,** 10 (1993) 1247–56

743 **Anderson, R M,** Mathematical models of the potential demographic impact of AIDS in Africa, *AIDS,* **5,** 1 (1991) 37–44

744 **Ankrah, E M,** The impact of HIV/AIDS on the family and other significant relationships: the African clan revisited, *AIDS care,* **5,** 1 (1993) 5–22

745 **Badji, B,** *La folie en Afrique: une rivalité pathologique.* Paris: Harmattan, 1993, 211pp

746 **Berkeley, S,** Parenteral transmissions of HIV in Africa, *AIDS,* **5,** 1 (1991) 87–92

747 **Bertozzi, S M,** Combating HIV in Africa: a role for economic research, *AIDS,* **5,** 1 (1991) 45–54

748 **Caldwell, J C,** African families and AIDS: context, reactions and potential interventions, *Health transition review,* **3,** (1993) supplementary issue, 1–16

749 **Collignon, R,** A propos des troubles des conduites alimentaires: 1. du pica des médecins à la géophagie des géographes, des voyageurs et des ethnologues, *Psychopathologie africaine,* **24,** 3 (1992) 385–398

750 **Decock, K M, et al,** Clinical research, prophylaxis, therapy and care for HIV disease in Africa, *American journal of public health,* **83,** 10 (1993) 1385–89

751 **Feldmeier, H, et al,** A synoptic inventory of needs for research on women and topical parasitic diseases. II: Gender-related biases in the diagnosis and morbidity assessment of schistosomiasis in women, *Acta tropica,* **55,** 3 (1993) 139–69

752 **Fleming, A,** Lessons from tropical Africa for addressing the HIV/AIDS epidemic in South Africa, in Cross, S & Whiteside, A (eds), *Facing up to AIDS (item 4753),* 295–317

753 **Fredland, R A,** The politics of AIDS, a comparative perspective: South Africa and other Africa, *Proteus,* **9,** 2 (1992) 35–40

754 **Garnett, G P, et al,** No reason for complacency about the potential demographic impact of AIDS in Africa, *Transactions of the Royal Society of Tropical Medicine and Hygiene,* **87,** 1 (1993) 19–22

755 **Gbesemete, K P, Jonsson, D,** A comparison of empirical models on determinants of infant mortality: a cross-national study on Africa, *Health policy,* **24,** 2 (1993) 155–74

756 **Green, E C,** Sexually transmitted disease, ethnomedicine and health policy in Africa, *Social science and medicine,* **35,** 2 (1992) 121–30

757 **Heymann, D L, Edstrom, K,** Strategies for AIDS prevention and control in subsaharan Africa, *AIDS,* **5,** 1 (1991) 197–208

758 **Heymann, S J,** Modelling the efficacy of prophylactic and curative therapies for preventing the spread of tuberculosis in Africa, *Transactions of the Royal Society of Tropical Medicine and Hygiene,* **87,** 4 (1993) 406–11

759 **Horburgh, C R, Pozniak, A,** Epidemiology of tuberculosis in the era of HIV, *AIDS,* **7,** 1 (1993) 109–114

760 **Hudson, C P,** Concurrent partnerships could cause AIDS epidemics, *International journal of STD & AIDS,* **4,** 5 (1993) 249–53

761 **Hunter, D J,** AIDS in subsaharan Africa: the epidemiology of heterosexual transmission and the prospects for prevention, *Epidemiology,* **4,** 1 (1993) 63–72

762 **Jager, H, et al,** Safe blood transfusions in Africa, *AIDS,* **5,** 1 (1991) 163–68

763 **Katabira, E T, Wabitsch, K R,** Management issues of patients with HIV infection in Africa, *AIDS,* **5,** 1 (1991) 149–55

764 **Kaufmant, A M,** Africa: the healer's art, *Unesco courier,* March 1993 30–33

765 **Lamboray, J L, Elmendorf, A E,** *Combatting AIDS and other sexually transmitted diseases in Africa: a review of the World Bank's agenda*

for action. Washington: World Bank, 1992, 35pp

766 **Lamptey, P, Goodridge, G A W,** Condom issues and AIDS prevention in Africa, *AIDS,* **5,** 1 (1991) 183–191

767 **Livingston, I L,** The international perspective: health promotion and HIV-AIDS in Africa - implications for women and children, *Pediatric AIDS and HIV infection,* **4,** 5 (1993) 344–57

768 **Lucas, S B,** The pathology of severe morbidity and mortality caused by HIV infection in Africa, *AIDS,* **5,** 1 (1991) 143–48

769 **Mboya, M M,** Development and initial validation of a perceived parental behaviour inventory for African adolescents, *Perceptual and motor skills,* **76,** 3 (1993) 1003–1108

770 **Miller, E M,** Could R-selection account for the African personality and life style?, *Personality and individual differences,* **15,** 6 (1993) 665–75

771 **Nkowane, B M,** Prevalence and incidence of HIV infection in Africa: a review of data published in 1990, *AIDS,* **5,** 1 (1991) 7–15

772 **Palmberg, M** (ed), *AIDS in Afrika.* Uppsala: Scandinavian Institute of African Studies, 1993, 236pp

773 **Perriens, J H, et al,** Tuberculosis and HIV-infection - implications for Africa, *AIDS,* **5,** 1 (1991) 127–33

774 **Piot, P, et al,** AIDS in Africa: the first decade and challenges for the future, *AIDS,* **5,** 1 (1991) 1–5

775 **Rey, J L,** Le SIDA en Afrique: aperçu d'une situation épidémioloique d'extrème gravité, *Orstom actgualités,* 35 (1992) 12–16

776 **Ryder, R W,** The effect of HIV–1 infection during pregnancy and the perinatal period on maternal and child health in Africa, *AIDS,* **5,** 1 (1991) 75–85

777 **Seidel, G,** The competing discourses of HIV/AIDS in subsaharan Africa: discourses of rights and empowerment vs discourses of control and exclusion, *Social science and medicine,* **36,** 3 (1993) 175–94

778 **Tayeh, A, Cairncross, S,** Dracunculiasis eradication by 1995: will endemic countries meet the target?, *Health policy and planning,* **8,** 3 (1993) 191–207

779 **van der Hoeven, F P C,** *Afrika in duel mer AIDS.* Kampen: Kok, 1992, 72pp

780 **Westley, D,** *Mental health and psychiatry in Africa: an annotated bibliography.* Oxford: Zell, 1993, 205pp

781 **Williams, A O,** *AIDS: an African perspective.* Boca Raton: CRC Press, 1991, 363pp

782 **Wilson, D, Lavelle, S,** HIV/AIDS-STD in Africa, *AIDS care,* **4,** 4 (1992) 438–43

783 **Wilson, D, Mehryar, A,** The role of AIDS knowledge, attitudes, beliefs and practices: research in subsaharan Africa, *AIDS,* **5,** 1 (1991) 177–81

784 **Zimba, C G, Buggie, S E,** An experimental study of the placebo effect in African traditional medicine, *Behavioural medicine,* **19,** 3 (1993) 103–109

Natural resources

785 **Adams, J C, McShane, T O,** *The myth of wild Africa: conservation without illusion.* New York: Norton, 1992, 266pp

786 **Anon,** Wood energy consumption and forest conservation in Africa, *Rural progress,* **12,** 1 (1993) 58–74

787 **Baumann, M** (ed), *Bäuerinnen and Bauern erhalten die biologische Viehalt: Biespiele aus dem Suden.* Berne: Swissaid/Genetic Resources Action International, 1991, 174pp

788 **Bhagavan, M R, Karekezi, S** (eds), *Energy management in Africa.* London: Zed, 1992, 180pp

789 **Bhagavan, M R, Karekezi, S,** Introduction, in Bhagavan, M R & Karekezi, S (eds), *Energy managment (Item 788)*, 1–6

790 **Bonner, R,** *At the hand of man: peril and hope for Africa's wildlife.* New York: Knopf, 1993, 322pp

791 **Borota, J,** *Tropical forests: some African and Asian case studies of composition and structure.* Amsterdam: Elsevier, 1991, 274pp

792 **Dang, H,** Fuel substitution in subsaharan Africa, *Environmental management,* **17,** 3 (1993) 283–88

793 **Davidson, O, Karekezi, S,** A new, environmentally sound energy strategy for the development of subsaharan Africa, in Karekezi, S & Mackenzie, G A (eds), *Energy options (Item 796)*, 8–22

794 **Dei, G J S,** Indigenous African knowledge systems: local traditions of sustainable forestry, *Singapore journal of tropical geography,* **14,** 1 (1993) 28–41

795 **Kadzombe, E D,** Use, conservation and management of forest resources, *Malawian geographer,* 29 (1991) 1–5

796 **Karekezi, S, Mackenzie, G A** (eds), *Energy options for Africa: environmentally sustainable alternatives.* London: Zed, 1993, 184pp

797 **Karekezi, S, Mackenzie, G A,** Introduction, in Karekezi, S & Mackenzie, G A (eds), *Energy options (Item 796)*, 1–7

798 **McNeely, J A,** Economic incentives for conserving biodiversity: lessons for Africa, *Ambio,* **22,** 2–3 (1993) 144–50

799 **Murphree, M W,** *Research on the institutional contexts of wildlife utilisation on communal areas of eastern and southern Africa.* Harare: CASS, University of Zimbabwe, 1990, 9pp

800 **Musa, E S,** The role of the African Development Bank in energy development, in Karekezi, S & Mackenzie, G A (eds), *Energy options (Item 796)*, 86–94

801 **Mwangi wa Githini, Perrings, C,** Social and economic sustainability in the use of biotic resources in subsaharan Africa, *Ambio,* **22,** 2–3 (1993) 110–116

802 **Newsom, M,** *Land, water and development.* London: Routledge, 1992; see pp 145–66,

803 **Roussel, B, Juhé-Beaulaton, D,** Les plantes americaines en Afrique tropicale, *Cahiers d'outre-mer,* **45,** 179/80 (1992) 373–86

804 **Sarfoh, J A,** *Energy in the development of West Africa: a selected bibliography.* New York: Greenwood, 1992, 114pp

Planning

See also: 1156

805 **Moughtin, C, et al,** *Who needs development? Planning with the poor in Third World countries.* Nottingham: Institute of Planning Studies, Nottingham University, 1992, 127pp

Politics

See also: 30, 34, 109, 132, 140, 163, 246, 277, 314, 322, 333, 475, 527, 555, 634, 652, 727, 734, 753, 958, 960, 961, 986, 1001, 1008, 1012, 1048, 2993, 2995, 2995, 5137

806 **Adam, H M,** Frantz Fanon as a democratic theorist, *African affairs,* **92,** 369 (1993) 499–518

807 **Adamife, E N, Warhola, J W,** Africa's political boundaries: colonial cartography, the OAU and the advisability of ethno-national adjustment, *International journal of*

politics, culture and society, **6,** 4 (1993) 533–54
808 Adeniji, O, Regionalism in Africa, *Security dialogue,* **24,** 2 (1993) 211–20
809 Adesina, J O, Critique and anti-critique in the 'governance in Africa' discourse, *Codesria bulletin,* 2 (1993) 24–27
810 Aidoo, A, Africa: democracy without human rights, *Human rights quarterly,* **15,** 4 (1993) 703–15
811 Ake, C, As Africa democratises, *Africa forum,* **1,** 2 (1991) 13–16
812 Ake, C, *The feasibility of democracy in Africa.* Ibadan: Ibadan University, 1992, 10pp
813 Ake, C, The unique case of African democracy, *International affairs,* **69,** 2 (1993) 239–44
814 Amoah, P, The African Charter on Human and Peoples' Rights - an effective weapon for human rights?, *African journal of international and comparative law,* **4,** 1 (1992) 226–240
815 Anyang' Nyong'o, P A, The African awakening, *Southern Africa political and economic monthly,* **4,** 9 (1991) 5–8
816 Arms Project, *Landmines: a deadly legacy.* New York: Human Rights Watch, 1993, 510pp
817 Arnold, G, *Political and economic encyclopaedia of Africa.* Harlow: Longman, 1993, 342pp
818 Arnold, G, Wars of Africa, *Africa forum,* **2,** 1 (1992) 30–33
819 Asibuo, S K, Inertia in African public administration: an examination of some causes in remedies, *Africa development,* **17,** 4 (1992) 67–80
820 Austin, D, reflections on African politics: Prospero, Ariel and Caliban, *International affairs,* **69,** 2 (1993) 203–22
821 Ayittey, G B N, *Africa betrayed.* Basingstoke: Macmillan, 1993, 412pp
822 Ayittey, G, Les blocages du développement africain, *Afrique 2000,* 12 (1993) 75–97
823 Bakary, T D, Des militaires aux avocats: une autre forme de coup d'état, *Géopolitique africaine,* **15,** 2 (1992) 7pp
824 Balogun, M J, The African civil service within the context of structural adjustment and structural transformation: a review and a synthesis of contending reform strategies for the 1990s, *African management development forum,* **2,** 1 (1991) 27–35
825 Baloro, J, International humanitarian law and situations of internal armed conflicts in Africa, *African journal of international and comparative law,* **4,** 2 (1992) 449–471
826 Bangoura, D, Armées et défis démocratiques en Afrique, *Afrique 2000,* 12 (1993) 111–22
827 Bayart, J F, Les églises chrétiennes et la politique du ventre, in Bayart, J F (ed), *Réligion et modernité politique (item 960)*, 129–60
828 Bayart, J F, *The state in Africa: the politics of the belly.* London: Longman, 1993, 370pp
829 Baynham, S, The subordination of African armies to civilian control: theory and praxis, *Africa insight,* **22,** 4 (1992) 259–63
830 Beckman, B, The liberation of civil society: neoliberal ideology and political theory, *Review of African political economy,* 58 (1993) 20–33
831 Bennett, T W, Human rights and the African cultural tradition, in Schmale, W (ed), *Human rights and cultural diversity* (Goldbach: Kiep, 1993), 269–80
832 Bienen, H, Leaders, violence and the absence of change in Africa, *Political science quarterly,* **108,** 2 (1993) 271–82

833 **Blaney, D L, Pasha, M K,** Civil society and democracy in the Third World: ambiguities and historical possibilities, *Studies in comparative international development,* **28,** 1 (1993) 3–24

834 **Boillot, F,** L'église catholique face aux processus de changement politique du début des années quatre-vingt-dix, *Année africaine 1992/93,* 115–44

835 **Boulaga, F E,** *Les conférences nationales: une affaire à suivre.* Paris: Karthala, 1993, 229pp

836 **Bouvier, P,** L'Afrique politique face à son devenir, *Civilisations,* **40,** 2 (1992) 232–252

837 **Breum, M,** *Menneskeret i Afrika.* Copenhagen: Dansk Center for Menneskerettigheder, 1993, 144pp

838 **Buijtenhuis, R, Rijnierse, E,** *Democratisation in subsaharan Africa: an overview of the literature.* Leiden: Afrikastudiecentrum, 1993, 97pp

839 **Busia, N K A,** The right to self-determination, the state and the quest for democracy in Africa: an exploratory analysis, *Annual conference (African Society of International and Comparative Law),* **4,** (1992) 29–48

840 **Clapham, C,** Democratisation in Africa: obstacles and prospects, *Third world quarterly,* **14,** 3 (1993) 423–38

841 **Clark, J F,** Theoretical disarray and the study of democratisation in Africa, *Journal of modern African studies,* **31,** 3 (1993) 529–34 (review article)

842 **Cohen, R, et al** (eds), *Human rights and governance in Africa.* Gainesville: University Press of Florida, 1993, 285pp

843 **Crocker, C A,** Afterword: strengthening African peacemaking and peacekeeping, in Smock, D R (ed), *Making war and waging peace (Item 409),* 263–70

844 **Danopoulos, C P** (ed), *Civilian rule in the developing world.* Boulder: Westview, 1992, 273pp

845 **Decalo, S,** Democracy in Africa: toward the 21st century, in Vanhanen, T (ed), *Strategies of democratisation* (New York: Crane Russak, 1992), 131–42

846 **DeLancey, M** (ed), *Handbook of political science research on subsaharan Africa.* New York: Greenwood, 1992, 427pp

847 **Depelchin, J,** Beyond elite politics: a comment on Ernest Wamba-dia-Wamba's essay 'Beyond elite politics of democracy in Africa', *Quest,* **7,** 2 (1993) 100–105

848 **Diarra, A** (ed), *Demokratisierung und Entwicklungsprobleme in Afrika.* Saarbrucken: Breitenbach, 1992, 200pp

849 **Dowden, R,** Reflections on democracy in Africa, *African affairs,* **92,** 369 (1993) 607–613 (review article)

850 **Dumont, R,** *Démocratie pour l'Afrique: la longue marche pour l'Afrique noire vers la liberté.* Paris: Seuil, 1993, 344pp

851 **Eboh, M P,** Democracy with an African flair: a reply to Wamba-dia-Wamba, *Quest,* **7,** 2 (1993) 92–99

852 **Ekwe-Ekwe, H,** *Africa 2001: the state, human rights and the people.* Reading: International Institute for Black Research, 1993, 121pp

853 **Ellis, S,** Democracy in Africa: achievements and prospects, in Rimmer, D (ed), *Action in Africa (Item 525),* 133–43

854 **Fowler, A,** Non-governmental organisations as agents of democratisation: an African perspective, *Journal of international development,* **5,** 3 (1993) 325–39

855 **Gaud, M, Porgès, L,** Les presidents de l'alternance, *Afrique contemporaine,* 167 (1993) 29–39
856 **Geisler, G,** Fair? What has fair got to do with it? Vagaries of election observations and democratic standards, *Journal of modern African studies,* **31,** 4 (1993) 613–37
857 **Global Coalition for Africa,** *Democracy and democratisation in Africa: final report.* The Hague: Institute of Social Studies, 1993, 126pp
858 **Gonideç, P F,** Démocratie et développement en Afrique: perspectives internationale et nationales, *Afrique 2000,* 14 (1993) 49–60
859 **Gupta, V,** Africa: the post Cold War era, *Indian journal of African studies,* **5,** 1 (1992) 1–13
860 **Hamrell, S, Nordberg, O** (eds), *The state and crisis in Africa: in search of a second liberation. Report of the Mweya Conference in Uganda, May 12–17, 1990.* Uppsala: Dag Hammarskjöld Foundation, 1992, 32pp
861 **Harding, J,** *Small wars, small mercies: journeys in Africa's disputed nations.* London: Viking, 1993, 441pp
862 **Harsch, E,** Accumulators and democrats: challenging state corruption in Africa, *Journal of modern African studies,* **31,** 1 (1993) 31–48
863 **Hawthorn, G,** Subsaharan Africa, in Held, D (ed), *Prospects for democracy* (Oxford: Polity, 1993), 330–54
864 **Haynes, J,** The state, governance, and democracy in subsaharan Africa, *Journal of modern African studies,* **31,** 3 (1993) 535–39 (review article)
865 **Healey, J, et al,** Will political reform bring about improved economic management in subsaharan Africa?, *IDS bulletin,* **24,** 1 (1993) 31–38
866 **Hebinck, P,** Democratisering in Afrika, *Derde Wereld,* **11,** 3 (1992) 4–11
867 **Howard, R E,** Communitarianism and liberalism in the debates on human rights in Africa, *Journal of contemporary African studies,* **11,** 1 (1992) 1–21
868 **Ibeanu, O O,** The state and the market: reflections on Ake's analysis of the state in the periphery, *Africa development,* **18,** 3 (1993) 117–131
869 **Ihonvbere, J O,** Is democracy possible in Africa? The elites, the people and civil society, *Quest,* **6,** 2 (1992) 84–108
870 **Irung Tshitambal'a Mulang,** La démocratie en Afrique actuelle, *Zaire Afrique,* 270 (1992) 591–98
871 **Jeffries, R,** The state, structural adjustment and good government in Africa, *Journal of Commonwealth and comparative politics,* **31,** 1 (1993) 20–35
872 **Jokobeit, C,** Das externe wirtschaftliche Umfeld der afrikanischen Demokratisierungsbemhungen: zwischen Schuldenfalle, Rohstoffpreisverfall, nachlassender Entwicklungshilfe, zerstörerischer Nahrungsmittelhilfe und ungebrochenem Protektionismus des Nordens, *Afrika Jahrbuch 1992,* 46–56
873 **Jones, M L, Blunt, P,** Organisational development and change in Africa, *International journal of public administration,* **16,** 11 (1993) 1735–65
874 **Joseph, R,** Governance and peacemaking, *Africa forum,* **2,** 3/4 (1992) 46–52
875 **Kalu, A U, Osinbajo, Y** (eds), *Perspectives on human rights.* Lagos: Federal Ministry of Justice, 1992, 318pp
876 **Kamto, M,** *L'urgence de la pensée: réflexions sur une précondition*

de la développement en Afrique. Paris: Mandara, 1993, 209pp

877 **Kihoro, W** (ed), *Towards Africa's second liberation: democracy, popular participation and human rights in Africa.* London: International Institute for Human Rights and Democracy in Africa, 1991, 39pp

878 **Klein, M A,** Back to democracy: Presidential address to the 1991 annual meeting of the African Studies Association, *African studies review,* **35,** 3 (1992) 1–12

879 **Kobia, S,** *The quest for democracy in Africa.* Nairobi: National Christian Council for Kenya, 1993, 60pp

880 **Konings, P,** Vakbonden, structurele aanpassing en democratisering in Afrika, *Internationale spectator,* **47,** 2 (1993) 113–117

881 **Kposowa, A J, Jenkins, J G,** The structural sources of military coups in postcolonial Africa 1957–1984, *American journal of sociology,* **99,** 1 (1993) 126–63

882 **Lancaster, C,** Democratisation in subsaharan Africa, *Survival,* **35,** 3 (1993) 38–50

883 **Legum, C,** The dynamics of African political societies in transition, in Siddiqui, R A (ed), *Subsaharan Africa (item 15),* 11–18

884 **Leonard, D K,** Professionalism and African administration, *IDS bulletin,* **24,** 1 (1993) 74–79

885 **MacCorquodale, R,** Self-determination beyond the colonial context and its potential impact on Africa, *African journal of international and comparative law,* **4,** 3 (1992) 592–608

886 **Mahmud, S S,** The state and human rights in Africa in the 1990s: perspectives and prospects, *Human rights quarterly,* **15,** 3 (1993) 485–98

887 **Mavila, J C,** L'État africain: quelles perspectives de changement des institutions politiques?, *Annual conference (African Society of International and Comparative Law),* **4,** (1992) 153–168

888 **Mayall, J, Simpson, M,** Ethnicity is not enough: reflections on protracted secessionism in the Third World, *International journal of comparative sociology,* **33,** 1/2 (1992) 5–25

889 **Mazrui, A A,** Planned governance and the liberal revival in Africa: the paradox of anticipation, *Cornell international law journal,* **25,** 3 (1992) 541–53

890 **Mbaku, J M,** Political democracy and the prospects of development in post-Cold War Africa, *Journal of social, political and economic studies,* **17,** 3/4 (1992) 345–71

891 **Mbaku, J M,** Political democracy, military expenditures and economic growth in Africa, *Scandanavian journal of development alternatives,* **12,** 1 (1993) 49–64

892 **Mbaye, K,** *Les droits de l'homme en Afrique.* Paris: Pedone, 1993, 312pp

893 **Mbembe, A,** Diagnostique sur les dérapages de la transition démocratique en Afrique (interview), *Afrique 2000,* 12 (1993) 57–64

894 **Mbembe, A,** Traditions de l'autoritarisme et problèmes de gouvernement en Afrique subsaharienne, *Africa development,* **17,** 1 (1992) 37–64

895 **Mbuyi Kabunda, Ngoie Tshibambe,** El preceso de democratizacion en Africa negra: producto de la perestroika o de la autenticidad Africana?, *Estudios Africanos,* **6,** 10/11 (1991/92) 61–71

896 **Médard, J F** (ed), *Etats d'Afrique noire: formation, mécanismes et crise.* Paris: Karthala, 1991, 405pp

897 **Médard, J F,** L'état neo-patrimoniale en Afrique noire, in Médard, J F (ed), *Etats d'Afrique noire (Item 896)*, 323–53
898 **Medhanie, T,** Les modèles de transition démocratique, *Afrique 2000,* 14 (1993) 61–69
899 **Metena M'nteba,** Les conférences nationales africaines et la figure politique de l'évêque-président, *Zaire-Afrique,* **33,** 276 (1993) 361–72
900 **Michalon, T,** Autoritarisme et hyper-centralisation: l'état africain contre les libertés, *Annual conference (African Society of Comparative and International Law),* **3,** (1991) 78–88
901 **Michalon, T,** L'État africain à la recherche d'une nouvelle légitimité, *Annual conference (African Society of International and Comparative Law),* **4,** (1992) 265–277
902 **Mohammed, N A L, Gyimah-Brempong, K,** Defence spending and economic growth in subsaharan Africa: comment (and reply), *Journal of peace research,* **30,** 1 (1993) 95–99
903 **Monnier, L,** Démocratie et développement en Afrique noire: quels termes pour quel débat?, *Informations et commentaires,* 78 (1992) 27–32
904 **Mouelle Kombi II, N,** Pour une approche prospective des problèmes politiques et internationaux en Afrique, *Afrique 2000,* 13 (1993) 29–38
905 **Moukoko Mbonjo, P,** Pluralisme socio-politique et démocratie en Afrique, *Afrique 2000,* 15 (1993) 39–54
906 **Moukoko Mbonjo, P,** Régimes militaires et transition démocratique en Afrique: à la recherche d'un cadre d'analyse politique, *Afrique 2000,* 13 (1993) 39–58
907 **Munslow, B,** Democratisation in Africa, *Parliamentary affairs,* **46,** 4 (1993) 478–91
908 **Museveni, Y,** A revolutionary with a cause (interview), *Africa forum,* **1,** 2 (1991) 8–12
909 **Mutahaba, G, et al,** *Vitalising African public administration for recovery and development.* West Hartford: Kumarian, 1993, 119pp
910 **Mutahaba, H,** The challenges of development in the 1990s: are the public/civil services combat ready?, *African management development forum,* **2,** 1 (1991) 3–7
911 **Nana Sinkam, S C,** Démocratie et développement en Afrique: peut-on les réussir, *Afrique 2000,* 14 (1993) 71–82
912 **Neocosmos, M,** *The agrarian question in Africa and the 'concept from below': economics and politics in the struggle for democracy.* Uppsala: Scandinavian Institute of African Studies, 1993, 79pp
913 **Njage-Rwito, L M,** Contextual issues in the search for optimum size of the public/civil service in managing the development challenges of the 1990s, *African management development forum,* **2,** 1 (1991) 7–14
914 **Nsereko, D D N,** The police, human rights and the constitution: an African perspective, *Human rights quarterly,* **15,** 3 (1993) 465–84
915 **Nyang'oro, J E,** The evolving role of the African state under structural adjustment, in Nyang'oro, J E & Shaw, T M (eds), *Beyond structural adjustment (Item 179),* 11–27
916 **Nyang'oro, J E,** National security and defence expenditure in Africa: a political and economic analysis, *Africa development,* **17,** 4 (1992) 5–28
917 **Nzombe, S,** *Democracy, human rights and constitutionalism in post-colonial Africa.* Harare: Sapes books, 1992, 11pp

918 **Obasanjo, O,** Reclaiming Africa's democratic roots, *Choices,* **2,** 1 (1993) 18–21
919 **Okamba, E,** L'analyse systémique des conférences nationales, *Afrique 2000,* 15 (1993) 21–37
920 **O'Kane, R H T,** Coup d'etat in Africa: a political economy approach, *Journal of peace research,* **30,** 3 (1993) 251–70
921 **O'Kane, R H T,** The ladder of abstraction: the purpose of comparison and the practice of comparing African coups d'etat, *Journal of theoretical politics,* **5,** 2 (1993) 169–93
922 **Osaghae, E E,** From benevolence to greater benevolence: the state and the politics of structural adjustment in rural Africa, *Africa quarterly,* **33,** (1993) 77–106
923 **Pollard, R,** La démocratie ambigue, *Année africaine 1992/93,* 17–57
924 **Reyntjens, P,** The winds of change: political and constitutional evolution in francophone Africa, *Journal of African law,* **35,** 1/2 (1991) 44–55
925 **Rijnierse, E,** Democratisation in subsaharan Africa? Literature overview, *Third world quarterly,* **14,** 3 (1993) 147–64
926 **Robertson, P,** Monitoring African elections, in Rimmer, D (ed), *Action in Africa (Item 525),* 154–57
927 **Roussillon, H** (ed), *Les nouvelles constitutions africaines: la transition démocratique.* Toulouse: Institut d'études politiques, 1993, 191pp
928 **Rudebeck, L,** Conditions of people's development in postcolonial Africa, in Galli, R E, et al *Rethinking the Third World* (New York: Crane Russak, 1992), 29–87
929 **Sandbrook, R,** *The politics of Africa's economic recovery.* Cambridge: CUP, 1993, 170pp
930 **Sandbrook, R, Halfani, M** (eds), *Empowering people: building a community, civil associations, and legality in Africa.* Toronto: Toronto University, Centre for Urban and Community Studies, 1993, 209pp
931 **Sangmpam, S N,** Neither soft nor dead: the African state is alive and well, *African studies review,* **36,** 2 (1993) 73–94
932 **Saxena, S C,** *Politics in Africa.* Delhi: Kalinga, 1993, 424pp
933 **Scarritt, J R,** Communal conflict and contention for power in Africa South of the Sahara, in Gurr, T R (ed), *Minorities at risk* (Washington: US Institute of Peace, 1992), 252–89
934 **Schatzberg, M G,** Power, legitimacy and 'democratisation' in Africa, *Africa,* **63,** 4 (1993) 445–61
935 **Semilinko, S,** Collective exorcism, *Africa forum,* **1,** 3 (1991) 12–16
936 **Shivji, I G,** *Fight my beloved continent: new democracy in Africa.* Harare: Sapes, 1992 (rev. ed'n), 46pp
937 **Sklar, R H,** The African frontier for political science, in Bates R H et al (eds), *Africa and the disciplines (item 3),* 83–110
938 **Smoke, P, Olowu, D,** 'Successful African local government': methodological and conceptual issues reconsidered, *Public administration and development,* **13,** 5 (1993) 507–14
939 **Suliman, M, Verney, P,** *The state of war and peace in Africa 1992.* Bonn: Stiftung Entwicklung und Frieden, 1993, 35pp
940 **Tetzlaff, R** (ed), *Perspektiven der Demokratisierung in Entwicklungsländern.* Hamburg: Deutches Ubersee-Institut, 1992, 287pp

941 **Tetzlaff, R,** Staatszerfall und staatliche Neugliederung: Perspektiven der zukünftigen Staatenstruktur in Afrika, *Afrika Jahrbuch 1992,* 22–33
942 **Therkildsen, O,** 'Successful African local government': some methodological and conceptual issues, *Public administration and development,* **13,** 5 (1993) 501–506
943 **Thompson, B,** The ombudsman and human rights: African versions of a European institution, *Annual conference (African Society of Comparative and International Law),* **3,** (1991) 10–18
944 **Tiangaye, N,** Crise de légitimité du pouvoir de l'État et conférences nationales en Afrique, *African journal of international and comparative law,* **4,** 3 (1992) 609–629
945 **Tshiwula, J M M,** *La conférence nationale en Afrique et ses secrètes mystiques.* Kinshasa: ed SCIEDI, 1992, 188pp
946 **Tshiyembe, M,** Résistance actuelles à la démocratisation en Afrique, *Afrique 2000,* 14 (1993) 39–48
947 **Turok, B,** What does the World Bank mean by 'empowering ordinary people', in Onimode, B (ed), *The African response (Item 186),* 46–57
948 **United Nations Centre for Human Rights,** *African seminar on international human rights standards and the administration of justice.* New York: United Nations, 1992, 45pp
949 **Van Hoek, F, Bossuyt, J,** Democracy in subsaharan Africa: the search for a new institutional set-up, *African development review,* **5,** 1 (1993) 81–92
950 **Wani, I J,** The rule of law and economic development in Africa, *East African journal of peace and human rights,* **1,** 1 (1993) 52–79
951 **Williams, D,** Liberalism and 'development discourse', *Africa,* **63,** 3 (1993) 419–29
952 **Wiseman, J A,** Democracy and the new political pluralism in Africa: causes, consequences and significance, *Third world quarterly,* **14,** 3 (1993) 439–49
953 **Wiseman, J A,** Leadership and personal danger in African politics, *Journal of modern African studies,* **31,** 4 (1993) 657–60
954 **Woods, D,** Civil society in Europe and Africa: limiting state power through a public sphere, *African studies review,* **35,** 2 (1992) 77–100
955 **Young, T,** Elections and electoral politics in Africa, *Africa,* **63,** 3 (1993) 299–312
956 **Zolberg, A R,** The spectre of anarchy: African states verging on dissolution, *Dissent,* **39,** 3 (1992) 303–311

Religion, philosophy

See also: 10, 48, 50, 233, 654, 827, 834

957 **Achermann, E,** *Schrei, geliebtes Afrika! Ein Kontinent braucht Hilfe.* Solothurn: Walter, 1993, 261pp
958 **Ahanotu, A M** (ed), *Religion, society and state in contemporary Africa: Nigeria, Sudan, South Africa, Zaire and Mozambique.* New York: Lang, 1992, 208pp
959 **Alkali, N, et al** (eds), *Islam in Africa: proceedings of the Islam in Africa Conference.* Ibadan: Spectrum, 1993, 454pp
960 **Bayart, J F** (ed), *Religion et modernité politique en Afrique noire.* Paris: Karthala, 1993, 312pp
961 **Bayart, J F,** La cité culturelle en Afrique noire, in Bayart, J F (ed), *Réligion et modernité politique (item 960),* 299–310
962 **Bediako, K,** New paradigms on ecumenical cooperation: an

African perspective, *International review of mission,* **81,** 323 (1992) 375–79
963 **Brenner, L** (ed), *Muslim identity and social change in subsaharan Africa.* London: Hurst, 1993, 250pp
964 **Brenner, L,** Muslim representations of identity and differences in the African discourse, in Brenner, L (ed), *Muslim identity (item 963)*, 1–20
965 **Carew, G M,** A critique of John S Mbiti's traditional African ontology, *Quest,* **7,** 1 (1993) 78–91
966 **Chrétien, J P** (ed), *L'invention religieuse en Afrique.* Paris: Karthala, 1993, 492pp
967 **Echeruo, M J C,** Negritude and history: Senghor's argument with Frobenius, *Research in African literatures,* **24,** 4 (1993) 3–13
968 **Echeruo, M J C,** Post-négritude: the odour of grandfathers, *Journal of modern African studies,* **31,** 4 (1993) 719–24 (review article)
969 **Ekechi, F K,** Religion, race and nationalism, *Canadian journal of African studies,* **26,** 1 (1992) 125–31 (review article)
970 **Esonwanne, U,** The nation as contested referent, *Research in African literatures,* **24,** 4 (1993) 49–62
971 **Eze, E,** Truth and ethics in African thought, *Quest,* **7,** 1 (1993) 4–18
972 **Gbadegesin, S,** Bioethics and culture: an African standpoint, *Bioethics,* **7,** 2–3 (1993) 257–62
973 **Hasenhüttl, G,** *Schwarz bin ich und schön: der theologische Aufbruch Schwarzafrikas.* Darmstadt: Wissenschaftliche Buchgesellschaft, 1991, 177pp
974 **Heijke, J,** African Synod: colonization of Africa?, *Exchange,* **21,** 3 (1992) 177–230
975 **Heising, J,** *Entwicklung und moderne Philosophie in Schwarzafrika: Wege zu einer unbekannten geisteswissenschaftlichten Tradition.* Frankfurt: Verlag für Interkulturelle Kommunikation, 1990, 193pp
976 **Hoffman, G R,** European attitudes to African philosophy, *Quest,* **7,** 1 (1993) 44–55
977 **Horton, R,** *Patterns of thought in Africa and the West: essays on magic, religion and science.* Cambridge: CUP, 1993, 471pp
978 **Hunwick, J O** (ed), *Religion and national integration in Africa.* Evanston: Northwestern University Press, 1992, 176pp
981 **Kabasele-Lumbala, F,** *Le christianisme et l'Afrique: une chance réciproque.* Paris: Karthala, 1993, 128pp
982 **Kalu, O U,** African church historiography, in Falola, T (ed), *African historiography (Item 385)*, 166–79
983 **Kimmerle, H,** *Philosophie in Afrika.* Frankfurt: Campus, 1991, 245pp
984 **ma Mpolo, J M, Mwachuku, D** (eds), *Pastoral care and counselling in Africa today.* Frankfurt: Lang, 1991, 194pp
985 **Mafeje, A,** *African philosophical projections and prospects for the indigenisation of political and intellectual discourse.* Harare: Sapes books, 1992, 29pp
986 **Mafeje, A,** *In search of an alternative: a collection of essays on revolutionary theory and politics.* Harare: Sapes, 1992, 121pp
986a **Mana, K,** *Foi chrétienne, crise africaine et reconstruction de l'Afrique.* Yaoundé: Cle, 1992, 220pp
987 **Mana, K,** *L'Afrique va't-elle mourir? Essai d'ethique politique.* Paris: Karthala, 1993, 221pp
988 **Mana, K,** *Théologie africaine pour temps de crise: christianisme et*

reconstruction de l'Afrique. Paris: Karthala, 1993, 205pp

989 **Manus, U C,** *Christ, the African king: New Testament Christology.* Frankfurt: Lang, 1993, 280pp

990 **Masolo, M A,** An archaeology of African knowledge: a critique of V Y Mudimbe's The invention of Africa, *Makerere historical journal,* **5,** 1/2 (1990/91) 60–85

991 **Mbembe, A,** La prolifération du divin en Afrique subsaharienne, in Kepel, G (ed), *Les politiques de Dieu* (Paris: Seuil, 1993), 177–201

992 **Miller, C L,** Response to Esonwanne: alien nation?, *Research in African literatures,* **24,** 4 (1993) 63–68

993 **Mudimbe, V Y, Appiah, K A,** The impact of African studies on philosophy, in Bates R H et al (eds), *Africa and the disciplines (item 3),* 113–38

994 **Mudimbe, V Y** (ed), *The surreptitious speech: Présence africaine and the politics of otherness, 1947–1987.* Chicago: University of Chicago Press, 1992, 463pp

995 **Nagl-Docekal, H, Wimmer, F M** (eds), *Postkoloniales Philosophieren, Afrika.* Vienna: Oldenbourg, 1992, 252pp

996 **Neugebauer, C (ed),** *Philosophie, Ideologie und Gesellschaft in Afrika.* Frankfurt: Lang, 1991, 212pp

997 **Nthamburi, Z,** *The African church at the crossroads: a strategy for indigenisation.* Nairobi: Uzima, 1991, 151pp

998 **Nyamiti, C,** Some moral implications of African ancestral Christology, *African christian studies,* **8,** 3 (1992) 36–51

999 **Nyerere, J K,** Socialism, democracy and development in Africa, in Sandbrook, R & Halfani, M (eds), *Empowering people (Item 930),* 23–32

1000 **Okafor, F U,** Issues in African philosophy reexamined, *International philosophical quarterly,* **33,** 1 (1993) 91–99

1001 **Osaghae, E E,** Colonialism and African political thought, *Ufahamu,* **19,** 2/3 (1990/1991) 22–38

1002 **Otayek, R** (ed), *Le radicalisme islamique au sud du Sahara: da'wa, arabisation et critique de l'Occident.* Paris: Karthala, 1993, 264pp

1003 **Pilaszewicz, S,** The heritage of traditional African religions in Afro-Christian churches, *Africana bulletin,* 40 (1992) 73–92

1004 **Platvoet, J G,** Programmatic statements from Africa, 1982–1992, *Numen,* **40,** 3 (1993) 322–42

1005 **Pobee, J S** (ed), *Exploring Afro-Christology.* Frankfurt: Lang, 1992, 155pp

1007 **Pobee, J S,** *Skenosis: Christian faith in an African context.* Gweru: Mambo, 1992, 174pp

1008 **Ramose, M B,** African democratic tradition: oneness, consensus and openness, a reply to Wamba-dia-Wamba, *Quest,* **6,** 2 (1992) 62–83

1009 **Ranger, T O,** New approaches to the study of mission Chistianity, in Falola, T (ed), *African historiography (Item 385),* 180–94

1010 **Rasmussen, L,** *Christian-Muslim relations in Africa.* London: Routledge, 1993, 132pp

1011 **Ruel, M,** Passages and the person, *Journal of religion in Africa,* **23,** 2 (1993) 98–124

1012 **Sanneh, L,** Religion, politics and national integration: a comparative African perspective, in Hunwick, J O (ed), *Religion and national integration (Item 978),* 131–66

1013 **Schreiter, F J** (ed), *Faces of Jesus in Africa.* Maryknoll: Orbis, 1991, 181pp

1014 **Senghor, L S,** *Le dialogue des cutlures.* Paris: Seuil, 1993, 295pp

1015 **Serpa, E,** Islam in subsaharan Africa, *Africa insight,* **22,** 4 (1992) 235–43

1016 **Shank, D A,** *Ministry in partnership with African independent churches.* Elkhart, Ind.: Mennonite Board of Missions, 1991, 436pp

1017 **ter Haar, G, et al,** *African traditional religions in religious education: a resource book with special reference to Zimbabwe.* Utrecht: Utrecht University, 1992, 224pp

1018 **Thomas, L V, Luneau, R,** *La terre africaine et ses réligions: traditions et changements.* Paris: Harmattan, 1992, 336pp

1019 **Ustorf, W,** *Christianised Africa - de-Christianised Europe? Missionary enquiries into the polycentric epoch of Christian history.* Amersbeck: Verlag an der Lottbek, 1992, 157pp

1020 **Utuk, E,** *From New York to Ibadan: the impact of African questions on the making of ecumenical mission mandates, 1900–1958.* New York: Lang, 1991, 350pp

1021 **van Hook, J M,** African philosophy: its quest for identity, *Quest,* **7,** 1 (1993) 28–43

1022 **Wienecke, W A,** *Die Bedeutung der Zeit in Afrika in den traditionellen Religionen und in der missionarischen Verkündigung.* Frankfurt: Lang, 1992, 363pp

1023 **Young, J U,** African traditional religion and African theology, in Cohn-Sherbrook, D (ed), *World religions and human liberation* (Maryknoll: Orbis, 1992), 93–112

Rural economy

See also: 193, 212, 222, 228, 245, 251, 254, 257, 273, 279, 289, 315, 334, 341, 348–50, 463, 482, 805, 5287

1024 **Anderson, D M,** Cow power: livestock and the pastoralist in Africa, *African affairs,* **92,** 366 (1993) 121–33 (review article)

1025 **Anon,** The dynamics of privatization of land resources in Africa, *Rural progress,* **11,** 1 (1992) 49–62

1026 **Anon,** Poverty alleviation and structural adjustment in rural Africa: some reflections on practical measures, *Rural progress,* **12,** 1 (1993) 10–24

1027 **Askley, J,** Oil seeds, in Rowland, J R J (ed), *Dryland farming (Item 1078),* 240–59

1028 **Bassett, T J** (ed), *Land in African agrarian systems.* Madison: University of Wisconsin Press, 1993, 418pp

1029 **Behnke, R H, et al,** *Range ecology at disequilibrium: new models of natural variability and pastoral adaptation in African savannas.* Coulder: Westview, 1993, 248pp

1030 **Berry, S,** *No condition is permanent: the social dynamics of agrarian change in subsaharan Africa.* Madison: University of Wisconsin Press, 1993, 258pp

1031 **Berry, S,** Understanding agricultural policy in Africa: the contribution of Robert Bates, *World development,* **21,** 6 (1993) 1055–62

1032 **Bourenane, N,** Introduction, *Africa development,* **17,** 3 (1992) 5–33

1033 **Bryceson, D F,** *De-agrarianisation and rural employment generation in subsaharan Africa: process and prospects.* Leiden: Afrikastudiecentrum, 1993, 51pp

1034 **Burnage, T,** *New tractors for old: an analysis of the rehabilitation of agricultural mechanisation systems in subsaharan Africa.* Norwich: University of East Anglia, School of Development Studies, 1992, 62pp

1035 **Camilleri, J L,** *Dialogue avec la brousse: village, ethnie et développement.* Paris: Harmattan, 1993, 154pp

1036 **Carter, R,** Small-scale irrigation in subsaharan Africa, in *Proceedings of the Conference on priorities for water resources allocation and management, Southampton, 1992* (Reading: Natural Resources Institute, 1993), 103–116

1037 **Cleaver, K M,** *A strategy to develop agriculture in subsaharan Africa and a focus for the World Bank.* Washington: World Bank, 1993, 140pp

1038 **Cloete, F,** Comparative lessons for land reform in South Africa, *Africa insight,* **22,** 4 (1992) 249–58

1039 **Coleman, J R, et al,** *How policy changes affected cocoa sectors in subsaharan African countries.* Washington: World Bank, 1993, 71pp

1040 **Croll, E, Parkin, D** (eds), *Bush base: forest farm.* London: Routledge, 1992, 263pp

1041 **Cross, N,** Talking back: the role of oral testimony in participatory development, in Slim, H & Thompson, P (eds), *Listening for a change* (London: Panos, 1993), 126–38

1042 **Darkoh, M B K, Ould-May, M,** Cash crops versus food crops in Africa: a conflict between dependency and autonomy, *Transafrican journal of history,* 21 (1992) 36–50

1043 **Development Cooperation Information Department,** *Sustainable development in semi-arid subsaharan Africa.* The Hague: Ministry of Foreign Affairs, 1992, 100pp

1044 **Duncan, A, Jones, S,** Agricultural marketing and pricing reform: a review of experience, *World development,* **21,** 9 (1993) 1495–1514

1045 **Dupriez, H,** Cultivation systems and environment: the heat and heaviness of the fields, in Dellière, R & Symoens, J J (eds), *Agricultural intensification and environment in the tropical areas* (Brussels: Académie royale des sciences d'outre-mer, 1991), 33–47

1046 **Edwards, R,** Traditional farming systems and farming system research, in Rowland, J R J (ed), *Dryland farming (Item 1078),* 95–108

1047 **Ehui, S, Polson, R,** A review of the economic and ecological considerations on animal draft cultivation in subsaharan Africa, *Soil and tillage research,* **27,** 1–4 (1993) 195–210

1048 **Ehui Koffi, B,** *Le pouvoir de la brousse: ni démocratie, ni développement en Afrique noire sans les paysans organisés.* Paris: Harmattan, 1993, 314pp

1049 **Eponou, T,** *Partners in agricultural technology: linking research and technology transfer to serve farmers.* The Hague: International Service for National Agricultural Reseach, 1993, 85pp

1050 **Fair, D,** Aid to African agriculture: lessons from two decades of donors' experience, *Africa insight,* **23,** 1 (1993) 55–59

1051 **Gellen, K,** Africa's rural poor: partners in growth, *African farmer,* Nov. 1993 34–38

1052 **Gibbon, P, et al,** *A blighted harvest: the World Bank and African agriculture in the 1980s.* London: Currey, 1993, 168pp

1053 **Gray, J,** Maize pricing policy in eastern and southern Africa, *Food policy,* **17,** 6 (1992) 409–419

1054 **Harsch, E,** Farmers recovering from Africa's wars, *African farmer,* Nov. 1993 2–7

1055 **Houtkamp, J A, van der Laan, H L,** *Commodity auctions in tropical Africa: a survey of the African* *tea, tobacco and coffee auctions.* Leiden: Afrikastudiecentrum, 1993, 93pp

1056 **Jamal, V,** Surplus extraction and the African agrarian crisis in a historical perspective, in Singh, A Tabatabai H (eds), *Economic crisis and Third World agriculture* (Cambridge: CUP, 1993), 65–90

1057 **Jarvis, L S,** Overgrazing and range degradation in Africa: is there need and scope for government control of livestock numbers?, *Eastern Africa economic review,* **7,** 1 (1991) 95–116

1058 **Kinsey, B H, Binswanger, H P,** Characteristics and performance of resettlement programmes: a review, *World development,* **21,** 9 (1993) 1477–94

1059 **Kumar, V, Rowland, J R J,** The dryland farming environment, in Rowland, J R J (ed), *Dryland farming (Item 1078),* 19–45

1060 **Leonard, D K,** Structural reform of the veterinary profession in Africa and the New Institutional Economics, *Development and change,* **24,** 2 (1993) 227–67

1061 **Mace, R,** Transition between cultivation and pastoralism in subsaharan Africa, *Current anthropology,* **34,** 4 (1993) 363–82

1062 **Mackenzie, F,** Exploring the connections; structural adjustment, gender and the environment, *Geoforum,* **24,** 1 (1993) 71–87

1063 **Mafeje, A,** Peasant organisations in Africa: a potential debate between economists and sociologists, *Codesria bulletin,* 1 (1993) 14–17

1064 **Maganya, E,** The World Bank's new agricultural policy for subsaharan Africa, in Onimode, B (ed), *The African response (Item 186),* 76–84

1065 **Makonnen, T,** Planning issues in the development of subsistence farming, in Chole, E (ed), *Food crisis (Item 275),* 203–24

1066 **Meyns, P,** Policy implementation in African rural development: some practical observations and proposals, in Chole, E (ed), *Food crisis (Item 275),* 184–202

1067 **Morris, M L, Byerlee, D E,** Narrowing the wheat gap in subsaharan Africa: a review of consumption and production issues, *Economic development and cultural change,* **41,** 4 (1993) 737–61

1068 **Mrema, G C,** *Agricultural mechanisation policies and strategies in Africa: case studies from Commonwealth African countries.* London: Commonwealth Secretariat, 1991, 322pp

1069 **Nett, B, et al** (eds), *Agricultural transformation and social change in Africa.* Frankfurt: Lang, 1992, 252pp

1070 **Nindi, B C,** Dilemmas of development in rural institutions in subsaharan Africa, *Journal of eastern African research and development,* 22 (1992) 49–59

1071 **Okai, M,** Contrasts in policy implementation and management of food and agricultural projects, in Chole, E (ed), *Food crisis (Item 275),* 155–83

1072 **Oyejide, T A,** Effects of trade and macroeconomic policies on African agriculture, in Bautista, R M & Valdés, A (eds), *The bias against agriculture* (Washington: IFPRI, 1993), 241–62

1073 **Place, F, Hazell, P,** Productivity effects of indigneous land tenure systems in subsaharan Africa, *American journal of agricultural economics,* **75,** 1 (1993) 10–19

1074 **Richards, P,** Cultivation: knowledge or performance?, in Hobart, M (ed), *An anthropological critique of development: the growth of* *ignorance* (London: Routledge, 1993), 61–78

1075 **Roalkvam, G,** *Samvirke: et alternativ i Afrika.* Skjetten: Det Kgl. Selskap for Norges Vel, 1993, 122pp

1076 **Rowland, J R J,** Agricultural development in dryland Africa, in Rowland, J R J (ed), *Dryland farming (Item 1078)*, 1–18

1077 **Rowland, J R J,** Cereal crops, in Rowland, J R J (ed), *Dryland farming (Item 1078)*, 218–39

1078 **Rowland, J R J (ed),** *Dryland farming in Africa.* Basingstoke: MacMillan, 1993, 336pp

1079 **Rowland, J R J,** Grain legumes, in Rowland, J R J (ed), *Dryland farming (Item 1078)*, 260–84

1080 **Rowland, J R J,** Root crops, in Rowland, J R J (ed), *Dryland farming (Item 1078)*, 185–94

1081 **Rowland, J R J, Whiteman, P,** Principles of dryland farming, in Rowland, J R J (ed), *Dryland farming (Item 1078)*, 68–94

1082 **Russell, N C, Dowswell, C R** (eds), *Africa's agricultural development in the 1990s: can it be sustained?* Geneva: Centre for Applied Studies in International Negotiation, 1992, 208pp

1083 **Russell, N C, et al** (eds), *Policy options for agricultural development in subsaharan Africa.* Mexico, D F: Centre for Applied Studies in International Negotiations, 1993, 192pp

1084 **Saran, R,** Implications of changes in the international trade environment for agricultural policies in subsaharan Africa, *Food policy,* **18,** 5 (1993) 439–44

1085 **Seckler, D** (ed), *Agricultural transformation in Africa.* Arlington: Winrock International, 1993, 208pp

1086 **Sherikova, I,** Agricultural policy in Africa: facing the challenge of the 90s, in Nett, B et al (eds), *Agricultural transformation (Item 1069)*, 185–20

1087 **Sihana, P M, Kerven, C K,** *The impact of commercialisation on the role of labour in African pastoral societies.* London: ODI, 1991, 34pp

1088 **Stroud, A,** The use of animal draught, in Rowland, J R J (ed), *Dryland farming (Item 1078)*, 205–217

1089 **Tadesse Zerihun,** Survival economics: structural adjustment, agricultural marketing and sustainable development in Africa, in Nett, B et al (eds), *Agricultural transformation (Item 1069)*, 201–22

1090 **Underhill, H W,** *Small scale irrigation in Africa in the context of rural development.* Bedford: Cranfield Press, 1990, 90pp

1091 **UNECA,** Role of African leadership in its rural structural transformation and development, *Rural progress,* **11,** 2 (1992) 61–90

1092 **UNECA,** Some thoughts on the process of rural deterioration in Africa, *Rural progress,* **11,** 2 (1992) 51–60

1093 **UNECA,** Towards sustainable agricultural production by Africa's small-scale farmers, *Rural progress,* **11,** 1 (1992) 1–30

1094 **van Imschoot, M,** Water as a source of employment, *International labour review,* **131,** 1 (1992) 125–37

1095 **von der Lühe, N,** Zur Bedeutung des Rapid Rural Appraisal für die landwirtschaftliche Beratung in Afrika, *Afrika spektrum,* 1 (1993) 37–52

1096 **Wellard, K, Copestake, J C** (eds), *Non-governmental organisations and the state in Africa: rethinking roles in sustainable agricultural development.* London: Routledge, 1993, 331pp

1097 **Wellard, K, Copestake, J C,** Introduction, in Wellard, K & Copestake, J C (eds), *NGOs and the state (Item 1096)*, 1–12

Science & technology

See also: 57, 211, 220, 235, 337, 655

1098 Chander, R, *Information systems and basic statistics in subsaharan Africa.* Washington: World Bank, 1990, 47pp

1099 Charakupa, R, Physics education and African development, *African journal of science and technology. Series C, General,* **2,** 2 (1991) 11–15

1100 Emereole, H U, Secondary school physics and technological development in Africa, *African journal of science and technology. Series C, General,* **2,** 2 (1991) 42–51

1101 Forster, D, Snow, B, Using microcomputers for rapid data collection in developing countries, *Health policy and planning,* **7,** 1 (1992) 67–71

1102 Malu wa Kalenga, *Science et technologie en Afrique (histoire, leçons et perspectives).* Brussels: Académie royale des sciences d'outre-mer, 1992, 266pp

1103 Odhiambo, T R, Responsibilities of a scientist in the developing world, *Whydah,* **3,** 3 (1993) 1–9

1104 Vitta, P B, Short of target: why in Africa research rarely reaches use, *Canadian journal of development studies,* **14,** 2 (1993) 245–60

1105 Woherem, E, *Information technology in Africa: challenges and opportunities.* Nairobi: ACTS, 1993, 180pp

1106 Zymelman, M, *Science, education and development in subsaharan Africa.* Washington: World Bank, 1990, 66pp

Sociology

See also: 180, 342, 651, 744, 748

1107 Adepoju, A (ed), *Impact of structural adjustment on the population of Africa.* London: Currey, 1993, 148pp

1108 Akiwowo, A, Responses to Makinde/Lawuyi & Taiwo, *International sociology,* **6,** 2 (1991) 243–52

1109 Bardem, I, L'emancipation des jeunes: un facteur négligé des migrations interafricains, *Cahiers des sciences humaines,* **29,** 2/3 (1993) 375–93

1110 Bulterys, M, et al, Multiple sexual partners and mother-to-child transmission of HIV–1, *AIDS,* **7,** 12 (1993) 1639–45

1111 Carael, M, et al, Overview and selected findings of sexual behaviour surveys, *AIDS,* **5,** 1 (1991) 65–74

1112 Cernea, M M, Guggenheim, S E (eds), *Anthropological approaches to resettlement: policy, practice and theory.* Boulder: Westview, 1993, 406pp

1113 Chalmers, B, *African birth: childbirth in cultural transition.* River Club, South Africa: Berev Publications, 1990, 140pp

1114 Clignet, R, Continuités et discontinuités des liens entre héritage et développement, *Cahiers des sciences humaines,* **29,** 1 (1993) 165–93

1115 Farah, N, Homing in on the pigeon, *Index,* **22,** 5/6 (1993) 16–20

1116 Farwer, C, *Afrikanische Flüchtlinge: Vertreibung und internationale Migration: eine auswahlbibliographie.* Hamburg: Deutsches Ubersee-Institut, 1993, 106pp

1117 Febiri, F A, Marxism, socal class, ethnic and gender inequalities in contemporary African societies, *African review,* **18,** 1/2 (1991) 39–56

1118 Garnett, G P, Anderson, R M, Factors controlling the spread of HIV in heterosexual communities in developing countries: patterns of mixing between different age and sexual activity classes, *Philosophical transactions of the Royal Society of London, Series: biological sciences,* **342,** 1300 (1993) 137–59

1119 **Granqvist, R,** Introduction: African culture - an estimate, in Granqvist, R (ed), *Culture in Africa (item 10)*, 5–13

1120 **Ki-Zerbo, L,** Youth factor, *Africa forum,* **1,** 4 (1991) 28–31

1121 **Kohnert, D,** 'Wer hat Angst vorm Schwarzen Mann'?: afrikanische Fluchting in Europa - Spielball der Politiker, *Afrika Jahrbuch 1992,* 65–76

1122 **Le Roy, E,** La culture commune comme réponse à la crise de l'état et des économies en Afrique francophone, in Rist, G (ed), *La culture, otage du développement?* (Paris, Harmattan, 1993), 99–118

1123 **Locoh, T,** Les familles africaines face à la crise, *Afrique contemporaine,* 166 (1993) 3–14

1124 **Mahieu, F R,** Le système communautaire des droits et obligations en Afrique, in Mappa, S (ed), *Ambitions et illusions de la coopération Nord-Sud: Lomé IV* (Paris: Harmattan, 1990), 187–203

1125 **Maja-Pearce, A,** In search of Achebe's dignity: or, the cauliflower episode, in Granqvist, R (ed), *Culture in Africa (item 10)*, 123–29

1126 **Makinda-Adebusoye, P,** Labour migration and female-headed households, in Federici, N (ed), *Women's position and demographic change* (Oxford: Clarendon, 1993), 319–38

1127 **Meekers, D,** The process of marriage in African societies: a multiple indicator approach, *Population and development review,* **18,** 1 (1992) 61–78

1128 **Njoku, J E E,** *African childhood: poor social and economic environment.* Lewiston: Mellen, 1993, 156pp

1129 **Oppong, C,** Traditional family systems in rural settings in Africa, in Berquo, P X (ed), *Family systems and cultural change* (Oxford: Clarendon, 1992, 69–86

1130 **Orubuloye, I O, et al,** Diffusion and focus in sexual networking: identifying partners and partner's partners, *Studies in family planning,* **23,** 6 (1992) 343–51

1131 **Richter, R,** *Flüchtlingsfragen in Afrika: Zwangmigrationen in Rahmen grösserer Entwicklungsprozesse.* Baden Baden: Nomos, 1992, 393pp

1132 **Sahli, S J,** *Les problèmes de la limitation des naissances dans les pays du Maghreb.* Tunis: Faculté des sciences humaines et sociales, Université de Tunis 1, 1992, 484pp

1133 **Suhrke, A,** A crisis diminished: refugees in the developing world, *International journal,* **48,** 2 (1993) 215–39

1134 **Touré, M,** Croissance rapide de la population, urbanisation et migration en Afrique, *African development review,* **4,** 2 (1992) 236–72

1135 **Zaman, M A,** The risk of uprising, *Africa forum,* **2,** 3/4 (1992) 24–27

Social welfare

1136 **Dangana, M, Berte, A,** Decentralisation and deconcentration of social security institutions in Africa, *Social security documentation - African servies,* 12 (1991) 133–67

1137 **Jolly, R,** Challenges and hopes for the 1990s, in Rimmer, D (ed), *Action in Africa (Item 525)*, 165–75

1138 **Mouyema, H E K, Mulozi, S K,** Economic aspects of social security in Africa, *Social security documentation - African series,* 12 (1991) 11–95

1139 **Nouira, A, Dei, H G,** Social welfare actions of social security institutions within the framework of the global policy of health care in Africa, *Social security documentation - African series,* 12 (1991) 97–132

1140 **Oiga, A, Oudghiri, M,** Problems arising in the application of social security conventions concerning migrant workers, *Social security documentation - African series,* 12 (1991) 169–95

1141 **Osei-Hwedie, K,** The challenge of social work in Africa: starting the indigenisation process, *Journal of social development in Africa,* **8,** 1 (1993) 19–30

Urban studies

See also: 89, 608, 1134

1142 **Becker, C M, Morrison, A R,** Observational equivalence in the modelling of African labour markets and urbanisation, *World development,* **21,** 4 (1993) 535–54

1143 **Bertrand, M,** Plaidoyers pour lers centres urbains secondaires en Afrique au sud du Sahara, *Tiers Monde,* **34,** 133 (1993) 117–38

1144 **Girard, C,** Costruzione e creazione fondiaria, *Storia urbana,* **17,** 63 (1993) 153–65

1145 **Godard, X** (ed), *Enseignements de dix ans d'histoire des transports collectifs urbain en Afrique subsaharienne: synthèse de six études de case - Abidjan, Bamako, Brazzaville, Conakry, Dakar et Pointe Noire.* Arcueil: INRETS, 1991, 101pp

1146 **Hammond, A A,** Housing in Africa, problems, prospects and strategies, *Journal of the Network of African Countries on Local Building Materials and Technologies,* **1,** 4 (1991) 1–6

1147 **Jaglin, S, Dubresson, A** (eds), *Pouvoirs et cités d'Afrique noire: décentralisation en question.* Paris: Karthala, 1993, 312pp

1148 **Le Roy, E,** Un diritto al di fuori della legge? Irregolarita e illegalita fondiarie in alcune citta dell'Africa nera, *Storia urbana,* **17,** 63 (1993) 203–22

1149 **Oyebande, L,** Aspects of urban hydrology and the challenges for African urban environments, *African urban quarterly,* **5,** 1/2 (1990) 39–68

1150 **Pinsky, B,** Settlements Information Network Africa (SINA), *Environment and urbanisation,* **5,** 1 (1993) 155–61

1151 **Rogerson, C M,** Feeding Africa's cities: the potential for urban agriculture, *Africa insight,* **22,** 4 (1992) 229–34

1152 **Sanders, D,** Eurocentric bias in the study of African urbanisation, *Antipode,* **24,** 3 (1992) 203–213

1153 **Sierig, J** (ed), *Halbformeller Wohnungsbau in Afrika.* Stuttgart: Informationszentrum Raum und Bau, 1990, 66pp

1154 **Sierig, J** (ed), *Kostenfrahen in Wohnungsbau in Afrika.* Stuttgart: Informationszentrum Raum und Bau, 1990, 54pp

1155 **Sierig, J** (ed), *Sanierung von Slums und Squattersiedlungen in Afrika.* Stuttgart: Informationszentrum Raum und Bau, 1991, 71pp

1156 **Sierig, J** (ed), *Town planning and town development in Africa.* Stuttgart: Informationszentrum Raum und Bau, 1991, 60pp

1157 **Sierig,** J, *Spontanseidlungen in Africa.* Stuttgart: Informationszentrum Raum und Bau, 1992 (2nd edn), 138pp

1158 **Sihana, P M, Kerven, C K** (ed), *Stadt und Siedlungsgeschichte in Afrika.* Stuttgart: Informationszentrum Raum und Bau, 1992, 83pp

1159 **Tipple, A G, Willis, K G** (eds), *Housing the poor in the developing world.* London: Routledge, 1991, 287pp

1160 **UN Centre for Human Settlements,** *The management of secondary cities in subsaharan Africa: traditional and modern institutional arrangements.* Nairobi: the Centre, 1991, 154pp

1161 **Vennetier, P** (ed), *Urbanisation et développement dans les pays tropicaux.* Talence: Centre d'études de géographie tropicale, 1991, 198pp

LUSOPHONE AFRICA

General

1162 **Pélissier, R,** *Don Quichotte en Afrique.* Orgeval: Pélissier, 1992, 175pp

Economic and social history

1163 **Estêvão, J,** *Moeda e sistema monetario colonial.* Lisbon: Escher, 1991, 208pp

Economy - Development

1164 **de Sa, L M, Brot, J,** Les pays africains de langue officiel portugaise (PALOP), *Mondes en développement,* **20,** 77/78 (1992) 159–68

History, C20th

1165 **Chabal, P,** Emergencies and nationalist wars in Portuguese Africa, *Journal of imperial and Commonwealth history,* **21,** 3 (1993) 235–49

International economic relations

1166 **Hamilton, K A,** *Lusophone Africa, Portugal and the United States.* Washington: CSIS, Georgetown University, 1992, 57pp

1167 **Neto, A M,** Portugal und die Länder Afrikas mit Portugiesisch als offizieller Sprache (PALOP): Zusammenarbeit auf wissenschaftlichem, technichem, un sozialem Gebiet, *DASP-Hefte,* 35/6 (1992) 71–110

Language

1168 **Massa, J M,** Pouvoir et culture en Afrique de langue portugais, *Les langues modernes,* **86,** 4 (1992) 15–27

Literature

1169 **Laranjeira, P,** *De letra em rite: identidade, autonomia e outras questiones nas literaturas de Angola, Cabo Verde, Moçambique et São Tomé e Principe.* Porto: Afrontamento, 1992, 105pp

1170 **Moser, G M, Ferreira, M,** *A new bibliography of the lusophone literatures of Africa.* Oxford: Zell, 1993, 432pp

Politics

1171 **Chabal, P,** The postcolonial state in Portuguese-speaking Africa, *Portuguese studies,* **8,** (1992) 189–202

1172 **Chabal, P,** Some reflections on the post-colonial state in Portuguese-speaking Africa, *Africa insight,* **23,** 3 (1993) 129–35

1173 **Hermele, K,** Strukturanpassung und politische Bündnisse in Angola, Guinea-Bissau und Mosambik, in Meyns, P (ed), *Demokratie und Strukturreformen (Item 1174),* 25–34

1174 **Meyns, P** (ed), *Demokratie und Strukturreformen im portugiesischsprachigen Afrika.*

Freiburg: Arnold Bergstrasser Institut, 1992, 303pp

1175 **Meyns, P,** Einleitung: ein neuer Aufgang für die portugiesischsprachigen Afrika?, in Meyns, P (ed), *Demokratie und Strukturreformen (Item 1174)*, 3–24

NORTH AFRICA

General

1176 **Zartman, I W,** Habeeb, W M (eds), *Polity and society in colonial North Africa.* Boulder: Westview, 1993, 285pp

Agriculture, scientific

1177 **Janssen, W G,** Economic and agricultural development in West Asia and North Africa: the need for agricultural research, *Food policy,* **18,** 6 (1993) 507–22

Anthropology

See also: 1192, 1193

1178 **Bourgeot, A,** Identité touarègue: de l'aristocratie à la revolution, *Etudes rurales,* 120 (1990) 129–62

1179 **de Chassey, F,** *L'étrier, la houe et le livre: 'sociétés traditionelles' au Sahara et au Sahel occidental.* Paris: Harmattan, 1993, 312pp

1180 **Ferrie, J N,** La naissance de l'aire culturelle méditerranéenne dans l'anthropologie physique de l'Afrique du nord, *Cahiers d'études africaines,* **33,** 129 (1993) 139–51

1181 **Harrak, A** (ed), *Contacts between cultures. Vol. 1: West Asia and North Africa.* Lewiston: Mellen, 1992, 493pp

Arts

See also: 1181

1182 **Sraieb, N** (ed), *Pratiques et résistance culturelles au Maghreb.* Paris: CNRS, 1992, 386pp

Demography

1183 **Moghadam, V M,** *Development and patriarchy: the Middle East and North Africa in economic and demographic transition.* Helsinki: WIDER, 1992, 63pp

1184 **Tabutin, D,** Evolution comparée de la mortalité en Afrique du nord de 1960 à nos jours, *Social science and medicine,* **36,** 10 (1993) 1257–65

Economy - Development

See also: 1183

1185 **Niblock, T, Murphy, E** (eds), *Economic and political liberalisation in the Middle East.* London: Tauris, 1993, 302pp

Education

1186 **El-Sanabary, N,** The Middle East and North Africa, in King, E M & Hill, M A (eds), *Women's education in developing countries* (Baltimore: Johns Hopkins University Press, 1993), 136–74

Food

1187 **El Ghonemy, M R,** Food security and rural development in North Africa, *Middle eastern studies,* **29,** 3 (1993) 445–66

Gender

See also: 1186

1188 Camps, G, *L'Afrique du nord au féminin: héroines du Maghreb et du Sahara.* Paris: Perrin, 1992, 333pp

1189 Rouach, D, *'Imma, ou rites, coutumes et croyances chez la femme juive en Afrique du nord.* Paris: Maisonneuve & Larose, 1990, 227pp

History, general

No entry. *See also:* 1188

History, early

See also: 1190

1190 Ministère de l'éducation nationale et de la culture (ed), *Histoire et archéologie de l'Afrique du nord: spectacles, vie portuaire, religions.* Paris: Comité des travaux historiques et scientifiques, 1992, 487pp

1191 Schuster, A M H, Ancient Nubia: Egypt's rival in Africa, *Archaeology,* **46,** 1 (1993) 60–63

History, C19th

1192 Boetsch, G, Egypte noire et Berbérie blanche: la rencontre manquée entre la biologie et la culture, *Cahiers d'études africaines,* **33,** 129 (1993) 73–98

1193 Boetsch, G, Ferrie, J N, L'impossible objet de la raciologie: prologue à une anthropologie physique de nord de l'Afrique, *Cahiers d'études africaines,* **33,** 129 (1993) 5–18

History, C20th

1194 Burke, E (ed), *Struggle and survival in the modern Middle East.* London: Tauris, 1993, 400pp

Industry & trade

1195 Marghani, ABD, *Ghibli: a study of the geography and politics of air transport in Libya and North Africa.* Wisbech: Middle East and North African Studies Press, 1991, 198pp

International economic relations

1196 Agate, P S, Coopération CEE-UMA: alternative or morcellement, *Annuaire de l'Afrique du nord,* **28,** (1990) 113–25

International relations

1197 Obdeijn, H J M, Europa en Noord-Afrika: goede buren?, *Internationale spectator,* **47,** 9 (1993) 502–507

Politics

1198 Ibrahim, S E, Crises, elites and democratisation in the Arab world, *Middle East journal,* **47,** 2 (1993) 292–306

1199 Lopez Garcia, B, et al (eds), *Elecciones, participacion y transiciones politicas en el Norte de Africa.* Madrid: Agencia Espagñola de Cooperacion Internacional, 1991, 319pp

Religion, philosophy

1200 Valderrama Martinez, F, El Islam en el mundo bereber, *Boletin de la Asociacion Espagñola de Orientalistas,* 27 (1991) 5–24

Rural economy

See also: 1187

1201 El-Ghonemy, M R, *Land, food and rural development in North Africa.* London: IT Publications, and Boulder: Westview, 1993, 192pp

MAGHREB

General

1202 **Filali-Ansary, A,** L'idée du Maghreb à travers les sciences sociales, *Annuaire de l'Afrique du nord,* **28,** (1990) 185–90

1203 **Tozy, M,** Orient et Occident dans l'imaginaire politique d'un babouchier de Fes: essai de lectures sur un mur d'images, *Annuaire de l'Afrique du nord,* **28,** (1990) 237–49

Anthropology

See also: 1215–17

1204 **Dachmi, A,** La séduction maternelle négative: approche anthropo-analytique du phénomène de la persécution au Maghreb, *Cahiers de sociologie économique et culturelle,* 17 (1992) 103–131

1205 **Ferrié, J N, Boetsch, G,** Du Berbère aux yeux clairs à la race eurafricaine: la Méditerrannée des anthropologues physiques, *Annuaire de l'Afrique du nord,* **28,** (1990) 191–207

1206 **Grandguillaume, G,** Par delà les frontières et les langues, *Annuaire de l'Afrique du nord,* **28,** (1990) 263–68

1207 **Shinar, P,** Some observations on the role of red in northwest Africa (the Maghrib), in Harrak, A (ed), *Contacts between cultures (Item 1181),* 383–90

Economic and social history

1208 **Longuenesse, E (ed),** *Bâtisseurs et bureaucrates: ingenieurs et société au Maghreb et au Moyen-Orient.* Lyon: Maison de l'Orient, 1990, 437pp

1209 **Martinez Sanz, J L,** Ciencia i colonialismo español en el Maghreb: el estudio cientifico de las colonias españolas y sus posibilidades economicas, *Estudios Africanos,* **6,** 10/11 (1991/92) 109–139

Economy - Development

See also: 1248

1210 **Helmschrott, H, et al,** Zur politischen Okonomie ordungspolitischer Reformen: Wirtschaftspolitik im Spannungsfeld politischer Machtprozesse: die Biepspiele Tunisien und Algerien, in their *Stagnation in der Dritten Welt* (Munich: IFO, 1992), 220–26

1211 **Sid Ahmed, A,** La crise des économies maghrébines: les politiques redistributives en question, *Tiers Monde,* **33,** 135 (1993) 565–83

Environment

1212 **Zaimeche, S E,** Environmental degradation and the threat of desertification in three north African countries: Morocco, Algeria, Tunisia, *Bulletin of francophone Africa,* 2 (1993) 86–101

Gender

1213 **Kaye, J,** Islam, islamisation and women in the Maghreb, *Bulletin of francophone Africa,* 2 (1993) 2–13

Geography, human

1214 **Perennes, J J,** *L'eau et les hommes au Maghreb.* Paris: Karthala, 1993, 637pp

History, C19th

1215 **Haoui, K,** Classifications linguistiques et anthropologiques de la Société d'anthropologie de Paris au XIXe siècle, *Cahiers d'études africaines,* **33,** 129 (1993) 51–72

1216 **Pouillon, F,** Simplification ethnique en Afrique du nord: Maures, Arabes et Berbères (XVIIIe-XIX siecles), *Cahiers d'études africaines,* **33,** 129 (1993) 37–50

1217 **Thomson, A,** La classification raciale de l'Afrique du nord au début du XIXe siècle, *Cahiers d'études africaines,* **33,** 129 (1993) 19–36

History, C20th

See also: 1244

1218 **Harmon, S J,** Shaykh Ma al-Aynan: armed resistance and French policy in northwest Africa, 1900–1910, *Jusur,* 8 (1992) 1–22

1219 **Müller, H L,** *Islam, gihad ('heiliger Kreig') und Deutsches Reich: ein Nachspiel zur wilheminischen Weltpolitik im Maghreb.* Frankfurt: Lang, 1991, 453pp

Industry & trade

1220 **Bernard, C (ed),** *Nouvelles logiques marchands au Maghreb: l'informel dans les années 80.* Paris: CNRS, 1991, 264pp

International economic relations

1221 **Balta, P, L'**UMA et le défi de la CEE, in Lopez Garcia, B, et al (eds), *Transiciones politicas (Item 1199),* 29–38

1222 **Bensidoun, I, Chevallier, A,** Europe-Méditerranée: fractures et rapprochements, *Politique africaine,* 49 (1993) 47–59

1223 **Blin, L, Parisot, B,** Les relations économiques entre la CEE et les pays Maghreb, *Annuaire de l'Afrique du nord,* **28,** (1990) 57–95

1224 **Kahder, B,** *Le grand Maghreb et l'Europe: enjeux et perspective.* Paris: Publisud, 1992, 264pp

1225 **Mahiou, A,** Le Maghreb et la CEE: entre la crainte et l'espoir, *Annuaire de l'Afrique du nord,* **28,** (1990) 27–37

1226 **Sid Ahmed, A,** Les relations économiques entre l'Europe et le Maghreb, *Tiers Monde,* **33,** 136 (1993) 759–80

1227 **Talha, L,** Relations Europe-Maghreb: la question des investissements directs, *Tiers Monde,* **33,** 136 (1993) 927–35

1228 **Weidnitzer, E,** *L'Union du Maghreb arabe: problèmes de la coopération maghrébine et le recherche d'un nouveau partenaire avec la CE.* Berlin: German Development Institute, 1992, 121pp

International relations

See also: 1246

1229 **Basfao, K,** Arrêt sur images: les rapports franco-maghrébins au mirior de la bande dessinée, *Annuaire de l'Afrique du nord,* **28,** (1990) 225–35

1230 **Basfao, K, Henry, J R,** Introduction: le Maghreb, l'Europe et la France, *Annuaire de l'Afrique du nord,* **28,** (1990) 3–13

1231 **Biad, A,** Le Maghreb et la guerre du Golfe, *Annuaire de l'Afrique du nord,* **28,** (1990) 439–52

1232 **Bistolfi, R,** La politique maghrébine de la Communauté: quels développements?, *Annuaire de l'Afrique du nord,* **28,** (1990) 17–25

1233 **de Larramendi, M H,** Perception espagnole du Maghreb et politique étrangère de l'Espagne démocratique, *Annuaire de l'Afrique du nord,* **28,** (1990) 153–69

1234 **Gobe, E,** Autour du Forum méditerranéen: valses, hesitations et enjeux, *Annuaire de l'Afrique du nord,* **28,** (1990) 97–106

1235 **Laafifi, A,** Quels nouveaux enjeux culturels pour la France et le Maroc face aux stratégies d'union en Europe et au Maghreb?, *Annuaire de l'Afrique du nord,* **28,** (1990) 269–74

1236 **Lopez-Garcia, B,** L'Espagne entre le Maghreb et l'Europe: imaginaire et interférences de l'opinion dans la politique maghrébine de l'Espagne, *Annuaire de l'Afrique du nord,* **28,** (1990) 139–52

1237 **Miyaji, K,** Le rapport Europe-Maghreb vu du Japon, *Annuaire de l'Afrique du nord,* **28,** (1990) 127–35

1238 **Rufins, O,** The Maghreb and the Persian Gulf crisis, *Revista de Africa y Medio Oriente,* **4,** 1 (1992) 24–40

1239 **Vasconcelos, A, et al,** *Européens et maghrebins: une solidarité obligée.* Paris: Karthala, 1993, 183pp

Law

1240 **Ebert, H G,** Familiengesetze im Maghreb: das Spannungsverhältnis von islamischrechtlicher Tradition und soziokulturen Wandel, *Orient,* **33,** 1 (1992) 61–79

Literature

1241 **Arnaud, J, et al (eds),** *Littératures maghrébines.* Paris: Harmattan, 1990, 2 vols.,

1242 **Bonn, C, Kachoukh, F,** *Bibliographie de la littérature maghrébine 1980–1990.* Vanves: Edicef, 1992, 96pp

1243 **Déjeux, J,** *La littérature maghrébine d'expression française.* Paris: PUF, 1992, 127pp

1244 **Mrani, N E,** A propos d'un refoulé de la littérature maghrébine de langue française: l'anthropologie et la littérature coloniale, *IBLA,* 169 (1992) 71–87

1245 **Pantucek, S,** Die Gestaltung der magribinischen Nationalliteraturen in der 1. Hälfte des 20. Jahhunderts, *Archiv orientalni,* **60,** 2 (1992) 134–46

Media

1246 **Geisser, V, Le Troquer, Y,** Guerre et presse: la presse maghrébine d'expression française et le crise du Golfe, *Annuaire de l'Afrique du nord,* **28,** (1990) 417–37

Politics

See also: 1239

1247 **Camau, M,** Démocratisation et changement des régimes au Maghreb, in Lopez Garcia, B, et al (eds), *Transiciones politicas (Item 1199),* 67–77

1248 **Spencer, C,** *The Maghreb in the 1990s: political and economic development in Algeria, Morocco and Tunisia.* London: International Institute of Strategic Studies, 1993, 64pp

Religion, philosophy

No entry. *See also:* 1213

Rural economy

No entry. *See also:* 1214

ALGERIA

General

1249 **Allouache, M, Colonna, F (eds),** *Algérie, 30 ans: les enfants de l'indépendance.* Paris: Autrement, 1992, 205pp

1250 **Anon,** Auswahlbibliographie Algerien (ab Erscheinungsjahr 1980 bis Juni 1992), *Wuqûf,* 6 (1992) 471–88

1251 **Ruhe, E,** *Algerien-Bibliographie:*

Publikationen aus der Bundesrepublik Deutschland, Osterreich und der Schweiz 1962–1989. Weisbaden: Harrassowitz, 1990, 181pp

Anthropology

1252 **Mohia-Navet, N,** *Les thérapies traditionelles dans la société Kabylie: pour une anthropologie psychanalytique.* Paris: Harmattan, 1993, 268pp

1253 **Rivière, T, Faublée, J,** Dans le sud de l'Aurès en 1935: circoncisions, mariages et *hiji* chez les Ouled Ahderrahman, *Etudes et documents berbères,* 8 (1991) 63–77

1254 **Cominardi, F,** Au coeur des Monts des Ksour: le Ksar de Chellala Dahrania, *Etudes et documents berbères,* 8 (1991) 135–58

Architecture

No entry. *See also:* 1263

Arts

See also: 1297

1255 **Elsner, j,** Zur Darstellung der algerischen Musik auf der ersten Konferenz für arabische Musik, Kairo 1932, in Elsner, J & Jähnichen, G (eds), *Studies in ethnomusicology. Vol. 3: Africa and Asia* (Berlin: Humbolt University, 1993), 111–36

1256 **Pouillon, F,** Exotisme, modernisme, identité; la société algérienne en peinture, *Annuaire de l'Afrique du nord,* **28,** (1990) 209–24

Current affairs

1257 **Beker, M,** Algerije in een patstelling: islamisten, militairen en de strijd in een politieke leegte, *Internationale spektator,* **47,** (1993) 248–52

1258 **Benamadi, Z, Akeb, F,** Interview mit Mohamed Boudiaf, Präsident des algerischen Staatrates (14.1–29.6.1992), *Wuqûf,* 6 (1992) 79–96

1259 **Lamchichi, A,** La démocratie en suspens, *Confluences Méditerranée,* 3 (1992) 27–41

1260 **Mortimer, R A,** Algeria: the clash between Islam, democracy, and the military, *Current history,* **92,** 570 (1993) 37–41

1261 **Younessi, B,** L'état contre la nation, *Confluences Méditerranée,* 3 (1992) 122–129

Demography

1262 **Kouaouci, A,** Migrations des femmes et fécondité en Algérie, *Revue du monde musulman et de la Méditerranée,* 65 (1992) 165–73

Economic and social history

1263 **Amamra, A A,** Fentress, E, Sétif: évolution d'un quartier, in *La casa hispano-musulmana: aportaciones de la arqueologia* (Granada: Patronata de la Alhambra y Generalife, 1990), 163–76

1264 **Arnaudies, F,** *Esquisses anecdotiques et historiques du vieil Alger.* Avignon: Barthélemy, 191, 241pp

1265 **Bergeret, A,** Discours et politiques forestières coloniales en Afrique et à Madagascar, *Revue française d'histoire d'outre-mer,* **80,** 298 (1993) 23–47

1266 **Crespo, G, Jordi, J J,** *L'immigration espagnole dans l'Algérie de 1830 à 1914.* Versailles: Atlanthrope, 1991, 181pp

1267 **Lahouel, B,** Euro-Algerian commercial relations (eighteenth to beginning of nineteenth centuries), *Bulletin of francophone Africa,* 4 (1993) 1–15

1268 **Laoust-Chantréaux, G** (ed. C Lacoste-Dujardin), *Kabylie côté* *femmes: la vie feminine à Aït Hichem 1937–1939. Notes d'ethnographie.* Aix en Provence: Edisud, 1990, 304pp

1269 **Mannoni, P,** *Les français d'Algérie: vie, moeurs, mentalités.* Paris: Harmattan, 1993, 288pp

Economy - Development

1270 **Benachenou, A,** Inflation et chômage en Algérie: les aléas de la démocratie et des réformes économiques, *Maghreb-Machrek,* 139 (1993) 28–41

1271 **Brahimi, A,** *Stratégies de développement pour l'Algérie: défis en enjeux.* Paris: Economica (2nd, revised edn), 1991, 425pp

1272 **Corm, G,** La réforme économique algérienne: une réforme mal aimée, *Maghreb-Machrek,* 139 (1993) 9–27

1273 **Mattes, H,** Der algerische 'Grand Sud': politische und ökonomische Entwicklung im Saharaum und grenzüberschrietende Einflussfaktoren, *Wuqûf,* 6 (1992) 169–258

1274 **Moussa, Z,** La problématique du développement local en Algérie: une tentative d'approche, *African journal of international and comparative law,* **4,** 4 (1992) 892–904

Education

No entry. *See also:* 1278

Environment

See also: 1321

1275 **Khaoula, M M,** Environnement et droits de l'homme en Algérie, *Annual conference (African Society of Comparative and International Law),* **3,** (1991) 32–39

Finance

1276 **Beltas, A, Jones, T,** Money, inflation and causality in a financially pressed economy: Algeria, 1970–88, *Applied economics,* **25,** 4 (1993) 473–80

Gender

See also: 1268

1277 **Amrabe, D,** *Les femmes algériennes dans la guerre.* Paris: Plon, 1991, 298pp

1278 **Benhassine-Miller, A,** Education et scolarisation des filles en Algérie, *Bulletin of francophone Africa,* 2 (1993) 29–36

1279 **Gacemi, B,** La longue marche des femmes algériennes, *Confluences Méditerranée,* 3 (1992) 87–94

1280 **Ladjah, M,** Conception, contraception: do Algerian women really have a choice?, in Turshen, M (ed), *Women and health (Item 343),* 125–41

History, early

1281 **Coye,** N, Préhistoire et protohistoire en Algérie au XIXe siècle: les significations du document archéologique, *Cahiers d'études africaines,* **33,** 129 (1993) 99–137

History, C18th

1282 **Brett, M,** Ibn Khaldun and the dynastic approach to local history: the base of Biskra, *Al Qantara,* **12,** 1 (1991) 157–80

1283 **Hunwick, J O,** The right of dhimmis to maintain a place of worship: a 15th century fatwa from Tlemcen, *Al Qantara,* **12,** 1 (1991) 133–55

History, C19th

1284 **Clancy-Smith, J,** The Shaykh

and his daughter: coping in colonial Algeria, in Burke, E (ed), *Struggle and survival (Item 1194)*, 145–63

1285 **Prochaska, D,** Tales of the city: between *Algérie française* and *Algérie algérienne*, in Segal, D (ed), *Crossing cultures: essays in the displacement of Western civilisations* (Tucson: University of Arizona Press, 1992), 182–225

History, C20th

See also: 1323, 1352

1286 **Brulé, J C,** Pouvoirs, sociétés et remodelages administratife: le cas de l'est algérien, *Cahiers de l'URBAMA,* 4 (1990) 49–60

1287 **Dahlab, S,** *Mission accomplie.* Alger: ed. Dahlab, 1990, 364pp

1288 **de Person, J,** *Un médecin au Sahara: Jacques de Person, 1911–13.* Brinon sur Sauldre: Grandvaux, 1992, 48pp

1289 **Delerive, R,** *Forts sahariens des territoires du sud.* Paris: Geuthner, 1990, 278pp

1290 **Establet, C,** *Etre caïd dans l'Algérie coloniale.* Paris: CNRS, 1991, 385pp

1291 **Faath, S,** Malek Bennabi: politischer Schriftsteller, Gesellschaftkriktiker, Visionär einer 'islamischen Zivilisation' im kolonisierten und unabhängigen Algerian, *Wuqûf,* 6 (1992) 133–52

1292 **Fabre, T,** France-Algérie: questions de mémoire, *Annuaire de l'Afrique du nord,* **28,** (1990) 353–60

1293 **Gervereau, L, et al** (eds), *La France en guerre d'Algérie.* Nanterre: Bibliothèque de documentation internationale contemporaine, 1992, 320pp

1294 **Guilhaume, J F,** *Les mythes fondateurs de l'Algérie française.* Paris: Harmattan, 1993, 331pp

1295 **Hébrad, J L, Hébrad, M C,** *L'Algérie autre-fois.* Le Coteau: Horvath, 1990, 143pp

1296 **Jauffret, J C,** The origins of the Algerian war: the reaction of France and its army to the emergencies of 8 May 1945 and 1 November 1954, *Journal of imperial and Commonwealth history,* **21,** 3 (1993) 17–29

1297 **Kasbadji, N,** Résistance et ambiguités dans l'Algérie coloniale: musique- théâtre-littérature, in Harrak, A (ed), *Contacts between cultures. Vol. 1: West Asia and North Africa* (Lewiston: Mellen, 1992), 59–65

1298 **Katz, J,** *L'honneur d'un général: Oran 1962.* Paris: Harmattan, 1993, 368pp

1299 **Khane, M,** Perceptions of Algerian identity in the 1950s: *Le Monde*'s treatment of intellectuals' views, *Bulletin of francophone Africa,* 4 (1993) 47–75

1300 **Lustick, I S,** *Unsettled states, disputed lands: Britain and Ireland, France and Algeria, Israel and the West Bank.* Ithaca: Cornell University Press, 1993, 576pp

1301 **Morizot, J,** *L'Aurès ou le mythe de la montagne rebelle.* Paris: Harmattan, 1991, 273pp

1302 **Mowitt, J,** Algerian nation: Fanon's fetish, *Cultural critique,* 22 (1992) 165–86

1303 **Pervillé, G,** *1962: la paix en Algérie.* Paris: Documentation française, 1992, 95pp

1304 **Roberts, H,** Historical and unhistorical approaches to the study of identity in Algeria, *Bulletin of francophone Africa,* 4 (1993) 79–92

1305 **Roux, M,** *Les harkis, ou les oubliés de l'histoire.* Paris: La Découverte, 1991, 420pp

1306 **Santo-Marino, R,** Une guerre en question: le contingent dans la guerre d'Algérie: retour à une enquête des organisations de jeunesse, *Annuaire de l'Afrique du nord,* **28,** (1990) 281–301

1307 **Stora, B,** Algeria: the war

without a name, *Journal of imperial and Commonwealth history,* **21,** 3 (1993) 208–216

1308 Stora, B, Pendant la guerre d'Algérie: le problème de l'Europe, *Annuaire de l'Afrique du nord,* **28,** (1990) 303–308

Industry & trade

See also: 460, 1376

1309 Benachenou, A, L'aventure de la désétatisation en Algérie, *Revue du monde musulman et de la Méditerranée,* 65 (1992) 175–85

1310 Benakli, A, *Die algerische Industrialisierungspolitik: Konzeption, Regulierung, Ausbau und Rückwirkungen auf die Landwirtschaft.* Frankfurt: Land, 1992, 289pp

1311 Benissad, H, *Micro-entreprises et cadre institutionnel en Algérie.* Paris: OECD Development Centre, 1993, 92pp

1312 Khennas, S, Industrialisation and energy policy: the Algerian case, in Khennas, S (ed), *Industrialisation (item 454)*, 112–26

1313 Mattes, H, Algeriens Nuklearambitionen zwischen Realität und 'Feindpropaganda', *Wuqûf,* 6 (1992) 311–31

International relations

1314 el-Kenz, A, *Algerian reflections on Arab crises.* Austin: Centre for Middle Eastern Studies, University of Texas, 1991, 116pp

1315 Henry, J R, L'univers mental des rapports franco-algériens, *Annuaire de l'Afrique du nord,* **28,** (1990) 369–77

1316 Hösel, J, Das Algerien-Bild der ehemaligen DDR: Versuch einer Aufarbeitung anhand wissenschaftlicher Publikationen aus den 80er Jahren, *Wuqûf,* 6 (1992) 373–83

1317 Mattes, H, Die algerische Afrikapolitik 1962–92: politische Grundsätze, praktische Umsetzung und präsidiale Arbeitsstile, *Wuqûf,* 6 (1992) 333–72

Labour & manpower

1318 Bernard, C, *L'auto-emploi urbaine en Algerie.* Geneva: ILO, 1990, 63pp

1319 Müller, H, Jugendarbeitslosigkeit in Algerien, *Wuqûf,* 6 (1992) 259–67

Language

1320 Steinhardt, E, Quelques réflexions sur la politique algérienne d'arabisation de la fin des années quatre-vingts, *Annuaire de l'Afrique du nord,* **28,** (1990) 275–79

Law

See also: 1275

1321 Kahloula, M M, Environnement et droits de l'homme en Algerie, *Annual conference (African Society of Comparative and International Law),* **3,** (1991) 32–39

1322 Lazhari, B, The Algerian constitutional experiment and human rights, *Annual conference (African Society of Comparative and International Law),* **3,** (1991) 40–50

Literature

See also: 3916

1323 Arab, S I, La guerre de libération dans quelques romans algérien d'expression francaise, *Bulletin of francophone Africa,* 3 (1993) 15–25

1324 Arab, S I, Three views of the desert in the French language novel of Algeria, *Bulletin of francophone Africa,* 4 (1993) 34–44

1325 **Aresu, B**, *Counterhegemonic discourse from the Maghreb: the poetics of Kateb's fiction.* Tubingen: Gunter Narr, 1993, 314pp

1326 **Bonn, C,** L'irrégularité de l'écrivain maghrébin francophone: Nedjma de Kateb Yacine dans le contexte des années cinquante, *Revue de l'Institut de sociologie,* 1990/91 129–38

1327 **Chaker, S,** La naissance d'une littérature écrite: le cas berbère (Kabylie), *Bulletin des études africaines de I'INALCO,* **9,** 17/18 (1992) 7–21

1328 **de la Hogue, J, Nerbonne, S,** *Mémoire écrite de l'Algérie depuis 1950: les auteurs et leurs oeuvres.* Paris: Maisonneuve et Larose, 1992, 231pp

1329 **Heller-Goldenberg, L,** Die jüdisch-algerische Literatur - eine Exilliteratur, *Wuqûf,* 6 (1992) 413–20

1330 **Ibnlfassi, L,** The evolution of the mother in the works of Driss Chraibi, *Bulletin of francophone Africa,* 4 (1993) 16–29

1331 **Keil, R,** 'Ein Vogelfänger wurde Kulturminister...': Anmerkungen zu Habib Tengour, *Wuqûf,* 6 (1992) 393–400

1332 **Tamba, S**, *Kateb Yacine.* Paris: Seghers, 1992, 221pp

1333 **Walter, H**, *Widerschein Afrikas: zu einer algerischen Literaturgeschichte - Themes und Motive.* Wiesbaden: Harrassowitz, 1990, 187pp

1334 **Woodhull, W,** Rereading Nedjma: feminist scholarship and North African women, *Sub-Stance,* 69 (1992) 46–63

Media

1335 **Byrne, E,** Dialogue suspended, *Index on censorship,* **22,** 2 (1993) 21–23

1336 **Ihaddaden, Z,** The postcolonial policy of Algerian broadcasting in Kabyle, in Riggins, S H (ed), *Ethnic minority media: an international perspective* (Newbury Park: Sage, 1992), 243–55

Politics

See also: 940, 1335, 1340, 1354, 1358, 1365, 1369, 1371

1337 **Anciaux, R,** Le poids de la variable islamique dans la construction politique de l'Algérie, *Civilisations,* **40,** 2 (1992) 154–169

1338 **Babadji, R,** Le FIS et héritage du FLN: la gestion des communes, *Confluences Méditerranée,* 3 (1992) 105–113

1339 **Benchikh, M,** Les obstacles au processus de démocratisation en Algérie, *African journal of international and comparative law,* **4,** 2 (1992) 473–485

1340 **Boudjedra, R**, *FIS de la haine.* Paris: Denoel, 1992, 141pp

1341 **Carlier, O,** De l'islahisme à l'islamisme: la thérapie politico-religieuse du FIS, *Cahiers d'études africains,* **32,** 126 (1992) 185–219

1342 **Chagnollaud, J-P,** Le militaire, le démocrate et l'islamiste, *Confluences Méditerranée,* 3 (1992) 7–18

1343 **Chaker, S,** La question berbère dans l'Algérie indépendante: la fracture inévitable?, *Revue du monde musulman et de la Méditerranée,* 65 (1992) 97–105

1344 **Cheikh, S,** Les élections locales en Algérie à l'ère du multipartisme, in Lopez Garcia, B, et al (eds), *Transiciones politicas (Item 1199)*, 247–86

1345 **Dunn, M C,** Revivalist Islam and democracy: thinking about the Algerian quandary, *Middle East policy,* **1,** 2 (1992) 16–22

1346 **Entelis, J P, Arone, L J,** Algeria in turmoil: Islam, democracy and the state, *Middle*

East policy, **1,** 2 (1992) 23–35
1347 **Faath, S,** Mohamed Boudiaf, *Orient,* **33,** 1 (1992) 22–28
1348 **Faath, U,** Militär und Demokratie in Algerien, *Wuqûf,* 6 (1992) 11–77
1349 **Fontaine, J,** Quartiers défavorisés et vote islamiste à Alger, *Revue du monde musulman et de la Méditerranée,* 65 (1992) 141–64
1350 **Frégosi, F,** Islam et état en Algérie: du gallicisme au fondamentalisme d'état, *Revue du monde musulman et de la Méditerranée,* 65 (1992) 61–76
1351 **Kapil, A,** L'évolution du régime authoritaire en Algérie: le 5 Octobre et les réformes politiques de 1988–89, *Annuaire de l'Afrique du nord,* **28,** (1990) 499–534
1352 **Lakehal, M** (ed), *Algérie, de l'indépendance à l'état d'urgence.* Paris: Harmattan, 1992, 284pp
1353 **Lavenue, J J,** *Algérie, la démocratie interdit.* Paris: Harmattan, 1993, 279pp
1354 **Lavenue, J-J,** L'armée algérienne et les institutions: de la constitution du 23 février 1989 à l'assassinat de Mohamed Boudiaf de 29 juin 1992, *Revue du droit public,* Jan-Feb 1993 101–139
1355 **Leca, J,** L'Algérie: démocratie, politiques économiques et demandes sociales, *Maghreb Machrek,* 139 (1993) 3–8
1356 **Leverrier, I,** Le Front islamique de salut entre la hâte et la patience, in Kepel, G (ed), *Les politiques de Dieu* (Paris: Seuil, 1993), 25–69
1357 **Meynier, G,** Émigration, armée, culture et démocratie en Algérie, *Confluences Méditerranée,* 3 (1992) 43–58
1358 **Mimouni, R,** *De la barbarie en général et de l'intégrisme en particulier.* Paris: Le Pré aux Clercs-Belfond, 1992, 173pp
1359 **Monbeig, F,** Algérie 1990–1993: la démocratie confisquée?, *Revue du monde musulman et de la Méditerranée,* 65 (1992) 29–60
1360 **Moussa, Z,** Évaluation de la décentralisation territorial en Algérie (1967–1988), *African journal of international and comparative law,* **4,** 2 (1992) 395–418
1361 **Rouadjia, A,** Die algerischen Islamisten, *Wuqûf,* 6 (1992) 101–22
1362 **Sutton, K, Aghrout, A,** Multiparty elections in Algeria: problems and prospects, *Bulletin of francophone Africa,* 2 (1993) 61–85
1363 **Tcheho, I C,** Cheikh Anta Diop et le monde arabo-africain: quelques images algériennes, *Ethiopiques,* 56 (1992) 47–61
1364 **Tzschaschel, J,** Algeria torn between fundamentalism and democracy, *Aussenpolitik,* **44,** 1 (1993) 23–34
1365 **Vogt, U, Benyoucef, B,** Algerien: alternative Islam? Alternativer Islam?, *Wuqûf,* 6 (1992) 123–31
1366 **Yefsah, A,** L'armée au pouvoir en Algérie de 1962 à 1992, *Revue du monde musulman et de la Méditerranée,* 65 (1992) 77–95
1367 **Yefsah, T,** Arabisch-islamische Ideologie und Berbertum in Algeria, *Wuqûf,* 6 (1992) 153–67

Religion, philosophy

1368 **Assouline, F,** *Musulmanes: une chance pour l'Islam.* Paris: Flammarion, 1992, 223pp
1369 **Harbi, M,** *L'Algérie et son destin: croyants ou citoyens.* Paris: Arcantère, 1992, 248pp
1370 **Lamchichi, A,** *L'islamisme en Algérie.* Paris: Harmattan, 1992, 251pp
1371 **Sharif, I A,** *Algerien: vom Populismus zum Islam.* Vienna: Sharif 1992, 189pp

Rural economy

1372 **Amara, H A,** La terre et ses enjeux en Algérie, *Revue du monde musulman et de la Méditerranée,* 65 (1992) 186–96

1373 **Brulé, J C,** Attentisme et spéculation dans des campagnes algériennes, *Maghreb-Machrek,* 139 (1993) 42–52

1374 **Guillermou, Y,** Survie et ordre social au Sahara: les oasis du Touat-Gourara-Tidikelt en Algérie, *Cahiers des sciences humaines,* **29,** 1 (1993) 121–38

1375 **Sutton, K, Aghrout, A,** Agricultural policy in Algeria in the 1980s: progress towards liberalisation, *Canadian journal of African studies,* **26,** 2 (1992) 250–73

Science & technology

1376 **Benashenou, A,** Algeria, in Patel, S J (ed), *Technological transformation in the Third World. Vol. 2* (Aldershot: Avebury, 1993), 1–94

Sociology

See also: 1256

1377 **Bahloul, J,** *La maison du mémoire: ethnologie d'une demeure judéo-arabe en Algérie (1937–61).* Paris: Métailié, 1992, 246pp

1378 **Lebveau, R, Ruf, W** (eds), *Migration und Staat: inner- und intergesellschaftliche Prozesse am Beispeil Algerian, Türkei, Deutschland und Frankreich.* Munster: Lit, 1991, 258pp

1379 **Mattes, H, et al,** Algerien im Spiegel ausgewählter Sozialreportagen, *Wuqûf,* 6 (1992) 269–310

EGYPT

Arts

1380 **Anderson, A A,** The Egyptian art theatre, *Theatre survey,* **33,** 2 (1992) 132–43

1381 **Bergmann, K,** *Filmkultur und Filmindustrie in Agypten.* Darmstadt: Wissenschaft Buchgesellschaft, 1993, 304pp

Demography

1382 **El Shalakani, M H, Suchindran, C M,** Estimation of fecundity and secondary sterility from survey data on birth intervals in Egypt, *Human biology,* **65,** 1 (1993) 59–70

Economic and social history

1383 **Booth, M,** Biography and feminist rhetoric in early twentieth ecntury Egypt: Mayy Ziyada's studies of three women's lives, *Journal of women's history,* **3,** 1 (1991) 38–64

1384 **Laskier, M M,** *The Jews of Egypt: in the midst of zionism, anti-semitism and the Middle East conflict.* New York: New York University Press, 1993, 326pp

1385 **Solihin, S H,** *Copts and Muslims in Egypt: a study on harmony and hostility.* Leicester: Islamic Foundation, 1991, 120pp

1386 **Stepniewska-Holzer, B,** Slaves in the 19th-century Egypt, *Africana bulletin,* 40 (1992) 65–72

1387 **Toledano, E R,** Shemsigal: a Circassian slave in mid-nineteenth century Cairo, in Burke, E (ed), *Struggle and survival (Item 1194),* 59–74

Economy - Development

See also: 124

1388 Beshai, A, Interpretations and misinterpretations of the Egyptian economy, in Tripp, C (ed), *Contemporary Egypt (Item 1432)*, 132–41

1389 Hinnebusch, R A, The politics of economic reform in Egypt, *Third world quarterly,* **14,** 1 (1993) 159–71

1390 Moustafa, N M, *The economic and political dimensions of Egyptian external debt: a political review of the literature.* Cairo: Cairo University, Faculty of Economics, 1990, 189pp

1391 Nassar, H A, *The economic and political dimensions of Egyptian external debt, part I: an economic review of the literature.* Cairo: Cairo University, Faculty of Economics, 1990, 101pp

1392 Roy, D A, The hidden economy in Egypt, *Middle Eastern studies,* **28,** 4 (1992) 689–711

1393 Springborg, R, Egypt, in Niblock, T & Murphy, E (eds), *Economic and political liberalisation in the Middle East* (London: Tauris, 1993), 145–65

Education

No entry. *See also:* 1447

Environment

1394 Dinham, B, *The pesticide hazard: a global health and environmental audit.* London: Zed, 1993, 228pp

Finance

1395 Anon, Development of the capital market in Egypt, *Economic bulletin (National Bank of Egypt),* **45,** 1/2 (1992) 8–24

1396 Galloux, M, Egypte: réforme bancaire et finance islamique, *Maghreb Machrek,* 141 (1993) 53–62

Gender

See also: 1383

1397 Abu-Lughod, L, Migdim: Egyptian Bedouin matriarch, in Burke, E (ed), *Struggle and survival (Item 1194)*, 271–89

1398 Early, E A, *Baladi women of Cairo: playing with an egg and a stone.* Boulder: Lynne Reinner, 1993, 217pp

1399 el Sheikh, M, Laczynski, P A, Cultural variability in stress and control: an investigation of Egyptian middle class, countryside and inner-city girls, *Journal of cross-cultural psychology,* **24,** 1 (1993) 81–98

1400 Faust, K, et al, Young women members of the Islamic revival movement in Egypt, *Muslim world,* **82,** 1 (1992) 55–65

1401 Harrison, G G, et al, Breastfeeding and weaning in a poor urban neighbourhood in Cairo, Egypt: maternal beliefs and expectations, *Social science and medicine,* **36,** 8 (1993) 1063–69

1402 Younis, N, et al, A community study of gynecological and related morbidities in rural Egypt, *Studies in family planning,* **24,** 3 (1993) 175–86

Geography, human

1403 Ayeb, H, La vallée du Nil: un grand axe géopolitique, *Maghreb Machrek,* 138 (1992) 64–73

1404 Degg, M, The 1992 'Cairo earthquake': cause, effect and response, *Disasters,* **17,** 3 (1993) 226–38

1405 Gilhar, Y, Egypt's northeastern boundary in Sinai, *Middle Eastern studies,* **29,** 1 (1993) 135–48

Health & welfare services

No entry. *See also:* 379

History, early

See also: 1191, 3691

1406 **Assman, J,** When justice fails: jurisdiction and imprecation in ancient Egypt and the near East, *Journal of Egyptian archaeology,* 78 (1992) 149–62

1407 **Bagnall, R S,** Landholding in late Roman Egypt: the distribution of wealth, *Journal of Roman studies,* **82,** (1992) 128–49

1408 **Bowman, A K, Rathbone, D,** Cities and administration in Roman Egypt, *Journal of Roman studies,* **82,** (1992) 107–27

1409 **Green, A R W,** The identity of So of Egypt; an alternative interpretation, *Journal of near eastern studies,* **52,** 2 (1993) 99–108

1410 **Harrison, T P,** Economics with an entrepreneurial spirit: early Bronze trade with late predynastic Egypt, *Biblical archaeologist,* **56,** 2 (1993) 81–93

1411 **Jansen-Winklen, K,** The career of the Egyptian high priest Bakenkhons, *Journal of near eastern studies,* **52,** 3 (1993) 221–25

1412 **Keita, S O Y,** Studies and comments on Ancient Egyptian biological relationships, *History in Africa,* **20,** (1993) 129–54

1413 **Mackenzie, N D,** *Ayyubid Cairo: a topographical study.* Cairo: American University in Cairo Press, 1992, 209pp

1414 **McGovern, P E, et al,** The Late Bronze Egyptian garrison at Beth-Shan: glass and faience production and importation in the late New Kingdom, *Bulletin of the American Schools of Oriental Research,* 290–91 (1992) 1–27

1415 **Stocks, D A,** Making stone vessels in ancient Mesopotamia and Egypt, *Antiquity,* **67,** 256 (1993) 596–603

1416 **Trigger, B G,** *Early civilisations: ancient Egypt in context.* Cairo: American University of Cairo Press, 1993, 158pp

1417 **Ward, W A,** The present status of Egyptian chronology, *Bulletin of the American Schools of Oriental Research,* 288 (1992) 53–66

History, C19th

1418 **Fedorak, C J,** The French capitulation in Egypt and the preliminary Anglo-French treaty of peace in October 1801: a note, *International history review,* **15,** 3 (1993) 525–34

History, C20th

See also: 1440, 1464

1419 **Al-Hadidy, A al-D,** Mustafa al-Nahhas and political leadership, in Tripp, C (ed), *Contemporary Egypt (Item 1432)*, 72–88

1420 **Beinin, J,** *Was the red flag flying there? Marxist politics and the Arab-Israeli conflict in Egypt and Israel 1948–1965.* London: Tauris, 1990, 317pp

1421 **Cole, J R I,** *Colonialism and revolution in the Middle East: social and cultural origins of Egypt's Urabi movement.* Princeton: Princeton University Press, 1993, 341pp

1422 **Dabous, S,** Nasser and the Egyptian press, in Tripp, C (ed), *Contemporary Egypt (Item 1432)*, 100–121

1423 **Dubois, C,** Avant-première: Suez, un cas de migration forcée (1956–57), *Civilisations,* **40,** 2 (1992) 128–153

1424 **El-Feki, M,** Makram Ebeid: politician of the majority party, in Tripp, C (ed), *Contemporary Egypt (Item 1432)*, 22–44

1425 **Goldschmidt, A** (ed), *The*

memoirs and diaries of Muhammed Farid, an Egyptian nationalist leader (1868–1919). San Francisco: Mellen University Research Press, 1992, 540pp

1426 **Kehdar, A,** The political press in Egypt, 1882–1914, in Tripp, C (ed), *Contemporary Egypt (Item 1432)*, 1–21

1427 **Kent, J,** The Egyptian base and the defence of the Middle East, 1945–54, *Journal of imperial and Commonwealth history,* **21,** 3 (1993) 45–65

1428 **Lefebvre, J A,** The United States and Egypt - confrontation and accommodation in northeast Africa, 1956–60, *Middle Eastern studies,* **29,** 2 (1993) 321–38

1429 **Rainero, R H, Serra, L** (eds), *L'Italia e l'Egitto: dalla rivolta di Arabi Pascia all'avvento del fascismo.* n.p.: Mazorati, 1991, 463pp

1430 **Sayed-Ahmed, M A al W,** Relations between Egypt and the United States of America in the 1950s, in Tripp, C (ed), *Contemporary Egypt (Item 1432)*, 89–99

1431 **Tripp, C,** Ali Mahir and the politics of the Egyptian army, 1936–42, in Tripp, C (ed), *Contemporary Egypt (Item 1432)*, 45–71

1432 **Tripp, C** (ed), *Contemporary Egypt: through Egyptian eyes.* London: Routledge, 1993, 156pp

Industry & trade

1433 **Abdel-Latif, A M,** The non-price determinants of export success or failure: the Egyptian readymade garment industry, 1975–89, *World development,* **21,** 10 (1993) 1677–84

1434 **Central Bank of Egypt,** The role of tourism in the Egyptian economy, *Economic review (Central Bank of Egypt)*, **30,** 1 (1989/1990) 69–90

1435 **Hassan, R, et al,** *Effective protection in the Egyptian agricultural sector.* Nottingham: Nottingham University, Centre for Research in Economic Development and International Trade, 1991, 22pp

1436 **Waterbury, J,** *Exposed to innumerable delusions: public enterprise and state power in Egypt, India, Mexico and Turkey.* Cambridge: CUP, 1993, 342pp

International economic relations

See also: 507, 1433

1437 **Miklaszewska, E,** The Egyptian experience with open-door policies, *Africana bulletin,* 40 (1992) 117–21

International relations

See also: 1405, 1440

1438 **Boutros-Ghali, B,** Egyptian diplomacy: East-West detente and North-South dialogue, in Tripp, C (ed), *Contemporary Egypt (Item 1432)*, 142–50

1439 **El-Gamasy, M A G,** *The October War: memoirs of Field-Marshall el-Gamasy of Egypt.* Cairo: American University in Cairo Press, 1993, 430pp

1440 **Morris, B,** *Israel's border wars.* New York: OUP, 1993, 451pp

1441 **Parker, R B,** *The politics of miscalculation: the Middle East.* Bloomington: Indiana University Press, 1993, 273pp

1442 **Zaki, M Y, Doss, M A,** The Egyptian-Sudanese integration scheme: an appraisal, *Middle Eastern studies,* **29,** 2 (1993) 275–91

Labour & manpower

1443 **Bayat, A,** Populism, liberalisation and popular participation: industrial democracy in Egypt, *Economic and industrial democracy,* **14,** 1 (1993) 65–87

1444 **Hinchliffe, K,** Manpower forecasting and rapid labour market analysis: the demand for technical school graduates in Egypt, *The vocational aspects of education,* **45,** 3 (1993) 39–50

Language

No entry. *See also:1448*

Law

1445 **Middle East Watch,** *Prison conditions in Egypt.* New York: Human Rights Watch, 1993, 154pp

Library - documentation

1446 **Dimitroff, A,** Information access in a developing country: special libraries in Egypt, *Special libraries,* **84,** 1 (1993) 25–29

1447 **Halwagy, A S,** Recent changes in library education in Egypt, *Journal of education for library and information science,* **33,** 3 (1992) 255–59

1448 **Khaled, M,** Information manpower development program in Egypt, *Journal of information science,* **18,** 6 (1992) 463–69

Literature

1449 **al Kadi, G,** L'émigration dans la littérature égyptienne contemporaine, *Cahiers des sciences humaines,* **29,** 2/3 (1993) 299–311

1450 **Mahfuz, N, Ghitany, G,** *Mahfouz par Mahfouz.* Paris: Sindbad, 1991, 168pp

Media

1451 **Abu-Lughod, L,** Finding a place for Islam: Egyptian television serials and the national interest, *Public culture,* **5,** 3 (1993) 493–513

Medical

See also: 1399, 1402

1452 **Wachs, T D, et al,** Relation of rearing environment to adaptive behaviour of Egyptian toddlers, *Child development,* **64,** 2 (1993) 586–604

1453 **Wachs, T D, et al,** Relations between nutrition and cognitive performance in Egyptian toddlers, *Intelligence,* **17,** 2 (1993) 151–72

1454 **Watts, D M,** Prevalence of HIV infection and AIDS in Egypt over four years of surveillance (1986–1990), *Journal of tropical medicine and hygiene,* **96,** 2 (1993) 113–117

Natural resources

1455 **Briggs, J, et al,** Sustainable development and resource management in marginal environments: natural resouces and their use in the Wadi Allagi region of Egypt, *Applied geography,* **13,** 3 (1993) 259–84

1456 **Stewart, J L, et al,** Screening of non-industrial tree species on reclaimed desert land in Middle Egypt, *Journal of arid environments,* **25,** 4 (1993) 375–85

Politics

1457 **Al-sayyid, M K,** A civil society in Egypt?, *Middle East journal,* **47,** 2 (1993) 228–42

1458 **Barnett, M N,** *Confronting the costs of war: military power, state and society in Egypt and Israel.* Princeton: Princeton University Press, 1992, 378pp

1459 **Kazziha, W,** Egypt in the balance, in Tripp, C (ed), *Contemporary Egypt (Item 1432),* 122–31

1460 **Makram-Ebeid, M,** From the single party rule to the one party domination: some aspects of pluralism without democracy, in Lopez Garcia, B, et al (eds), *Transiciones politicas (Item 1199)*, 121–32

1461 **Moharram, S,** The process of controlled decentralisation in Egyptian local finance, *Developing economies,* **30,** 4 (1992) 450–81

1462 **Reed, S,** The battle for Egypt, *Foreign affairs,* **72,** 4 (1993) 94–107

1463 **Singer, H F,** *The Socialist Labour Party: a case study of a contemporary Egyptian opposition party.* Cairo: American University, 1993, 70pp

Religion, philosophy

See also: 1400, 1451

1464 **Dajani, Z R,** *Egypt and the crisis of Islam.* New York: Lang, 1990, 255pp

1465 **Sagiv, D,** Ashmawi and militant Islam in Egypt, *Middle eastern studies,* **28,** 3 (1992) 531–46

Rural economy

See also: 1466, 1472

1466 **Barondi, S,** Egyptian agricultural exports since 1973, *Middle East journal,* **47,** 1 (1993) 63–76

1467 **Belal, A E,** Sustainable development in Wadi Allagi in Egypt, *Desertification control bulletin,* 23 (1993) 39–43

1468 **Löfgren, T,** Liberalising Egypt's agriculture: a quadratic programming anaysis, *Journal of African economics,* **2,** 2 (1993) 238–62

1469 **Reichert, C,** Labour migration and rural development in Egypt: a study of return migration in six villages, *Sociologica ruralis,* **33,** 1 (1993) 42–60

1470 **Varangis, P N, et al,** *Risk management prospects for Egyptian cotton.* Washington: World Bank, 1993, 26pp

1471 **World Bank,** *Arab Republic of Egypt: an agricultural strategy for the 1990s.* Washington: World Bank, 1993, 124pp

Sociology

See also: 1449, 1457, 1469

1472 **Adams, R H,** The economic and demographic determinants of international migration in rural Egypt, *Journal of development studies,* **30,** 1 (1993) 146–67

1473 **Nelson, G L, et al,** Egyptian and American compliments: a cross-cultural study, *International journal of intercultural relations,* **17,** 1 (19093) 293–313

LIBYA

General

1474 **Simons, G,** *Libya: the struggle for survival.* Basingstoke: Macmillan, 1993, 396pp

Anthropology

No entry. *See also:* 4516

Gender

1475 **Graeff-Wassink, M,** *Women at arms: is Ghaddafi a feminist?* London: Darf, 1993, 262pp

1476 **Simon, R,** *Change within tradition among Jewish women in Libya.* Seattle: University of Washington Press, 1992, 221pp

Geography, human

No entry. *See also:* 1484

Geography, physical

1477 **Gale, S J, et al,** Late Holocene environmental change in the Libyan pre-desert, *Journal of arid environments,* **24,** 1 (1993) 1–19

History, early

1478 **Van Albada, A,** Van Albada, A M, Chasseurs et pasteurs du Messak Settafet (Fezzan-Libye), *Préhistoire anthropologie méditerranéennes,* **1,** (1992) 99–104

History, C20th

1479 **Anderson, L,** Ramamdan al-Suwayhli: hero of the Libyan resistance, in Burke, E (ed), *Struggle and survival (Item 1194),* 114–28

1480 **Martel, A,** *La Libye 1835–1990: essai de géopolitique historique.* Paris: PUF, 1991, 247pp

Industry & trade

1481 **Bergs, R,** Der libysche Raffinerie- und Petrochemiesektor, *Orient,* **33,** 2 (1992) 243–51

International relations

No entry. *See also:* 1474, 1480, 1483

Politics

See also: 1475

1482 **Djaziri, M,** Pouvoir gestionnaire, pouvoir révolutionnaire, *Confluences Méditerranée,* 3 (1992) 145–157

Religion, philosophy

1483 **Mattes, H,** La da'wa libyenne entre le Coran et le Livre vert, in Otayek, R (ed), *Radicalisme islamique (Item 1002),* 37–73

Rural economy

1484 **Bukechiem, A A,** Utilisation of groundwater in Jerbel et Akhdar, northeast Libya, as a basis of agricultural improvement with special emphasis on the El Marj Plain, *Libyan studies,* **24,** (1993) 121–42

MOROCCO

Agriculture, scientific

No entry. *See also:*1532

Anthropology

1485 **Bakker, J,** The rise of female healers in the Middle Atlas, Morocco, *Social science and medicine,* **35,** 6 (1992) 819–29

1486 **Griffin, K,** The ritual of silent wishes: notes on the Moroccan sensorium, in Howes, D (ed), *The varieties of sensory experience* (Toronto: University of Toronto Press, 1991), 210–20

1487 **Guennoun, S,** Littérature des Berbères de la Haute Moulouya, *Etudes et documents berbères,* 8 (1991) 113–34

1488 **Kraus, W,** *Die Ayt Hdiddu: Wirtschaft und Gesellschaft im zentralen Hohen Atlas. Ein Beitrag zur Duskussione segemtärer Systeme in Marokko.* Vienna: Ostereichische Akakdemie der Wissenschaften, 1991, 114pp

1489 **Munson, H,** Rethinking Gellner's segmentary analysis of Morocco's Ait 'Atta, *Man,* **28,** 2 (1993) 267–80

1490 **Tauveron, A,** Le propre et le sale vus par les habitants de Fès (Maroc), *Cahiers de l'URBAMA,* 4 (1990) 5–13

1491 **Webber, S J,** *Romancing the real: folklore and ethnographic* *representation in North Africa.* Philadelphia: University of Pennsylvania Press, 1991, 293pp

Architecture

1492 **Boumaza, Z,** Une lecture par l'image d'un espace urbain maghrébin traditionnel: le vieux Mila, *L'ethnographie,* **89,** 2 (1993) 83–103

1493 **Erbati, E,** La maison de Tétouan, in *La casa hispano-musulmana: aportaciones de la arqueologia* (Granada: Patronata de la Alhambra y Generalife, 1990), 99–110

Current affairs

1494 **Clément, J-F,** Un nouveau lifting pour la "démocratie" hassanienne?, *Confluences Méditerranée,* 3 (1992) 137–144

Demography

1495 **Varea, C,** Marriage, age at last birth and fertility in a traditional Moroccan population, *Journal of biosocial science,* **25,** 1 (1993) 1–16

Economic and social history

1496 **Fernaud, P,** Estampas y visiones tangerinas, *Estudios Africanos,* **6,** 10/11 (1991/92) 83–107

1497 **Knibiehler, Y,** Des français au Maroc, *Ethnologie française,* **23,** 2 (1993) 185–91

1498 **Serels, M M,** *A history of the Jews of Tangiers in the 19th and 20th centuries.* New York: Sepher-Hermon, 1991, 326pp

1499 **Szymanski, E,** Les relations politiques et commerciales entre l'Europe et le le Maroc au 18ème siècle, *Africana bulletin,* 40 (1992) 53–64

Economy - Development

1500 **Azam, J P,** The agricultural minimum wage and wheat production in Morocco (1971–89), *Journal of African economics,* **1,** 2 (1992) 171–92

1501 **Leymarie, S, Tripier, J,** *Maroc: le prochain dragon.* Paris: Karthala, 1993, 230pp

Education

1502 **Essaki, A,** A changing literacy in Morocco: a contextal and pedagogical overview, *Journal of reading,* **37,** 2 (1993) 142–45

Gender

No entry. *See also:* 1485, 1495

Geography, human

See also: 1546

1503 **Swearingen, W D,** Drought hazard in Morocco, *Geographical review,* **82,** 4 (1992) 401–412

Health & welfare services

1504 **Abdmouleh, R,** Quelques recettes d'automédication familiale à Sfax, *IBLA,* 169 (1992) 3–16

History, general

See also: 1530

1505 **Munson, H,** *Religion and power in Morocco.* New Haven: Yale University Press, 1993, 232pp

History, C18th

1506 **Aguadé, J, Elyaacoubi, M,** Sidi Mhemmed u-Ye'cub y sus descendientes: estudio preliminar de la tradicion oral relativa a una familia marabutica en el sur de

Marruecos, *Al Qantara,* **12,** 2 (1991) 537–72

1507 **el Mansour, M,** *Morocco in the reign of Mawlay Sulayman.* Wisbech: Middle East and North African Studies Press, 1990, 248pp

1508 **Garcia-Arenal, M,** Mahdi Murabit, Sharif: l'avènement de la dynastie sa'dienne, *Studia islamica* (71) *1990,* 77–114

History, C19th

See also: 1489

1509 **Bendaoud, A, Maniar, M** (eds), *Tanger 1800–1956: contribution à l'histoire récente du Maroc.* Rabat: Faculté des Lettres, 1991, 249+292pp

1510 **Elboudrari, H,** Transmission du charisme et institutionnalisation: le cas de la *zawiya* d'Ouezzane, Maroc, 17è–19è siècles, *Al Qantara,* **12,** 2 (1991) 523–36

1511 **Schroeter, D,** Yashaq ben Ya'is Halewi: a Moroccan reformer, in Burke, E (ed), *Struggle and survival (Item 1194),* 44–58

History, C20th

See also: 1509

1512 **Ben Mlih, A,** *Structures politiques du Maroc colonial.* Paris: Harmattan, 1990, 396pp

1513 **Burke, E,** Mohand N'Hamoucha: Middle Atlas Berber, in Burke, E (ed), *Struggle and survival (Item 1194),* 100–113

1514 **Clayton, A,** Emergency in Morocco, 1950–56, *Journal of imperial and Commonwealth history,* **21,** 3 (1993) 129–47

1515 **Emmery, G, et al** (comp), *Des Français au Maroc: la presence et le mémoire (1912–1956).* Paris: Denoel, 1992, 412pp

1516 **Guérin, D,** *Ben Barka, ses assassins.* Paris: Syllepse/Periscope, 1991 (rev. edn), 343pp

1517 **Laurent, E,** *Hassan II.* Paris: Plon, 1993, 304pp

1518 **Le Tourneau, R,** *Histoire du Maroc moderne.* Aix en Provence: Université de Provence, 1992, 345pp

1519 **Seddon, D,** Muhammed el Merid: the man who became *qaid,* in Burke, E (ed), *Struggle and survival (Item 1194),* 211–23

1520 **Violet, B,** *L'affaire Ben Barka.* Paris: Fayard, 1991, 506pp

Industry & trade

1521 **Aouad, A,** The impact of the mining industry on industrialisation in Morocco, in Khennas, S (ed), *Industrialisation (item 454),* 20–46

1522 **Haddad, M,** *How trade liberalisation affected productivity in Morocco.* Washington: World Bank, 1993, 40pp

1523 **Tangeaoui, S,** *Les entrepreneurs marocains.* Paris: Karthala, 1993, 325pp

International economic relations

1524 **Haddad, M, Harrison, A,** Are there positive spillovers from direct foreign investment? Evidence from panel data for Morocco, *Journal of development economics,* **42,** 1 (1993) 51–74

1525 **McMurray, D,** Haddou: a Moroccan migrant worker, in Burke, E (ed), *Struggle and survival (Item 1194),* 377–93

1526 **Zejly, A,** Commerce extérieur, taux de change et protection tarifaire, *African development review,* **5,** 1 (1993) 16–31

International relations

See also: 1536, 3798

1527 **Berramdane, A,** Le Maroc et

l'Europe: un destin commun, *Annuaire de l'Afrique du nord,* **28,** (1990) 39–56

Labour & manpower

No entry. *See also:* 1500

Law

1528 **Mir-Hosseini, Z,** Paternity, patriarchy and matrilocality in the Sharia and social practice: the cases of Morocco and Islam, *Cambridge anthropology,* **16,** 2 (1993) 22–40

Library - documentation

1529 **Benjelloun-Laroui, L,** *Les bibliothèques au Maroc.* Paris: Maisionneuve et Larose, 1990, 413pp

1530 **Vilar, J B,** *Mapas, planos y fortificaciones hispanicos de Marruecos (s.XVI-XX).* Madrid: Agencia Espagñola de Cooperación Internacional, 1992, 605pp

Literature

1531 **van den Heuvel, P,** Innovations maghrébines: le discours extatique: Le livre du sang d'Abdelkadir Khatibi, *Revue de l'Institut de sociologie,* 1990/91 139–53

Planning

1532 **Collion, M H,** Kissi, A, Learning by doing: developing a programme planning method in Morocco, *Public administration and development,* **13,** 3 (1993) 261–70

Politics

See also: 1505

1533 **Damis, J,** Sources of political stability in modernising monarchical regimes: Jordan and Morocco, in Danopoulos, C P (ed), *Civilian rule (Item 844),* 23–51

1534 **Daure-Serfaty, C,** *Tazmamart: une prison de la mort au Maroc.* Paris: Stock, 1992, 239pp

1535 **de Mas, P,** Pouvoir et migration au maroc: dynamiques électorales divergentes dans le Rif et le Sous, in Lopez Garcia, B, et al (eds), *Transiciones politicas (Item 1199),* 79–94

1536 **Moha, G,** *Les 'amis' des peuples: réponse à Giles Perrault.* Paris: Picollec, 1991, 205pp

1537 **Sa'af, 'A,** Sur les agitations de l'état marocain: entre l'état 'profond' et l'état 'variable', in Lopez Garcia, B, et al (eds), *Transiciones politicas (Item 1199),* 175–99

1538 **Santucci, J C,** Processus électoraux et légitimation du pouvoir: réflexions sur l'expérience marocaine, in Lopez Garcia, B, et al (eds), *Transiciones politicas (Item 1199),* 287–93

1539 **Sehimi, M,** Maroc: partis politiques et stratégies électorales, in Lopez Garcia, B, et al (eds), *Transiciones politicas (Item 1199),* 217–30

1540 **Serfaty, A, Daure, C,** *La mémoire de l'autre.* Paris: Stock, 1993, 336pp

Rural economy

1541 **Blanc, F P, Sen,** C (eds), *Perspectives pour une réforme des chambres de agriculture au Maroc.* Perpignan: Presses Universitaire de Perpignan, 1992, 169pp

1542 **Bourguignon, F, et al,** *Adjustment and the rural sector: a counterfactual analysis of Morocco.* Paris: DELTA, 1991, 31pp

1543 **Khrouz, D,** Effets de l'aide internationale sur l'agriculture africaine: le cas du Maroc, *Africa development,* **17,** 3 (1992) 99–138

1544 **Rafsnider, G T, et al,** Theory and application of risk analysis in an agricultural development setting: a Moroccan case study, *European review of agricultural economics,* **20,** 4 (1993) 471–89

Sociology

See also: 1525

1545 **Hansen, C D,** Culture, cognition and literacy: tales from Morocco, *International journal of intercultural relations,* **17,** 3 (19093) 271–93

Urban studies

See also: 1490, 1492

1546 **Erickson, E C, Young, F W,** Urban hierarchies and regional development in Morocco: a graphical technique for monitoring and assessment, *Journal of developing societies,* **8,** 2 (1992) 160–78

1547 **McPhail, A,** Overlooked market for water connections on Rabat's shantytowns, *Journal of water resources planning and management,* **119,** 3 (1993) 388–403

TUNISIA

Anthropology

1548 **Halouani, R,** La dimension symbolique de la maladie: son impact et son importance dans l'acte de santé, *IBLA,* 169 (1992) 17–30

Economy - Development

1549 **Alaya, H,** *Monnaie et financement en Tunisie.* Tunis: Cérès, 1991, 414pp

1550 **Marks, J,** Tunisia, in Niblock, T & Murphy, E (eds), *Economic and political liberalisation in the Middle East* (London: Tauris, 1993), 166–76

Education

1551 **Bousnina, M,** *Développement scolaire et dispartités régionales en Tunisie.* Tunis: Université de Tunis 1, 1991, 2 vols, 471pp

1552 **Gill, H,** Educational reform in post-colonial Tunisia: approaches and problems, *Bulletin of francophone Africa,* 2 (1993) 14–28

1553 **Mahfoudh, D,** L'égalité des chances par l'éducation, *Confluences Méditerranée,* 3 (1992) 59–73

1554 **Sraieb, N,** Khérédine et l'enseignement: une nouvelle conception du savoir en Tunisie, *Revue du monde musulman et de la Méditerranée,* 63/64 (1992) 203–210

Environment

1555 **Camus, H, Missaoui, H,** Protection de l'environnement et développement rural: l'exemple de la Tunisie semi-aride, *Orstom actualités,* 39 (1993) 13–17

Finance

1556 **Vittas, D,** *Options for pension reform in Tunisia.* Washington: World Bank, 1993, 32pp

Food

1557 **Shaw, J, Clay, E,** Tunisia: food deficits and food aid in a middle income country, in their *World food aid: experiences of recipients and donors* (London: Currey, 1993), 98–107

Gender

See also: 1575

1558 **Abu-Zahra, N,** The Tunisian

personal status code: national policy and the homogenisation of the population, *Cambridge anthropology,* **16,** 2 (1993) 41–53

1559 El Amouri Institute, Women's role in the informal sector in Tunisia, in Massiah, J (ed), *Women in developing economies: making visible the invisible* (Oxford: Berg, 1993), 135–66

History, general

No entry. *See also:* 1570

History, early

1560 Ferchiou, N, Habitats fortifiés pré-impériaux en Tunisie antique, *Antiquités africaines,* **26,** (1990) 43–86

History, C19th

1561 Mestiri, S, *Moncef Bey. Tome II: chronique des années d'exil.* Tunis: Arcs, 1990, 339pp

History, C20th

See also: 1565

1562 Bertotti, R, *Un soldat italien en Afrique du Nord: une guerre méconnue - la Tunisie 1942–1943.* Paris: Harmattan, 1993, 128pp

1563 Brown, K, Muhammed Ameur: a Tunisian comrade, in Burke, E (ed), *Struggle and survival (Item 1194)*, 251–67

1564 Kraiem, M, *Pouvoir colonial et mouvement national: la Tunisie des années trente - crise et renouveau.* (Tunis): Alif, (1990), 355pp

1565 Mestiri, S, *Le ministère Chénik à la poursuite de l'autonomie interne: de la déclaration de Thionville à l'exil de Kebili.* Tunis: Arcs, 1991, 284pp

Industry & trade

See also: 1559

1566 Poirier, R, Wright, S, Tunisia: political economy of tourism, *Journal of modern African studies,* **31,** 1 (1993) 149–62

International relations

1567 Brondino, M, L'Italie au croisement des rapports euro-maghrébins: le cas tunisien, *Annuaire de l'Afrique du nord,* **28,** (1990) 171–84

Labour & manpower

1568 Ahmed, E, Schaar, S, M'hammed Ali: Tunisian labour organiser, in Burke, E (ed), *Struggle and survival (Item 1194)*, 191–210

Law

See also: 1558

1569 Moussa, F, La stratégie de lutte contre "le recul de la terre": le cas tunisien, *African journal of international and comparative law,* **4,** 3 (1992) 678–713

Library - documentation

1570 Vilar, J B, *Mapas, planos y fortificaciones hispanicos de Tunez (s.XVI-XX).* Madrid: Agencia Espagñola de Cooperación Internacional, 1991, 489pp

Literature

1571 Omri, M S, 'Literature of the nineties in Tunisia': making sense of the fin de siècle, *Jusur,* 8 (1992) 91–97

Politics

See also: 940, 1342

1572 **Kraiem, M,** Système totalitaire et pluralisme en Tunisie (fondements socio-culturels et évolution), in Lopez Garcia, B, et al (eds), *Transiciones politicas (Item 1199)*, 97–119

Religion, philosophy

1573 **Bahri, J,** Le lycée de Radaka: une filière de formation pour les arabisants d'Afrique noire en Tunisie, in Otayek, R (ed), *Radicalisme islamique (Item 1002)*, 75–95

1574 **Kilani, M,** *La construction de la mémoire: le lignage et la sainteté dans l'oasis d'el-Ksar.* Geneva: Labor et Fides, 1992, 337pp

1575 **Tjomsland, M,** *'The educated way of thinking': individualisation and islamism in Tunisia.* Bergen: Chr. Michelsens Institute, 1993, 15pp

Rural economy

No entry. *See also:* 1555, 1563, 1569

Sociology

1576 **Boubakri, H, Lamine, R,** Migrations pendulaires autour de M'saken, *Revue tunisien de géographie,* 21/22 (1992) 11–29

1577 **Lamine, R,** Modifications ses champs migratoires internes dans le Sahel et immigration dans la ville de Sousse, *Revue tunisien de géographie,* 21/22 (1992) 97–119

Urban studies

See also: 1577

1578 **Belhedi, A,** Le système urbaine tunisien: croissance urbaine et structuration hiérarchique, *Revue tunisien de géographie,* 21/22 (1992) 177–91

1579 **Landeau, J F,** Ratio analysis: a study of mortage borrowers in Tunisisa, in Tipple, A G & Willis, K G (eds), *Housing the poor (item 1159)*, 113–25

1580 **Schiffler, M,** Uberlebensökonomie, Wohnungsbau und informelle Kredite in einem tunesischen Armverteil, *Orient,* **33,** 1 (1992) 81–96

NORTH EAST AFRICA

Anthropology

1581 **Lewis, I M,** Parental terms of reference: a patrilineal kinship puzzle, *Australian journal of anthropology,* **1,** 2/3 (1990) 83–95

1582 **Pelizzari, E,** Due riti di possessione a confronto: il culto di Sheekh Xussen e il Mingis, *Africa (Rome),* **47,** 3 (1992) 355–374

Economic and social history

1583 **Garad, A,** *Harar: Wirtschaftgeschichte eines Emirats im Horn von Afrika.* Frankfurt: Lang, 1990, 299pp

1584 **Kropp, M,** La corne orientale de l'Afrique chez les géographes arabes, *Bulletin des études africaines de l'INALCO,* **9,** 17/18 (1992) 161–97

Environment

No entry. *See also:* 1595

Food

See also: 1595

1585 **Duffield, M,** NGOs, disaster relief and asset transfer in the Horn: political survival in a permanent emergency, *Development and change,* **24,** 1 (1993) 131–57

Gender

1586 **Hicks, E K,** *Infibulation: female genital mutilation in Islamic northeastern Africa.* New Brunswick: Transition, 1993, 298pp

Geography, human

No entry. *See also:* 1584

International relations

See also: 1593

1587 **Iyob, R,** Regional hegemony: domination and resistance in the Horn of Africa, *Journal of modern African studies,* **31,** 2 (1993) 257–76

1588 **Schraeder, P J,** US intervention in the Horn of Africa amidst the end of the Cold War, *Africa today,* **40,** 2 (1993) 7–27

1589 **Sheth, V S,** Changing international relations and conflict resolution in the Horn, *African currents,* 11 (1990) 48–57

Politics

See also: 1198, 1585

1590 **Clapham, C,** The Horn of Africa: consequences of insurgency, *Africa insight,* **23,** 4 (1993) 184–89

1591 **Lancaster, C J,** The Horn of Africa, in Lake, A et al *After the wars* (New Brunswick: Transaction, 1990), 168–90

1592 **Legum, C,** *The Horn of Africa: prospects for political transformation.* London: Research Institute for the Study of Conflict and Terrorism, 1992, 21pp

1593 **Woodward, P,** A new map of

Africa? Reflections on the Horn, *Africa insight,* **23,** 1 (1993) 6–16

Rural economy

1594 Ahmed, A G M, Beyond national boundaries: the integration of rural production systems in the some countries in the Horn of Africa, in Nett, B et al (eds), *Agricultural transformation (Item 1069)*, 173–84

1595 Hutchison, R A (ed), *Fighting for survival: people and the environment in the Horn of Africa.* Gland: IUCN, 1991, 181pp

1596 Markakis, J (ed), *Conflict and decline of pastoralism in the Horn of Africa.* Basingstoke: Macmillan, 1993, 165pp

1597 Unruh, J D, Refugee resettlement on the Horn of Africa: the integration and host and refugee land use patterns, *Land use policy,* **10,** 1 (1993) 49–66

1598 Unruh, J D, Restocking refugee pastoralists in the Horn of Africa, *Disasters,* **17,** 4 (1993) 305–20

Sociology

See also: 1597

1599 UNRISD, *Refugees returning home: report on the symposium for the Horn of Africa on the social and economic aspects of mass voluntary return movements of refugees.* Geneva: UNRISD, 1993, 34pp

DJIBOUTI

Health & welfare services

1600 Rondy, P, Duprat, M, Socio-économie et clinique pédiatrique au SMI2 en République de Djibouti, *Revue de l'ISERT,* 6/7 (1991) 81–84

History, C20th

1601 Elmi Osman, M, Djibouti et la Seconde guerre mondiale, *Revue de l'ISERT,* 6/7 (1991) 11–19

Industry & trade

1602 Guedda Mohamed, M, L'avenir d'une tradition: le dromadaire, *Revue de l'ISERT,* 6/7 (1991) 21–27

International relations

1603 Clarke, W S, The 'Esayi dream: a footnote to the Ogaden war, *Northeast African studies,* **13,** 1 (1991) 29–38

Law

1604 Leclercq, C, La Constitution de la République de Djibouti du 15 septembre 1992, *Revue juridique et politique,* **47,** 1 (1993) 71–77

Medical

1605 Morand, J J, et al, La tuberculose de l'enfant en République de Djibouti: aspects épidemiologiques et cliniques, *Revue de l'ISERT,* 6/7 (1991) 37–62

Politics

1606 Schraeder, P J, Ethnic politics in Djibouti: from 'eye of the hurricane' to 'boiling cauldron', *African affairs,* **92,** 367 (1993) 203–21

ERITREA

Current affairs

1607 Anon, Eritrea: birth of a nation, *Review of African political economy,* 57 (1993) 110–114

1608 Hubbell, S, Eritrea nascent: the next fight for independence, *Nation,* **256,** 21 (1993) 732–35

1609 Orr, D, Eritrea's turn for development, *Choices,* **2,** 3 (1993) 4–11

1610 Pausewang, S, Surkhe, A (eds), *The referendum on independence for Eritrea: report of the Norwegian Observer Group in UNOVER.* Oslo: Norwegian Institute of Human Rights, 1993, 87pp

Economic and social history

1611 Bausi, A, et al, Materiali di studio dal Sära'e (Eritrea): le istituzioni monastiche a la struttura della proprieta fondiaria, *Africa (Rome),* **48,** 3 (1993) 446–63

Economy - Development

1612 Gebre Hiwey Tesfagiorgis, *Emergent Eritrea: challenges of economic development - proceedings of a conference.* Washington: Eritreans for Peace and Democracy in North America, 1992, 282pp

History, early

No entry. *See also:* 1675

International relations

See also: 1700

1613 Pateman, R, The people the world forgot: the United Nations and Eritrea, *Horn of Africa,* **13/14,** 3–4/1–2 (1990/1991) 26–37

Politics

See also: 861, 1616

1614 Connell, D, *Against all odds: a chronicle of the Eritrean revolution.* Trenton: Red Sea Press, 1993, 309pp

1615 Okbazghi Yohannes, Eritrea: a country in transition, *Review of African political economy,* 57 (1993) 7–28

1616 Pool, D, Eritrean independence: the legacy of the Derg and the politics of reconstruction, *African affairs,* **92,** 368 (1993) 389–402

1617 Suther, D, Freedom's just another word, *Executive,* Dec. 1992-Jan. 1993, 53–58

1618 Tsegezab Gebregergis, *Eritrea: an account of an Eritrean political exile on his visit to liberated Eritrea.* Amsterdam: Liberation Books, 1993, 115pp

Rural economy

1619 Vallely, P, *Promised lands: stories of power and poverty in the Third World.* London: Fount, 1992, 159pp

Social welfare

No entry. *See also:* 1879

Sociology

No entry. *See also:* 1877

ETHIOPIA

General

1620 Pankhurst, R, Beyene, T (eds), *Silver jubilee anniversary of the Institute of Ethiopian Studies: proceedings of the Symposium, Addis Ababa, November 24–26, 1988.* Addis Ababa: Addis Ababa University, 1990, 122pp

1621 Pankhurst, R, et al (eds), *Proceedings of the first national conference of Ethiopian studies: Addis Ababa, April 11–12, 1990.* Addis Ababa: Institute of Ethiopian Studies, 1990, 534pp

Agriculture, scientific

1622 **Fichtl, R,** Bienenhaltung und Ressourcenschutz, in Hopp, J (ed), *Wüstenwind und Tropenregen* (Berlin: Reimer, 1993), 143–61

Anthropology

See also: 1661, 1712, 2035

1623 **Abbink, J,** Ch'at in popular culture, a prayer from Harar, Ethiopia, *Sociology ethnology bulletin,* **1,** 2 (1992) 89–93

1624 **Abbink, J,** Reading the entrails: analysis of an African divination discourse, *Man,* **28,** 4 (1993) 705–26

1625 **Amborn, H,** *Differenzierung und Integration: vergleichende Untersuchungen zu Spezialisten und Handwerken in südäthiopischen Agrargesellschaften.* Munich: Trickster, 1990, 476pp

1626 **Eleni Tedla,** Indigenous African education as means for understanding the fullness of life: Amara traditional education, *Journal of Black studies,* **23,** 1 (1992) 7–26

1627 **Getie, G,** Our visit to the Gamo Highlands, and the elders' blessing in Doko market, *Sociology ethnology bulletin,* **1,** 2 (1992) 4–8

1628 **Lydall, J,** The jab, medicine or sacrifice?, *Sociology ethnology bulletin,* **1,** 2 (1992) 80–85

1629 **Marco, B,** Institutional forgiveness in Borana assemblies, *Sociology ethnology bulletin,* **1,** 2 (1992) 50–54

1630 **Pankhurst, A,** Settling strife in a resettlement setting, symbolic sanctions?, *Sociology ethnology bulletin,* **1,** 2 (1992) 73–79

1631 **Solomon, G,** Conflict resolution in traditional Amhara society, *Sociology ethnology bulletin,* **1,** 2 (1992) 55–60

1632 **Sumner, C,** Ethiopian wisdom literature, *Journal of humanities,* 5 (1991) 87–107

1633 **Tadesse, W,** The death and burial of Kalla Qänazmach Kayoté, a ritual leader of the Konso people of southern Ethiopia, *Sociology ethnology bulletin,* **1,** 2 (1992) 12–21

1634 **Teferi, A,** Resource use in Konso, *Sociology ethnology bulletin,* **1,** 2 (1992) 22–25

1635 **Vecchiato, N L,** Illness, therapy, and change in Ethiopian possession cults, *Africa,* **63,** 2 (1993) 176–96

Arts

See also: 70

1636 **Hecht, E D,** Basketwork of Harar, *African study monographs (supplementary issue),* 18 (1992) 1–39

Current affairs

1637 **Harbeson, J W,** The future of the Ethiopian state after Mengistu, *Current history,* **92,** 574 (1993) 208–212

Demography

See also: 1662, 1704

1638 **Lindtjorn, B, et al,** Population growth, fertility, mortality and migration in drought-prone areas in Ethiopia, *Transactions of the Royal Society of Tropical Medicine and Hygiene,* **87,** 1 (1993) 24–28

1639 **Mammo, A,** Factors responsible for childhood mortality variation in rural Ethiopia, *Journal of biosocial science,* **25,** 2 (1993) 223–38

1640 **Shamebo, D, et al,** The Butajira project in Ethiopia: a nested case-referent study of under-five mortality and its public health determinants, *Bulletin of the World Health Organisation,* **71,** 3/4 (1993) 389–96

Economic and social history

1641 Jalata, A, The modern world-economy, Ethiopian settler colonialism and the Oromos, 1880s–1930s, *Horn of Africa,* **13/14,** 3–4/1–2 (1990/1991) 59–80

Economy - Development

See also: 196

1642 Befekadu Degefe, *Growth and foreign debt: the Ethiopian experience, 1964–86.* Nairobi: African Economic Research Consortium, 1992, 50pp

1643 Hansson, G, Ethiopia: away from socialism, in Blomström, M & Lundahl, M (eds), *Economic crisis (Item 119),* 285–321

Education

1644 Abraham, H, A comparative study on the preparation of senior secondary school teachers in Ethiopia, *Ethiopian journal of education,* **12,** 1 (1991) 1–40

1645 Girma, Z, Degree of preparation of secondary school students in Addis Ababa for the Ethiopian School Leaving Certificate examination: an empirical study, *Ethiopian journal of education,* **12,** 2 (1991) 1–35

1646 Searle, C, *A blindfold removed: Ethiopia's struggle for literacy.* London: Karia Press, 1991, 112pp

1647 Tilahun, W, Ethiopian pioneering in adult education: Berhane Zare New Institute (1948–1978), *Ethiopian journal of education,* **12,** 2 (1991) 36–87

Environment

No entry. *See also:* 1634, 2035

Finance

1648 Befekadu, D, The exchange rate of the birr: recent experience and policy options, *Ethiopian journal of development research,* **13,** 1 (1991) 1–37

Food

See also: 1703, 1749

1649 Alemayehu Lirenso, *Socio-economic constraints to the production of 'belg' crops in Ethiopia: a case study of three peasant associations.* New York: Social Science Research Council, Project on African Agriculture, 1991, 34pp

1650 Brons, M, Some political factors affecting food security in Jijiga Awraja, Ethiopia, in Nett, B et al (eds), *Agricultural transformation (Item 1069),* 1–15

1651 Derseh Endale, *The Ethiopian famines, entitlements and governance.* Helsinki: WIDER, 1993, 56pp

1652 Derseh Endale, *External imbalances, famines and entitlements: a case study.* Helsinki: WIDER, 1993, 62pp

1653 Derseh Endale, *Rural markets, food-grain prices and famines: a study on selected regions in Ethiopia.* Helsinki: WIDER, 1993, 28pp

1654 Kelly, M, Operational value of anthropometric surveillance in famine early warning and relief: Wollo Region, Ethiopia, 1987–88, *Disasters,* **17,** 1 (1993) 48–55

1655 Kiros, F, *The subsistence crisis in Africa: the case of Ethiopia.* Addis Ababa: OSSREA, 1993, 224pp

1656 Nyangabyaki Bazaara, Coming to terms with the famine and food question in Ethiopia, *Africa development,* **17,** 4 (1992)

102–112 (review article)

1657 Solberg, R, *Miracle in Ethiopia: a partnership response to famine.* New York: Friendship Press, 1991, 208pp

1658 Villumsted, S, Hendrie, B, New policy direction in disaster preparedness and response in Ethiopia, *Disasters,* **17,** 2 (1993) 122–32

1659 Webb, P, Coping with droughts and food insecurity in Ethiopia, *Disasters,* **17,** 1 (1993) 33–47

1660 Webb, P, et al, *Famine and drought mitigation in Ethiopia during the 1990s.* Washington: IFPRI, 1992, 213pp

Gender

See also: 1670

1661 Abbink, J, Gender and power, male and female in a Me'en homicide compensation ceremony, *Sociology ethnology bulletin,* **1,** 2 (1992) 67–72

1662 Assela, B, Projection of Addis Ababa (Ethiopia) female population, 1984: an application of matrix method, *Sinet,* **13,** 1 (1990) 1–13

1663 Taye, M, Farming and cooking: the value of home activities in the grain-plough culture of Ethiopia, *Ethiopian journal of development research,* **12,** 1 (1990) 47–65

1664 Terefe, A, Larson, C P, Modern contraception use in Ethiopia - does involving husbands make a difference?, *American journal of public health,* **83,** 11 (1993) 1567–71

1665 Tsehai Berhane-Selassie (ed), *Gender issues in Ethiopia.* Addis Ababa: Institute of Ethiopian Studies, 1991, 155pp

Geography, human

No entry. *See also:* 1403, 1717

Geography, physical

1666 Laike, M A, Seismicity and earthquake risk in the Addis Ababa region, *Sinet,* **13,** 1 (1990) 15–35

Health & welfare services

See also: 379

1667 Bitran-Dicowsky, R, Dunlop, D W, The determinants of hospital costs: an analysis of Ethiopia, in Mills, A & Lee, K (eds), *Health economics research in developing countries* (Oxford: OUP, 1993), 250–71

1668 Derege, K, Tigest, K, Medical students attitudes towards community health, *Ethiopian journal of health development,* **4,** 1 (1990) 35–43

1669 Kloos, H, Buying drugs in Addis Ababa: a quantitative analysis, in van der Geest, S & Whyte, S R (eds), *The context of medicines in developing countries* (Amsterdam: Spinhuis, 1991), 81–106

1670 Materia, E, et al, A community survey on maternal and child health services utilisation in rural Ethiopia, *European journal of epidemiology,* **9,** 5 (1992) 511–16

1671 Tesfaye, S, Survey of immunisation levels and factors affecting programe participation in Kaffa, southwestern Ethiopia, *Ethiopian journal of health development,* **4,** 1 (1990) 51–59

1672 Zein, Z A, Kloos, H (eds), *The ecology of health and disease in Ethiopia.* Boulder: Westview, 1993, 540pp

History, general

1673 Hassen, M, The historian Bahrey and the importance of his 'History of the Galla', *Horn of Africa,* **13/14,** 3–4/1–2 (1990/1991) 90–106

1674 **Quirin, J,** Oral traditions as historical sources in Ethiopia: the case of the Beta Israel (Falashas), *History in Africa,* **20,** (1993) 297–312

History, early

1675 **Fattovich, R,** L'archeologia en Etiopia ed Eritrea: aspetti, problemi et prospettive, *Africa (Rome),* **48,** 3 (1993) 464–69

History, C18th

1676 **Chernetsov, S B,** *Efiopskaia feodal'naia monarkhiaa v XVII veke.* Moscow: Nauka, 1990, 326pp
1677 **Diop, B,** Un lutte pour l'hégémonie à la fin de l'antiquité: l'enjeu africain et l'arme de l'exégèse, *Annales de la Faculté des lettres et sciences humaines (Dakar),* 21 (1991) 141–54
1678 **Pankhurst, R,** Peace negotiations in the land of Däwaro in 1531: a page from the history of Ahmäd Grän, *Sociology ethnology bulletin,* **1,** 2 (1992) 61–64
1679 **Taddesse Tamrat,** *Church and state in Ethiopia: 1270–1527.* Oxford: Clarendon, 1972, 327pp
1680 **Tedeschi, S,** L'Etiopia di Poggio Bracciolini, *Africa (Rome),* **48,** 3 (1993) 333–58
1681 **Wagner, E,** The genealogy of the later Walashama' sultans of Adal and Harar, *Zeitschrift der deutschen morgenländischen Gesellschaft,* **141,** 2 (1991) 376–86

History, C19th

See also: 417
1682 **Ahmad, A H,** Emperor Yohannis' campaign in Gojjam, August 1888 to February 1989, *Northeast African studies,* **13,** 1 (1991) 1–7
1683 **Gascon, A, Hirsch, B,** Les espaces sacrés comme lieux de confluence religieuse en Ethiopie, *Cahiers d'études africaines,* **32,** 128 (1992) 689–704

History, C20th

See also: 1711
1684 **Bahru Zewde,** The Ethiopian intelligentsia and the Italo-Ethiopian War, 1935–41, *International journal of African historical studies,* **26,** 2 (1993) 271–95
1685 **Davis, R,** Mesentente cordiale: the failure of the Anglo-French alliance. Anglo-French relations during the Ethiopian and Rhineland crises, *European history quarterly,* **23,** 4 (1993) 513–28
1686 **Dore, G,** Etnologica e storia nella ricercai di Giovanni Ellero, *Africa (Rome),* **48,** 1 (1993) 35–46
1687 **Eshete, T,** The root causes of the political problems in the Ogaden, 1942–1960, *Northeast African studies,* **13,** 1 (1991) 9–28
1688 **Jalata, A,** *Oromia and Ethiopia: state formation and ethnonational conflict, 1868–1992.* Boulder: Lynne Reinner, 1993, 233pp
1689 **Kurimoto, E,** Natives and outsiders: the historical experience of the Anywaa of Western Ethiopia, *Journal of Asian and African studies* (Tokyo), 43 (1992) 1–43
1690 **Marcus, H G,** Translating the Emperor's words: Volume II of Haile Selassie's My life and Ethiopia's progress, *History in Africa,* **20,** (1993) 413–20
1691 **Scott, W R,** *The sons of Sheba's race: African-Americans and and the Italo-Ethiopian war, 1935–41.* Bloomington: Indiana University Press, 1992, 288pp
1692 **Taddia, I,** Un funzionario tra ricerca scietifica e colonialismo: Giovanni Ellero, *Africa (Rome),* **48,** 1 (1993) 24–34

Industry & trade

1693 Aydagnehum Geleta, Problems of pharmaceutical production in Ethiopia, *Science, technology and development,* **11,** 1 (1993) 26–35

1694 Chole, E, Privatisation and deregulation in Ethiopian industry: problems, prospects and impact on economy, *Journal of Ethiopian studies,* **26,** 1 (1993) 33–58

1695 Keleta, E, Application and interpretation of Probit analysis in identifying factors influencing decision making in production in small scale enterprises of Ethiopia, *Eastern Africa economic review,* **7,** 1 (1991) 39–44

1696 Mbogoh, S G, The concept of marketing efficiency, applications and policy implications: a case of dairy marketing in Addis Ababa, Ethiopia, *Discovery and innovation,* **4,** 4 (1992) 85–95

1697 Mengistu Tefera, The case of Ethiopia, in Bhagavan, M R & Karekezi, S (eds), *Energy managment (Item 788)*, 42–84

1698 Mengistu Tefera, Maintaining Ethiopia's power sector, in Karekezi, S & Mackenzie, G A (eds), *Energy options (Item 796)*, 51–67

International economic relations

No entry. *See also:* 1642

International relations

See also: 602

1699 Baissa, L, Ethiopian-Sudanese relations, 1956–91: mutual deterrence through mutual blackmail?, *Horn of Africa,* **13/14,** 3–4/1–2 (1990/1991) 1–25

1700 Henze, P, Ethiopia and Eritrea: the defeat of the Derg and the establishment of new governments, in Smock, D R (ed), *Making war and waging peace (Item 409)*, 53–77

1701 Patman, R G, Soviet-Ethiopian relations: the horns of dilemma, in Light, M (ed), *Troubled friendships: Moscow's Third World ventures* (London: British Academic Press, 1993), 110–39

Library - documentation

1702 Gupta, S, Development of the library profession and education in Ethiopia, *International information and library review,* **25,** 1 (1993) 73–83

Media

1703 Sorenson, J, *Imagining Ethiopia: struggles for history and identity in the Horn of Africa.* New Brunswick: Rutgers University Press, 1993, 216pp

Medical

See also: 1628, 1693

1704 Desta, S, Mothers' perceived cause of death: a survey of infant mortality in Butajira, Ethiopia, *Ethiopian journal of health development,* **4,** 1 (1990) 15–20

1705 Lindtjørn, B, Nutritional status and risk of infection among Ethiopian children, *Journal of tropical pediatrics,* **39,** 2 (1993) 76–82

Natural resources

1706 Fekade, T, Technical and managerial aspects of environmental and health impact assessment of water resource development projects, the Ethiopian experience, *Ethiopian journal of health development,* **4,** 1 (1990) 61–68

1707 **Girmaye, K,** The Mago national park and the people in its vicinity: conflict or coexistence?, *Sociology ethnology bulletin,* **1,** 2 (1992) 35–40

1708 **Melaku Worede,** Ethiopia: a genebank working with farmers, in Cooper, D et al (ed), *Growing diversity: genetic resources and local food security* London: Intermediate Technology Publications, 1992, 78–94

Planning

1709 **Getahun Tadesse,** *Methodology of social planning within a framework of national development planning: a review of the Ethiopian Ten Year Plan.* London: Centre of Ethiopian Studies, 1992, 55pp

Politics

See also: 1651, 1700

1710 **Abbas Hadji,** *L'état et les crises de l'integration nationale en Ethiopie contemporaine.* Talence: Bordeaux University, CEAN, 1993, 30pp

1711 **Abbas Haji,** L'Éthiopie va-t-elle éclater? Conflits politiques, économie et société en pays Arssi (1900–1935), *Cahiers d'études africains,* **32,** 126 (1992) 239–284

1712 **Abbink, J,** Ethnic conflict in the 'tribal zone': the Dizi and Suri in southern Ethiopia, *Journal of modern African studies,* **31,** 4 (1993) 675–82

1713 **Allen, H,** After Mengistu: the political geography of Ethiopia since 1991, *Geography,* **78,** 341 (1993) 445–58

1714 **Andargachew Tiruneh,** *The Ethiopian revolution 1974–1987: a transformation from an aristocratic to a totalitarian autocracy.* Cambridge: CUP, 1993, 435pp

1715 **Bereket Habte Selassie,** *Riding the whirlwind.* Trenton: Red Sea Press, 1993, 331pp

1716 **Clapham, C,** How many Ethiopias?, *Africa,* **63,** 1 (1993) 118–28 (review article)

1717 **Donham, D L,** A note on space in the Ethiopian revolution, *Africa,* **63,** 4 (1993) 583–90

1718 **Engedayehu Walle,** Ethiopia: democracy and the politics of ethnicity, *Africa today,* **40,** 2 (1993) 29–52

1719 **Eshete, A,** Implementing human rights and a democratic constitution in Ethiopia, *Issue,* **21,** 1/2 (1993) 8–13

1720 **Harbeson, J W,** The Ethiopian crisis: alternative scenarios for change, *Horn of Africa,* **13/14,** 3–4/1–2 (1990/1991) 121–131

1721 **Hasselblatt, G, et al,** *Das geheime Lachen in Bambuswald: wom Freiheitkampf der Oromo in Athiopien.* Stuttgart: Radius, 1990, 153pp

1722 **Kane, T L,** Excerpts from the prison dairy of Ahadu Saboure, *Northeast African studies,* **13,** 1 (1991) 59–71

1723 **Sheckler, A C,** Creating democratic traditions in an undemocratic State: mass organisations in Ethiopia, *Horn of Africa,* **13/14,** 3–4/1–2 (1990/1991) 81–89

1724 **Tekle, A,** Military rule in Ethiopia (1974–87): the balance sheet, *Horn of Africa,* **13/14,** 3–4/1–2 (1990/1991) 38–58

1725 **Welch, C E,** The military and social integration in Ethiopia, in Dietz, H et al (eds), *Ethnicity, integration and the military* (Boulder: Westview, 1991), 151–78

Religion, philosophy

See also: 1683, 1746

1726 **Pelizzari, E,** L'Islam popolare

in Etiopia: il pelligrinaggio di Shaykh Husayn, *Africa (Rome)*, **48,** 3 (1993) 382–95

Rural economy

See also: 1025, 1649, 1663

1727 **Abbink, J,** Famine, gold and guns: the Suri of southwestern Ethiopia 1985–91, *Disasters,* **17,** 3 (1993) 218–25

1728 **Agneta, F, et al,** The dynamics of social and economic adaptation during resettlement: the case of Beles valley in Ethiopia, in Cernea, M M & Guggenheim, S E (eds), *Anthropological approaches to resettlement (item 1112)*, 251–82

1729 **Aredo, D,** The *iddir* : a study of an indigenous informal institution in Ethiopia, *Savings and development,* **17,** 1 (1993) 77–90

1730 **Aspen, H,** *Competition and co-operation: North Ethiopian peasant households and their resource base.* Trondheim: Trondheim University, 1993, 106pp

1731 **Bassi, M,** Sviluppo partecipante e sistemi tradizionali: il caso dei Borana dell'Etiopia, *Africa (Rome),* **47,** 3 (1992) 317–335

1732 **Dejene Aredo,** Developmental aid and agricultural development policies in Ethiopia, 1957–1987, *Africa development,* **17,** 3 (1992) 209–237

1733 **Dessalegn Rahmato,** Agrarian change and agrarian crisis: state and peasantry in post-revolution Ethiopia, *Africa,* **63,** 1 (1993) 36–55

1734 **Gamaledin, M,** The decline of Afar pastoralism, in Markakis, J (ed), *Conflict and the decline of pastoralism (item 1596)*, 45–62

1735 **Gezahegu, A,** Financial returns, economic efficiency and pricing policy in state farming in Ethiopia: the case of the middle Awash cotton farms, *Ethiopian journal of development research,* **13,** 1 (1991) 39–54

1736 **Hogg, R,** Continuity and change among the Boran in Ethiopia, in Markakis, J (ed), *Conflict and the decline of pastoralism (item 1596)*, 63–82

1737 **Holden, S J, Coppock, D L,** Effects of distance to market, season and family wealth on pastoral dairy marketing in Ethiopia, *Journal of arid environments,* **23,** 3 (1993) 321–34

1738 **Kidane Asmerom,** Determinants of multiple cropping in Ethiopia: an application of qualitative response model, *Eastern African economic review,* **8,** 1 (1992) 75–80

1739 **Pickett, J,** *Economic development in Ethiopia: agriculture, the market, and the state.* Paris: OECD Development Centre, 1991, 176pp

1740 **Poluha, E, et al,** *Concern and responsibility: an evaluation of the Dodota water supply project in Ethiopia.* Stockholm: SIDA, 1990, 75pp

1741 **Stiles, D,** The Gabbra: traditional social factors in aspects of land-use management, *Nomadic peoples,* 30 (1992) 41–52

1742 **Storck, H, et al,** *Farming systems and farm management practices of smallholders in the Haraghe highlands: a baseline survey.* Kiel: Vauk, 1991, 195pp

1743 **Tenkir Bonger,** The state, the peasantry and rural class formation in prerevolutionary Ethiopia, *Africa development,* **17,** 2 (1992) 89–114

1744 **Wegenie, Y,** The development problems of agricultural producers' cooperatives in Ethiopia, *Ethiopian journal of development research,* **12,** 1 (1990) 67–109

Science & technology

1745 **Adane Bistegne Woldu,** *Science and technology for development of Ethiopia: lessons from experience of South Korea and India.* London: Centre of Ethiopian Studies, 1991, 117pp

Sociology

See also: 1638, 1730

1746 **Darge Wole,** The reactions of social science first year students in Addis Ababa to moral dilemmas related to academic matters, *Journal of Ethiopian studies,* **26,** 1 (1993) 1–32

1747 **Kebede, D, Ketsela, T,** Suicide attempts in Ethiopian adolescents in Addis Ababa high schools, *Ethiopian medical journal,* **31,** 2 (1993)

1748 **Moss, W, Ephrem, D,** Child abuse: case presentation and discussion of medical and legal issues in Ethiopia, *Ethiopian medical journal,* **30,** 1 (1992) 37–41

1749 **Asmerom, H K,** Bureaucracy and poverty-alleviation programme in Ethiopia: an assessment, in Asmerom, H K, et al (eds), *Bureacracy and developmental policies (Item 109)*, 35–59

Urban studies

1750 **Tesseme Ta'a,** The process of urbanisation in Wollega, western Ethiopia: the case of Nekemte, *Journal of Ethiopian studies,* **26,** 1 (1993) 59–72

SOMALIA

General

1751 **Adam, H M,** Geshekter, C L (eds), *Proceedings of the First International Congress of Somali Studies.* Atlanta: Scholars Press, 1992, 923pp

Anthropology

1752 **Aguilar, M L,** The role of the *Sarki* dance in Waso Boorana/Somali symbiosis and conflict, *Anthropos,* **88,** 1/2 (1993) 184–90

1753 **Mohamed-Abdi, M,** *Anthropologie somalienne: actes du deuxième colloque des études somaliennes (Besançon, 8–11 octobre 1990).* Paris: Belles Lettres, 1993, 275pp

1754 **Rirache, M A,** Somali oral poetry as a vehicle for understanding disequilibrium and conflicts in a pastoral society, *Nomadic peoples,* 30 (1992) 114–21

Economic and social history

1756 **Kapteijns, L, Spaulding, J,** From slaves to coolies: two documents from the 19th century Somali coast, *Sudanic Africa,* 3 (1992) 1–8

Economy - Development

1757 **Samatar, A I,** Structural adjustment as development strategy: bananas, boom and poverty in Somalia, *Economic geography,* **69,** 1 (1993) 25–43

1758 **Tommasoli, M,** Aggiustamento strutturale e sviluppo in Somalia: il negoziato con le istituzioni finanziarie internazionali, *Africa (Rome),* **47,** 4 (1992) 475–502

Gender

See also: 1763

1759 **Arbesman, M, et al,** Assesment of the impact of female circumcision on the gynecological, genitourinary and obstetrical health problems of women from Somalia: literature review and case series, *Women and health,* **20,** 3 (1993) 27–42

1760 **Kapteijns, L,** *Women and the Somali pastoral tradition: corporate kinship and capitalist transformation in northern Somalia.* Boston: African Studies Center, Boston University, 1991, 13pp

1761 **van der Kwaak, A,** Besnijdenis bij Somalische vrouwen: de stilte doorbroken?, *Medische antropologie,* **3,** 2 (1991) 210–235

Health & welfare services

1762 **LaFond, S A,** Deterrents to immunisation in Somalia: a survey of mothers' attitudes, *Development in practice,* **3,** 1 (1993) 27–35

1763 **LaFond, S A,** Why an immunisation programme failed to make its mark on women: Somalia, in Slim, H & Thompson, P (eds), *Listening for a change* (London: Panos, 1993), 95–103

1764 **Serkkola, A,** *Medeicine, pharmacy and family: triplicity of self-medication in Mogadishu.* Helsinki: Helsinki University, IDS, 1990, 23pp

1765 **Serkkola, A,** *Organizational diversity of health services in Mogadishu, Somalia.* Helsinki: Helsinki University, IDS, 1992, 122pp

History, early

1766 **Ali, I,** *Origin and history of the Somali people, Vol. 1.* Cardiff: Panite Books, 1993, 168pp

History, C20th

1767 **Morin, D,** Reconstruire la Somalie, *Politique africaine,* 49 (1993) 117–31

1768 **Sheik-Abdi, A,** *Divine madness: Mohammed Abdulle Hassan of Somalia (1856–1920).* London: Zed, 1993, 226pp

International relations

See also: 605, 3010

1769 **African Rights,** *Somalia: human rights abuses by the United Nations' forces.* London: African Rights, 1993, 35pp

1770 **Baynham, S,** Somalia: Operation 'Restore hope', *Africa insight,* **23,** 1 (1993) 17–23

1771 **Clark, J,** Debacle in Somalia, *Foreign affairs,* **72,** 1 (1993) 109–23

1772 **Makinda, S M,** *Seeking peace from chaos: humanitarian intervention in Somalia.* Boulder: Lynne Reinner, 1993, 92pp

1773 **Michler, W,** *Somalia: ein Volk stirbt - die Bürgerkrieg und das Versagen des Auslands,* Bonn, Dietz: 1993, 128pp

1774 **Rifrac, S,** Somalie: aide humanitaire ou intérêt stratégique?, *Cahiers du communisme,* **69,** 3 (1993) 116–118

1775 **Stevenson, J,** Hope restored in Somalia?, *Foreign policy,* 91 (1993) 138–54

Politics

See also: 816, 172, 1754, 1794

1776 **African Rights,** *Somalia. Operation Restore Hope: a preliminary assessment.* London: African Rights, 1993, 59pp

1777 **African Rights, Mines Advisory Group,** *Violent deeds live on: landmines in Somalia and Somaliland.* London: African Rights, 1993, 82pp

1778 **Ahmed, A I,** Somalia: roots of anarchy, *Indian journal of African studies,* **5,** 1 (1992) 14–26

1779 **Bradbury, M,** *The Somali conflict: prospects for peace.* Oxford: Oxfam, 1993, 149pp

1780 **Compagnon, D,** Dynamiques de mobilisation, dissidence armée et rébellion populaire: le cas du Mouvement national somali, *Africa (Rome)*, **47,** 4 (1992) 503–530

1781 **Compagnon, D,** Somalie: de l'état en formation à l'état en pointillé, in Médard, J F (ed), *Etats d'Afrique noire (Item 896)*, 145–69

1782 **de Waal, A,** *Somalia: no mercy in Mogadishu, the human cost of the conflict and the struggle for relief.* New York: Physicians for Human Rights/Africa Watch, 1992, 25pp

1783 **Doornbos, M,** Pasture and polis: the roots of political marginalisation of Somali pastoralism, in Markakis, J (ed), *Conflict and the decline of pastoralism (item 1596)*, 100–121

1784 **Ehlers, P, Witzke, A,** *Somalia: bakgrund och framtid.* Uppsala: Scandinavian Institute of African Studies, 1992, 96pp

1785 **Farah, A Y, Lewis, I M,** *Somalia: the roots of reconciliation. Peace making attempts of contemporary lineage leaders: a survey of grassroots peace conferences in 'Somaliland'.* London: Actionaid, 1993, 89pp

1786 **Lewis, I M,** Misunderstanding the Somali crisis, *Anthropology today,* **9,** 4 (1993) 1–3

1787 **Lewis, I M,** *Understanding Somalia.* London: Haan, 1993, 115pp

1788 **Michaelson, M,** Somalia: the painful road to reconciliation, *Africa today,* **40,** 2 (1993) 53–73

1789 **Prunier, G,** A candid view of the Somali National Movement, *Horn of Africa,* **13/14,** 3–4/1–2 (1990/1991) 107–120

Religion, philosophy

1790 **Mohamed-Abdi, M,** *Histoire des croyances en Somalie: religions traditionelles et religion du Livre.* Besançon: Université de Besançon, Centre de recherches d'histoire ancienne, 1992, 163pp

Rural economy

See also: 1760, 1783

1791 **Besteman, C,** *Land tenure in the Middle Juba Valley, Somalia: customary tenure and the effect of land registration.* Madison: Land Tenure Centre, University of Wisconsin, 1990, 106pp

1792 **Branca, S, D'Arca, R** (eds), *Salute per tutti? Esperienze e valutazioni da un'area rurale della Somalia.* Milan: Angeli, 1992, 334pp

1793 **Herren, U J,** Cash from camel milk: the impact of commercial camel milk sales on Garre and Gaaljacel camel pastoralism in southern Somalia, *Nomadic peoples,* 30 (1992) 97–113

1794 **Omaar, R, de Waal, A,** *Land tenure, the creation of famine, and the prospects for peace in Somalia.* London: African Rights, 1993, 20pp

Sociology

No entry. *See also:* 1115, 2194

SUDAN

Agriculture, scientific

No entry. *See also:* 1806

Anthropology

See also: 1801, 1817, 1818, 1871, 3818

1795 **Moszynski, P,** Crushing a culture, *Focus on Africa,* **4,** 4 (1993) 12–17

1796 **Palmisano, A L,** *Ethnicity: the Beja as representation.* Berlin: Das Arabische Buch, 1991, 135pp

Current affairs

1797 **Foreign and Commonwealth Office,** *Sudan.* London: FCO, 1992, 7pp

1798 **Medani, K,** Sudan human and political crisis, *Current history,* **92,** 574 (1993) 203–207

Demography

1799 **Taha, T el T,** Family planning practice in central Sudan, *Social science and medicine,* **37,** 5 (1993) 685–89

Economic and social history

1800 **Hofheinz, A,** Sons of a hidden imam: the genealogy of the Mirghani family, *Sudanic Africa,* 3 (1992) 9–27

1801 **Hutchinson, S,** The cattle of money and the cattle of girls among the Nuer, 1930–1983, *American ethnologist,* **19,** 2 (1992) 294–316

1802 **Perkins, K J,** *Port Sudan: the evolution of a colonial city.* Boulder: Westview, 1993, 264pp

1803 **Spaulding, J,** The birth of an African private epistolography, Echo Island 1862–1901, *Journal of African history,* **34,** 1 (1993) 115–41

Economy - Development

See also: 124

1804 **Abdel Ati, H A,** The development impact of NGO activities in the Red Sea Province of Sudan: a critique, *Development and change,* **24,** 1 (1993) 103–30

1805 **Taha, E A, et al,** *Towards alternative economic policies for Sudan.* Bremen: University of Bremen, Sudan Economic Research Group, 1990, 90pp

Environment

1806 **Fadl, O A A,** Hydro-agricultural schemes and their effects on agricultural production and environment: the case of the irrigation in Sudan Gezira, in Dellière, R & Symoens, J J (eds), *Agricultural intensification and environment in the tropical areas* (Brussels: Académie royale des sciences d'outre-mer, 1991), 79–89

1807 **Hussein, S G,** Environmental degradation in a semi-arid rangeland in northern Sudan, *Desertification control bulletin,* 19 (1991) 29–32

Finance

1808 **Kevane, M,** In the *shiel* a shill? Informal credit in rural Sudan, *Journal of developing areas,* **27,** 4 (1993) 515–34

Food

See also: 1816, 1873

1809 **Gray, L, Kevane, M,** For whom is the drought economy resilient? Initial effects of drought in western Sudan, *Development and change,* **24,** 1 (1993) 159–76

1810 **Harrison, G G,** Nutrition and child feeding patterns in the Sudan, *Ahfad journal,* **9,** 2 (1992) 4–22

1811 **Locke, C G, Ahmadi-Esfahani, F Z,** Famine analysis: a study of entitlements in Sudan, 1984–85, *Economic development and cultural change,* **41,** 2 (1993) 363–76

1812 **Ogbe, G,** *Ernährungssicherungspolitik in Schwarzafrika: ökonomische Analyse und Entwicklungs strategien am Beispiel des Sudans.* Frankfurt: Lang, 1991, 200pp

1813 **Pyle, A S, Gabbar, O A,** *Household vulnerability to famine:*

survival and recovery strategies among Zasghawa and Berti migrants in northern Darfur, Sudan, 1982–1989. New York: Social Science Research Council, Project on African Agriculture, 1990(?), 33pp

Gender

See also: 1822, 1844

1814 **Bernal, V,** *Gender, culture and capitalism in the Islamic revival (Sudan).* Boston: African Studies Center, Boston University, 1992, 23pp

1815 **Grawert, E,** Impacts of male outmigration on women: a case study of Kutum/northern Darfur/Sudan, *Ahfad journal,* **9,** 2 (1992) 37–60

1816 **Gray, L,** The effect of drought and economic decline on rural women in western Sudan, *Geoforum,* **24,** 1 (1993) 89–98

1817 **Grotberg, E H,** Mental health aspects of 'zar' for women in Sudan, in Rothblum, E D & Cole, E (eds), *Women's mental health (item 338),* 15–24

1818 **Katz, C,** Growing girls/closing circles: limits on the spaces of knowing in rural Sudan and US cities, in Katz, C & Monk, J (eds), *Full circle: geographies of women over the life cycle,* 88–106

1819 **Khider, M, Beshir, L O,** Policies and strategies for integrating women in agriculture and rural development, *Ahfad journal,* **9,** 2 (1992) 61–83

1820 **Parker, M,** Bilharzia and the boys: questioning common assumptions, *Social science and medicine,* **37,** 4 (1993) 481–92

Geography, physical

1821 **Lehmann, J,** Danzer, J, Soil evaluation on the western slopes of Jebel Marra, Darfur, Sudan, with special reference to plantation forestry and agroforestry, *Applied geography and development,* 40 (1992) 89–111

Health & welfare services

1822 **el Hiday, M M, Zumrawi, F Y,** The effects of nutrition education programme on pregnant women attending a Khartoum model clinic, *Ahfad journal,* **9,** 2 (1992) 23–36

History, general

See also: 1803

1823 **Allen, T,** Histories and contexts: using pasts in the present in Sudan, *Bulletin of the John Rylands University Library of Manchester,* **73,** 3 (1991) 63–91

History, early

1824 **Garcea, E A A,** Early Khartoum mesolithic settlements in the Geili-Kabbashi area, Sudan, *Journal of field archaeology,* **20,** 4 (1993) 519–22

1825 **Garcea, E A A,** Indagine sulla diffusione dell'orizzonte 'Early Khartoum' nella media e alta valle del Nilo (Sudan), *Africa (Rome),* **48,** 2 (1993) 184–98

1826 **Haaland, R,** Fish, pots and grain: Early and Mid-Holocene adaptations in the Central Sudan, *African archaeological review,* **10,** (1992) 43–64

1827 **Krzyzaniak, L,** *Schlek pradziejow w srodkowym Sudanie.* Poznam: Archaeological Museum, 1992, 256pp

History, C18th

1828 **Bjorkelo, A, Abou Shouk, A I,** A sultanic charter from Sinnar, *Sudanic Africa,* 3 (1992) 29–39

1829 Lobban, R A, Using Nubian genealogies in historical reconstruction, in Harrak, A (ed), *Contacts between cultures (Item 1181)*, 38–44

History, C19th

See also: 417

1830 Bleuchot, H, Les institutions du Soudan au XIXe siècle, *Arab historical review for Ottoman studies,* 1/2 (1990) 65–82

1831 Johnson, D H, Deng Laka and *mut roal*: fixing the date of a unknown battle, *History in Africa,* **20,** (1993) 119–28

1832 Kramer, R S, The capitulation of the Omdurman notables, *Sudanic Africa,* 3 (1992) 41–55

1833 O'Fahey, R S, A prince and his neighbours, *Sudanic Africa,* 3 (1992) 57–93

1834 Robson, B, *Fuzzy-Wuzzy: the campaigns in the eastern Sudan 1884–85.* Tunbridge Wells: Spellmount, 1993, 228pp

History, C20th

1836 Lea, C A E (ed. M W Daly), *On trek in Kordofan: the diaries of a British District Officer in the Sudan, 1931–1933.* London: British Academy/OUP, 1993, 304pp

1837 Okeny, K, The 1947 Juba conference, *Northeast African studies,* **13,** 1 (1991) 39–59

1838 Warburg, G R, The Condominium revisited: the Anglo-Egyptian Sudan 1934–1956 - a review article, *Bulletin of SOAS,* **56,** 1 (1993) 1–12

Industry & trade

1839 Speece, M, Trade, marketing and economic integration in Kordofan, Sudan, in Harrak, A (ed), *Contacts between cultures (Item 1181)*, 447–50

International economic relations

No entry. *See also:* 2555

International relations

See also: 602, 1442, 1699

1840 Lefebvre, J A, Globalism and regionalism: US arms transfers to Sudan, *Armed forces and society,* **17,** 2 (1991) 211–27

1841 Lesch, A M, External involvement in the Sudanese civil war, in Smock, D R (ed), *Making war and waging peace (Item 409)*, 79–105

Labour & manpower

1842 Mohammed Nur, E I T, The impact of malaria on labour use and efficiency in the Sudan, *Social science and medicine,* **37,** 9 (1993) 1115–1119

Law

1843 Köndgen, O, *Das islamische Strafrecht des Sudan: von seiner Einführung 1983 bis Juli 1992.* Hamburg: Deutsches Orient-Institut, 1993, 145pp

Medical

See also: 1820

1844 Parker, M, Reassessing disability: the impact of schistosomal infection on daily activities among women in Gezira Province, Sudan, *Social science and medicine,* **35,** 7 (1992) 877–90

Natural resources

See also: 1821

1845 Dijk, J A V, Ahmed, M H,

Opportunities for expanding water harvesting in subsaharan Africa: the case of the teras of Kassala. London: International Institute for Environment and Development, 1993, 17pp

1846 **Livingstone, A, McPherson, H J,** Management strategies for rural water development: a case study from Sudan, *Natural resources forum,* **17,** 4 (1993) 294–301

Politics

See also: 1841, 1843, 1864, 1867, 1878

1847 **An-Naim, A A,** Islam and national integration in the Sudan, in Hunwick, J O (ed), *Religion and national integration (Item 978)*, 11–38

1848 **de Waal, A,** Sudan: searching for the origins of absolutism and decay, *Development and change,* **24,** 1 (1993) 177–202 (review article)

1849 **Deng, F M,** Negotiating identity: dishonoured agreements in the Sudanese conflict, in de Silva, K M & Samarasinghe, S W (eds), *Peace accords and ethnic conflict* (London: Pinter, 1992), 60–82

1850 **Deng, F M,** Sudan: a nation in search of identity, *Africa forum,* **1,** 4 (1991) 11–15

1851 **Deng, F M,** A three-dimensional approach to the conflict in the Sudan, in Hunwick, J O (ed), *Religion and national integration (Item 978)*, 39–61

1852 **Hassan, S,** The Sudan National Democratic Alliance: the quest for peace, unity and democracy, *Issue,* **21,** 1/2 (1993) 14–25

1853 **Kaballo, S,** Sudan: over four years of fundamentalist rule, *Review of African political economy,* 58 (1993) 106–109

1854 **Kocjok, D D M,** The Malual Dinka-Baqqara border conflict and the impact on national integration in the Sudan, *Northeast African studies,* **13,** 1 (1991) 73–83

1855 **Kok, P N,** Hasan Abdallah al-Turabi, *Orient,* **33,** 2 (1992) 185–92

1856 **Lesch, A M,** Negotiations in Sudan, in Smock, D R (ed), *Making war and waging peace (Item 409)*, 107–138

1857 **Mitchell, C,** The process and stages of mediation: two Sudanese cases, in Smock, D R (ed), *Making war and waging peace (Item 600)*, 139–59

1858 **Mohammed, N A L,** Militarism in Sudan: trends and determinants, *Armed forces and society,* **19,** 3 (1993) 411–33

1859 **Nhial, A A J, et al,** Human rights abuses in the Sudan, *Review of African political economy,* 58 (1993) 110–118

1860 **Prunier, G,** Les Frères musulmans soudanais: une nouvelle diplomatie révolutionnaire, *Islam et sociétés au Sud du Sahara,* 6 (1992) 5–16

1861 **Salih, M A M,** Pastoralists and the war in southern Sudan: the Ngok Dinka/Humr conflict in south Kordofan, in Markakis, J (ed), *Conflict and the decline of pastoralism (item 1596)*, 16–29

1862 **Thomas, G F,** *Sudan: struggle for survival.* London: Darf, 1993, 263pp

1863 **Yongo-Bure, S,** *The nationalities question and national unity or disintegration in Sudan.* Bremen: University of Bremen, Sudan Economic Research Group, 1990, 19pp

Religion, philosophy

See also: 1814,1847, 1851

1864 **Al-Karsani, A A-S,** Beyond sufism: the case of millenial Islam in the Sudan, in Brenner, L (ed), *Muslim identity (item 963)*, 135–53

1865 Grandin, N, Al-Merkaz al-islami al-ifriqi bi'l-Khartoum: la République du Soudan et la propagation de l'islam en Afrique noire, in Otayek, R (ed), *Radicalisme islamique (Item 1002)*, 97–120

1866 Oevermann, A, *Die 'Republikanischen Brüder' im Sudan: eine islamische Reformbewegung in Zwanzigsten Jahrhundert.* Frankfurt: Lang, 1993, 172pp

1867 O'Fahey, R S, Islamic hegemonies in the Sudan: sufism, mahdism and islamism, in Brenner, L (ed), *Muslim identity (item 963)*, 21–35

Rural economy

See also: 1201, 1808, 1819, 1861

1868 Abdelmagid, S A, *The economic impact of faba bean introduction in smallholdings: a case study of the Gezira Scheme.* Kiel: Vauk, 1992, 92pp

1869 Bascom, J, The peasant economy of refugee resettlement in eastern Sudan, *Annals of the Association of American Geographers,* **83,** 2 (1993) 320–46

1870 Bontkes, T E S, Dynamics of rural development in southern Sudan, *System dynamics,* **9,** 1 (1993) 1–21

1871 Dombrowski, K, Some considerations for the understanding of small herd dynamics in East African arid zones: the long term consequences of bridewealth exchange networks, *Human ecology,* **21,** 1 (1993) 23–50

1872 Elmekhi, A, Baker, J, Marketing, politics and agarian crisis in Sudan, *IDS bulletin,* **24,** 3 (1993) 68–74

1873 Morton, J, Pastoral decline and famine: the Beja case, in Markakis, J (ed), *Conflict and the decline of pastoralism (item 1596)*, 30–44

1874 Salem-Murdock, M, Involuntary resettlement: a plea for the host population, in Cernea, M M & Guggenheim, S E (eds), *Anthropological approaches to resettlement (item 1112)*, 307–20

1875 Salih, M S M, Agro-pastoralists' response to agricultural policies: the predicament of the Baggara, western Sudan, in Nett, B et al (eds), *Agricultural transformation (Item 1069)*, 153–72

1876 Sultan, D H, Merchants and a bankrupt state: reflections on contextual imperatives and the genesis of a predicament in Kordofan, *African studies review,* **36,** 3 (1993) 75–94

Sociology

1877 Bascom, J, The political economy of refugee resettlement in eastern Sudan, *Annals of the Association of American Geographers,* **83,** 2 (1993) 320–46

1878 Scott-Villiers, A, et al, Repatriation of 150,000 Sudanese refugees from Ethiopia: the manipulation of civilians in a situation of civil conflict, *Disasters,* **17,** 3 (1993) 202–17

Social welfare

1879 Simon, B, Flüchtlinge und Integration: eritreische Flüchtlinge im Sudan, *Paideuma,* **38,** (1992) 249–67

Urban studies

No entry. *See also:* 1802, 3818

EAST AFRICA

General

1880 **Gibbon, P (ed)**, *Social change and economic reform in Africa.* Uppsala: Scandinavian Institute of African Studies, 1993, 381pp

Anthropology

See also: 1901

1881 **Ahr, C,** *Fruchtbarkeit und 'Respekt': filmethnologische Untersuchung eines Geschlechterkonflikts un ein Ritual bei den Maasai.* Gottingen: Re, 1991, 128pp

1882 **Galaty, J G,** 'The eye that wants a person, where can it not see?' Inclusion, exclusion and boundary shifters in Maasai identity, in Spear, T & Waller, R (eds), *Becoming Maasai (Item 1885)*, 174–94

1883 **Klumpp, D, Kratz, C,** Aesthetics, expertise and ethnicity: Okiek and Maasai perspectives in personal ornaments, in Spear, T & Waller, R (eds), *Being Maasai (Item 1885)*, 195–221

1884 **Rigby, P,** Objectification and alienation: some Maasai views of peripheral capitalism, in Gailey, C W (ed), *Dialectical anthropology: essays in honour of Stanley Diamond, Vol. 1* (Gainesville: University Press of Florida, 1992), 303–31

1885 **Spear, T, Waller, R** (eds), *Being Maasai: ethnicity and identity in East Africa.* London: Currey, 1993, 322pp

1886 **Spencer, P,** Becoming Maasai, being in time, in Spear, T & Waller, R (eds), *Being Maasai (Item 1885)*, 140–56

Demography

No entry. *See also:* 3942

Economic and social history

1887 **Ault, D E, Rutman, G L,** Land scarcity, property rights and resource allocation in agriculture: eastern and southern Africa, *South African journal of economics,* **61,** 1 (1993) 32–44

1888 **Galaty, J G,** Maasai expansion and the new East African pastoralism, in Spear, T & Waller, R (eds), *Being Maasai (Item 1885)*, 61–86

1889 **Gregory, R G,** *South Asians in East Africa: an economic and social history.* Boulder: Westview, 1993, 410pp

1890 **Thomas, K,** The adventures of H & G Simmonds Ltd in Malta and East Africa, *Business archives,* **61,** (1991) 40–54

1891 **White, L,** *Cars out of place: vampires, technology, and labor in East and Central Africa.* Johannesburg: University of Witwatersrand, African Studies Institute, 1993, 28pp

1892 **Wright, M,** *Strategies of slaves and women: life-stories from East/Central Africa.* London: Currey, 1993, 238pp

Economy - Development

See also: 1880, 1896

1893 Green, C, Murinde, V, The potency of stabilisation policy in developing economies: Kenya, Tanzania and Uganda, *Journal of policy modelling,* **15,** 4 (1993) 427–62

1894 Murinde, V, *Macroeconomic policy modelling for developing countries.* Aldershot: Avebury, 1993, 442pp

Education

1895 Saki, K M O, Instructional strategies (teaching methodology) courses in East African universities: a reappraisal, *Papers in education and development,* 14 (1990) 36–45

Environment

No entry. *See also:* 1897

Finance

1896 Harvey, C, *The role of commercial banking in recovery from economic disaster in Ghana, Tanzania, Uganda and Zambia.* Brighton: Institute of Development Studies, 1993, 33pp

Food

1897 Homewood, J K, Development and the ecology of Maasai food and nutrition, *Ecology of food and nutrition,* **29,** 1 (1992) 61–80

Gender

See also: 1881, 1892

1898 Due, J M, Policies to overcome the negative effects of structural adjustment programs on African female-headed households, in Gladwin, C H (ed), *Structural adjustment and African women farmers (Item 315),* 103–27

History, general

1899 Allen, J de V, *Swahili origins: Swahili culture and the Shungwaya phenomenon.* London: Currey, 1993, 272pp

1900 Sutton, J E G, Becoming Maasailand, in Spear, T & Waller, R (eds), *Being Maasai (Item 1885),* 38–60

1901 Waller, R, Conclusions, in Spear, T & Waller, R (eds), *Becoming Maasai (Item 1885),* 290–302

History, early

1902 Schoenbrun, D L, We are what we eat: ancient agriculture between the Great Lakes, *Journal of African history,* **34,** 1 (1993) 1–31

1903 Stewart, K A, Iron Age ceramic studies in Great Lakes eastern Africa: a critical and historiographical review, *African archaeological review,* **11,** (1993) 21–37

1904 Virgin, K, *Urban origins in eastern Africa.* Stockholm: SAREC, 1993, 54pp

History, C18th

1905 Pouwels, R L, Reflections on historiography and pre-nineteenth century history from the Pate 'chronicles', *History in Africa,* **20,** (1993) 263–96

1906 Schoenbrun, D L, Cattle lands and banana gardens: the historical geography of the western Great Lakes region, ca. AD 800–1500, *African archaeological review,* **11,** (1993) 39–72

1907 Sutton, J E G, The antecedents of the Interlacrustine kingdoms, *Journal of African history,* **34,** 1 (1993) 33–64

History, C19th

No entry. *See also:* 1885

History, C20th

1908 **Gregory, R G,** *The quest for equality: Asian politics in East Africa, 1900–1967.* Hyderabad: Orient Longman, 1993, 231pp

Industry & trade

See also: 1934

1909 **Juneja, J S,** The role of small enterprises in industrial development of East Africa: an integrated approach, *African currents,* 12 (1990) 27–49

International economic relations

See also: 3950, 4425

1910 **Närman, A,** East African attempts at regional cooperation, in Siddiqui, R A (ed), *Subsaharan Africa (item 15)*, 261–86

International relations

No entry. *See also:* 2893

Language

1911 **Mazrui, A M, Mazrui, A A,** Dominant languages in a plural society: English and Kiswahili in postcolonial East Africa, *International political science review,* **14,** 3 (1993) 275–92

1912 **Sommer, G, Vossen, R,** Dialects, sectiolects and simply lects? The Maasai language in time perspective, in Spear, T & Waller, R (eds), *Becoming Maasai (Item 1885)*, 25–37

1913 **Tanner, R E S,** East African ethical ideas and translation: some possible consequences of a bilateral process, *Anthropos,* **88,** 1/2 (1993) 29–37

Literature

1914 **Imbuga, F,** East African literature in the 1980s, *Matatu,* 10 (1993) 121–35

1915 **Mulokozi, M M,** A survey of Kiswahili literature: 1970–1988, *Afrika focus,* **8,** 1 (1992) 49–61

Media

No entry. *See also:* 734

Medical

See also: 1918, 1935, 1936

1916 **Colebunders, R L, Latif, A S,** Natural history and clinical presentation of HIV–1 infection in adults, *AIDS,* **5,** 1 (1991) 103–112

Politics

1917 **Constation, F,** Leadership, muslim identities and East African politics: tradition, bureaucratisation and communication, in Brenner, L (ed), *Muslim identity (item 963)*, 36–58

1918 **Lanegran, K, Hyden, G,** Mapping the politics of AIDS: illustrations from East Africa, *Population and environment,* **14,** 3 (1993) 245–63

1919 **M'Siri, K,** Retour à la paix dans la sous région: un défi permanent pour la CEPGL, *Grands lacs,* (1991) 4–13

1920 **Okullu, H,** Church, state, and society in East Africa, *Southern Africa political and economic monthly,* **4,** 11 (1991) 4–10

1921 **Zeleza, T,** African social scientists and the struggle for academic freedom, *Journal of* *eastern African research and development,* **22,** (1992) 11–32

Religion, philosophy

See also: 1913, 1920

1922 Balda, J L, The role of Kiswahili in East African Islam, in Brenner, L (ed), *Muslim identity (item 963)*, 226–38

1923 Bellagamba, A, Priestly and religious formation in eastern Africa: its missionary dimension, *African christian studies,* **8,** 3 (1992) 52–73

Rural economy

See also: 1052

1924 Barampama, A, *Le manioc en Afrique de l'Est.* Paris: Karthala, 1993, 285pp

1925 Baxter, P T W, The 'new' East African pastoralist: an overview, in Markakis, J (ed), *Conflict and the decline of pastoralism (item 1596)*, 143–62

1926 Bevan, D, et al, *Agriculture and the policy environment: Tanzania and Kenya.* Paris: OECD, 1993, 103pp

1927 Dietz, T, The state, the market and the decline of pastoralism: challenging some myths, with evidence from western Pokot in Kenya/Uganda, in Markakis, J (ed), *Conflict and the decline of pastoralism (item 1596)*, 83–99

1928 Eisemon, T O, The impact of primary schooling on agricultural thinking and practices in Kenya and Burundi, in Mades, G G (ed), *Primary school agriculture (item 222)*, 31–37

1929 Helland, J, Finding a new sustainable pastoralism or sustaining pastoralists? The dilemma facing East African pastoralists, *Forum for utviklungstudier,* 2 (1990) 167–82

1930 Hogg, R, NGOs, pastoralists and the myth of community: three case studies of pastoral development from East Africa, *Nomadic peoples,* 30 (1992) 122–46

1931 Kategile, J A, Mubi, S (eds), *Future of livestock industries in eastern and southern Africa: proceedings of the workshop held at Kadoma Ranch Hotel, Zimbabwe, 20–23 July 1992.* Addis Ababa: International Livestock Centre for Africa, 1993, 227pp

1932 Schwettman, J, Cooperatives in economies under reconstruction: Cameroon, Tanzania and Uganda, *Yearbook of cooperative enterprise 1993,* 69–81

1933 Turner, B L (ed), *Population growth and agricultural change in Africa.* Gainesville: University Press of Florida, 1993, 461pp

Sociology

1934 Klein, C G, Die indische Händlerminorität in Ostafrika: Ursachen und Verlauf einer ungelösten Konflikts, *Sociologus,* **43,** 1 (1993) 46–67

1935 Valleroy, L A, et al, The consequences of HIV/AIDS in eastern Africa on mothers, children and orphans, *Population and environment,* **14,** 3 (1993) 301–305

1936 Way, P O, Stanecki, K, How bad will it be: modelling the AIDS epidemic in eastern Africa, *Population and environment,* **14,** 3 (1993) 265–78

Urban studies

1937 Hughes, G, Cost-benefit analysis: housing and squatter upgrading in East Africa, in Tipple, A G & Willis, K G (eds), *Housing the poor (item 1159)*, 234–57

BURUNDI

Demography

1938 **Makinson, C,** Estimates of adult mortality in Burundi, *Journal of biosocial science,* **25,** 2 (1993) 169–80

Economic and social history

No entry. *See also:* 4156

Economy - Development

See also: 1953
1939 **Egger, U, Stockli, B,** *Vershuldung, Anpassung and Entwicklung: Analyse von Strukturanpassungsprogrammen am Beispiel Burundis und weltwirtschatliche Konsequenzen einer integralen Entwicklunspolitik.* Keil: Vauk, 1990, 77pp

Education

See also: 1928
1940 **Eisemon, T O, et al,** Can schooling make a better farmer? Primary schooling and agriculture in Burundi, in Mades, G G (ed), *Primary school agriculture (item 222),* 129–40

Finance

1941 **Zodrow, G K,** Capital income taxation in Burundi, *Journal of African economics,* **2,** 3 (1993) 348–80

Gender

1942 **Ntampaka, C,** Femme, des inégalités consacrées, *Dialogue,* 161 (1992) 3–22

Geography, human

1943 **Ndayishimiye, J P, et al,** Geography in Burundi, *Professional geographer,* **44,** 2 (1992) 219–23

History, general

1944 **Chrétien, J P,** *Burundi, l'histoire retrouvée: 25 ans de metier d'historien.* Paris: Karthala, 1993, 512pp

History, C20th

1945 **Dickerman, C,** African courts under the colonial regime: Usumbura, Ruanda-Urundi, 1938–62, *Canadian journal of African studies,* **26,** 1 (1992) 55–69

Industry & trade

No entry. *See also:* 1958

International economic relations

1946 **Willame, J C,** Les manipulations du développement: ajustement, cogestion et démocratisation au Burundi, *Cahiers du CEDAF,* 5 (1992) 1–182

International relations

No entry. *See also:* 1946

Law

No entry. *See also:* 1945

Medical

1947 **Anon,** Epidémiologie de SIDA au Burundi, *Au coeur de l'Afrique,* **60,** 1 (1992) 129–40

Politics

See also: 1944, 1946

1948 Lemarchand, R, Burundi in comparative perspective: dimensions of ethnic strife, in McGarry, J & O'Leary, B (eds), *The politics of ethnic conflict regulation* (London: Routledge, 1993), 151–71

1949 National Democratic Institute, *NDI elections advisory mission to the Republic of Burundi, December 13–19, 1992.* Washington: the Institute, 1992, 16pp

1950 Ndegeya, V, *Repression au Burundi: journal d'un prisonnier vainquer.* Paris: Harmattan, 1993, 135pp

1951 Pabanel, J P, Burundi: un état d'origine traditionelle, in Médard, J F (ed), *Etats d'Afrique noire (Item 896)*, 277–90

1952 Reyntjens, F, The proof of the pudding is in the eating: the June 1993 elections in Burundi, *Journal of modern African studies,* **31,** 4 (1993) 563–83

1953 Rutake, P, *Développement décentralisé: mutations politiques, pouvoir local et développement communal au Burundi.* Paris: Publisud, 1992, 145pp

Religion, philosophy

1954 Feltz, G, Christianisation et mentalités au Burundi: innovations et permanences des comportments socio-culturels en milieu rural, *History in Africa,* **20,** (1993) 27–42

Rural economy

See also: 1928, 1940

1955 Verhaegen, E, Degand, J, *L'évolution des systèmes agricoles au Burundi: une dynamique conflictuelle.* Louvain-la-neuve: CIDEP, 1993, 100pp

Sociology

See also: 1954

1956 Mbonimpa, M, *Hutu, Tutsi, Twa: pour une société sans castes au Burundi.* Paris: Harmattan, 1993, 109pp

Urban studies

1957 Calcio-Gaudino, C, Urbanisation et déséquilibre de l'occupation de l'espace au Burundi, in Vennetier, P (ed), *Urbanisation et développement (Item 1161)*, 27–43

1958 Sirven, P, La polarisation des transports par la capitale au Burundi, in Vennetier, P (ed), *Urbanisation et développement (Item 1161)*, 147–59

KENYA

General

1959 Friedrich Naumann Stiftung, *Blueprint for a new Kenya: post election action programme.* Nairobi: Friedrich Naumann Stiftung, 1992, 255pp

1960 Orora, J HO, Doing qualitative research in Kenya: reflections on some problems and strategies of three qualitative research methods, *Maseno journal of education, arts and science,* **1,** 1 (1992) 31–46

Agriculture, scientific

1961 Barrow, E G G, *Tree rights in Kenya: the case of Turkana.* Nairobi: ACTS, 1992, 26pp

1962 Evans, M I, Choice of species for social forestry in Kenya, in Kiriro, A & Juma, C (eds), *Gaining ground (item 2025)*, 177–202

1963 Groothenhuis, J G, Olubayo,

R O, Disease research in the wildlife-livestock interface in Kenya, *Veterinary quarterly,* **15,** 2 (1993) 55–59

Anthropology

See also: 1988, 2035, 2061, 2142

1964 Bernardi, B, Old Kikuyu religion 'igongona' and 'mambura': sacrifice and sex - rereading Kenyatta's ethnography, *Africa (Rome),* **48,** 2 (1993) 167–83

1965 Fratkin, E, Maa-speakers of the northern Desert: recent developments in Ariaal and Rendille identity, in Spear, T & Waller, R (eds), *Being Maasai (Item 1885),* 273–89

1966 Harkness, S, Super, C M, The cultural foundations of fathers' roles: evidence from Kenya and the United States, in Hewlett, B S (ed), *Father-child relations* (New York: Aldine de Gruyter, 1992), 191–211

1967 Krabbe, G, Mayer, H P, *Die schwarze Familie: wie Entwicklungshilfe die schwarzafrikanische Familie und die Rollen ihrer Mitgleider verändert hat.* Frankfurt: Lang, 1991, 359pp

1968 Kratz, C A, 'We've always done it like this ... except for a few details': tradition and innovation in Okiek ceremonies, *Comparative studies in society and history,* **35,** 1 (1993) 30–65

1969 Little, M A, et al, Growth of nomadic and settled Turkana infants of northwest Kenya, *American journal of physical anthropology,* **92,** 3 (1993) 273–89

1970 McGivney, J, Is she a wife or a mother?: social order, respect, and address in Mijikenda, *Language in society,* **22,** 1 (1993) 19–39

1971 Peatrik, A M, 'Age, generation et temps' chez les Meru Tigania-Igembe du Kenya, *Africa,* **63,** 2 (1993) 241–60

1972 Peatrik, A M, *Ages de la vie, temps de la société: le dilemme de sociétés à système d'age et de génération d'Afrique orientale.* Nairobi: Institut francais de recherche en Afrique, 1993, 21pp

1973 Sato, S, The camel trust system in the Rendille society of northern Kenya, *African study monographs,* **13,** 2 (1992) 69–89

1974 Schlee, G, Inter-ethnic clan identities, ethnicity, centrism and biases: a response to Paul Spencer, *Africa,* **63,** 4 (1993) 591–600

1975 Sottas, B, *Afrika entwickeln und modernisierung: Paradigmen, Identitätsbildung und kleinbäuerische Uberlebensstrategie.* Freiburg: Freiburg University, 1992, 322pp

Current affairs

1976 Ajulu, R, The 1992 Kenya general elections: a preliminary assessment, *Review of African political economy,* 56 (1993) 98–102

1977 Andreassen, B-A, et al, *A hobbled democracy: the Kenya general elections 1992.* Bergen: Chr Michelsen Institute, 1993, 46pp

1978 Bourmaud, D, Les elections au Kenya: victoire ou répit?, *Politique africaine,* 49 (1993) 141–46

1979 Chege, M, Mwangale's turn, *Society,* **2,** 16 (1992) 8–12

1980 Commonwealth Secretariat, Observer Group, *The presidential, parliamentary and civic elections in Kenya: 29 December, 1992.* London: The Secretariat, 1993, 71pp

1981 Gatabaki, N, An interview with Raila, *Finance,* 30.12.92 42–45

1982 Gatabaki, N, Musyoka wa Kyendo, How minorities won, *Finance,* 31.1.93 12–20

1983 Muriithi, E, KANU versus the opposition: what prospects?, *Nairobi law monthly,* 43 (1992) 14–17

1984 **Muriithi, E, Mburu, C,** Economic and human rights issues: case study, KANU v FORD, *Nairobi law monthly,* 43 (1992) 18–23

1985 **National Election Monitoring Unit,** *The multi-party general elections in Kenya: 29 December, 1992.* Nairobi: NEMU, 1993, 262pp

1986 **Owuor, G,** Scaring Moi, *Society,* **2,** 13 (1992) 32–35

Demography

1987 **Hyatt, D E, Milne, W J,** Determinants of fertility in urban and rural Kenya: estimates and a simulation of the impact of education policy, *Environment and planning, Series A,* **25,** 3 (1993) 371–82

1988 **Roth, E A,** A reexamination of Rendille population regulation, *American anthropologist,* **95,** 3 (1993) 597–611

1989 **Uitto, J I,** Fertility transition and socio-economic change in western Kenya, *African study monographs,* **13,** 4 (1992) 185–201

Economic and social history

See also: 2026,2050

1990 **Anderson, D M,** The 'crisis of capitalism' and Kenya's social history: a comment, *African affairs,* **92,** 367 (1993) 285–90

1991 **Campbell, D J,** Land as ours, land as mine: economic, political and ecological marginalisation in Kajiado District, in Spear, T & Waller, R (eds), *Being Maasai (Item 1885)*, 258–72

1992 **Cooper, F,** Colonizing time: work rhythms and labour conflict in colonial Mombasa, in Dirks, N B (ed), *Colonialism and culture* Ann Arbor: University of Michigan Press, 1992, 209–45

1993 **Ensminger, J,** *Making a market: the institutional transformation of an African society.* Cambridge: CUP, 1992, 212pp

1994 **Mnjama, N M,** Railway records as sources of information for the study of Kenya history, *African research and documentation,* 63 (1993) 1–12

1995 **Munene, J M,** Historical perspective on ethnic relations in Kenya, *Wajibu,* **7,** 3 (1992) 2–6

1996 **Rutten, M M E M,** *Selling wealth to buy poverty: the process of individualisation of land ownership among the Maasai pastoralists of Kajiado District, Kenya, 1890–1990.* Saarbrucken: Breitenbach, 1992, 510pp

1997 **Tiffen, M,** *Environmental change and dryland management in Machakos district, Kenya, 1930–90: farming and incomes systems.* London: Overseas Development Institute, 1991, 81pp

Economy - Development

See also: 180, 2157

1998 **Bevan, D, et al,** Anatomy of a temporary trade shock: the Kenyan coffee boom of 1976–9, *Journal of African economics,* **1,** 2 (1992) 271–305

1999 **Bigsten, A,** Regulation versus price reforms in crisis management: the case of Kenya, in Blomström, M & Lundahl, M (eds), *Economic crisis (Item 119)*, 61–74

2000 **Fielding, D,** Determinants of investment in Kenya and Côte d'Ivoire, *Journal of African economics,* **2,** 3 (1993) 299–328

2001 **Hetherington, P,** Explaining the crisis of capitalism in Kenya, *African affairs,* **92,** 366 (1993) 89–103

2002 **Himbara, D,** Myths and realities of Kenyan capitalism, *Journal of modern African studies,* **31,** 1 (1993) 93–107

2003 **Hoddinott, J,** Modelling remittance flows in Kenya, *Journal of African economics,* **1,** 2 (1992) 206–32

2004 **Juma, C,** Sustainable development and economic policy in Kenya, in Kiriro, A & Juma, C (eds), *Gaining ground (item 2025)*, 51–86

2005 **Kimenyi, M S,** The civil service and the economy, *Finance,* 31.7.92 39–43

Education

See also: 1928, 1987, 2048, 2053, 2088, 2090

2006 **Ayodo, T M O,** Educational opportunities and services for expanding Eldoret, *Maseno journal of education, arts and science,* **1,** 1 (1992) 58–72

2007 **Davison, J,** School attainment and gender: attitudes of Kenyan and Malawian parents toward educating girls, *International journal of educational development,* **13,** 4 (1993) 331–38

2008 **Eshiwani, G S,** *Education in Kenya since independence.* Nairobi: EAEP, 1993, 229pp

2009 **Gravenir, F Q,** An assessment of trends in public financing of education in Kenya, *Kenya journal of education,* **5,** 1 (1991) 1–17

2010 **Kerre, B W,** Vocational and technical education and training in Kenya: the past, present and future, *Kenya journal of education,* **5,** 1 (1991) 18–45

2011 **Knight, J B, et al,** Is the rate of return of primary schooling really 26 per cent?, *Journal of African economics,* **1,** 2 (1992) 192–205

2012 **Legère, K** (ed), *The role of language in primary education in eastern Africa with special reference to Kiswahili.* Bonn: Zentralstelle für Erziehung, Wissenschaft und Dokumentation, 1992, 503pp

2013 **Mosoti Obae, R, Gravenir, F Q,** Achieving full enrollment in secondary education in Kenya: a projection, *Maseno journal of education, arts and science,* **1,** 1 (1992) 47–57

2014 **Mwiria, K,** Kenyan women adult literacy learners: why their motivation is difficult to sustain, *International review of education,* **39,** 3 (1993) 183–92

2015 **Namaswa, G B,** Education and urban/rural integration: issues, problems and prospects in Kenya, *Maseno journal of education, arts and science,* **1,** 1 (1992) 12–20

2016 **Okech, J G,** Curriculum problems in Kenya and their influence on teachers' decision making about subject matter to be taught, *Journal of eastern African research and development,* **22,** (1992) 105–119

2017 **Osler, A,** Education for development and democracy in Kenya: a case study, *Educational review,* **45,** 2 (1993) 165–73

2018 **Sperling, D C,** Rural *madrasas* of the southern Kenya coast, 1971–92, in Brenner, L (ed), *Muslim identity (item 963)*, 198–209

Environment

See also: 251, 1961, 2044, 2047, 2050–52, 2055, 2059, 2066, 2116, 2126, 2137, 2186

2019 **Arum, G,** Kenya Energy and Environment Organisation (1981–90), in Wellard, K & Copestake, J C (eds), *NGOs and the state (Item 1096)*, 145–58

2020 **Baker, R,** Environmental degradation in Kenya: two conflicting 'explanations', in his *Environmental management in the tropics: an historical perspective* (Boca Raton: CRC Press, 1993), 153–66

2021 **Blankenship, L H, et al,** *Game cropping in East Africa: the*

Kekopey experiment. College Station: Texas Agricultural Experiment Station, 1990, 128pp

2022 **Darkoh, M B K,** Land degradation and resource management in Kenya, *Desertification control bulletin,* 19 (1991) 61–72

2023 **de Groot, P, et al,** *Taking root: revegetation in semi-arid Kenya.* Nairobi: ACTS, 1992, 105pp

2024 **Kabereri-Macharia, J W,** Women and environmental law in Kenya, in Khasiani, S A (ed), *Groundwork (item 2051)*, 91–100

2025 **Kiriro, A, Juma, C** (eds), *Gaining ground: institutional innovations in land-use management in Kenya.* Nairobi: ACTS, 1991, 228pp

2026 **Korir-Koech, M,** History of environmental management in Kenya, in Kiriro, A & Juma, C (eds), *Gaining ground (item 2025)*, 21–34

2027 **Liniger, H,** A study of the effects of land use on water and soil resources on the slopes of Mount Kenya, in Hudson, N & Cheatle, R J (eds), *Working with farmers (Item 245)*, 208–211

2028 **Medley, K F,** Patterns of forest diversity along the Tana river, *Journal of tropical ecology,* **8,** 4 (1992) 353–71

2029 **Mukabi-Kabira, W,** Story-tellers and the environment, in Khasiani, S A (ed), *Groundwork (item 2051)*, 67–73

2030 **Munene, M J,** Grass-roots environmental research in Kenya, *Nature and resources,* **28,** 2 (1992) 14–21

2031 **Mung'ala, P M,** Government experience of collaboration with NGOs in rural afforestation, in Wellard, K & Copestake, J C (eds), *NGOs and the state (Item 1096)*, 118–35

2032 **Oba, G,** *Ecological factors in land use conflicts, land administration and food insecurity in Turkana, Kenya.* London: Overseas Development Institute, 1992, 23pp

2033 **Oba, G,** Environmental education for sustainable development among the nomadic peoples: the UNESCO-IPAL experience in northern Kenya, *Nomadic peoples,* 30 (1992) 53–73

2034 **Rauch, D,** Mobilizing farmers to counter desertification in Nyanza District, Kenya, in Hudson, N & Cheatle, R J (eds), *Working with farmers (Item 245)*, 190–96

2035 **Schlee, G,** Ritual topography and ecological use: the Gabbra of the Kenya/Ethiopia borderlands, in Croll, E & Parkin, D (eds), *Bush base, forest farm* (London: Routledge, 1992), 110–28

2036 **Thomas, D B,** Choosing conservation measures for cropland on smallholdings in Kenya, in Hudson, N & Cheatle, R J (eds), *Working with farmers (Item 245)*, 117–26

2037 **Wamalwa, B N,** Indigenous knowledge and ecological management, in Kiriro, A & Juma, C (eds), *Gaining ground (item 2025)*, 35–49

Finance

2038 **Adam, C,** On the dynamic specification of money demand in Kenya, *Journal of African economics,* **1,** 2 (1992) 233–70

2039 **Kimenyi, M S,** Inflation, money and economic growth, *Finance,* 30.12.92 34–37

2040 **Mullei, A K,** Determining the international competitive value of the Kenya shilling, *Eastern Africa economic review,* **7,** 2 (1991) 17–25

Food

No entry. *See also:* 2032

Gender

See also: 337, 1970, 2007, 2014, 2024, 2109, 2127, 2138, 2139, 5508

2041 Ahawo, D O, *Kenyan women in socioeconomic development.* Nairobi: Women's Bureau, 1990, 74pp

2042 Amisi, B (ed), *Women and democracy in Kenya.* Nairobi: AFARD, 1992, 18pp

2043 Björkman, I, Oppression and liberation of Kenyan women: on orature and modern women's literature, in Granqvist, R (ed), *Culture in Africa (item 10)*, 109–22

2044 Chiuri, W, Nzioli, A, Women: invisible managers of natural resources, in Khasiani, S A (ed), *Groundwork (item 2051)*, 19–25

2045 Ensminger, J, Structural transformation and its consequences for Orma women pastoralists, in Gladwin, C H (ed), *Structural adjustment and African women farmers (Item 315)*, 281–300

2046 Freeman, D B, Survival strategy or business training ground? The significance of urban agriculture for the advancement of women in urban Africa, *African studies review,* **36,** 3 (1993) 1–22

2047 Hyma, B, Nyamwange, P, Women's role and participation in farm and community tree-growing activities in Kaimbu district, Kenya, in Momsen, J H & Kinnaird, V (eds), *Different places, different voices (Item 332)*, 30–45

2048 Juma, M N, Some factors determining women participation in non-formal education: a study of Mombasa North, Kenya, *Kenya journal of education,* **5,** 1 (1991) 46–74

2049 Kabira, W M, Nzioki, E A, *Celebrating women's resistance: a case study of women's groups movement in Kenya.* Nairobi: African Women's Perspective, 1993, 108pp

2050 Kanogo, T, Women and environment in history, in Khasiani, S A (ed), *Groundwork (item 2051)*, 7–17

2051 Khasiani, S A (ed), *Groundwork: African women as environmental managers.* Nairobi: ACTS, 1992, 131pp

2052 Khasiani, S A, Women in soil and water conservation projects: an assessment, in Khasiani, S A (ed), *Groundwork (item 2051)*, 27–39

2053 Kithinji, C T, Education of women in Kenya before and after the women's decade, *Wajibu,* **7,** 4 (1992) 5–8

2054 Mann, E, Kibwezi Women's Integrated Rural Development Programme, in *Human ecology, environmental education and sustainable development, Vol. 1* (Edinburgh: Edinburgh University, Centre for Human Ecology, 1991), 104–113

2055 Mbote, P K (ed), *African women as environmental managers.* Nairobi: ACTS, 1992, 34pp

2056 McCormick, D, Gender and work: women in Nairobi's small enterprise, *Wajibu,* **7,** 4 (1992) 12–15

2057 Musyoki, A, Orodho, J A, Urban women workers in the informal sector and economic change in Kenya in the 1980s, in Gibbon, P (ed), *Social change and economic reform (item 1880)*, 106–33

2058 Nzomo, M, The gender dimension of democratisation in Kenya: some international linkages, *Alternatives,* **18,** 1 (1993) 61–73

2059 Nzomo, M, Policy impacts on women and environment, in Khasiani, S A (ed), *Groundwork (item 2051)*, 101–117

2060 Robertson, C, Traders and urban struggle: ideology and the creation of a militant female underclass in Nairobi 1960–1990,

Journal of women's history, **4,** 3 (1993) 9–42

2061 **Teleia Chieni, Spencer, P,** The world of Telelia: reflections of a Maasai woman in Matapato, in Spear, T & Waller, R (eds), *Being Maasai (Item 1885)*, 157–73

2062 **von Bülow, D, Sørensen, A,** Gender and contract farming: tea outgrower schemes in Kenya, *Review of African political economy,* 56 (1993) 38–52

2063 **Wanyoni, B,** Gender planning for development in Kenya, *Yearbook of cooperative enterprise 1993,* 143–52

Geography, human

2064 **Fox, R,** The impact of space: land division and urban development in Kenya and South Africa, *International regional science review,* **15,** 1 (1992) 39–49

2065 **Kisovi, L M,** Changing land-use policy and population problems in Kitui District, Kenya, *Journal of eastern African research and development,* 22 (1992) 91–104

Geography, physical

2066 **Grunblat, J, et al,** A GIS approach to desertification assessment and mapping, *Journal of arid environments,* **23,** 1 (1992) 81–102

Health & welfare services

2067 **Ajode, K, et al,** *Maintaining health: an evaluation/in-depth review of the maintenance project for rural health facilities in Kenya.* Stockholm: SIDA, 1992, 83pp

2068 **Bloom, G, et al,** *Expenditure and financing of the health sector in Kenya: abridged report of a study performed for the Ministry of Health and the World Bank.* Brighton: Institute of Development Studies, 1993, 130pp

2069 **Brainard, J M,** *Health and development in a rural Kenyan community.* New York: Lang, 1991, 218pp

2070 **Huber, J H,** Ensuring access to health care with the introduction of user fees: a Kenyan example, *Social science and medicine,* **36,** 4 (1993) 485–94

2071 **Johnson, B R, et al,** Costs and resource utilisation for the treatment of incomplete abortion in Kenya and Mexico, *Social science and medicine,* **36,** 11 (1993) 1443–53

2072 **Lackritz, E M, et al,** Blood transfusion practices and blood-banking services in a Kenyan hospital, *AIDS,* **7,** 7 (1993) 995–99

2073 **Oyugi, W,** Bureaucracy and the management of health services in Kenya, in Asmerom, H K, et al (eds), *Bureacracy and developmental policies (Item 109)*, 221–36

History, general

2074 **Dietler, M, Herbich, I,** Living on Luo time: reckoning sequence, duration, history and biography in a rural African society, *World archaeology,* **25,** 2 (1993) 248–60

History, early

2075 **Marean, C W,** Hunter to herder: large mammal remains from the hunter-gatherer occupation at Enkapune ya Muto rock shelter, Central Rift, Kenya, *African archaeological review,* **10,** (1992) 65–127

History, C18th

2076 **Walsh, M,** Mijikenda origins: a

review of the evidence, *Transafrican journal of history,* 21 (1992) 1–18

History, C19th

See also: 418

2077 **Lamphear, J,** Aspects of 'becoming Turkana': interaction and assimilation between Maa- and Ateker-speakers, in Spear, T & Waller, R (eds), *Becoming Maasai (Item 1885)*, 87–104

2078 **Sobania, N,** Defeat and dispersal: the Laikipiak and their neighbours at the end of the nineteenth century, in Spear, T & Waller, R (eds), *Becoming Maasai (Item 1885)*, 105–119

History, C20th

2079 **Anderson, J,** Black mischief: crime, protest and resistance in colonial Kenya, *Historical journal,* **36,** 4 (1993) 851–77

2080 **Aseka, E,** *Makers of history, 1: Jomo Kenyatta.* Nairobi: East Africa Educational Publishers, 1993, 103pp

2081 **Aseka, E,** *Makers of history, 2: Ronald Ngala.* Nairobi: East Africa Educational Publishers, 1993, 36pp

2082 **Chevenix-Trench, C P,** *Men who ruled Kenya: the Kenya administration, 1892–1963.* London: Radcliffe, 1993, 316pp

2083 **Duder, C J,** 'Men of the officer class': the participants in the 1919 soldier settlement scheme in Kenya, *African affairs,* **92,** 366 (1993) 69–87

2084 **Gächter, A,** Akteure in Aufstad: über Versuche, Mau Mau zu erklären, in Feldbauer, P & Puhle, H J (eds), *Bauern in Widerstand* (Vienna: Bohlau, 1992), 175–96

2085 **Kubai, A,** The early muslim communities of Nairobi, *Islam et sociétés au Sud du Sahara,* 6 (1992) 33–44

2086 **Maloba, W O,** *Mau Mau and Kenya: an analysis of a peasant revolt.* Bloomington: Indiana University Press, 1993, 228pp

2087 **Maxon, R M,** *Struggle for Kenya: the loss and reassertion of imperial initiative, 1912–1923.* London: Associated University Presses, 1993, 351pp

2088 **Mwiria, K,** Education for subordination: African education in colonial Kenya, *History of education,* **20,** 3 (1991) 261–72

2089 **Okoth, G P,** Intermittent tensions in Uganda-relations: historical perspectives, *Transafrican journal of history,* 21 (1992) 69–92

2090 **Whitehead, C,** Education for subordination? Some reflections on Kiemi Mwiria's account of African education in colonial Kenya, *History of education,* **20,** 3 (1991) 85–93

Industry & trade

See also: 1998, 2056, 2057

2091 **Chakrabarti, S K, Ali, J A,** *Prices in Kenya: an empirical investigation.* Cambridge, Mass.: Harvard Institute for International Development, 1992, 22pp

2092 **Collinson, S,** Constraints on the transfer of manufacturing technology: a British-Kenyan comparison, *Science, technology and development,* **11,** 2 (1993) 113–43

2093 **Gitau, L G,** Fake gold exports, *Society,* **2,** 16 (1992) 42–47

2094 **House, W J, et al,** Urban self-employment in Kenya: panacea or viable strategy?, *World development,* **21,** 7 (1993) 1205–23

2095 **Kimuyu, P K,** Urbanisation and consumption of petroleum products in Kenya, *Energy policy,* **21,** 4 (1993) 403–407

2096 Kremer, E M, *Die Träume des Ali M. Tourismus zwischen Europe und Afrika.* Lucerne: Rex, 1992, 150pp

2097 Little, K, On safari: the visual politics of a tourist representation, in Howes, D (ed), *The varieties of sensory experience* (Toronto: University of Toronto Press), 148–63

2098 Mbugua, M, The sugar story..., *Executive,* Feb. 1992 5–8

2099 Mwega, F M, Import demand elasticities and stability during trade liberalisation: a case study of Kenya, *Journal of African economics,* **2,** 3 (1993) 381–416

2100 Nyoike, P M, National industrial energy conservation: perspectives from Kenya, in Karekezi, S & Mackenzie, G A (eds), *Energy options (Item 796),* 128–38

2101 Nyoike, P M, Olech, B A, The case of Kenya, in Bhagavan, M R & Karekezi, S (eds), *Energy managment (Item 788),* 87–123

2102 Ogonda, R T, The regionalisation of the road network systems in Kenya, *Maseno journal of education, arts and science,* **1,** 1 (1992) 84–98

2103 Olindo, P, The old man of nature tourism: Kenya, in Whelan, T (ed), *Nature tourism* (Washington: Island Press, 1991), 23–38

2104 Raikes, P, *Business as usual: national and local food marketing in Kenya.* Copenhagen: Centre for Development Research, 1993, 29pp

International economic relations

See also: 507

2105 Hazlewood, A, Foreign aid and economic development in Kenya, in Lele, U & Nabi, I (eds), *Transitions in development* San Francisco: ICS Press, 1991, 125–49

2106 Ramchandani, R R, Biswas, A, India-Africa economic relations: the case of bilateral relations between India and Kenya, *African currents,* 11 (1990) 58–85

International relations

2107 Biswas, A, India-Kenya relations 1947–1977, *African currents,* 13 (1991) 18–43

Labour & manpower

See also: 1992

2108 Wilson, L S, Kenyanisation and African capacity 'shuffling', *Public administration and development,* **13,** 5 (1993) 489–500

Language

See also: 624, 2012

2109 Omondi, L N, The role of language in rural development, in Khasiani, S A (ed), *Groundwork (item 2051),* 75–90

Law

See also: 648, 1961, 2024

2110 Kuria, G K, An open letter to the Registrar General over the Islamic Party of Kenya, *Nairobi law monthly,* 46 (1992) 40–43

2111 Kuria, G K, Restructuring the Kenya constitution, *Nairobi law monthly,* 44 (1992) 34–43

2112 Kuria, G K, Vazquez, A M, Judges and human rights: the Kenyan case, *Journal of African law,* **35,** 1/2 (1991) 142–73

2113 Mburu, C, The Julie Ward murder cover-up: a father's search for elusive justice, *Nairobi law monthly,* 44 (1992) 14–20,22,30

2114 M'Inoti, K, Enforcement of

fundamental rights in Kenya: righting some of the initial wrongs, *Nairobi law monthly,* 42 (1992) 33–38

2115 **Ojwang, J B,** Constitutional law and political change: recent developments in Zambia and Kenya, *African journal of international and comparative law,* **4,** 2 (1992) 325–352

2116 **Ojwang, J B,** *Environmental law and political change in Kenya.* Nairobi: ACTS, 1992, 30pp

Library - documentation

2117 **Durrani, S,** Libraries, communication and development in Kenya: the missing political factor, in Wise, M & Olden, A (eds), *Information and libraries (item 672),* 159–70

2118 **Were, J,** Computerisation of library services: developments in Kenya, in Wise, M & Olden, A (eds), *Information and libraries (item 672),* 59–82

Literature

See also: 699, 2043, 3443

2119 **Amidu, A,** Lessons from Kimondo: an aspect of Kiswahili culture, *Nordic journal of African studies,* **2,** 1 (1993) 34–56

2120 **Frederiksen, B F,** Living in the neighbourhood of one's dreams: the role of popular writing in the creation of the ordinary, in Granqvist, R (ed), *Culture in Africa (item 10),* 87–107

2121 **Ndigirgi, G,** Character names and types in Ngugi's Devil on the cross, *Ufahamu,* **19,** 2/3 (1991) 96–111

2122 **Ochillo, Y H,** Weep not, child and the need to believe, *CLA journal,* **36,** 3 (1993) 270–79

Media

See also: 5508

2123 **Chakava, H,** Private enterprise publishing in Kenya: a long struggle for emancipation, *Logos,* **4,** 3 (1993) 130–35

2124 **Hobbs, R, Frost, R,** Comprehension of transitional editing conventions by African tribal villages, in Korzenny, F et al (eds), *Mass media effects across cultures* (Newbury Park: Sage, 1993), 110–29

2125 **Omolo Ochilo, P J,** Press freedom and the role of the media in Kenya, *Africa media review,* **7,** 3 (1993) 19–33

Medical

See also: 2200, 2184

2126 **Bifani, P,** *Turkana dogs and diseases; traditional lifestyles and health.* Dakar: ENDA, 1992, 84pp

2127 **Garland, M, et al,** Knowledge of AIDS and other sexually-transmitted diseases among women attending a family-planning clinic in Nairobi, Kenya, *American journal of preventive medicine,* **9,** 1 (1993) 1–5

2128 **Leslie, P W,** Pregnancy loss in nomadic and settled women in Turkana, Kenya: a prospective study, *Human biology,* **65,** 2 (1993) 237–54

2129 **Mwabu, G, et al,** Quality of medical care and choice of medical treatment in Kenya: an empirical analysis, *Journal of human resources,* **28,** 4 (1993) 838–62

2130 **Rogstad, K E, et al,** Knowledge of HIV transmission and risk behaviour in Kenyan health-care workers, *International journal of STD & AIDS,* **4,** 4 (1993) 200–203

2131 **Schutz-Bergdort, V,** 'Fremde' Medizinen, Heilerwissen und Kaufmännischen Verhalten eines Heilers in Lamu-Stadt (Kenya), *Sociologus,* **42,** 1 (1992) 72–87

Natural resources

2132 **Berger, D J,** *Wildlife extension: participatatory conservation by the Maasai of Kenya.* Nairobi: ACT, 1993, 194pp

2133 **Bradley, P N, Huby, M** (eds), *Woodfuel, women and woodlots. Vol. 2: The Kenya Woodfuel Development Programme.* Basingstoke: Macmillan, 1993, 274pp

2134 **Juma, C,** Managing biological diversity in Kenya, in Kiriro, A & Juma, C (eds), *Gaining ground (item 2025)*, 125–54

2135 **Marekia, E N,** Managing wildlife in Kenya, in Kiriro, A & Juma, C (eds), *Gaining ground (item 2025)*, 155–76

2136 **Milukas, M V,** Energy for secondary cities: the case of Nakuru, Kenya, *Energy policy,* **21,** 5 (1993) 543–58

2137 **Okoth-Ogendo, H W O,** Managing watersheds in Kenya, in Kiriro, A & Juma, C (eds), *Gaining ground (item 2025)*, 115–23

2138 **Omosa, M,** Women and the management of domestic energy, in Khasiani, S A (ed), *Groundwork (item 2051)*, 41–54

2139 **Sunny, G,** Women's role in the supply of fuelwood, in Khasiani, S A (ed), *Groundwork (item 2051)*, 55–65

Politics

See also: 913, 1959, 2042, 2058, 2060, 2108, 2110, 2113, 2119, 4048

2140 **Africa Watch,** *Divide and rule: state sponsored ethnic violence in Kenya.* New York: Africa Watch, 1993, 97pp

2141 **Andreassen, B A, et al,** *A hobbled democracy: the Kenya general elections 1992.* Bergen: Chr Michelsen Institute, 1993, 46pp

2142 **Bollig, M,** Intra- and interethnic conflict in northwest Kenya, *Anthropos,* **88,** 1/2 (1993) 176–84

2143 **Bourmaud, D,** L'état centrifuge au Kenya, in Médard, J F (ed), *Etats d'Afrique noire (Item 896)*, 241–75

2144 **Cohen, J M,** Importance of public service reform: the case of Kenya, *Journal of modern African studies,* **31,** 3 (1993) 449–476

2145 **Gillies, D W, Makau wa Mutua,** *A long road to Uhuru: human rights and political participation in Kenya.* Montreal: International Centre for Human Rights and Democratic Development; London: Westminster Foundation for Democracy, 1993, 43pp

2146 **Gitau, L G,** Elusive peace, *Society,* **2,** 14 (1992) 19–22

2147 **Harris, C,** The persistence and fragility of civilian rule on Kenya, in Danopoulos, C P (ed), *Civilian rule (Item 844)*, 125–40

2148 **Haugerud, A, Njogu, K,** *State voices in the countryside: politics and the Kenyan baraza.* Boston: African Studies Center, Boston University, 1991, 46pp

2149 **International Republican Institute,** *Kenya: the December 29, 1992, elections.* Washington: the Institute, 1993, 57 +21pp

2150 **Kanyinga, K,** The social-political context of the growth of non-governmental organisations in Kenya, in Gibbon, P (ed), *Social change and economic reform (item 1880)*, 53–77

2151 **Kuria, G K,** Restructuring the Kenya constitution, part 2, *Nairobi law monthly,* 45 (1991) 30–36

2152 **Lehmann, H P,** The paradox

of state power in Africa: debt management policies in Kenya and Zimbabwe, *African studies review,* **35,** 2 (1992) 1–34

2153 Mawhood, P, Wallis, M, Ethnic minorities in eastern Africa: Kenya and Tanzania, *Regional politics and policy,* **3,** 1 (1993) 170–89

2154 Mukalo wa Kwayera, Courting revolt, *Society,* **2,** 18 (1992) 8–12

2155 Musyoka wa Kyendo, The Kalenjin, *Finance,* 31.7.92 10–14

2156 Mwangi, P, Police brutality in Kenya, the inside story, *Kenya jurist,* Jan 1992 15–19

2157 Ngunyi, M G, Gathiaka, K, State-civil institutions relations in Kenya in the 1980s, in Gibbon, P (ed), *Social change and economic reform (item 1880)*, 28–52

2158 Oruka, H O, *Oginga Odinga: his philosophy and beliefs.* Nairobi: Initiatives, 1992, 188pp

2159 Sande, G M, Muthoga, L G, The presidency and the impeachment, *Finance,* 15.11.92 32–35

2160 Smoke, P, Local government fiscal reform in developing countries: lessons from Kenya, *World development,* **21,** 6 (1993) 901–23

2161 Throup, D, Elections and political legitimacy in Kenya, *Africa,* **63,** 3 (1993) 371–96

2162 Tomkys, R, Implementing Africa's second liberation: the case of Kenya, in Rimmer, D (ed), *Action in Africa (Item 525)*, 144–51

Religion, philosophy

See also: 2018, 2168

2163 Franke, P J L, *Siku y mwaka*: New Year's Day in Swahililand (with special reference to Mombasa), *Journal of religion in Africa,* **23,** 2 (1993) 125–35

Rural economy

See also: 1030, 1928, 1996, 2004, 2015, 2025, 2036, 2045, 2054, 2062, 2067, 2109, 2195, 2398, 3954

2164 Adams, M, Slow progress with Integrated Rural Development Programmes in Kenya's arid and semi-arid lands, *Land degradation and rehabilitation,* **2,** 2 (1990) 285–99

2165 Akabwai, D M, *Extension and livestock development: experience from among the Turkana pastoralists of Kenya.* London: Overseas Development Institute, 1992, 16pp

2166 Barasa, T N, et al, Economic analysis of smallholder cotton production in Kenya: a linear programming case study of Funyula Division, Busia District, *Eastern African economic review,* **8,** 2 (1992) 142–58

2167 Bekure, S, et al (ed), *Maasai herding: an analysis of the livestock production systems of Maasai pastoralists in eastern Kajiado District, Kenya.* Addis Ababa: International Livestock Centre for Africa, 1991, 154pp

2168 Bergman, J, *Christentum und sozioökonomische Entwicklung: eine empirische Untersuchung im ruralen Kenia.* Aachen: Alano/Herodot, 1992, 326pp

2169 Buch, L E, Development of participatory approaches for promoting agroforestry ... (1980–91), in Wellard, K & Copestake, J C (eds), *NGOs and the state (Item 1096)*, 118–35

2170 Charles, R A, Wellard, K, Agricultural activities of government and NGOs in Siaya District, in Wellard, K & Copestake, J C (eds), *NGOs and the state (Item 1096)*, 100–110

2171 Cheatle, R J, Njoroge, S N J, Smallholder adaptation of some land husbandry practices in Kenya, in Hudson, N & Cheatle, R J (eds), *Working with farmers (Item 245)*, 130–41

2172 **Copestake, J C,** Kenya: country overview, in Wellard, K & Copestake, J C (eds), *NGOs and the state (Item 1096)*, 87–98

2173 **Galaty, J G,** 'The land is yours': social and economic factors in the privatisation, sub-division and sale of Maasai ranches, *Nomadic peoples,* 30 (1992) 26–40

2174 **Getahun, A, et al,** *Agroforestry for development in Kenya: an annotated bibliography.* Nairobi: International Council for Research in Agroforestry, 1991, 228pp

2175 **Gibbon, P,** A failed agenda? African agriculture under structural adjustment, with special reference to Kenya and Ghana, *Journal of peasant studies,* **20,** 1 (1992) 50–96

2176 **Goldman, A,** Agricultural innovation in three areas of Kenya: neo-Boserupian theories and regional characterisation, *Economic geography,* **69,** 1 (1993) 44–71

2177 **Hedlund, H,** *Coffee cooperatives and culture: an anthropological study of a coffee cooperative in Kenya.* Nairobi: OUP, 1992, 205pp

2178 **Ikiara, G K, et al,** Agricultural decline, politics and structural adjustment in Kenya, in Gibbon, P (ed), *Social change and economic reform (item 1880)*, 78–105

2179 **Jama, M A,** Smallholder farmers credit repayment performance in Lugari Division, Kakamega District, Kenya, *Eastern African economic review,* **8,** 2 (1992) 85–91

2180 **Kakili, J,** NGO involvement in agricultural activities in Machakos District, in Wellard, K & Copestake, J C (eds), *NGOs and the state (Item 1096)*, 111–117

2181 **Kiambi, M, Opole, M,** Promoting traditional trees and food crops in Kenya, in Cooper, D et al (ed), *Growing diversity: genetic resources and local food security* London: Intermediate Technology Publications, 1992, 53–66

2182 **Kibera, F N,** Communication and modernisation in central Kenya, an experiment, *Business management review,* **2,** 2 (1991) 71–84

2183 **Kimuyu, P K,** Determinants of fertilizer use on smallholder coffee and maize in Murang'a District, Kenya, *Eastern Africa economic review,* 7, 1 (1991) 45–49

2184 **Mang'ombe, J K, Mwabu, G M,** Agricultural land use patterns and malaria conditions in Kenya, *Social science and medicine,* **37,** 9 (1993) 1121–30

2185 **Mucai-Kattambo, V,** *Cooperatives: formation, management and settlement of disputes.* Nairobi: OUP, 1992, 142pp

2186 **Mutiso, C C,** Manging arid and semi-arid areas in Kenya, in Kiriro, A & Juma, C (eds), *Gaining ground (item 2025)*, 87–114

2187 **Opile, W R,** Coffee development and research in Kenya, *Aproma,* 27–29 (1992) 41–48

2188 **Orvis, S,** The Kenyan agrarian debate: a reappraisal, *African studies review,* **36,** 3 (1993) 23–48

2189 **Rostom, R S, Mortimore, M,** *Environmental change and dryland management in Machakos district, Kenya, 1930–90: land use profile.* London: Overseas Development Institute, 1991, 44pp

2190 **Sharma, K L,** Aggregate farm supply response in Kenya, *Eastern African economic review,* **8,** 2 (1992) 92–101

2191 **Sottas, B, Wiesmann, U,** Ausmass, Richtung und Gewichtung von

Unterstützungleistungen bei Kleinbauern im kenianischen Hochland, *Anthropos,* **88,** 3/4 (1993) 375–92

2192 Suda, C A, Towards an understanding of small-holder agriculture in western Kenya: an analysis of the factors influencing crop production, *Discovery and innovation,* **4,** 4 (1992) 15–23

2193 Waller, R, Acceptees and aliens: Kikuyu settlement in Maasailand, in Spear, T & Waller, R (eds), *Being Maasai (Item 1885),* 226–57

Science & technology

No entry. *See also:* 2134

Sociology

2194 African Rights, *The nightmare continues: abuses against Somali refugees in Kenya.* London: African Rights, 1993, 54pp

2195 Francis, E, Hoddinott, J, Migration and differentiation in western Kenya: a tale of two sub-locations, *Journal of development studies,* **30,** 1 (1993) 115–45

2196 Khasiani, S A, A model of migration motivations: migration valuations and migration dispositions among rural youth in Kenya, *Eastern Africa economic review,* **7,** 2 (1991) 27–38

2197 Kilbride, P R, Unwanted children as a consequence of delocalisation in modern Kenya, in Poggie, J J, et al (eds), *Anthropological research* (Albany: SUNY Press, 1992), 185–203

2198 Mählmann, P, The role of sport in the process of modernisation, the Kenyan case, *Journal of eastern African research and development,* 22 (1992) 120–31

2199 Mwega, F M, Kabugo, J W, Kenya, in Adepoju, A (ed), *Impact of structural adjustment (Item 1107),* 25–39

2200 Plummer, F A, et al, The importance of core groups in the epidemiology and control of HIV–1 infection, *AIDS,* **5,** 1 (1991) 169–76

2201 Weisz, J R, et al, Parent reports of behavioral and emotional problems among children in Kenya, Thailand the United States, *Child development,* **64,** 1 (1993) 98–109

Social welfare

No entry. *See also:* 5508

Urban studies

See also: 2046, 2064, 2094, 2095, 2136

2202 Menon, P A, Lee-Smith, D, Urban agriculture in Kenya, *Canadian journal of African studies,* **27,** 1 (1993) 25–42

2203 Mitullah, W V, *State policy and urban housing in Kenya: the case of low income housing in Nairobi.* Nairobi: Institute of Development Studies, 1992, 61pp

2204 Rodriguez-Torres, D, *Le développement urbain à Nairobi hier et aujourd'hui.* Nairobi: CREDU, 1992, 40pp

2205 Syagga, P M, Promoting the use of appropriate building materials in shelter provision in Kenya, *Habitat international,* **17,** 3 (1993) 125–36

2206 Wangui, E E, Darkoh, M B K, A geographical study of Kibera as an example of an uncontrolled settlement, *Journal of eastern African research and development,* 22 (1992) 75–91

RWANDA

Anthropology

2207 **Godding, J P,** Gisenyi, intégration des Batwa au développement, *Dialogue,* 155 (1992) 17–25
2208 **Ngirinshuti, D,** Impunyu, quatrième ethnie du Rwanda?, *Dialogue,* 155 (1992) 3–16

Current affairs

2209 **Hitiyise, F,** De la dictature à la démocratie, *Dialogue,* 152 (1992) 3–9

Demography

2210 **Karagwira, A,** Famine, fécondité, développement: cas de Rwanda, *Famille, santé, développement,* 24 (1992) 20–30

Economic and social history

No entry. *See also:* 4156

Economy - Development

2211 **Waller, D,** *Rwanda: which way now?* Oxford: Oxfam, 1993, 64pp

Education

2212 **Freyens-Martin, M,** Que pensent les enseignants du secondaire de leur métier?, *Dialogue,* 150 (1992) 21–26
2213 **Karemangingo, A, Bingiwiki, A,** Primary school agriculture in Rwanda, in Mades, G G (ed), *Primary school agriculture (item 222)*, 16–30
2214 **Mugabonake, G,** Les problèmes de l'enseignement technique au Rwanda, *Dialogue,* 151 (1992) 13–18
2215 **Rutsindura, A,** Education scolaire et démocratie, *Dialogue,* 156 (1992) 3–14

Environment

2216 **Kabagmbe, J B,** Raisons écologiques du dépeuplement du lac Muhazi, *Dialogue,* 156 (1992) 23–28

Food

2217 **Bakundakwita, C,** Autosuffisance alimentaire, *Dialogue,* 150 (1992) 3–12
2218 **Pottier, J,** Taking stock: food marketing reform in Rwanda, 1982–89, *African affairs,* **92,** 366 (1993) 5–30

Gender

See also: 1942, 2226, 2242, 2255
2219 **Allen, S, et al,** Pregnancy and contraception use among urban Rwandan women after HIV teaching and counselling, *American journal of public health,* **83,** 5 (1993) 705–710

Health & welfare services

2220 **Habimana, P, Bulterys, M,** Continuation et abandon de la planification familiale au Centre universitaire de santé publique, *Famille, santé, développement,* 24 (1992) 34–40
2221 **Shepard, D S, et al,** Household participation in financing of health care at government health centres in Rwanda, in Mills, A & Lee, K (eds), *Health economics research in developing countries* (Oxford: OUP, 1993), 140–64

History, C20th

2222 **Nahimana, F,** *Rwanda: émergence d'un état.* Paris: Harmattan, 1993, 346pp

2223 **Newbury, C,** The cohesion of oppression: clientship and ethnicity in Rwanda 1860–1960, *Mankind quarterly,* **33,** 3 (1993) 359–64

Industry & trade

No entry. *See also:* 2218

International relations

2224 **Mutaganzwa, C,** La diplomatie rwandaise réduite au tatonnement, *Dialogue,* 152 (1992) 13–17

Labour & manpower

See also: 2257

2225 **Muligo, T,** Aperçu sur les principaux aspects de l'emploi au Rwanda, *Famille, santé, développement,* 24 (1992) 13–19

Language

2226 **Kimenyi, A,** Why is it that women in Rwanda cannot marry?, in Hall, K, et al (eds), *Locating power, Vol. 2* (Berkeley: University of California, 1992), 300–311

Law

2227 **Bouveir, O L,** Magistrature; sous le diktat de l'exécutif, *Dialogue,* 162 (1993) 3–24

2228 **Ngarambe, J,** Plaidoyer pour la justice sociale, *Dialogue,* 151 (1992) 37–42

2229 **Ntampaka, C,** Pour les lois promotrices des libertés, *Dialogue,* 159 (1992) 9–24

2230 **Rubaduka, J,** Le pouvoir judiciare, gardien des droits et libertés publics, *Dialogue,* 154 (1992) 23–28

Media

2231 **Bart, A,** L'aventure d'une revue d'élites, *Dialogue,* 153 (1992) 13–26

2232 **Higiro, J V,** Kinyamateka sous la 2e République, *Dialogue,* 155 (1992) 29–39

2233 **Higiro, J V,** La presse, miroir de la société, *Dialogue,* 156 (1992) 15–21

2234 **Higiro, J V,** Rwanda, la voix de son maître, *Dialogue,* 154 (1992) 29–37

2235 **Mukene, P,** Faut-il avoir peur de la TV?, *Dialogue,* 163 (1993) 19–28

2236 **Nsengiyaremye, T,** SOS, notre presse se meurt, *Dialogue,* 163 (1993) 41–46

2237 **Nshimyimana, E,** Dialogue à travers ses themes, *Dialogue,* 153 (1992) 33–39

2238 **Ntamahungiro, J,** Pour une radio libre rurale, *Dialogue,* 152 (1992) 25–33

Medical

2239 **Gotanegre, J F,** Analyse géographique de l'incidence du VIH et du SIDA au Rwanda en 1990, *Cahiers d'outre-mer,* **46,** 183 (1993) 233–52

2240 **Keiner, H,** Le SIDA au Rwanda: un défi à nos églises, *Dialogue,* 158 (1992) 31–41

2241 **Lepage, P, Hitimana, D G,** Natural history and clinical presentation of HIV-1 infection in children, *AIDS,* **5,** 1 (1991) 117–25

2242 **Moore, P S, et al,** Role of nutritional status and weight loss in HIV seroconversion among Rwandan women, *Journal of AIDS,* **6,** 6 (1993) 611–616

2243 **Ntamahungiro, J,** SIDA, cri

d'alarme, *Dialogue,* 160 (1992) 19–30

2244 Rwangabo, P C, *La médécine traditionnel au Rwanda.* Paris: Karthala, 1993, 261pp

Natural resources

2245 Micha, J C, Frank, V, Ressources et charactéristiques piscicoles des lacs rwandais (bassin nilotique), *Bulletin des séances,* **37,** 3 (1991) 379–98

Politics

See also: 2215, 2222, 2227

2246 Féderation international des droits de l'homme, et al, *Rapport de la Commission internationale d'enquête sur les violations des droits de l'homme au Rwanda depuis le 1er octobre 1990.* Paris: the Federation, 1993, 99pp

2247 Funga, F, A la recherche de la démocratie, *Dialogue,* 161 (1992) 23–29

2248 Habimana, J, Rwanda, difficile processus démocratique, *Dialogue,* 157 (1992) 33–41

2249 Karinganire, J, Le mal politique rwandaise, *Dialogue,* 162 (1993) 25–38

2250 Nkubito, A, Rwanda, violation des droits de l'homme, *Dialogue,* 152 (1992) 19–24

2251 Nsengimana, J, Le Rwanda est-il une nation?, *Dialogue,* 162 (1993) 39–52

2252 Ntakarutimana, E, Eglise et politique, *Dialogue,* 153 (1992) 51–59

Religion, philosophy

See also: 2240, 2252

2253 Ntakarutimana, E, L'histoire d'une Eglise africaine à la remorque du temps, *Dialogue,* 154 (1992) 39–46

Rural economy

2254 Godding, J P, Le premier séminaire sur le développement des Batwa forestiers, *Dialogue,* 162, (1992) 13–16

2255 Pottier, J, Nkundabashaka, A, Intolerable environments: towards a cultural reading of agrarian practice and policy in Rwanda, in Croll, E & Parkin, D (eds), *Bush base: forest farm (Item 1040),* 146–68

2256 Sebureze, D, Innnovation and agricultural development in Rwanda: a socioeconomic analysis, in Nett, B et al (eds), *Agricultural transformation (Item 1069),* 135–52

Sociology

See also: 2472

2257 Casas, J, *L'enfant des milles collines.* Paris: Cerf, 1991, 150pp

2258 Clay, D C, Vander Haar, J E, Patterns of intergenerational support and childbearing in the Third World, *Population studies,* **47,** 1 (1993) 67–84

2259 Groha, G, Historische Wurzeln der kriegerischen Auseinandersetzungen in Rwanda, *Afrika Jahrbuch 1990,* 66–70

2260 Guichoua, A, *Le problème des refugiés rwandais et des populations banyarwande dans le region des Grands Lacs.* Geneva: UNHCR, 1992, 54pp

2261 Mugabo, M, L'absurdité de l'ethnisme à la Rwandaise, *Dialogue,* 151 (1992) 3–7

2262 Ntamahungiro, L, Le problème des refugiés rwandais, *Dialogue,* 158 (1992) 3–12

2263 Valmajo, J, Lettre d'un enfant déplacé de guerre, *Dialogue,* 156 (1992) 45–50

TANZANIA

Agriculture, scientific

2264 **Ravnborg, H M,** *Planning and priority setting in agricultural research: the case of Tanzania.* Copenhagen: Centre for Development Research, 1993, 44pp

Anthropology

See also: 2270, 2361, 2395

2265 **Carlson, R G,** Hierarchy and the Haya divine kingship: a structural and symbolic reformulation of Frazer's thesis, *American ethnologist,* **20,** 2 (1993) 312–35

2266 **Erdtsieck, J,** *Spiritual forces in illness and healing: the role of 'Pepo' in the life and healing practice of a female healer in the southwestern highlands of Tanzania.* Nijmegen: Catholic University of Nijmegen, Third Word Centre, 1992, 147pp

2267 **Wagner-Glenn, D,** *Searching for a baby's calabash: a study of Arusha Maasai fertility songs as crystallised expression of central culutural values.* Ludwigsburg: Philipp, 1992, 251pp

2268 **Weiss, B,** Plastic teeth extraction: the iconography of Haya gastro-sexual affiction, *American ethnologist,* **19,** 3 (1992) 538–52

Architecture

2269 **Battle, S,** Zanzibar revisited, *Mimar,* 41 (1991) 26–33

Arts

No entry. *See also:* 70

Demography

See also: 2410

Economic and social history

2270 **Bluton Jones, N G, et al,** Demography of the Hadza, an increasing and high density population of savanna foragers, *American journal of physical anthropology,* **89,** 2 (1992) 159–71

2271 **Daley, P,** From the kipande to the kibali: the incorporation of refugees and labour migrants in western Tanzania, 1900–87, in Black, R & Robinson, V (eds), *Geography and refugees* (London: Belhaven, 1993), 17–32

2272 **Giblin, J L,** *The politics of environmental control in northeastern Tanzania, 1840–1940.* Philadelphia: University of Pennsylvania Press, 1992, 209pp

2273 **Grove, A,** Water use by the Chagga of Kilimanjaro, *African affairs,* **92,** 368 (1993) 431–48

2274 **Little, M,** Colonial policy and subsistence in Tanganyika 1925–45, *Geographical review,* **81,** 4 (1991) 375–88

2275 **Paul, J L,** Avant les paysans: agriculture et écologie dans une société agraire: l'exemple des Waluguru (Tanzanie), *Tiers Monde,* **34,** 134 (1993) 263–80

2276 **Shao, I F,** *The political economy of land reform in Zanzibar.* Dar es Salaam: Dar es Salaam University Press, 1992, 106pp

2277 **Sunseri, T,** Slave ransoming in German east Africa, 1885–1922, *International journal of African historical studies,* **26,** 3 (1993) 481–511

2278 **Tominaga, C,** British colonial policy and agricultural credit in Zanzibar, 1890–1963, in Austin, G & Sugihara, K (eds), *Local suppliers* *of credit in the Third World, 1750–1960* (Basingstoke: Macmillan, 1993), 229–253

Economy - Development

See also: 196, 2317, 2322

2279 Bukuku, E S, *The Tanzanian economy: income distribution and economic growth.* Westport: Praeger, 1993, 219pp

2280 Due, J M, Liberalisation and privatisation in Tanzania and Zambia, *World development,* **21,** 12 (1993) 1981–88

2281 Eriksson, G, Lundahl, M, Economic recovery under institutional constraints: Tanzania facing the economic crisis, in Blomström, M & Lundahl, M (eds), *Economic crisis (Item 119),* 268–87

2282 Hyden, G, Karlström, B, Understanding structural adjustment: Tanzania in comparative perspective, in Blomström, M & Lundahl, M (eds), *Economic crisis (Item 119),* 41–60

2283 Kiondo, A, The nature of economic reforms in Tanzania, *Taamuli,* **1,** 1/2 (1990) 26–45

2284 Musonda, F M, The consequences of the 1976–7 coffee boom on the Tanzanian economy: a test of the Dutch disease model, *Eastern Africa economic review,* **7,** 2 (1991) 1–16

2285 Mwanza, A, Structural adjustment programmes in Tanzania and Zambia: some lessons for late-starters in SADCC, *Southern Africa political and economic monthly,* **4,** 7 (1991) 4–11

2286 Ngasongwa, J, *Foreign-assisted regional integrated development projects in Tanzania: a case for rehabilitation.* Norwich: School of Development Studies, University of East Anglia, 1991, 43pp

2287 Nordas, H K, *MACMOD - a macroeconomic model for the Tanzania economy: documentation.* Bergen: Chr Michelsen Institute, 1993, 36pp

2288 Poget, J L, Tanzanie: 20 ans de politique économique autocentrée at 5 ans d'ajustement structurel: de l'utopie à la déception, *Revue Madagascar, océan Indien,* 7/8 (1991) 61–83

2289 Shao, I A, Structural adjustment programmes and liberalisation policies in Tanzania, in Siddiqui, R A (ed), *Subsaharan Africa (item 15),* 75–99

2290 Shao, I F, et al, *Structural adjustment in a socialist country: the case of Tanzania.* Harare: Sapes books, 1992, 46pp

2291 Stein, H, The economics of the state and the IMF in Tanzania, *Taamuli,* **1,** 1/2 (1990) 1–25

Education

See also: 213, 2366

2292 Galabawa, J C J, Innovations in higher education: a case study of the Musoma Resolutions policy, *Papers in education and development,* 14 (1990) 23–35

2293 Lugalla, J L P, Structural adjustment policies and education in Tanzania, in Gibbon, P (ed), *Social change and economic reform (item 1880),* 184–214

2294 Mbilinyi, M, Mbughuni, P (eds), *Education in Tanzania with a gender perspective.* Stockholm: SIDA, 1991, 115pp

2295 Mosha, H J, The relevance of higher educational systems to the Tanzanian development process, *Papers in education and development,* 14 (1990) 54–65

2296 Mtonga, H L, Comparing the role of education in serving socioeconomic and political development in Tanzania and

Cuba, *Journal of Black studies,* **23,** 3 (1993) 382–402

2297 **Pendaeli, J,** Reflections on ten years of University Teaching and Learning Improvement (UTLIP) at the University of Dar es Salaam, *Papers in education and development,* 14 (1990) 1–12

2298 **Roy Campbell, Z M,** Education, ideology and the crisis in Tanzania, *Papers in education and development,* 14 (1990) 13–22

2299 **Shivji, I G,** The jurisprudence of the Dar es Salaam Declaration on Academic Freedom, *Journal of African law,* **35,** 1/2 (1991) 128–34 (and135–41)

Environment

See also: 2275

2300 **Homewood, K M, et al,** Maasailand ecology: pastoralist development and wildlife conservation in Ngorongoro, Tanzania, *Systems practice,* **6,** 5 (1993) 567–72

2301 **Jensen, F P, Jensen, S B,** The forest avifauna of the Uzungwa Mountains, Tanzania, *Scopus,* **15,** 2 (1992) 65–83

2302 **Kaihura, F B S, Mowo, J G,** Soil and water conservation in Tanzania, in Hudson, N & Cheatle, R J (eds), *Working with farmers (Item 245)*, 29–33

2303 **Monela, G C, et al,** Socioeconomic aspects of charcoal consumption and environmental consequences along the Dar es Salaam-Morogoro highway, Tanzania, *Forest ecology and management,* **58,** 3/4 (1993) 249–58

2304 **Nshubemuki, L,** Desertification control in semi-arid parts of Tanzania: 'what is' and 'what ought to be', *Desertification control bulletin,* 19 (1991) 73–76

Finance

2305 **Fanger, U,** Finanzpolitik und Steuerverwaltung in Tansania während der "verlorenen Entwicklungsdekade", *Verfassung und Recht in Übersee,* **25,** 3 (1992) 303–326

2306 **Hyuda, M, et al,** *Scope, structure and policy implications of informal financial markets in Tanzania.* Nairobi: African Economic Research Consortium, 1993, 38pp

2307 **Kapalatu, S S,** The exchange rate regime, macroeconomic instability, and trade liberalisation in Tanzania, *IFM journal of financial management,* **1,** 1 (1992) 56–71

2308 **Kavura, R M,** The marketing of financial services in Tanzania: the challenge of the 1990s, *IFM journal of financial management,* **1,** 1 (1992) 28–55

2309 **Killaganne, Y S M,** Inflation and financial accounting practices in Tanzania, *Acountant,* **4,** 1 (1991) 7–15

2310 **Lyakurwa, W,** The fiscal impact of trade reforms in Tanzania in the 1980s, *World economy,* **16,** 5 (1993) 621–38

2311 **Moshi, F, Shirima, L L,** Organisational constraints in enhancing accountability in parastatals, the Tanzanian case, *IFM journal of finance management,* **1,** 1 (1992) 17–27

2312 **Osoro, N E,** Revenue productivity of the tax system in Tanzania 1979–89, *Journal of African economics,* **1,** 3 (1992) 395–416

2313 **Osoro, N E,** *Revenue productivity implications of tax reform in Tanzania.* Nairobi: African Economic Research Consortium, 1993, 34pp

Food

See also: 2338, 2350, 2405

2314 **Bryceson, D F,** Urban bias revisited: staple food pricing in Tanzania, in Hewitt de Alcantara, C (ed), *Real markets: social and political issues of food policy reform* (London: Cass, 1993), 82–106

2315 **Mtalo, C N,** The Iringa Integrated Nutrition Programme In Tanzania; research and development, in Kotler, N G (ed), *Sharing innovation* (Washington: Smithsonian Institution Press, 1990), 124–39

2316 **Rindstedt, C,** *Children, feeding and attitudes in Iramba, Tanzania: report from a minor field study.* Stockholm: Stockholm University, Development Studies Unit, 1991, 55pp

2317 **Shaw, J, Clay, E,** Tanzania: self reliance, economic growth and equity, in their *World food aid: experiences of recipients and donors* (London: Currey, 1993), 130–42

2318 **Wandel, M, Holmboe-Ottesen, G,** Food availability and nutrition in a seasonal perspective: a study from the Rukwa region in Tanzania, *Human ecology,* **20,** 1 (1992) 89–107

Gender

See also: 2266, 2294, 2357, 2417

2319 **Bujra, J,** Gender, class and empowerment: a tale of two Tanzanian servants, *Review of African political economy,* 56 (1993) 68–78

2320 **Caplan, P,** Learning gender: fieldwork in a Tanzanian coastal village 1965–85, in Bell, D et al (eds), *Gendered fields: women, men and ethnography* (London: Routledge, 1993), 168–81

2321 **Meena, R,** Bibi Titi, traitor or heroine of uhuru?, *Southern Africa political and economic monthly,* **5,** 7 (1992) 45–48

2322 **Meena, R,** The impact of structural adjustment programs on rural women in Tanzania, in Gladwin, C H (ed), *Structural adjustment and African women farmers (Item 315),* 169–90

2323 **Tanzania Media Women's Association,** Violence against women in Tanania, *Review of African political economy,* 56 (1993) 111–116

Health & welfare services

2324 **Abel-Smith, P, Rawal, P,** Can the poor afford free health services: a case study of Tanzania, *Health policy and planning,* **7,** 4 (1992) 329–41

2325 **Cooksey, B, et al,** *The provision and acceptability of child immunisation services in Tanzania.* Dar es Salaam: TADREG, 1992, 52pp

2326 **Heidenberger, K, Flessa, S,** A system dynamic model for AIDS policy support in Tanzania, *European journal of operational research,* **70,** 2 (1993) 167–76

History, general

2327 **Knappert, J,** Pemba, *Annales aequatoria,* 13 (1992) 39–52

2328 **Knappert, J,** A short history of Zanzibar, *Annales aequatoria,* 13 (1992) 15–37

2329 **Willis, J,** Feedback as a 'problem' in oral history: an example from Bonde, *History in Africa,* **20,** (1993) 353–60

History, C19th

2330 **Spear, T,** Being 'Maasai' but not 'people of cattle': Arusha agricultural Maasai in the nineteenth century, in Spear, T & Waller, R (eds), *Being Maasai (Item 1885)*, 120–36

History, C20th

See also: 2321, 2369, 4602

2331 **Haenger, P,** *Die Militärstation Mpapua, 1900–1904: Akten des Kaiserlichen Gouvernements von Deutsch-Ostafrika.* Basle: Baseler Afrika Bibliographien, 1992, 12pp

2332 **Itandala, B,** African response to German colonialism in East Africa: the case of Usukuma, 1890–1918, *Ufahamu,* **20,** 1 (1991/92) 3–29

2333 **Othman, H,** *Zanzibar's political history: the past haunting the present?* Copenhagen: Centre for Development Research, 1993, 15pp

2334 **Willis, J,** The administration of Bonde, 1920–60: a study of the implementation of indirect rule in Tanganyika, *African affairs,* **92,** 366 (1993) 53–67

2335 **Willis, J,** The allure of mission community: the Universities Mission to Central Africa in Bonde, *Past and present,* 140 (1993) 127–54

Industry & trade

See also: 2307, 2310, 2354, 2397, 2414, 3955, 4320, 4409, 5472

2336 **Bagachwa, M S D,** An agenda for sustainable growth of non-traditional exports in Tanzania, *Tanzanian economic trends,* **5,** 3/4 (1992/93) 41–51

2337 **Bol, D,** Non-traditional exports in Tanzania: trends and prospects, *Tanzanian economic trends,* **5,** 3/4 (1992/93) 4–40

2338 **Bryceson, D,** *Liberalising Tanzania's food trade: the public and private faces of urban marketing policy 1939–88.* London: Currey, 1993, 306pp

2339 **Coulter, J,** Cereal marketing liberalization in Tanzania, *Food policy,* **17,** 6 (1992) 420–430

2340 **DeRosa, D A,** Protection and own-funds window in Tanzania: an analytical framework and estimates of the effects of trade liberalisation, *Journal of African economics,* **2,** 1 (1993) 24–48

2341 **Hyman, E L,** *Local agro-processing with sustainable technology: sunflowerseed oil in Tanzania.* London: International Institute for Environment and Development, 1992, 15pp

2342 **Koda, B,** Small scale industries and the informal sector in Tanzania, in Onimode, B (ed), *The African response (Item 186)*, 32–36

2343 **Makaba, J W,** Public control and public enterprise performance in subsaharan Africa: the case of Tanzania and Zambia, *Africa development,* **18,** 3 (1993) 37–59

2344 **Mbatia, K S,** Constraints to the growth of non-traditional exports: incentives schemes, *Tanzanian economic trends,* **5,** 3/4 (1992/93) 52–63

2345 **Mbelle, A,** Foreign exchange and efficiency in Tanzanian industry: a short-run industry production function approach, *Eastern Africa economic review. New series,* **7,** 1 (1991) 31–38

2346 **Moshi, H P B,** Development and mineral resources in Africa: the case of Tanzania, in Khennas, S (ed), *Industrialisation (item 454)*, 47–80

2347 **Nditi, N N,** The plight of consumer cooperative ventures in Tanzania: legal and practical problems involved, *Eastern Africa law review,* **17,** 1 (1990) 1–17

2348 **Okoso Amaa, K,** The use of forecasting methods in Tanzanian firms, an exploratory survey, *Business management review,* **2,** 2 (1991) 102–28

2349 Rustayisire, L W, An empirical analysis of public enterprises' performance in Tanzania's manufacturing sector and some suggestions for improvement, *Eastern Africa economic review,* **7,** 1 (1991) 13–30

2350 Santorum, A, Trading responses to food market liberalization in Tanzania, *Food policy,* **17,** 6 (1992) 431–442

2351 Shaidi, L P, Trade liberalisation and the law, *Taamuli,* **1,** 1/2 (1990) 46–55

International economic relations

See also: 507, 2400

2352 Collier, P, Aid and economic performance in Tanzania, in Lele, U & Nabi, I (eds), *Transitions in development* (San Francisco: ICS Press, 1991), 151–71

2353 Faraji, A C, Tanzanian debt, aid and foreign investment, in Rimmer, D (ed), *Action in Africa (Item 525),* 119–29

2354 Folke, S, et al, Transfer of technology in South-South trade: India's export of capital goods to Tanzania, in their *South-South trade and development: manufactures in the new international division of labour* (Basingstoke: Macmillan, 1993), 189–215

2355 Mmbaga, W D S, Is institutional development and sustainability in development assistance necessary?, *Accountant,* **44,** 1 (1991) 27–33

Labour & manpower

See also: 609

2356 Lwoga, C M F, Human resources deployment and urban unemployment in Dar es Salaam, Tanzania: a symptom of a perverse socioeconomic structure, *Journal of eastern African research and development,* 22 (1992) 60–74

2357 Mbilinyi, M, Structural adjustment and agribusiness in Tanzania: struggles over the labour of women peasants and farm workers, *Taamuli,* **1,** 1/2 (1990) 76–102

Law

See also: 2299, 2347, 2390

2358 Fimbo, G M, CCM and the executive in Tanzania's constitutional structure, *Eastern Africa law review,* **17,** 2 (1990) 183–204

2359 Fimbo, G M, Public participation in judicial proceedings in Tanzania, *Eastern Africa law review,* **17,** 1 (1990) 18–33

2360 Kees van Donge, J, The arbitrary state in the Uluguru mountains: legal arenas and land disputes in Tanzania, *Journal of modern African studies,* **31,** 3 (1993) 431–48

2361 Kees van Donge, J, Legal insecurity and land conflicts in Mgeta, Uluguru mountains, Tanzania, *Africa,* **63,** 2 (1993) 197–218

2362 Lugakingira, K S K, Personal liberty and judicial attitude: the Tanzanian case, *Eastern Africa law review,* **17,** 1 (1990) 107–33

2363 Nyange, H H, Legislative and judicial implementation of the norm against torture, *Eastern Africa law review,* **17,** 1 (1990) 64–106

2364 Peter, C M, Five years of the Bill of Rights in Tanzania: drawing a balance-sheet, *African journal of international and comparative law,* **4,** 1 (1992) 131–167

2365 Shivji, I G, Contradictory developments in the teaching and practice of human rights law in Tanzania, *Journal of African law,* **35,** 1/2 (1991) 116–27

2366 Shivji, I G, Rights-struggle,

class-struggle and the law: reflections on experiences at the University of Dar es Salaam, in Adelman, S & Paliwala, A (eds), *Law and crisis in the Third World* (London: Zell, 1993), 127–48

2367 Wambali, M K B, Freedom of movement under the Tanzanian constitution: some operational observations, *Eastern Africa law review,* **17,** 1 (1990) 34–63

Library - documentation

2368 Kimbangu, T M, The CCM library and research services for Tanzania's politicians, in Wise, M & Olden, A (eds), *Information and libraries (item 672)*, 171–81

Literature

2369 Biersteker, A, *The significance of the Swahili literary tradition and interpretation of early twentieth-century political poetry.* Boston: African Studies Centre, Boston University, 1990, 28pp

2370 Blommaert, J, Intercultural communication and African popular literature: on a reading a Swahili pulp novel, *African languages and cultures,* **6,** 1 (1993) 21–36

2371 Ohly, R, *The Zanzibarian challenge: Swahili prose in the years 1975–1981.* Windhoek: University of Namibia, 1990, 186pp

Medical

See also: 2417

2372 Cegielski, J P, et al, Intestinal parasites and HIV infection in Tanzanian children with chronic diarrhoea, *AIDS,* **7,** 2 (1993) 213–21

2373 Justesen, A, et al, Abortions in a hospital setting: hidden realities in Dar es Salaam, Tanzania, *Studies in family planning,* **23,** 5 (1992) 325–29

2374 Kaijage, F J, AIDS control and the burden of history in northwestern Tanzania, *Population and environment,* **14,** 3 (1993) 279–300

2375 Lwihula, G, et al, AIDS epidemic in Kagera Region, Tanzania: the experiences of local people, *AIDS care,* **5,** 3 (1993) 347–57

Natural resources

See also: 791

2376 Boberg, J, Competition in Tanzanian woodfuel markets, *Energy policy,* **21,** 5 (1993) 474–90

2377 Jerve, A M, What sustains sustainable development? Natural resource management and popular participation in Tanzania, *Forum for utviklungstudier,* 1 (1990) 85–103

2378 Massawe, E T, Assessment of the state of chimpanzee populations in western Tanzania, *African study monographs,* **13,** 1 (1992) 35–55

2379 Mwandosya, M J, Luhanga, M L, Energy and development in Tanzania: issues and perspectives, *Energy policy,* **21,** 5 (1993) 441–53

Politics

See also: 2153, 2299, 2311, 2368

2380 Bagenda, M, *A contribution to the debate on political pluralism in Tanzania.* Dar es Salaam: Friedrich-Ebert Foundation, 1991, 111pp

2381 Campbell, H, The politics of demobilisation in Tanzania: beyond nationalism, *Taamuli,* **1,** 1/2 (1990) 56–75

2382 Hartmann, J, The state in Tanzania, yesterday, today and tomorrow, in Mappa, S (ed), *Ambitions et illusions de la coopération*

Nord-Sud: Lomé IV (Paris: Harmattan, 1990), 333–57

2383 Hyden, G, Karlström, B, Structural adjustment as a policy process: the case of Tanzania, *World development,* **21,** 9 (1993) 1395–1404

2384 Kiondo, A S Z, Structural adjustment and non-governmental organisations in Tanzania: a case study, in Gibbon, P (ed), *Social change and economic reform (item 1880),* 161–83

2385 Martin, D C, La Tanzanie et le multipartisme, *Afrique contemporaine,* 167 (1993) 3–13

2386 Mmuya, M, Chaligha, A, *Towards multiparty politics in Tanzania: a spectrum of the current opposition and the CCM response.* Dar es Salaam: Friedrich-Ebert Foundation, 1992, 167pp

2387 Omari, A H, Beyond the civil military dichotomy in Africa: the case of Tanzania, in Siddiqui, R A (ed), *Subsaharan Africa (item 15),* 19–48

2388 Othman, H, *Succession politics and the union presidential elections.* Bergen: Chr. Michelsen Institute, 1993, 18pp

2389 Othman, H, *Tanzania: the withering away of the union?* Bergen: Chr. Michelsen Institute, 1993, 40pp

2390 Shivji, I G, Minimum legal conditions to begin the process of democratisation in Tanzania, *Eastern Africa law review,* **17,** 2 (1990) 134–82

2391 Shivji, I G, The politics of liberalisation in Tanzania: notes on the crisis of ideological hegemony, *Taamuli,* **1,** 1/2 (1990) 138–52

2392 Shivji, I G, *State coercion and freedom in Tanzania.* Roma: Institute of Southern African Studies, 1990, 107pp

2393 Zirker, D, The preservation of civilian rule in Tanzania, in Danopoulos, C P (ed), *Civilian rule (Item 844),* 107–23

Religion, philosophy

2394 Herterich-Akinpelu, I, *Ethnizität und Stratifikation an Biespiel islamischer Organisationen und ihren Praktiken Tansania.* Würzburg: Ergon, 1991, 110pp

2395 Lamburn, R G P (& Fiedler, K), *Robin Lamburn - from a missionary's notebook: the Yao of Tunduru and other essays.* Saarbrucken: Breitenbach, 1991, 240pp

2396 Watschinger, H, *'Gib die Hoffnung nicht auf': ein Leben im Dienst der Maasai.* Mödling: St Gabriel, 1992, 215pp

Rural economy

See also: 3954, 3955

2397 Amani, H K R, Policies to promote an effective private trading system in farm products and farm inputs in Tanzania, *Tanzania economic trends,* **4,** 3/4 (1992) 36–54

2398 Bevan, D, *Agriculture and the policy environment: Tanzania and Kenya.* Paris: OECD Development Centre, 1993, 103pp

2399 Boesen, J, Ravnborg, H M, *Peasant production in Iringa district, Tanzania.* Copenhagen: Centre for Development Research, 1993, 75pp

2400 Bruijsten, P, *Mashine za maendeleo?: Netherland's funded grinding mill projects and the development of Tanzania.* Nijmegen: Catholic University of Nijmegen, Third Word Centre, 1993, 143pp

2401 Chachage, C S L, Forms of accumulation, agriculture and structural adjustment in Tanzania, in Gibbon, P (ed), *Social change*

and economic reform (item 1880), 215–43

2402 Dercon, S, Peasant supply responses and macroeconomic policies: cotton in Tanzania, *Journal of African economics*, **2,** 2 (1993) 157–94

2403 Eriksson, G, *Peasant response to price incentives in Tanzania: a theoretical and empirical investigation.* Uppsala: Scandinavian Institute of African Studies, 1993, 84pp

2404 Havnevik, K J, *Tanzania: the limits to development from above.* Uppsala: Scandinavian Institute of African Studies, 1993, 343pp

2405 Hyman, E L, Production of edible oils for the masses and by the masses: the impact of the ram press in Tanzania, *World development*, **21,** 3 (1993) 429–43

2406 Kashuliza, A K, Perception and role of informal rural finance in developing countries: the example of Tanzania, *Journal of rural studies*, **9,** 2 (1993) 163–74

2407 Maganya, E N, The structural adjustment programmes and the agricultural sector: the case of Tanzania, *Taamuli*, **1,** 1/2 (1990)

2408 Masawe, J L, Farming systems and agricultural production among small farmers in the Uluguru mountain area, Morogoro region, Tanzania, *African study monographs*, **13,** 3 (1992) 171–83

2409 Mshana, R R, *Insisting on people's knowledge to resist developmentalism: peasant communities as producers of knowledge for social transformation in Tanzania.* Frankfurt: Verlag für Interkulturelle Kommunikation, 1992, 330 + 36pp

2410 Mulder, M B, Demography of pastoralists: preliminary data on the Datoga of Tanzania, *Human ecology*, **20,** 4 (1992) 383–405

2411 Potts, D, Rehabilitation of export-oriented estate agriculture in Tanzania, in Kirkpatrick, C (ed), *Project rehabilitation (Item 164)*, 75–100

2412 Taube, G, *Wirtschaftliche Stabilisierung und Strukturanpassung in Tansania: die Auswirkungen des Economic Recovery Programme 1986–1989 im ländlichen Bereich - Fallstudie West-Usambara-Berge, Distrikt Lushoto.* Hamburg: Institut für Afrika-Kunde, 1992, 241pp

2413 Waters, T, Lifeworld and system: of water systems and grain mill development in rural Tanzania, *African studies review*, **35,** 2 (1992) 35–54

Science & technology

2414 Wangwe, S M, Tanzania, in Patel, S J (ed), *Technological transformation in the Third World. Vol. 2* (Aldershot: Avebury, 1993), 95–142

Sociology

See also: 2319

2415 Aschenbrenner-Wellman, B, Veränderungen der Ethnizität in Tanzania, *Sociologus*, **42,** 2 (1992) 113–31

2416 Evans, R, Pride and prejudice, *Focus on Africa*, **4,** 3 (1993) 33–37

2417 Weiss, B, 'Buying her grave': money, movement and AIDS in north-west Tanzania, *Africa*, **63,** 1 (1993) 19–35

Urban studies

2418 Hosier, R H, Urban energy systems in Tanzania: a tale of three cities, *Energy policy*, **21,** 5 (1993) 510–23

2419 Hosier, R H, et al, Future energy development in Tanzania: the energy costs of urbanisation, *Energy policy*, **21,** 5 (1993) 524–42

2420 **Hosier, R H, Kipondya, W,** Urban househould energy use in Tanzanaia: prices, subsitutes and poverty, *Energy policy,* **21,** 5 (1993) 454–73

2421 **Kironde, J M L,** Rent control legislation and the National Housing Corporation in Tanzania, *Canadian journal of African studies,* **26,** 2 (1992) 306–27

2422 **Loire, G,** *Gens de mer à Dar es Salaam.* Paris: Karthala, 1993, 231pp

2423 **Lusugga Kironde, J M,** Will Dodoma ever be the new capital of Tanzania?, *Geoforum,* **24,** 4 (1993) 435–53

UGANDA

Anthropology

No entry. *See also:* 2458, 2460

Economic and social history

2424 **Hansen, H B,** Forced labour in a missionary context: a study of *kaswuru* in early twentieth century Uganda, *Slavery and abolition,* **14,** 1 (1993) 186–206

2425 **Mamdani, M,** The Uganda Asian expulsion twenty years after, *Economic and political weekly,* **28,** 3/4 (1993) 93–96

Economy - Development

2426 **Bibangambah, J R,** The cooperative movement in Uganda's transition to a free market economy, *Yearbook of cooperative enterprise 1993,* 83–91

2427 **Brett, E A,** Voluntary agencies as development organisations: theorising the problem of efficiency and accountability, *Development and change,* **24,** 2 (1993) 269–303

2428 **Granberg, P,** *Micro-economic effects of development plan expenditures: a framework for analysis, with special reference to Uganda.* Bergen: Chr Michelsen Institute, 1993, 51pp

2429 **Kayizzi-Mugerwa, S,** Urban bustle/rural slumber: dilemmas of uneven economic recovery in Uganda, in Blomström, M & Lundahl, M (eds), *Economic crisis (Item 119),* 181–201

2430 **Laishley, R,** Uganda: turning growth into prosperity, *Africa recovery,* **7,** 2 (1993) 16–21

2431 **Murinde, V,** Budgetary and financial policy potency amid structural bottlenecks: evidence from Uganda, *World development,* **21,** 5 (1993) 841–59

2432 **Okoth, P H,** Africa's development nightmare, Uganda's case, *Journal of eastern African research and development,* 22 (1992) 132–49

2433 **Sepehri, A, Loxley, J,** Uganda: constraints on economic growth, *African development review,* **4,** 1 (1992) 29–46

Education

See also: 2449, 3684

2434 **Eisemon, T O, et al,** *Strengthening Uganda's policy environment for investing in university development.* Washington: World Bank, 1993, 68pp

2435 **Oloka-Onyango, J,** The legal control of tertiary institutions in East Africa: the case of Makerere University, *Africa development,* **17,** 4 (1992) 47–65

Environment

2436 **Tukahirwa, E M, Veit, P,** Community soil conservation in Kabale, Uganda, in Hudson, N & Cheatle, R J (eds), *Working with farmers (Item 245),* 162–65

Finance

No entry. *See also:* 2431

Food

See also: 2470

2437 **Nisimbambi, A,** Politics and food policy in Uganda, in Chole, E (ed), *Food crisis (Item 275)*, 76–97

Gender

2438 **Kisekka, M N,** AIDS in Uganda as a gender issue, in Rothblum, E D & Cole, E (eds), *Women's mental health (item 338)*, 35–53

2439 **McGrath, J W, et al,** Anthropology and AIDS: the cultural context of sexual risk behaviour among urban Baganda women in Kampala, Uganda, *Social science and medicine,* **36,** 4 (1993) 429–40

2440 **Ntege, H,** Women and urban housing crisis: imact of public policies and practices in Uganda, *Economic and political weekly,* **28,** 44 (1993) WS46–62

Geography, human

No entry. *See also:* 2469

Health & welfare services

2441 **Cotinovis, I, et al,** Construction of a socio-economic index to facilitate analysis of health data in developing countries, *Social science and medicine,* **36,** 8 (1993) 1087–97

2442 **Whyte, S R,** Pharmaceuticals as folk medicine: transformations in the social relations of health care in Uganda, *Culture, medicine and psychiatry,* **16,** 2 (1992) 163–86

History, C19th

2443 **Rowe, J A,** Erieza Kintu's Sulutani Anatoloka: a nineteenth-century historical memoir from Buganda, *History in Africa,* **20,** (1993) 313–319

History, C20th

See also: 2089

2444 **Rowe, J A,** *'Okukkera Ngomuzungu', to talk nonsense like a whiteman: the use of proverbs in Luganda historical writing.* Boston: African Studies Centre, Boston University, 1991, 9pp

2445 **Twaddle, M,** *Kakungulu and the creation of Uganda 1868–1928.* London: Currey, 1993, 310pp

International economic relations

2446 **Gupta, V,** Land-locked Uganda: constraints on political economy, *Ind-Africana,* **4,** 2 (1991) 1–14

International relations

2447 **Khadiagala, G L,** Uganda's domestic and regional security since the 1970s, *Journal of modern African studies,* **31,** 2 (1993) 231–55

Labour & manpower

2448 **Baingaba, E,** Performance appraisal in the civil service of Uganda: pitfalls and remedies, *African management development forum,* **2,** 2 (1991) 11–19

Library - documentation

2449 **Kigongo-Bukenya,** I M N, Combating illiteracy in Uganda through the public library services, in Wise, M & Olden, A (eds),

Information and libraries (item 672), 124–43

Literature

2450 **Ruganda, J,** *Telling the truth laughingly: the politics of Francis Imbuga's drama.* Nairobi: EAEP, 1992, 204pp

2451 **Sicherman, C,** Individual and community in Timothy Wangusa's Upon this mountain, *International fiction review,* **20,** 1 (1993) 48–53

Medical

See also: 2438, 2439, 2473

2452 **Kalecha, N, et al,** *We miss you all. Noerine Kaleba: AIDS in the family.* Harare: Women and AIDS Support Network, 1991, 103pp

2453 **Kigadye, R M, et al,** Sentinel surveillance for HIV–1 among pregnant women in a developing country: three years experience and comparison with a population serosurvey, *AIDS,* **7,** 6 (1993) 849–55

2454 **Konde-Lule, J, et al,** Focus group interviews about AIDS in Rakai district of Uganda, *Social science and medicine,* **37,** 5 (1993) 679–84

2455 **Obbo, C,** HIV transmission through social and geographical networks in Uganda, *Social science and medicine,* **36,** 7 (1993) 949–55

2456 **Wabinga, H R, et al,** Cancer in Kampala, Uganda, in 1989–91: changes in the era of AIDS, *International journal of cancer,* **54,** 1 (1993) 731–43

2457 **Wagner, H U, et al,** General and HIV–1 associated morbidity in a rural Ugandan community, *AIDS,* **7,** 11 (1993) 1461–67

2458 **Whyte, S R,** The power of medicines in East Africa, in van der Geest, S & Whyte, S R (eds), *The context of medicines in developing countries* (Amsterdam: Spinhuis, 1991), 217–33

Natural resources

2459 **Turyareeba, P,** Mobilising local financial resources: the case of Uganda, in Karekezi, S & Mackenzie, G A (eds), *Energy options (Item 796)*, 68–85

Politics

See also: 908, 2447

2460 **Behrend, H,** Krieg als Aufstand der natur: die Holy-Spirit-Bewegung und die Mächte der Natur im norden Ugandas, *Anthropos,* **88,** 1/2 (1993) 39–46

2461 **Jamison, M,** *Idi Amin and Uganda: an annotated biliography.* New York: Greenport, 1992, 145pp

2462 **Kabumba, I,** *The contribution of managers to the survival of dictatorship in Uganda.* Kampala: Nyoni, 1992, 58pp

2463 **Okema, M,** The political crises in Uganda, in Siddiqui, R A (ed), *Subsaharan Africa (item 15)*, 49–71

2464 **Oloka-Onyango, J,** The dynamics of corruption control and human rights enforcement in Uganda, *East African journal of peace and human rights,* **1,** 1 (1993) 23–51

2465 **Oloka-Onyango, J,** Governance, democracy and development in Uganda today: a socio-legal examination, *African study monographs,* **13,** 2 (1992) 91–109

2466 **Tumwesigya, J,** The system of councils and committees in Uganda, in Sandbrook, R & Halfani, M (eds), *Empowering people (Item 930)*, 155–59

Rural economy

2467 **Brett, E A,** *Providing for the rural poor: institutional decay in Uganda.* Brighton: Institute of Development Studies, 1992, 91pp

2468 **Nabuguzi, E,** Peasant response to economic crisis in Uganda: rice farmers in Busoga, *Review of African political economy,* 56 (1993) 53–67

2469 **Nyakaana, J B,** The impact of distance and accessibility on fish marketing in Uganda, *Maseno journal of education, arts and science,* **1,** 1 (1992) 114–29

2470 **Olokoa-Onyango, J, et al,** *Pastoralism, crisis and transformation in Karamoja.* London: International Institute for Environment and Development, 1993, 19pp

2471 **Roth, M, et al,** *Tenure security, credit use, and farm investment in the Rujumbura pilot land registration scheme, Rukungiri District, Uganda.* Madison: Land Tenure Centre, University of Wisconsin, 1993, 46pp

Sociology

See also: 2455

2472 **Prunier, G,** L'Ouganda et le FPR, *Dialogue,* 163 (1993) 3–19

2473 **Schopper, D, et al,** Sexual behaviour relevant to HIV transmission in a rural African population. How much can a KAP survey tell us?, *Social science and medicine,* **37,** 3 (1993) 401–12

Urban studies

See also: 2440, 2453

2474 **Maxwell, D, Zzima, S,** *Urban farming in Africa: the case of Kampala.* Nairobi: ACTS, 1992, 74pp

WEST AFRICA

Agriculture, scientific

2475 Péhaut, Y, L'arachide en Afrique occidentale, *Cahiers d'outre-mer,* **45,** 179/80 (1992) 387–406

2476 Pieri, C J, *Fertility of soils: a future for farming in the West African savanna.* Berlin: Springer, 1992, 348pp

2477 Uzo Mokwunye, A (ed), *Alleviating soil fertility constraints to increased crop production in West Africa.* Dordrecht: Kluwer, 1991, 244pp

Anthropology

See also: 2528

2478 Azarya, V, Sedentarisation and ethnic identity among the Fulbe: a comparative view, *Senri ethnological studies,* 35 (1993) 35–60

2479 Bognolo, D, Les *taari* du *baba, Arts d'Afrique noire,* 84 (1992) 9–16

2480 Dehoux, V, Gessain, M, La musique bassari: un parcours obligé, *Cahiers de musiques traditionelles,* 5 (1992) 17–35

2481 Fiéloux, M, Lombard, J (eds), *Images d'Afrique et sciences sociales: les pays Lobi, Birifir et Dagara.* Paris: Karthala, 1993, 567pp

2482 Frantz, C, Are the Mbororo'en boring, and are the Fulbe finished?, *Senri ethnological studies,* 35 (1993) 11–34

2483 Kassibo, B, La géomancie ouest-africaine: formes endogènes et emprunts exterieuries, *Cahiers d'études africaines,* **32,** 128 (1992) 541–96

2484 Kawada, J, *Boucle du Niger: approches multidisciplinaires.* Tokyo: Institute for Research on the Languages and Cultures of Asian and Africa, 1988–1992, 3 vols

2485 Kesteloot, L, La poésie orale dans l'ouest africain, *Ethiopiques,* 56 (1992) 65–86

2486 Savary, C, Le symbolisme de l'eau en Afrique de l'ouest, *Newsletter (Société suisse d'études africaines),* 1 (1993) 15–22

2487 Schott, R, 'La femme enceinte éventrée': variabilité et contexte socioculturel d'un type de conte ouest-africain, in Görög-Karady, V (ed), *D'un conte ... à l'autre (item 38),* 327–38

2488 Sow, A A, Fulani poetic genres, *Research in African literatures,* **24,** 2 (1993) 61–77

2489 Zubko, G V, Ethnic and cultural characteristics of the Fulbe, *Senri ethonological studies,* 35 (1993) 201–13

Architecture

2490 Oguntoyinbo, J S, Climatology and building design in West Africa, *African urban quarterly,* **5,** 1/2 (1990) 104–117

Arts

2491 Horner, A E, Tourist arts in

Africa before tourism, *Tourism research,* **20,** 1 (1993) 52–63

2492 Konaré, A, Les dramaturges négro-africains et l'histoire: une pédagogie de la responsabilité, *Ethiopiques,* **7,** 2 (1991) 115–131

Economic and social history

See also: 2475, 2478, 2519, 2520

2493 Arnalte, A, Noticias sobre comercio espagñol en la costa de Africa a mediados del siglo XIX, *Estudios Africanos,* **6,** 10/11 (1991/92) 35–49

2494 Austin, G, Indigenous credit institutions in West Africa, c.1750-c.1960, in Austin, G & Sugihara, K (eds), *Local suppliers of credit in the Third World, 1750–1960* (Basingstoke: Macmillan, 1993), 93–159

2495 Bernard, C, Les débuts de la politique de reboisement dans la vallée du fleuve Sénégal (1920–1945), *Revue française d'histoire d'outre-mer,* **80,** 298 (1993) 49–82

2496 Cowen, M P, Shenton, R W, Finance capital and peasants in colonial west Africa: a reply to August Gachter, *Journal of peasant studies,* **20,** 4 (1993) 681–87

2497 Everaert, J, De Wilde, C, Pindanoten voor de ontluikende industriële revolutie: een alternative kijk op de Belgische commerciële expansie in West-Afrika (1844–1861), *Bulletin des séances,* **37,** 3 (1991) 317–48

2498 Gachter, A, Finance capital and peasants in colonial west Africa: a comment on Cowen and Shenton, *Journal of peasant studies,* **20,** 4 (1993) 669–80

2499 Inikori, J E, The volume of the British slave trade, 1655–1807, *Cahiers d'études africaines,* **32,** 128 (1992) 643–88

2500 Inikori, J E, Engerman, S L (eds), *The Atlantic slave trade: effects on economies, societies and peoples in Africa, the Americas and Europe.* Durham, N C: Duke University Press, 1992, 412pp

2501 Iroko, A F, Les hommes et les incendies à la côte des esclaves durant la période précoloniale, *Africa (Rome),* **48,** 3 (1993) 396–423

2502 Law, R, The historiography of the commercial transition in West Africa, in Falola, T (ed), *African historiography (Item 385)*, 91–115

2503 Law, R, The Royal African Company of England's West African correspondence, 1681–1699, *History in Africa,* **20,** (1993) 173–84

2504 Lovejoy, P E, *Mugu*: the wages of slavery in the Western Sudan, *Slavery and abolition,* **14,** 1 (1993) 168–85

2505 Ly, A, *La Compagnie du Sénégal.* Paris: Karthala, 1993, 448pp

2506 Lynn, M, British business archives and the history of business in 19th century West Africa, *Business archives,* **62,** (1991) 28–39

2507 Manning, P, The slave trade: the formal demography of a global system, in Inikori, J E & Engerman, S L (eds), *The Atlantic slave trade (Item 2500)*, 117–41

2508 McIntosh, R J, The pulse model: genesis and accommodation of specialisation in the Middle Niger, *Journal of African history,* **34,** 2 (1993) 181–220

2509 Roberts, R, Guinée cloth: linked transformations in production within France's empire in the nineteeth century, *Cahiers d'études africaines,* **32,** 128 (1992) 597–627

2510 Searing, J F, *West African slavery and Atlantic commerce: the Senegal River valley, 1700–1860.* Cambridge: CUP, 1993, 252pp

2511 **van der Laan, H L,** Migration, mobility and settlement of the Lebanese in West Africa, in Hourani, A & Shehadi, N (eds), *The Lebanese in the world* (London: Tauris, 1992), 531–47

2512 **Webb, J L A,** the horse and slave trade between the western Sahara and Senegambia, *Journal of African history,* **34,** 2 (1993) 221–46

Economy - Development

See also: 158

2513 **Biao, B,** Aspects économiques et socio-politiques des programmes d'ajustement structurel en Afrique centrale et occidentale, *Études et statistiques (BEAC),* 195 (1992) 251–267

2514 **Fair, D,** West Africa's economic islands of development: thirty years on, *Africa insight,* **23,** 3 (1993) 141–48

2515 **Roy, S,** Aspects of structural adjustment in west Africa and southeast Asia, *Economic and political weekly,* **28,** 37 (1993) 1937–49

Environment

2516 **Cleaver, K, et al (eds),** *Conservation of West and Central African rainforests.* Washington: World Bank, 1992, 353pp

2517 **Emearole, P O,** Training of environmental health officers in anglophone West Africa: how adequate for environmental monitoring?, *Journal of the Royal Society of Health,* **113,** 1 (1993) 17–23

Finance

No entry. *See also:* 2558, 2561

Food

2518 **Savané, M A (ed),** *Populations et gouvernements face aux problèmes alimentaires: regards sur les zones de l'Afrique de l'ouest.* Geneva: UNRISD, 1992, 389pp

Gender

2519 **Berns, M C, Art,** history and gender: women and clay in West Africa, *African archaeological review,* **11,** (1993) 129–48

2520 **Birkett, D,** The 'white woman's burden' in the 'white man's grave': the introduction of British nurses in colonial West Africa, in Chauduri, N & Strobel, M (eds), *Western women and imperialism* (Bloomington: Indiana University Press, 1992), 177–88

2521 **Last, M,** The importance of extremes: the social implications of intra-household variation in child mortality, *Social science and medicine,* **35,** 6 (1992) 799–810

Geography, human

2522 **Médard, C,** *Les représentations de l'Afrique orientale dans les géographies universelles françaises de XIXe et XXe siécles.* Talence: Bordeaux University, CEAN, 1993, 108pp

Geography, physical

2523 **Mahé, G,** *Les écoulements fluviaux sur la façade atlantique de l'Afrique.* Paris: Orstom, 1993, 438pp

Health & welfare services

2524 **Maine, D, et al,** Barriers to the treatment of obstetric emergencies in rural communities of West Africa, *Studies in family planning,* **23,** 5 (1993) 279–91

2525 Muller, A S, The control of river blindness in West Africa: the role of the Onchocerciasis Control Programme and the endemic countries, *Bulletin des séances,* **37,** 4 (1991) 619–27

2526 Wigg, D, *And then forgot to tell us why ... A look at the campaign against river blindness in West Africa.* Washington: World Bank, 1993, 44pp

History, general

2527 Ardouin, C D, Quels models pour les musées africains? Perspectives ouest-africains/What models for African museums: West African prosects, *WAMP bulletin,* 4 (1993) 14–28

2528 Barreteau, D, Tourneux, H (eds), *Actes du IIIème Congrès Mega-Tchad, Paris, ORSTOM, 1986: relations interethniques et culture matérielle dans le bassin du Lac Tchad.* Paris: ORSTOM, 1990, 266pp

2529 Barreteau, D, von Graffenreid, C (eds), *Datation et chronologie dans le bassin du lac Tchad/Dating and chronology in the Lake Chad basin.* Paris: Orstom, 1993, 292pp

2530 Dilley, R, Interpreting Tukulor oral literature: the myth of origin of the nine *mabube* clan names, *Bulletin of the John Rylands University Library of Manchester,* **73,** 3 (1991) 25–36

2531 Nanni, S, Fonti missionarie per la storia dell'Africa occidentale, in Turco, A (ed), *Anno d'Africa (Item 17)*, 217–56

History, early

2532 Andah, B W, African paleoanthropological studies: which way forward?, in Andah, B W, et al (eds), *Imprints of West Africa's past (Item 2534)*, 2–10

2533 Andah, B W, Bagodo, O B, Research and theory in archaeology since the 1960s: an assessment of the African, especially West African, scene, *West African journal of archaeology,* **23,** (1993) 1–23

2534 Andah, B W, et al (eds), *Imprints of West Africa's past.* Ibadan: Wisdom, 1993, 314pp

2535 Andah, B W, Folorunso, C A, Pioneers of archaeological work in West Africa, in Andah, B W et al (eds), *Imprints of West Africa's past (Item 2534)*, 12–24

2536 Hart, W A, Fyfe, C, The stone sculptures of the upper Guinea coast, *History in Africa,* **20,** (1993) 71–87

History, C18th

See also: 407

2537 Blum, C, Fisher, H, Love for three oranges, or, the *Askiya*'s dilemma: the *Askiya*, Al-Maghili and Timbuktu, C.1500 AD, *Journal of African history,* **34,** 1 (1993) 65–91

2538 Cressier, P, Archéologie de la dévotion soufi, *Journal des Africanistes,* **62,** 2 (1992) 69–90

2539 Farrar, T, When African kings became 'chiefs': some transformations in European perceptions of West African civilisation, c.1450–1800, *Journal of Black studies,* **23,** 2 (1992) 258–78

2540 Hair, P E H, On editing Barbot, *History in Africa,* **20,** (1993) 53–59

2541 Hunwick, J O, Studies in the Tarikh al-fattash, II: an alleged charter of privilege issued by Askiya al-hajj Muhammed to the descendants of Mori Hawgaro, *Sudanic Africa,* 3 (1992) 133–48

2542 Johnson, J W (ed), *The epic of Son-Jara: a West African tradition.*

Bloomington: Indiana University Press, 1993, 242pp

2543 **Lange, D,** Ein vernacklässigtes Forschungsgebiet: die Geschichte des westafrikanischen Mittelalters, *Saeculum,* **43,** 4 (1992) 291–306

2544 **Watta, O,** *Rosary, mat and molo: a study in the spiritual epic of Omar Seku Tal.* New York: Lang, 1993, 217pp

History, C19th

2545 **Birkett, D,** *Mary Kingsley (1862–1900): a biographical bibliography.* Bristol: Bristol University, 1993, 30pp

2546 **Gomez, M A,** *Pragmatism in the age of jihad: the precolonial state of Bundu.* Cambridge: CUP, 1992, 252pp

2547 **Jenkins, P,** The earliest generation of missionary photographers in West Africa and the portrayal of indigenous people and culture, *History in Africa,* **20,** (1993) 89–118

2548 **Klein, M A,** The impact of the Atlantic slave trade on the societies of the Western Sudan, in Inikori, J E & Engerman, S L (eds), *The Atlantic slave trade (Item 2500),* 25–47

2549 **Shimada, Y,** Jihad as dialectical movement and formation of Islamic identity among the Fulbe, *Senri ethnological studies,* 35 (1993) 87–117

History, C20th

2550 **Miles, W F S,** Colonial Hausa idioms: toward a West African ethno-history, *African studies review,* **36,** 2 (1993) 11–30

Industry & trade

See also: 2491, 2557

2551 **Grégoire, E, Labazée, P** (eds), *Grands commercants de l'Afrique de l'ouest.* Paris: Karthala, ORSTOM, 1993, 264pp

2552 **Kaka, A,** Entreprises étrangères et activités industrielles en Afrique de l'ouest, *Africa development,* **18,** 2 (1993) 79–95

International economic relations

See also: 2552, 3805

2553 **Abutudu, I,** Fund versus Secretariat: the struggle for the management of extraversion in ECOWAS, *Quarterly journal of administration,* **25,** 3/4 (1991) 260–72

2554 **Abutudu, I,** Regime change, political instability and economic integration in West Africa: the experience of Ecowas, *Nigerian journal of international affairs,* **16,** 1 (1990) 90–107

2555 **Badiane, O,** External trade pessimism and the role of regional markets in the groundnut trade by AGC countries, *Journal of African economics,* **2,** 1 (1993) 1–23

2556 **Coussy, J, Hibou, B,** *Variantes de politiques nationales des échanges extérieures et marchés céréaliers en Afrique de l'ouest: analyse comparative dans le sous-espace ouest.* Paris: IRAM, 1991, 97pp

2557 **Gebremariam, Y,** Obstacles to trade liberalization and economic cooperation among West African states, *Journal of international development,* **5,** 1 (1993) 79–92

2558 **Guidy Wandja, J,** Peut-on dévaluer le franc CFA?, *Afrique 2000,* 15 (1993) 75–82

2559 **Iheduru, O C,** Competing nationalism, regional cooperation and the politics of international shipping in West Africa, *Ocean development and international law,* **24,** 2 (1993) 123–53

2560 **Madden, P**, *Brussels beef carve-up: EC beef dumping in West Africa.* London: Christian Aid, 1993, 22pp

2561 **Monga, C,** Monnaie et politique en Zone Franc, *Afrique 2000,* 15 (1993) 65–74

2562 **Moukoko Mbonjo, P,** Intégration régionale et construction de l'état en Afrique de l'Ouest: un essai d'interpretation, *Afrique 2000,* 12 (1993) 5–42

2563 **Samen, S,** Intégration économique dans les pays de l'UDEAC et de l'UMOA: leçons de l'histoire, fondements théoriques et perspectives pour les années 90, *Etudes et statistiques (BEAC),* 201 (1993) 127–43

2564 **Unilag Consult**, *The potential effects of the 1992 Single European Market on member states of Ecowas.* Lagos: University of Lagos Press, 1991, 63pp

International relations

No entry. *See also:* 3390

Labour & manpower

No entry. *See also:* 2517

Language

2565 **Sosu, A E,** Multilingualism and problems of choice of official indigenous languages in the West African subregion, *Africa development,* **17,** 1 (1992) 113–28

Literature

2566 **Amuzu, K,** Landscape as an expression of alienation: Armah, Awoonor, Soyinka, *English in Africa,* **20,** 1 (1993) 77–89

2567 **Dieng, B,** Les genres narratifs et les phénomènes intertextuels dans l'espace soudanais (mythes, épopées et romans), *Annales de la Faculté des lettres et sciences humaines (Dakar),* **21,** (1991) 77–93

2568 **Dieng, S,** La technique littérare des chansons de geste et des épopées peules, *Annales de la Faculté des lettres et sciences humaines (Dakar),* **21,** (1991) 65–76

2569 **Palmer, E,** West African literature in the 1980s, *Matatu,* 10 (1993) 61–84

2570 **Seydou, C,** Unité et diversité du monde peul à travers sa production littéraire: quelques aperçus, *Senri ethnological studies,* 35 (1993) 163–79

2571 **Wehrs, D R,** Colonialism, polyvocality and Islam in L'aventure ambigue and Le devoir du violence, *Modern language notes,* **107,** 5 (1992) 1000–1027

Medical

See also: 2521

2572 **Decock, K M, et al,** HIV-1 and HIV-2 infections and AIDS in West Africa, *AIDS,* **5,** 1 (1991) 21–28

Natural resources

2573 **de Bie, S,** *Wildlife resources of the West African savanna.* Wageningen: Wageningen Agricultural University, 1991, 266pp

2574 **Falconer, J** (ed. Koppell, C R S), *The major significance of 'minor' forest products: the local use and value of forests in the West African humid firest zone.* Rome: FAO, 1990, 232pp

Politics

2575 **Plane, P,** Des la crise à l'assainissement: le difficile cheminement des services publiques africains (Cameroun,

Niger et Sénégal), *Mondes en développement,* **20,** 77/78 (1992) 149–57

Religion, philosophy

2576 **Hamès, C,** Entre recette magique d'al-Buni et prière islamique d'al-Ghazali: textes talismaniques d'Afrique occidentale, *Systèmes de pensée en Afrique noire,* 12 (1993) 187–223

2577 **Roger, S,** La conception Dagara de dieu en question, *Papers in Dagara studies,* **1,** 3 (1991) 30–43

2578 **Schulze, R,** La da'wa saoudienne en Afrique de l'Ouest, in Otayek, R (ed), *Radicalisme islamique (Item 1002),* 21–35

2579 **Thayer, J S,** Pilgrimage and its influence on West African Islam, in his *Sacred journeys: the anthropology of pilgrimage* (New York: Greenwood, 1992), 169–87

Rural economy

2580 **Adams, W M,** Indigenous use of wetlands and sustainable development in West Africa, *Geographical journal,* **159,** 2 (1993) 209–218

2581 **Anon,** Agricultural policies and income distribution: a challenge for a maximum economic growth, *Rural progress,* **11,** 1 (1992) 31–48

2582 **Bernus, E,** Le nomadisme pastoral en question, *Etudes rurales,* 120 (1990) 41–52

2583 **Dvorak, A,** Resource management by West African farmers and the economics of shifting cultivation, *American journal of agricultural economics,* **74,** 3 (1992) 809–15

2584 **Fafchamps, M,** Sequential labour decisions under uncertainty: an estimable household model of West African farmers, *Econometrica,* **61,** 5 (1993) 1173–97

2585 **Floret, C, Serpantie, G** (eds), *La jachère en Afrique de l'Ouest.* Paris: Orstom, 1993, 496pp

2586 **Grut, M, et al,** *Forest pricing and concession policies: managing the high forests of West and Central Africa.* Washington: World Bank, 1991, 77pp

2587 **Kumar, V,** Crop production in the West African drylands, in Rowland, J R J (ed), *Dryland farming (Item 1078),* 109–141

2588 **McMillan, D E, et al,** *Settlement and development in the river blindness control zone.* Washington: World Bank, 1992, 109pp

2589 **Park, T K** (ed), *Risk and tenure in arid lands: the political ecology of development in the Senegal River basin.* Tucson: University of Arizona Press, 1993, 383pp

2590 **Votz, A,** *Traditionnelle Anbaustrategien westafrikanischer Bauerkulturen.* Munster: Lit, 1990, 243pp

Sociology

2591 **Desai, S,** Children at risk: the role of family structure in Latin America and West Africa, *Population and development review,* **18,** 4 (1992) 689–717

2592 **Onuoha, N,** Nuptiality patterns in two West African states, *Journal of biosocial science,* **25,** 1 (1993) 33–43

2593 **Vimard, P,** Modernité et pluralité familiales en Afrique de l'ouest, *Tiers Monde,* **34,** 133 (1993) 89–115

Urban studies

2594 **James, V U, Nwomonoh, J,** Urban development in West Africa, *African review,* **18,** 1/2 (1991) 20–28

SAHEL

Agriculture, scientific

See also: 2476

2595 Bosc, P M, et al, *Le développement agricole au Sahel. Tome 1: milieux et défis.* Montpellier: CIRAD, 1992, 342pp

Anthropology

See also: 1179

2596 Gaudio, A, *Les populations du Sahara occidental.* Paris: Karthala, 1993, 357pp

Economic and social history

See also: 2598

2597 Dupuy, C, Trois milles ans d'histoire pastorale au sud du Sahara, *Préhistoire anthropologie méditerranénnes,* **1,** (1992) 105–26

Environment

See also: 2612

2598 Barker, R, Documenting oral history in the African Sahel, in Johnson, M (ed), *Lore: capturing traditional environmental knowledge* (Hay River: Dene Cultural Institute, 1992), 113–35

2599 Bernus, E, et al, Le Sahel oublié, *Tiers Monde,* **34,** 134 (1993) 305–26

2600 Boureima, A G, Ecologie et histoire: concepts et conceptions traditionnels sur les sécheresses, famines, et épidémies du Sahel, *Canadian journal of African studies,* **27,** 2 (1993) 260–70

2601 Guichoua, A, Employment and environmental rehabilitation in the Sahel, *International labour review,* **131,** 1 (1992) 111–23

2602 Suhrke, A, *Pressure points: environmental degradation, migration and conflict.* Toronto: University of Toronto, 1993, 67pp

Food

No entry. *See also:* 276, 284, 2600

Gender

2603 van de Walle, F, van de Walle, E, Urban women's autonomy and natural fertility in the Sahel region of Africa, in Federici, N (ed), *Women's position and demographic change* (Oxford: Clarendon, 1993), 61–79

Geography, physical

2604 Lambin, E F, et al, Agricultural production monitoring in the Sahel using remote sensing: present possibilities and research needs, *Journal of environmental management,* **38,** 4 (1993) 301–22

2605 Lebel, T, et al, Hapex-Sahel: vers une meilleure compréhension des mécanismes du climat, *Orstom actualités,* 39 (1993) 7–12

2606 Tauer, W, Humborg, G, *Runoff irrigation in the Sahel zone: remote sensing and geographical information systems for determing potential sites.* Weikersheim: Margraf, 1992, 192pp

History, early

2607 Milburn, N, Inaccurate reporting of cultural information: a growing threat to Saharan studies, in Andah, B W, et al (eds), *Imprints of West Africa's past (Item 2534),* 71–77

International economic relations

2608 Brandt, H, Lembke, H H, Problems and prospects of development aid to Sahelian countries, *Economics,* 43 (1991) 79–90

Literature

2609 **Dieng, B,** Narrative genres and intertextual phenomena in the Sahelian region (myths, epics, and novels), *Research in African literatures,* **24,** 2 (1993) 33–45

Natural resources

2610 **Vedeld, T,** *Local institution building and resource management in the West African Sahel.* London: Overseas Development Institute, 1992, 32pp

Planning

No entry. *See also:* 2611

Rural economy

See also: 1041, 2580, 2604, 2610

2611 **Berthome, J, Mercoiret, J,** *Méthode de planification locale pour les organisations paysannes d'Afrique sahelienne.* Paris: Harmattan, 1993, 349pp

2612 **Horowitz, M M,** Donors and deserts: the political ecology of destructive development in the Sahel, *African environment,* **7,** 25–28 (1990) 185–209

2613 **Marty, A,** La gestions des terroirs et les éleveurs: un outil d'exclusion ou de négociation?, *Tiers Monde,* **34,** 134 (1993) 327–44

2614 **Painter, T M,** *Getting it right: linking concepts and action for improving the use of natural resources in Sahelian West Africa.* London: International Institute for Environment and Development, 1993, 39pp

2615 **Powell, J, Williams, T,** *Livestock, nutrient recycling and sustainable agriculture in the West African Sahel.* London: International Institute for Environment and Development, 1993, 13pp

2616 **Reardon, T,** Cereals demand in the Sahel and potential impacts of regional cereal protection, *World development,* **21,** 1 (1993) 17–35

2617 **Spiers, A, Olsen, O,** *Indigenous integrated farming systems in the Sahel.* Washington: World Bank, 1992, 80pp

2618 **van den Brink, R, et al,** *The economics of Cain and Abel: agropastoral property rights in the Sahel.* Washington: Cornell Food and Nutrition Policy Program, 1991, 37pp

FRANCOPHONE WEST AFRICA

Anthropology

2619 **Gattinari, G C C,** *I Tuareg attraverso la loro poesia orale.* Rome: Consiglio Nazionale delle Recherche, 1992, 760pp

Economic and social history

2620 **Fall, B,** *Le travail forcé en Afrique Occidentale Française (1900–1946).* Paris: Karthala, 1993, 336pp

Finance

2621 **Julienne, R,** L'évolution de la monnaie en AOF de 1955 à 1975, *Mondes et cultures,* **50,** 2–4 (1990) 274–85

History, C20th

2622 **Bernus, E, et al,** *Nomades et commandants: administration et sociétés nomades dans l'ancienne AOF.* Paris: Karthala, 1993, 248pp

2623 **Lambert, M C,** From

citizenship to negritude: making a difference in elite ideologies of colonized French West Africa, *Comparative studies in society and history,* **35,** 2 (1993) 239–62

International economic relations

2624 M'Bet, A, Niamkey, A M, *European economic integration and the Franc zone: the future of the CFA franc after 1996. Part 1: historical background and a new evaluation of monetary cooperation in the CFA countries.* Nairobi: African Economic Research Centre, 1993, 78pp

Library - documentation

2625 Mbaye, S, *Guide des archives de l'Afrique occidentale francaise.* Dakar: Imprimerie Saint-Paul, 1990, 205pp

Literature

2626 Gasster, S, Inside looking out: the journal novel in West African francophone literature, *Modern language studies,* **23,** 3 (1993) 60–72

BENIN

General

2627 Passot, B, *Le Bénin.* Paris: Harmattan, 1993, 335pp

Anthropology

See also: 2643, 2658

2628 Bierschenk, T, The ethnicisation of Fulani society in the Borgou Province of Benin by the ethnologist, *Cahiers d'études africains,* **32,** 127 (1992) 509–520

2629 Iroko, A F, Hommes à queue et traditions en République du Bénin, *Africa (Rome),* **47,** 3 (1992) 413–423

2630 Morton-Williams, P, A Yourba woman remembers servitude in a palace of Dahomey, in the reigns of Kings Glélé and Behanzin, *Africa,* **63,** 1 (1993) 102–117

2631 Palau Marti, M, *Nom, famille et lignage chez les Sabé (République du Bénin).* Paris: Masonneuve et Larose, 1992, 369pp

2632 Tingbé-Azalou, A, Rites funéraires et exhibitionnisme social en milieu Fon du Bénin, *Anthropos,* **88,** 1/2 (1993) 163–69

Architecture

2633 Sinou, A, La valorisation du patrimoine architectural et urbain: l'exemple de la ville de Ouidah au Bénin, *Cahiers des sciences humaines,* **29,** 1 (1993) 33–51

Arts

2634 Adandé, J C E, Histoire de l'art et histoire nationale, *Afrika Zamani,* NS 1 (1993) 23–52

Economic and social history

2635 Adandé, A, Les origines lointaines des peuples de la République du Bénin: problématique et perspectives, *Afrika Zamani,* NS 1 (1993) 65–92

2636 Codo, B, Régime colonial, crises économiques et mutations socio-économique à Ouidah (1927–1937), *Afrika Zamani,* NS 1 (1993) 175–89

2637 Debourou, D, Importance de la vallée du Niger dans l'explication du peuplement du Bargu, *Afrika Zamani,* NS 1 (1993) 149–60

2638 Manning, P, Structure économique et politique économique dans l'histoire du Bénin, *Afrika Zamani,* NS 1 (1993) 163–73

2639 Videgla, M D K, Le 'tramway' de Porto-Novo, Sakété-Pobé (1901–1914) une nouvelle dimension de l'économie coloniale du Dahomey, *Afrika Zamani,* NS 1 (1993) 191–220

Economy - Development

2640 Attolou, A, Problématique du développement à la base au Bénin, *Review of African political affairs,* **4,** 1/2 (1990) 21–41

2641 Collange, G, et al, L'ajustment structurel et les hommes: le cas du Bénin, *Afrique contemporaine,* 167 (1993) 14–28

Education

No entry. *See also:* 2644

Food

2642 Shaw, J, Clay, E, Benin: the multipurpose approach in action, in their *World food aid: experiences of recipients and donors* (London: Currey, 1993), 108–117

Geography, human

No entry. *See also:* 2648

Health & welfare services

2643 Lux, T, *Gespräche mit afrikanischen Krankenpflegern und Heilern: Bilder von Krankheit im Mikrocosmos von Malanville, Benin.* Frankfurt: Lang, 1991, 312pp

History, general

2644 Amoussou, J, Les problèmes de l'enseignement de l'histoire nationale en République du Bénin, *Afrika Zamani,* NS 1 (1993) 265–74

2645 Bagodo, O, Jalons et perspectives pour une approche des problèmes de chronologie dans l'histoire du Baruwu (Bargu) precoloniale, *Afrika Zamani,* NS 1 (1993) 125–48

2646 N'Tia, R, Géopolitiqie de l'Atakora précolonial, *Afrika Zamani,* NS 1 (1993) 107–24

2647 Palau Marti, M, *L'histoire de Sabé et de ses rois (République du Bénin).* Paris: Maisonneuve & Larose, 1992, 343pp

2648 Tchitchi, T Y, Toponymie et histoire nationale, *Afrika Zamani,* NS 1 (1993) 53–64

2649 Tiando, E, L'historiographie du Bénin précolonial septentrional: l'état de la questiom, *Afrika Zamani,* NS 1 (1993) 95–106

History, early

2650 Bagodo, O B, Pour une approche archéologique du peuplement ancienne du Baruwa, in Andah, B W, et al (eds), *Imprints of West Africa's past (Item 2534),* 277–94

History, C18th

2651 Stewart, M H, *Borgu and its kingdoms: a reconstruction of a Western Sudanese polity.* Lewiston: Mellen, 1993, 503pp

History, C19th

2652 Bonfils, J, La mission catholique en République du Bénin: la préfecture apostolique du Dahomey, de 1883 à 1895, *Nouvelle revue de science missionnaire,* **48,** 3 (1992) 203–21

2653 Law, R, The 'amazons' of Dahomey, *Paideuma,* **39,** (1993) 245–60

History, C20th

2654 **Bierschenk, T,** The creation of a tradition: Fulani chiefs in Dahomey/Benin from the late nineteenth century, *Paideuma,* **39,** (1993) 217–44

2655 **Georgy, G,** *L'oiseau sorcier.* Paris: Flammarion, 1993, 330pp

Industry & trade

2656 **Macdonaldo, I,** Building networks: an experiment in support to small urban producers in Benin, *International labour review,* **132,** 2 (1993) 245–64

2657 **Minvielle, J P,** Realisation en coopération d'un système national d'information sur les prix au Bénin, *Orstom actualités,* 37 (1992) 20–23

International economic relations

No entry. *See also:* 3385

International relations

No entry. *See also:* 2655

Literature

2658 **Mediohouan, G,** Vodoun et littérature au Bénin, *Canadian journal of African studies,* **27,** 2 (1993) 245–58

Medical

2659 **Hounsa, A M,** et al, An application of Ajzen's theory of planned behaviour to predict mothers' intention to use oral rehydration therapy in a rural area of Benin, *Social science and medicine,* **37,** 2 (1993) 253–62

Politics

See also: 2654, 3787

2660 **Heilbrunn, J R,** Social origins of national conferences in Benin and Togo, *Journal of modern African studies,* **31,** 2 (1993) 277–99

2661 **Laloupo, P,** La conférence nationale du Bénin: un concept nouveau de changement de régime politique, *Année africaine 1992/93,* 89–114

2662 **Nzouankeu, J M,** The role of the national conference in the transition to democracy in Africa; the cases of Benin and Mali, *Issue,* **21,** 1/2 (1993) 44–50

2663 **Vittin, T E,** Bénin: du 'système Kérékou' au renoveau démocratique, in Médard, J F (ed), *Etats d'Afrique noire (Item 896),* 93–115

Rural economy

2664 **Dissou, M,** L'aide et les priorités internes des politiques agricoles nationales et sa place dans secteur agricole: le cas du Bénin, *Africa development,* **17,** 3 (1992) 139–69

2665 **Kamuanga, M, Murinda, V M,** The value of agroclimatic conditions and farmers' resources level in determing farm typologies; the case of northern Benin, *Singapore journal of tropical geography,* **14,** 1 (1993) 58–71

2666 **Koudokpon, V** (ed), *Pour une recherche participative: stratégie et développement d'une approche de recherche avec les paysans au Bénin.* Amsterdam: KIT, 1993, 96pp

Social welfare

No entry. *See also:* 2641

BURKINA FASO

General

2667 **Aicardi de St Paul, M,** *De la Haute Volta au Burkina Faso: tradition et modernité au pays des hommes intégrés.* Paris: Albatros, 1993, 176pp

2668 **Association 'Decouverte du Burkina',** *Decouverte du Burkina. Tome 1.* Saint Maur: Sepia, 1993, 237pp

Anthropology

See also: 2481, 1674, 2816

2669 **Cros, M,** *Anthropologie du sang en Afrique: essai d'hématologie symbolique chez les Lobi du Burkina Faso et de Côte d'Ivoire.* Paris: Harmattan, 1990, 298pp

2670 **Dacher, M,** Représentation de la paternité dans une société matrilinéaire: les Goin du Burkina Faso, *Journal des Africanistes,* **63,** 2 (1993) 25–49

2671 **Fiéloux, M,** *Biwanté: récit autobiographique d'un Lobi du Burkina Faso.* Paris: Karthala, 1993, 246pp

2672 **Reisman, P, et al,** *First find your child a good mother: the construction of self in two African communities.* New Brunswick: Rutgers University Press, 1992, 241pp

2673 **Ritz-Müller, U,** Bäume des Lebens: zum Naturverständnis is der Westafrikanischen Savanne (Burkina Faso), *Paideuma,* **39,** (1993) 163–76

Arts

2674 **Morganti, N,** L'Africa mediante il cinema: il film 'Wend Kuuni' nella storia e nella cultura dei *mosi* del Burkina Faso, *Afriche,* 17 (1993) 1–47

Current affairs

2675 Mouvement burkinabe des droits de l'homme, *Mission d'observation des élections legisatives du 24 Mai 1992: rapport générale.* Ougadougou: the Movement, 1992, 23pp

Demography

No entry. *See also:* 2682

Economic and social history

2676 **Kiethéga, J B,** Etat des recherches sur la production traditionelle du fer au Burkina Faso, *Afrika Zamani,* NS 1 (1993) 221–46

Environment

See also: 251

2677 **Atampugre, N,** *Behind the lines of stone: the social impact of a soil and water conservation project in the Sahel.* Oxford: Oxfam, 1993, 168pp

2678 **Knierim, A,** *Wahrnehmung von Umweltveränderung: eine Fallstudie bei den Fulbe im Sahel von Burkina Faso.* Bochum: Universität Bochum, Institut für Entwicklungsforschung und Entwicklungspolitik, 1993, 120pp

Gender

See also: 2579

2679 **Dijkman, H, van Dijk, M P,** Female entrepreneurs in the informal sector of Ougagdougou, *Development policy review,* **11,** 3 (1993) 273–88

2680 **Kers, J,** Vrouwen en voedingsvoorlichting: een case-study uit Burkina Faso, *Medische antropologie,* **3,** 2 (1991) 263–275

2681 **Waibel, G,** *Frauen in Burkina Faso: Lebensevrhältnisse, Handlungsperspektiven und Organisationsformen.* Saarbrucken: Breitenbach, 1992, 144pp

2682 **Wollast, E, et al,** Detecting maternal morbidity and mortality by traditional birth attendants in Burkina Faso, *Health policy and planning,* **8,** 2 (1993) 161–68

Geography, physical

2683 **Claude, J,** et al, *Une espace sahélien: la mare d'Oursi, Burkina Faso.* Paris: ORSTOM, 1991, 241pp

Health & welfare services

See also: 379

2684 **Askew, I, et al,** Quality of care in family planning programmes: a rapid assessment in Burkina Faso, *Health policy and planning,* **8,** 1 (1993) 19–32

2685 **Unger, J P, Yada, A,** Should medicines be distributed by health services or pharmacies - a preliminary evaluation of the Boulgou project in Burkina Faso, *Health policy and planning,* **8,** 3 (1993) 240–46

History, general

2686 **Izard, M,** Centralisation du pouvoir: la preuve par la toponymie, *Journal des Africanistes,* **63,** 2 (1993) 5–24

History, early

2687 **Millogo, K A,** Prehistoric researches in Burkina Faso, *Anthropologie,* **97,** 1 (1993) 97–118

2688 **Père, M,** Vers la fin du mystère des ruines du Lobi, *Journal des Africanistes,* **62,** 1 (1992) 79–93

Industry & trade

See also: 2679

2689 **Blanc, F P, et al,** *Les entreprises publiques au Burkina Faso.* Toulouse: Presses de l'IEP, 1990, 189pp

2690 **Cosaert, P,** Le transport en commun urbain au Burkina Faso, in Vennetier, P (ed), *Urbanisation et développement (Item 1161),* 161–69

Law

See also: 2699

2691 **Toe, J Y,** Le rôle du droit dans l'organisation économique: le cas du Burkina Faso, *Revue burkinabè de droit,* 22 (1992) 211–246

Library - documentation

2692 **Gervais, R R,** Archival documents on Upper Volta: here, there and everywhere, *History in Africa,* **20,** (1993) 379–84

Medical

2693 **Curtis, V,** et al, Structured observations on hygiene behaviours in Burkina Faso: validity, variability and utility, *Bulletin of the WHO,* **71,** 1 (1993) 23–32

2694 **Legrand, T K, Mbacke, C S M,** Teenage pregnancy and child health in the urban Sahel, *Studies in family planning,* **24,** 3 (1993) 137–49

2695 **Prazuck, T, et al,** HIV infection and severe malnutrition; a clinical and epidemiologic study in Burkina Faso, *AIDS,* **7,** 1 (1993) 103–108

Politics

See also: 2705

2696 **Banegas, R,** *Insoumissions populaires et révolution au Burkina*

Faso. Talence: Bordeaux University, CEAN, 1993, 140pp

2697 **Mouvement burkinabe des droits de l'homme,** *Démocratie, droits de l'homme et développement: contribution au Forum de reconciliation nationale, Ougadougou, 1992.* Ougadougou: the Movement, 1992, 12,23pp

2698 **Otayek, R,** Une relecture islamique du projet révolutionnaire de Thomas Sankara, in Bayart, J F (ed), *Réligion et modernité politique (item 960)*, 101–27

2699 **Yonaba, S,** La "conférénce nationale" et le droit: les leçons de l'expérience burkinabè, *Revue juridique et politique,* **47,** 1 (1993) 78–108

2700 **Yonaba, S,** Les élections législatives du mai 1992 et la polémique autour de la 'fraude électorale', *Revue burkinabe de droit,* 23 (1993) 11–32

Religion, philosophy

See also: 2698

2701 **Otayek, R,** L'affirmation élitaire des arabisants au Burkina Faso: enjeux et contradictions, in Otayek, R (ed), *Radicalisme islamique (Item 1002)*, 229–52

2702 **van Duc, J,** Quelques apercus relatifs aux pèlerins de la Mecque: les cas des Voltaiques-Burkinabe, *Paideuma,* **39,** (1993) 135–44

Rural economy

See also: 2581, 2677, 2707

2703 **Faure, A,** Niaogho versus Beghedo: un conflit foncier à la veille de la révolution burkinabe, *Cahiers des sciences humaines,* **29,** 1 (1993) 105–119

2704 **Guillaud, D,** *L'ombre du mil: un système agropastoral sahélien en Aribina (Burkina Faso).* Paris: Orstom, 1993, 322pp

2705 **Jacob, J P,** *Relations entre l'administration locale et les organisations locales au Burkina Faso: étude sur le rôle des collectivités publiques locales dans le développement rural.* Vissoie: Association suisse pour le service aux régions et communes, 1992, 140pp

2706 **McMillan, D E, et al,** *Settlement and development in the river blindness control zone: case study - Burkina Faso.* Washington: World Bank, 1993, 160pp

Science & technology

2707 **Pöschl, J,** *Angepasste Technologie für die afrikanische Landwirtschaft: Studie zu einem Mechanierungsprojekt in Burkina Faso.* Frankfurt: Brandes und Apsel, 1992, 151pp

Sociology

2708 **Gorgen, R,** Problems related to schoolgirl pregnancies in Burkina Faso, *Studies in family planning,* **24,** 5 (1993) 283–94

Urban studies

See also: 2690

2709 **Jaglin, S,** Logische fondiarie pubbliche e azioni dei cittadini nella periferia di Ouagadougou, *Storia urbana,* **17,** 63 (1993) 73–98

2710 **Neuvry, G,** L'eau de consommation au Burkina Faso, in Vennetier, P (ed), *Urbanisation et développement (Item 1161)*, 171–90

CHAD

Agriculture, scientific

2711 **Yosko,** I, et al, Essai d'étude des interrelations entre les facteurs de la production dans un système pastoral sahélien du Tchad (Région du Bahr-el-Ghazal), *Revue scientifique du Tchad,* **3,** 1 (1993) 19–27

Anthropology

2712 **Kraton, S,** *La chefferie chez les Ngama.* Paris: Harmattan, 1993, 125pp

2713 **Yosko, I,** Ethnoterritoralité Kréda et dynamique socio-spatiale nationale actuelle, *Revue scientifique du Tchad,* **3,** 1 (1993) 28–31

Current affairs

2714 **Aicardi de St Paul, M,** La Conférence nationale souveraine du Tchad, 15 janvier - 7 avril 1993, *Afrique contemporaine,* 167 (1993) 41–44

Economic and social history

2715 **Creach, P,** *Se nourrir au Sahel: l'alimentation au Tchad, 1937–1939.* Paris: Harmattan, 1993, 167pp

Education

No entry. *See also:* 2716

Gender

2716 **Kouma, C,** The situation surrounding literacy work among the Chadian women, *Journal of the African Association for Literacy and Adult Education,* **6,** 1 (1992)

Health & welfare services

2717 **Lippeveld, T J, et al,** *Transforming health facility-based reporting systems into management information systems: lessons from the Chad experience.* Cambridge, Mass.: Harvard Institute for International Development, 1992, 26pp

2718 **Milleliri, J M, et al,** Le programme élargi de vaccination dans la ville de Sarh (Tchad): bilan de 12 mois d'activités (1988–1989) avec deux enquêtes de couverture vaccinale, *Revue scientifique du Tchad,* **3,** 1 (1993) 72–76

History, C19th

2719 **Vikr, K,** The Sanusi letters: a checklist, *Sudanic Africa,* 3 (1992) 149–62

History, C20th

2720 **Lanne, B,** Résistances et mouvements anticoloniaux au Tchad (1914–1940), *Revue française d'histoire d'outre-mer,* **80,** 300 (1993) 425–42

2721 **Malval, J,** *Ma pratique médicale au Tchad 1926–1928.* Paris: Harmattan, 1993, 136pp

2722 **N'gangbet Kosnaye, M,** *Tribulations d'un jeune tchadien: de l'école coloniale à la prison de l'indépendance.* Paris: Harmattan, 1993, 179pp

Natural resources

2723 **Baroin, C,** Pret, P F, Le palmier de Borkou, végetal social total, *Journal des Africanistes,* **63,** 1 (1993) 5–20

Politics

See also: 2722

2724 **Amnesty International,** *Chad: never again?: killings continue into the 1990s.* London: Amnesty International, 1993, 31pp

2725 **Buijtenhuijs, R,** *La conférence national souveraine du Tchad.* Paris: Karthala, 1993, 216pp

2726 **Magnant, J P,** Tchad: crise de

l'état ou crise de gouvernement?, in Médard, J F (ed), *Etats d'Afrique noire (Item 896)*, 173–203

Rural economy

See also: 2723

2727 **Bruggerman, H,** *Pastoral associations in Chad: experiences from a Oxfam project.* Oxford: Oxfam, 1993, 39pp

2728 **Mahamat, A D, Assegninou, S,** Développement de l'arachide au Tchad, *Revue scientifique du Tchad,* **3,** 1 (1993) 36–38

2729 **Yosko, I, et al,** Un 'modele' de gestion de l'espace pastoral dans la région du Bahr-el-Ghazal (programme de recherche), *Revue scientifique du Tchad,* **3,** 1 (1993) 14–18

COTE D'IVOIRE

Agriculture, scientific

2730 **Leouff, L,** et al (eds), *Environnement et resources aquatiques de Côte d'Ivoire. T 1: le mileu marin.* Paris: Orstom, 1993, 592pp

Anthropology

See also: 2481, 2669

2731 **Adams, M,** To deny death: succession rites among the Wè/Guérê, Canton Boo, Western Côte d'Ivoire, *Zeitschrift fur Ethnologie,* 117 (1992) 89–116

2732 **Coulibaly, M,** Musique et excision chez les Djimini (Côte d'Ivoire), *Cahiers de musiques traditionelles,* 5 (1992) 37–52

2733 **Deluz, A,** Etude longditudinale de villages en Côte d'Ivoire, in *De village en village: espace communitaires de développement* (Paris: PUF, 1992), 75–85

2734 **Deluz, A,** Le meutre de la mère dans le culte du Zamble, *Journal des Africanistes,* **62,** 2 (1992) 183–91

2735 **Haxaire, C,** La palmier à huile chez les Gouro de Côte d'Ivoire, *Journal des Africanistes,* **62,** 1 (1992) 55–77

2736 **Monnet, A,** Poetic idiom among the Akyé of Côte d'Ivoire: the *agnanda nou, Research in African literatures,* **24,** 2 (1993) 109–116

2737 **Ofner, U,** *Modernität als Tradition: von der Crew-men der Küstenboote zur 'Ethnie' der Kru.* Saarbrucken: Breitenbach, 1992, 108pp

2738 **Perrot, C H,** Prophétisme et modernité en Côte d'Ivoire: un village Eotilé et le culte Gbahié, in Bayart, J F (ed), *Réligion et modernité politique (item 960)*, 215–75

2739 **Röhrich, L,** La morale de l'immoralité: à mi-chemin entre la farce et l'histoire moralisante, in Görög-Karady, V (ed), *D'un conte ... à l'autre (item 38)*, 315–25

Demography

No entry. *See also:* 2775

Economic and social history

2740 **Harding, L, Kipre, P** (eds), *Commerce et commerçants en Afrique de l'ouest. Vol. 2: le Côte d'Ivoire.* Paris: Harmattan, 1993, 327pp

2741 **Ibo, G J,** La politique coloniale de protection de la nature en Côte-d'Ivoire (1900–1958), *Revue française d'histoire d'outre-mer,* **80,** 298 (1993) 83–104

2742 **Labazée, P,** Crise, mobilité professionnelle, conversion identitaire. L'exemple du commerce de l'igname à Korhogo (Côte d'Ivoire), *Cahiers d'études africains,* **32,** 127 (1992) 455–468

2743 **Le Pape, M,** L'attraction urbaine: soixante-cinq ans d'observations sur Abidjan, *Cahiers des sciences humaines,* **29,** 2/3 (1993) 333–48

2744 **Rapley, J,** *Ivorien capitalism: African entrepreneurs in Côte d'Ivoire.* Boulder: Lynnne Reinner, 1993, 198pp

2745 **Schwartz, A,** *Sous-peuplement et développement dans le sud-ouest de la Côte d'Ivoire: cinq siècles d'histoire économique et sociale.* Paris: ORSTOM, 1993, 490pp

Economy - Development

See also: 2000

2746 **Bigo, D,** The Lebanese community in the Ivory Coast: a non-native network at the heart of power?, in Hourani, A & Shehadi, N (eds), *The Lebanese in the world* (London: Tauris, 1992), 509–30

2747 **Chamley, C,** Côte d'Ivoire: the failure of structural adjustment, in Thomas, V et al (eds), *Restructuring economies in distress* (Oxford: OUP, 1991), 287–305

2748 **Grootaert, C, Kanbur, R,** *The lucky few amidst economic decline: distributional change in Côte d'Ivoire as seen through panel data sets, 1985–88.* Washington: World Bank, 1993, 36pp

2749 **Jarret, M F, Mahieu, F R,** Ajustement structurel, croissance et répartition: l'exemple de la Côte d'Ivoire, in Mappa, S (ed), *Ambitions et illusions de la coopération Nord-Sud: Lomé IV* (Paris: Harmattan, 1990), 90–114

2750 **Jarret, M F, Mahieu, R,** Structural adjustment, growth and distribution: the case of the Ivory Coast, *African environment,* **7,** 25–28 (1990) 107–33

Education

2751 **Serie, R T,** Une exemple de recherche sur les pratiques de lecture des étudiants Abidjanais, *Africa media review,* **7,** 1 (1993) 73–85

2752 **Vijverberg, P M,** Educational investment and returns for women and men in Côte d'Ivoire, *Journal of human resources,* **28,** 4 (1993) 933–74

Environment

See also: 2730, 2741

2753 **de Rouw, SA,** Regeneration by sprouting in slash and burn cultivation, Tai rain forest, Côte d'Ivoire, *Journal of tropical ecology,* **9,** 3 (1993) 387–401

2754 **van den Breemer, J P M,** Ideas and usage: environment in Aouan society, Ivory Coast, in Croll, E & Parkin, D (eds), *Bush base: forest farm (Item 1040)*, 97–109

Finance

2755 **Ridler, N B,** Fixed exchange rates and structural adjustment programmes: Côte d'Ivoire, *Journal of modern African studies,* **31,** 2 (1993) 301–308

2756 **Togba, Z,** Crise financière et système fiscal: analyse qualitative et quantitative du cas ivoirien (1980–1990), *African journal of international and comparative law,* **4,** 1 (1992) 84–130

Food

2757 **Budd, J W,** Changing food prices and rural welfare: a nonparametric examination of the Côte d'Ivoire, *Economic development and cultural change,* **41,** 3 (1993) 587–603

Gender

See also: 2752

2758 **Gottlieb, A,** Rethinking female pollution: the Beng case, in Sanday, P R & Goodenough, R G (eds), *Beyond the second sex* (Philadelphia: University of Pennsylvania Press, 1990), 113–38

2759 **Guillaume, A,** Women, children and health in Côte d'Ivoire, in Turshen, M (ed), *Women and health (Item 343)*, 169–86

Geography, human

See also: 2863

2760 **Velenchik, A D,** Cash seeking behaviour and migration: a place-to-place migration function for Côte d'Ivoire, *Journal of African economics,* **2,** 3 (1993) 329–47

Health & welfare services

See also: 2759

2761 **Dor, A, van der Gaag, J,** Quantity rationing and the demand of adults for medical care in rural Côte d'Ivoire, in Mills, A & Lee, K (eds), *Health economics research in developing countries* (Oxford: OUP, 1993), 193–213

2762 **Kouame, E K, Sia, J N,** Les formes de communication traditionelles en Côte d'Ivoire et leur utilisation en matière d'éducation pour la santé, *Africa media review,* **7,** 2 (1993) 17–29

History, general

2763 **Boutillier, J L,** *Bouna, royaume de la savanne ivoirienne.* Paris: Karthala, 1993, 399pp

2764 **Derive, J,** Gestion de la variabilité des récits historiques dans une communauté dioula de Côte d'Ivoire, in Görög-Karady, V (ed), *D'un conte ... à l'autre (item 38)*, 291–300

History, early

2765 **Biot, B,** Problematique des sites 'mesoneolithiques' du Baoule-sud, in Andah, B W, et al (eds), *Imprints of West Africa's past (Item 2534)*, 220–42

2766 **Fofana, L,** Problematique de la metallurgie ancienne du fer en Côte d'Ivoire precoloniale, in Andah, B W, et al (eds), *Imprints of West Africa's past (Item 2534)*, 257–76

History, C20th

2767 **Grah Mel, F,** *Marcel Treich-Laplène, précurseur de la Côte d'Ivoire.* Abidjan: Université nationale de la Côte d'Ivoire, 1991, 207pp

Industry & trade

See also: 451

2768 **Baha-Bi, Y,** Les P.M.E. ivoiriennes, difficile promotion des entreprises nationales, *Cahiers de sociologie économique et culturelle,* 18 (1992) 115–130

2769 **Boone, C,** Commerce in Côte d'Ivoire: ivoirianisation without Ivoirian traders, *Journal of modern African studies,* **31,** 1 (1993) 67–92

2770 **Marcel, K B,** Restructuration et évolution de l'emploi dans le secteur public et para-public en Côte d'Ivoire, *Africa development,* **17,** 1 (1992) 93–112

International economic relations

2771 **Tuho, C V,** *L'économie ivoirienne et la Communauté économique européene.* Abidjan: CEDA, 1992, 288pp

Labour & manpower

2772 **Grootaert, C,** The position of migrants in the urban informal labour markets in Côte d'Ivoire, *Journal of African economics,* **1,** 3 (1992) 416–45

Law

2773 **Goffri-Lawson, M F,** La protection des droits de l'homme par la constitution: le cas de la Côte d'Ivoire, *Annual conference (African Society of Comparative and International Law),* **3,** (1991) 51–56

Media

2774 **Kourouma, M,** Dix ans de contentieux électoral municipal en Côte d'Ivoire (1981–1991), *Penant,* **103,** 813 (1993) 292–322

Medical

2775 **Koné, H,** Recherche en communication en matière de population: cas d'un projet de communication en planification familiale, *Africa media review,* **7,** 1 (1993) 51–71

2776 **Buehler, J W, et al,** Surveillance definitions for AIDS, *AIDS,* **7,** 1 (1993) 73–81

2777 **Caprara, A, et al,** The perception of AIDS in the Bété and Baoulé of the Ivory Coast, *Social science and medicine,* **36,** 9 (1993) 1229–35

2778 **Cowley, P,** Preliminary cost-effectiveness analysis of an AIDS vaccine in Abidjan, Ivory Coast, *Health policy,* **24,** 2 (1993) 145–53

2779 **Decock, R M, et al,** Epidemiology and transmission of HIV–2: why there is no HIV–2 pandemic, *Journal of the American Medical Association,* **270,** 17 (1993) 2083–86

2780 **Deniaud, F,** SIDA, préservatifs et jeunesse urbaine en Côte d'Ivoire: un essai d'ethnoprevention, *Bulletin liaison CNDT,* no. spécial (1991) 49–69

2781 **Dozon, J P, Vidal, L** (eds), *Les sciences sociales face au SIDA: cas africains autour de l'exemple ivoirien.* Abidjan: ORSTOM, 1993, 391pp

2782 **Lucas, S B, et al,** The mortality and pathology of HIV infection in a West African city, *AIDS,* 7, 12 (1993) 1569–79

2783 **Msellati, P, et al,** *Bibliographie des travaux sur le SIDA en Côte d'Ivoire.* Abidjan: ORSTOM, 1993, var pag.

2784 **Sibili, Y, et al,** *Aspects socio-culturels du SIDA dans le milieu urbain périphérique d'Abidjan (Côte d'Ivoire): rapport final.* Abidjan: Comité national de lutte contre le SIDA, 1991, 102pp

2785 **Various authors,** *Séminaire national pour la mobilisation de l'Eglise dans la lutte contre le SIDA.* Abidjan: Caritas, 1993, 100pp

Politics

See also: 2774, 2790

2786 **Bakary, T D,** Côte d'Ivoire: l'étatisation de l'état, in Médard, J F (ed), *Etats d'Afrique noire (Item 896),* 53–91

2787 **Fauré, Y,** Democracy and realism: reflections on the case of Côte d'Ivoire, *Africa,* **63,** 3 (1993) 313–29

2788 **Loucou, J N,** *Le multipartisme en Côte d'Ivoire.* Abidjan: Neter, 1992, 213pp

Rural economy

See also: 2581, 2742, 2863, 2944

2789 **Delaunay, K,** Bodwiche Aïvi:

un filet, deux filets, trois filets...: biographie d'un pêcheur ghanéen en Côte d'Ivoire, *Plein sud,* 1 (1991) 4147

2790 **Niho, O,** Conflits fonciers dans les forêts classées: le cas du périmètre papetier du Rapide Grah et du Monogaga dans le sud-ouest de la Côte d'Ivoire, *African journal of international and comparative law,* **4,** 2 (1992) 353–368

2791 **Paton, J,** *The intra-household allocation of resources in the Côte d'Ivoire: is there evidence of gender bias?* Oxford & Turin: International Development Centre & Centro Studi Luca d'Agliano, 1993, 37pp

2792 **Widner, J A,** The origins of agricultural policy in Côte d'Ivoire, *Journal of development studies,* **29,** 4 (1993) 25–59

Social welfare

2793 **Ainsworth, M,** *Economic aspects of child fostering in Côte d'Ivoire.* Washington: World Bank, 1993, 43pp

Urban studies

See also: 1145, 2863

2794 **Dubresson, A,** Decentramento e problemi fondiari nelle citta interne della Costa d'Avorio, *Storia urbana,* **17,** 63 (1993) 99–118

2795 **Grégoire, E, Labazée, P,** Mobilité marchande et urbanisation: les cas de Kohogo (Côte d'Ivoire) et de Maradi (Niger), *Cahiers des sciences humaines,* **29,** 2/3 (1993) 527–46

GAMBIA

Agriculture, scientific

2796 **Owens, S,** Catholic Relief Services in the Gambia: evolution from agricultural research to community-based experimentation, in Wellard, K & Copestake, J C (eds), *NGOs and the state (Item 1096)*, 239–50

2797 **Sarch, M T,** Case study of the Farmer Innovation and Technology Testing Programme in the Gambia, in Wellard, K & Copestake, J C (eds), *NGOs and the state (Item 1096)*, 225–38

Anthropology

2798 **Beckerley, S,** The interplay of precedence and patronage in Mandinka village politics, *Cambridge anthropology,* **16,** 1 (1992) 45–60

Economy - Development

No entry. *See also:* 3705

Gender

2799 **Barrett, H, Browne, A,** The impact of labour-saving devices on the lives of rural African women: grain mills in the Gambia, in Momsen, J H & Kinnaird, V (eds), *Different places, different voices (Item 332)*, 52–62

2800 **Pickering, H, Wilkins, H A,** Do unmarried women of Africa have to sell sex, or is it a mater of choice?, *Health transition review,* **3,** (1993) supplementary issue, 17–27

2801 **Schroeder, R A,** Shady practice: gender and political ecology of resource stabilisation in Gambian garden/orchards, *Economic geography,* **69,** 4 (1993) 349–65

Geography, physical

2802 **Anyadike, R N C,** Patterns and variations of rainfall over Banjul, Gambia, *Singapore journal of tropical geography,* **14,** 1 (1993) 1–14

Health & welfare services

See also: 2870

2803 **Robertson, R L, et al,** Cost-effectiveness of immunisation: the Gambia revisited, *Health policy and planning,* **7,** 2 (1992) 111–22

Industry & trade

2804 **Dieke, P O C,** Tourism in the Gambia: some issues in development policy, *World development,* **21,** 2 (1993) 277–83

International relations

No entry. *See also:* 3705

Labour & manpower

See also: 609

2805 **Murrell, K L,** Evaluation as action research: the case of the Management Development Institute in the Gambia, West Africa, *International journal of public administration,* **16,** 3 (1993) 341–56

Law

2806 **Hunt, P,** Children's rights in West Africa; the case of the Gambia's *almudos, Human rights quarterly,* **15,** 3 (1993) 499–532

Politics

See also: 2798

2807 **Fye, S M B,** Experience in administrative reform with particular reference to structural adjustment programme (SAP) - the case of Gambia, *African administrative studies,* 39 (1992) 35–57

2808 **Sall, E,** La Gambie: un état exigu et enclavé, in Médard, J F (ed), *Etats d'Afrique noire (Item 896),* 15–52

Rural economy

See also: 2801

2809 **Rawlings, P, et al,** Ownership patterns and management of small ruminants, equines and pigs in the Gambia, *African livestock research,* **1,** 2 (1992) 50–56

2810 **Sarch, M T, Copestake, J C,** The Gambia: country overview, in Wellard, K & Copestake, J C (eds), *NGOs and the state (Item 1096),* 213–24

2811 **Ulijaszek, S J,** Influence of birth interval and child labour on family energy requirements and dependency ratios in two traditional subsistence economies in Africa, *Journal of biosocial science,* **25,** 1 (1993) 79–86

GHANA

General

2812 **Drucker-Brown, S,** Mamprusi witchcraft, subversion and changing gender relations, *Africa,* **63,** 4 (1993) 531–49

Agriculture, scientific

2813 **Kolbilla, D, Wellard, K,** Langbensi Agricultural Station: experience of agricultural research, in Wellard, K & Copestake, J C (eds), *NGOs and the state (Item 1096),* 202–210

Anthropology

See also: 2481, 2812, 2929

2814 **Dzakpasu, C C K,** *Some aspects of tradition and culture among the Anlo and Dzodze Ewe.* Kumasi: Dela, 1991, 18pp

2815 **McLeod, M D,** L'arte nel quotidiano. L'artigianato degli Asante del Ghana, techniche, uso practico e valore simbolico, *Afriche,* 19 (1993) 6–32

2816 **Scott, R,** Le caillou et la boue: les traditions orales en tant que légitimation des autorités traditionelles chez les Bulsa (Ghana) et les Lyéla (Burkina Faso), *Paideuma,* **39,** (1993) 145–62

2817 **Tengan, E,** *The land as being and cosmos: the institution of the earth cult among the Sisala of northwestern Ghana.* Frankfurt: Lang, 1991, 243pp

2818 **Wiredu, K,** African philosophical tradition: a case study of the Akan, *Philosophical forum,* **24,** 1 (1993) 35–62

Arts

2819 **Agovi, K E,** The origin of literary theatre in Ghana, *Research review (Legon),* **6,** 1 (1990) 1–23

Current affairs

2820 **Commonwealth Secretariat,** Observer Group, *The presidential election in Ghana: 3 November, 1992.* London: The Secretariat, 1992, 144pp

Demography

2821 **Sichona, F J,** The polygyny-fertility hypothesis revisited: the situation in Ghana, *Journal of biosocial science,* **25,** 4 (1993) 473–82

Economic and social history

2822 **Agbodeka, F,** *An economic history of Ghana from the earliest times.* Accra: Ghana Universities Press, 1993 (dated 1992), 182pp

2823 **Dumett, R,** Disease and mortality among gold miners of Ghana: colonial government and mining company attitudes and policies, 1900–1938, *Social science and medicine,* **37,** 2 (1993) 213–32

2824 **Nováky, G,** Small company trade and the Gold Coast: the Swedish Africa Company 1650–1663, *Itinerario,* **16,** 1 (1992) 57–76

2825 **Rathbone, R,** Some aspects of the prehistory of the Ghanaian economy, *Journal of Commonwealth and comparative politics,* **31,** 1 (1993) 7–19

Economy - Development

See also: 1896, 2930

2826 **Anyemedu, K,** The economic policies of the PNDC, in Gyimah-Boadi, E (ed), *Ghana under PNDC rule (item 2927),* 13–47

2827 **Baffoe, J K,** Income distribution and poverty profile in Ghana 1987–1988, *African development review,* **4,** 1 (1992) 1–28

2828 **Boachie-Danquah, Y,** Structural adjustment programmes and welfare interventions: the case of Ghana, *Africa insight,* **22,** 4 (1992) 244–48

2829 **Goldman, R H, et al,** *Ghana's development: strategic lessons from Asia.* Cambridge, Mass.: Harvard Institute for International Development, 1992, 113pp

2830 **Gordon, D V, Sakyi-Bejoe, K,** Testing the export-growth hypothesis: some parametric and non-parametric results for Ghana, *Appled economics,* **25,** 4 (1993) 553–63

2831 **Kimble, H,** The impact of structural adjustment on Ghana's economy, in Nett, B et al (eds), *Agricultural transformation (Item 1069)*, 17–50

2832 **Kusi, N K,** Macroeconomic adjustments, economic growth and the balance of payments in Ghana 1983–1988, *Journal of international development,* **4,** 5 (1992) 541–59

2833 **Leechor, C,** Ghana: ending chaos, in Thomas, V et al (eds), *Restructuring economies in distress* (Oxford: OUP, 1991), 309–38

2834 **Leith, J C, Lofchie, M F,** The political economy of structural adjustment in Ghana, in Bates, R H & Krueger, A O (eds), *Political and economic interactions in economic policy reform* (Oxford: Blackwell, 1993), 225–93

2835 **Otubusin, P O,** The Ghanaian economy as a test case: an application of competing theories, in his *Exploitation, unequal exchange and dependency* (New York: Lang, 1992), 135–53

2836 **Sams, A H,** Household welfare during crisis and adjustment in Ghana, *Journal of African economics,* **2,** 2 (1993) 195–237

2837 **Younger, S,** *Ghana: economic recovery programme: a case study of stabilization and structural adjustment in subsaharan Africa.* Washington: World Bank, 1990, 58pp

2838 **Lloyd, C B, Brandon, A J,** *Does sibsize matter?: the implications of family size for children's education in Ghana.* New York: Population Council, 1992, 45pp

Education

No entry. *See also:* 213, 2960

Environment

2839 **Dei, G J S,** A forest beyond the trees: tree-cutting in rural Ghana, *Human ecology,* **20,** 1 (1992) 57–88

2840 **Hogg, D,** *The SAP in the forest: the environmental and social impacts of structural adjustment programmes in the Phillipines, Ghana and Guyana.* London: Friends of the Earth, 1993, 165pp

2841 **Oppong, J E,** Desertification in northern Ghana, *Desertification control bulletin,* 23 (1993) 44–49

2842 **Osie, W Y,** Woodfuel and deforestation: answers for a sustainable environment, *Journal of environmental management,* **37,** 1 (1993) 51–62

2843 **Schmidt-Wulffen, W,** Environmental perception of African peasants and European experts - acting between fiction and reality: a case study of Ghana, *Geographische Zeitschrift,* **80,** 3 (1992) 160–73

Finance

See also: 1896

2844 **Atyeetey, E, Gockel, F,** *Mobilising domestic resources for capital formation in Ghana: the role of informal financial sectors.* Nairobi: Initiatives, 1991, 67pp

2845 **Botchway, K,** Deregulating the foreign exchange market in Ghana, in Rimmer, D (ed), *Action in Africa (Item 525)*, 34–39

2846 **Gyimah-Brempong, K,** Exchange control and black market exchange rate in Ghana: a simultaneous equation approach, *Eastern African economic review,* **8,** 1 (1992) 41–53

2847 **Younger, S D,** Testing the link between devaluation and inflation: time series evidence from Ghana, *Journal of African economics,* **1,** 3 (1992) 369–94

Food

2848 Alderman, H, Intercommodity price transmittal: analysis of food markets in Ghana, *Oxford bulletin of economics and statistics,* **55,** 1 (1993) 43–64

2849 Devereux, S, Goats before ploughs, dilemmas of household response sequencing during food shortages, *IDS bulletin,* **24,** 4 (1993) 52–59

2850 Ferguson, E L, Seasonal food consumption patterns and dietary diversity of rural preschool Ghanaian and Malawian childfen, *Ecology of food and nutrition,* **29,** 3 (1993) 219–34

2851 Manu, F A, The state and marketing in Africa: a case study of Ghana, *Journal of international food and agribusiness marketing,* **4,** 2 (1992) 67–82

Gender

2852 Abudulai, S, Bawka East Women's Development Association (BEWDA), *Yearbook of cooperative enterprise 1993,* 195–205

2853 Ampofo, A A, Controlling and punishing women: violence against Ghanaian women, *Review of African political economy,* 56 (1993) 102–110

2854 Ardayfio-Schandorf, E, Household energy supply and rural women's work in Ghana, in Momsen, J H & Kinnaird, V (eds), *Different places, different voices (Item 332),* 15–29

2855 Asimeng, M, Women in Ghana: their integration in socioeconomic development, *Research review (Legon),* **6,** 1 (1990) 57–68

2856 Awusabo-Asare, K, et al, Women's control over their sexuality and the spread of STDs and HIV/AIDS in Ghana, *Health transition review,* **3,** (1993) supplementary issue, 69–84

2857 Clark, G, Women traders in Ghana and the structural adjustment program, in Gladwin, C H (ed), *Structural adjustment and African women farmers (Item 315),* 217–36

2858 Ghartey, N K T, *The training of women for managerial capabilities in the modern economy of Ghana.* Bradford: University of Bradford. Development and Project Planning Centre, 1992, 44pp

2859 Kost, T K, Callenius, C, *Ghanaische Frauen erzählen aus ihrem Alltage: Problemanalyse aus der Sicht von Frauen eines Dorfes in Nord-Ghana.* Hamburg: Institut für Afrika-Kunde, 1992, 214pp

2860 Lloyd, C B, Gage-Brandon, A, Women's role in maintaining households: family welfare and sexual inequality in Ghana, *Population studies,* **47,** 1 (1993) 115–32

2861 Manuh, T, Women, the state and society under the PNDC, in Gyimah-Boadi, E (ed), *Ghana under PNDC rule (item 2927),* 176–95

2862 Okine, V, The survival strategies of poor families in Ghana and the role of women therein, in Massiah, J (ed), *Women in developing economies: making visible the invisible* (Oxford: Berg, 1993), 167–94

Geography, human

2863 Schaaf, T, Manshard, W, The significance of towns as central places for rural development in the border region of Ghana and the Ivory Coast, *Applied geography and development,* 40 (1992) 39–50

2864 Songsore, J, McGranahan, G, Environment, wealth and health: toward an analysis of interurban differentials within Greater Accra Metropolitan Area, Ghana, *Environment and urbanisation,* **5,** 2 (1993) 10–34

Health & welfare services

See also: 2864

2865 Bermejo, A, Bekui, A, Community participation in disease control, *Social science and medicine,* **36,** 9 (1993) 1145–50

2866 Cassels, A, Janovsky, K, A time of change: health policy, planning and organisation in Ghana, *Health policy and planning,* **7,** 2 (1992) 144–54

2867 Eades, C A, Traditional birth attendants and maternal mortality in Ghana, *Social science and medicine,* **36,** 11 (1993) 1503–1507

2868 Ego, M L, Moran, M, HIV/AIDS counselling program: a rural Ghana experience, *Health transition review,* **3,** (1993) supplementary issue, 85–92

2869 Fosu, G B, The use of injections for treating childhood diseases: determinants and consequences for preventive health care in developing countries, *Sociological focus,* **25,** 4 (1992) 329–44

2870 Issaka-Tionorgah, A, Waddington, C, Encouraging efficiency through programme and functional budgeting: lessons from experience in Ghana and the Gambia, in Mills, A & Lee, K (eds), *Health economics research in developing countries* (Oxford: OUP, 1993), 335–50

2871 Kirby, J P, The islamic dialogue with African traditional religion: divination and health care, *Social science and medicine,* **36,** 3 (1993) 237–48

2872 Lavy, V, Quigley, J M, *Willingness to pay for the quality and intensity of medical care: low-income households in Ghana.* Washington: World Bank, 1993, 39pp

2873 Nkrumah, F K, *The quality of child life and health: an indictment against society.* Accra: Ghana Universities Press, 1992, 13pp

History, general

2874 Carmichael, J, *African eldorado: Ghana from Gold Coast to independence.* London: Duckworth, 1993, 224pp

History, early

2875 Nunoo, R, Thurstan Shaw and West African archaeology: the case of Ghana, in Andah, B W, et al (eds), *Imprints of West Africa's past (Item 2534),* 25–32

History, C18th

2876 Decorse, C R, Culture contact, continuity, and change on the Gold Coast, AD 1400–1900, *African archaeological review,* **10,** (1992) 163–196

2877 Decorse, C R, The Danes on the Gold Coast: culture change and European presence, *African archaeological review,* **11,** (1993) 148–73

History, C19th

2878 Baku, K, History and national development: the case of John Mensah Sarbah and the reconstruction of Gold Coast history, *Research review (Legon),* **6,** 1 (1990) 36–48

2879 Wilks, I, *Forests of gold.* Athens, Ohio: Ohio University Press, 1993, 388pp

2880 Wilson, L E, *The Krobo people of Ghana to 1892: a political and social history.* Athens, Ohio: Ohio University, Centre for

International Studies, 1992, 253pp

History, C20th

2881 **Allman, J M,** *The quills of the porcupine: Asante nationalism in an emergent Ghana.* Madison: Wisconsin University Press, 1993, 263pp

2882 **Gilbert, M,** The Cimmerian darkness of intrigue: Queen Mothers, Christianity and truth in Akuapem history, *Journal of religion in Africa,* **23,** 1 (1993) 2–43

2883 **Gocking, R,** British justice and the Native Tribunals of the southern Gold Coast Colony, *Journal of African history,* **34,** 1 (1993) 91–113

2884 **Israel, A M,** The Afrocentric perspective in African journalism: a case study of the *Ashanti Pioneer,* 1939–1957, *Journal of Black studies,* **23,** 2 (1992) 411–28

2885 **Kramer, R S,** Two Tidjani scholars of Kumasi, Ghana: biographical notes, *Islam et sociétés au Sud du Sahara,* 6 (1992) 71–74

2886 **Lentz, C,** Histories and political conflict: a case study of chieftancy in Nandom, northwestern Ghana, *Paideuma,* **39,** (1993) 177–215

2887 **Rathbone, R,** Police intelligence in Ghana in the late 1940s, *Journal of imperial and Commonwealth history,* **21,** 3 (1993) 107–28

Industry & trade

See also: 2857, 2948

2888 **Chigabatia, L Y,** Information system on state-owned enterprises in Ghana, *Public enterprise,* **12,** 3–4 (1992) 251–262

2889 **Dawson, J,** Development of small-scale industry in Ghana: a case study of Kumasi, in Thomas, H et al (eds), *Small-scale production: strategies for industrial restructuring* (London: Intermediate Technology Publications, 1991), 173–207

2890 **Eades, J S,** *Strangers and traders: Yoruba migrants, markets and the state in northern Ghana.* Edinburgh: Edinburgh University Press, 1993, 234pp

2891 **Jebuni, C D, et al,** *Diversifying exports: the supply response of non-traditional exports to Ghana's Economic Recovery Programme.* London: Overseas Development Institute, 1992, 64pp

2892 **Technology Transfer Centre,** *Report on capital goods sector: strengthening the national capacity for the transfer, utilisation and development of technology.* Accra: Technology Transfer Centre, 1990, 113pp

International economic relations

No entry. *See also:* 2930

International relations

2893 **Agyeman, O,** *Nkrumah's Ghana and East Africa: panafricanism and African interstate relations.* Rutherford: Farleigh Dickinson University Press, 1992, 234pp

2894 **Boafo-Arthur, K,** Ghana's external relations since 31 December 1981, in Gyimah-Boadi, E (ed), *Ghana under PNDC rule (item 2927)*, 135–53

Labour & manpower

See also: 2858

2895 **Aboagye, A A,** *Employment in the urban informal sector in Ghana: report of a survey of informal sector enterprises in Accra, Kumasi and Tema.* Addis Ababa: ILO, JASPA, 1992, 84pp

2896 **Gyimah-Boadi, E, Essuman-Johnson, A,** The PNDC and organised labour: the anatomy of political control, in Gyimah-Boadi, E (ed), *Ghana under PNDC rule (item 2927)*, 196–212

2897 **Ofei-Nkansah, K,** Empowering self-employed rural workers: the role of the General Agricultural Workers Union in Ghana, in Sandbrook, R & Halfani, M (eds), *Empowering people (Item 930)*, 76–81

Law

See also: 2883

2898 **Dankwa, E V O,** Implementation of international human rights instruments: Ghana as an illustration, *Annual conference (African Society of Comparative and International Law)*, **3,** (1991) 57–64

2899 **Gyimah, S,** Legal aid and human rights: the case of Ghana, in Sandbrook, R & Halfani, M (eds), *Empowering people (Item 930)*, 52–56

2900 **Oquaye, M,** Law, justice and the revolution, in Gyimah-Boadi, E (ed), *Ghana under PNDC rule (item 2927)*, 154–75

2901 **Wallace-Bruce, N L,** Ghana's legal aid scheme: a worthy beginning, *African journal of international and comparative law,* **4,** 4 (1992) 905–926

Library - documentation

2902 **Akotia, P,** Judicial and legal records in the National Archives of Ghana/Accra: an introduction for users, *History in Africa,* **20,** (1993) 361–67

2903 **Akussah, H,** A calendar of Kwame Nkrumah papers in the Documentation Centre of the Institute of African Studies, University of Ghana, 1935–1848, *African research and documentation,* 61 (1993) 12–25

2904 **Alemna, A A,** Libraries in research and scholarship in Ghana, *African research and documentation,* 57 (1991) 6–14

2905 **Alemna, A A,** Professional education and subsequent careers: a follow-up study of former students of the Department of Library and Archival Studies, University of Ghana, Legon, *Education for information,* **11,** 1 (1993) 57–63

2906 **Amissah-Arthur, M,** New dimensions of library services in Ghana, *African research and documentation,* 58 (1992) 16–19

Literature

2907 **Kolawole, M E M,** Kofi Awoonor as a prophet of conscience, *African languages and cultures,* **5,** 2 (1992) 125–32

2908 **Kropp Dakubu, M E,** Search sweet country and the language of authentic being, *Research in African literatures,* **24,** 1 (1993) 19–35

2909 **Ogede, O S,** The rhetoric of revolution in Armah's The healers: form as experience, *African studies review,* **36,** 1 (1993) 43–58

2910 **Sarr, N,** The use of sensory imagery in The beautyful one's are not yet born, *Université, recherche et développement,* 1 (1993) 93–99

2911 **Wright, D** (ed), *Critical perspectives on Ayei Kwesi Armah.* Washington: Three Continents Press, 1992, 354pp

2912 **Wright, D,** Man and his Teacher: a note on double-narrative, *World literature written in English,* **31,** 2 (1991) 78–83

Media

See also: 2884

2913 **Dekutsey, W A,** Ghana: a case study in publishing development, *Logos,* **4,** 2 (1993) 66–73

Medical

See also: 2856

2914 **Agyepong, I A,** Malaria: ethnomedical perceptions and practice in an Adangbe farming community and implications for control, *Social science and medicine,* **35,** 2 (1992) 131–37

2915 **Anarfi, J K,** Sexuality, migration and AIDS in Ghana - a socio-behavioural study, *Health transition review,* **3,** (1993) supplementary issue, 45–67

2916 **Chinery, W A,** *Impact of socio-economic development on populations of of some parasites and vectors in Ghana.* Accra: Ghana Universities Press, 1993 (dated 1990), 55pp

2917 **Hunter, J M,** Elephantiasis: a disease of development in northeast Ghana, *Social science and medicine,* **35,** 5 (1992) 627–49

Natural resources

See also: 791, 2839, 2842

2918 **Gyasi, E,** Emergence of a new oil palm belt in Ghana, *Tidschrift voor economische en sociale geografie,* **83,** 1 (1992) 39–49

2919 **Wereko-Bobby,** Innovative energy policy instruments and institutional reform: the case of Ghana, in Karekezi, S & Mackenzie, G A (eds), *Energy options (Item 796)*, 23–38

Politics

See also: 1896, 2899

2920 **Ampaw, A,** The contribution of NGOs to democratic transition in Ghana, in Sandbrook, R & Halfani, M (eds), *Empowering people (Item 930)*, 189–97

2921 **Asibuo, S K,** Military regime performance in decentralisation and local administration for development: a Ghanaian case study, *Africa insight,* **22,** 4 (1992) 283–87

2922 **Asibuo, S K,** The performance of local government: lessons from Ghana, an experiment that failed, *African management development forum,* **2,** 2 (1991) 38–41

2923 **Asibuo, S K,** The Provisional National Defence Council (PNDC) and the District Assemblies in Ghana: an analysis of the new Local Government Law, 1988 (PNDCL 207), *African review,* **18,** 1/2 (1991) 10–19

2924 **Ayee, J R A,** Decentralisation and local government under the PNDC, in Gyimah-Boadi, E (ed), *Ghana under PNDC rule (item 2927)*, 114–34

2925 **Ayee, J R A,** Decentralization under Ghana's Fourth Republican Constitution, *Verfassung und Recht in Übersee,* **25,** 4 (1992) 394–406

2926 **Folson, K G,** Ideology, revolution and development: the years of J J Rawlings, in Gyimah-Boadi, E (ed), *Ghana under PNDC rule (item 2927)*, 74–99

2927 **Gyimah-Boadi, E** (ed), *Ghana under PNDC rule.* Dakar: Codesria, 1993, 221pp

2928 **Gyimah-Boadi, E,** The search for economic development and democracy in Ghana: from Limann to Rawlings, in Gyimah-Boadi, E (ed), *Ghana under PNDC rule (item 2927)*, 1–12

2929 **Haynes, J A,** Sustainable democracy in Ghana? Problems and prospects, *Third world quarterly,* **14,** 3 (1993) 451–68

2930 **Herbst, J,** *The politics of reform in Ghana, 1982–1991.* Berkeley: University of California Press, 1993, 180pp

2931 **Jeffries, R, Thomas, C,** The Ghanaian elections of 1992, *African affairs,* **92,** 368 (1993) 331–66

2932 **Laryea, E O,** The rejuvenation of local government in Ghana, in Sandbrook, R & Halfani, M (eds), *Empowering people (Item 930),* 146–50

2933 **Ninsin, K A,** Some problems in Ghana's transition to democratic governance, *Africa development,* **18,** 2 (1993) 5–22

2934 **Ninsin, K A,** Strategies of mobilisation under the PNDC government, in Gyimah-Boadi, E (ed), *Ghana under PNDC rule (item 2927),* 100–113

2935 **Ninsin, K A, Drah, F K** (eds), *Political parties and democracy in Ghana's Fourth Republic.* Accra: Woeli, 1993, 258pp

2936 **Petchenkine, Y,** *Ghana in search of stability, 1957–1992.* Westport: Praeger, 1992, 242pp

2937 **Rawlings, J J,** Leadership in defiance (interview), *Africa forum,* **2,** 2 (1992) 10–17

Religion, philosophy

See also: 2885

2938 **da Silva, J A,** African independent churches: origin and development, *Anthropos,* **88,** 3/4 (1993) 393–402

2939 **Kirby, J P,** Anthropology of knowledge and the christian dialogue with African traditional religions, *Missiology,* **20,** 3 (1992) 323–41

2940 **Owusu-Mensa, K,** *Saturday God and adventism in Ghana.* Frankfurt: Lang, 1993, 102pp

2941 **Yoda, L,** The influence of the USA on the political ideas of Kwame Nkrumah, *Round table,* **82,** 326 (1993) 187–98

Rural economy

See also: 1030, 1052, 2175, 2859, 2863, 2897

2942 **Addo, N O, Kwegyir, A E K,** *Short-term circular migration in the context of socio-economic development in rural Ghana: the case of rice farmers in some selected rural communities in the north-eastern Volta region.* Geneva: ILO, 1991, 135pp

2943 **Adu-Aryee, V Q,** Resettlement in Ghana: from Akasombo to Kpong, in Cernea, M M & Guggenheim, S E (eds), *Anthropological approaches to resettlement (item 1112),* 133–51

2944 **Alpine, R W L, Pickett, J,** *Agriculture, liberalisation and economic growth in Ghana and Côte d'Ivoire: 1960–1990.* Paris: OECD Development Centre, 1993, 137pp

2945 **Amanor, K, et al,** Ghana: country overview, in Wellard, K & Copestake, J C (eds), *NGOs and the state (Item 1096),* 183–94

2946 **Anyimadu, A,** Some institutional aspects of agricultural development policy under the PNDC, in Gyimah-Boadi, E (ed), *Ghana under PNDC rule (item 2927),* 60–73

2947 **Dorm-Adzobu, C, et al,** Agroforestry by mobisquads in Ghana, in Hudson, N & Cheatle, R J (eds), *Working with farmers (Item 245),* 165–69

2948 **Edusah, S, Tribe, M,** *Rural small-scale industries in Ghana's economic development: an agenda for research.* Bradford: University of Bradford. Development and Project Planning Centre, 1992, 30pp

2949 **Fosu, K Y,** Domestic public policy and Ghana's agriculture, 1982–89, in Gyimah-Boadi, E (ed), *Ghana under PNDC rule (item 2927),* 48–59

2950 **Koney, E B M,** *Livestock production and health in Ghana.* Accra: Advent Press, 1992, 158pp

2951 **Lebiyika, M,** The Association of Church Development Projects (ACDEP) in northern Ghana, in Wellard, K & Copestake, J C (eds), *NGOs and the state (Item 1096)*, 195–201

2952 **Schmidt-Wulffen, W D,** Ghanaische Kleinbauern zwischen Agrarmodernisierung und standortgerechtem Landbau, *Afrika spektrum,* 1 (1993) 54–72

2953 **Sefa Dei, G J,** The renewal of a Ghananian rural economy, *Canadian journal of African studies,* **26,** 1 (1992) 24–53

2954 **Swaminathan, M S,** *Agricultural growth and human welfare.* Accra: Ghana Universities Press, 1993, 95pp

2955 **Tripp, R,** Invisible hands, indigenous knowledge and inevitable fads: challenges to public sector agricultural research in Ghana, *World development,* **21,** 12 (1993) 2003–16

Science & technology

2956 **Gyasi, E A,** Science policy priorities and implementation strategies in subsaharan Africa: the experience of Ghana, *African development review,* **4,** 1 (1992) 87–101

Sociology

See also: 1915

2957 **Achanfuo-Yeboah, D,** Grounding a theory of African migration in recent data on Ghana, *International sociology,* **8,** 2 (1993) 215–26

2958 **Anarfi, J K, Awusabo-Asare, K,** Experimental research on sexual networking in some selected areas of Ghana, *Health transition review,* **3,** (1993) supplementary issue, 29–43

2959 **Ankomah, A,** Premarital sexual relationships in Ghana in the era of AIDS, *Health policy and planning,* **7,** 2 (1992) 135–43

2960 **Dodoo, F N A,** Education and changing reproductive behaviour in Ghana, *Sociological perspectives,* **36,** 3 (1993) 241–56

2961 **Ezeh, A C,** The influence of spouses over each other's contraceptive attitudes in Ghana, *Studies in family planning,* **24,** 3 (1993) 163–74

2962 **Nukunya, G K,** *Tradition and change in Ghana: an introduction to sociology.* Accra: Ghana Universities Press, 1993, 283pp

2963 **Sowa, N K,** Ghana, in Adepoju, A (ed), *Impact of structural adjustment (Item 1107)*, 7–24

Urban studies

See also: 2863

2964 **Whittington, D, et al,** Household sanitation in Kumasi, Ghana, *World development,* **21,** 5 (1993) 733–48

2965 **Whittington, D, et al,** Household demand for improved sanitation services in Kumasi, Ghana: a contingent valuation study, *Water resources research,* **29,** 6 (1993) 1539–60

2966 **Willis, K G,** Regression analysis: determinants of overcrowding and house condition in Ghanaian housing markets, in Tipple, A G & Willis, K G (eds), *Housing the poor (item 1159)*, 143–68

2967 **Willis, K G, Tipple, A G,** Discriminant analysis: tenure choice and demand for housing services in Kumasi, Ghana, in Tipple, A G & Willis, K G (eds), *Housing the poor (item 1159)*, 126–42

GUINEA

General

2968 **Botte, R,** Guinée: mise au jour du patrimoine ou retour aux sources, *Journal des Africanistes,* **63,** 1 (1993) 93–138

Education

No entry. *See also:* 2970

Environment

2969 **Rossi, G,** Evolution politique, démographie et dynamique de l'environnement en Guinée forestière, *Cahiers d'outre-mer,* **46,** 183 (1993) 253–72

Gender

2970 **Sow, D,** Women and literacy in Guinea, *Journal of the African Association for Literacy and Adult Education,* **6,** 1 (1992) 6–14

History, general

2971 **Iffono, A G,** *Lexique historique de la Guinée-Conakry.* Paris: Harmattan, 1993, 234pp

History, C20th

2972 **Kaba, L,** *The 'non' de la Guinée à de Gaulle.* Paris: Chaka, 1990, 190pp

Industry & trade

2973 **Campbell,** B, Le secteur de la bauxite en République de Guinée: ajustement structurel et restructuration internationale de l'industrie de l'aluminium, *Tiers Monde,* **34,** 133 (1993) 187–208

2974 **Souare, O, et al,** Mineral and energy resources and their impact on industrialisation in Guinea, in Khennas, S (ed), *Industrialisation (item 454)*, 127–53

International economic relations

No entry. *See also:* 2973

Library - documentation

2975 **Conrad, D C,** Archival research in Guinea-Conakry, *History in Africa,* **20,** (1993) 369–78

2976 **Sugiyama, Y, Koman, J,** The flora of Bossou: its utilisation by chimpanzees and humans, *African study monographs,* **13,** 3 (1992) 127–69

Rural economy

2977 **Clapp, J A,** Interpreting agricultural performance in Guinea under structural adjustment, *Canadian journal of African studies,* **27,** 2 (1993) 173–95

2978 **Gassiat-Sanguinet, A,** Quel avenir pour l'arachide en haute-Guinée? Les consequences des interventions sur la production et la commercialisation d'une culture de rente, *Cahiers d'outre-mer,* **46,** 183 (1993) 273–95

2979 **Nett, B,** Agriculture in Guinea (Conakry), in Nett, B et al (eds), *Agricultural transformation (Item 1069)*, 51–78

Urban studies

No entry. *See also:* 1145

GUINEA BISSAU

Anthropology

2980 **Henry, C,** Les 'arebuko' des Bijogo (Guinée-Bissau): culte de possession, objets de puissance, *Systèmes de pensée en Afrique noire,* 12 (1993) 39–64

2981 **Journet, O,** Le harpon et le baton, *Systèmes de pensée en Afrique noire,* 12 (1993) 17–37

2982 **Scamtamburio, L,** *Etnologia dos Bijagos da ilha de Bubaque.* Lisbon: Instituto de Investigacão Centifica Tropical, 1991, 109pp

Economic and social history

2983 **Bigman, L,** *History and hunger in West Africa.* New York: Greewood, 1993, 148pp

Economy - Development

See also: 2988

2984 **Bentsi-Enchill, N K,** Guinea-Bissau struggles for development, *Africa recovery,* **7,** 1 (1993) 22–25

2985 **Rudebeck, L,** Entwicklung oder Abwicklung? Politik und Strukturanpassung in einen westafrikanischen Dorf, in Meyns, P (ed), *Demokratie und Strukturreformen (Item 1174)*, 169–86

2986 **Scheifer, U, Sigrist, C,** Von der fiktiven Planwirtschaft zur simulierten Markwirtschaft - Betrachtungen zur Wirtschaftsreform in Guinea Biussau, in Meyns, P (ed), *Demokratie und Strukturreformen (Item 1174)*, 121–39

Food

2987 **Gunnlaugsson, G,** Einarsdottir, J, Colostrum and ideas about bad milk: a case study from Guinea-Bissau, *Social science and medicine,* **36,** 3 (1993) 283–88

Gender

2988 **Achinger, G,** Die Auswirkungen des Strukturellen Anpassungsprogramme (SAP) in Guinea Bissau auf die wirtschaftliche und soziale Situation der Frauen auf den Lande, in Meyns, P (ed), *Demokratie und Strukturreformen (Item 1174)*, 152–68

International economic relations

2989 **de Vylder, S,** *Aid and macroeconomics: an evaluation of Swedish import support to Guinea-Bissau, Mozambique, Nicaragua and Vietnam.* Stockholm: SIDA, 1993, 62pp

Medical

See also: 2779, 2987

2990 **Andreasson, P A, et al,** A prospective study of vertical transmission of HIV–2 in Bissau, Guinea-Bissau, *AIDS,* **7,** 7 (1993) 989–93

2991 **Naucler, A, et al,** Sexually transmitted diseases and sexual behaviour as risk factors for HIV–2 infection in Bissau, Guinea-Bissau, *International journal of STD and AIDS,* **4,** 4 (1993) 217–21

2992 **Poulson, A G, et al,** HIV–2 infections in Bissau, West Africa: incidence, prevalences, and routes of transmission, *Journal of AIDS,* **6,** 8 (1993) 941–48

Politics

See also: 928

2993 **Davidson, B,** Remembering Cabral, *Review of African political economy,* 58 (1993) 78–85

2994 **Dhada, M,** *Warriors at work: how Guinea was set free.* Niwot: University of Colorado Press, 1993, 324pp

2995 **Ishemo, S,** Amilcar Cabral's thought and practice; some lessons for the 1990s, *Review of African political economy,* 58 (1993) 71–78

2996 **Rudebeck, L,** Reading Cabral in 1993, *Review of African political economy,* 58 (1993) 63–70

Rural economy

2997 **Alvesson, M,** Zejan, M, Guinea-Bissau: impact of the structural adjustment programme on the welfare of smallholder farmers, in Blomström, M & Lundahl, M (eds), *Economic crisis (Item 119)*, 202–18

2998 **Cardoso, C,** Subsistenz und Markt: sur Reform der Agrarproduktion in Guinea Bissau, in Meyns, P (ed), *Demokratie und Strukturreformen (Item 1174)*, 140–51

2999 **Lea, J D Z,** Applied policy analysis of the rice marketing subsector of Guinea Bissau, *Journal of international food and agribusiness marketing,* **4,** 4 (1992) 23–40

LIBERIA

Anthropology

See also: 3016

3000 **Ofri-Scheps, D M,** *On the object of ethnology: apropos of the Vai culture in Liberia.* Bern: Lang, 1993, 780pp

Current affairs

3001 **Kappel, R, Korte, W,** Liberia vor der Zerfall?, *Afrika Jahrbuch 1990,* 56–65

Economic and social history

3002 **Konneh, A,** Mandingo integration into the Liberian political economy, *Liberian studies journal,* **18,** 1 (1993) 44–62

Economy - Development

3003 **NARDA,** *A report of the round table conference on strategies and direction for a reconstruction and development of Liberia.* Monrovia: New African Research and Development Agency, 1992, 66pp

Education

3004 **Mason, M J,** et al, Higher education in Liberia: yesterday, today and tomorrow, *Liberian studies journal,* **18,** 1 (1993) 1–20

Health & welfare services

3005 **Gray, R H,** et al, Evaluation of natural family planning programs in Liberia and Zambia, *Journal of biosocial science,* **25,** 2 (1993) 249–58

History, C20th

3006 **Sawyerr, A,** *The emergence of autocracy in Liberia: tragedy and challenge.* San Francisco: Institute for Contemporary Studies, 1992, 418pp

Industry & trade

3007 **Atta, J,** The consequences of high oil prices for non-fuel mining countries in tropical Africa: the case of Liberia, in Khennas, S (ed), *Industrialisation (item 454)*, 232–77

3008 **Pereira-Lunghu, J,** A simulation model of investment planning and industrial expansion for Liberia, *Liberian studies journal,* **18,** 1 (1993) 63–87

International economic relations

No entry. *See also:* 3020

International relations

See also: 3017

3009 Conteh-Morgan, E, Ecowas: peace-making or meddling in Liberia?, *Africa insight,* **23,** 1 (1993) 36–41

3010 Eikenberg, K, Korner, P, Bewaffnete Humanität oder Interessenpolitik? Militärinterventionen in Liberia und Somalia, *Afrika Jahrbuch 1992,* 34–45

3011 Kerry, G I, *His brother's keeper: the travails of an ECOMOG soldier.* Lagos: Okey Okwechime, 1993, 73pp

3012 Kieh, G K, *Dependency and the foreign policy of a small power: the Liberian case.* San Francisco: Mellen Research University Press, 1992, 204pp

3013 N'Diaye, T M, Conflict prevention and conflict resolution in the African context: peacekeeping in Liberia, *Issue,* **21,** 1/2 (1993) 70–73

3014 Tarr, S B, The Ecomog initiative in Liberia: a Liberian perspective, *Issue,* **21,** 1/2 (1993) 74–83

3015 Yoroms, G J, Ecomog and West African regional security: a Nigerian perspective, *Issue,* **21,** 1/2 (1993) 84–91

Medical

3016 Green, E C, The anthropology of sexually transmitted disease in Liberia, *Social science and medicine,* **35,** 12 (1992) 1457–68

Politics

See also: 3019

3017 Gershoni, Y, From ECOWAS to ECOMOG: the Liberian crisis and the struggle for political hegemony in West Africa, *Liberian studies journal,* **18,** 1 (1993) 21–43

3018 Unoke, E, *The untold story of the Liberian civil war.* Enugu: ABIC, 1993, 109pp

Religion, philosophy

3019 Gifford, P, *Christianity and politics in Doe's Liberia.* Cambridge: CUP, 1993, 349pp

Rural economy

3020 Brautigan, D, South-South technology transfer: the case of China's Kpatawee rice project in Liberia, *World development,* **21,** 12 (1993) 1989–2001

Sociology

3021 Ruiz, H A, *Uprooted Liberians: casualties of a brutal war.* Washington: US Committee for Refugees, 1992, 32pp

MALI

Anthropology

See also: 2484, 3059

3022 Cissé, O, La circoncision au Khasso: rôle et place des différents actants, *Etudes maliennes,* 46 (1992) 34–56

3023 Couloubaly, P B, The narrative genre among the Bamana of Mali, *Research in African literatures,* **24,** 2 (1993) 47–60

3024 Jonckers, D, Autels sacrificiels et puissances religieuses: le Manyan (Bamana-Minyanka, Mali), *Systèmes de pensée en Afrique noire,* 12 (1993) 65–101

3025 Kante, N, Erny, P, *Forgerons d'Afrique noire: transmission des savoirs traditionels en pays malinké.* Paris: Harmattan, 1993, 269pp

3026 Makolo Muswaswa, Amadou

Hampaté Ba: l'avocat de l'humanisme sacré et intégral, *Zaire-Afrique,* **33,** 275 (1993) 313–317

3027 **Randall, S C,** Blood is hotter than water: popular use of hot and cold in Kel Tamasheq illness management, *Social science and medicine,* **36,** 5 (1993) 673–81

3028 **Seydou, C,** 'La fille recluse': variations sur un thème, in Görög-Karady, V (ed), *D'un conte ... à l'autre (item 38)*, 503–19

3029 **Songore, I,** L'observation traditionelle des météores en milieu Bamanan, *Etudes maliennes,* 46 (1992) 57–66

Demography

See also: 2603

3030 **Brown, E, Cazes, M H,** Differences de mortalité chez les Dogon de Boni, *Social science and medicine,* **36,** 10 (1993) 1291–96

3031 **Cazes, M H,** Les Dogon de Boni: approche démogénetique d'un isolat de Mali, *Population,* **48,** 2 (1993) 473–80

3032 **Cazes, M H,** *Les Dogon de Boni: approche démogénetique d'un isolat de Mali.* Paris: INED/PUF, 1993, 306pp

Economic and social history

3033 **Camara, S,** Les Numun et la métallurgie ancienne du fer au Manden, *Etudes maliennes,* 46 (1992) 5–33

3034 **Warms, R L,** Merchants, muslims and Wahhabiyya: the elaboration of islamic identity in Sikasso, Mali, *Canadian journal of African studies,* **26,** 3 (1992) 485–507

Economy - Development

No entry. *See also:* 3060

Education

See also: 3041, 3067

3035 **Antonioli, A,** *Le droit d'apprendre: une école pour tous en Afrique.* Paris: Harmattan, 1993, 185pp

Environment

See also: 251, 3073

3036 **Benjaminsen, T A,** Fuelwood and desertification: Sahel orthodoxies discussed on the basis of field data from the Gourma Region in Mali, *Geoforum,* **24,** 4 (1993) 397–409

3037 **MacLain, R J,** *Recomendations for a new Malian forest code: observations from the Land Tenure Centre's study of land and tree tenure in Mali's Fifth Region.* Madison: Land Tenure Centre, University of Wisconsin, 1992, 45pp

3038 **Turner, M,** Overstocking the range: a critical analysis of the environmental science of Sahelian pastoralism, *Economic geography,* **69,** 4 (1993) 403–21

3039 **van Driel, A,** *Planter un arbre, c'est préparer l'avenir: femmes et arbres en Afrique occidentale - le cas d'un village au Mali-Sud.* Amsterdam: Royal Tropical Institute, 1993, 39pp

Food

3040 **Adams, A,** Food insecurity in Mali: exploring the role of the moral economy, *IDS bulletin,* **24,** 4 (1993) 41–51

Gender

See also: 2603, 3039

3041 **Barka, L B,** Women literacy programme in Mali, *Journal of the African Association for Literacy and Adult Education,* **6,** 1 (1992) 15–27

3042 **Keita, R N,** *Le role de la femme dans le developement.* Bamako: Centre Djoliba, 1992, 13pp

3043 **Turritin, J,** Aoua Keita and the nascent women's movement in the French Soudan, *African studies review,* **36,** 1 (1993) 59–89

Geography, physical

No entry. *See also:* 3029

Health & welfare services

See also: 3027

3044 **Audibert, M, et al,** Social and epidemiological aspects of Guinea worm control, *Social science and medicine,* **36,** 4 (1993) 463–74

3045 **Brunet-Jailly, J, et al,** *Se soigner au Mali: une contribution de sciences sociales.* Paris: Karthala/ORSTOM, 1993, 344pp

History, general

3047 **de Moraes Farias, P,** The oral traditionalist as critic and intellectual producer: an example from contemporary Mali, in Falola, T (ed), *African historiography (Item 385),* 14–38

History, early

3048 **Dutour, O,** Palimpseste paléoanthropologique sur 'l'homme fossile d'Asselar' (Sahara), *Préhistoire anthropologie méditerranénnes,* **1,** (1992) 73–83

3049 **Georgeon, E, et al,** Paléoanthropologie du gisement lacustre néolithique de Kobadi (Mali), *Préhistoire anthropologie méditerranénnes,* **1,** (1992) 85–97

History, C20th

No entry. *See also:* 3043

Industry & trade

3050 **Diallo, S,** *Industrie et industrialisation au Mali: défis et contraintes.* Bamako: Centre Djoliba, 1990, 25pp

International economic relations

No entry. *See also:* 3072

Library - documentation

3051 **Hunwick, J O,** CEDRAB: the Centre de documentation et de recherches Ahmed Baba at Timbuktu, *Sudanic Africa,* 3 (1992) 173–81

Literature

3052 **McGuire, J R,** Narrating Mande heroism in the Malian novel: negotiating postcolonial identity in Diabaté's Le boucher de Kouta, *Research in African literatures,* **24,** 3 (1993) 35–57

Medical

See also: 2694

3053 **Collignon, R,** La santé mentale au Mali: éléments de bibliographie annotée, *Psychopathologie africaine,* **24,** 2 (1992) 243–287

3054 **Corin, E, et al,** Articulation et variations des systèmes de signes, de sens et d'action, *Psychopathologie africaine,* **24,** 2 (1992) 183–204

3055 **Corin, E, et al,** La place de la culture dans la psychiatrie africaine d'aujourd'hui: paramètres pour une cadre de référence, *Psychopathologie africaine,* **24,** 2 (1992) 149–181

3056 **Koumaré, B,** Définition d'un instrument de dépistage des troubles psychiques, *Psychopathologie africaine,* **24,** 2 (1992) 229–242

3057 Koumaré, B, L'assistance psychiatrique au Mali: à propos du placement des patients psychiatriques chroniques auprès de tradipraticiens, *Psychopathologie africaine,* **24,** 2 (1992) 135–148

3058 Miquel-Garcia, E, et al, Malnutrition et troubles relationnels mère-enfant en milieu urbain au Mali, *Psychopathologie africaine,* **24,** 2 (1992) 205–228

3059 van Beek, W E A, Banga, P M, The Dogon and their trees, in Croll, E & Parkin, D (eds), *Bush base: forest farm (Item 1040)*, 57–75

Planning

3060 Kano, K, *Le plan est-il un instrument efficace de developpement: le cas du Mali.* Bamako: Centre Djoliba, 1991, 17pp

Politics

See also: 2662

3061 Amselle, J L, La corruption et le clientélisme au Mali et en Europe de l'Est: quelques points de comparaison, *Cahiers d'études africaines,* **32,** 128 (1992) 629–41

3062 Le Roy, E, Mouvement paysan et transition démocratique dans le sud du Mali (Avril 1991-avril 1992), *Année africaine 1992/93,* 145–59

3063 Lelievre, P, *La revolution silencieuse des paysans: le cas du Mali.* Bamako: Centre Djoliba, 1990, 22pp

3064 Vengroff, R, Governance and the transition to democracy: political parties and the party system in Mali, *Journal of modern African studies,* **31,** 4 (1993) 541–62

Religion, philosophy

3065 Brenner, L, Constructing muslim identities in Mali, in Brenner, L (ed), *Muslim identity (item 963)*, 59–78

3066 Brenner, L, La culture arabo-islamique au Mali, in Otayek, R (ed), *Radicalisme islamique (Item 1002)*, 161–95

3067 Sanakoua, B, Brenner, L (eds), *L'enseignement islamique au Mali.* Bamako: Jamana, 1991, 153pp

Rural economy

See also: 3036, 3038

3068 Dante, G, Lelievre, P, *La revolution silenceuse des paysans: la cas du Mali.* Bamako: Centre Djoliba, 1990, 22pp

3069 de Bruijn, M, van Dijk, H, State formation and the decline of pastoralism: the Fulani in central Mali, in Markakis, J (ed), *Conflict and the decline of pastoralism (item 1596)*, 122–42

3070 Horowitz, M M, et al, Resettlement at Mamantali, Mali: short-term success, long-term problems, in Cernea, M M & Guggenheim, S E (eds), *Anthropological approaches to resettlement (item 1112)*, 229–50

3071 Kremer, A R, Lock, C, Where food is capital: labour allocation in cereals production, NW Mali, *Agricultural systems,* **41,** 1 (1993) 197–213

3072 Sarr, M, Les effets de l'aide bilatérale et multilatérale sur l'agriculture. L'aide-projet: le case de l'Opération arachide, *Etudes maliennes,* 46 (1992) 67–87

3073 van Beek, W E A, Processes and limitations of Dogon agricultural knowledge, in Hobart, M (ed), *An anthropological critique of development: the growth of ignorance* (London: Routledge, 1993), 43–60

3074 van Keulen, H, Veeneklaas, F R, Options for agricultural development: a case study from

Mali's Fifth Region, in Penning de Vries, F et al (eds), *Systems approaches for agricultural development* (Dordrecht: Kluwer, 1992), 367–80

Urban studies

See also: 1145

3075 **Bertrand, M,** Attorno a qualche 'sonsorobougou' nei centri urbani del Mali, *Storia urbana,* **17,** 63 (1993) 65–101

MAURITANIA

General

3076 **Ould Ahmedou, El G,** *Le genie des sables.* Nouakchott: Imprimerie du Maghreb, 1991, 136pp

Anthropology

3077 **Voisset, G M,** The tebra' of Moorish women from Mauritania: the limits (or essence) of the poetic act, *Research in African literatures,* **24,** 2 (1993) 79–88

Current affairs

3078 **Balta, P, A** l'heure du multipartisme, *Confluences Méditerranée,* 3 (1992) 130–136

Economic and social history

3079 **Santoir, C,** Le repli peul en Mauritanie à l'ouest de l'Assaba: l'évolution du peuplement peul sur la rive droit du fleuve Sénégal, *Cahiers d'outre-mer,* **46,** 183 (1993) 131–51

Economy - Development

3080 **MacKay, A,** *Profil du pauvreté en Mauritanie: partie descriptive.* Nouakchott: Projet Dimensions sociales de l'ajustement, Ministère du Plan, 1992, 88pp

Education

3081 **Ba, O M,** *Noirs et Beydanes mauritaniens: l'école, creuset de la nation?* Paris: Harmattan, 1993, 167pp

Gender

No entry. *See also:* 3077

History, C20th

3082 **Clausen, U,** Sidi Mohammed ould Boubabcar, *Orient,* **33,** 1 (1992) 13–21

Industry & trade

3083 **Charmes, J,** *La contribution du secteur informel à l'emploi et au produit national en Mauritanie 1977–1992.* Nouakchott: Projet Dimensions sociales de l'ajustement, Ministère du Plan, 1992, 94pp

Law

No entry. *See also:* 3088

Media

3084 **Roques, C,** Essor et difficultés d'une presse indépendante en Mauritanie (juillet 1991 - juillet 1992), *Revue de monde musulman et de la Méditerranée,* 63/64 (1992) 245–255

Politics

3085 **Baduel, P R,** La difficile sortie d'un régime autoritaire: Mauritanie 1990–1992, *Revue de monde musulman et de la Méditerranée,* 63/64 (1992) 225–243

3086 **Diallo, G,** *Mauritania: the other apartheid?* Uppsala: Scandinavian Institute of African Studies, 1992, 57pp
3087 **Wegemund, R,** Die Rückkehr zu pluralistischer Demokratie in Mauretanien, *Internationales Afrikaforum,* **28,** 4 (1992) 375–382

Rural economy

3088 **Leservoisier, O,** Le contexte de 'l'après-barrage' en Mauritanie: nouvelles lois foncières et nouveaux propriétaires dans le vallee du Sénégal, *Plein sud,* 1 (1991) 16–25
3089 **Villasante-de Beauvais, M,** Quelques aspects sociaux et fonciers de l'oasis de Kurudjel (région de l'Assaba, République islamique de Mauritanie), *Cahiers de l'URBAMA,* 6 (1990) 7–125
3090 **Santoir, C,** D'un rive à l'autre: les Peul mauritainiens réfugiés au Sénégal (départements de Dagana et de Podor), *Cahiers des sciences humaines,* **29,** 1 (1993) 195–229

Sociology

See also: 3081
3091 **Tijani, O K,** *Reintegration of the repatriates: recent achievements and future prospects.* Nouakchott: Agence Mauritainienne pour la communication et la diffusion, 1990, 58pp

NIGER

Agriculture, scientific

3092 **Price, T L,** Gestion 'scientifique' et connaissances locales: le projet pêches au Niger, *Arbres, forêts et communautés rurales,* 5 (1993) 37–44

Anthropology

See also: 3106
3093 **Anon,** Bibliographie de Suzy Bernus, *Journal des Africanistes,* **62,** 2 (1992) 235–38
3094 **Bernus, S,** Le mariage chez les Isawaghen d'In Gall (Niger): extraits des carnets d'enquête, *Journal des Africanistes,* **62,** 2 (1992) 219–33
3095 **Bisilliat, J, Laya, B,** Le système familial Songhai-Zarma, *Journal des Africanistes,* **62,** 2 (1992) 161–81
3096 **Calame-Griaule, G,** Variations stylistique dans un conte touareg, in Görög-Karady, V (ed), *D'un conte … à l'autre (item 38),* 83–102
3097 **Caron, B,** *Le haoussa de l'Ader.* Berlin: Reimer, 1991, 387pp
3098 **Claudot-Hawad, H,** Gani: la politique touaregue en spectacle, *Revue de monde musulman et de la Méditerranée,* 63/64 (1992) 211–224
3099 **Echard, N,** Les mémoires de l'oubli, *Journal des Africanistes,* **62,** 2 (1992) 23–29
3100 **Olivier de Sardan, J P,** La surinterprétation politique: les cultes de possession *hawka* du Niger, in Bayart, J F (ed), *Réligion et modernité politique (item 960),* 163–213
3101 **Rasmussen, S J,** Reflections on *tamazai,* a Tuareg idiom of suffering, *Culture, medicine and psychiatry,* **16,** 3 (1992) 337–65
3102 **Rouch, J,** Le salut d'irrémediable à Suzy Bernus, *Journal des Africanistes,* **62,** 2 (1992) 15–22
3103 **Vidal, L,** La possession par les génies chez les Peul (Niger): de la parole à l'invention du rituel, *Archives des sciences sociales des réligions,* 79 (1992) 69–85

Architecture

3104 **Calame-Griaule,** D, Manoirs

d'argile: note sur l'habitat à In Gall, *Journal des Africanistes,* **62,** 2 (1992) 131–52

Arts

3105 Gouletquer, P, Bijoux d'Agadez et In Gall, *Journal des Africanistes,* **62,** 2 (1992) 115–30

Economic and social history

3106 Spittler, G, *Les Touregs face aux sécheresses et aux famines: les Kel Ewey de l'Aïr (Niger).* Paris: Karthala, 1993, 424pp

Economy - Development

3107 Azam, J P, et al, *Le Niger: la pauvreté en période d'ajustement.* Paris: Harmattan, 1993, 222pp

3108 Chambas, G, *Les effets des politiques macro-économiques sur la pauvreté au Niger (1982–1990).* Niamey: Ministère du plan, 1991, 163pp

3109 Gervais, M, Les enjeux politiques des ajustements structurels au Niger, *Canadian journal of African studies,* **26,** 2 (1992) 226–4

3110 Tankoano, A, Les contrats programme entre l'état nigérien et les entreprises publiques, *African journal of international and comparative law,* **4,** 4 (1992) 854–873

Education

3111 Bergmann, H, Yahouza, I, *Niger: étude sectorielle sur éducation de base.* Eschborn: Deutsche GTZ, 1992, 121pp

Finance

See also: 3136

3112 Barlow, R, Synder, F, Taxation in Niger: problems and proposals, *World development,* **21,** 7 (1993) 1179–89

Food

No entry. *See also:* 3106

Gender

3113 Geadah, Y, *L'influence de l'Islam sur les femmes dans les projects de développement au Niger.* Hull: Canadian International Development Agency, 1992, 38pp

Geography, human

3114 Hauzer, J, Pellé, L, Fleuve Niger: toponymie et géographie récente du W (de Kirtachi à Boumba), *Journal des Africanistes,* **63,** 1 (1993) 35–66

Geography, physical

3115 Poncet, Y, Mémoire d'images: la région d'Agadez vue à travers les images satellitaires, *Journal des Africanistes,* **62,** 2 (1992) 91–103

Health & welfare services

3116 Juncker, T, Cost recovery for drugs provided at the rural dispensary: an experiment in Niger, *Annales de la Société belge de médecine tropical,* **73,** 3 (1993) 235–46

History, general

3117 Mounkaïla, F, Ancestors from the East in Sahelo-Sudanese myth: Dinga Soninké, Zabarkane Zarma, and others, *Research in African literatures,* **24,** 2 (1993) 13–21

History, early

3118 Paris, F, Chin Tafidet, village

néolithique, *Journal des Africanistes,* **62,** 2 (1992) 33–54

3119 Paris, F, et al, Les débuts de la métallurgie au Niger septentrional, *Journal des Africanistes,* **62,** 2 (1992) 55–68

History, C19th

3120 Hamini, D, Stratégies politiques et règles de succession de l'Ayar précolonial, *Journal des Africanistes,* **62,** 2 (1992) 105–112

History, C20th

3121 Bakary, D, *'Silence! On décolonise...'. Itinéraire politique et syndicale d'un miltant africain.* Paris: Harmattan, 1993, 297pp

3122 Koudize, A K, *Chronologie politique du Niger de 1900 à nos jours.* Naimey: Imprimerie nationale, 1991, 70pp

3123 Mayaki, A, *Les parties politiques nigeriens de 1946 à 1958: documents et temoinages.* Niamey: Imprimerie nationale, 1991, 111pp

Industry & trade

3124 Grégoire, E, Islam and the identity of merchants in Maradi (Niger), in Brenner, L (ed), *Muslim identity (item 963)*, 106–115

3125 Oumarou Ibrahim, et al, Direct and indirect effects of the mining and energy sectors on industrialisation: the Niger experience, in Khennas, S (ed), *Industrialisation (item 454)*, 182–231

International relations

No entry. *See also:* 3391

Law

3126 Mahamadou, L K, Les lacunes juridiques de l'acte fondamental no. 21 portant organisation des pouvoirs publics au Niger, *Revue juridique et politique,* **47,** 1 (1993) 109–119

Literature

3127 Tandina, O, Sarraounia, an epic?, *Research in African literatures,* **24,** 2 (1993) 23–32

Politics

See also: 2575, 3100

3128 Commission nationale preparatoire de la Conférence nationale souveraine, *Resultat des travaux.* Niamey: ANFANI, 1991, 105pp

3129 Conférence nationale souveraine, *Conférence national du Niger, Niamey, 19 juillet à 3 novembre 1991. Vol. 1: travaux.* Niamey: Imprimerie nationale, 1991, 3 vols,

3130 Ministère du plan, *Contribution presentée par le Ministère du plan pour la preparation de la Conférence nationale.* Niamey: Imprimerie nationale, 1991, 284pp

Religion, philosophy

See also: 3113, 3124

3131 Niandou Souleye, A, Les 'licenciés du Caire' et l'état au Niger, in Otayek, R (ed), *Radicalisme islamique (Item 1002)*, 213–27

Rural economy

3132 Croce, D, Faggi, P, Dal fiume al deserto: viaggio nell'irragazione nigerina, in Turco, A (ed), *Anno d'Africa (Item 17)*, 111–44

3133 Heston-Demirel, V, *The Keita integrated development project.* Rome: FAO, 1990, 25pp

3134 Lund, C, *Waiting for the rural*

code: perspectives on a land tenure reform in Niger. London: International Institute for Environment and Development, 1993, 26pp

3135 **Shapiro, B I, et al,** Evaluating and adapting new technologies in a high-risk agricultural system: Niger, *Agricultural systems*, **42,** 1 (1993) 153–71

3136 **Tinguiri, K L,** Finances rurales au Sahel: le cas des tontines et gardes-monnaies villageois au Niger, *African administrative studies*, 38 (1992) 31–43

Urban studies

No entry. *See also:* 2795

NIGERIA

General

3137 **Nnoli, O (ed),** *Deadend to Nigerian development: an investigation on the social, economic and political crisis in Nigeria*. Dakar: Codesria, 1993, 250pp

3138 **Toye, B O,** *Nigerian theses: a list of theses on Nigerian subjects and of theses by Nigerians*. Ibadan: Ibadan University Press, 1992, 257pp

Agriculture, scientific

See also: 3250

3139 **Isichei, A O, Muoghalu, J I,** The effects of tree canopy cover on soil fertility in a Nigerian savanna, *Journal of tropical ecology*, **8,** 3 (1992) 329–38

3140 **Okocha, K F, Odi, A,** Qualitative and quantitative factors concerning scientific information in agricultural research: a case study of southeastern Nigeria, *International information and library review*, **24,** 4 (1992) 315–27

Anthropology

See also: 2484, 3171, 3292, 3310, 3580, 3582

3141 **Aboyade, B O,** *Yoruba culture and civilisation: an introductory bibliography (1845–1976)*. Ibadan: Fountain, 1991, 89pp

3142 **Adekola, O O, Alamu, O,** *Oke'badan: discussions on the significance of Oke'badan festival*. Ibadan: Kolapo, 1991, 36pp

3143 **Adelberger, J,** The problem of 'Wurkun': new evidence for the clarification of an enigma in northern Nigerian ethnography and linguistics, *African languages and cultures*, **5,** 1 (1992) 1–9

3144 **Aguwa, J C U,** 'Agwu' possession: belief and experience in traditional Igbo society, *Paideuma*, **39,** (1993) 279–89

3145 **Aguwa, J C U,** Taboos and purification of ritual pollutions in Igbo traditional society, *Anthropos*, **88,** 3/4 (1993) 539–46

3146 **Amali, I O O,** Indigenous Nigerian oral drama as an instrument of social regulation: a study of Ogbollo secret society of Idoma, *Ufahamu*, **20,** 1 (1991/92) 56–67

3147 **Barber, K,** Multiple discourses in Yoruba oral literature, *Bulletin of the John Rylands University Library of Manchester*, **73,** 3 (1991) 11–24

3148 **Didam, E,** *Synopsis on the Kagoro tribe*. Fadan Kagoro: Ezedam Enterprises, 1991, 113pp

3149 **Egudu, R N,** *African poetry of the living dead: Igbo masquerade poetry*. Lewiston: Mellen, 1992, 231pp

3150 **Folorunso, C A,** Ethnoarchaeology, its methods and practice: the Tiv example, *West African journal of archaeology*, **23,** (1993) 92–103

3151 **Folorunso, C A,** La poterie du Tiv: étude ethnographique à Ushungo, in Andah, B W, et al (eds), *Imprints of West Africa's past (Item 2534)*, 165–77

3152 **Kwami, R,** Songs from the Akwa Ibom and Cross River States of Nigeria, *African languages and cultures,* **5,** 2 (1992) 133–556

3153 **Lowe, J** (ed), *Yoruba culture.* Ibadan: Nigerian Field Society, 1992, 64pp

3154 **Madu, R O,** *African symbols, proverbs and myths.* New York: Lang, 1992, 327pp

3155 **Nwoye, O G,** Body based metaphors in Igbo, *Journal of Asian and African studies (Tokyo),* 44 (1992) 167–77

3156 **Okanlawon, T,** Variability in African oral literature: some theses for newly collected materials from Nigeria, in Görög-Karady, V (ed), *D'un conte ... à l'autre (item 38)*, 233–44

3157 **Okpoko, A I,** Traditional methods of disposal of the dead in parts of Nigeria, *West African journal of archaeology,* **23,** (1993) 104–21

3158 **Osifo, N G,** *A system of traditional health care. Vol. 2.* Benin City: Neraso, 1992, 65pp

3159 **Rom Kalilu, R O,** Costumes and the origins of Egungun, *African studies,* **52,** 1 (1993) 55–69

3160 **Salamone, F A, Salamone, V A,** *Kikki*: a core concept of Hausa culture, *Africa (Rome),* **48,** 3 (1993) 359–81

3161 **VerEecke, C,** Subnational Fulbe identity in Nigeria?: responses to political change in post-independence times, *Senri ethnological studies,* 35 (1993) 139–61

3162 **Verger, P,** O deus supremo Iorubá: uma revisão das fontes, *Afro-Asia,* 15 (1992) 18–35

3163 **Yai, O B,** In praise of metonymy: the concepts of 'tradition' and 'creativity' in the transmission of Yoruba artistry over time and space, *Research in African literatures,* **24,** 4 (1993) 29–37

3164 **Yalwa, L D,** Sociocultural and linguistic implications of abusive expressions in Hausa, *Ufahamu,* **20,** 1 (1991/92) 68–84

Architecture

3165 **Imah, M R,** The museum audience: the Old Residency experience, *WAMP bulletin,* 4 (1993) 33–38

Arts

See also: 70

3166 **Adesanya, A** (ed), *The Nigerian film/TV index.* Lagos: A-Productions Nigeria, 1992, 128pp

3167 **Bello, S** (ed), *Culture and decision making in Nigeria.* Lagos: National Council for Arts and Culture, 1991, 218pp

3168 **Boyd, R, Fardon, R,** Bisiweeri: the songs and times of a Muslim Chamba woman (Adamawa State, Nigeria), *African languages and cultures,* **5,** 1 (1992) 11–41

3169 **Coker, A,** The context and development of Ola Rotimi at the Iri Olokun theatre, *Journal of Black studies,* **23,** 1 (1992) 60–74

3170 **Furniss, G,** Burlesque in Hausa: 'And my text for today is food', said Mister Matches, *Bulletin of the John Rylands University Library of Manchester,* **73,** 3 (1991) 37–62

3171 **Götrick, K,** The actor, the art of acting and liminality, in Granqvist, R (ed), *Culture in Africa (item 10)*, 145–71

3172 **Hassan, S M,** *Art and islamic literacy among the Hausa of northern*

Nigeria. Lewiston: Mellen, 1992, 373pp

3173 Kelly, B M, *Nigerian artists: a who's who and bibliography.* Oxford: Zell, 1993, 600pp

3174 Menke, K, *Kunst und Kultur im gesellschaftlichen Wandel eines Entwicklunglandes, dargestellt am Beispiel Nigerias.* Munich: Tuduv, 1991, 355pp

3175 Simmonds, D, A review of pottery techniques in Nigeria (1969–70) in a West African context, in Andah, B W, et al (eds), *Imprints of West Africa's past (Item 2534)*, 147–58

3176 Ukpokodu, I P, Plays, possession and rock and roll: political theater in Africa, *Tulane drama review,* **36,** 4 (1992) 28–53

Current affairs

3177 Okoroji, J C, The Nigerian presidential elections, *Review of African political economy,* 58 (1993) 123–31

Demography

See also: 74

3178 Egunjobi, L, Spatial distribution of mortality from leading notifiable diseases in Nigeria, *Social science and medicine,* **36,** 10 (1993) 1267–72

3179 Hollos, M, Larsen, U, Fertility differences among the Ijo in southern Nigeria: does urban residence make a difference?, *Social science and medicine,* **35,** 9 (1992) 1199–1210

3180 Isingo-Abanike, V C, et al, Urban nuptiality patterns and marital fertility in Nigeria, *Journal of biosocial science,* **25,** 4 (1993) 483–98

3181 Shah, V P, Trends in health, nutrition, and socio-economic status in Nigeria, India, and Brazil (1960–1990), *Journal of tropical pediatrics,* **39,** 2 (1993) 118–127

3182 Udjo, E O, Age distribution and mis-reporting among some Kanuri of northeast Nigeria, *Annals of Borno,* **6/7,** (1989/1990) 68–76

Economic and social history

See also: 3255, 3351, 3576

3183 Adebayo, A G, Precolonial institutional frameworks for moneylending and loan repayments among the Yoruba, *Paideuma,* **38,** (1992) 163–76

3184 Aluk, J O, *Osomalo: the early exploits of the Ijesha entrepreneurs.* Ibadan: Book Builders, 1993, 75pp

3185 Andah, B W, *Nigeria's indigenous technology.* Ibadan: Ibadan University Press, 1992, 141pp

3186 Falola, T, 'My friend the Shylock': money-lenders and their clients in south-western Nigeria, *Journal of African history,* **34,** 3 (1993) 403–23

3187 Guyer, J I, 'Toiling ingenuity': food regulation in Britain and Nigeria, *American ethnologist,* **20,** 4 (1993) 797–817

3188 Hunwick, J O, Falkeiana II: a letter from the Amir of Mafara to the Amir of Zamfara, *Sudanic Africa,* 3 (1992) 95–108

3189 Iwo, O G, *A social history of Degema.* Port Harcourt: Don Sun Communications, 1991, 145pp

3190 Kriger, C, Textile production and gender in the Sokoto Caliphate, *Journal of African history,* **34,** 3 (1993) 361–401

3191 Last, M, The traditional muslim intellectual in Hausaland: the background, in Falola, T (ed), *African historiography (Item 385)*, 116–31

3192 Lovejoy, P E, Hogendorn, J S, *Slow death for slavery: the course of abolition in northern Nigeria,*

1897–1936. Cambridge: CUP, 1993, 391pp

3193 **Naanen, B,** Economy within an economy: the manilla currency, exchange-rate instability and social conditions in southeastern Nigeria, *Journal of African history,* **34,** 3 (1993) 426–46

3194 **Okonkwo, R,** The Nigerian Civil Service Union, 1919–1922, *International journal of African historical studies,* **26,** 3 (1993) 609–22

3195 **Oriji, J N,** *Ngwa history: a study of social and economic changes in Igbo mini-states in time perspective.* New York: Lang, 1991, 176pp

3196 **Singer, H W, Roy, S,** *Economic progress and prospects in the Third World: lessons of development experience since 1945.* Aldershot: Edward Elgar, 1993, 187pp

3197 **Ubah, C N,** The colonial administration in northern Nigeria and the problem of free slave children, *Slavery and abolition,* **14,** 3 (1993) 208–33

3198 **Ubah, C N,** Hope for the despondent: a colonial health care scheme at Uzuakoli, eastern Nigeria, *Transafrican journal of history,* 21 (1992) 51–68

3199 **Umoren, U E,** The Port Harcourt City cemetery: an archaeological site of socioreligious symbolism, *West African journal of archaeology,* **23,** (1993) 122–44

Economy - Development

See also: 3137, 3258, 3278, 3471, 3625

3200 **Agunbiade, A O,** *Regional problem in Nigeria: a survey of regional resource profiles and socio-economic indicators, phase 1.* Ibadan: NISER, 1991, 90pp

3201 **Ajene, O G,** The significance of glasnost and perestroika for political and economic development in Nigeria, *Nigerian journal of international affairs,* **16,** 2 (1990) 42–60

3202 **Ariyo, A,** An assessment of the sustainability of Nigeria's fiscal deficit, *Journal of African economics,* **2,** 2 (1993) 263–83

3203 **Dike, E,** Nigeria: the political economy of the Buhari regime, *Nigerian journal of international affairs,* **16,** 2 (1990) 86–116

3204 **Dozie, P, Bickersteth, O** (eds), *Report on the first Nigerian Economic Summit.* Ibadan: Spectrum, 1993, 128pp

3205 **Ekpo, A H,** Unemployment and inflation under structural adjustment: the Nigerian experience, *Eastern African economic review,* **8,** 2 (1992) 102–113

3206 **Ezeala-Harrison, F,** From structural maladjustment to structural re-adjustment in Nigeria, *Scandanavian journal of development alternatives,* **12,** 1 (1993) 15–31

3207 **Ezeala-Harrison, F,** Structural re-adjustment in Nigeria: diagnosis of a severe Dutch disease syndrome, *American journal of economics and sociology,* **52,** 2 (1993) 193–208

3208 **Forrest, T,** *Politics and economic development in Nigeria.* Boulder: Westview, 1993, 254pp

3209 **Gavin, M,** Adjusting to the terms of trade shock: Nigeria 1972–88, in Doornbosch, R (ed), *Policymaking in the open economy* (Oxford: OUP, 1993), 172–219

3210 **Giwa, R F,** *Thoughts on the Nigerian economy: an industrialist's perspective.* Lagos: Mednet, 1992, 263pp

3211 **Mensah, S N-A,** Structural adjustment programmes in Africa: lessons from Ghana and Nigeria, *Africa insight,* **23,** 2 (1993) 72–78

3212 **Nnoli, N,** Nigeria: the failure of a neocolonial society, in Nnoli,

O (ed), *Deadend to Nigerian development (item 3137)*, 1–26

3213 **Nnoli, O,** Deadend to Nigerian development, in Nnoli, O (ed), *Deadend to Nigerian development (item 3137)*, 219–38

3214 **Nnoli, O,** Reactionary twist to the class struggle in Nigeria, in Nnoli, O (ed), *Deadend to Nigerian development (item 3137)*, 97–123

3215 **Nwachukwu, C B,** The structural adjustment programme in Nigeria, *Wisssenschaftliche Beiträge,* **25,** 4 (1990) 3–12

3216 **Nyatepe-Coo, A A,** External disturbances, domestic policy responses and debt accumulation in Nigeria, *World development,* **21,** 10 (1993) 1621–31

3217 **Okigbo, P N C,** *Change and crisis in the management of the Nigerian economy.* Enugu: Fourth Dimension, 1993, 406pp

3218 **Okigbo, P N C,** *Growth and structure of the Nigerian economy.* Enugu: Fourth Dimension, 1993, 286pp

3219 **Okigbo, P N C,** *Lectures on the structural adjustment programme.* Enugu: Fourth Dimension, 1993, 292pp

3220 **Okowa, W J,** *The political economy of development planning in Nigeria.* Port Harcourt: Pam Unique, 1991, 146pp

3221 **Olashore, O,** *Challenges of Nigeria's economic reform.* Ibadan: Fountain, 1992, 331pp

3222 **Olowo, T A, Akinwumi, J A** (eds), *Proceedings of the national conference of the Ibadan Socio-Economic Group on Development Strategies in 21st Century Nigeria.* Ibadan: University of Ibadan, 1992, 271pp

3223 **Oshikoya, T W,** *The Nigerian economy: a macroeconomic and input-potput model.* New York: Praeger, 1990, 192pp

3224 **Oyemakinde, W,** *Strategies for revamping the Nigerian economy.* Ibadan: Sunlight Institute, 1991, 84pp

3225 **Toby, A J,** Structural adjustment and economic development in Nigeria, *Indian journal of African studies,* **5,** 1 (1992) 27–32

3226 **Zwingina, J S,** *Capitalist development in an African economy.* Ibadan: Ibadan University Press, 1992, 286pp

Education

See also: 2637, 3287, 3300, 3410, 3432, 3437, 3470, 3500, 3518, 3608

3227 **Agboola, A T,** Nigerian government publications on education, *Government information quarterly,* **10,** 3 (1993) 357–64

3228 **Akinnaso, F N,** Policy and experiment in mother tongue literacy in Nigeria, *International review of education,* **39,** 4 (1993) 255–85

3229 **Ali, A, Akubue, A,** Winning students over to science, *Discovery and innovation,* **5,** 2 (1993) 101–105

3230 **Banu, D P,** The contributions of the Church of the Brethren Mission to the development of Western education in Borno and Gongola States, *Annals of Borno,* **6/7,** (1989/1990) 46–55

3231 **Ekpo, O E,** Institutional objectives and the pursuit of higher education in Nigeria, *Journal of further and higher education,* **15,** 2 (1991) 36–46

3232 **Ezenibe, S,** *Education and religion: the Nigerian situation. A sociological analysis.* Bern: Lang, 1992, 124pp

3233 **Fadayomi, T O,** Nigeria; consequences for education, in Adepoju, A (ed), *Impact of structural adjustment (Item 1107)*, 98–104

3234 **Fajonyomi, A A,** The impact of locational differences on the effectiveness of adult literacy centres in Borno State, Nigeria, *Annals of Borno,* **6/7,** (1989/1990) 35–45

3235 **Mordi, C,** Student achievement in science: a cross-cultural comparison of the Second International Science Study (SISS) results in Nigeria, *International journal of science education,* **15,** 6 (1993) 685–91

3236 **Obidi, S S,** A study of the reactions of secondary grammar school students to indigenous moral values in Nigeria, *Journal of Negro education,* **62,** 1 (1993) 82–90

3237 **Osiyale, A,** *Teacher preparation and participation in curriculum improvement.* Lagos: Lagos University Press, 1991, 53pp

3238 **Osiyale, A,** *Teacher preparation and participation in curriculum improvement.* Lagos: University of Lagos Press, 1992, 53pp

3239 **Reichmuth, S,** Islamic learning and its interaction with 'western' education in Ilorin, Nigeria, in Brenner, L (ed), *Muslim identity (item 963)*, 179–98

3240 **Tahir, G** (ed), *Education and pastoralism in Nigeria.* Zaria: Ahmadu Bello University Press, 1991, 186pp

3241 **Tsuma, O G K,** The problems of the Nigerian integrated science curriculum, *Kenya journal of education,* **5,** 1 (1991) 106–22

3242 **Ukeje, B O, et al,** *Educational administration.* Enugu: Fourth Dimension, 1992, 444pp

3243 **Watkins, D, Akande, A,** Student evaluations of teaching effectiveness: a Nigerian investigation, *Higher education,* **24,** 4 (1992) 453–63

3244 **Yahaya, A D, Akinyele, C I** (ed), *Human resources development and utilisation: policies and issues.* Ibadan: Spectrum, 1992, 268pp

Environment

See also: 3655, 3656

3245 **Adams, W M,** Development's deaf ear: downstream users and water releases from the Bakalori dam, Nigeria, *World development,* **21,** 9 (1993) 1405–16

3246 **Adewule, O,** The right of the individual to environmental protection: a case study of Nigeria, *Environment and urbanisation,* **4,** 2 (1992) 176–83

3247 **Akingbade, T,** *Nigeria: on the trail of the environment.* Lagos: Triple E Systems Associates, 1991, 155pp

3248 **Ekwue, E I,** Survey of soil erosion features in Borno State: a detailed study of former Biu Local Government Area, *Annals of Borno,* **6/7,** (1989/1990) 221–230

3249 **Odemerho, F O,** Land degradation impacts on tropical agricultural basins and their management: the Nigerian example, *Geoforum,* **23,** 4 (1992) 499–506

3250 **Odemerho, F O, Arwunodiogba, A,** The effects of changing cassava management practices on soil loss: a Nigerian example, *Geographical journal,* **159,** 1 (1993) 63–69

3251 **Osemeobo, G J,** Land use issues on wild plant conservation in Nigeria, *Journal of environmental management,* **36,** 1 (1992) 17–26

Finance

See also: 3210, 3272

3252 **Ajayi, A,** *The regulation of banks and financial institutions.* Lagos: Greyhouse African Professional Resource Development Project, 1991, 287pp

3253 **Anao, A R, Atomatofa,** The problems and prospects of sales tax administration in Nigeria: a Bendel

State study, *Quarterly journal of administration,* **25,** 3/4 (1991) 231–47

3254 Asabia, S O, *Essays in money and banking.* Ibadan: Fountain, 1992, 232pp

3255 Asechemie, D P S, *A history of accounting in Nigeria.* Port Harcourt: University of Port Harcourt Press, 1992, 175pp

3256 Falegan, S B, *The naira exchange rate.* Ibadan: Fountain, 1991, 29pp

3257 Ikhide, S I, Alawode, A A, Impact of stabilisation programs on the growth of the money market in Nigeria, *Developing economies,* **31,** 2 (1993) 220–40

3258 Ndekwu, E C, *Interest rates, bank deposits and growth of the Nigerian economy.* Ibadan: NISER, 1991, 65pp

3259 Ndekwu, E C, *Monetary development and management in Nigeria: a study of monetary theories, policies and realities in the management of Nigeria's economy.* Ibadan: NISER, 1990, 326pp

3260 Nnadi, G S, Impact of computers on governmental auditing: a comparative study of three Nigerian States, *Annals of Borno,* **6/7,** (1989/1990) 77–87

3261 Ojo, M O, *The evolution and performance of monetary policy in Nigeria in the 1980s.* Lagos: Central Bank of Nigeria, 1992, 38pp

3262 Oshisami, K, *Government accounting and financial control.* Ibadan: Spectrum, 1992, 231pp

3263 Sote, G A, Delay and waiting problems in some Nigerian banks, *Scandanavian journal of development alternatives,* **12,** 1 (1993) 65–80

3264 Soyibo, A, Adekanye, F, *Financial system regulation, deregulation and savings mobilisation in Nigeria.* Nairobi: African Economic Research Consortium, 1992, 32pp

3265 Soyibo, A, Adekanye, F, *The Nigerian banking system in the context of policies of financial regulation and deregulation.* Nairobi: African Economic Research Consortium, 1992, 31pp

3266 Various authors, *Deregulation in the Nigerian banking industry: directions, challenges, problems and prospects.* Lagos: Financial Institutions Training Centre, 1991, 168pp

Food

See also: 3187

3267 Aboyade, O, Perspectives on African food policy and agricultural development in the 1990s; a Nigerian perspective, in Kotler, N G (ed), *Sharing innovation* (Washington: Smithsonian Institution Press, 1990), 1–14

3268 Guptill, K S, et al, Evaluation of a face-to-face weaning food intervention in Kwara State, Nigeria: knowledge, trial, and adoption of a home-prepared weaning food, *Social science and medicine,* **36,** 5 (1993) 665–72

3269 Kolawole, A, et al, Agricultural transformation, food crisis and the Accelerated Wheat Production Program in Nigeria: the case of Kano and Kaduna, in Nett, B et al (eds), *Agricultural transformation (Item 1069)*, 111–34

Gender

See also: 3168, 3303, 3334, 3354, 3422, 3478, 3481, 3488, 3495, 3570, 3587, 3596, 3607, 3636

3270 Abdullah, H, The democratic process and the challenge of gender in Nigeria, *Review of African political economy,* 56 (1993) 27–41

3271 Abiola, L T, *Tyalode Hunmuani Alade: the embodiment of*

truth. Ibadan: Famlod, 1990, 64pp

3272 **Anyanwu, J C,** Women, education, and the use of bank credit in Nigeria: challenges for the twenty-first century, *Ufahamu,* **19,** 2/3 (1990/1991) 130–145

3273 **Barnes, S T,** Women, property and power, in Sanday, P R & Goodenough, R G (eds), *Beyond the second sex* (Philadelphia: University of Pennsylvania Press), 1990, 253–80

3274 **Dare, F O, et al,** Biosocial factors affecting menarche in a mixed Nigerian population, *Central African journal of medicine,* **38,** 2 (1992) 77–81

3275 **Ekejuiba, F,** *Women's participation in the democratisation process in Nigeria.* Boston: African Studies Center, Boston University, 1992, 22pp

3276 **Elabor-Idemudia, P,** The impact of structural adjustment programs on women and their households in Bendel and Ogun States, Nigeria, in Gladwin, C H (ed), *Structural adjustment and African women farmers (Item 315)*, 128–50

3277 **Guyer, J I,** Women's agricultural work in a multimodal rural economy: Ibarapa District, Oyo State, Nigeria, in Gladwin, C H (ed), *Structural adjustment and African women farmers (Item 315)*, 257–80

3278 **Ijere, M O** (ed), *Women in Nigerian economy.* Enugu: Acena, 1991, 216pp

3279 **Johnson-Odim, C,** On behalf of women and the nation: Funmilayo Ransome-Kuti and the struggles for Nigerian independence and women's equality, in Johnson-Odim, C & Strobel, M (eds), *Expanding the boundaries of women's history* (Bloomington: Indiana University Press, 1992), 144–57

3280 **Mabogunje, A L,** *Women in business and agribusiness in Nigeria.* Ibadan: Institute of African Studies, Ibadan University, 1991, 11pp

3281 **Mbata, J N,** The role of women in traditional agriculture: a case study of women in food crops production in Rivers State, Nigeria, *Discovery and innovation,* **5,** 1 (1993) 81–87

3282 **Mebrahtu, S,** Women, work and nutrition in Nigeria, in Turshen, M (ed), *Women and health (Item 343)*, 89–106

3283 **Odujinrin, O,** Wife battering in Nigeria, *International journal of gynecology and obstetrics,* **41,** 2 (1993) 159–64

3284 **Ogbuagu, S C,** The deteriorating condition of women in Nigeria, in Nnoli, O (ed), *Deadend to Nigerian development (item 3137)*, 203–218

3285 **Ogunleye, B,** The empowerment of rural women: the experience of the Country Women's Association of Nigeria, in Sandbrook, R & Halfani, M (eds), *Empowering people (Item 930)*, 104–110

3286 **Onunwa, U R,** Feminity in African cosmology: paradoxes and ambiguities, *Journal of Asian and African studies (Tokyo),* 44 (1992) 131–43

3287 **Osuala, J D C,** Nigerian women's quest for role fulfillment, in Rothblum, E D & Cole, E (eds), *Women's mental health (item 338)*, 89–98

3288 **Shettima, K, et al** (eds), *Women in the transition to democracy in Nigeria.* Samaru: Women in Nigeria, 1993, 78pp

3289 **Trager, L,** New women's organisations in Nigeria: one response to structural adjustment, in Gladwin, C H (ed), *Structural adjustment and African women farmers (Item 315)*, 339–58

3290 **VerEecke, C,** 'It is better to die than be shamed': cultural and moral dimensions of women's trading in an Islamic Nigerian society, *Anthropos,* **88,** 3/4 (1993) 403–17

3291 **VerEecke, C,** Muslim women traders of northern Nigeria: perspectives for the city of Yola, *Ethnology,* **32,** 3 (1993) 217–36

3292 **Weisser, G,** *Frauen in Männerbünden: zur Bedeutung der frauen in den Bünden der Yoruba.* Saarbrucken: Breitenbach, 1992, 164pp

Geography, human

3293 **Ayeni, B, Faniran, A (eds),** *Geographical perspectives on Nigeria's development: a collection of presidential addresses to the Nigerian Geographical Association.* Lagos: Nigerian Geographical Association, 1990, 335pp

3294 **Guyer, J I, Lambin, E F,** Land use in an urban hinterland; ethnography and remote sensing in the study of African intensification, *American anthropologist,* **95,** 4 (1993) 839–59

3295 **Phillips-Howard, K D,** Indirect mineland reclamation on the Jos Plateau, Nigeria: the basis for a viable policy, *Land use policy,* **10,** 1 (1993) 2–15

Geography, physical

3296 **Ojo, O,** Aspects of the urban climate of Lagos, Nigeria, *African urban quarterly,* **5,** 1/2 (1990) 76–90

3297 **Sholanke, O O,** Delimiting the territorial sea between Nigeria and Cameroon: a rational approach, *International and comparative law quarterly review,* **42,** 2 (1993) 398–411

Health & welfare services

See also: 379, 3282, 3570, 3645

3298 **Adeykoya, A, Bishop, C S,** The failure of environmental health programs in Nigeria: a concern for health planners in the developing nations, *International journal of environmental health research,* **2,** 4 (1992) 167–70

3299 **Akinniyi, J A,** Rural resources and national development (part 1): a case for the recognition of African traditional medicine in Nigeria, *Annals of Borno,* **6/7,** (1989/1990) 279–293

3300 **Akpala, C O,** Medical education and primary health care in Nigeria: the Sokoto University experience, *Central African journal of medicine,* **37,** 11 (1991) 374–77

3301 **Aregbeyen, J B O,** *Economic implications of preventive health care: the case of environmental sanitation in Nigeria.* Ibadan: NISER, 1991, 69pp

3302 **Bamgboye, E A, Ladipo, O A,** Oral contraceptive marketing in Ibadan, Nigeria, *Social science and medicine,* **35,** 7 (1992) 903–906

3303 **Nwakoby, B N,** The influence of new maternal care facilities in rural Nigeria, *Health policy and planning,* **7,** 3 (1992) 269–78

3304 **Oshiname, F O, Brieger, W R,** Primary care training for patent medicine vendors in rural Nigeria, *Social science and medicine,* **35,** 12 (1992) 1477–84

3305 **Popoola, D,** Nigeria; consequences for health, in Adepoju, A (ed), *Impact of structural adjustment (Item 1107)*, 92–97

History, general

3306 **Danmole, H O, Falola, T,** The documentation of Ilorin by Samuel Ojo Bada, *History in Africa,* **20,** (1993) 1–13

3307 **Doortmont, M R,** The roots of Yoruba historiography: classicism, traditionalism and pragmatism, in Falola, T (ed), *African historiography (Item 385)*, 52–63

3308 **Erim, E O,** The use of migration tradition in reconstructing Idoma culture history, in Andah, B W, et al (eds), *Imprints of West Africa's past (Item 2534)*, 78–84

3309 **Fiberisima, J A,** *Okrika in search of an ancestry.* Ibadan: Evans, 1990, 220pp

3310 **Gwom, S L,** *The Berom tribe of Plateau State of Nigeria.* Jos: Fab Education Books, 1992, 304pp

3311 **Ibrahim, S,** *The Nupe and their neighbours.* Ibadan: Heinemann Educational, 1992, 152pp

3312 **Ojuade, J S,** The issue of *Oduduwa* in Yoruba genesis: the myths and realities, *Transafrican journal of history,* 21 (1992) 139–58

3313 **Westley, D,** *Hausa oral traditions: an annotated bibliography.* Boston: African Studies Center, Boston University, 1991, 22pp

History, early

See also: 1416, 2650, 3150

3314 **Aleru, J O,** Archaeological sites in Igbominaland, north central Yorubaland, Kwara State, Nigeria: the need for systematic archaeological research, *West African journal of archaeology,* **23,** (1993) 37–50

3315 **Andah, B W,** Thurstan Shaw at Ogbo-Ukwu; the limits of rescue archaeology, in Andah, B W et al (eds), *Imprints of West Africa's past (Item 2534)*, 33–39

3316 **Anozie, F N,** Ogbo-Ukwu after Thurstan Shaw, in Andah, B W, et al (eds), *Imprints of West Africa's past (Item 2534)*, 40–46

3317 **Fatusin, A,** A late Stone Age site in Kagoro, in Andah, B W, et al (eds), *Imprints of West Africa's past (Item 2534)*, 243–56

3318 **Gundu, Z A, Igirgi, A D,** Oral traditions in the Middle Benue Valley; some archaeological perspectives, in Andah, B W, et al (eds), *Imprints of West Africa's past (Item 2534)*, 85–96

3319 **Ibeanu, A M,** Pottery function: an indispensable criterion in Igbo pottery classification, in Andah, B W, et al (eds), *Imprints of West Africa's past (Item 2534)*, 159–64

3320 **Jemkur, J F,** *Aspects of the Nok culture.* Zaria: Ahmadu Bello University Press, 1992, 103pp

3321 **Ogundele, S O,** Archaeological reconnaissance and excavations in parts of Tivland, *West African journal of archaeology,* **23,** (1993) 67–91

3322 **Oriji, J N,** *Traditions of Igbo origin: a study of precolonial population movements in Africa.* New York: Lang, 1990, 199pp

History, C18th

See also: 2651

3323 **Lange, D,** Die Hausa-Traditionen in ihrer Abhängigkeit von Kanem-Borno und Nubien, *Anthropos,* **88,** 1/2 (1993) 47–76

3324 **Lange, D,** Ethnogenesis from within the Chadic state: some thoughts on the history of Kanem-Bornu, *Paideuma,* **39,** (1993) 261–77

3325 **Soper, R,** The palace at Oyo Ife, Western Nigeria, in Andah, B W, et al (eds), *Imprints of West Africa's past (Item 2534)*, 295–311

History, C19th

3326 **Akinwumi, O D,** The Oyo-Borgu military alliance of 1835: a case study in the precolonial military history, *Transafrican journal of history,* 21 (1992) 159–70

3327 **Falola, T,** Ade Ajayi on Samuel Johnson: filling the gaps, in Falola, T (ed), *African historiography (Item 385)*, 80–90

3328 **Farias, P F de M,** A letter from Ki-Toro Mahamman Gaani, King of Busa (Borgu, northern Nigeria) about the 'Kisra' stories of origin (C.1910), *Sudanic Africa,* 3 (1992) 109–132

3329 **Hallam, W K R,** Rabih and the European powers in the Chad Basin, 1891–1901, *Annals of Borno,* **6/7,** (1989/1990) 23–34

3330 **Kani, A M, Gandi, K A** (eds), *State and society in the Sokoto Caliphate.* Sokoto: Usman dan Fodio University, 1990, 340pp

3331 **Lovejoy, P E, Kanya-Forstner, S,** Collaborative research in the recovery of documentation on the conquest of the Sokoto Caliphate, *Sudanic Africa,* 3 (1992) 165–72

3332 **Mohammed, A R,** The popular phase of Islam in Ebiraland, Nigeria: the roles of Sheikh Ahmad Rufai and el-Hajj Abdulmalik, *Islam et sociétés au Sud du Sahara,* 6 (1992) 47–63

3333 **Musa, S,** Leadership in Islam: a case study of the leadership qualities of Sultan Muhammed Bello, *Hamdard islamicus,* **15,** 3 (1992) 33–46

3334 **Ogbomo, O W, Ogbomo, Q O,** Women and society in precolonial Iyede, *Anthropos,* **88,** 3/4 (1993) 431–41

3335 **Olukoju, A,** Oral traditions and the political history of Oka-Akoko, *History in Africa,* **20,** (1993) 249–62

3336 **Raji, R A,** The 'Ishriniyat' of Al-Fazazi: an aspect of the precedence of the Kanem-Borno empire in Arabic and Islamic scholarship, *Annals of Borno,* **6/7,** (1989/1990) 1–10

3337 **Rowlands, M,** The good and bad death: ritual killing and historical transformation in a West African kingdom, *Paideuma,* **39,** (1993) 291–301

History, C20th

See also: 3271, 3279, 3475, 3853

3338 **Achebe, C,** A letter, in Gailey, C W (ed), *Dialectical anthropology: essays in honour of Stanley Diamond, Vol. 1* (Gainesville: University Press of Florida, 1992), 133–36

3339 **Adebayo, A G,** *Embattled federalism: history of revenue allocation in Nigeria, 1946–1990.* New York: Lang, 1993, 265pp

3340 **Adeyanju, T,** *The Rev. Israel Oluditun Ransome-Kuti: teacher and nation builder.* Abeokuta: Litany Nigeria, 1993, 232pp

3341 **Afolabi, M O,** A bibliography of the Nigerian governments' commissions of inquiry reports and accompanying white papers from 1920 to 1986, *Government publications review,* **20,** 3 (1993) 297–358

3342 **Ajayi, R,** Politics and traditional institutions in Nigeria: a historical overview, *Transafrican journal of history,* 21 (1992) 124–38

3343 **Akinyele, R,** A Western Niger Province, or constitutional safeguards: the search for an effective remedy to the fears of the Igbo West of the Niger, 1941–54, *Immigrants and minorities,* **11,** 2 (1992) 156–70

3344 **Apata, Z O,** Lugard and the creation of provincial administration, northern Nigeria 1900–1918, *Transafrican journal of history,* 21 (1992) 111–23

3345 **Aronson, L,** *Weaving and the British presence in southeastern Nigeria after 1900.* Boston: African Studies Centre, Boston University, 1991, 17pp

3346 **Ayandele, E A,** *The Ijebu of Yorubaland, 1850–1950: politics, economy and society.* Ibadan: Heinemann, 1992, 356pp

3347 **Ehindero, S G,** *The constitutional development of Nigeria 1849–1989.* Jos: Ehindero, 1991, 368pp

3348 **Elegbede-Fernandez, A D,** *Lagos: a legacy of honour. Dosumu (1861) - Babangida (1991).* Ibadan: Spectrum, 1992, 203pp

3349 **Falola, T** (ed), *Modern Nigeria: a tribute to G O Olusanya.* Lagos: Modelor, 1990, 248pp

3350 **Falola, T,** Ibadan power elite and the search for political order, 1893–1939, *Africa (Rome),* **47,** 3 (1992) 336–354

3351 **Falola, T,** 'Salt is gold': the management of salt scarcity in Nigeria during World War II, *Canadian journal of African studies,* **26,** 3 (1992) 412–36

3352 **Hogendorn, J, Lovejoy, P E,** Keeping slaves in place: the secret debate on the slavery question in northern Nigeria, 1900–1904, in Inikori, J E & Engerman, S L (eds), *The Atlantic slave trade (Item 2500),* 49–75

3353 **Huydecoper van Nigtevecht, J L R, van Emden, A,** *Honger als wapen: de Biafraoorlog 1967–1970.* 's-Gravenhage: Sdu Uitgeverij Koninginnegracht, 1992, 88pp

3354 **Ina, K E,** The tax crisis of 1929 in Ibibioland, *Transafrican journal of history,* 21 (1992) 171–81

3355 **Kirk-Greene, A H M,** Nigeria: a constitutional chronology and documentary calendar, 1919–1989, *African research and documentation,* 57 (1991) 1–5

3356 **Ludwig, F,** *Kirche im kolonialen Kontext: anglikanische Missionare und afrikanische Propheten im südöstlichen Nigeria, 1879–1918.* Frankfurt: Lang, 1992, 405pp

3357 **Mason, M,** The history of Mr Johnson: progress and protest in northern Nigeria 1900–1921, *Canadian journal of African studies,* **27,** 2 (1993) 196–217

3358 **Misra, D M,** Public reaction to the Lebanese presence in Nigeria during the colonial period, in Hourani, A & Shehadi, N (eds), *The Lebanese in the world* (London: Tauris, 1992), 565–78

3359 **Oduyoye, M A,** *Leadership development in the Methodist Church Nigeria, 1842–1962.* Ibadan: Sefer, 1992, 107pp

3360 **Oduyoye, M A,** *The Wesleyan presence in Nigeria, 1842–1962: an exploration of power, control and partnership in mission.* Ibadan: Sefer, 1992, 160pp

3361 **Ottenberg, S,** *Colonialism and the individual: a Nigerian life history.* Boston: African Studies Centre, Boston University, 1992, 26pp

3362 **Saaed, A G,** British fears over mahdism in northern Nigeria: a look at Bormi 1903, Satiru 1906 and Dumbulwa 1923, *Frankfurter afrikanistische Blätter,* 4 (1992) 34–46

3363 **Tignor, R L,** Political corruption in Nigeria before independence, *Journal of modern African studies,* **31,** 2 (1993) 175–202

3364 **Yakubu, A M,** Coercing old guard emirs in northern Nigeria: the abdication of Yakubu III of Bauchi, 1954, *African affairs,* **92,** 369 (1993) 593–604

Industry & trade

See also: 460, 3214, 3280, 3290, 3291, 3409, 3626, 3629

3365 **Adubifa, O A,** Technology policy in national development: a comparative study of the automobile industry in Nigeria and Brazil, *Journal of Asian and African studies,* **28,** 1/2 (1993) 42–53

3366 **Akarakiri, J B, et al,** A study of coal production in Nigeria, *Materials and society,* **15,** 4 (1991) 255–71

3367 **Chukwujekwu, S,** Development of design and manufacturing capabilities in a small Nigerian company, in Bhalla, A S (ed), *Small and medium enterprises* (London: Intermediate Technology, 1992), 175–81

3368 **Dikke, E, Ihuoma, A A,** Some aspects of technological capacity in the Nigerian leather industry: results from a field survey, *Science, technology and development,* **11,** 2 (1993) 144–65

3369 **Fadahunsi, A, Igwe, B U N** (eds), *Capital goods, technological change and accumulation in Nigeria.* London: Codesria, 1990, 204pp

3370 **Gebert, D, et al** (eds), *Traditionsorientierung und unternehmerischer Erfolg: Studien zum Selbverständnis nigerianischer Geschäftsleute.* Saarbrucken: Breitenbach, 1992, 410pp

3371 **Hathaway, J T,** 'Go-slow': the political economy of urban transport in Nigeria with an emphasis on Ado-Ekiti, *Geoforum,* **24,** 2 (1993) 165–82

3372 **Mba, H C,** The transport system and socioeconomic development, in Taylor, R W (ed), *Urban development in Nigeria (Item 3657),* 72–82

3373 **Moseley, K P,** Seizing the chance: economic crisis and industrial restructuring in Nigeria, in Nyang'oro, J E & Shaw, T M (eds), *Beyond structural adjustment (Item 179),* 119–47

3374 **Ogunrinola, O,** Determinants of entrepreneurship development in the urban informal sector of Lagos, *Africa development,* **17,** 4 (1992) 81–97

3375 **Okoroafo, S C,** Firm performance in a liberalised environment: empirical evidence from a developing country, *Journal of business research,* **28,** 3 (1993) 175–89

3376 **Oluwasanmi, A J,** Road accident trends in Nigeria, *Accident analysis and prevention,* **25,** 4 (1993) 485–87

3377 **Onwuka, R I,** *A political economy of the control of transnational corporations in Nigeria.* Owerri: International Universities Press, 192, 155pp

3378 **Soremekun, K, Obi, C,** The changing pattern of private foreign investments in Nigerian oil industry, *Africa development,* **18,** 3 (1993) 5–20

3379 **Uniamikogbo, S O,** The state of the capital goods industry in a developing economy: the case of Nigeria, *Indian journal of economics,* **72,** 286 (1992) 319–34

3380 **Wilfert, A,** *Die strategien nigerianischer Unternehmer bei wechselnden ökonomischen Rahmenbedindigung: eine empirische Analyse des Wirkungen des Strukturanpassungsprogrammes.* Fuchsstadt: Wilfer, 1992, 283pp

International economic relations

See also: 3201, 3378, 3425, 3593

3381 **Abutudu, M I M,** Nigerian-European Community economic relations: an appraisal, in Obadan, M I (ed), *The Single European Market (Europe 1992) and the developing countries* (Benin City: University of Benin, 1992), 42–57

3382 **Adebayo, A G,** South-South aid: a survey of Nigeria's financial and technical assistance to African countries in the 1980s, *Nigerian journal of international affairs,* **16,** 1 (1990) 20–48

3383 **Agene, C E,** *Foreign exchange and international trade in Nigeria.* Lagos: Gene Publications, 1991, 220pp

3384 **Alade, J A,** The role of multinational corporations in economic development: the Nigerian experience, *Quarterly journal of administration,* **25,** 3/4 (1991) 291–306

3385 **Asiwaju, A I,** *The Nigeria/Benin transborder trade, border control, and the Nigerian structural adjustment program.* Boston: African Studies Center, Boston University, 1991, 25pp

3386 **Badejo, B A,** Nigeria's economic relationship with Brazil and India: an assessment of South-South cooperation, *Nigerian journal of international affairs,* **16,** 1 (1990) 73–89

3387 **Mordi, K,** Nigeria and the EEC: an association of mutul advantage?, in Obadan, M I (ed), *The Single European Market (Europe 1992) and the developing countries* (Benin City: University of Benin, 1992), 58–69

International relations

See also: 567, 3015, 3472

3388 **Adefuye, A,** *Culture and foreign policy: the Nigerian example.* Lagos: NIIA, 1992, 230pp

3389 **Adelusi, U,** An application of the concept of independence to the study of bilateral relations: the case of Nigeria and France, in Jacob, H J & Omar, M (eds), *France and Nigeria (Item 3395)*, 92–104

3390 **Akinrinade, O,** From hostility to accomodation: Nigeria's West African policy 1984–90, *Nigerian journal of international affairs,* **18,** 1 (1992) 47–77

3391 **Asiwaju, A I, Barkindo, B M** (eds), *The Nigerian-Niger transborder cooperation.* Lagos: Malthouse, 1993, 517pp

3392 **Fawole, W A,** Babangida and Nigeria's foreign policy: reality and pragmatism in external relations, *Review of African political affairs,* **4,** 1/2 (1990) 5–20

3393 **Inamete, U B,** The conceptual framework of Nigerian foreign policy, *Australian journal of politics and history,* **39,** 1 (1993) 72–87

3394 **Izah, P P,** *Continuity and change in Nigerian foreign policy.* Zaria: Ahmadu Bello University Press, 1991, 153pp

3395 **Jacob, H J, Omar, M** (eds), *France and Nigeria: issues in comparative studies.* Ibadan: CREDU, 1992, 180pp

3396 **Jolaoso, O,** *In the shadows: reflections of a pioneer diplomat.* Lagos: Malthouse, 1993, 236pp

3397 **Nwuneli, O, et al,** Media use, knowledge of world affairs, and image of nations among Nigerian youth, *Africa media review,* **7,** 1 (1993) 33–49

3398 **Owoeye, J** (ed), *Nigeria in international institutions.* Ibadan: College Press, 1993, 200pp

Labour & manpower

See also: 3634

3399 **Aduaka, E E,** Constraints on succession planning: the Nigerian public service experience, *African administrative studies,* 38 (1992) 47–60

3400 **Agbola, T,** Manpower problems in the building industry, in Taylor, R W (ed), *Urban development in Nigeria (Item 3657)*, 145–53

3401 **Fashoyin, T,** Nigeria; consequences for employment, in Adepoju, A (ed), *Impact of structural adjustment (Item 1107)*, 78–91

3402 **Gbosi, A N,** The impact of wage commissions on labour-management relations in Nigeria, 1964–84, *Quarterly journal of administration,* **25,** 3/4 (1991) 307–23

3403 Gbosi, A N, Nigeria's contemporary industrial relations policies: a critical review, *Indian journal of industrial relations,* **28,** 3 (1993) 248–57

3404 Nnoli, O, The deteriorating condition of the Nigerian working class, in Nnoli, O (ed), *Deadend to Nigerian development (item 3137),* 154–79

3405 Okunla, P O, *High level manpower utilisation in the new local government structure: a case study of Oyo State.* Ibadan: NISER, 1991, 54pp

3406 Olugbemi, S O, *Labour productivity and the Nigerian public service.* Ikeja: Pumark, 1990, 26pp

3407 Omaji, P O, The state and industrial relations: background to the adoption of compulsory arbitration law in Australian and Nigeria, *British journal of industrial relations,* **31,** 1 (1993) 37–55

3408 Otobo, D (ed), *Further readings in Nigerian industrial relations.* Ikeja: Malthouse, 1992, 198pp

3409 Sawyerr, O O, Environmental uncertainty and environmental scanning activities of Nigerian manufacturing executives: a comparative analysis, *Strategic management journal,* **14,** 4 (1993) 287–99

3410 Uno, J U, *New approaches to training: a preliminary review of Nigeria's national open apprenticeship scheme (NOAS).* Geneva: ILO, 1990, 21pp

Language

See also: 618

3412 Brann, C M B, Democratisation of language use in public domains in Nigeria, *Journal of modern African studies,* **31,** 4 (1993) 639–56

3413 Mann, C C, The sociolinguistic status of Anglo-Nigerian pidgin: an overview, *International journal of the sociology of language,* 101–101 (1993) 167–78

3414 Nwoye, O G, Linguistic politeness and sociocultural variations of the notion of face, *Journal of pragmatics,* 18 (1992) 309–28

Law

See also: 3297, 3377, 3407, 3491, 3615

3415 Aduba, J N, Overcrowding in Nigerian prisons: a critical appraisal, *Journal of criminal justice,* **21,** 2 (1993) 185–91

3416 Ajetunmob, M A, Reorganisation of legal system in northern Nigeria: appraisal of 1958 recommendations, *Islamic and comparative law quarterly,* 10/11 (1990/91) 96–108

3417 Alemika, E E O, Trends and conditions of imprisonment in Nigeria, *International journal of offender therapy and comparative criminology,* **37,** 2 (1993) 147–62

3418 Guobadia, A, Constitutional instability and legitimacy in Africa: issues, conflicts and solutions - the Nigerian experience, *Annual conference (African society of international and comparative law),* **4,** (1992) 112–140

3419 Gye-Wado, O, Nigerian law and the toxic waste question: another dimension of the limits of international law?, *Nigerian journal of international affairs,* **16,** 2 (1990) 61–85

3420 Inocent, C, *The Nigerian police and individual liberties.* Lagos: Civil Liberties Organisation, 1993, 30pp

3421 Jegede, O, Book scarcity, law libraries and the legal profession in Nigeria, *International information and library review,* **25,** 2 (1993) 141–64

3422 Nnabue, U S F, Towards the

liberalisation of abortion laws in Nigeria, *Lawyers' journal,* **1,** 2 (1990) 65–69

3423 Obot, I S, Ethical and legal issues in the control of drug abuse and drug trafficking: the Nigerian case, *Social science and medicine,* **35,** 4 (1992) 481–93

3424 Odinkaly, A C, *Justice denied: the area courts system in the northern states of Nigeria.* Lagos: Kraft, 1992, 157pp

3425 Osinbajo, Y, Sovereign immunity in international commercial arbitration: the Nigerian experience and emerging state practice, *African journal of international and comparative law,* **4,** 1 (1992) 1–25

3426 Osinbajo, Y, Kalu, A (eds), *Democracy and the law: papers presented at the second conference of the Body of Attorneys General in the Federation.* Lagos: Federal Ministry of Justice, 1991, 338pp

3427 Read, J S, Nigeria's new constitution for 1992: the Third Republic, *Journal of African law,* **35,** 1/2 (1991) 174–93

3428 Udo, R K, *Land use policy and land ownership in Nigeria.* Lagos: Ebieakwa Ventures, 1990, 166pp

3430 Yadudu, A H, Colonialism and the transformation of islamic law in the northern states of Nigeria, *Journal of legal pluralism and unofficial law,* 32 (1992) 103–39

Library - documentation

See also: 3421

3431 Adeniran, O R, et al, The use of microcomputers in Nigerian libraries and information centres, *Journal of information science,* **19,** 3 (1993) 239–46

3432 Agboola, A T, Third-generation Nigerian university libraries, *International information and library review,* **25,** 1 (1993) 43–59

3433 Hair, P E H, The Nigerian Records Survey remembered, *History in Africa,* **20,** (1993) 391–94

3434 Heap, S, The Nigerian National Archives, Kaduna: an introduction for users and a summary of holdings, *History in Africa,* **20,** (1993) 395–407

3435 Ifidon, S E, The effects of government funding on university libraries in Nigeria, in Wise, M & Olden, A (eds), *Information and libraries (item 672),* 90–106

3436 Nwokocha, U, Resources utilisation by adults in Nigeria: the case of two public libraries, *International information and library review,* **25,** 1 (1993) 85–91

3437 Ochogwu, M G, Producing the basic competences in information science education in Nigeria, *Education for information,* **11,** 2 (1993) 147–54

3438 Ogunbameru, A, Acquisition of government publications: the Nigerian experience, *Government publications review,* **20,** 5 (1993) 515–21

3439 Okojie, V O, Review of automated library and information services in Nigeria, *Program-automated library and information systems,* **27,** 2 (1993) 191–95

3440 Tiamiyu, M A, The realities of developing modern information resources management systems in government organisations in developing countries with particular reference to Nigeria, *Journal of information science,* **19,** 3 (1993) 189–97

3441 Tiamiyu, M A, Source use by Nigerian civil servants and their organisational and information exposure characteristics, *Journal of information science,* **19,** 5 (1993) 339–47

Literature

See also: 700

3442 **Awodiya, D M** (ed), *Excursions in drama and literature: interviews with Femi Osofisan.* Lagos: Kraft, 1993, 144pp

3443 **Bardolph, J,** Des littératures populaires de langue anglaise: Nigeria, Kenya, *Bulletin des études africaines de l'INALCO,* **9,** 17/18 (1992) 23–41

3444 **Ezeigbo, T A,** *Fact and fiction in the literature of the Nigerian civil war.* Ojo: Unity, 1991, 202pp

3445 **Gingell, S,** Controlling communication: Wole Soyinka's Death and the king's horseman, in Whitlock, G & Toffin, H (eds), *Re-siting Queen's English: text and tradition in post-colonial literature* (Amsterdam: Rodolpi, 1992), 103–115)

3446 **Griswold, W,** The writing on the mud wall: Nigerian novels and the imaginary village, *American sociological review,* **57,** 6 (1992) 709–24

3447 **Hogg, P, Sternberg, I,** *Market literature from Nigeria: a checklist.* London: British Library, 1990, 125pp

3448 **Iji, E M,** *Three radical dramatists: Brecht, Artaud, Soyinka.* Lagos: Kraft, 1991, 129pp

3449 **Iji, E M,** *Understanding Brecht and Soyinka.* Lagos: Kraft, 1991, 216pp

3450 **Kolawole, G,** On the making of Wole Soyinka's poetry: a literary inquiry into his sources, *Journal of Asian and African studies (Tokyo),* 44 (1992) 119–30

3451 **Lindfors, B,** Amos Tutuola: oral tradition and the motif-index, *Current bibliography on African affairs,* **24,** 3 (1992/1993) 229–249

3452 **Maduakor, O,** The political content of Wole Soyinka's plays, *Journal of Commonwealth literature,* **28,** 1 (1993) 82–96

3453 **Muoneke, R O,** *Art and redemption: a reading of the novels of Chinua Achebe.* New York: Lang, 1993, 186pp

3454 **Mwachukwu, J O J,** The eighties and the return to oral cadence in Nigerian poetry, *Matatu,* 10 (1993) 85–105

3455 **Ogundele, W,** Criticism and the tradition of political poetry in Africa: the example of Wole Soyinka, *Ufahamu,* **19,** 2/3 (1990/1991) 51–66

3456 **Oko, A,** *The tragic paradox: a study of Wole Soyinka.* Lagos: Kraft, 1992, 116pp

3457 **Palmer, E,** Isidore Okpewho's The last duty, *International fiction review,* **20,** 1 (1993) 22–32

3458 **Rhoads, D A,** Culture in Chinua Achebe's Things fall apart, *African studies review,* **36,** 2 (1993) 61–72

3459 **Simola, R,** The Flute, The Drum and How the Leopard got his Claws by Chinua Achebe, *Nordic journal of African studies,* **2,** 1 (1993) 87–102

3460 **ten Kortenaar, N,** 'Only connect': Anthills of the savannah and Achebe's trouble with Nigeria, *Research in African literatures,* **24,** 3 (1993) 59–72

3461 **Williams, A,** Ritual and the political unconscious: the case of Death and the king's horseman, *Research in African literatures,* **24,** 1 (1993) 67–79

3462 **Wright, D,** *Wole Soyinka revisited.* New York: Twayne, 1993, 219pp

Media

3463 **Agbaje, A,** Beyond the state: civil society and the Nigerian press under military rule, *Media, culture and society,* **15,** 3 (1993) 455–72

3464 **Agbaje, A A B,** *The Nigerian press: hegemony and the social construction of legitimacy 1960–1983.* Lewiston: Mellen, 1992, 333pp

3465 **Amienyi, O P,** Adult attitudes towards mass media in Nigeria, *Africa media review,* **7,** 1 (1993) 19–32

3466 **Bosompra, K,** Television, sexual behaviour and attitudes towards AIDS: a study in cultivation analysis, *Africa media review,* **7,** 3 (1993) 35–62

3467 **Hayatu, H** (ed), *Fifty years of truth: the story of Gaskiya Corporation, Zaria, 1939–1991.* Zaria: Gaskiya, 1991, 190pp

3468 **Ibrahim, M,** *The radio as a campaign instrument.* Maiduguri: University of Maiduguri Press, 1991, 21pp

3469 **Igbarumah, M,** *Ideology: the mass media and journalism.* Jos: Jos University Press, 1990, 47pp

3470 **Jimada, U,** Eurocentric media training in Nigeria; what alternative?, *Journal of Black studies,* **23,** 2 (1992) 366–79

3471 **Nwokeafor, C, Nwanko, R N,** Development information content in the African mass media: a study of two Nigerian dailies, *Africa media review,* **7,** 3 (1993) 75–90

3472 **Okere, L C,** Nigerian press and the expulsion of West African aliens, 1983, *International studies,* **29,** 2 (1992) 327–38

3473 **Okoye, I,** Video in the lives of Nigerian children, *Africa media review,* **7,** 3 (1993) 63–74

3474 **Oso, L,** Agriculture on Nigerian television: a critique of current practice, *Africa media review,* **7,** 2 (1993) 31–43

3475 **Ugochukwu, F,** La guerre de Biafra à la radio: situation militaire et livraisons d'armes en 1968–1969, *Peuples noirs, peuples africains,* **14,** 80 (1991) 60–76

Medical

See also: 3466

3476 **Abiodun, O A,** Emotional illness in a pediatric population in Nigeria, *Journal of tropical pediatrics,* **39,** 1 (1993) 49–57

3477 **Abiodun, O A,** A study of mental morbidity among primary care patients in Nigeria, *Comprehensive psychiatry,* **34,** 1 (1993) 10–13

3478 **Abiodun, O A, et al,** Psychiatric morbidity in a pregnant population in Nigeria, *General hospital psychiatry,* **15,** 2 (1993) 125–28

3479 **Adamson, T A,** Psychiatric illness in first-degree relatives of Nigerian schizophrenic and surgical control patients, *Tropical and geographical medicine,* **45,** 2 (1993) 73–76

3480 **Adelekan, M L, et al,** Psychsocial correlates of alcohol, tobacco and cannabis use: findings from a Nigerian university, *Drug and alcohol dependence,* **33,** 3 (1993) 247–56

3481 **Aderibigbe, Y A, et al,** Postnatal emotional disorders in Nigerian women: a study of antecedents and associations, *British journal of psychiatry,* **163,** Nov. (1993) 645–50

3482 **Adewuyi, J O,** Current prevalence and some clinical associations of childhood anaemia in urban and rural communities of central Nigeria, *Central African journal of medicine,* **38,** 2 (1992) 66–72

3483 **Akpala, C O,** Perinatal mortality in a northern Nigerian rural community, *Journal of the Royal Society of Health,* **113,** 3 (1993) 124–27

3484 **Baiyewu, O,** The effect of demographic and health variables on a modified form of mini-mental state examination scores in Nigerian elderly community residents, *International journal of geriatric psychiatry,* **8,** 6 (1993) 503–10

3485 **Chikwem, J O, et al** (eds), *AIDS prevention and control.* Kaduna: Gbakeks, 1990, 136pp

3486 **Chikwem, J O, et al,** Factors affecting the seroprevalence of human immunodeficiency virus (HIV) infection in female prostitutes in Borno State of Nigeria, *Annals of Borno,* **6/7,** (1989/1990) 273–278

3487 **Hamidu, L J,** Guinea worm (Dracunculus medinensis) infection in Mafi and Kawaram, Borno State, *Annals of Borno,* **6/7,** (1989/1990) 106–114

3488 **Hollos, M, Richards, F,** Gender-associated development of formal operations in Nigerian adolescents, *Ethos,* **21,** 1 (1993) 24–52

3489 **Igun, U A,** Knowledge of AIDS and preventive behaviour in Maiduguri, Borno State, *Annals of Borno,* **6/7,** (1989/1990) 88–98

3490 **McLennan, J, et al,** Death anxiety and death denial: Nigerian and Australian students' metaphors of personal death, *Journal of psychology,* **127,** 4 (1993) 399–407

3491 **Ogungbemi, K, Ahmed, M H,** Psychosocial aspects of murder in Nigeria, *Forensic science international,* **59,** 2 (1993) 157–62

3492 **Ohaeri, J U, Odejide, O A,** Admissions for drug and alcohol-related problems in Nigerian psychiatric care facilities in one year, *Drug and alcohol dependence,* **31,** 2 (1993) 101–109

3493 **Okonofua, F E, et al,** Maternal mortality in ife-Ife, Nigeria: a study of risk factors, *Studies in family planning,* **23,** 5 (1992) 319–24

3494 **Olaleye, O D, et al,** Prevalence of HIV type–1 and type–2 infections in Nigeria, *Journal of infectious diseases,* **167,** 3 (1993) 710–714

3495 **Orubuloye, L O, et al,** African women's control over their sexuality in an era of AIDS: a study of the Yoruba of Nigeria, *Social science and medicine,* **37,** 7 (1993) 859–72

Natural resources

3496 **Ayedelo, A I,** Energy development and utilisation within the subsidisation policy in Africa: the Nigerian case, in Khennas, S (ed), *Industrialisation (item 454),* 81–111

3497 **Hyman, E L,** Forestry policies and programmes for fuelwood supply in northern Nigeria, *Land use policy,* **10,** 1 (1993) 26–43

3498 **Oseogbo, G J,** Agricultural land use in Nigerian forestry reserves: towards a solution to problems or conflict in biotic conservation, *Land use policy,* **10,** 1 (1993) 44–48

Planning

See also: 3592, 3648, 3657

3499 **Adeniji, K,** Physical planning framework: an overview, in Taylor, R W (ed), *Urban development in Nigeria (Item 3657),* 57–62

3500 **Adeniji, K, Oyeneye, O Y,** Training town planners in a depressed economy, in Taylor, R W (ed), *Urban development in Nigeria (Item 3657),* 95–100

3501 **Barimah, A A,** Integrated agricultural development project planning in Nigeria, *Journal of rural development,* **11,** 6 (1992) 713–28

3502 **Egunjobi, T O,** Economic planning and physical planning: an integrated approach, in Taylor, R

W (ed), *Urban development in Nigeria (Item 3657)*, 63–71

3503 **Egunjobi, T O,** Regional planning and rural development, in Taylor, R W (ed), *Urban development in Nigeria (Item 3657)*, 83–94

3504 **Olujimi, J A B,** The administration of physical planning in Nigeria: the Ondo State experience, *Landscape and urban planning,* **25,** 1 (1993) 115–26

Politics

See also: 833, 3176, 3203, 3208, 3270, 3275, 3288, 3339, 3349, 3395, 3399, 3412, 3418, 3426, 3429, 3441, 3455, 3464, 3573, 3574, 3577

3505 **Adedeji, O,** Communication barriers in Nigerian Local Government Areas, *Quarterly journal of administration,* **25,** 3/4 (1991) 324–32

3506 **Adedeji, O,** Understanding Nigerian political office holders and their cold attitude to public accountability, *Review of African political affairs,* **6,** 1/2 (1992) 71–80

3507 **Adenuga, O K O,** *Modern local government administration in Ogun State of Nigeria (1976–1992).* Onitsha: Africana-FEP, 1991, 89pp

3508 **Adewale, I A** (ed), *Issues on the practice of local government in Nigeria.* Ikeja: Comfort Press, 1990, 172pp

3509 **Agbakoba, O,** Loosening legal and political constraints on NGOs: the case of Nigeria, in Sandbrook, R & Halfani, M (eds), *Empowering people (Item 930)*, 120–24

3510 **Aguwa, J C U,** *Religious dichotomy in Nigerian politics.* Enugu: Fourth Dimension, 1993, 32pp

3511 **Ahamba, M I,** *Twin pillars of unity: freedom and justice.* Enugu: Fourth Dimension, 1990, 93pp

3512 **Akindele, S T,** The reinstatement of Local Government Service Commission in Nigeria: an examination of its effects on local government autonomy, *Review of African political affairs,* **6,** 1/2 (1992) 5–21

3513 **Amadife, E N,** The challenge of democratisation in Nigeria: involvement or alienation of the military?, *Ufahamu,* **20,** 1 (1991/92) 30–43

3514 **Aminu, L S,** *Nigeria's weapons procurement process: its implications for her defence policy.* Lagos: Nigerian Institute for International Affairs, 1992, 64pp

3515 **Amuwo, K,** Treetop politics versus grassroots democracy in Nigeria: some theoretical and methodological queries, *Africa (Rome)*, **47,** 4 (1992) 617–626

3516 **Aniagolu, A N,** *The making of the 1989 constitution of Nigeria.* Ibadan: Spectrum, 1993, 307pp

3517 **Arogbofa, J O,** *The man marches on.* Ibadan: Spectrum, 1992, 145pp

3518 **Babatope, E,** *Student power in Nigeria (1956–1980).* Lagos: Ebino Topsy, 1991, 193pp

3519 **Barnes, K D,** The ban on corporate political donations in Nigerian law and the prospects of enforcement, *Review of African political affairs,* **4,** 1/2 (1990) 42–52

3520 **Bassey, C O,** Defence planning in the Nigerian armed forces modernisation process (1970–1991): an institutional analysis, *Armed forces and society,* **19,** 2 (1993) 253–77

3521 **Blaney, D L, Pasha, M K,** Civil society and democracy in the Third World: ambiguities and historical possibilities, *Studies in comparative international development,* **28,** 1 (1993) 3–24

3522 **Civil Liberties Organisation,** *Executive lawlessness in the*

Babangida regime. Lagos: Civil Liberties Organisation, 1991, 19pp

3523 **Daloz, J P,** Nouvelle République, nouvelle réplique? Velléités transformatrices et perpétuation des comportments politiques au Nigeria, *Année africaine 1992/93,* 59–88

3524 **Dare, L O,** *The praetorian trap: the problems and prospects of military disengagement.* Ile Ife: Obafemi Awolowo University Press, 1991, 31pp

3525 **Duyile, D,** *Profiles of selected ministers of information of Nigeria (1956–1992) and the Federal Ministry of Information.* Ibadan: Ororo, 1992, 148pp

3526 **Egwu, S G,** Ethnicity, economic crisis and national development in Nigeria, in Nnoli, O (ed), *Deadend to Nigerian development (item 3137),* 44–78

3527 **Egwurube, J,** Local power in France and Nigeria compared, in Jacob, H J & Omar, M (eds), *France and Nigeria (Item 3395),* 119–36

3528 **Egwurube, J,** Nigeria and France: problems of the comparative method, in Jacob, H J & Omar, M (eds), *France and Nigeria (Item 3395),* 1–10

3529 **Eleanyu, L U,** *Great lessons for the Third Republic.* Enugu: Auto-Century, 1991, 137pp

3530 **Fadahunsi, O,** Reforming the Nigerian civil service for the economic recovery programme of the 1990s and beyond, *African management development forum,* **2,** 1 (1991) 15–23

3531 **Fajonyomi, S O,** A review of December 8 local government election in Nigeria, *African review,* **18,** 1/2 (1991) 1–9

3532 **Gambari, I,** The role of religion in national life: reflections on recent experiences in Nigeria, in Hunwick, J O (ed), *Religion and national integration (Item 978),* 85–99

3533 **Hart, C,** The Nigerian elections of 1983, *Africa,* **63,** 3 (1993) 397–418

3534 **Ibrahim, J,** Le développement de l'état nigerian, in Médard, J F (ed), *Etats d'Afrique noire (Item 896),* 141–72

3535 **Ibrahim, J,** Political party corruption in Nigeria and in France, in Jacob, H J & Omar, M (eds), *France and Nigeria (Item 3395),* 137–50

3536 **Ifowodo, O** (ed), *Human rights in retreat: a report on seven years of human rights violations by the miliary regime of General Ibrahim Babangida, August 1985 to August 1992.* Lagos: Civil Liberties Organisation, 1993, 204pp

3537 **Kieh, G K, Agbese, P O,** From politics back to the barracks in Nigeria: a theoretical exploration, *Journal of peace research,* **30,** 4 (1993) 409–36

3538 **Kwarteng, C O,** Nigeria's elusive search for nationhood, *Africa insight,* **23,** 1 (1993) 24–35

3539 **Lawuyi, O B,** Honorary chieftancy title award as perspective to the administrative culture in the Yoruba society, *Quarterly journal of administration,* **25,** 3/4 (1991) 333–46

3540 **Layonu, T, et al,** *Reflections on leadership in Nigeria.* Ibadan: Laytal Communications, 1993, 254pp

3541 **Mustapha, A R,** Ever decreasing circles: democratic rights in Nigeria, in Nnoli, O (ed), *Deadend to Nigerian development (item 3137),* 79–96

3543 **Nwabueze, B O,** *Military rule and social justice in Nigeria.* Ibadan: Spectrum, 1993, 310pp

3544 **Nwankwo, A A,** *Nigeria, the political transition and the future of democracy.* Enugu: Fourth Dimension, 1993, 404pp

3545 Ogbemudia, S O, *Years of challenge.* Ibadan: Heinemann, 1991, 266pp

3546 Ohadike, D, Muslim-Christian conflict and political instability, in Hunwick, J O (ed), *Religion and national integration (Item 978)*, 101–24

3547 Okeke, C C S (ed), *Defence, patriotism and national development.* Onitsha: Veritas, 1990, 246pp

3548 Okigbo, C, Horserace and issues in Nigerian elections, *Journal of Black studies,* **22,** 3 (1992) 349–65

3549 Okoye, I K, *Soldiers and politics in Nigeria.* Enugu: New Age, 1991, 126pp

3551 Olagungu, T, et al, *Transition to democracy in Nigeria, 1985–1993.* Ibadan: Spectrum, 1993, 278pp

3552 Olowu, D, The Nigerian experience in administrative reform, *African administrative studies,* 39 (1992) 1–32

3553 Olowu, D, et al (eds), *Nigerian public administration: past, present and future.* Ibadan: Shaneson, 1991, 120pp

3554 Oludumi, O, The provision and financing of social services by local governments in rural Nigeria, *Quarterly journal of administration,* **25,** 3/4 (1991) 248–59

3555 Omar, M, The state of local government functionaries in France and Nigeria: a comparative analysis, in Jacob, H J & Omar, M (eds), *France and Nigeria (Item 3395)*, 169–80

3556 Osaghae, E E, The status of state governments in Nigeria's federalism: a study of the changing phases, *Indian journal of political science,* **52,** 2 (1991) 242–61

3557 Osogwa, J, *C C Onoh: politics and power in eastern Nigeria.* Enugu: Idika, 1991, 219pp

3558 Reno, W, Old brigades, money bags, new breeds, and the ironies of reform in Nigeria, *Canadian journal of African studies,* **27,** 1 (1993) 66–87

3559 Sanda, A O, *Essays in public administration.* Ibadan: Fact Finders International, 1991, 163pp

3560 Sanusi, H U, *Public policy coordination in Nigeria.* Kuru: National Institute for Policy and Strategic Studies, 1992, 182pp

3561 Shettima, K A, Structural adjustment and the student movement in Nigeria, *Review of African political economy,* 56 (1993) 83–91

3562 Sil, N P, Ideology, intellectuals and development in Nigeria: problems and prospects, *Africa (Rome)*, **48,** 1 (1993) 47–69

3563 Sil, N P, Nigerian intellectuals and socialism: retrospect and prospect, *Journal of modern African studies,* **31,** 3 (1993) 361–85

3564 Tamuno, T N, *Peace and violence in Nigeria: conflict resolution in society and the state.* Lagos: Federal Government Printer, 1991, 676pp

3565 Taylor, R W, The historical context, in Taylor, R W (ed), *Urban development in Nigeria (Item 3657)*, 25–43

3566 Tobi, N, *Understanding the 1989 constitution better: the citizens companion.* n.p.: Forward Press and Bookshop, 1992, 156pp

3567 Uba, U B, Umezurike, C, Ideology and national development, in Nnoli, O (ed), *Deadend to Nigerian development (item 3137)*, 27–43

3568 Wright, S, State consolidation and social integration in Nigeria: the military's search for the elusive, in Dietz, H et al (eds), *Ethnicity, integration and the military* (Boulder: Westview, 1991), 179–207

3569 Yahaya, A D, Akinyele, C I (eds), *Effective leadership: proceedings of the ministerial workshops on the Nigerian civil service*

reforms (1988). Ibadan: Spectrum, 1992, 180pp

Religion, philosophy

See also: 3232, 3239, 3362, 3510, 3532, 3546, 3567, 3620, 3637

3570 Adetunji, J A, Church-based obstetric care in a Yoruba community, Nigeria, *Social science and medicine,* **35,** 9 (1992) 1171–78

3571 Aigbe, S A, *Theory of social involvement: a case study in the anthropology of religion, state and society.* Lanham: University Press of America, 1993, 266pp

3572 Barkindo, B M, Growing islamisation in Kano city since 1970: causes, forms and implications, in Brenner, L (ed), *Muslim identity (item 963)*, 91–105

3573 Birai, U M, Islamic *tajdid* and the political process in Nigeria, in Marty, M E & Appleby, R S (eds), *Fundamentalism and the state* (Chicago: University of Chicago Press, 1993), 211–42

3574 Coulon, C, Les itinéraires politiques de l'islam au Nord-Nigeria, in Bayart, J C (ed), *Religion et modernité politique (item 960)*, 19–62

3575 Ebhomielen, P O, *Forty years of Nigerian Baptist Convention missions.* Benin City: Christian Network Organisation, 1993, 82pp

3576 Familusi, M M, *Methodism in Nigeria (1842–1992).* Ibadan: NPS Educational, 1992, 315pp

3577 Makinde, J A K, Religion and the modern state: comparative analysis of religion in civil society in Nigeria and France, in Jacob, H J & Omar, M (eds), *France and Nigeria (Item 3395)*, 151–68

3578 Mohammed, A R, The influence of the Niass Tijaniyya in the Niger-Benue confluence area of Nigeria, in Brenner, L (ed), *Muslim identity (item 963)*, 116–34

3579 Okafor, G M, *Development of christianity and Islam in modern Nigeria.* Würzberg: Echter, 1992, 240pp

3580 Onoh, C O, *Christianity and the Igbo rites of passage: the prospects of inculturation.* Frankfurt: Peter Lang, 1992, 263pp

3581 Peel, J D Y, An Africanist revisits *Magic and the millenium,* in Barker, E et al (eds), *Secularisation, rationalism and sectarianism* (Oxford: Clarendon, 1993), 81–100

3582 Rasmussen, L, *Religion and property in northern Nigeria: socio-economic development and Islamic and Christian influence in northern Nigeria, with special reference to the rights and views of property among the Birom and Kilba.* Copenhagen: Akademisk, 1990, 290pp

3583 Ray, B C, Aladura Christianity: a Yoruba religion, *Journal of religion in Africa,* **23,** 3 (1993) 266–91

3584 Umar, M S, Changing islamic identity in Nigeria from the 1960s to the 1980s: from sufism to anti-sufism, in Brenner, L (ed), *Muslim identity (item 963)*, 154–78

3585 Wambutda, D N, *A study of conversion among the Angas of Plateau State of Nigeria with emphasis on Christianity.* Frankfurt: Lang, 1991, 238pp

Rural economy

See also: 1030, 1933, 3245, 3249, 3269, 3277, 3281, 3474, 3501, 3503

3586 Adedeji, O, Participatory democracy for rural development and its constraints in Nigeria today, *Review of African political affairs,* **4,** 1/2 (1990) 62–75

3587 Adeyeye, V A, *Group farming in Oyo State, Nigeria: a comparison*

of male and female participants. Ibadan: NISER, 1991, 84pp

3588 **Arene, C J,** Comparative economics of maize and rice production among resource-poor farmers in Anambra State of Nigeria, *African development review,* **4,** 1 (1992) 102–113

3589 **Arene, C J,** Farm production credit use among smallholder farmers in rural Nigeria, *Journal of rural development,* **12,** 3 (1993) 275–80

3590 **Awotunden, J S,** Importance of agriculture and its integral role in rural development, *Review of African political affairs,* **4,** 1/2 (1990) 53–61

3591 **Ayo, S B,** *Focus on Niger River Basin Development Authority.* Ife-Ife: Obafemi Awolowo University, 1991, 41pp

3592 **Braimah, A A,** Integrated agricultural development project planning in Nigeria, *Journal of rural development,* **11,** 6 (1993) 713–28

3593 **Ekong, E E,** The role of the World Bank in Nigerian agricultural policy, *Africa development,* **17,** 3 (1992) 65–98

3594 **Ewuola, S O,** Agriculture in Nigeria's development process, *Journal of rural development,* **12,** 3 (1993) 269–73

3595 **Ibeanu, O,** The deteriorating condition of the Nigerian peasantry, in Nnoli, O (ed), *Deadend to Nigerian development (item 3137),* 124–53

3596 **Idowu, O, Guyer, J,** *Commercialisation and the harvest work of women, Ibarapa, Oyo State, Nigeria.* Ibadan: Institute of African Studies, Ibadan University, 1991, 35pp

3597 **Igodan, C O, Olawoye, J E,** Planning and execution of a pilot project on rural development: lessons from Badeku, Nigeria, *Journal of rural development and administration,* **24,** 3 (1992) 1–17

3598 **Kolajo, E F,** Financing peasant agriculture: the case of agricultural credit guarantee system in Nigeria, *Savings and development,* **17,** 1 (1993) 39–60

3599 **Kolawole, A,** Structural adjustment programmes and large scale irrigation systems in Nigeria, *Review of African political affairs,* **5,** 1/2 (1991) 5–16

3600 **Madu, E N, Umebali, E E,** Self help approach to rural transformation in Nigeria, *Community development journal,* **28,** 2 (1993) 141–53

3601 **Mohammed, J B,** The mediation of dependence: development communication planning for agricultural development in northern Nigeria, *Africa media review,* **7,** 2 (1993) 1–16

3602 **Odejide, A F,** *Case of Hadejia-Jama'are River Basin Development Authority, Kano.* Ife-Ife: Obafemi Awolowo University, 1991, 38pp

3603 **Ogunfiditimi, T O,** A survey of the socio-cultural and economic characteristics of the nomads in the arid zone agriculture of Nigeria, *Annals of Borno,* **6/7,** (1989/1990) 155–168

3604 **Ogunwale, S A,** Applicable structural adjustment programme strategies for improved irrigation systems management in Nigeria, *Review of African political affairs,* **5,** 1/2 (1991) 17–25

3605 **Okoiwak, E A,** Rural transformation: the key to poverty alleviation in Nigeria, in Asmerom, H K, et al (eds), *Bureacracy and developmental policies (Item 109),* 75–95

3606 **Okorji, E C, Obeichina, C O B,** The role of seed yam procurement arrangements in the smallholder cropping system on Anambra State, Nigeria, *African* *development review,* **5,** 1 (1993) 70–80

3607 **Olatubi, W O, et al,** *Special aspects of rural development in Nigeria.* Geissen: Justis Leibig University, 1991, 75pp

3608 **Olayiwole, C B,** The role of home economics agents in rural development programs in northern Nigeria: impacts of structural adjustment, in Gladwin, C H (ed), *Structural adjustment and African women farmers (Item 315),* 359–72

3609 **Olofson, H,** Eating the dry season in Funtua (1970–71): an ethnographer's view, *Anthropos,* **88,** 3/4 (1993) 419–29

3610 **Olomola, A S, Nwosu, A C** (eds), *Rural development strategies in Nigeria: proceedings of the sixth annual conference of the Nigerian Rural Sociological Association.* n.p.: Nigerian Rural Sociological Association, 1992, 273pp

3611 **Osemeobo, G J,** The hazards of rural poverty: decline of common property resources in Nigerian rain forest ecosystems, *Journal of environmental management,* **38,** 3 (1993) 201–212

3612 **Osemeobo, G J,** Land tenure issues on changing patterns of smallholder farming systems in Nigeria, *Journal of rural development,* **12,** 4 (1993) 403–12

3613 **Oyejide, T A,** The oil boom, macroeconomic policies and Nigerian agriculture: analysis of a 'Dutch disease' phenomenon, in Bautista, R M & Valdés, A (eds), *The bias against agriculture* (Washington: IFPRI, 1993), 77–92

3614 **Remi, A, Oyewole, A,** An evaluation of saving and investment behaviour of coperative fishermen in the riverine area of Nigeria, *Journal of environmental management,* **36,** 1 (1992) 27–34

3615 **Sa'ad, A,** Mode of production and informal law and justice in Kilba, Mumuye and Jukun communities of Gongola state, Nigeria, *Annals of Borno,* **6/7,** (1989/1990) 56–67

3616 **Shimada, S,** Economic change and labour migration in rural Nigeria, *Geographical review of Japan (series B),* **64,** 2 (1991) 79–97

3617 **Swindell, K, Iliya, M A,** *Accumulation, consolidation and survival: non-farm incomes and agrarian change in northwest Nigeria.* New York: Social Science Research Couincil, Project on African Agriculture, 1992, 25pp

3618 **Ukpong, E A,** The constraints of NGOs' operational flaws on rural development initiatives in Nigeria, *Journal of social development in Africa,* **8,** 1 (1993) 51–72

Science & technology

See also: 3229, 3235, 3241, 3260

3619 **Adeniyi, I F,** The prevalence of thunder and its effect on rainwater quality at Ile-Ife, southwest Nigeria, *Discovery and innovation,* **4,** 4 (1992) 41–51

3620 **Nwoko, M I,** *Philosophy of technology and Nigeria.* Owerri: Claretian Institute of Philosophy, 1992, 177pp

Sociology

See also: 1125, 3423, 3495, 3595

3621 **Ademola, A,** The living and the dead: the burial practice in some Nigerian communities, *Ind-Africana,* **4,** 2 (1991) 69–78

3622 **Ajila, C O,** Causes of drug abuse among in-school adolescents in Ondo State, Nigeria, *Review of African political affairs,* **6,** 1/2 (1992) 45–55

3623 **Alali, A O,** Management of death and grief in obituary and in-memoriam pages of Nigerian newspapers, *Psychological reports,* **73,** 3 (1993) 835–42

3624 **Assobie, H A,** The pauperisation of the Nigerian petty bourgeoisie, in Nnoli, O (ed), *Deadend to Nigerian development (item 3137)*, 180–202

3625 **Ihonvbere, J O,** Economic crisis, structural adjustment and social crisis in Nigeria, *World development,* **21,** 1 (1993) 141–53

3626 **Iyun, B F, Oke, E A,** The impact of contraceptive use among urban traders in Nigeria: Ibadan traders and modernisation, in Momsen, J H & Kinnaird, V (eds), *Different places, different voices (Item 332)*, 63–73

3627 **Kalu, W,** Bereavement and stress in career women, in Rothblum, E D & Cole, E (eds), *Women's mental health (item 338)*, 75–87

3628 **Lawuyi, O B,** Driving sign exchange and social change: the cultural utility of transport as a mirror of social relations in a Nigerian university community, *Semiotica,* **95,** 1–2 (1993) 63–74

3629 **Lawuyi, O B,** Time, identity and Nigerian business ethos: reflections from bush-taxi and banking interactions, *Anthropos,* **88,** 1/2 (1993) 99–107

3630 **Makinwa-Adebusoye, P K,** *Adolescent reproductive behaviour in Nigeria: a study of five cities.* Ibadan: NISER, 1991, 96pp

3631 **Ogbuagu, S C, Charles, J O,** Survey of sexual networking in Calabar, *Health transition review,* **3,** (1993) supplementary issue, 105–119

3632 **Ojile, E,** Juvenile delinquency in the northern states of Nigeria, *Journal of social psychology,* **133,** 3 (1993) 255–85

3633 **Okafor, T R U,** Death education in the Nigerian home: the mother's role, *Omega: journal of death and dying,* **27,** 4 (1993) 271–80

3634 **Oloko, B A,** Children's street work in urban Nigeria as adaptation and maladaptation to changing socioeconomic circumstances, *International journal of behavioural development,* **16,** 3 (1993) 465–82

3635 **Oloko, B, Omobiye, A O,** Sexual networking among some Lagos State adolescent students, *Health transition review,* **3,** (1993) supplementary issue, 151–57

3636 **Omorodion, F I,** Sexual networking among market women in Benin City, Bendel State, Nigeria, *Health transition review,* **3,** (1993) supplementary issue, 159–59

3637 **Orobuloye, I O, et al,** The role of religious leaders in changing sexual behaviour in southwest Nigeria in an era of AIDS, *Health transition review,* **3,** (1993) supplementary issue, 93–104

3638 **Oyeneye, O Y, Kawonise, S,** Sexual networking in Ijebu-Ode, Nigeria: an exploratory study, *Health transition review,* **3,** (1993) supplementary issue, 171–83

3639 **Peel, J D Y,** Between Crowther and Ajayi: the religious origins of the modern Yoruba intellectuals, in Falola, T (ed), *African historiography (Item 385)*, 64–79

3640 **Renne, E P,** Changes in adolescent sexuality and the perception of virginity in a southwestern Nigerian village, *Health transition review,* **3,** (1993) supplementary issue, 121–33

3641 **Salamone, F A, Salamone, V A,** Erikson in Nigeria: exploring the universality of the theory of psychosocial development, *Anthropos,* **88,** 1/2 (1993) 87–98

3642 **Women in Nigeria,** *Child abuse.* Samaru Zaria: Women in Nigeria, 1992, 46pp

Social welfare

See also: 3543

3643 Adejumobi, A, *Processes and problems of community organisation for self reliance.* Ibadan: NISER, 1991, 42pp

3644 Anyanwu, C N, *Community development: the Nigerian perspective.* Ibadan: Gabesther, 1992, 335pp

Urban studies

See also: 3296, 3348, 3371

3645 Aina, T A, Housing and health in Olaleye-Iporiri, a low-income settlement in Lagos, Nigeria, in Hardoy, J E, et al (eds), *The poor die young: housing and health in Third World cities* (London: Earthscan, 1990), 56–88

3646 Arimah, B C, Housing attributes in determining housing values: a case study of metropolitan Ibadan, Nigeria, *Indian geographical journal,* **66,** 2 (1991) 106–119

3647 Awotona, A, The urban poor's perception of housing conditions, in Taylor, R W (ed), *Urban development in Nigeria (Item 3657)*, 130–44

3648 Braimah, A A, Urban planning and development, in Taylor, R W (ed), *Urban development in Nigeria (Item 3657)*, 47–56

3649 Enyolu, E 'B, *Nigeria's urban housing markets: structure and growth.* New York: Vantage, 1991, 172pp

3650 Gyuse, T N, Socio-cultural dimensions of public housing, in Taylor, R W (ed), *Urban development in Nigeria (Item 3657)*, 154–65

3651 Izeogu, C V, Public poverty and affordable housing for the urban poor in Nigeria: a study of squatter redevelopment programmes in Port Harcourt, *Habitat international,* **17,** 2 (1993) 21–38

3652 Mba, H C, Public housing policies and programmes: an analysis, in Taylor, R W (ed), *Urban development in Nigeria (Item 3657)*, 117–29

3653 Morah, E U, Housing development in Nigeria's new capital at Abuja, *African development review,* **4,** 1 (1992) 64–86

3654 Okolocha, C F, The evolution of a land policy, in Taylor, R W (ed), *Urban development in Nigeria (Item 1107)*, 189–95

3655 Olu Sule, R A, Housing facilities and urban environmental quality, in Taylor, R W (ed), *Urban development in Nigeria (Item 3657)*, 166–74

3656 Olu Sule, R A, The tropical environment and housing comfort, in Taylor, R W (ed), *Urban development in Nigeria (Item 3657)*, 175–85

3657 Taylor, R W (ed), *Urban development in Nigeria.* Aldershot: Avebury, 1993, 245pp

3658 Taylor, R W, The policy context, in Taylor, R W (ed), *Urban development in Nigeria (Item 3657)*, 13–24

3659 Umeh, L C, The building of a new capital city: the Abuja experience, in Taylor, R W (ed), *Urban development in Nigeria (Item 3657)*, 215–28

3660 Umeh, L C, Urbanisation trends and housing, in Taylor, R W (ed), *Urban development in Nigeria (Item 3657)*, 103–116

SENEGAL

General

3661 Lowerve, S, *Under the neem tree.* Seattle: University of Washington Press, 1991, 255pp

Agriculture, scientific

3662 Dugue, P, The Senegalese Institute for Agricultural Research (ISRA) and the Fatick Region Farmers Association (ARAF), in Wellard, K & Copestake, J C (eds), *NGOs and the state (Item 1096)*, 270–82

Anthropology

See also: 3702

3663 Ogawa, R, Ethnic identity and social interaction: a reflection on Fulbe identity, *Senri ethnological studies,* 35 (1993) 119–37

3664 Robinson, D, Ethnography and customary law in Senegal, *Cahiers d'études africains,* **32,** 126 (1992) 221–237

3665 Syllan, A, *Le Lébou de la presqu'ile du Cap-Vert.* Dakar: Nouvelles editions africaines, 1992, 135pp

3666 Tidiane Ndione, C A, *Woyi céét*: traditional marriage songs of the Lebu, *Research in African literatures,* **24,** 2 (1993) 89–100

Architecture

3667 Bourdier, J P, Triangles of light: Tokolor dwellings, *Mimar,* 43 (1992) 68–75

Arts

See also: 70

3668 Gouard, C, Dynamiques de la création picturale sénégalaise contemporarine, *Anthropos,* **88,** 1/2 (1993) 77–86

3669 Pallister, J L, From La noire de... to Milk and honey: portraits of the alienated African woman, *Modern language studies,* **22,** 4 (1992) 76–87

3670 Zimmer, W, Frankophones Theater in Senegal, *Anthropos,* **88,** 1/2 (1993) 172–75

Demography

3671 Onuoha, N, Contributions of the proximate determinants to fertility change in Senegal, *Social science and medicine,* **35,** 10 (1992) 1317–20

3672 Salem, G, Géographie de la mortalité et de la natalité à Pikine (Sénégal): interêts et limites des données d'état civil dans les villes africaines, *Social science and medicine,* **36,** 10 (1993) 1297–1311

Economic and social history

See also: 2510

3673 Barry, B, Harding, L (eds), *Commerce et commerçants en Afrique de l'ouest. Vol. 1: le Sénégal.* Paris: Harmattan, 1993, 378pp

3674 Boone, C, Rise and decline of Senegal's light industry: the merchant-capital logic of accumulation, *Année africaine 1992/93,* 269–82

3675 Boumedouha, S, Change and continuity in the relationship between the Lebanese in Senegal and their hosts, in Hourani, A & Shehadi, N (eds), *The Lebanese in the world* (London: Tauris, 1992), 549–63

3676 de Benoist, J R, Camara, A, *Gorée: the island and the museum.* Dakar: IFAN, 1993, 67pp

3677 McIntosh, S K, McIntosh, R S, Field survey in the tumulus zone of Senegal, *African archaeological review,* **11,** (1993) 73–107

3678 Moitt, B, Slavery, flight and redemption in Senegal, 1819–1905, *Slavery and abolition,* **14,** 2 (1993) 70–86

3679 Sinou, A, *Comptoirs et villes coloniales du Sénégal: Saint-Louis, Gorée, Dakar.* Paris: Karthala/ORSTOM, 1993, 344pp

3680 Thompson, J M, When the fires are lit: the French Navy's recruitment and training of Senegalese mechanics and stokers, 1864–1887, *Canadian journal of African studies,* **26,** 2 (1992) 274–303

Economy - Development

See also: 3705

3681 Jacquemot, P, State disengagement: the case of Senegal, *African environment,* **7,** 25–28 (1990) 153–64

Education

See also: 3090, 3585, 3706, 3711

3682 Bensalah, K, Education for all between wish and reality: the example of a Human Resource Development Project in Senegal, *UNESCO-Africa,* 6 (1993) 7–11

3683 Carton, M, et al, *Ajustement structurel, éducation et formation au Sénégal.* Geneva: ILO, 1993, 67pp

3684 Eisemon, T O, Salmi, J, African universities and the state: prospects for reform in Senegal and Uganda, *Higher education,* **25,** 2 (1993) 151–68

Food

No entry. *See also:* 3733

Gender

See also: 3740, 3741

3685 Mbow, P, Illiteracy and poverty among women: the case of Senegal, *UNESCO-Africa,* 6 (1993) 21–25

3686 Reveyrand-Coulon, O, Les énonces féminins de l'islam, in Bayart, J F (ed), *Réligion et modernité politique (item 960),* 63–100

3687 Sow, F, *La decennie des Nations Unis pour la femme (1975–1985) au Sénégal: bilan et perspectives.* Bamako: Centre Djoliba, 1990, 22pp

3688 Sow, F, Les initiatives féminines au Sénégal: une réponse à la crise?, *Africa development,* **18,** 3 (1993) 89–115

Geography, physical

3689 Frederiksen, P, et al, NOAA-AVHRR and GIS-based monitoring of fire activity in Senegal: a provisional methodology and potential applications, in Goldhammer, J G (ed), *Fire in the tropical biota* (Berlin: Springer, 1990), 400–417

History, general

3690 Heckmann, H, Amadou Hampâté Bâ et la récolte des traditions orales, *Journal des Africanistes,* **63,** 2 (1993) 53–56

History, early

3691 Lam, A M, Les migrations entre le Nil et le Sénégal: les jalons de Yoro Dyao, *Annales de la Faculté des lettres et sciences humaines (Dakar),* **21,** (1992) 117–39

History, C19th

See also: 3664

3692 Ka, T, Al-Hajj Mukhtar Touré de Ndiaye-Ndiaye Wolof (1983–1918), un marabout méconnu, *Islam et sociétés au Sud du Sahara,* 6 (1992) 65–69

3693 Midiohouan, G, La Révolution francaise et l'émergence du nationalisme, *Université, recherche et développement,* 1 (1993) 79–92

3694 Robinson, D, *Colonial politics and historical texts: the case of the Umarian narratives.* Boston:

African Studies Centre, Boston University, 1991, 13pp

History, C20th

3695 Baum, R M, *Diola land/European country: religious representation of the French in twentieth century Senegal.* Boston: African Studies Centre, Boston University, 1992, 28pp

3696 Devey, M, *Hampate Ba, l'homme de la tradition.* Dakar: Nouvelles editions africaines, and Paris: Livre Sud, 1993, 191pp

3697 Samb, D, *Cheikh Anta Diop.* Dakar: Nouvelles éditions africaines, 1992, 144pp

Industry & trade

See also: 445, 3673, 3674, 3724

3698 Alioune, S, La politique industrielle: controverses et démarche stratégique en Afrique au sud du Sahara: le cas du Sénégal, *Africa development,* **18,** 3 (1993) 61–88

3699 Assunção, P T B, et al, Intensives Institution Building sur Förderung von Kleinbetrieben: Beispiele aus Senegal und Sambia, in their *Internationale Organisationen, Entwicklungsverwaltung und Kleingewerfördung in der Dritten Welt* (Baden-Baden: Nomos, 1993), 192–231

3700 Diemé, M, et al, Energy and industrialisation in Senegal, in Khennas, S (ed), *Industrialisation (item 454),* 154–81

3701 Galand, P, Les entrepreneurs sénégalais face aux contraintes d'un environnement précaire, *Année africaine 1992/93,* 299–322

3702 Join-Lambert, A, Ba, A S, Stratégies commerciales et identité peule: le 'tee-fankaagal' au Sénégal, *Etudes rurales,* 120 (1990) 53–69

3703 Valette, A, Enjeux et réalités d'une politique publique: la Nouvelle Politique Industrielle (NPI) sénégalaise, *Année africaine 1992/93,* 283–297

International economic relations

See also: 507

3704 Freud, C, Aid and development in Senegal, in Lele, U & Nabi, I (eds), *Transitions in development* (San Francisco: ICS Press, 1991), 173–93

International relations

3705 Diouf, B, Problèmes actuels, politiques et économiques au Sénégal, *Mondes et cultures,* **50,** 2–4 (1990) 501–14

Labour & manpower

3706 Engelhard, P, Some reflections on employment and training: the case of Senegal, *African environment,* **7,** 25–28 (1990) 373–93

3707 Lubell, H, *Urban self-employment in Senegal.* Geneva: ILO, 1990, 26pp

3708 Niang, A, Le secteur informel en milieu urbain au Sénégal, un recours à la crise, *Université, recherche et développement,* 1 (1993) 25–47

Language

3709 Irvine, J T, Mastering African languages: the politics of linguistics in nineteenth century Senegal, *Social analysis,* 33 (1993) 27–46

3710 Prinz, M F, *Die kulturtragenden Institutionen Senegals: zwischen kolonialen Erbe und Unabhängigkeit.* Saarbrucken: Breitenbach, 1992, 232pp

Literature

3711 **Arungwa, C I,** Fiction and progressivism in children's education: a study of Aminata Sow-Fall's L'appel des arènes, *African languages and cultures,* **6,** 1 (1993) 11–19

3712 **Baritaud, B,** De *Dakar-Matin* au *Soleil*: les avatars de la page littéraraire d'un quotidien national, *Revue de l'Institut de sociologie,* 1990/91 183–90

3713 **Giercsynski-Bocandé, U,** *Cheikh Aliou Ndao: ein senegalischer Schriftsteller im Spannungsfeld zweier Sprachen: Französisch und Wolof.* Frankfurt: Lang, 1992, 428pp

3714 **Petroni, L,** Senghor, sensuel et plurivalent poète civil: identité, émotion, universalité, *Ethiopiques,* 56 (1992) 5–16

3715 **Seydou, C,** L'oeuvre littéraire de Amadou Hampâté Bâ, *Journal des Africanistes,* **63,** 2 (1993) 57–60

3716 **Smith, C V,** The stereography of class, race and nation in God's bits of wood, *Research in African literatures,* **24,** 1 (1993) 51-

Media

No entry. *See also:* 3712

Medical

3717 **Badji, B,** *La folie en Afrique: une rivalité pathologique: le cas des pyschoses puerpérales en milieu sénégalais.* Paris: Harmattan, 1992, 221pp

3718 **Beiser, M, et al,** Puubuq lanq: la géophagie chez les Sereer du Sénégal, *Psychopathologie africaine,* **24,** 3 (1992) 349–366

3719 **Donnelly, C, et al,** Comparison of transmission rates of HIV-1 and HIV-2 in a cohort of prostitutes in Senegal, *Bulletin of mathematical biology,* **55,** 4 (1993) 731–43

Natural resources

See also: 3700

3720 **van den Breemer, J P M, et al** (eds), *La foresterie rurale au Sénégal: participation villageoise et gestion locale.* Leiden: Vakgroep Culturele Antropologie en Sociologie der Niet-Westerse Samenlevingen, 1993, 162pp

Politics

See also: 2575, 3745

3721 **Diouf, M,** Senegal's Feb. 1993 elections: new factors in the political arena, *Codesria bulletin,* 2 (1993) 4–7

Religion, philosophy

See also: 967, 3686, 3731

3722 **Biondi, J P,** *Senghor ou la tentation de l'universel.* Paris: Denoël, 1993, 197pp

3723 **Bousbina, S,** Musa Kamara, le savant 'autodidacte', *Islam et sociétés au Sud du Sahara,* 6 (1992) 75–78

3724 **Diop, M C, Diouf, M,** Notes sur la reconversion des marabouts mourides dans l'économie urbaine, *Anné africaine 1992/93,* 323–32

3725 **Fall, M,** Les arabisants au Sénégal: contre-élite ou courtiers?, in Otayek, R (ed), *Radicalisme islamique (Item 1002),* 197–212

3726 **Ndao, A,** La pensée humaniste du président Léopold Sédar Senghor, *Ethiopiques,* 56 (1992) 17–30

3727 **Villalon, L A,** Charisma and ethnicity in political context: a case study in the establishment of a Senegalese religious clientele, *Africa,* **63,** 1 (1993) 80–101

Rural economy

See also: 3688

3728 Beye, M, Eychenne, D, *La palmeraie de Casamance: quel avenir? Les paysans parlent.* Dakar: ENDA, 1991, 103pp

3729 Dansokho, M, Les effets de l'aide bilatérale et multilatérale sur l'agriculture africaine: l'exemple du Sénégal, *Africa development,* **17,** 3 (1992) 171–208

3730 Diop, A M, Rodale Institute/Rodale International/CRAR Senegal, in Wellard, K & Copestake, J C (eds), *NGOs and the state (Item 1096),* 264–69

3731 Diop, M C, Diouf, M, L'administration sénégalaise, les confréries réligeuses et les paysanneries, *Africa development,* **17,** 2 (1992) 65–87

3732 ENDA, *La ressource humaine, avenir des terriors: recherches paysannes au Sénégal.* Paris: Karthala, 1993, 318pp

3733 Goetz, S J, Interlinked markets and the cash crop-food crop debate in land-abundant tropical agriculture, *Economic development and cultural change,* **41,** 2 (1993) 342–61

3734 Guèye, M B, Senegal: country overview, in Wellard, K & Copestake, J C (eds), *NGOs and the state (Item 1096)*, 253–63

3735 Lèye, N, *Writing from experience: grassroots work in Senegal.* London: International Institute for Environment and Development, 1993, 13pp

3736 Sall, B, *De la modernité paysanne en Afrique noire: le Sénégal (pour une sociologie de la norme et de la ruse).* Paris: Harmattan, 1993, 253pp

3737 Weicker, M, *Nomades et sédentaires au Sénégal.* Dakar: ENDA, 1993, 161pp

3738 Woodhouse, P, Ndiaye, I, *Structural adjustment and irrigated food farming in Africa: the 'disengagement' of the state in the Senegal River valley.* New York: Social Science Research Council, Project on African Agriculture, 1991, 31pp

Sociology

See also: 3727

3739 Kane, K, Senegal, in Adepoju, A (ed), *Impact of structural adjustment (Item 1107)*, 60–68

3740 Lachenmann, G, Civil society and social movements in Africa: the case of the peasant movement in Senegal, *European journal of development research,* **5,** 2 (1993) 68–100

3741 Werner, J F, *Marges, sexe et drogues à Dakar: enquête ethnographique.* Paris: Karthala, 1993, 296pp

3742 Werner, J F, Urbanisation et déviance: études anthropologiques sur la drogue au Sénégal, *Cahiers des sciences humaines,* **29,** 1 (1993) 3–32

Social welfare

3743 Ndione, E S, *Dakar, une société en grappe.* Paris: Karthala, 1993, 232pp

Urban studies

See also: 1145, 1148, 3679, 3741

3744 Bonnardel, R, *Saint-Louis de Sénégal: mort ou naissance?* Paris: Harmattan, 1992, 423pp

3745 Diop, M C, Diouf, M, Enjeux et contraintes politiques de la gestion municipale au Sénégal, *Canadian journal of African studies,* **26,** 1 (1992) 1–23

3746 Gaye, M, The self-help production of housing and the living environment in Dakar, Senegal, *Environment and urbanisation,* **4,** 2 (1992) 101–108

3747 **Hesseling, G,** Pratiche fondiarie all'ombra della legge: l'applicazione del diritto fondiario a Ziguinchor, Senegal, *Storia urbana,* **17,** 63 (1993) 23–44

3748 **Mainet, G,** La conquête urbaine au Sénégal, in Vennetier, P (ed), *Urbanisation et développement (Item 1161)*, 17–26

3749 **Ndione, E S,** *Le don et la recours: ressorts de l'économie urbaine.* Dakar: ENDA, 1992, 210pp

SIERRA LEONE

Anthropology

No entry. *See also:* 3761, 3773

Current affairs

3750 **Tosterin, M,** Sinking to the depths, *Focus on Africa,* **4,** 3 (1993) 23–26

3751 **Zack-Williams, A, Riley, S,** Sierra Leone; the coup and its consequences, *Review of African political economy,* 56 (1993) 91–98

Economic and social history

3752 **Abdullah, I,** Profit versus social reproduction: labour protests in the Sierra Leonean iron-ore mines, 1933–38, *African studies review,* **35,** 3 (1992) 13–41

3753 **Cline-Cole, R,** Wartime forest energy policy and practice in British West Africa: social and economic impact on the labouring classes 1939–45, *Africa,* **63,** 1 (1993) 56–79

3754 **Leighton, N O,** Lebanese immigration: its effect on the political economy of Sierra Leone, in Hourani, A & Shehadi, N (eds), *The Lebanese in the world* (London: Tauris, 1992), 579–601

Economy - Development

3755 **Zack-Williams,** A B, Sierra Leone: the deepening crisis and survival strategies, in Nyang'oro, J E & Shaw, T M (eds), *Beyond structural adjustment (Item 179)*, 149–68

Environment

No entry. *See also:* 3756

Gender

3756 **Bledsoe, C,** School fees and the marriage process for Mende girls in Sierra Leone, in Sanday, P R & Goodenough, R G (eds), *Beyond the second sex* Philadelphia: University of Pennsylvania Press, 1990, 281–309

3757 **Leach, M,** Women's crops in women's spaces: gender relations in Mende rice farming, in Croll, E & Parkin, D (eds), *Bush base: forest farm (Item 1040)*, 76–96

History, C18th

3758 **Hair, P E H,** Davies, J D, Sierra Leone and the Grand Duke of Tuscany, *History in Africa,* **20,** (1993) 61–69

History, C19th

3759 **Adeloye, A,** *Dr James Africanus Beale Horton: West African medical scientist of the nineteenth century.* Pittsburgh: Dorrance, 1992, 59pp

3760 **Sillah, M B,** Edward Blyden and Islam in Sierra Leone: a study of African intellectual response to British colonialism, *Hamdard islamicus,* **14,** 4 (1991) 23–42

History, C20th

3761 **Yambasu, S J,** Order and disorder: the Mende and the missionary case, *Paideuma,* **39,** (1992) 111–34

Industry & trade

3762 **Davies, C, et al,** *Training opportunities in the informal sector of Freetown.* Freetown: University Research and Development Services Bureau, University of Sierra Leone, 1991, 188pp

Law

3763 **Thompson, B,** Illegitimacy in Sierra Leone law: a lingering anachronism: comparative perspectives, *African journal of international and comparative law,* **4,** 3 (1992) 728–738

Library - documentation

3764 **Dillsworth, G E,** The Sierra Leone national library service, in Wise, M & Olden, A (eds), *Information and libraries (item 672)*, 107–23

Medical

3765 **Amin, R, et al,** Immunisation coverage, infant morbidity and infant mortality in Freetown, Sierra Leone, *Social science and medicine,* **35,** 7 (1992) 851–56

3766 **Bledsoe, C H, Goubaud, M F,** The reinterpretation and distribution of western pharmaceuticals: an example from the Mende of Sierra Leone, in van der Geest, S & Whyte, S R (eds), *The context of medicines in developing countries* (Amsterdam: Spinhuis, 1991), 253–76

Politics

See also: 3755

3767 **Daramy, S B,** *Constitutional developments in the post-colonial state of Sierra Leone, 1961–1984.* Lewiston: Mellen, 1993, 303pp

3768 **Kpundeh, S J,** Prospects in contemporary Sierra Leone, *Corruption and reform,* **7,** 3 (1992/93) 237–47

3769 **Mukonweshuro, E G,** *Colonialism, class formation and underdevelopment in Sierra Leone.* Lanham: University Press of America, 1993, 257pp

Rural economy

No entry. *See also:* 3757, 3771

Sociology

3770 **Elliot, J W,** Sierra Leone, in Adepoju, A (ed), *Impact of structural adjustment (Item 1107)*, 40–59

3771 **Leach, M,** *Dealing with displacement: refugee-host relationships, food and forest resources in Sierra Leonean Mende communties during the Liberian influx, 1990–91.* Brighton: Institute of Development Studies, 1992, 51pp

Social welfare

3772 **Gboka, M,** Community development in Sierra Leone, *Community development journal,* **28,** 2 (1993) 167–75

Urban studies

3773 **Hardin, K L,** *The aesthetics of action: continuity and change in a West African town.* Washington: Smithsonian Institution Press, 1993, 314pp

TOGO

General

3774 **Curkeet, A A,** *Togo: portrait of a West African francophone republic in the 1980s.* Jefferson: McFarland, 1993, 216pp

3775 **de Menthon, J,** *A la rencontre du … Togo.* Paris: Harmattan, 1993, 269pp

3776 **Francois, Y,** *Le Togo.* Paris: Karthala, 1993, 189pp

Anthropology

3777 **de Surgy, A,** Les ingrédients de fétiches, *Systèmes de pensée en Afrique noire,* 12 (1993) 103–43

3778 **Gayibor, N L,** Rôle et importance des 'tashinon' (dignitaires) au sein de la société Aja (Togo), *Afrika Zamani,* NS 1 (1993) 247–58

3779 **Hahn, H P,** *Die materielle Kultur der Bassar (Nord-Togo).* Stuttgart: Steiner, 1991, 237pp

3780 **Piot, C D,** Secrecy, ambiguity, and the everyday in Kabre culture, *American anthropologist,* **95,** 2 (1993) 353–70

Current affairs

3781 **Pilon, M,** La transition togolaise dans l'impasse, *Politique africaine,* 49 (1993) 136–40

Economic and social history

3782 **de Haan, L,** *La régime des savannes au Togo.* Paris: Karthala, 1993, 360pp

History, general

3783 **Quarcoopone, N O,** Notse's ancient kingship: some archaeological and art-historical considerations, *African archaeological review,* **11,** (1993) 109–28

History, early

3784 **Aguigah, D,** Les pavements en tessons de poterie, organisation de l'espace dans les régions du Golfe du Bénin: la cas du Togo, in Andah, B W, et al (eds), *Imprints of West Africa's past (Item 2534),* 133–44

Language

3785 **Marx, R M,** *Sprachpraxis und Diskurs über Sprache: Französisch und Ewe im südlichen Togo.* Vienna: VWGO, 1991, 330pp

Media

See also: 3793

Natural resources

3786 **Tanzidani, T K T,** Les problèmes sociaux dans les réserves de faune et de flore du Togo, *Cahiers d'outre-mer,* **46,** 181 (1993) 61–73

Politics

See also: 2660

3787 **Berthiane, C,** Togo: a crisis like no other, *Refugees,* 93 (1993) 24–27

3788 **Ellis, S,** Rumour and power in Togo, *Africa,* **63,** 4 (1993) 462–76

3789 **Toulabor, C,** Le culte Eyadéma au Togo, in Bayart, J F (ed), *Réligion et modernité politique (item 960),* 277–97

3790 **van Rouveroy van Nieuwaal, E A B,** Nationale Commissie voor Mensenrechten en volkshoofden in Togo: een rechtsantropologisch perspectief, *Antropologische Verkenningen,* **11,** 4 (1992) 49–65

3791 **van Rouveroy van Nieuwaal, E,** The Togolese chiefs: caught between Scylla and Charybdis?, *Journal of legal pluralism and unofficial law,* 32 (1992) 19–46

Rural economy

See also: 3786

3792 **Olschewski, M,** *Landwirtschftspolitiks in Togo 1967–1987 und ihre Aufwirkung auf die Kleinbauern.* Munster: Lit, 1993, 391pp

3793 **Wendl, T,** Film, Ethnologie und Entwicklungshilfe: ein westafrikanischen Beispiel, *Sociologus,* **42,** 1 (1992) 59–72

Urban studies

3794 **Marguerat, Y,** *Les études urbaines au Togo: bibliographie thématique des origines à 1991.* Lomé: HaHo, 1992, 44pp

3795 **Marguerat, Y, Pelei, T,** *Si Lomé m'était conté.* Lomé: HaHo, 1992, 248pp

WESTERN SAHARA

International relations

See also: 1536

3796 **Damis, J,** The UN settlement plan for the Western Sahara: problems and prospects, *Middle East policy,* **1,** 2 (1992) 36–46

3797 **Durch, W J,** United Nations Mission for the Referendum in Western Sahara, in Durch, W J (ed), *The evolution of UN peacekeeping* (New York: St Martin's Press, 1993), 406–34

3798 **Smith de Cherif, T K,** Western Sahara: a Moroccan-style election?, *Review of African political economy,* 58 (1993) 99–105

3799 **Zoubir, Y H, Volman, D** (eds), *International dimensions of the Western Sahara conflict.* New York: Praeger, 1993, 258pp

Politics

See also: 861, 1536

3800 **de Pineis, J,** *La descolonizacion del Sahara: un tema sin concluir.* Madris: Espasa Calpa, 1990, 236pp

WEST CENTRAL AFRICA

Anthropology

3801 **Hewlett, B S,** Husband-wife reciprocity and the father-infant relationship among Aka pygmies, in Hewlett, B S (ed), *Father-child relations* (New York: Aldine de Gruyter, 1992), 153–76

3802 **Kirschbaum, S** (ed), *Deforestation and the forest peoples of central Africa.* Mönchengladbach: Institut für Okologie und angewande Ethnologie, 1990, 67pp

Economic and social history

3803 **Guyer, J I,** Wealth in people and self-realization in equatorial Africa, *Man,* **28,** 2 (1993) 243–65

Economy - Development

No entry. *See also:* 2513

Gender

3804 **Villien, F,** Urbanisation et évolution du sort de la femme en Afrique centrale, in Vennetier, P (ed), *Urbanisation et développement (Item 1161)*, 117–30

International economic relations

3805 **Barbier, J P,** L'intégration régional en Afrique du centre et de l'ouest, *Afrique contemporaine,* 166 (1993) 27–38

3806 **Boungou Bazika, J C,** Spécialisation et intégration économique en Afrique centrale, *Etudes et statistiques (BEAC),* 201 (1993) 144–58

3807 **Kitchen, R,** *Problems in regional integration in Africa: the UDEAC.* Bradford: Bradford University Project Planning Centre, 1990, 23pp

3808 **Tamba, I,** Intégration régionale en Afrique, zone franc: les cas de l'UDEAC dans la sous-region Afrique centrale, *Etudes et statistiques (BEAC),* 196 (1992) 289–99

Politics

3809 **Monnier, L,** Non-démocratisation des autres: démocratie et factions en Afrique centrale, *Revue nouvelle,* Jan-Feb (1993) 122–31

Rural economy

No entry. *See also:* 2586

Urban studies

3810 **Piermay, J L,** *Citadins en quête du sol dans les villes d'Afrique centrale.* Paris: Harmattan, 1993, 579pp

3811 **Piermay, J L,** Disparita nel prezzo dei suoli urbani in Africa centrale: la consuetudine in aiuto della modernita, *Storia urbana,* **17,** 63 (1993) 167–75

CAMEROUN

General

3812 **Salmon, P, Symoens, J J** (eds), *La recherche en sciences humaines au Cameroun.* Brussels: Academie royale des sciences d'outre mer, 1991, 145pp

Anthropology

See also: 3845

3813 **Abega, S C,** La bru tueuse, *Journal des Africanistes,* **62,** 1 (1992) 95–106

3814 **Baeke, V,** L'anthropologie dans les Grassfields: systèmes de guérison traditionels chez les Wuli-Mfumte, in Salmon, P & Symoens, J J (eds), *Sciences humaines au Cameroun (item 3812),* 121–33

3815 **Eguchi, P K,** 'Fulbe-ness' in Fulbe oral literature of Cameroon, *Senri ethonological studies,* 35 (1993) 181–200

3816 **Elouga, M,** Semiologie des motifs décoratifs de la céramique actuelle d'un groupe bantou du sud Cameroun: les Beti de la Lekie, in Andah, B W, et al (eds), *Imprints of West Africa's past (Item 2534),* 178–89

3817 **Fowler, I,** African sacred kings: expectations and performance in the Cameroun grassfields, *Ethnology,* **32,** 3 (1993) 253–68

3818 **Hino, S,** Fulbe people in African urban society: a comparative study of Cameroon and the Sudan, *Senri ethonological studies,* 35 (1993) 61–95

3819 **Masquelier, B M,** Descent, organisational strategy, and polity formation in the Cameroon Highlands (Bamenda Grassfields), *Anthropos,* **88,** 3/4 (1993) 443–58

3820 **Masquelier, B,** Parler la maladie: querelles et language chez les Ide de Cameroun, *Journal des Africanistes,* **63,** 1 (1993) 21–33

3821 **Nsamenang, B A,** Perceptions of parenting among the Nso of Cameroun, in Hewlett, B S (ed), *Father-child relations* New York: Aldine de Gruyter, 1992, 321–43

3822 **Ongoum, L M,** Erotic poetry of the grasslands, *Research in African literatures,* **24,** 2 (1993) 101–108

3823 **Pradelles de Latour, C H,** 'La crâne qui parle', ou la réversabilité de la parole, in Görög-Karady, V (ed), *D'un conte ... à l'autre (item 38),* 563–70

3824 **Warnier, J P,** The king as a container in the Cameroon Grassfields, *Paideuma,* **39,** (1992) 303–319

3825 **Zeitlyn, D,** Spiders in and out of court, or, 'the long legs of the law': styles of spider divination in their sociological context, *Africa,* **63,** 2 (1993) 219–40

Current affairs

3826 **Ngome, V E,** Things fall apart, *Focus on Africa,* **4,** 1 (1993) 29–32

Demography

3827 **Lee, B S, Pol, L G,** The influence of rural-urban migration on migrants' fertility in Korea, Mexico and Cameroon, *Population research and policy review,* **12,** 1 (1993) 3–26

3828 **Ngatchou, R D, et al,** Les inégalités géographiques de la mortalité au Cameroun, *Social science and medicine,* **36,** 10 (1993) 1285–90

Economic and social history

See also: 3831, 3856

3829 **Diduk, S,** European alcohol,

history and the state in Cameroun, *African studies review,* **36,** 1 (1993) 1–42

Economy - Development

3830 Bekolo Ebem, B, Dynamique nouvelle de financement et sortie de crise au Cameroun, *Mondes en développement,* **20,** 77/78 (1992) 101–118

3831 Gankou, J M, *La politique économique du Cameroun: son impact sur le croissance depuis 1960.* Neuchatel: Centre de recherche sur la développement, 1991, 79pp

3832 Geschiere, P, Konings, P (eds), *Itinéraires d'accumulation au Cameroun.* Paris: Karthala, 1993, 368pp

3833 Mbaku, J M, Foreign aid and economic growth in Cameroon, *Applied economics,* **25,** 10 (1993) 1309–1314

3834 Tabetsing, C, *Cameroun: sursault ou suicide?* n.p.: Arthaud, 1991, 143pp

Education

See also: 3840

3835 Nkili, R, La recherche en enseignement au Cameroun, in Salmon, P & Symoens, J J (eds), *Sciences humaines au Cameroun (item 3812),* 9–36

3836 Smith, S, Taylor, B, Curriculum planning for women and agricultural households: the case of Cameroon, in Gladwin, C H (ed), *Structural adjustment and African women farmers (Item 315),* 373–86

Environment

See also: 3858

3837 Tschawa, P, La dégradation des sols dans le Bamiléké méridional, conditions naturelles et facteurs anthropiques, *Cahiers d'outre-mer,* **46,** 181 (1993) 75–104

Finance

3838 Deverajan, S, et al, External shocks, purchasing power parity and the equilibrium real exchange rate, *World Bank economic review,* **7,** 1 (1993) 45–53

Gender

See also: 3836, 3872, 4035

3839 Westermann, V, *Women's disturbances: der Anlu-Aufstand bei den Kom (Kamerun), 1958–1960.* Munster: Lit, 1990, 190pp

3840 Woodhouse, H, Ndongko, T M, Women and science education in Cameroon: some critical reflections, *Interchange,* **241/2,** (1993) 131–58

Health & welfare services

3841 Essomba, R O, et al, The reorientation of primary health care in Cameroon: rationale, obstacles and constraints, *Health policy and planning,* **8,** 3 (1993) 232–39

3842 Litvak, J I, Bodart, C, User fees plus quality equals improved access to health care: results of a field experiment in Cameroun, *Social science and medicine,* **37,** 3 (1993) 369–83

History, general

3843 Maceachern, S, Selling the iron for their shackles: Wandala-*Montagnard* interactions in northern Cameroon, *Journal of African history,* **34,** 2 (1993) 247–70

History, early

3844 de Maret, P, La recherche archéologique au Cameroun, in

Salmon, P & Symoens, J J (eds), *Sciences humaines au Cameroun (item 3812)*, 37–51

3845 Elouga, M, Semiologie des motifs decoratifs de la céramique actuelle d'un groupe bantu du sud-Cameroun: les Beti de la Lekie, *Nsi,* 10/11 (1992) 17–24

History, C19th

3846 Kosack, G, Aus der Zeit der Sklaverei (Nordkamerun): alte Mafa erzählen, *Paideuma,* **38,** (1992) 177–94

3847 Mzeka, P N, *Four Fons of Nso: 19th and early 20th century kingship in the western grassfields of Cameroon.* Bamenda: Spider, 1990, 141pp

3848 Zeitlyn, D, Un fragment de l'histoire des Mambila: un texte de Duabang, *Journal des Africanistes,* **62,** 1 (1992) 135–50

History, C20th

See also: 3839

3849 Austen, R A, Tradition, invention and history: the case of the Ngondo, (Cameroon), *Cahiers d'études africains,* **32,** 126 (1992) 285–309

3850 Fohtung, M G, Self-portrait of a Cameroonian, *Paideuma,* **38,** (1992) 219–48

3851 Geschiere, P, Chiefs and colonial rule in Cameroon: inventing chieftaincy, French and British style, *Africa,* **63,** 2 (1993) 151–75

3852 Weber, C W, *International influences and Baptist mission in West Cameroun: German-American missionary endeavour under international mandate and British colonialism.* Leiden: Brill, 1993, 176pp

3853 Yearwood, P J, 'In a casual way with a blue pencil': British policy and the partition of Kamerun, 1914–1919, *Canadian journal of African studies,* **27,** 2 (1993) 218–44

Industry & trade

3854 Cook, A, Quelques réflexions sur le tourisme au Cameroun, *Bulletin of francophone Africa,* 3 (1993) 37–55

3855 Courcelle, M, et al, *Le secteur privé au Cameroun.* Paris: OECD, 1990, 95pp

3856 Mouafo, D, La production camérounaise de caoutchouc naturel: évolution et perspectives de commercialisation, *Canadian journal of African studies,* **26,** 1 (1992) 92–116

3857 Warnier, J P, *L'esprit d'entreprise au Cameroun.* Paris: Karthala, 1993, 307pp

3858 Wilkie, D S, et al, Mechanised logging, market hunting, and a bank loan in Congo, *Conservation biology,* **6,** 4 (1992) 570–80

International economic relations

No entry. *See also:* 3833, 3859

International relations

3859 Beti, M, *La France contre l'Afrique: retour au Cameroun.* Paris: La Découverte, 1993, 207pp

3860 Mabe, J E, *Deutsche Entwicklungspolitik in Kamerun.* Frankfurt: Peter Lang, 1993, 218pp

3861 Sindjoun, L, L'action internationale de l'Assemblé nationale du Cameroun: éléments d'analyse politique, *Etudes internationales,* **24,** 4 (1993) 813–44

Labour & manpower

3862 Konings, P, *Labour resistance in Cameroon: managerial strategies*

and labour resistance in the agro-industrial plantations of the CDC 1947–1987. London: Currey, 1993, 203pp

Language

3863 Janssens, B, Les langues du Cameroun hier et aujourd'hui, in Salmon, P & Symoens, J J (eds), *Sciences humaines au Cameroun (item 3812)*, 53–73

3864 Mbangwana, P, Some instances of linguistic and literary resource in certain humorous Cameroonianisms, *Humor,* **6,** 2 (1993) 195–222

3865 Tangwa, G, Colonial legacy and the language situation in Cameroon, *Quest,* **6,** 2 (1992) 24–43

Law

No entry. *See also:* 3297

Literature

See also: 3876

3866 Ellerman, E, The passion of Perpetua: a generic approach to Beti's Perpetué, *Research in African literatures,* **24,** 3 (1993) 25–34

3867 Lobe Ewane, M, Mongo Beti: itinéraire d'un écrivain engagé, *Afrique 2000,* 14 (1993) 125–32

Media

3868 Nga Ndongo, V, *Les médias au Cameroun: mythes et délires d'une société en crise.* Paris: Harmattan, 1993, 228pp

3869 Nyamnjoh, F B, Contrôle de l'information au Cameroun: implication pour la recherche en communication, *Afrika spektrum,* 1 (1993) 93–115

Medical

See also: 3893

3870 Nsamenang, A B, Lamb, M E, The acquisition of sociocognitive competence by Nso children in the Bamenda grassfields of northwest Cameroon, *International journal of behavioural development,* **16,** 3 (1993) 429–41

3871 van der Geest, S, The articulation of formal and informal medicine distribution in South Cameroun, in van der Geest, S & Whyte, S R (eds), *The context of medicines in developing countries* (Amsterdam: Spinhuis, 1991), 131–48

3872 Zekeng, L, et al, Barrier contraceptive use and HIV-infection among high risk women in Cameroon, *AIDS,* **7,** 5 (1993) 725–31

Politics

See also: 940, 2575, 3851, 3859, 3861, 3869

3873 Abwa, D, *André-Marie Mbida, Premier ministre camerounais (1917–1980).* Paris: Harmattan, 1993, 275pp

3874 Banock, M, *Le processus de démocratisation en Afrique: la cas camerounais.* Paris: Harmattan, 1992, 252pp

3876 Breitinger, E, 'Lamentations patriotiques': writers, censors and politics in Cameroon, *African affairs,* **92,** 369 (1993) 557–75

3877 Daissala, D, *Libre derrière les barreaux.* Paris: Jaguar, 1993, 283pp

3878 Gobata, R, *The past tense of shit.* Limbe: Mooremac, 1993, 191pp

3879 Mehler, A, *Kamerun in der Ara Biya: Bedingungen, erste Schritte und Blockaden einer demoktratischen Transition.* Hamburg: Institut für Afrika-Kunde, 1993, 451pp

3880 Mukong, A, *My stewardship in the Cameroon struggle.* n.p.: (?London): the author, 1992, 222pp

3881 Muna, B, *Cameroun: face au défi du 21ème siècle.* Yaoundé: Tama Books, 1993, 186pp

3882 Ndendi Penda, P, *Le pouvour aux deux visages: la terreur et la prosperité.* n.p.: Galaxie, 1992(?), 78pp

3883 Ndi Mbarga, V, *Ruptures et continuités au Cameroun.* Paris: Harmattan, 1993, 297pp

3884 Ngniman, Z, *Cameroun: la démocratie emballée.* Yaoundé: Clé, 1993, 315pp

3885 Sipa, J B, *Outrage à la République. Tome I: une transition manquée.* Douala: SEPEC, 1992, 80pp

3886 Takougang, J, The demise of Biya's new deal in Cameroon, 1982–1992, *Africa insight,* **23,** 2 (1993) 91–101

3887 Torimiro, F B, Personal rule and the search for political pluralism in Cameroon, in Danopoulos, C P (ed), *Civilian rule (Item 844)*, 89–106

Rural economy

See also: 1932, 3862, 4035

3888 Bray, M, The problems that arise in relation to local communities and the state in contemporary West Africa: the case of the Bamiléké in Cameroun, *Bulletin of francophone Africa,* 3 (1993) 26–36

3889 Diduk, S, The paradoxes of changing land tenure in Kedjom chiefdoms, Northwest Province, Cameroon, *Paideuma,* **38,** (1992) 195–217

3890 Douffisa, A, *L'élevage bovin dans le Mbéré (Adamaoua camerounais).* Paris: Orstom, 1993, 282pp

3891 Jean, N A, Développement rurale au Cameroun: et si les paysans le concevaient autrement?, *Africa development,* **17,** 4 (1992) 29–45

3892 Mbuagbaw, T, *Problems of rural development: the case of Manyu Division, West Cameroon, and SWELA leadership.* Douala: Georges Frères, 1992(?), 28pp

Sociology

See also: 3827, 3889

3893 Beat-Songue, P, *SIDA et prostitution aux Cameroun.* Paris: Harmattan, 1993, 99pp

3894 Iyebi-Mandjek, O, Les migrations saisonnières chez les Mafas, montagnards du Nord-Cameroun: une solution au surpeuplement et un frein à l'émigration, *Cahiers des sciences humaines,* **29,** 2/3 (1993) 419–41

3895 Lee, B S, The influence of rural-urban migration on migrants' fertility in Cameroon, *International migration review,* **26,** 4 (1992) 1416–47

3896 Ndongko, W A, Cameroon, in Adepoju, A (ed), *Impact of structural adjustment (Item 1107)*, 119–29

3897 Savage, O M N, Artifical donor insemination in Yaoundé: some socio-cultural considerations, *Social science and medicine,* **35,** 7 (1992) 907–913

3898 Tsala Tsala, J-P, Souffrance familiale et famille en souffrance: la famille camerounaise entre le village et la ville, *Cahiers de sociologie économique et culturelle,* 18 (1992) 99–113

Urban studies

See also: 3818

3899 Frenay, P, De quelques faits nouveaux de la dynamique urbaine au Cameroun, in Salmon, P &

Symoens, J J (eds), *Sciences humaines au Cameroun (item 3812)*, 75–102

CENTRAL AFRICAN REPUBLIC

General

3900 **Kalck, P,** *Central African Republic.* Oxford: Clio, 1993, 155pp

Anthropology

See also: 3902

3901 **Sarno, L,** *Song from the forest.* London: Bantam, 1993, 288pp

Arts

3902 **Furniss, S,** Les instruments de musique de Centrafrique au Musée de l'Homme: collections et collecteurs, *Journal des Africanistes,* **63,** 2 (1993) 81–119

Politics

3903 **Lique, R J,** *Bokassa 1er: la grande mystification.* Paris: Chaka, 1993, 191pp

Sociology

3904 **Somse, P, et al,** Multiple sexual partners - results of national HIV/AIDS survey in the Central African Republic, *AIDS,* **7,** 4 (1993) 579–83

CONGO

General

3905 **Ballif, N,** *Le Congo.* Paris: Karthala, 1993, 215pp

Anthropology

3906 **Hagenbucher-Sacripanti, F,** Fonctions du discours dans la représentation de l'au-delà: réflexion générale et comparative, *Cahiers des sciences humaines,* **29,** 1 (1993) 53–72

3907 **Hagenbucher-Sacripanti, F,** Introduction à l'étude des techniques de discours dans une secte thérapeutique du Congo méridional, *Cahiers des sciences humaines,* **29,** 1 (1993) 73–103

3908 **Sato, H,** Notes on the distribution and settlement patterns of hunter-gatherers in northwestern Congo, *African study monographs,* **13,** 4 (1992) 203–16

Demography

3909 **Anglade, F,** La fécondité à Brazzaville et dans les centres urbains: modèle congolais de demain?, in Vennetier, P (ed), *Urbanisation et développement (Item 1161)*, 131–45

Economic and social history

3910 **Martin, P,** *The social history of leisure and sport in colonial Brazzaville.* Boston: African Studies Centre, Boston University, 1990, 11pp

Economy - Development

3911 **Friedman, K E,** Afromarxism and its disastrous effects on the economy: the Congolese case, in Blomström, M & Lundahl, M (eds), *Economic crisis (Item 119)*, 219–45

Food

3912 **Cornu, A, et al,** *Enquête nationale sur l'état nutrionnel des* *enfants d'âge préscholaire au Congo.* Paris: ORSTOM, 1990, 337pp

History, early

3913 Pincon, B, Archéologie des plateaux et collines Teke (République populaire du Congo): de nouvelles données, *Nsi,* 8/9 (1991) 24–32

History, C20th

No entry. *See also:* 3932

Law

3914 Ahoungou, J G, La problématique des principes généraux du droit en droit congolais, *Revue congolaise de droit,* 10 (1991) 41–53

Literature

3915 Anyinefa, K, Intertextuality in Dongala's Un fusil dans la main, un poème dans la poche, *Research in African literatures,* **24,** 1 (1993) 5–17

3916 Martin-Granel, N, Corps, pouvoir, écriture dans deux romans africains, *Cahiers d'études africains,* 126 (1992) 311–340

3917 Wright, K, Satire and censorship in Tchicaya U Tam'si's Le destin glorieux du maréchal Mnikon Nniku, prince qu'on sort, *Ufahamu,* **19,** 2/3 (1991) 80–95

Medical

3918 Mock, N B, et al, Socioeconomic, environmental, demographic and behavioural factors associated with occurrence of diarrhoea in young children in Republic of Congo, *Social science and medicine,* **36,** 6 (1993) 807–16

Natural resources

No entry. *See also:* 791

Politics

3918a Bazanquisa, R (Bazenguissa, R), La Sape et la politique au Congo, *Journal des Africanistes,* **62,** 1 (1992) 151–57

3919 Breton, J-M, La transition vers la démocratie au Congo: (juillet 89 - décembre 1990), *Revue congolaise de droit,* 10 (1991) 13–40

3920 Menga, H G, *Congo, la transition escamotée.* Paris: Harmattan, 1993, 217pp

3921 Weissman, F, *Election présidentielle de 1992 au Congo: entreprise politique et mobilisation électorale.* Talence: Bordeaux University, CEAN, 1993, 150pp

Urban studies

See also: 1145

3922 Gourgand, M, et al, Morphodynamique et urbanisation à Brazzaville (Congo), in Vennetier, P (ed), *Urbanisation et développement (Item 1161),* 69–80

3923 Ziavoula, R E, La scena fondiaria di Brazzaville, *Storia urbana,* **17,** 63 (1993) 139–52

EQUATORIAL GUINEA

Agriculture, scientific

3924 Gamarra, R, Morales, R, Investigaciones agronomicas en Fernando Poo (Guinea Espagñol), *Estudios Africanos,* **6,** 10/11 (1991/92) 157–64

Gender

No entry. *See also:* 3926

History, C19th

3925 **Vaz, T,** Pensamiento y accion misionera de Jeronimo Usera en la Guinea Espagñola, *Estudios Africanos,* **6,** 10/11 (1991/92) 7–34

History, C20th

3926 **Negrin Fajardo,** O, La educacion de la mujer en los comienzos de la colonizacion de Guiné espagñola (1884–1910), *Estudios Africanos,* **6,** 10/11 (1991/92) 51–60

Politics

3927 **Liniger-Goumaz, M,** *Who's who de la dictature de Guinée Equatoriale: les Nguemistes, 1979–1993.* Geneva: ed du Temps, 1993, 351pp

GABON

Agriculture, scientific

3928 **Tutin, C E G,** Fernandez, M, Relationships between temperature and fruit production in some tropical forest trees in Gabon, *Journal of tropical ecology,* **9,** 2 (1993) 241–48

Economy - Development

3929 **Zomo Yebe, G,** *Comprendre la crise de l'économie gabonaise.* Paris: Harmattan, 1993, 268pp

History, early

3930 **Oslisly, R,** Peyrot, B, L'arrivée des premiers métallurgistes sur l'Oguée, Gabon, *African archaeological review,* **10,** (1992) 129–38

History, C19th

3931 **Merlet, A,** *Vers les plateaux de Masuku (1866–1890): histoire des peuples du bassin de l'Ogooué, de Lambarene au Congo, au temps de Brazza et ses factoreries.* Libreville: Centre culturel français, 1990, 492pp

History, C20th

3932 **Dupré, M C,** La guerre de l'impôt dans les monts du Chaillu, Gabon, Moyen Congo (1909–1920), *Revue française d'histoire d'outre-mer,* **80,** 300 (1993) 409–23

Law

3933 **Rémondo, M,** Le cour constitutionnelle gabonaise, *Penant,* **103,** 813 (1993) 275–91

Politics

3934 **Bouchard, J C D,** *La longue marche de la démocratie gabonaise.* Libreville: Gabédip, 1992, 159pp

3935 **Edzodzomo-Ela, M,** *De la démocratie au Gabon.* Paris: Karthala, 1993, 279pp

3936 **Hillebrand, E,** Demoktisierung als Eliten-Recycling: das Beispiel Gabuns, *Afrika spektrum,* 1 (1993) 73–92

3937 **Kombila-Iboanga, F,** L'expérimentation des mécanismes de la réforme administrative au Gabon: contribution à l'étude de la science administrative en Afrique, *Penant,* **102,** 810 (1992/1993) 309–325 and 103, 811(1993) 78–92

3938 **Rossatanga-Rignault, G,** Les

partis politiques gabonais: un essai d'analyse, *Afrique 2000,* 14 (1993) 107–23

Urban studies

No entry. *See also:* 1145

CENTRAL AFRICA

General

3939 Musambachime, M C, The University of Zambia's Institute for African Studies and social science research in Central Africa, 1938–1988, *History in Africa,* **20,** (1993) 237–48

Anthropology

See also: 4362

3940 Bahuchet, S, L'invention des pygmées, *Cahiers d'études africaines,* **33,** 129 (1993) 153–81

3941 Janzen, J M, *Ngoma: discourses of healing in central and southern Africa.* Berekeley: University of California Press, 1992, 241pp

Demography

3942 Murara, J, Le problème démographique dans la sous-région, *Au coeur de l'Afrique,* **60,** 1 (1992) 45–58

Economic and social history

No entry. *See also:* 1891, 1892, 4729, 4731

Economy - Development

3943 Chakaodza, A M, *Structural adjustment in Zambia and Zimbabwe: reconstructive or destructive?* Harare: Third World Publishing House, 1993, 116pp

Education

3944 Shabani, J, Coopération régionale dans le domain de la formation, *Au coeur de l'Afrique,* **60,** 1 (1992) 96–112

Environment

No entry. *See also:* 2516

Food

3945 Ndikumana, J, Pour une stratégie de sécurité alimentaire dans la sous-région des grands lacs, *Au coeur de l'Afrique,* **60,** 1 (1992) 84–95

Gender

No entry. *See also:* 1892, 1898

Geography, human

No entry. *See also:* 3952

Health & welfare services

3946 Alexandre, Y, Actions communes à mener dans la lutte contre le SIDA et les autres maladies sexuelles transmissibles dans le sous-région, *Au coeur de l'Afrique,* **60,** 1 (1992) 113–28

History, early

No entry. *See also:* 1904

History, C20th

3947 **Darwin, J,** The Central African emergency, 1959, *Journal of imperial and Commonwealth history,* **21,** 3 (1993) 217–34

3948 **Hannecart, K,** *'Intrepid sowers': from Nyasa to Fort Jameson 1889–1946 - some historical notes.* Roma: Missionari d'Africa, Historical Dept., 1991, 237pp

Industry & trade

See also: 3955, 3956

3949 **Koester, U,** Policies for promoting regional agricultural trade, *Food policy,* **18,** 4 (1993) 355–65

International economic relations

3950 **Girukwigomba, A,** Intégration économique dans la sous-région/Economic integration in the sub-region, *Au coeur de l'Afrique,* **60,** 1 (1992) 59–83

Medical

3951 **Horsburgh, C R,** Pozniak, A, Epidemiology of tuberculosis in the era of AIDS, *AIDS,* **7,** 1 (1993) 109–114

3952 **Tessier, S F, et al,** The frontline of HIV–1 diffusion in the Central African region: a geographical and epidemiological perspective, *International journal of epidemiology,* **22,** 1 (1993) 127–34

Religion, philosophy

3953 **Bududira, B,** Rôle de l'église face aux problèmes socioéconomiques et politiques sans les pays des Grands Lacs, *Au coeur de l'Afrique,* **60,** 1 (1992) 4–12

Rural economy

3954 **Fair, T J D,** *African rural development: policy and practice in six countries.* Pretoria: Africa Institute, 1992, 78pp

3955 **Quiroz, J Valdes, A,** Agricultural incentives and international competitiveness: governmental interventions and exogenous shocks in four East African countries, *Food policy,* **18,** 4 (1993) 342–54

3956 **Valdes, A, Muir-Leresche, K** (eds), *Agricultural polcy reforms and regional market integration in Malawi, Zambia and Zimbabwe.* Washington: IFPRI, 1993, 347pp

Sociology

3957 **Gapangwa, N,** Les problèmes des émigrés et des réfugiés dans la sous-région des Grands Lacs, *Au coeur de l'Afrique,* **60,** 1 (1992) 31–37

3958 **Mgulunde, M,** The problems of refugees and migrants, *Au coeur de l'Afrique,* **60,** 1 (1992) 21–30

ANGOLA

General

3959 **Tvedten, I,** *Country analysis: Angola.* Stockholm: SIDA, 1992, 144pp

Anthropology

3960 **Lima, M,** *Os Kyaka de Angola: vol. 3, organização politica e territoriale.* Lisbon: Tavola Redonda, 1992, 407pp

Current affairs

3962 **Awosu, A,** Dreams of peace, *Focus on Africa,* **4,** 1 (1993) 39–42

3963 Campbell, H, Peace, democracy and elections in Angola, *Southern Africa political and economic monthly,* **5,** 12 (1992) 8–11

3964 Egero, B, Efforts in democracy: Angola's uneasy election, *Choices,* **2,** 1 (1993) 13–17

3965 Gonçalves, J, Uncertain road ahead, *Southern Africa political and economic monthly,* **5,** 9 (1992) 35–39

3966 Marcum, J A, Angola - war again, *Current history,* **92,** 574 (1993) 218–23

3967 Nkeita, T, Angola: a too distant hope, *Southern Africa political and economic monthly,* **7,** 2 (1993) 14–17

3968 Orr, D, Death, starvation and agony in Kuito, *Southern Africa political and economic monthly,* **7,** 2 (1993) 5–10

Economic and social history

3969 von Krosigk, K, Kontakte durch deutsche Pflanzer und Unternehmer in Angola, *DASP-Hefte,* 35/6 (1992) 120–34

Economy - Development

3970 Aguilar, R, Zejan, M, Angola on the verge of economic reforms, in Blomström, M & Lundahl, M (eds), *Economic crisis (Item 119)*, 243–67

3971 Hodges, T, *Angola to 2000: prospects for recovery.* London: Economist Intelligence Unit, 1993, 170pp

3972 Hodges, T, Looking to Angola's future: rebuilding the economy, *Africa insight,* **23,** 3 (1993) 159–67

3973 Rela, J M Z, *Angola: entre o presente e o futura.* Lisbon: Escher, 1992, 498pp

Gender

3974 Campbell, H, Angolan women and the electoral process in Angola, 1992, *Africa development,* **18,** 2 (1993) 23–63

Health & welfare services

3975 Björck, M, et al, Improving the quality of primary care services in Angola, *Health policy and planning,* **7,** 3 (1992) 290–95

History, C18th

See also: 4182

3976 Heitze, B, Gefährdetes Asyl: Chancen und Konsequenzen der Flucht angolanischer Sklaven im 17. Jahrhunderts, *Paideuma,* **39,** (1993) 321–41

3977 Miller, J C, The numbers, origins and destinations of slaves in the eighteenth-century Angolan slave trade, in Inikori, J E & Engerman, S L (eds), *The Atlantic slave trade (Item 2500)*, 77–115

History, C19th

No entry. *See also:* 4193

History, C20th

3978 Correia, P P, *Descolonização de Angola: ajóia da coroa do império português.* Lisbon: Inquérito, 1991, 198pp

3979 Mabeko Tali, J M, 'Tribalisme' 'régionalisme' et lutte de libération nationale: la question 'tribale' dans la dissidence au sein du MPLA dans l'est angolais en 1969–1974, *Année africaine 1992/93,* 463–86

Industry & trade

No entry. *See also:* 460

International economic relations

3980 **Hippmann, P,** Fortlaufende, von der ermahligen DDR begonnene Projekte und Kontakte: Angola, *DASP-Hefte,* 35/6 (1992) 19–30

International relations

3981 **Belikov, I,** Soviet-Angolan relations: venture into southern Africa, in Light, M (ed), *Troubled friendships: Moscow's Third World ventures* (London: British Academic Press, 1993), 52–81

3982 **Campbell, H,** The delegitimisation of the liberation struggles in Africa: the experience of Angola, *Southern Africa political and economic monthly,* **7,** 2 (1993) 42–45

3983 **Campbell, H,** The United Nations and Angola, *Southern Africa political and economic monthly,* **7,** 2 (1993) 46–49

3984 **Fortna, V P,** United Nations Angola Verification Mission II, in Durch, W J (ed), *The evolution of UN peacekeeping* (New York: St Martin's Press, 1993), 388–405

3985 **Papp, D S,** The Angolan civil war and Namibia: the role of external intervention, in Smock, D R (ed), *Making war and waging peace (Item 600)*, 161–96

3986 **Pereira, A W,** Peace in the Third World: the case of Angola, *Dissent,* **40,** 3 (1993) 291–94

3987 **Vines, A,** *One hand tied: Angola and the UN.* London: CIIR, 1993, 46pp

3988 **Williams, A,** Negotiations and the end of the Angolan civil war, in Smock, D R (ed), *Making war and waging peace (Item 600)*, 197–217

3989 **Zischg, R,** *Die Politik der Sowjetunion gegenüber Angola und Mosambik.* Baden Baden: Nomos, 1990, 333pp

Library - documentation

3990 **da Conceiçao Tali,** M, Factors which affect the development of libraries in Angola, *Information trends,* **5,** 3 (1992) 93–96

Politics

See also: 861, 3974, 3979, 3982, 4462

3991 **Africa Watch,** *Land mines in Angola.* New York: Africa Watch, 1993, 69pp

3992 **Amnesty International,** Angola: will the new government protect human rights?, *Southern Africa political and economic monthly,* **5,** 12 (1992) 14–19

3993 **Makombé, J B F,** Un pays écartelé: l'Angola, *Afrique 2000,* 13 (1993) 107–114

3994 **Mohanty, S,** *Political development and ethnic identity in Africa: a study of Angola since 1960.* London: Sangam, 1992, 246pp

3995 **Pössinger, H,** Angola: ein Neuanfang?, in Meyns, P (ed), *Demokratie und Strukturreformen (Item 1174)*, 97–117

3996 **Ptak, H P,** *Angola: vom Bürgerkreig zur neuer Ordnung: eine Unterrichtung anlässlich des Waffenstillstandes von Lissabon.* Bammental: Klemmerberg, 1991, 59pp

3997 **Sellstrom, T,** *Observer's report on the Angolan elections, 29–30 September 1992.* Windhoek: Namibian Economic Policy Research Unit, 1992, 7pp

3998 **Siddiqui, R A,** Conflict creation in Angola and UNITA destabilisation, in Siddiqui, R A (ed), *Subsaharan Africa (item 15)*, 190–208

3999 **Somerville, K,** The failure of democratic reform in Angola and Zaire, *Survival,* **35,** 3 (1993) 53–77

4000 **Tvedten, I,** The Angolan

debacle, *Journal of democracy,* **4,** 2 (1993) 108–118

Religion, philosophy

4001 Henderson, L W, *The church in Angola: a river of many currents.* Cleveland: Pilgrim Press, 1992, 448pp

MALAWI

General

See also: 4054

4002 Research and Publications Committee (ed), *Research and development: proceedings of a conference held at Bunda College of Agriculture, Lilongwe, Malawi, 1th–10th April, 1992.* Zomba: Univerity of Malawi, n.d., 290pp

Agriculture, scientific

See also: 4055

4003 Cromwell, E, Zambezi, B, *The performamce of the seed sector in Malawi: an analysis of the influence of organisational structure.* London: Overseas Development Institute, 1993, 192pp

4004 Green, D A G, Ngongola, D H, Factors affecting fertilizer adoption in less-developed countries: an application of multivariate logistic analysis in Malawi, *Journal of agricultural economics,* **44,** 1 (1993) 99–109

4005 Singh, U, et al, Maize modelling in Malawi: a tool for soil fertility research and development, in Penning de Vries, F et al (eds), *Systems approaches for agricultural development* (Dordrecht: Kluwer, 1992), 253–73

4006 Smale, M, Heisey, P W, Simultaneous estimation of seed-fertilizer adoption decisions: an application to hybrid maize in Malawi, *Technological forecasting and social change,* **43,** 3/4 (1993) 353–68

Anthropology

4007 Van Alstyne, G, The unvoiced text: allusion in Malawian sung poetry, *Journal of the Anthropological Society of Oxford,* **24,** 1 (1993) 13–32

Current affairs

4008 Chipeta, M, Malawi, turning point or political paralysis?, *Southern Africa political and economic monthly,* **5,** 8 (1992) 3–7

Demography

See also: 4036

4009 Kalipeni, E, Determinants of infant mortality in Malawi: a spatial perspective, *Social science and medicine,* **37,** 2 (1993) 183–98

4010 Srivastava, M L, The demographic profile of Malawi in 1990, *Tizame,* 3 (1992) 23–27

Economic and social history

See also: 4042

4011 Baker, C, *Seeds of trouble: government policy and land rights in Nyasaland, 1946–1964.* London: British Academic Press, 1993, 215pp

4012 Chriwa, W C, Child and youth labour in the Nyasaland plantations 1890–1953, *Journal of southern African studies,* **19,** 3 (1993) 662–8-

4013 Davison, J, Tenacious women: clinging to *Banja* household production in the face of changing gender relations in Malawi, *Journal of southern African studies,* **19,** 3 (1993) 405–21

4014 Kalinga, O J M, The Master Farmers' Scheme in Nyasaland, 1950–62: a study of a failed attempt to create a 'yeoman' class, *African affairs,* **92,** 368 (1993) 367–87

4015 King, M S, King, E, *The story of medicine and disease in Malawi: the 130 years since Livingstone.* Blantyre: Montfort Press, (1992?), 183pp

4016 Power, J, Race, class, ethnicity and Anglo-Indian trade rivalry in colonial Malawi, 1910–1945, *International journal of African historical studies,* **26,** 3 (1993) 575–607

Economy - Development

See also: 4059

4017 Chipeta, C, Economic policy framework, in Mhone, G C Z (ed), *Malawi at the crossroads (Item 4020)*, 90–134

4018 Kalemba, E, Non-governmental organisations (NGOs) working in Malawi and their developmental importance, *Tizame,* 3 (1992) 55–69

4019 Kaluwa, B, et al, *The structural adjustment programme in Malawi: a case of successful adjustment?* Harare: Sapes books, 1992, 61pp

4020 Mhone, G C Z (ed), *Malawi at the crossroads: the post-colonial political economy.* Harare: Sapes Books, 1992, 380pp

4021 Mhone, G C Z, The political economy of Malawi: an overview, in Mhone, G C Z (ed), *Malawi at the crossroads (Item 4020)*, 1–33

4022 Mhone, G, The political economy of Malawi, *Southern Africa political and economic monthly,* **5,** 8 (1992) 8–17

4023 Simukonda, P, The non-governmental sector in Malawi's socio-economic development, in Mhone, G C Z (ed), *Malawi at the crossroads (Item 4020)*, 298–348

4024 van Frausum, Y, Sahn, D E, An econometric model for Malawi: measuring the effects of external shocks and policies, *Journal of policy modelling,* **15,** 3 (1993) 313–27

Education

See also: 2007

4025 Chimombo, J P, Educational research in Malawi: problems of data collection, in *Research and development (Item 4002)*, 207–217

4026 Dubbey, J M, How effective is our university? A study of graduates from the University of Malawi, *Higher education quarterly,* **45,** 3 (1991) 219–33

4027 Moyo, C, Education policy and development strategy in Malawi, in Mhone, G C Z (ed), *Malawi at the crossroads (Item 4020)*, 265–97

4028 Murphy, P, Costs of an alternative form of second level education in Malawi, *Comparative education review,* **37,** 2 (1993) 107–22

4029 Pausewang, S, Pausewang, E A, *Prepared for returning? An evaluation of NRC vocational training programmes for refugees in Malawi.* Oslo: Norwegian Refugee Council, 1993, 35pp

Environment

4030 Barbier, E, *The role of smallholder producer prices in land degradation: the case of Malawi.* London: International Institute for Environment and Development, 1991, 33pp

4031 Bweya, L A C, Mukenga, N J, Sustainable soil and water management in Malawi, in Hudson, N & Cheatle, R J (eds), *Working with farmers (Item 245)*, 21–29

4032 **Hyde, W F, Seve, J E,** The economic role of wood products in tropical deforestation: the severe example of Malawi, *Forest ecology and management,* **57,** 1/4 (1993) 283–300

4033 **Kasweswe, W M K,** Shelter and the living environment: the case of Malawi, *Malawian geographer,* 29 (1991) 99–114

Food

No entry. *See also:* 2850

Gender

See also: 2007, 4013, 4056, 4073

4034 **Davison, J,** Changing relations of production in southern Malawi's households: implications for involving rural women in development, *Journal of contemporary African studies,* **11,** 1 (1992) 72–84

4035 **Gladwin, C H,** Fertilizer subsidy removal programs and their potential impacts on women farmers in Malawi and Cameroun, in Gladwin, C H (ed), *Structural adjustment and African women farmers (Item 315),* 191–216

Geography, human

4036 **Mmanga, W R,** Implications of population growth on land availability in Malawi, *Malawian geographer,* 29 (1991) 78–98

Health & welfare services

4037 **Chimbwete, C E K,** The impact of immunisation on the survival of the child in Malawi, in *Research and development (Item 4002),* 198–206

4038 **Helitzer-Allen, D L, et al,** Malaria chemoprophylaxis compliance in pregnant women: a cost effectiveness analysis of alternative treatments, *Social science and medicine,* **36,** 4 (1993) 403–407

4039 **Tembo, K C,** Village Health Committees as instruments for primary health care promotion, *Society of Malawi journal,* **46,** 1 (1993) 38–42

History, general

4040 **Msiska, A W C,** Malawi's hidden bibliographies: a preliminary survey of some earlier volumes, *African research and documentation,* 57 (1991) 15–20

History, C20th

See also: 4064

4041 **Newell, J,** 'How the English gentlemen makes war in the colonies': securing naval supremacy on Lake Malawi, 1914–1916, *Society of Malawi journal,* **46,** 1 (1993) 1–37

Industry & trade

4042 **Kalinga, O J M,** Early attempts at aquaculture in Malawi and implications for future projects, *Journal of Asian and African studies,* **28,** 3/4 (1993) 145–61

4043 **Kaluma, B,** Malawian industry: policies, performance and problems, in Mhone, G C Z (ed), *Malawi at the crossroads (Item 4020),* 205–40

4044 **Mtawali, K M,** Trade, price and market reform in Malawi: current status, proposals and constraints, *Food policy,* **18,** 4 (1993) 30–307

4045 **Safalaoh, A C L,** A review of poultry production in Malawi, constraints and possible solutions, *Tizame,* 3 (1992) 15–22

4046 Silumbu, E B D, External trade strategy in Malawi since 1964: selected issues, in *Research and development (Item 4002)*, 260–73

4047 Silumbu, E, Foreign trade policies and performance in Malawi, 1965–1990, in Mhone, G C Z (ed), *Malawi at the crossroads (Item 4020)*, 135–67

International economic relations

See also: 4046

4048 Robinson, M, Will political conditionality work?, *IDS bulletin,* **24,** 1 (1993) 58–66

Labour & manpower

4049 Msiska, F W G, School leavers' skewed occupational preferences and choices and their unemployment in Malawi, in *Research and development (Item 4002)*, 219–33

Law

See also: 644

4050 Kamchedzera, G, Land tenure relations, the law and development in Malawi, in Mhone, G C Z (ed), *Malawi at the crossroads (Item 4020)*, 188–204

4051 Maluwa, T, The legal regimes for the protection of refugees in Malawi, in Mhone, G C Z (ed), *Malawi at the crossroads (Item 4020)*, 349–71

4052 Nzunda, M, Security for advances to farmers of livestock and of food crops, in *Research and development (Item 4002)*, 250–56

Library - documentation

4053 Lweysa, K W, Appraisal standards in non-governmental records in Malawi, suggestions for improvement, *Tizame,* 3 (1992) 50–54

4054 Msiska, A W C, *An annotated bibliography of theses and dissertations held by Chancellor College Library, University of Malawi as at May 1992.* Zomba: University of Malawi Library, 1992, 113pp

4055 Ngwira, M, Nkhata, B, Information provision for research in Malawi, local and international sources (with particular reference to agriculture and the life sciences), in *Research and development (Item 4002)*, 281–86

Medical

See also: 4074

4056 Dallabetta, G A, et al, High socioeconomic status is a risk factor for HIV-1 infection but not for sexually-transmitted diseases in women in Malawi: implications for HIV-1 control, *Journal of infectious diseases,* **167,** 1 (1993) 36–42

Natural resources

4057 Mkanda, F X, Possible solutions for the encouragement of positive public attitudes towards national parks and game reserves in Malawi, *Nyala,* **15,** 1 (1991) 25–37

4058 Teplitz-Sembitzky, W, Zieroth, G, *The Malawi Charcoal Project: experience and lessons.* Washington: World Bank, 1990, 63pp

Planning

4059 Kaunda, J, The administrative organisation and process of national development planning in Malawi, in Mhone, G C Z (ed), *Malawi at the crossroads (Item 4020)*, 50–89

Politics

See also: 4048

4060 **Amnesty International,** Human rights abuse in Malawi, *Southern Africa political and economic monthly,* **5,** 12 (1992) 31–34

4061 **Chipeta, M,** The political process, civil society and the state, in Mhone, G C Z (ed), *Malawi at the crossroads (Item 4020)*, 34–49

4062 **Hirshmann, D,** Institutional development in the era of economic policy reform: concerns, contradictions and illustrations from Malawi, *Public administration and development,* **13,** 2 (1993) 113–28

4063 **L'Hoiry, P,** L'état au Malawi: l'Afrique disciplinée, in Médard, J F (ed), *Etats d'Afrique noire (Item 896)*, 291–304

4064 **Lwanda, J L,** *Kamuzu Banda of Malawi: a study in promise, power and paralysis.* Glasgow: Dudu Nsomba Publications, 1993, 374pp

Religion, philosophy

4065 **Thorold, A,** Metamorphoses of the Yao muslims, in Brenner, L (ed), *Muslim identity (item 963)*, 79–90

Rural economy

See also: 4014, 4020, 4034, 4035, 4050, 4052

4066 **Diacou, D,** The rural housing programme of Malawi, an example of the successful provision of rural low-cost housing, *Review of rural and urban planning in southern and eastern Africa,* 1 (1992) 117–27

4067 **Ferguson, A E, et al,** The new development rhetoric and Lake Malawi, *Africa,* **63,** 1 (1993) 1–18

4068 **Mangoche, S,** The problems of communication in development: the Malawi rural case, *Tizame,* 3 (1992) 37–44

4069 **Mkandawire, R,** The land question and agarian change in Malawi, in Mhone, G C Z (ed), *Malawi at the crossroads (Item 4020)*, 171–87

4070 **Ngwira, A,** The impact of small-scale rural non-farm agro-industries on employment and household income, in Mhone, G C Z (ed), *Malawi at the crossroads (Item 4020)*, 241–61

4071 **Simukonda, P H,** Contradictions and dilemmas in Malawi rural (agricultural) development, in *Research and development (Item 4002)*, 239–49

Sociology

See also: 4029

4072 **Chipeta, C,** Malawi, in Adepoju, A (ed), *Impact of structural adjustment (Item 1107)*, 105–118

4073 **Kalipeni, E, Zulu, E M,** Gender differences in knowledge and attitudes toward modern and traditional methods of child spacing in Malawi, *Population research and policy review,* **12,** 2 (1993) 103–21

4074 **Tembo, K C, Phiri, T B,** Sexually based cultural practices implicated in the transmission of AIDS, *Society of Malawi journal,* **46,** 1 (1993) 43–48

Urban studies

See also: 4033

4075 **Mwafongo, W M K,** Shelter and the living environment: the case of Malawi, *Malawian geographer,* 29 (1991) 99–114

MOZAMBIQUE

Agriculture, scientific

4076 **Gaifami, A,** Developing local seed production in Mozambique, in Cooper, D et al (ed), *Growing diversity: genetic resources and local food security* (London: Intermediate Technology Publications, 1992), 97–105

Current affairs

4077 **Isaacs, D,** Clean sweep, *Focus on Africa,* **4,** 4 (1993) 32–37
4078 **Isaacs, D,** Friend or foe?, *Focus on Africa,* **4,** 1 (1993) 25–28

Economic and social history

4079 **Lehmann, D,** Einblicke in das Leben deutscher Siedler in Mosambik, *DASP-Hefte,* 35/6 (1992) 135–45
4080 **White, L,** *Bridging the Zambesi: a colonial folly.* Basingstoke: Macmillan, 1993, 223pp

Economy - Development

See also: 4116
4081 **Kössler, R,** Zwischen Rationalität und 'Anarchie': Beobachtungen zu Plan und Markt in sowjetischen Modell und in der Erfahrung Mosambiks, in Meyns, P (ed), *Demokratie und Strukturreformen (Item 1174)*, 35–48
4082 **Mhone, G,** Mozambique, structural adjustment in a war economy, *Southern Africa political and economic monthly,* **5,** 10 (1992) 14–17
4083 **Roesch, O,** Economic reforms in Mozambique: notes on stabilisation, war and class formation, *Taamuli,* **1,** 1/2 (1990) 116–37
4084 **Schoeller, W,** Mosambik in der 'Structurellen Anpassung', in Meyns, P (ed), *Demokratie und Strukturreformen (Item 1174)*, 51–75
4085 **Thomas, S,** Sustainability in NGO relief and development work: further thoughts from Mozambique, *Development in practice,* **2,** 1 (1993) 37–46

Education

4086 **Marshall, J,** *Literacy, power and democracy in Mozambique.* Boulder: Westview, 1993, 313pp
4087 **Robinson, E,** The effect of family background on pupils' academic achievement in Mozambique, *International journal of educational development,* **13,** 3 (1993) 289–94

Environment

See also: 4127
4088 **Ellegard, A,** The Maputo coal stove project: environmental assessment of a new household fuel, *Energy policy,* **21,** 5 (1993) 598–614

Gender

4089 **Cliffe, J,** The war on women in Mozambique: health consequences of South African destabilisation, economic crisis, and structural adjustment, in Turshen, M (ed), *Women and health (Item 343)*, 15–34
4090 **Madzokere, C,** Gender and work - past, present and future: the situation of rural Mozambican women at Mazowe River Bridge camp in Zimbabwe, *Journal of social development in Africa,* **8,** 2 (1993) 23–32
4091 **Women and Law in Southern Africa Research Project,** *Women and law in Mozambique.* Harare: Women and

Law in Southern Africa Trust, 1992, 204pp

Health & welfare services

See also: 379, 4089, 4092

4092 **Cliff, J,** Donor dependence or donor control? The case of Mozambique, *Community development journal,* **28,** 3 (1993) 237–44

4093 **Cliff, J, Noormohammed, A R,** The impact of war on children's health in Mozambique, *Social science and medicine,* **36,** 7 (1993) 843–48

History, C20th

4094 **Serapião, L B,** Mozambique Liberation Front (Frelimo) and religion in Mozambique, 1962–88, *Africa (Rome),* **48,** 1 (1993) 110–24

4095 **Silva, T, José, A,** Eduardo Mondlane: pontos para uma periodização da trajectoria de um nacionalista (1940–1961), *Estudos Mozambicanos,* 9 (1991) 73–121

Industry & trade

4096 **Anon,** Rehabilitation of Mozambican railway lines, *Zimbabwe engineer,* **57,** 7 (1992) 5–11,13–15

4097 **Johnston, A,** *Formação no sector construção e aguas, Moçambique.* Uppsala: Scandinavian Institute of African Studies, 1991, 68pp

4098 **Levene, V,** LAM: mais voos, *Economia,* 7 (1991) 15–21

International economic relations

See also: 2989

4099 **Groth, D,** Staatliche Entwicklungszusammenarbeit mit Mosambik, *DASP-Hefte,* 35/6 (1992) 7–18

4100 **Plank, D N,** Aid, debt and the end of sovereignity: Mozambique and its donors, *Journal of modern African studies,* **31,** 3 (1993) 407–30

International relations

See also: 3989

4101 **Adam, I,** Portugal-Moçambique, a procura de uma relação, *Estudos Moçambicanos,* 9 (1991) 37–72

4102 **Harsch, E, Lashley, R,** *Mozambique: out of the ruins of war.* New York: United Nations, 1993, 20pp

Law

See also: 4091

4103 **Hall, M, Young, T,** Recent constitutional developments in Mozambique, *Journal of African law,* **35,** 1/2 (1991) 102–115

Media

4104 **Darch, C,** The book trade and publishing in Mozambique, *African book publishing record,* **19,** 1 (1993) 9–12

Medical

4105 **Coolins, A,** Environmental influences on the distribution of the incidence of cholera: a case study in Quelimane, Mozambique, *Disasters,* **17,** 4 (1993) 321–40

Planning

4106 **Sidaway, J D,** Urban and regional planning in Mozambique, *International journal of urban and regional research,* **17,** 2 (1993) 241–59

Politics

See also: 816, 861, 928, 4094, 4462, 5543

4107 **Adam, E,** Reform in Mosambik: eine Rückkehr zu den 'wahren' Zielen der Befreiung?, in Meyns, P (ed), *Demokratie und Strukturreformen (Item 1174)*, 76–94

4108 **Alden, C, Simpson, M,** Mozambique: a delicate peace, *Journal of modern African studies,* **31,** 1 (1993) 109–30

4109 **Cahen, M,** Check on socialism in Mozambique: what check? What socialism?, *Review of African political economy,* 57 (1993) 46–59

4110 **De Waal, A, Vines, A,** Conspicuous destruction: war, famine, and the reform of process in Mozambique, *Southern Africa political and economic monthly,* **5,** 10 (1992) 9–13

4111 **Deve, T,** Which way Mozambique?, *Southern Africa political and economic monthly,* **5,** 11 (1992) 39–42

4112 **Gonçalves, F,** Mozambique, the winding road to peace, *Southern Africa political and economic monthly,* **5,** 9 (1992) 39–44

4113 **Gonçalves, F,** Peace in Mozambique, to October 1, *Southern Africa political and economic monthly,* **5,** 12 (1992) 27–30

4114 **Gonçalves, F,** Peace in sight?, *Southern Africa political and economic monthly,* **5,** 10 (1992) 5–9

4115 **Graham, L S,** The dilemmas of managing transitions in weak states: the case of Mozambique, *Public administration and development,* **13,** 4 (1993) 409–22

4116 **Isaacman, A,** Conflicts in southern Africa: the case of Mozambique, in Hunt Davis, R (ed), *Apartheid unravels (Item 4677)*, 182–212

4117 **McCormick, S H,** Mozambique's cautious steps toward lasting peace, *Current history,* **92,** 574 (1993) 224–48

4118 **Nilsson, A,** From pseudo-terrorists to pseudo-guerillas: the MNR in Mozambique, *Review of African political economy,* 57 (1993) 60–71, & 58 (1993) 34–42

4119 **Roesch, O,** Renamo and the peasantry in southern Mozambique, *Canadian journal of African studies,* **26,** 3 (1992) 462–84

4120 **Saul, J,** Rethinking the Frelimo state, *Socialist register 1993,* 139–65

4121 **Schneidman, W W,** Conflict resolution in Mozambique, in Smock, D R (ed), *Making war and waging peace (Item 409)*, 219–38

4122 **Simpson, M,** Foreign and domestic factors in the transformation of Frelimo, *Journal of modern African studies,* **31,** 2 (1993) 309–37

Religion, philosophy

No entry. *See also:* 4094

Rural economy

See also: 1052

4123 **Lima, F,** Mozambicans return to their fields, *African farmer,* Nov 1993, 8–11

4124 **Marshall, J, Roesch, O,** The 'green zones' agricultural cooperatives of Nampula City: a new phase in the Mozambican cooperative movement?, *Journal of southern African studies,* **19,** 2 (1993) 240–72

4125 **Myers, G, West, H G,** *Land tenure security and state farm divestiture in Mozambique: case studies in Nhamatanda, Manica and Montepuez Districts.* Madison: Land Tenure Centre, University of Wisconsin, 1993, 2 vols, 87pp, 492pp

4126 **Profe, B,** Erfahrungen aus mehrjähriger Tätigkeit im Agrarsektor der Republik Mocambique, *DASP-Hefte,* 35/6 (1992) 40–51

4127 **Tanner, C, et al,** *Land disputes and ecological degradation in an irrigation scheme: a case study of state farm divestiture in Chokwe, Mozambique.* Madison: Land Tenure Centre, University of Wisconsin, 1993, 72pp

Sociology

See also: 4083, 5590

4128 **Boothby, N,** Reuniting unaccompanied children and families in Mozambique: an effort to link networks of community volunteers to a national programme, *Journal of social development in Africa,* **8,** 2 (1993) 11–22

4129 **Korstad, R R,** Documentary projects for refugee and displaced children in southern Africa, *Journal of social development in Africa,* **8,** 2 (1993) 61–72

4130 **Phiri, S, Duncan, J W,** Substitute family placements of unaccompanied Mozambican refugee children, *Journal of social development in Africa,* **8,** 2 (1993) 73–81

ZAIRE

General

4131 **Kankwenda Mbaya (ed),** *Zaire: what destiny?* Dakar: Codesria, 1993, 376pp

4132 **Kankwenda, M,** Conclusion: what destiny?, in Kankwenda, M (ed), *Zaire: what destiny? (item 4131),* 357–61

4133 **Omasombo, J** (ed), *Le Zaire à l'épreuve de l'histoire immédiate.* Paris: Karthala, 1993, 312pp

Anthropology

See also: 3802

4134 **Bockie, S,** *Death and the invisible powers: the world of Kongo belief.* Bloomington: Indiana University Press, 1993, 157pp

4135 **Devisch, R,** De *mbwoolu* genezingscultus bij de Yaka van Zaire, *Bulletin des séances,* **37,** 3 (1991) 273–95

4136 **Dupré, M C,** Les structures sociales sont-elles nécessairement inconscientes?, *Canadian journal of African studies,* **26,** 3 (1992) 393–411

4137 **Fabian, J,** *Time and the work of anthropology: critical essays 1971–1991.* Chur: Harwood, 1991, 299pp

4138 **Friedman, K E,** *Catastrophe and creation: the transformation of an African culture.* Chur: Harwood, 1991, 271pp

4139 **Goblet-Vanormelingen, V,** La maison du *mibombo*; rite thérapeutique pour les enfants à haut risques dans le Zaire rural, *Social science and medicine,* **37,** 2 (1993) 241–52

4140 **Hulstaert, G,** Institutions coûtoumières Mongo, *Annales aequatoria,* **12,** (1992) 529–38

4141 **Kalombo Mpolesha,** Note sur la dynamique des biens matrimoniaux chez les Baluba du Kasai: essai d'explication, *Frankfurter afrikanistische Blätter,* 4 (1992) 5–15

4142 **Kimura, D,** Daily activities and social association of the Bongando in central Zaire, *African study monographs,* **13,** 1 (1992) 1–33

4143 **Mananiah, K,** *La maladie et la guérison en mileu Kongo.* Kinshasa: Kalombo Diyoka, 1993, 211pp

4144 **Meurant, G,** Les dessins des Mbuti de l'Ituri, *Arts d'Afrique noire,* 78 (1991) 15–22

4145 **Miller, T R,** The evidence of

(musical) instruments, *Anthropology and humanism quarterly,* **17,** 2 (1992) 49–60

4146 Misago, K, Recherches ethnoarchéologiques à Ikenge, Région de l'Equateur, Zaire, *Nsi,* 10/11 (1992) 41–46

4147 Morelli, G A, Tronick, E Z, Male care among Efe foragers and Lese farmers, in Hewlett, B S (ed), *Father-child relations* (New York: Aldine de Gruyter, 1992), 231–61

4148 Theuws, J A, Space, travel and ritual among the Luba, *Africana Gandensia,* **7,** (1992) whole issue (119pp)

4149 van den Beken, A, *Proverbes Yaka du Zaire.* Paris: Karthala, 1993, 352pp

4150 Walle Sombo Bolene, Essai de bibliographie de la Basse Lomami, *Annales aequatoria,* **13** (1992) 475–87

Arts

See also: 63

4151 Buputu Kitok Mwan, Il teatro populare degle Ekonda, Zaire, *Africa (Rome),* **48,** 2 (1993) 199–215

4152 Jans, P, Alphonse Walschap, MSC (1903–1938), *Annales aequatoria,* **13** (1992) 505–16

Demography

See also: 4256

4153 Chahnazarian, A, et al, Impact of selective primary care on childhood mortality in a rural health zone in Zaire, *International journal of epidemiology,* **22,** 1 (1993) 32–41

4154 Taylor, W R, et al, Mortality and the use of health services surveys in rural Zaire, *International journal of epidemiology,* **22,** 1 (1993) 15–19

Economic and social history

See also: 4171, 4200

4155 Dibwe dia Mwembu, Les fonctions des femmes africaines dans les camps des travailleurs de l'Union Minière du Haut Katanga (1925–1960), *Zaire Afrique,* **33,** 272 (1993) 105–118

4156 Drachoussof, V, et al, *Le développement rurale en Afrique centrale, 1890–1960/62 - synthèse et réflexions.* Brussels: Fondation Roi Baudoin, 1991, 2 vols, 1,203pp

4157 Kangene, C, Les marchés dans le Bushi précoloniale, *Journal of Asian and African studies (Tokyo),* 44 (1993) 215–219

4158 Verbeek, L, L'histoire des chants et les danses populaires: la zone culturelle Bemba du Haut-Shaba (Zaire), *Enquêtes et documents d'histoire africaine,* 10 (1992) 1–137

Economy - Development

See also: 4225, 4235

4159 Kankwenda, M, The problem of the accumulation model, in Kankwenda, M (ed), *Zaire: what destiny? (item 4131),* 243–63

4160 Konate, I, *Le role des ONG locales dans l'assistance au developpement: le cas du Zaire.* Bamako: Centre Djoliba, 1992, 60pp

4161 Lukasa dia Bondo, Les conditions minimales de redressement de l'économie zairoise, *Zaire Afrique,* 270 (1992) 583–90

4162 Mokoli, M M, *State against development: the experience of post–1965 Zaire.* New York: Greenwood, 1992, 147pp

4163 Muhinduka Di-Kuruba, Aperçu de la politique économique zairoise et perspectives, *Zaire-Afrique,* **33,** 276 (1993) 333–52

4164 **Mutamba Lukusa,** *Déséquilibre macroéconomique et ajustements au Zaire 1876–1987.* Kinshasa: Presses Universitaire du Zaire, 1990, 215pp

4165 **Ngoie Tshibambe,** Discours politiques et jugements populaires: la dialectique de survie au Zaire, *Estudios Africanos,* **6,** 10/11 (1991/92) 73–81

Education

See also: 4173, 4188, 4199, 4257

4166 **Bongeli, Y Y A, Myumba, L,** Universities, research and underdevelopment in Zaire, in Kankwenda, M (ed), *Zaire: what destiny? (item 4131)*, 160–96

4167 **Ekwa bis Isal, M,** Quel avenir pour l'école zairoise?, *Zaire-Afrique,* **33,** 277 (1993) 399–416

4168 **Kabeya, N,** Continuing education: strong points and stress lines, in Kankwenda, M (ed), *Zaire: what destiny? (item 4131)*, 219–41

4169 **Kisangani, E,** Education and society, in Kankwenda, M (ed), *Zaire: what destiny? (item 4131)*, 129–59

4170 **Mukoko, N, Mulambu, M,** The study of humanities in Zaire, in Kankwenda, M (ed), *Zaire: what destiny? (item 4131)*, 197–218

Finance

See also: 4251

4171 **Rwanyindo, R,** Vicissitudes of the Zairean exchequer since 1960, in Kankwenda, M (ed), *Zaire: what destiny? (item 4131)*, 264–87

Food

4172 **Aunger, R,** The nutritional consequences of rejecting food in the Ituri forest of Zaire, *Human ecology,* **20,** 3 (1992) 263–91

Gender

See also: **4155,** 4219–21

4173 **Katana, B G,** Conscientizing adult education and community development: the experiences of the Elimu Association in women literacy, Uvira, Zaire, *Journal of the African Association for Literacy and Adult Education,* **6,** 1 (1992) 29–32

4174 **Lannoy, D, Lambinet, F,** Entrepreneuriat féminin au Zaire, *Cahiers du CEDAF,* 3/4 (1992) 195–205

4175 **Schoepf, B G, et al,** Gender, power and risk of AIDS in Zaire, in Turshen, M (ed), *Women and health (Item 343)*, 187–204

4176 **Schoepf, B, et al,** Women and structural adjustment in Zaire, in Gladwin, C H (ed), *Structural adjustment and African women farmers (Item 315)*, 151–68

Geography, physical

4177 **Bruneau, J C,** Flouriot, J, Etude des espaces urbains et péri-urbains par télédétection: exemples de Lubumbashi et Mbuji-Mayi (Zaire), in Vennetier, P (ed), *Urbanisation et développement (Item 1161)*, 55–68

Health & welfare services

4178 **Criel, V, van Balen, H,** Paying for the Kasongo hospital in Zaire: a conceptual framework, *Health policy and planning,* **8,** 1 (1993) 61–71

4179 **Mock, N B, et al,** The utility of case control methods for health policy and planning analysis - an illustration from Kinshasa, Zaire, *Evaluation and program planning,* **16,** 3 (1993) 199–205

4180 **Vernon, A S, et al,** Changes in the use of health services in a rural health zone in Zaire,

International journal of epidemiology, **22,** 1 (1993) 20–31

History, general

4181 Hulstaert, G, La linguistique et l'histoire, *Annales aequatoria,* **13,** (1992) 53–66

History, C18th

4182 Mukuna, M, La question des esclaves d'église détenus par les Pères Capuchins au Kongo et Angola (1645–1835), *Revue africaine de théologie,* **15,** 30 (1991) 163–79

History, C19th

See also: 417

4183 Nsondé, J, Christianisme et religion traditionelle en pays Koongo aux 18e–19e siècles, *Cahiers d'études africaines,* **32,** 128 (1992) 705–11

4184 Vinck, H, Chefs et patriarches de Mbandanka (1883–1893), *Annales aequatoria,* **13** (1992) 517–28

History, C20th

See also: 4138, 4215, 4245, 4247

4185 Benot, Y, *La mort du Lumumba (ou la tragédie congolaise).* Paris: Chaka, 1991, 190pp

4186 Comhaire, J, Souvenirs sur l'information de guerre au Congo-Belge, *Bulletin des séances,* **37,** 3 (1991) 301–308

4187 Dembour, M B, La chicote comme symbole de colonialisme belge?, *Canadian journal of African studies,* **26,** 2 (1992) 205–25

4188 Depaepe, M, et al, Missionary education in the Belgian Congo during the colonial period (1908–1960), *Nouvelle revue de science missionnaire,* **48,** 4 (1992) 265–80

4189 Eelen, G, Authority in international political discourse: a pragmatic analysis of UN documents on the Congo crisis, *Text,* **13,** 1 (1993) 29–63

4190 Gibbs, D N, Dag Hammarskjöld, the United Nations and the Congo crisis of 1960–1, *Journal of modern African studies,* **31,** 1 (1993) 163–74

4191 Hulstaert, G, Note sur la politique de la relégation, *Annales aequatoria,* **13,** (1992) 538–45

4192 Kambayi Buatshia, *Blancs et noirs face à la décolonisation du Congo Belge.* Kinshasa: Kalomba Diyoka, 1992, 265pp

4193 Longo Mbenza, *Kasa-Vubu, père de l'indépendance du Congo-Zaire.* Kinshasa: Kalomba Diyoka, 1993, 201pp

4194 Lufungula Lewono, Ernest Itela, Chef du CEC de Coquilhatville, *Annales aequatoria,* 13 (1992) 499–504

4195 Lumuna Sando, K, *Nord-Katanga, 1960–1964: de la sécession à la guerre civile, le meutre des chefs.* Paris: Harmattan, 1993, 222pp

4196 Rösiö, B, The Ndola crash and the death of Dag Hammarsjköld, *Journal of modern African studies,* **31,** 4 (1993) 661–71

4197 Turner, T, Patrice Lumumba: review article, *African studies,* **52,** 1 (1993) 103–111

4198 Vinck, H, Charles Lemaire de passage à Mbandaka (1895–1900–1902), *Annales aequatoria,* **13** (1992) 67–124

Industry & trade

See also: 4174

4199 Gasibirege, S, Education informelle et développement des petits métiers de l'artisanat au Zaire, *Cahiers du CEDAF,* 3/4 (1992) 207–16

4200 **Kankwenda, M,** Mineral resources, the state and industrialisation in Zaire, in Kankwenda, M (ed), *Zaire: what destiny? (item 4131)*, 319–56

4201 **Leclercq, H,** L'économie populaire informelle de Kinshasa: approche macroéconomique, *Cahiers du CEDAF,* 3/4 (1992) 139–60

4202 **Leclercq, H,** L'économie populaire informelle de Kinshasa: approache macroéconomique, *Zaire Afrique,* **33,** 271 (1993) 17–36

4203 **Lokota, E P,** L'économie informelle à Kinshasa: fait nouveau ou permanent?, *Cahiers du CEDAF,* 3/4 (1992) 161–78

4204 **Mananiah, K,** *Les coopératives au Zaire.* Kinshasa: Kalombo Diyoka, 1993, 133pp

4205 **Mbwinga Bila,** Secteur informel et marché intérieur de consommation de masse au Zaire, *Cahiers du CEDAF,* 3/4 (1992) 179–93

4206 **Muamba Ngalula,** Synthèse de récits de vie de petits entrepreneurs, *Cahiers du CEDAF,* 3/4 (1992) 109–36

4207 **Muamba Ngalula,** Trajectoires et profils de quelques acteurs de la petite économie marchande à partir de récits de vie, *Cahiers du CEDAF,* 3/4 (1992) 97–107

4208 **Omasombo Tshonda,** Economie populaire, état, capitalisme, *Cahiers du CEDAF,* 3/4 (1992) 19–31

4209 **Omasombo Tshonda,** Exclus de prêts bancaires, ils sort ailleurs, *Cahiers du CEDAF,* 3/4 (1992) 81–96

4210 **Omasombo Tshonda, et al,** Les *khadifi*: revendeurs 'non-officiels' de carburant, *Cahiers du CEDAF,* 3/4 (1992) 61–80

4211 **Sumata, C,** Les spécifités de entreprise informelle zairoise et son mode de financement, *Année africaine 1992/93,* 333–49

4212 **Verhaegen, B,** La petite économie marchande à Kisangali, *Cahiers du CEDAF,* 3/4 (1992) 33–47

4213 **Vwakyanakazi, M,** Creuseurs d'or et crise socio-économique au Nord-Kivu en République du Zaïre, *Africa (Rome),* **47,** 3 (1992) 375–391

4214 **Willems, M,** Un recensement des petite activités marchandise à Kabondo, *Cahiers du CEDAF,* 3/4 (1992) 49–60

International relations

See also: 4235

4215 **Durch, W J,** The UN operation in the Congo, in Durch, W J (ed), *The evolution of UN peacekeeping* (New York: St Martin's Press, 1993), 315–52

4216 **Gibbs, D N,** International influences on Third World development: the case of Mobutu's Zaire, *Nytt fran Nodiska Afrikainstitutet,* 29 (1992) 12–22

Library - documentation

4217 **Vinck, H,** Le microfilmage des Archives Aequatoria, *History in Africa,* **20,** (1993) 423–27

Literature

4218 **Cailler, B,** The impossible ecstasy: an analysis of V Y Mudimbe's Déchirures, *Research in African literatures,* **24,** 4 (1993) 15–2

Media

No entry. *See also:* 4186

Medical

See also: 4175, 4253

4219 **Csete, J,** Health-seeking behaviour of Rwandan women, *Social science and medicine,* **37,** 11 (1993) 1285–92

4220 **Heyward, W L, et al,** Impact of HIV counselling and testing among child-bearing women in Kinshasa, Zaire, *AIDS,* **7,** 12 (1993) 1633–37

4221 **Schoepf, B G,** AIDS action-research with women in Kinshasa, Zaire, *Social science and medicine,* **37,** 11 (1993) 1401–13

4222 **Thea, D M, et al,** A prospective study of diarrhoea and HIV-1 infection among 429 Zairian infants, *New England journal of medicine,* **329,** 23 (1993) 1696–1702

4223 **Tonglet, R, et al,** Can improvements in water supply reduce childhood diarrhoea?, *Health policy and planning,* **7,** 3 (1992) 260–68

Natural resources

4224 **Terashima, H, et al,** Ethnobotany of the Lega in the tropical rain forest of estern Zaire: part 2, Zone de Walikale, *African study monographs (supplementary issue),* 19 (1992) 1–60

Politics

See also: 1919, 3999

4225 **Askin, S, Collins, C,** External collusion with kleptocracy: can Zaire recapture its stolen wealth?, *Review of African political economy,* 57 (1993) 72–85

4226 **Biaya, T K,** Ethnicity: the root of nationalist ideology, in Kankwenda, M (ed), *Zaire: what destiny? (item 4131),* 2–16

4227 **de Saint-Moulin, L,** Le mouvement de démocratisation dans la zone de Ngaba à Kinshasa, *Zaire-Afrique,* **33,** 274 (1993) 225–43

4228 **Digekisa Piluka, V,** *Le massacre de Lubumbashi, Zaire, 11–12 Mai 1990: dossier d'un témoin-accusé.* Paris: Harmattan, 1993, 414pp

4229 **Elliott, J M, Dymally, M M,** *Voices of Zaire: rhetoric or reality.* Washington: Washington Institute Press, 1990, 175pp

4230 **Jewsiewicki, B,** *Naître et mourir au Zaire: récits de vie.* Paris: Karthala, 1993, 255pp

4231 **Kaleke-ya-Bila,** Regionalist ideologies, in Kankwenda, M (ed), *Zaire: what destiny? (item 4131),* 17–42

4232 **Kikassa Mwanalessa, F,** 'Expliquez-moi la démocratie', *Zaire Afrique,* **33,** 272 (1993) 83–95

4233 **Kinkela vi Kans'y,** Le rapport final des travaux de la Conférence nationale souveraine: texte intégral, *Zaire-Afrique,* **33,** 273 (1993) 131–99

4234 **Lawyers Committee for Human Rights,** *Zaire: repression as policy. A human rights report.* New York: the Committee, 1990, 232pp

4235 **Leslie, W J,** *Zaire: continuity and change in an oppressive state.* Boulder: Westview, 1993, 204pp

4236 **Longandjo, O,** State power under MPR control: an interpretive essay, in Kankwenda, M (ed), *Zaire: what destiny? (item 4131),* 83–96

4237 **Massamba, J,** *Reconstruire la nation: 400 propositions pour bâtir la Troisième République du Zaire.* Kinshasa: Kalomba Diyoka, 1993, 198pp

4238 **Monsengwo Pasinya, L,** La démocratisation au Zaire et ses protagonistes, *Zaire-Afrique,* **33,** 275 (1993) 275–85

4239 **Mulambu, M,** State and structure: the perennial search for stability, in Kankwenda, M (ed), *Zaire: what destiny? (item 4131)*, 43–82

4240 **Nkuku Kilombo,** *Plaidoyer pour une transition démocratiqe au Zaire.* Kinshasa: Kalomba Diyoka, 1993, 262pp

4241 **Otemikongo Mandefu Yahisule, Toengaho Lokungo,** Impératif de la démocratie pour une Territoriale de développement au Zaire, *Zaire Afrique,* 270 (1992) 599–618

4242 **Ruys, M,** Het fiasco van het mobutisme, *Internationale spectator,* **46,** 12 (1992) 725–730

4243 **Tshiyembe Mwayila, Bukasa Mayele,** *Invention de l'état de droit et projet de société democratique en Afrique: le cas du Zaire.* n.p.: Diane de Selliers, 1991, 220pp

4244 **Wamba-dia-Wamba,** National reconciliation in Zaire: reasons for the impasse, *Codesria bulletin,* 2 (1993) 10–13

Religion, philosophy

See also: 4226

4245 **Mackay, D, Ntoni-Nzinga, I D,** Kimbangu's interlocutor: Nyurudi's *Nsamu miangunza* (The story of the prophets), *Journal of religion in Africa,* **23,** 3 (1993) 232–65

4246 **Ngoy Kasukuti,** *Recht und Grenze der Inkulturation: Heilserfahrungen im Christentum Afrikas am Beispiel der Kimbanguistenkirche in Zaire.* Erlangen: Evangelisch Lutherischen Mission, 1991, 165pp

4247 **Pemberton, J,** The history of Simon Kimbangu, prophet, by the writers Nfinangani and Nzungu, 1921: an introduction and annotated translation, *Journal of religion in Africa,* **23,** 3 (1993) 194–231

Rural economy

4248 **Bidinkama Kupa Ngandu, Bilowa Bidiku,** Culture et usage actuels du maïs dans la Collectivité de Kafuba au Kasai-Occidental, *Zaire Afrique,* **33,** 271 (1993) 42–48

4249 **Fairhead, J,** Paths of authority: roads, the state and the market in eastern Zaire, in Hewitt de Alcantara, C (ed), *Real markets: social and political issues of food policy reform* (London: Cass, 1993), 17–35

4250 **Kankwenda, M,** The agricultural crisis: anatomy of a paradox, in Kankwenda, M (ed), *Zaire: what destiny? (item 4131)*, 288–318

4251 **Tshibaka, T B,** Agricultural pricing and the exchange rate in Zaire, in Bautista, R M & Valdés, A (eds), *The bias against agriculture* (Washington: IFPRI, 1993), 93–110

Sociology

4252 **Biaya, T K, Omassombo, T,** Social classes in Zaire today, in Kankwenda, M (ed), *Zaire: what destiny? (item 4131)*, 97–127

4253 **Brown, J E, et al,** Dry and tight; sexual practices and potential AIDS risk in Zaire, *Social science and medicine,* **37,** 8 (1993) 989–94

4254 **Kamjamachumbi, P,** *Les populations du Kivu et la loi sur la nationalité: vraie et fausse problème.* Kinshasa: Kalomba Diyoka, 1993, 273pp

4255 **Lututala, M, et al,** Zaire, in Adepoju, A (ed), *Impact of structural adjustment (Item 1107)*, 130–43

4256 **Mamdani, M, et al,** Fertility and contraceptive use in poor urban areas of developing countries, *Health policy and planning,* **8,** 1 (1993) 1–18

4257 **Ngub'Usim Mpey-Nka,** La récupération des jeunes de la rue par une éducation au travail productif, *Zaire Afrique*, 269 (1992) 537–44

Social welfare

4258 **Mukadi Boni,** *Quelle sécurité sociale pour la Troisième République du Zaire?* Kinshasa: Kalomba Diyoka, 1993, 136pp

4259 **Thibaud, A, et al,** Les villages Bondeko pour enfants handicapés à Kinshasa, *Zaire Afrique*, 269 (1992) 545–56

4260 **Toengaho Lokundo,** Pour une approche managériale dans le réalisation des projets de développement communitaire au Zaire, *Zaire Afrique*, **33,** 272 (1993) 97–103

Urban studies

See also: 3811, 4177, 4201, 4203

4261 **Codou, A, et al,** Urbanisation et difficultés de développement à Kikwit et au Kwilu (région de Bandundu - Zaire), in Vennetier, P (ed), *Urbanisation et développement (Item 1161)*, 45–54

4262 **Odio, O O,** Histoire de quelques avenues de Mbandaka, *Annales aequatoria*, **13,** (1992) 125–36

ZAMBIA

General

4263 **Sumaili, F K M, Lungwangwa, G** (ed), *Zambia in the 1990s.* Lusaka: 'Professors World Peace Academy of Zambia', 1991, 182pp

Anthropology

4264 **Luig, U,** Besessenheitsrituale als historische Charta: die Verarbeitung europäischer Einflusse in sambianischen Besessenheitskulten, *Paideuma*, **39,** (1993) 343–55

Current affairs

4265 **Holmes, T,** Letter from Lusaka, *Southern African review of books*, **5,** 2 (1993) 11–13

4266 **Kabwe, T C,** Kaunda bounces back?, *Southern Africa political and economic monthly*, **4,** 12 (1991) 26–30

4267 **Kamwambe, G T N,** *Frederick Chiluba: is he riding a tide of fortune?* Lusaka: n.p., 1991, 92pp

Economic and social history

See also: 4300, 4311

4268 **Hamalengwa, M,** *Class struggles in Zambia 1889–1989 (and: The fall of Kenneth Kaunda 1990–1991).* Lanham: University Press of America, 1992, 182pp

4269 **Kanduza, A M** (ed), *Socioeconomic change in eastern Zambia: precolonial to 1980s.* Lusaka: Historical Association of Zambia, 1992, 204pp

4270 **Lucheme, C,** Ethnic stereotypes, violence and labour in early colonial Zambia, 1889–1924, in Chipunga, S N (ed), *Guardians in their time (Item 4311)*, 30–49

4271 **Macmillan, H,** The historiography of transition on the Zambian Copperbelt: another view, *Journal of southern African studies*, **19,** 3 (1993) 681–712

4272 **Matongo, A B K,** Popular culture in a colonial society: another look at Mbeni and Kalela dances on the Copperbelt, 1930–64, in Chipunga, S N (ed), *Guardians in their time (Item 4311)*, 180–217

4273 **Musambichime, M C,** Colonialism and the environment

in Zambia, in Chipunga, S N (ed), *Guardians in their time (Item 4311)*, 8–29

4274 Seleti, Y N, Entrepreneurship in colonial Zambia, in Chipunga, S N (ed), *Guardians in their time (Item 4311)*, 147–79

Economy - Development

See also: 1896, 2280, 2285, 4337

4275 Anderson, P A, Kayizzi-Mugerwa, S, External shocks and the search for diversification in Zambia, in Blomström, M & Lundahl, M (eds), *Economic crisis (Item 119)*, 143–61

4276 Bates, R H, Collier, P, The politics and economics of policy reform in Zambia, in Bates, R H & Krueger, A O (eds), *Political and economic interactions in economic policy reform* (Oxford: Blackwell, 1993), 387–443

4277 Fradi, M A, Zambia: reform and reversal, in Thomas, V et al (eds), *Restructuring economies in distress* (Oxford: OUP, 1991), 332–52 (and see 352–8)

4278 Havnevik, K J, The failure of two decades of structural adjustment in Zambia, *Nytt fran Nodiska Afrikainstitutet,* 29 (1992) 23–41

4279 Mhone, G, MMD, behind the paralysis in economic policy, *Southern Africa political and economic monthly,* **5,** 11 (1992) 14–17

4280 Milimo, J T, The role of research in Zambia's development efforts in the 1990s, in Sumaili, F K M & Lungwangwa, G (eds), *Zambia in the 1990s (item 4263)*, 115–25

4281 Mwanza, A M, et al (eds), *The structural adjustment programme in Zambia: lessons from experince.* Harare: Sapes, 1992, 47pp

4282 Reinikka-Soininen, R, *Theory and practice in structural adjustment: the case of Zambia.* Helsinki: School,of Economics, Helsinki University, 1990, 106pp

Education

See also: 231

4283 Kaniki, A M, Continuing education programmes for library, documentation and information personnel in Zambia, *Zambia Library Association journal,* 20 (1992) 29–41

4284 Kasanda, C D, Problems of conducting educational research in Zambia, *Zimbabwe journal of educational research,* **5,** 2 (1993) 206–21

4285 Lungwangwa, G, From crisis to a meaningful educational policy in Zambia: suggestions for educational development in the 1990s, in Sumaili, F K M & Lungwangwa, G (eds), *Zambia in the 1990s (item 4263)*, 1–21

4286 Phiri, F A, Looking into Zambia's secondary school curriculum in the 1990s, in Sumaili, F K M & Lungwangwa, G (eds), *Zambia in the 1990s (item 4263)*, 43–64

4287 Pillai, V K, Yates, D L, Teenage sexual activity in Zambia: the need for a sex education policy, *Journal of biosocial science,* **25,** 3 (1993) 411–14

4288 Ronning, J A, Nabuzoka, D, Promoting social interaction and status of children with intellectual disabilities in Zambia, *Journal of special education,* **27,** 3 (1993) 277–305

4289 Sikwibele, A L, The political economy of financing education in Zambia: policies and challenges for the 1990s, in Sumaili, F K M & Lungwangwa, G (eds), *Zambia in the 1990s (item 4263)*, 23–41

Environment

See also: 4486

4290 **Mukanda, N, Mwiinga, R,** Soil and water management in Zambia, in Hudson, N & Cheatle, R J (eds), *Working with farmers (Item 245)*, 37–40

4291 **Mulwanda, M,** The need for new approaches to disaster management: the 1989 floods in Lusaka, Zambia, *Environment and urbanisation,* **5,** 2 (1993) 67–77

4292 **Sumaili, F K M, et al** (ed), *Population growth and the environment.* Nairobi: Masaki, 1990, 63pp

4293 **Sutherland, A J,** Integrating a socioeconomic perspective into soil and water management in Zambia, in Hudson, N & Cheatle, R J (eds), *Working with farmers (Item 245)*, 64–68

Finance

See also: 1896

4294 **Kamya, A,** Zambia's exchange rate policy in the 1990s, in Sumaili, F K M & Lungwangwa, G (eds), *Zambia in the 1990s (item 4263)*, 143–71

Food

4295 **Foster, S,** Maize production, drought and AIDS in Monze District, Zambia, *Health policy and planning,* **8,** 3 (1993) 247–54

4296 **Wandel, M, Holmboe-Ottesen, G,** Child malnutrition and development processes in two Zambian villages, *Health policy and planning,* **7,** 2 (1992) 123–34

Gender

See also: 4332, 4344

4297 **Geisler, G,** Moving with tradition: the politics of marriage amongst the Toka of Zambia, *Canadian journal of African studies,* **26,** 3 (1992) 437–61

4298 **Hansen, K T,** Body politics: sexuality, gender and domestic service in Zambia, *Journal of women's history,* **2,** 1 (1990) 120–42

4299 **Hansen, K T,** Body politics: sexuality, gender and domestic service in Zambia, in Johnson-Odim, C & Strobel, M (eds), *Expanding the boundaries of women's history* (Bloomington: Indiana University Press, 1992), 3–25

4300 **Hansen, K T,** White women in a changing world: employment, voluntary work, and sex in post-World War II Northern Rhodesia, in Chauduri, N & Strobel, M (eds), *Western women and imperialism* Bloomington: Indiana University Press, 1992), 247–68

4301 **Liatto-Katunda, B,** The women's lobby and gender relations in Zambia, *Review of African political economy,* 56 (1993) 79–83

4302 **Mulozi, L,** Women's participation in Zambian cooperatives, *Yearbook of cooperative enterprise 1993,* 179–84

4303 **Mumba, N M,** *A song in the night: personal memoir of widowhood in Zambia.* Lusaka: Multimedia, 1992, 90pp

Geography, human

4304 **Nag, P,** *Population, settlement and development in Zambia.* New Delhi: Concept, 1990, 232pp

Health & welfare services

See also: 3005

4305 **Chela, C M, Siankanga, Z C,** Home and community care: the

Zambia experience, *AIDS,* **5,** 1 (1991) 157–61

4306 Zondag, A M, et al, Immunisation and nutritional status of under-fives in rural Zambia, *Central African journal of medicine,* **38,** 2 (1992) 62–66

History, general

4307 Colson, E, *Zambia past and present: the history of Nampeyo.* Luska: Kenneth Kaunda Foundation, 1991, 76pp

History, C20th

4308 Carter, T D, *The Northern Rhodesian record: a history of the Northern Rhodesia police.* Worthing: White House, 1992, 222pp

4309 Chipunga, S N, Accumulation from within: the *boma* class and the Native Treasury in colonial Zambia, in Chipunga, S N (ed), *Guardians in their time (Item 4311)*, 74–96

4310 Chipunga, S N, African leadership under indirect rule in colonial Zambia, in Chipunga, S N (ed), *Guardians in their time (Item 4311)*, 50–73

4311 Chipunga, S N (ed), *Guardians in their time: experiences of Zambians under colonial rule 1890–1964.* Basingsoke: Macmillan, 1993, 223pp

4312 Gadsen, F, Education and society in colonial Zambia, in Chipunga, S N (ed), *Guardians in their time (Item 4311)*, 97–125

4313 Kanduza, A M, Towards a history of ideas in Zambia, in Chipunga, S N (ed), *Guardians in their time (Item 4311)*, 126–46

4314 Phiri, B J, The failure of multiracial 'liberal' parties in Northern Rhodesia/Zambia: prelude to the one-party state?, *Asian and African Studies (Haifa)*, **25,** 1 (1991) 55–80

Industry & trade

See also: 3669, 4334, 4349

4315 Assunção, P, *Makroökonomische und Institutionelle Grenzen einer Kleingewerbeförderungspolitik in sub-saharaischen Afrika: das Beispiel Sambias.* Konstanz: Hartung-Gorre, 1992, 166pp

4316 Assunção, P T B, et al, Begrenzung det finanziellen Förderung: die 'small-scale entreprise promotion' (SEP) und die sambische Entwicklungsbank, in their *Internationale Organisationen, Entwicklungsverwaltung und Kleingewerförderung in der Dritten Welt* (Baden-Baden: Nomos, 1993), 258–67

4317 Auty, R, Mismanaged mineral depletion in Zambia, 1970–1990, in his *Sustaining development in mineral economies* (London: Routledge, 1993), 220–38

4318 Bardouille, R, *An annotated bibliography of research on the informal sector in Zambia.* Lusaka: University of Zambia, 1991, 234pp

4319 Mpande, M M, The effect of the mining industry on the industrialisation of Zambia, in Khennas, S (ed), *Industrialisation (item 454)*, 278–327

4320 Osei-Hwedie, B Z, Osei-Hwedie, K, *Tanzania-Zambia Railroad (TAZARA): an analysis of Zambia's decision-making in transportation.* Lawrenceville: Brunswick, 1990, 117pp

4321 Shawa, J J, Trade, price and market reform in Zambia: current status and constraints, *Food policy,* **18,** 4 (1993) 294–99

International economic relations

4322 Allen, T, The law relating to private foreign investment in manufacturing in Botswana, Zambia and Zimbabwe, *African journal of international and comparative law,* **4,** 1 (1992) 44–83

Law

See also: 2115, 4297, 4322

4323 Mhlaba, L, Press freedom in Zambia, or the right of the political oppositon to be heard: Arthur Wina and others v. the Attorney General 1990/HP/1878, *Zimbabwe law review,* 7/8 (1989/90) 174–80

Library - documentation

See also: 4283

4324 Chisenga, J, Information technology and the Zambian librarian: preparations for the 21st century takeoff, *Zambia Library Association journal,* 20 (1992) 42–48

4325 Kakoma, A K, Library associations, an overlooked aspect in the development of librarianship in Zambia, *Zambia Library Association journal,* 20 (1992) 4–11

4326 Lungu, C B M, Exchange of publications in Zambian libraries, *Zambia Library Association journal,* 20 (1992) 21–28

4327 Mwanakatwe, J M, Funding for libraries, *Zambia Library Association journal,* 20 (1992) 12–20

4328 Nkoma, B P, Librarianship in Zambia, government policy, and training implications, *Information trends,* **5,** 3 (1992) 97–108

Literature

4329 Sumaili, F K M (ed), *Zambian writers talking.* Ndola: Printpak, 1991, 146pp

4330 Sumaili, F K M, Zambian literature in the 1990s, in Sumaili, F K M & Lungwangwa, G (eds), *Zambia in the 1990s (item 4263),* 65–84

Media

See also: 4323

4331 Nyirenda, J E, Development broadcasting in Zambia: challenges for the 1990s, in Sumaili, F K M & Lungwangwa, G (eds), *Zambia in the 1990s (item 4263),* 101–114

Medical

See also: 4295

4332 Peltzer, K, Likwa, R, Psychosocial effects of unwed pregnancy in Lusaka, Zambia, *International journal of mental health,* **21,** 4 (1993) 50–58

Natural resources

4333 Chidumayo, E N, Zambian charcoal production - Mlombo woodland recovery, *Energy policy,* **21,** 5 (1993) 586–97

Planning

4334 Ehie, I C, Benjamin, C O, An integrated multiobjective planning model: a case study of the Zambian copper-mining industry, *European journal of operational research,* **68,** 2 (1993) 160–72

Politics

See also: 4268, 4301

4335 Agyeman-Duah, B, Civilian control of the military in Africa: the case of Zambia, in Danopoulos, C P (ed), *Civilian rule (Item 844),* 141–59

4336 Chisala, B S, *Luchembe coup attempt.* Lusaka: Multimedia, 1991, 84pp

4337 Musiker, R, *Kaunda's Zambia 1964–1991: a selected and annotated*

bibliography. Braamfontein: SAIIA, 1993, 426pp

4338 **National Democratic Institute, Carter Center,** *The October 31, 1991, national elections in Zambia.* Washington: The Institute/Atlanta: the Center, 1992, 167pp

4339 **Rakner, L,** Political transition and economic reform: the role of labour in Zambian national politics, *Forum for development studies,* 2 (1993) 131–47

Religion, philosophy

4340 **Nagan, W P,** Africa's value debate: Kaunda on humanism and African humanism - a comment, *East African journal of peace and human rights,* **1,** 1 (1993) 103–114

4341 **Ogez, J M,** *Where it all began...* Lusaka: Missionaries of Africa: Zambian Region, 1991, 221pp

Rural economy

See also: 1030, 1052

4342 **Copestake, J C,** The contribution to agricultural technology development of the Gwembe Valley Agricultural Mission, in Wellard, K & Copestake, J C (eds), *NGOs and the state (Item 1096)*, 174–79

4343 **Copestake, J C,** Zambia: country overview, in Wellard, K & Copestake, J C (eds), *NGOs and the state (Item 1096)*, 161–73

4344 **Due, J M,** Does the T&V extension assist female-headed families?: some recent evidence from Zambia, *Eastern Africa economic review,* **7,** 1 (1991) 69–75

4345 **Kaonga, Y, Malayisha, E,** An agroforestry extension project in Mazabuku District, Zambia, in Hudson, N & Cheatle, R J (eds), *Working with farmers (Item 245)*, 203–206

4346 **Kokwe, M,** *Wetlands in drylands: the agroecology of savanna systems in Africa. Part 3e: the role of dambos in agricultural development in Zambia.* London: International Institute for Environment and Development, 1991, 35pp

4347 **Mäckel, R, Siebert, M,** Recent and potential types of use for the seasonally wet grasslands in Zambia, *Applied geography and development,* 40 (1992) 7–21

4348 **Musambachime, M C,** Rural settlement schemes as a strategy for rural development in Zambia in the 1990s, in Sumaili, F K M & Lungwangwa, G (eds), *Zambia in the 1990s (item 4263)*, 127–41

4349 **Shawa, J, et al,** Economic analysis of expanding agricultural exports: the case of cotton in Zambia, *Zambian journal of agricultural science,* **2,** 1 (1992) 7–18

Science & technology

4350 **Lungu, C B M,** The advent of information technology in Zambia: prospects for the 1990s, in Sumaili, F K M & Lungwangwa, G (eds), *Zambia in the 1990s (item 4263)*, 85–99

Sociology

4351 **Mwanalushi, M,** *Youth and society in Zambia: growing up in a changing society.* Lusaka: Multimedia, 1990, 86pp

4352 **Mwanamina, I,** Zambia, in Adepoju, A (ed), *Impact of structural adjustment (Item 1107)*, 69–77

4353 **Pillai, V K,** Men and family planning in Zambia, *Journal of biosocial science,* **25,** 1 (1993) 17–23

Urban studies

4354 **Schlyter, A,** Time series analysis: a londitudinal study of housing quality in Lusaka, in Tipple, A G & Willis, K G (eds), *Housing the poor (item 1159)*, 62–80

4355 **UN Centre for Human Settlements,** *Community participation in Zambia: the DANIDA/UNCHS training programme.* Nairobi: the Centre, 1992, 56pp

SOUTHERN AFRICA

General

No entry. *See also:* 4677

Anthropology

See also: 3941, 4469

4360 **Gordon, R J, Spiegel, A D,** Southern Africa revisited, *Annual review of anthropology,* **22,** (1993) 83–105

4361 **Hoff, A,** Die tradisionelle wereldbesoukouing van die Khoekhoen, *South African journal of ethnology,* **16,** 1 (1993) 1–9

4362 **Mphande, L,** Ngoni praise poetry and the Nguni diaspora, *Research in African literatures,* **24,** 4 (1993) 99–122

Arts

4363 **Chifunyise, S J,** SADC to boost cultural industries, *Southern Africa political and economic monthly,* **5,** 12 (1992) 45–56

4364 **Mda, Z,** *When people play people: development communication through theatre.* London: Zed, 1993, 250pp

Economic and social history

See also: 1887, 4464, 4731

4365 **Crush, J, Ambler, C,** *Liquor and labour in southern Africa.* Pietermaritzburg: University of Natal Press, 1993, 432pp

4366 **McAllister, P A,** Indigenous beer in southern Africa: functions and fluctuations, *African studies,* **52,** 1 (1993) 71–88

4367 **Miles, M, Crush, J N,** Personal narratives as interactive texts: collecting and interpreting migrant life-histories, *Professional geographer,* **45,** 1 (1993) 84–129

4368 **Nurse, G T,** Some biological concomitants of sociocultural hierarchies in southern Africa before the Mfecane, in Sperber, G H (ed), *From apes to man* (New York: Wiley, 1990), 17–25

4369 **Phoofolo, P,** Epidemics and revolutions: the rinderpest epidemic in late nineteenth-century southern Africa, *Past & present,* 138 (1993) 112–143

4370 **Schmidt, B,** Intermediäre ethnizistische Mobilisierungen: des Biespiel der Kalanga in Zimbabwe und Südafrika, *Saeculum,* **43,** 4 (1992) 273–90

Economy - Development

See also: 4457

4371 **Baiculescu, M, et al** (eds), *Kap der kleinen Hoffnung: das Südliche Afrika nach der Apartheid.* Vienna: Promedia, 1993, 224pp

4372 **Barnard, D** (ed), *Prodder's development directory...: an assesment and comprehensive survey of Southern African development agencies and organisations.* Braamfontein: Human Sciences Research Council, 1993, 614pp

4373 **Koester, U, et al,** *Demand-side constraints and structural adjustment in* *subsaharan African countries.* Washington: International Food Policy Research Institute, 1990, 90pp

4374 **Love, R,** The future of southern Africa, *Review of African political economy,* 57 (1993) 86–90

4375 **Mijere, N J,** SADCC, IMF economic adjustment programmes and regional economic cooperation, *Eastern African social science research review,* **6,** 1 (1990) 48–60

4376 **Mwanza, A,** The debt crisis in the SADCC region, *Southern Africa political and economic monthly,* **4,** 9 (1991) 16–20

4377 **Whiteside, A,** Introduction, in Cross, S & Whiteside, A (eds), *Facing up to AIDS (item 4753)*, 3–12

Education

See also: 4454

4378 **Mundy, K,** Toward a critical analysis of literacy in southern Africa, *Comparative education review,* **37,** 4 (1993) 389–411

4379 **Mungazi, D A,** *The challenge of educational innovation and national development in southern Africa.* New York: Lang, 1992, 200pp

Environment

4380 **Moyo, S, et al,** *The southern African environment: the environmental context of the SADC region.* London: Earthscan, 1993, 354pp

4381 **Rugumamu, W,** Outline of a research programme to combat desertification and promote food and energy production in the southern African sub-region, *Desertification control bulletin,* 22 (1993) 69–76

Finance

See also: 4417

4382 **Stuart, J G W,** An optimal currency area for South Africa and the BLS countries: comment, *South African journal of economics,* **61,** 1 (1993) 90–95

Food

See also: 4411

4383 **Collins, C,** *Famine defeated: southern Africa, UN win battle against drought.* New York: United Nations, 1993, 12pp

4384 **Green, R H,** The political economy of drought in southern Africa, *Health policy and planning,* **8,** 3 (1993) 255–66

4385 **Green, R H,** Southern Africa: that the people may be fed, *Food policy,* **17,** 6 (1992) 455–464

4386 **Shalott, F,** How southern Africa triumphed over famine, *African farmer,* Nov 1993, 19–22

Gender

4387 **Doran, J,** *A moving issue for women: low cost transport, an appropriate intervention to alleviate women's burden in southern Africa?* Norwich: School of Development Studies, University of East Anglia, 1990, 90pp

4388 **Gaidzanwa, R,** Bourgeois theories of gender and feminism and their shortcomings with reference to southern African countries, in Meena, R (ed), *Gender in southern Africa (item 4399)*, 92–125

4389 **Gaidzanwa, R,** Citizenship, nationality, gender and class in southern Africa, *Alternatives,* **18,** 1 (1993) 39–59

4390 **Geisler, G,** Silences speak louder than claims: gender, household and agricultural development in southern Africa, *World development,* **21,** 12 (1993) 1965–80

4391 **Jacobs, S M,** Give a thought to

Africa: black women missionaries in southern Africa, in Chaudhuri, N & Strobel, M (eds), *Western women and imperialism* (Bloomington: Indiana University Press, 1992), 207–28

4392 **Kazembe, J L,** Women and law in southern Africa, in Sandbrook, R & Halfani, M (eds), *Empowering people (Item 930)*, 92–96

4393 **Manana, T,** Conventional economic theories and gender analysis, in Meena, R (ed), *Gender in southern Africa (item 4399)*, 126–56

4394 **Mannathoko, C,** Feminist theories and the study of gender issues in southern Africa, in Meena, R (ed), *Gender in southern Africa (item 4399)*, 71–91

4395 **Mbilinyi, M,** Research methodologies in gender issues, in Meena, R (ed), *Gender in southern Africa (item 4399)*, 31–70

4396 **McNamara, E,** *Women and law in southern Africa: an annotated bibliography.* Harare: Women and Law in Southern Africa Trust, 1991, 98pp

4397 **Meena, R,** Conceptual issues of gender in southern Africa, *Southern Africa political and economic monthly,* **4,** 8 (1991) 36–38

4398 **Meena, R,** Do women have an agenda in the struggle for democracy in southern Africa?, *Southern Africa political and economic monthly,* **5,** 8 (1992) 39–42

4399 **Meena, R** (ed), *Gender in southern Africa: conceptual and theoretical issues.* Harare: Sapes, 1992, 201pp

4400 **Meena, R,** Gender research/studies in southern Africa: an overview, in Meena, R (ed), *Gender in southern Africa (item 4399)*, 1–30

Geography, physical

4401 **Coetzee, M, et al,** Distribution of mosquitos belonging to the anopholes-Gambiae complex, including malaria vectors, South of latitude 15 degrees, *South African journal of science,* **89,** 5 (1993) 227–31

Health & welfare services

See also: 4384

4402 **Beattie, A, et al,** Problems and prospects for health sector links in the southern African region: the role of South Africa, *Social science and medicine,* **37,** 7 (1993) 927–35

4403 **Hira, S K, et al,** Designing appropriate intervention strategies for HIV/AIDS in southern Africa, *Population and environment,* **14,** 3 (1993) 307–313

History, general

4404 **Nkiwane, S,** Military and political destabilisation in southern Africa: an historical perspective, in Siddiqui, R A (ed), *Subsaharan Africa (item 15)*, 169–89

History, early

4405 **Clark, J D,** The earliest cultural evidence of hominids in southern and south central Africa, in Sperber, G H (ed), *From apes to man* (New York: Wiley, 1990), 1–15

4406 **Lewis-Williams, D, et al,** Rock art and changing perceptions of southern Africa past: Ezeljagdspoort reviewed, *Antiquity,* **67,** 255 (1993) 273–91

4407 **Wadley, L,** The Pleistocene later Stone Age South of the Limpopo River, *Journal of world prehistory,* **7,** 3 (1993) 243–96

History, C18th

4408 Hall, M, The archaeology of colonial settlement in Southern Africa, *Annual review of anthropology,* **22,** (1993) 177–200

History, C19th

No entry. *See also:* 4391

Industry & trade

See also: 4387, 4467

4409 Mwase, N, *The future of TAZARA in post-apartheid southern Africa.* Bellville: University of the Western Cape. Centre for Southern African Studies, 1993, 28pp

4410 Nyoni, T S, Trade policy and development in the SADCC region, *Eastern African social science research review,* **6,** 1 (1990) 13–29

4411 Pinkney, T C, Is market liberalisation compatible with food security? Storage, trade and price policies for maize in southern Africa, *Food policy,* **18,** 4 (1993) 325–33

International economic relations

See also: 4447, 4958

4412 Cedergren, J, Swedish aid priorities for regional development in southern Africa, in Oden, B (ed), *Southern Africa after apartheid (Item 4447),* 240–46

4413 Ching'ambo, I, SADC, the rebirth of SADCC, *Southern Africa political and economic monthly,* **5,** 11 (1992) 22–25

4414 Cobbe, J, South Africa and SADCC: economics of the southern African region, in Hunt Davis, R (ed), *Apartheid unravels (Item 4677),* 165–81

4415 Davies, R, Emerging South African perspectives in regional cooperation and integration after apartheid, in Oden, B (ed), *Southern Africa after apartheid (Item 4447),* 71–86

4416 Gwaradzimba, F, SADCC and the future of southern African regionalism, *Issue,* **21,** 1/2 (1993) 51–59

4417 Harvey, C, Hudson, D, Post-apartheid regional financial and monetary cooperation, in Oden, B (ed), *Southern Africa after apartheid (Item 4447),* 108–29

4418 Isaksen, J, Prospects for SACU after apartheid, in Oden, B (ed), *Southern Africa after apartheid (Item 4447),* 182–200

4419 Leistner, E, *Designing the framework for a Southern African development community.* Pretoria: Africa Institute of South Africa, 1992, 31pp

4420 Magnusson, A, Swedish trade and investment links with southern Africa, in Oden, B (ed), *Southern Africa after apartheid (Item 4447),* 247–59

4421 Maphanyane, E M, SADCC - future challenges, in Oden, B (ed), *Southern Africa after apartheid (Item 4447),* 174–81

4422 McCarthy, C, The Southern African Customs Union in a changing economic and political environment, *Journal of world trade,* **26,** 4 (1992) 5–24

4423 Mehrota, S, Southern Africa Development Coordination Conference (SADCC): evaluating recent trends in regional cooperation, *International studies,* **28,** 4 (1991) 389–408

4424 Mfune, P, The future of SADCC, in Siddiqui, R A (ed), *Subsaharan Africa (item 15),* 287–303

4425 Mtengeti-Migiro, R, *Institutional arrangements for economic integration in eastern and southern Africa: a study of SADCC and the PTA, with experiences from*

the EEC. Konstanz: Hartung-Gorre, 1992, 220pp

4426 **Oden, B,** Factors affecting the flows of external capital to post-apartheid southern Africa, in Oden, B (ed), *Southern Africa after apartheid (Item 4447)*, 221–39

4427 **Odén, B,** *Om den regional integrationen i Södra Afrika.* Uppsala: Scandinavian Institute of African Studies, 1993, 11pp

4428 **Odén, B,** *Om nyregionalismens relevans för södra Afrika.* Göteborg: Göteborg University, 1993, 21pp

4429 **Ofstad, A,** Will PTA be relevant in the post-apartheid era?, in Oden, B (ed), *Southern Africa after apartheid (Item 4447)*, 201–217

4430 **Ostergaard, T,** Classical models of regional integration: what relevance for southern Africa?, in Oden, B (ed), *Southern Africa after apartheid (Item 4447)*, 27–47

4431 **Rogerson, C M,** British aid to South Africa: the role of the Commonwealth Development Corporation, *Africa insight,* **23,** 4 (1993) 209–218

4432 **Saasa, O S,** The effectiveness of regional transport networks in southern Africa: some post-apartheid perspectives, in Oden, B (ed), *Southern Africa after apartheid (Item 4447)*, 130–43

4433 **Tostensen, A,** What role for SADC(C) in the post-apartheid era?, in Oden, B (ed), *Southern Africa after apartheid (Item 4447)*, 142–73

International relations

See also: 4997

4434 **Baynham, S, Mills, G,** British military training assistance in southern Africa: lessons for South Africa, *Africa insight,* **22,** 3 (1992) 218–24

4435 **Black, D R,** Canada's role in the long term security of SADC(C) states, in Siddiqui, R A (ed), *Subsaharan Africa (item 15)*, 304–37

4436 **Ching'ambo, I,** Towards a defence alliance in southern Africa?, *Southern Africa political and economic monthly,* **5,** 8 (1992) 33–36

4437 **du Pisani, A,** Post-settlement South Africa and the future of southern Africa, *Issue,* **21,** 1/2 (1993) 60–69

4438 **Dudley, R O,** CODESA and the Frontline States: what of the future?, *Southern Africa political and economic monthly,* **5,** 9 (1992) 8–11

4439 **Keita, M,** Glasnost, perestroika, and the peace dividend: US/Soviet policy, the great thaw and its effects on southern Africa, *Ufahamu,* **19,** 2/3 (1991) 39–50

4440 **Laigy, I,** SADCC um modelo de cooperaçao regional, *Estudos Moçambicanos,* 9 (1991) 163–208

4441 **Lemon, A,** Apartheid as foreign policy: dimensions of international conflict in southern Africa, in Kliot, N & Waterman, S (eds), *The political geography of conflict and peace* (London: Belhaven, 1991), 166–83

4442 **Mandaza, I,** The Frontline States summit: a mission revived?, *Southern Africa political and economic monthly,* **5,** 11 (1992) 37–40

4443 **Mandaza, I,** SADC, an economic agenda or a mere political expression?, *Southern Africa political and economic monthly,* **5,** 11 (1992) 18–21

4444 **Mills, G,** *Plus ça change, plus c'est le même chose: South Africa and southern African security after apartheid.* Lancaster: Lancaster University, Centre for Defence and International Security, 1993, 107pp

4445 **Musoke, I K S,** Beyond summits and jet-setting: prospects for regional integration in southern

Africa, *Eastern Africa social science research review,* **6,** 1 (1990) 30–47

4446 Nkiwane, S M, *Regional security and confidence-building processes; the case of southern Africa in the 1990s.* New York: United Nations Institute for Disarmament Research, 1993, 57pp

4447 Oden, B (ed), *Southern Africa after apartheid: regional integration and external resources.* Uppsala: Scandinavian Institute of African Studies, 1993, 277pp

4448 Ohlson, T, The end of the Cold War and conflict resolution in southern Africa, in Siddiqui, R A (ed), *Subsaharan Africa (item 15),* 233–58

4449 Ohlson, T, Stedman, S J, Security in post-apartheid South Africa, *Security dialogue,* **24,** 4 (1993) 415–28

4450 Ohlson, T, Stedman, S J, Toward enhanced regional security in southern Africa?, in Oden, B (ed), *Southern Africa after apartheid (Item 4447),* 87–107

4451 Sparkes, A, War and peace, *Africa forum,* **1,** 4 (1991) 20–25

4452 Swatuk, L, Shaw, T M, Zimbabwe: security for development, in Siddiqui, R A (ed), *Subsaharan Africa (item 15),* 100–24

4453 Vale, P, Seven ways to change the balance of power in southern Africa, *Nigerian journal of international relations,* **18,** 1 (1992) 78–93

Labour & manpower

No entry. *See also:* 4367

Library - documentation

4454 Manaka, S, Library education in southern Africa, in Wise, M & Olden, A (eds), *Information and libraries (item 672),* 25–46

Literature

4455 Roberts, S, Sites of paranoia and taboo: Lessing's The grass is singing and Gordimer's July's people, *Research in African literatures,* **24,** 3 (1993) 73–85

Medical

No entry. *See also:* 4401

Natural resources

4456 Reynolds, N, Economic management of natural resources by rural communities, in Hudson, N & Cheatle, R J (eds), *Working with farmers (Item 245),* 77–81

Politics

See also: 4371, 4389, 4398

4457 Benjamin, L, Gregory, C (eds), *Southern Africa at the crossroads?: prospects for stability and development in the 1990s.* Rivonia: Justified Press, 1992, 287pp

4458 Chona, M C, Herbst, J I, Southern Africa, in Lake, A et al *After the wars* (New Brunswick: Transaction, 1990), 140–66

4459 Coker, C, Conclusion: experiencing Southern Africa in the twenty-first century, in Johnston, A, et al (eds), *Constitution making (Item 5194),* 252–66

4460 Denton, G, *Reconciliation and reconstruction in South and southern Africa.* London: HMSO, 1992, 37pp

4461 Mandaza, I, *Southern Africa in the 1990s: towards a research agenda.* Harare: Sapes, 1992, 33pp

4462 Sidaway, J, Simon, D, Geopolitical transition and state formation : the changing political geographies of Angola, Mozambique and Namibia, *Journal of southern African studies,* **19,** 1 (1993) 1–28

4463 **Viera, S, et al**, *How fast the wind? Southern Africa, 1975–2000.* Trenton: Africa World Press, 1993, 412pp

Religion, philosophy

See also: 4390

4464 **Hofmeyr, J W, et al**, *History of the church in southern Africa - a select bibliography. Vol. 3.* Pretoria: University of South Africa, 1993, 504pp

4465 **Oosthuizen, G C**, *The healer-prophet in Afro-Christian churches.* Leiden: Brill, 1992, 200pp

Rural economy

See also: 1931

4466 **Abel, N O J**, *What's in a number? The carrying capacity controvery on the communal rangelands of southern Africa.* Norwich: Overseas Development Group, University of East Anglia, 1993, 486pp

4467 **Muir-Leresche, K,** Liberalisation and regional agricultural trade in southern Africa, *Food policy,* **18,** 4 (1993) 366–74

Sociology

4468 **Balch, L A (ed)**, *Children of apartheid: international action for southern Africa's youth.* Amsterdam: African European Institute, 1993, 58pp

4469 **Seidman, J**, *In our own image: a cultural studies textbook for southern Africa.* Gaborone: Foundation for Education with Production, 1990, 161pp

BOTSWANA

Anthropology

See also: 4514

4470 **Gollbach, F**, *Leben und Tod bei die Tswana: das traditionelle Lebens- und Todesverständnis des Tswana im südlichen Afrika.* Berlin: Reimer, 1992, 279pp

4471 **Kent, S,** Sharing in an egalitarian Kalahari community, *Man,* **28,** 3 (1993) 479–514

4472 **Kuper, A,** Post-modernism, Cambridge and the Kalahari debate, *Social anthropology,* **1,** 1A (1992) 57–72

4473 **Lee, R B, Guenther, M,** Problems in Kalahari historical ethnography and the tolerance of error, *History in Africa,* **20,** (1993) 185–235

4474 **Valiente-Noailles, C**, *The Kua: life and soul of the central Kalahari Bushmen.* Rotterdam: Balkema, 1993, 232pp

Demography

4475 **Miller, H M,** The future population of Botswana, *Eastern Africa economic review,* **7,** 1 (1991) 85–91

4476 **Rutenberg, N, Diamond, I,** Fertility in Botswana: the recent decline and future prospects, *Demography,* **30,** 2 (1993) 143–57

4477 **Van der Post, C**, *Fertility in three contrasting villages in Botswana.* Gaborone: NIDRD, 1992,

Economy - Development

See also: 5407

4478 **Harvey, C,** Botswana: is the economic miracle over?, *Journal of African economics,* **1,** 3 (1992) 271–305

4479 **Jefferis, K,** Botswana and

diamond-dependent development, *Southern Africa political & economic monthly,* **4,** 10 (1991) 33–34

4480 **Norberg, H, Blomström, M,** Dutch disease and the management of windfall gains in Botswana, in Blomström, M & Lundahl, M (eds), *Economic crisis (Item 119),* 162–78

4481 **Parsons, N,** Botswana: an end to exceptionality?, *Round table,* **82,** 325 (1993) 73–82

4482 **Sjögren, A,** *Botswana after the diamond boom: facing a new phase of economic development.* Stockholm: SIDA, 1993, 50pp

4483 **Valentine, T R,** Mineral-led economic growth, drought relief, and incomes policy: income distribution in Botswana reconsidered, *American journal of economics and sociology,* **52,** 1 (1993) 31–49

Education

4484 **Adeyemi, B M,** Tabulawa, R, AIDS and related issues: the views of junior secondary teachers in Botswana, *Educational studies,* **19,** 2 (1993) 227–34

4485 **Meyer, J W, et al,** The expansion of mass education in Botswana: local and world society perspectives, *Comparative education review,* **37,** 4 (1993) 454–75

Environment

4486 **Børhaug, K,** *From policy guidelines to problem solving: a critical assessment of the national conservation strategies of Botswana and Zambia.* Bergen: Chr Michelsen Institute, 1993, 61pp

Food

4487 **Simmons, C,** Lyons, S, Rhetoric and reality: the management of Botswana's 1982–88 drought relief programme, *Journal of international development,* **4,** 6 (1992) 607–31

Gender

No entry. *See also:* 1898

Geography, physical

4488 **Thomas, D S G,** Shaw, P A, The evolution and characteristics of the Kalahari, southern Africa, *Journal of arid environments,* **25,** 1 (1993) 97–108

History, general

No entry. *See also:* 4473

History, C19th

4489 **Gulbrandsen, U,** The rise of the northwestern Tswana kingdoms: on the dynamics of interaction between internal relations and external forces, *Africa,* **63,** 4 (1993) 550–82

4490 **Gulbrandsen, U,** Missionaries and northern Tswana rulers: who used whom?, *Journal of religion in Africa,* **23,** 1 (1993) 44–83

Industry & trade

4491 **McCutcheon, R T,** Botswana: a description of the district roads labour-intensive improvement and maintenance programme, *Development southern Africa,* **9,** 3 (1992) 269–94

4492 **Rwelamila, P D,** The factors affecting productivity in the Botswana construction industry, the case of Gaberone, *Botswana journal of technology,* **1,** 1 (1992) 23–28

International economic relations

No entry. *See also:* 4322

International relations

See also: 4500, 4629

4493 **Dale, R,** Botswana's relations with Bophuthatswana: the politics of ethnicity, legitimacy and propinquity in southern Africa, *Journal of contemporary history,* **17,** 2 (1992) 1–19

Language

4494 **Andersson, L G,** Janson, T, Rich and poor languages in Botswana, in Granqvist, R (ed), *Culture in Africa (item 10)*, 73–85

Law

No entry. *See also:* 4322, 4502

Media

4495 **Obombwa-Jaswa, P,** *Mass media and AIDS in Botswana: what the newspapers say and their implications.* Gaborone: NIDRD, 1993, ??pp

Medical

No entry. *See also:* 4484, 4495

Natural resources

4496 **Diphaha, J B S,** Burton, R, Photovoltaics and solar water heaters in Botswana, in Karekezi, S & Mackenzie, G A (eds), *Energy options (Item 796)*, 139–53

4497 **Mordi, A R,** *Attitudes towards wildlife in Botswana.* New York: Garland, 1991, 217pp

Planning

4498 **Danevad, A,** *Development planning and the importance of democratic institutions in Botswana.* Bergen: Chr Michelsen Institute, 1993, 166pp

Politics

See also: 4481, 4498, 4509

4499 **Charlton, R,** The politics of elections in Botswana, *Africa,* **63,** 3 (1993) 330–70

4500 **Stedman, S J** (ed), *Botswana: the political economy of democratic development.* Boulder: Lynne Reinner, 1993, 213pp

4501 **Wallis, M,** Decentralisation and development: are there lessons to be learnt from Botswana?, *Journal of research,* 2 (1992) 1–26

Religion, philosophy

4502 **Nsereko, D D,** Religious liberty and the law in Botswana, *Journal of church and state,* **34,** 4 (1992) 843–62

Rural economy

See also: 2811

4503 **Dlamini, P M, Ditshipi, P P,** Analysis of demand, supply and marketing channels of grain sorghum in Botswana, *UNISWA research journal,* **6,** 1 (1992) 1–15

4504 **Hitchcock, R K, Holm, J D,** Bureaucratic domination of hunter-gatherer societies: a study of the San in Botswana, *Development and change,* **24,** 2 (1993) 305–338

4505 **Nteta, D, Hermans, J** (eds), *Sustainable rural development: proceedings of a workshop held by the Botswana Society.* Gaberone: Botswana Society, 1992, 280pp

4506 **Roe, E M,** Public service, rural development and careers in public management: a case study of expatriate advising and African land reform, *World development,* **21,** 3 (1993) 349–61

4507 **Sharma, K C,** Bureaucracy and coordination of rural development in Botswana, in Asmerom, H K, et al (eds), *Bureacracy and developmental policies (Item 109)*, 96–115

4508 **Valentine, T,** Drought, transfer entitlements, and income distribution: the Botswana experience, *World development,* **21,** 1 (1993) 109–26

Sociology

4509 **Good, K,** At the ends of the ladder: radical inequalities in Botswana, *Journal of modern African studies,* **31,** 2 (1993) 203–30

Social welfare

4510 **Fitzgerald, M,** Participatory community development in Botswana, *Community development journal,* **28,** 1 (1993) 11–18

4511 **Jacques, G,** Social work practice in Botswana: principles and relevance, *Journal of social development in Africa,* **8,** 1 (1993) 31–49

Urban studies

4512 **Mosha, A C,** The management and use of urban land in Botswana, an overview, *Botswana journal of technology,* **1,** 1 (1992) 37–40

4513 **Rapoport, A, Hardie, G,** Cultural change analysis: core concepts of housing for the Tswana, in Tipple, A G & Willis, K G (eds), *Housing the poor (item 1159)*, 35–61

4514 **van Binsbergen, W,** Making sense of urban space in Francistown, Botswana, in Nas, P J M (ed), *Urban symbolism* (Leiden: Brill, 1993), 184–228

LESOTHO

General

4515 **Ambrose, D,** An annotated bibliography of recent literature relevant to Lesotho research, *Journal of research,* 2 (1992) 183–203

Anthropology

4516 **Slotta, R, Skalli,** M (eds), *International symposium on preservation and presentation of the cultural heritage of Lesotho, Maseru, 1991.* Bochum: Deutsches Bergbau Museum, 1991, 81pp

Arts

No entry. *See also:* 4364

Current affairs

4517 **Commonwealth Secretariat,** Observer Group, *The general election in Lesotho: 27 March 1993.* London: Commonwealth Secretariat, Observer Group, 1993, 61pp

4518 **King Moshoeshoe II,** Crisis in Lesotho, *Southern Africa political and economic monthly,* **4,** 7 (1991) 26–29

4519 **Kolane, J T, Thuli, M D,** Constituent Assembly: Lesotho's return to parliamentary democracy, *Parliamentarian,* 74, 3 (1993) 130–36

4520 **Makoa, F K,** Lesotho after the fall of Lekhanya, *Southern Africa political and economic monthly,* **4,** 10 (1991) 24–28

Economic and social history

4521 **Ambrose, D,** *Maseru: an illustrated history.* Morija: Morija Museum, 1993, 256pp

Economy - Development

See also: 201, 4532

4522 **Ferguson, J, et al,** The anti-politics machine: a debate with James Ferguson, *Journal of research,* 2 (1992) 95–159

4523 **Gustafson, B, Makonnen, N,** Poverty and remittances in Lesotho, *Journal of African economics,* **2,** 1 (1993) 49–73

4524 **Neocosmos, M,** Towards a political economy of adjustment in a labour reserve economy: the case of Lesotho, in Gibbon, P (ed), *Social change and economic reform (item 1880)*, 134–60

4525 **Petersson, L,** Structural adjustment and economic management in a dependent economy: the case of Lesotho, in Blomström, M & Lundahl, M (eds), *Economic crisis (Item 119)*, 118–42

4526 **Matlosa, K,** The state, intelligentsia, and academic freedom in Lesotho, *Southern Africa political and economic monthly,* **4,** 7 (1991) 39–42

4527 **Monyooe, L A,** Perspective reports of corporal punishment by pupils in Lesotho, *Psychological reports,* **73,** 2 (1993) 515–518

4528 **Ntlhakana, L N, Nkheloane, T,** Primary school agriculture in subsaharan Africa: the Lesotho experience, in Mades, G G (ed), *Primary school agriculture (item 222)*, 208–211

Environment

4529 **Shaxson, T F,** A strategy for better land husbandry in Thabana Morena, in Hudson, N & Cheatle, R J (eds), *Working with farmers (Item 245)*, 126–30

4530 **Shone, G,** A programme for farm improvement with soil conservation in Lesotho (FISC), in Hudson, N & Cheatle, R J (eds), *Working with farmers (Item 245)*, 183–90

Finance

4531 **Ambrose, D,** A note on inflation in Lesotho, *Journal of research,* 2 (1992) 83–94

Food

4532 **Shaw, J, Clay, E,** Lesotho: sustaining development in in a small landlocked economy, in their *World food aid: experiences of recipients and donors* (London: Currey, 1993), 118–129

Gender

4533 **Baylies, C, Wright,** C, Female labour in the textile and clothing industry of Lesotho, *African affairs,* **92,** 369 (1993) 577–91

4534 **Epprecht, M,** Domesticity and piety in colonial Lesotho: the private politics of Basotho women's pious associations, *Journal of southern African studies,* **19,** 2 (1993) 202–24

4535 **Riley, P J, Krogman, N T,** Gender-related factors infuencing the viability of irrigation projects in Lesotho, *Journal of Asian and African studies,* **28,** 3/4 (1993) 162–79

History, early

4536 **Mitchell, PJ,** Archaeological research in Lesotho: a review, *African archaeological review,* **10,** (1992) 3–34

History, C20th

No entry. *See also:* 4534

Industry & trade

See also: 4541

4537 **Hunter, J P, Mokotimi, N,** *The development of Lesotho's wool and mohair marketing system: options for continued institutional change and policy reforms.* Roma: Institute of Southern African Studies, 1990, 35pp

4538 **Mochebelele, M,** *The economics of milk production and marketing in Lesotho.* Roma: Institute of Southern African Studies, 1990, 120pp

4539 **Mohapeloa,** The case of Lesotho, in Bhagavan, M R & Karekezi, S (eds), *Energy managment (Item 788)*, 9–41

4540 **Mokitimi, N,** *Analysis of the performance of the Lesotho grain marketing system.* Roma: Institute of Southern African Studies, 1990, 93pp

International economic relations

4541 **Matlosa, K T,** International labour migration in Lesotho: recent dimensions and context, in Siddiqui, R A (ed), *Subsaharan Africa (item 15)*, 125–48

Labour & manpower

See also: 4541

4542 **Matlosa, K,** Retrenchment of Basotho mineworkers in South Africa and the capacity of Lesotho rural 'informal sector' employment, *Journal of research,* 2 (1992) 27–48

4543 **Matlosa, K,** Structural adjustment programmes and the employment challenge in Lesotho, *Southern Africa political and economic monthly,* **4,** 7 (1991) 17–25

Planning

No entry. *See also:* 4547

Politics

4544 **Makoa, F K,** Lesotho political parties: focus on the Basutoland Congress Party (BCP), *Southern Africa political and economic monthly,* **5,** 10 (1992) 31–34

4545 **Tangri, R,** Foreign business and political unrest in Lesotho, *African affairs,* **92,** 367 (1993) 223–38

Religion, philosophy

No entry. *See also:* 4534

Rural economy

See also: 4528, 4535

4546 **Hunter, J P, Weaver, L C,** Developing sustainable grazing associations in Lesotho, in Hudson, N & Cheatle, R J (eds), *Working with farmers (Item 245)*, 212–219

Urban studies

See also: 4521

4547 **Kahimbaara, J A,** The convolution of urban planning with tradition in Lesotho, *Environment and planning, Series A,* **25,** 7 (1993) 1003–20

NAMIBIA

General

4548 **Brunborg, H, et al,** *Perspectives in the development of a statistical system for Namibia.* Windhoek: Namibian Economic Policy Research Unit, 1992, 149pp

4549 **Melber, H,** Sozio-kulturelle Länderkurzanalyse: Namibia,

Afrika spektrum, **27**, 3 (1992) 367–376

Anthropology

4550 **Crandall, D P,** The strength of the OvaHimba lineage, *Cimbebasia,* 13 (1991) 45–51
4551 **Draper, P, Buchanan, A,** If you have a child you have a life: demographic and cultural perspectives on fathering in old age in Kung society, in Hewlett, B S (ed), *Father-child relations* (New York: Aldine de Gruyter, 1992), 131–52
4552 **Schmidt, S,** Ideological changes in Nama and Dama folktales, in Görög-Karady, V (ed), *D'un conte ... à l'autre (item 38)*, 303–14
4553 **van Damme, P, van den Eyden, V,** Topnaar or Hottentot? The people on the top revisited, *Afrika focus,* **8**, 3/4 (1992) 215–21
4554 **Zinke, S,** Zu strukturellen Gestaltungselementen in Musikbogenliedern der Ovambo, in Elsner, J & Jähnichen, G (eds), *Studies in ethnomusicology, Vol. 3: Africa and Asia* (Berlin: Humboldt University, 1993), 3–32

Current affairs

4555 **Decraene, P,** La Namibie: une décolonisation ratée, *Mondes et cultures,* **50**, 2–4 (1990) 198–201 (and see 202–206)
4556 **Lindeke, W A,** Namibia's second year of independence, *Southern Africa political and economic monthly,* **5**, 8 (1992) 26–31
4557 **Willemot, Y,** Namibie drie jaar alter: politiek ontvoogd maar economisch wankel, *Afrika focus,* **8**, 3/4 (1992) 179–201

Demography

See also: 4595
4558 **Amutenya, P, et al,** *Population distribution and migration.* Windhoek: Namibian Economic Policy Research Unit, 1993, 18pp
4559 **Andima, J, et al,** *Population issues in Namibia.* Windhoek: Namibian Economic Policy Research Unit, 1993, 18pp

Economic and social history

4560 **Hishongwa, N S,** *The contract labour system and its effects on family and social life in Namibia: a historical perspectives.* Windhoek: Gamsberg, 1992, 116pp
4561 **Kinahan, J,** The historical archaeology of nineteenth century fisheries at Sandwich Harbour on the Namib coast, *Cimbebasia,* 13 (1991) 1–27
4562 **Lau, B, Reiner, P,** *One hundred years of agricultural development in colonial Namibia: a historical overview of visions and experiments.* Windhoek: Archives of Namibia, 1993, 94pp
4563 **Pennington, R, Harpending, H,** *The structure of an African pastoralist community: demography, history and ecology of the Ngamiland Herero.* Oxford: Clarendon, 1993, 288pp
4564 **Werner, W,** A brief history of land dispossession in Namibia, *Journal of southern African studies,* **19**, 1 (1993) 135–46

Economy - Development

See also: 4618
4565 **Aicardi de St-Paul, M,** L'économie de la Namibie à la veille de l'indépendance, *Mondes et cultures,* **50**, 2–4 (1990) 207–14
4566 **Brown, S,** *Assessment of popular participation in the formulation and*

implementation of development policies and programmes: a case study of Namibia. Windhoek: Namibian Economic Policy Research Unit, 1992, 32pp

4567 **Cole, K,** *Namibia, SWAPO and socialist development.* Norwich: School of Development Studies, University of East Anglia, 1990, 48pp

4568 **Fröhlich, C, Frayne, B,** *Hawking: an "informal" sector activity in Katutura, Windhoek.* Windhoek: NISER, 1991, 59pp

4569 **Gleichmann, C,** *Evaluation study of the follow-up programme of the Otto Benecke Fondation In Namibia.* Windhoek: Namibian Economic Policy Research Unit, 1993, 46pp

4570 **Hoffman, J,** *Review of FNDC projects in the Caprivi area.* Windhoek: Namibian Economic Policy Research Unit, 1992, 13pp

4571 **Isaksen, J, Moorsom, R,** *Comments on papers prepared for the donor pledging conference, June 1990.* Windhoek: Namibian Economic Policy Research Unit, 1992, 16pp

4572 **Ruffert, M,** Nicht-Regierungsorganisationen als Träger gesellschaftlicher Entwicklung in Namibia, *Afrika spektrum,* **27,** 3 (1992) 377–383

4573 **Sellström, T,** Namibia's economy a year after independence, *Southern Africa political and economic monthly,* **4,** 6 (1991) 4–7

4574 **Sellstrom, T,** *Some notes on the Namibian economy two years after independence.* Windhoek: Namibian Economic Policy Research Unit, 1992, 9pp

4575 **Sherbourne, R,** *Export processing zones and their relevance to Namibia.* Windhoek: Namibian Economic Policy Research Unit, 1993, 27pp

4576 **Stone, S,** *Poverty and income distribution in Namibia.* Windhoek: Namibian Economic Policy Research Unit, 1993, 23pp

4577 **van der Linden, E, Amutenya, P,** *The Namibia-Angola border fence and its socioeconomic implications: report of a fact-finding mission, 17–20 June 1992.* Windhoek: Namibian Economic Policy Research Unit, 1993, 24pp

4578 **World Bank,** *Namibia: poverty alleviation witrh sustainable growth.* Washington: World Bank, 1992, 165pp

Education

4579 **Breitenfeld, J (ed),** *Vocational training and reintegration.* Baden Baden: Nomos, 1992, 154pp

4580 **Mkandawire, D S J, Marira, C,** The evaluation of teacher professional competence in former non-white Namibian schools, *Zimbabwe journal of educational research,* **5,** 2 (1993) 124–35

4581 **Turner, J, et al,** The new system of higher education in Namibia, *Journal of southern African studies,* **19,** 1 (1993) 60–79

Environment

4582 **van Damme, P,** The natural environment of the Namib desert, *Afrika focus,* **8,** 3/4 (1992) 202–214

4583 **van Pinxteren, B,** *Environment and development in Namibia: the role of NGOs.* Nairobi: Environmental Liaison Centre International, 1990, 15pp

Finance

4584 **Chauvin, S,** *The monetary independence of Namibia.* Windhoek: Namibian Economic Policy Research Unit, 1992, 18pp

4585 **Gaomab, M,** *Prices and*

inflation in Namibia. Windhoek: Namibian Economic Policy Research Unit, 1993, 17pp

4586 **Sherbourne, R,** *The social dimensions of monetary, currency and credit policy in Namibia.* Windhoek: Namibian Economic Policy Research Unit, 1993, 24pp

4587 **Stone, S,** *The consumer price index and inflation in Namibia.* Windhoek: Namibian Economic Policy Research Unit, 1993, 34pp

4588 **van der Linden, E,** *Namibia's tax system.* Windhoek: Namibian Economic Policy Research Unit, 1992, 87pp

Gender

See also: 4638

4589 **Andima, J,** *The integration of women into the rural development process.* Windhoek: Namibian Economic Policy Research Unit, 1992, 32pp

4590 **Andima, J,** *Women's role in the development process with special reference to factors of production.* Windhoek: Namibian Economic Policy Research Unit, 1993, 15pp

4591 **Draper, P,** Remembering the past: !Kung life history narratives, in Johnson, P L (ed), *Balancing acts: women and the process of social change* (Boulder: Westview, 1992), 7–41

4592 **Gawanas, B,** Legal rights of Namibian women and affirmative action: the eradication of gender inequalities, *Review of African political economy,* 56 (1993) 116–22

4593 **Hubbard, D,** *Women and children in Namibia: the legal context.* Windhoek: NISER, 1990?, 25pp

4594 **Lewis, M, Van Rooy, G,** *A study of the prospects for training of young unemployed women in Katutura.* Windhoek: NISER, 1991, 56pp

4595 **Lindsay, J,** The politics of population control in Namibia, in Turshen, M (ed), *Women and health (Item 343)*, 143–88

4596 **Wildenthal, L,** 'She is the victor': bourgeois women, nationalist identities and the ideal of the independent woman farmer in German South West Africa, *Social analysis,* 33 (1993) 68–88

Geography, human

4597 **Kokkonen, P,** Religious and colonial realities: cartography of the Finnish Mission in Ovamboland, Namibia, *History in Africa,* **20,** (1993) 155–71

History, general

4598 **Heywood, A, et al,** *Warriors, leaders, sages and outcasts in the Namibian past: narratives collected from Herero sources for the MSORP 1985–1986.* Windhoek: Michael Scott Oral Records Project, 1992, 223pp

4599 **Komen, J, Pretorius, B,** A bibliography of the State Museum of Namibia, *Cimbebasia,* 13 (1991) 141–53

History, early

4600 **Sadler, K,** Gender ambiguity in primary source material: the case of southern African rock art, *Ufahamu,* **19,** 2/3 (1991) 112–29

History, C19th

4601 **Hayes, P,** Order out of chaos: Mandume ya Ndemufayo and oral history, *Journal of southern African studies,* **19,** 1 (1993) 89–114

History, C20th

See also: 4596, 4921

4602 **Cohen, C,** 'Our natives must

first become good workmen': formal education provision in German South West and East Africa compared, *Journal of southern African studies,* **19,** 1 (1993) 115–34

4603 **Dale, R,** Achieving Namibia's independence: the realities of international and regional politics, 1915–1990, *Journal of contemporary history,* **17,** 1 (1992) 36–51

4604 **Dale, R,** Melding war and politics in Namibia: South Africa's counterinsurgency campaign, 1966–1989, *Armed forces and society,* **20,** 1 (1993) 7–24

4605 **Dedering, T,** The German-Herero War of 1904: revision of genocide or imaginary historiography?, *Journal of southern African studies,* **19,** 1 (1993) 80–88

4606 **Gordon, R,** The impact of the Second World War on Namibia, *Journal of southern African studies,* **19,** 1 (1993) 147–65

4607 **Nujoma, S,** A fighter leader (interview), *Africa forum,* **2,** 1 (1992) 4–12

Industry & trade

See also: 4620

4608 **Amavilah, V H S,** The political economy of export processing zones (EPZS) in developing countries: implications foir the Arandis EPZ initiative in Namibia, *Natural resources forum,* **17,** 4 (1993) 273–87

4609 **Amutenya, P,** *Report on the present status of the rock lobster industry.* Windhoek: Namibian Economic Policy Rcsearch Unit, 1992, 12pp

4610 **Curry, S, Stoneman, C,** Problems of industrial development and market integration in Namibia, *Journal of southern African studies,* **19,** 1 (1993) 40–59

4611 **Gaomab, M,** *An analysis of the interim consumer price index.* Windhoek: Namibian Economic Policy Research Unit, 1993, 18pp

4612 **Isaksen, T, Shipoke, P,** *Some notes on an industrial policy for Namibia.* Windhoek: Namibian Economic Policy Research Unit, 1992, 16pp

4613 **Namibian Economic Policy Research Unit,** *Walvis Bay: report of a fact-finding mission, October 1990.* Windhoek: Namibian Economic Policy Research Unit, 1992, 25pp

4614 **van der Linden, E,** *African Development Bank proposal: 'Namibia - trade policy reform study' - an evaluation.* Windhoek: Namibian Economic Policy Research Unit, 1992, var pp

4615 **van der Linden, E,** *An evaluation of current methods of collecting trade statistics in Namibia.* Windhoek: Namibian Economic Policy Research Unit, 1993, 31pp

4616 **van der Linden, E,** *The informal sector in Namibia.* Windhoek: Namibian Economic Policy Research Unit, 1993, 23pp

4617 **van der Linden, E,** *Namibia's energy sector; a country review.* Windhoek: Namibian Economic Policy Research Unit, 1993, 41pp

International economic relations

See also: 4571, 4661

4618 **Isaksen, J,** *Comments on papers prepared for the donor pledging conference, June 1990.* Windhoek: Namibian Economic Policy Research Unit, 1992, 20pp

4619 **Isaksen, J,** *Namibia and the Southern African Customs Union.* Windhoek: Namibian Economic Policy Research Unit, 1992, 18pp

4620 **Moorsom, R, Goodison, P** (eds), *A fisheries agreement between the European Community and Namibia: workshop report.*

Windhoek: Namibian Economic Policy Research Unit, 1993, 92pp

4621 **Mwase, N,** Regional economic integration schemes in southern Africa: options for independent Namibia, *Eastern Africa economic review. New series,* **7,** 1 (1991) 51–68

4622 **Orford, J,** *Bilateral economic links between Namibia and South Africa.* Windhoek: Namibian Economic Policy Research Unit, 1992, 15pp

4623 **Orford, J, et al,** *Country report: Namibia's trade and investment climate.* Windhoek: Namibian Economic Policy Research Unit, 1993, 50pp

4624 **Shipoke, P,** *Namibia's external trade development prospects.* Windhoek: Namibian Economic Policy Research Unit, 1992, 30pp

International relations

See also: 3985, 4637

4625 **Anon,** Foreign policy perspectives of the Republic of Namibia: an overview, *Southern Africa political and economic monthly,* **4,** 6 (1991) 11–15

4626 **Evans, G,** A new small state with a powerful neighbour: Namibia-South Africa relations since independence, *Journal of modern African studies,* **31,** 1 (1993) 131–48

4627 **Fortna, V P,** United Nations Transition Assistance Group, in Durch, W J (ed), *The evolution of UN peacekeeping* (New York: St Martin's Press, 1993), 353–75

4628 **Kaela, L C W,** The Reagan administration and the decolonisation of Namibia, in Siddiqui, R A (ed), *Subsaharan Africa (item 15)*, 209–32

4629 **Maluwa, T,** Disputed sovereignity over Sidudu (or Kasikili) Island (Botswana-Namibia): some observations on the international legal aspects, *African journal of international and comparative law,* **5,** 1 (1993) 113–38

4630 **Schleicher, H-G,** UNTAG und der internationale Faktor im Unabhängigkeitsprozess Namibias, *Afrika spectrum,* **27,** 3 (1992) 327–341

Labour & manpower

See also: 4590, 4594

4631 **Bogosi, R, Orford, J,** *Report on the National Conference on Employment Strategies.* Windhoek: Namibian Economic Policy Research Unit, 1992, 9pp

Language

4632 **Rüdiger, K,** "Hart wie Kameldornholz": der Weg der Deutschsprachigen von Südwest nach Namibia, *Afrika spektrum,* **27,** 3 (1992) 343–365

Law

4633 **Akweenda, S,** Culture and justice revisited: African culture, human rights and law, *Annual conference (African Society of Comparative and International Law),* **3,** (1991) 89–96

4634 **Cottrell, J,** The constitution of Namibia, *Journal of African law,* **35,** 1/2 (1991) 56–78

4635 **Figueira, M,** AIDS, the Namibian constitution and human rights: an overview, *South African journal on human rights,* **9,** 1 (1993) 30–38

4636 **Gordon, R J,** *Vernacular law and the future of human rights in Namibia.* Windhoek: NISER, 1991, 35pp

4637 **Hill, R,** *Namibia: constitutional and international law issues.*

Pretoria: Centre for Public Law Studies, University of South Africa, 1991, 227pp

4638 **Hubbard, D,** *A critical discussion of the law on rape in Namibia.* Windhoek: NISER, 1991, 101pp

4639 **Parker, C,** Legal aspects of access to land and tenure in Namibia: a case of social inequality supported and regulated by the law, *Lesotho law journal,* **7,** 1 (1991) 93–106

Natural resources

4640 **van Damme, P, et al,** Plant uses by the Topnaar of the Kuiseb valley Namib desert, *Afrika focus,* **8,** 3/4 (1992) 223–52

4641 **van Damme, P, et al,** Plant uses by the Topnaar of the Sesfontein area (Namib desert), *Afrika focus,* **8,** 3/4 (1992) 253–81

Politics

See also: 861, 4462, 4692

4642 **Adouki, D E,** Le Protocole de Brazzaville et les Accords de New York: une étape décisoire pour l'indépendance de la Namibie, *Revue congolaise de droit,* 10 (1991) 123–151

4643 **du Pisani, A,** Namibia: the making of a new state in the region, in Johnston, A, et al (eds), *Constitution making (Item 5194),* 234–52

4644 **du Pisani, A,** *Rumours of rain: Namibia's post-independence experience.* Braamfontein: SAIRR, 1991, 51pp

4645 **Fosse, L J,** *The social construction of ethnicity and nationalism in independent Namibia.* Windhoek: NISER, 1992, 51pp

4646 **Kelly, S,** *The Namibia voter education project, October 15 - December 15, 1992: final report.* Washington: National Democratic Institute, 1992, 9pp

4647 **Kösler, R,** *Towards greater participation and equality? Some findings on the 1992 regional and local elections in Namibia.* Windhoek: Namibian Economic Policy Research Unit, 1993, 10pp

4648 **Lush, D,** *Last steps to uhuru: an eyewitness account of Namibia's transition to independence.* Windhoek: New Namibia Books, 1993, 346pp

4649 **Malan, J,** The foundations of ethnicity and some of its current ramifications in Namibia, *Africa insight,* **23,** 4 (1993) 205–208

4650 **Strand, P,** *SWAPO and nation building in Namibia, transfer of power in the post communist era.* Windhoek: NISER, 1991(?), 71pp

4651 **Tötemeyer, G,** *The reconstruction of the Namibian national, regional and local state.* Windhoek: NISER, 1992, 142pp

4652 **Weiland, H,** Demokratie und nationale Entwicklung in Namibia: eine Zwischenbilanz nach zweieinhalb Jahren Unabhängigkeit, *Afrika spektrum,* **27,** 3 (1992) 273–301

4653 **Wellmer, G,** Notas sobre a transição da Namibia para a independencia, *Estudos Moçambicanos,* 9 (1991) 123–62

Rural economy

See also: 4589

4654 **Adams, F, et al,** *The land issue in Namibia: an inquiry.* Windhoek: NISER, 1990, 186pp

4655 **Adams, M E,** *Grappling with land reform in pastoral Namibia.* London: Overseas Development Institute, 1992, 20pp

4656 **Adams, M E,** Options for land reform in Namibia, *Land use policy,* **10,** 3 (1993) 191–96

4657 **Adams, M E, Devitt, P,**

Grappling with land reform in pastoral Namibia. London: Overseas Development Institute, 1992, 20pp

4658 **Andima, J**, *Review of four UNDP base studies on Namibia.* Windhoek: Namibian Economic Policy Research Unit, 1992, 19pp

4659 **Elkan, W, et al**, *Namibian agriculture: policies and prospects.* Windhoek: Namibian Economic Policy Research Unit, 1992, 46pp

4660 **Kimble, H,** Agricultural transformation in Namibia after apartheid, in Nett, B et al (eds), *Agricultural transformation (Item 1069)*, 79–110

4661 **Lister, S**, *Notes on aid management, agriculture and rural development.* Windhoek: Namibian Economic Policy Research Unit, 1992, 16pp

4662 **Moorsom, R, et al**, *Socioeconomic survey of the southern communal areas, 1992: summary.* Windhoek: Namibian Economic Policy Research Unit, 1993, 31pp

4663 **NEPRU**, *Republic of Namibia, National Conference on Land Reform and the Land Question, Windhoek, 25 June - 1 July 1991. Vol. 1: research papers, addresses and concensus documents.* Windhoek: Namibian Economic Policy Research Unit, 1993, 350pp

4664 **Oates, P, Vigne, P**, *Rural development priorities in northern Namibia.* Windhoek: Namibian Economic Policy Research Unit, 1992, 50pp

4665 **Schade, K,** Die Ergebnisse der Landkonferenz in Namibia: eine Relativierung geweckter Hoffnungen?, *Afrika spektrum*, **27**, 3 (1992) 303–326

4666 **Tapscott, C**, *A preliminary evaluation of the socio-economic impact of the rural electrification project in the Ovamebo region.* Windhoek: NISER, 1992, 20pp

4667 **Yaron, Y, et al**, *Rural development in the Okavango region of Namibia: an assessment of needs, opportunities and constraints.* Windhoek: Gamsberg, 1992, 245pp

Sociology

4668 **Ahrenson-Pandikow, H,** *Survey of attitudes towards the use of contraceptives in Namibia.* Windhoek: NISER, 1992, 68pp

4669 **Botelle, A**, *Onaanda community-based road construction project, Western Owambo region: a base-line socio-economic survey.* Windhoek: NISER, 1992, 99pp

4670 **Pomuti, A, Eiseb, G**, *Alcohol abuse: a southern Namibian survey.* Windhoek: NISER, 1990, 18pp

4671 **Simon, D, Preston, R,** Return to the promised land: repatriation and resettlement of Namibian refugees,1989–1990, in Black, R & Robinson, V (eds), *Geography and refugees* (London: Belhaven, 1993), 47–63

4672 **Tamas, K**, *After return: repatriated exiles in independent Namibia.* Windhoek: NISER, 1992, 36pp

4673 **Tapscott, C,** National reconciliation, social equity and class formation in independent Namibia, *Journal of southern African studies*, **19,** 1 (1993) 29–39

Social welfare

4674 **Tapscott, C, Mulongeni, B,** *An evaluation of the welfare and future prospects of repatriated Namibians in Northern Namibia.* Windhoek: NISER, 1990, 55pp

Urban studies

4675 **Frayne, B,** *A discussion of housing issues in post-independence*

Windhoek. Windhoek: NISER, 1991, 61pp

SOUTH AFRICA

General

4676 **Darbon, D, et al,** *La République Sud-africaine: états des lieux.* Paris: Karthala, 1993, 248pp
4677 **Hunt Davis, R** (ed), *Apartheid unravels.* Gainesville: University of Florida Press, 1991, 251pp

Agriculture, scientific

4678 **Gosnell, R J,** Eberhard, A A, Photovoltaic water pumping in developing areas: a case study, *Development southern Africa,* **10,** 1 (1993) 85–100

Anthropology

See also: 4470, 4516, 4867, 4929
4679 **De Jongh, M,** A case of ambiguous identity: oral tradition and the Ba ga Seleka of Lephalala, *South African journal of ethnology,* **15,** 4 (1992) 101–108
4680 **Erlmann, V,** L'inachèvement d'un achèvement connu: à propos de la ritualisation en Afrique du Sud, *Cahiers de musiques traditionnelles,* 5 (1992) 3–16
4681 **Kaschula, R H,** *Imbongi* in profile, *English in Africa,* **20,** 1 (1993) 65–76
4682 **McAllister, P A,** Public oratory in Xhosa ritual: tradition and change, *Ethnology,* **32,** 3 (1993) 291–304
4683 **Wilmsen, E N,** *Auxiliary instruments of labour: the homogenization of diversity in the discourse of ethnicity.* Johannesburg: University of the Witwatersrand, African Studies Institute, 1993, 27pp
4684 **Zamani, N M,** *The world and the word: tales and observations from the Xhosa oral tradition.* Madison: University of Wisconsin Press, 1992, 499pp

Architecture

4685 **Chipkin, C,** *Johannesburg style: architecture and society, 1880's–1960's.* Cape Town: Philip, 1993, 346pp

Arts

4686 **Bruce, H J, Saks, D Y,** A new museum for a new South Africa, *Museum,* **44,** 4 (1992) 238–41
4687 **Degenaar, J J,** Art and culture in a changing South Africa, *South African journal of philosophy,* **12,** 3 (1993) 51–56
4688 **Hamm, C,** 'The constant companion of man': separate development, Radio Bantu and music, *Popular music,* **10,** 2 (1991) 147–63
4689 **Horn, P,** Njabulu Ndebele, *Southern African review of books,* **5,** 4 (1993) 13–15
4690 **Huskisson, Y,** *Black composers of South Africa.* Pretoria: HSRC, 1992, 110pp
4691 **Jackson, M,** Popular Indian South African music: division in diversity, *Popular music,* **10,** 2 (1991) 175–88
4692 **Oliphant, A W** (ed), *Culture and empowerment: debates, workshops, art and photography from the Zabalaza Festival.* Johannesburg: COSAW, 1993, 244pp
4693 **Steadman, I,** Performance and politics in process: practices of representation in South African theatre, *Theatre survey,* **33,** 2 (1992) 188–210

Current affairs

4694 **Ansprenger, F,** Südafrika nach der Freilassung Nelson Mandelas und der Legalisierung von ANC und PAC, *Afrika Jahrbuch 1990,* 46–55

4695 **Dexter, P,** The regime's election strategy, *African communist,* 135 (1993) 36–40

4696 **Macleod, S,** South Africa on the edge, *New York review of books,* **40,** 4 (1993) 24–28

4697 **Maja-Pearce, A,** Through the looking glass, *Index on censorship,* **22,** 7 (1993) 16–20

4698 **Mkondo, R,** *Reporting South Africa.* London: Currey, 1993, 194pp

4699 **O'Flaherty, J D,** Holding together South Africa, *Foreign affairs,* **72,** 4 (1993) 126–36

Demography

See also: 4595, 47–5, 5310

4700 **Brophy, G,** Modelling the demographic impact of AIDS: potential effects on the Black population of South Africa, in Cross, S & Whiteside, A (eds), *Facing up to AIDS (item 4753),* 113–34

4701 **Bureau of Market Research,** *Validation and adjustment of the 1991 population as counted.* Pretoria: the Bureau, 1993, 200pp

4702 **Chimeredan, O,** Population policy in South Africa, *Studies in family planning,* **24,** 1 (1993) 31–39

4703 **de Vos, M,** A theoretical perspective on population policy in South Africa, *Development southern Africa,* **9,** 3 (1992) 347–63

4704 **Doyle, P,** The demographic impact of AIDS on the South African population, in Cross, S & Whiteside, A (eds), *Facing up to AIDS (item 4753),* 87–112

4705 **Levin, M, du Plessis, A P,** *Population figures and economic indicators.* Diazland: Unit for Statistical Analysis, 1990, 94pp

4706 **Pelser, A J, et al,** Politics as an environmental factor in population development: reviewing the South African situation, *Development southern Africa,* **9,** 1 (1992) 65–73

Economic and social history

See also: 4841, 4885, 5301

4707 **Atkins, K,** *The moon is dead! Give us our money! The cultural origins of an African work ethic in Natal, c.1843–1900.* London: Currey, 1993, 190pp

4708 **Beinart, W,** La nuit du Chacal: moutons, pâturages et prédateurs en Afrique du Sud de 1900 à 1930, *Revue française d'histoire d'outre-mer,* **80,** 298 (1993) 105–29

4709 **Bhana, S** (ed), *Essays on indentured Indians in Natal.* Leeds: Peepal Press, 1990, 235pp

4710 **Bonner, P, Shapiro, K A,** Company town, company estate: Pilgrim's Rest, 1910–1932, *Journal of southern African studies,* **19,** 2 (1993) 171–201

4711 **Bouch, R,** Glen Grey before Cecil Rhodes: how a crisis of local colonial authority led to the Glen Grey Act of 1894, *Canadian journal of African studies,* **27,** 1 (1993) 1–24

4712 **Bundy, C,** Development and inequality in historical perspective, in Schrire, R (ed), *Wealth or poverty? (Item 4779),* 24–38

4713 **Dangor, S E,** The myth of the 1860 settlers, *Africa quarterly,* **33,** 1–4 (1992/93) 73–80

4714 **Drummond, J, Mason, A,** The rise and demise of African agricultural production in Dinokana Village, Bophuthatswa, *Canadian journal of African studies,* **27,** 3 (1993) 461–79

4715 **Duncan, D,** The regulation of working conditions for Africans in South Africa, 1919–1948, *African studies,* **52,** 1 (1993) 1–25

4716 **Garson, N,** *South Africa, imperial preference and Ottawa: 1925–1932.* Johannesburg: University of the Witwatersrand, African Studies Institute, 1993, 33pp

4717 **Gerstner, J,** *The thousand generation covenant: Dutch Reformed covenant theology and group identity in colonial South Africa, 1652–1914.* Leiden: Brill, 1991, 280pp

4718 **Jeeves, A H, Crush, J,** The failure of stabilisation experiments and the entrenchment of migrancy to the South Africa gold mines, *Labour, capital and society,* **25,** 1 (1992) 18–45

4719 **Johnson, D,** Aspects of a liberal education: late ninteenth century attitudes to race, from Cambridge to the Cape Colony, *History Workshop journal,* 36 (1993) 162–82

4720 **Jones, S, Müller, A,** *The South African economy, 1910–1990.* Basingstoke: Macmillan, 1992, 384pp

4721 **Kaplan, M, Robertson, M** (eds), *Founders and followers: Johannesburg Jewry 1887–1915.* Cape Town: Vlaeberg, 1991, 300pp

4722 **Krige, S,** *'Trustees and agents of the state?': missions and post-union policy formation towards African education 1910–1920.* Johannesburg: University of the Witwatersrand, African Studies Institute, 1993, 30pp

4723 **Leseuer, D, et al,** Historical perspective on the malaria problem in Natal with emphasis on the period 1928–1932, *South African journal of science,* **89,** 5 (1993) 232–39

4724 **Malherbe, C, Saunders, C,** *Struggle for the land.* Pietermaritzburg: Shuter & Shuter, 1990, 90pp

4725 **McCracken, D P,** Irish settlement and identity in South Africa before 1910, *Irish historical studies,* **28,** 110 (1992) 134–449

4726 **Morrell, R, et al,** Banking, credit and capital in colonial Natal, c.1850–1910, in Austin, G & Sugihara, K (eds), *Local suppliers of credit in the Third World, 1750–1960* (Basingstoke: Macmillan, 1993), 160–203

4727 **Murray, M,** *'Slave driving' and 'The poor man's friend': capitalist farming in Bethal district, ca. 1910–1940.* Johannesburg: University of Witwatersrand, African Studies Institute, 1993, 30pp

4728 **Nel, E L,** Racial segregation in East London, 1836–1948, *South African geographical journal,* **73,** 2 (1991) 60–68

4729 **Pachard, R M,** The invention of the 'tropical worker': medical research and the quest for central African labour on the South African gold mines, 1903–36, *Journal of African history,* **34,** 2 (1993) 271–92

4730 **Parnell, S M,** The ideology of African home-ownership: the establishment of Dube, Soweto, 1946–1955, *South African geographical journal,* **73,** 2 (1991) 69–76

4731 **Pirie, G,** Railways and labour migration to the Rand mines: constraints and significance, *Journal of southern African studies,* **19,** 3 (1993) 713–30

4732 **Pirie, G H,** Slaughter by steam: railway subjugation of ox-wagon transport in the eastern Cape and Transkei, 1886–1910, *International journal of African historical studies,* **26,** 2 (1993) 319–43

4733 **Redding, S,** Peasants and the creation of an African middle class in Umtata, 1880–1950, *International journal of African historical studies,* **26,** 3 (1993) 513–39

4734 Rich, P B, Bernard Huss and the experiment in African cooperatives in South Africa, 1926–1948, *International journal of African historical studies,* **26,** 2 (1993) 297–317

4735 Ross, R, Emanicipation and the economy of the Cape Colony, *Slavery and abolition,* **14,** 1 (1993) 131–48

4736 Russell, C, Lee, J, The MacArthur-Forrest: opportunists or saviours of the South African mining industry?, *Mining survey,* 1 (1991) 34–41

4737 Terblanche, H O, Die armblanke-vraagstuk in Port Elizabeth, 1916–1934: 'n verkennende studie, *Contree,* 33 (1993) 1–11

4738 van Sittert, L, 'Making like America': the industrialisation of the St Helena Bay fisheries c.1935-c.1956, *Journal of southern African studies,* **19,** 3 (1993) 422–47

4739 Vernon, G, 'A vague vision of a legion of Mephistopholes': the attitudes of four women to class and race on the Eastern Cape frontier, 1843–1878, *Contree,* 32 (1992) 16–23

Economy - Development

See also: 149

4740 Aicardi de St Paul, M, L'Afrique du Sud, géant de l'Afrique?, *Afrique contemporaine,* 165 (1993) 19–31

4741 Bethlehem, R, Economic restructuring in post-apartheid South Africa, in Johnston, A, et al (eds), *Constitution making (Item 5194)*, 138–53

4742 Bethlehem, R, Issues of economic restructuring, in Schrire, R (ed), *Wealth or poverty? (Item 4779)*, 524–47

4743 Bond, P, Scenario plundering, *Southern African review of books,* **5,** 4 (1993) 3–8

4744 Botha, J J B, et al, Index: papers and reviews, 1933–1992, *South African journal of economics,* **61,** 2 (1993) 1–129

4745 Brijlal, P, Restructuring for economic development and growth in post-apartheid South Africa, *Africa quarterly,* **33,** 1–4 (1992/93) 149–58

4746 Broomberg, J, Current research on the economic impact of HIV/AIDS; review of the international and South African literature, in Cross, S & Whiteside, A (eds), *Facing up to AIDS (item 4753)*, 34–57

4747 Broomberg, J, et al, The economic impact of the AIDS epidemic in South Africa, in Cross, S & Whiteside, A (eds), *Facing up to AIDS (item 4753)*, 158–90

4748 Brudgman, D H M, et al (eds), *South Africa's leading edge? A guide to the Western Cape economy.* Cape Town: WESGRO, 1992, 134pp

4749 Caldwell, D, *No more martyrs now: capitalism, democracy and ordinary people.* Craighall: Conrad Business Books, 1992, 270pp

4750 Chipasula, J, Chilivumbo, A (eds), *South Africa's dilemmas in the post-apartheid era.* Lanham: University Press of America, 1993, 193pp

4751 Coetzee, S, Reconciling structural adjustment and reconstruction, *Africa insight,* **23,** 4 (1993) 225–31

4752 Cross, S, A socio-economic analysis of the long-run effects of AIDS in South Africa, in Cross, S & Whiteside, A (eds), *Facing up to AIDS (item 4753)*, 137–57

4753 Cross, S, Whiteside, A (eds), *Facing up to AIDS: the socioeconomic*

impact in southern Africa. Basingstoke: Macmillan, 1993, 331pp

4754 **Dollery, B E,** A conceptual framework for the growth and redistribution debate in South Africa, *Development southern Africa,* **10,** 1 (1993) 23–31

4755 **Dollery, R E,** A note on contestability and the government supply of public goods in a post-apartheid economy, *Development southern Africa,* **9,** 1 (1992) 3–10

4756 **Eckert, J B, van Niekerk, L K,** The horns of a dilemma: economic discipline and economic development in South Africa, *Development southern Africa,* **10,** 1 (1993) 3–22

4757 **Frankel Max Pollak Vinderine Inc, et al,** A labour-intensive development strategy for South Africa, *South Africa international,* **23,** 4 (1992/3) 156–61

4758 **Friedman, S,** Beyond symbols? The politics of economic compromise, in Schrire, R (ed), *Wealth or poverty? (Item 4779),* 608–22

4759 **Geerdts, P J, et al,** *Information for development planning in Lebowa: income and expenditure patterns.* Pretoria: HSRC, 1990, 155pp

4760 **Godsell, B, Buys, J,** Growth and poverty: towards some shared goals, in Schrire, R (ed), *Wealth or poverty? (Item 4779)*, 635–56

4761 **Harris, L,** South Africa's economic and social transformation: from 'no middle road' to 'no alternative', *Review of African political economy,* 57 (1993) 91–103

4762 **Harvey, C, Jenkins, C,** *The unorthodox response of the South African economy to changes in macroeconomic policy.* Brighton: Institute of Development Studies, 1992, 40pp

4763 **Hilsenrath, P E,** Stages of growth revisited, *Development southern Africa,* **10,** 1 (1993) 101–110

4764 **Leistner, E,** South Africa's future: powerhouse or poorhouse?, *Africa insight,* **23,** 2 (1993) 85–90

4765 **Ligthelm, A A, Wilsenach, A,** Development, poverty and the environment with particular reference to the eastern Transvaal region, *Development southern Africa,* **10,** 1 (1993) 45–64

4766 **Lipton, M, Simpkins, C** (eds), *State and market in post-apartheid South Africa.* Johannesburg: Witwatersrand University Press, 1993, 463pp

4767 **Lundahl, M, Moritz, L,** Macroeconomic stagnation and structural weakness in the South African economy, in Blomström, M & Lundahl, M (eds), *Economic crisis (Item 119)*, 322–43

4768 **Maasdorp, G,** Meeting expectations: the policy environment facing the post-apartheid government, in Schrire, R (ed), *Wealth or poverty? (Item 4779)*, 584–607

4769 **Marx, A W,** The state, economy and self-determination in South Africa, *Political science quarterly,* **107,** 4 (1992) 655–75

4770 **McMillan, S M,** Economic growth and military spending in South Africa, *International interactions,* **18,** 1 (1992) 35–50

4771 **Moleketi, J,** Is a retreat from National Democratic Revolution to National Bourgeois Revolution imminent?, *African communist,* 133 (1993) 11–19

4772 **Moll, T,** *Macroeconomic policy in South Africa: apartheid and after.* London: SOAS, Dept. of Economics, 1992, 26pp

4773 **Morris, M,** Who's in, who's out?, *Work in progress,* 87 (1993) 6–9

4774 **Nattrass, N,** The ANC's economic policy: a critical perspective, in Schrire, R (ed), *Wealth or poverty? (Item 4779)*, 623–34

4775 **Naude, W A, Brixen, P,** On a provisional computable general equilibrium model for South Africa, *South African journal of economics,* **61,** 3 (1993) 153–65

4776 **Roux, A, Donaldson, A,** *Finance and development in South Africa.* Bellville: University of the Western Cape, Economic Policy Research Project, 1992, 32pp

4777 **Schlemmer, L,** Distribution and redistribution trade-offs, in Schrire, R (ed), *Wealth or poverty? (Item 4779)*, 565–83

4778 **Schrire, R,** The economic debate and the politics of unreason, *South Africa international,* **23,** 2 (1992/1993) 71–77

4779 **Schrire, R** (ed), *Wealth or poverty?: critical choices for South Africans.* Cape Town: OUP, 1992, 680pp

4780 **Singh, H,** Impact of sanctions and armed struggle on South African economy, *Africa quarterly,* **33,** 1–4 (1992/93) 127–47

4781 **Smit, B,** Secular trends in South African macroeconomic data, in Schrire, R (ed), *Wealth or poverty? (Item 4779)*, 39–58

4782 **Southall, H,** Inequity and resource allocation in South Africa: the case of Development Region D, *Journal of contemporary African studies,* **11,** 1 (1992) 85–103

4783 **Stadler, A W,** The political economy of post-apartheid South Africa, in Johnston, A, et al (eds), *Constitution making (Item 5194)*, 128–37

4784 **Stoneman, C,** The World Bank: some lessons for South Africa, *Review of African political economy,* 58 (1993) 87–98

4785 **Tanzer, M, Resnick, I,** Towards a socialist economy: observations from abroad, *African communist,* 132 (1993) 29–35

4786 **Terrebanche, S,** Equity and growth, in Schrire, R (ed), *Wealth or poverty? (Item 4779)*, 548–64

4787 **Thompson, J O,** New South Africa, new business prospects, *Optima,* **38,** 1 (1992) 30–39

4788 **Tran, M L,** Challenge for South Africa, *South African journal of economics,* **61,** 3 (1993) 194–204 (review article)

4789 **Trotter, G,** Some reflections on a human capital approach to the analysis of the impact of AIDS on the South African economy, in Cross, S & Whiteside, A (eds), *Facing up to AIDS (item 4753)*, 191–214

4790 **van der Valt, J T, de Wet, G L,** The constraining effects of limited foreign capital inflow on the economic growth of South Africa, *South African journal of economics,* **61,** 1 (1993) 3–12

4791 **Van Ryneveld, P,** *The economics of structures of decentralisation.* Bellville: University of the Western Cape, Economic Policy Research Project, 1992, 22pp

4792 **Van Ryneveld, P,** *Federalism and economic growth.* Bellville: University of the Western Cape, Economic Policy Research Project, 1992, 22pp

4793 **Van Ryneveld, P,** *Response to the De Loor commission report on development assistance.* Bellville: University of the Western Cape, Economic Policy Research Project, 1992, 19pp

Education

See also: 4722, 4842, 5044, 5110, 5234

4794 **Coetzee, D,** Training as an instrument to combat poverty and unemployment: a national and international perspective, *Development southern Africa,* **9,** 3 (1992) 295–315

4795 Collins, C B, Gillespie, R R, Education strategies for South Africa in a post-apartheid society, *International journal of educational development,* **13,** 1 (1993) 33–44

4796 Cross, M, *Resistance and transformation: education, culture and reconstruction in South Africa.* Braamfontein: Skotaville, 1992, 292pp

4797 Cross, M, Youths, culture, and politics in South African education: the past, present and future, *Youth and society,* **24,** 4 (1993) 377–98

4798 Curtin, T, The political economy of education in South Africa, *African affairs,* **92,** 368 (1993) 417–30

4799 Donaldson, A R, *Content, quality and flexibility: the economics of education system change.* Braamfontein: SAIRR, 1992, 12pp

4800 Donaldson, A, In search of affordable excellence: the future of tertiary education in South Africa, *Optima,* **39,** 1 (1993) 12–19

4801 Flanagan, W, A pedagogy for teacher education: cultivating the disposition to think, *Curriculum studies,* **1,** 2 (1993) 179–93

4802 Gaganakis, M, Language and ethnic group relations in non-racial schools, *English Academy review,* **9,** (1992) 46–55

4803 Haricombe, L J, Combining qualitative and quantitative methodologies to study the effects of an academic boycott on academics in South Africa, *Library quarterly,* **63,** 4 (1993) 508–27

4804 Herbstein, F H, Towards the new South Africa: equal opportunity policies at the University of Cape Town, *Higher education,* **25,** 2 (1993) 183–98

4805 Hofmeyr, J, McLennan, A, The challenge of equalising education, in Schrire, R (ed), *Wealth or poverty? (Item 4779),* 174–92

4806 Hosking, S G, The paradox of Black pupil enrollment in South African schools, *Development southern Africa,* **9,** 3 (1992) 317–29

4807 Kahn, M, Rollnick, M, Science education in the new South Africa, *International journal of science education,* **15,** 3 (1993) 261–72

4808 Kerfoot, C N, Participatory education in a South African context: contradictions and challenges, *Tesol quarterly,* **27,** 3 (1993) 431–47

4809 Kotze, J M A, Bridging the gap for the culturally disadvantaged, *Maseno journal of education, arts and science,* **1,** 1 (1992) 73–83

4810 Kraak, A, *Beyond the market: comprehensive institutional restructuring of South African labour markets, education, training and work.* Johannesburg: University of Witwatersrand, Educational Policy Unit, 1991, 98pp

4811 MacKenzie, C G, Academic standards and progressive university provision in a new South Africa: prospects for evolution in an African context, *African affairs,* **92,** 368 (1993) 403–16

4812 Mackenzie, C G, New models of school management in South Africa: licence for change or loophole for separatism?, *British journal of educational studies,* **41,** 3 (1993) 287–301

4813 Mncwabe, M P, *Post-apartheid education: towards non-racial, unitary and democratic socialisation in the new South Africa.* Lanham: University Press of America, 1993, 252pp

4814 Moulder, J, Education and distribution, in Schrire, R (ed),

Wealth or poverty? (Item 4779), 161–73

4815 **Nkabinde, Z P,** The role of special education in a changing South Africa, *Journal of special education,* **27,** 1 (1993) 107–114

4816 **Paterson, A, Hodge, D,** The paradox of black school enrollment growth rates in South African schools: a rejoinder, *Development southern Africa,* **10,** 1 (1993) 111–118

4817 **Penny, A, et al,** Just sort of fumbling in the dark: a case study of the advent of racial integration in South African schools, *Comparative education review,* **37,** 4 (1993) 412–33

4818 **Randall, S,** People's education and 'nation building' for a new South Africa, *Review of African political economy,* 58 (1993) 43–60

4819 **SACHED Trust,** *Back to learning: the National education conference 1992.* Johannesburg: Ravan, 1992, 84pp

4820 **Scourfield, J H D,** The classics after apartheid, *Classical journal,* **88,** 1 (1992) 43–54

4821 **Spangenberg, J P** (ed), *Education in South Africa: a regional overview.* Halfway House: Centre for Information Analysis, Development Bank of Southern Africa, 1992, 28pp

4822 **Steinberg, C, Suttner, M** (eds), *Never too old to learn! Towards formulating policy for adult basic education in a post-apartheid South Africa.* Johannesburg: Learn and Teach Publications, 1991, 157pp

4823 **Strydom, A H, Noruwana, J,** Academic standards in South African universities and proposals for quality assurance, *Higher education,* **25,** 4 (1993) 379–93

Environment

See also: 1394, 4765, 5053

4824 **Association for Rural Advancement,** *Maputaland; conservation and removals.* Pietermaritzburg: the Association, 1990, 60pp

4825 **Fuggle, R F, Rabie, M A** (eds), *Environmental management in South Africa.* Cape Town: Juta, 1992, 823pp

4826 **Fuls, E R,** Ecosystem modification created by patch-overgrazing in semi-arid grassland, *Journal of arid environments,* **23,** 1 (1992) 59–69

4827 **Garland, G, Broderick, D,** Changes in the extent of erosion in the Tugela catchment, 1944–1981, *South African geographical journal,* **74,** 2 (1992) 45–48

4828 **Harding, W R,** Fecal coliform densities and water quality criteria in three coastal receational lakes in the SW Cape, South Africa, *Water,* **19,** 3 (1993) 235–46

4829 **Van Horen, C, et al,** Energy, environment and urban poverty in South Africa, *Energy policy,* **21,** 5 (1993) 623–39

4830 **van Vilgen, B W, et al,** Fire management in southern Africa: some examples, in Goldhammer, J G (ed), *Fire in the tropical biota* (Berlin: Springer, 1990), 179–215

Finance

See also: 4858, 4957

4831 **Davis, D,** Taxation in post-aparthied South Africa, in Schrire, R (ed), *Wealth or poverty? (Item 4779)*, 105–20

4832 **Gaunt, J, Hamersma, A,** The financial sector: mechanisms of redistribution, in Schrire, R (ed), *Wealth or poverty? (Item 4779)*, 495–504

4833 **Gidlow, R,** Banking on economic growth in South Africa, *Optima,* **38,** 2 (1992) 80–87

4834 **Loots, L,** The post-apartheid challenge to fiscal policy, in

Schrire, R (ed), *Wealth or poverty? (Item 4779)*, 90–104

4835 **Rogni, J,** The response of private wealth to capital flight controls: South Africa as a case study, *Millenium,* **22,** 1 (1993) 1–24

4836 **Roux, A, Donaldson, A,** Development and the financial sector, in Schrire, R (ed), *Wealth or poverty? (Item 4779)*, 504–23

4837 **Schoombes, G A,** Die Ontwikkeling van die Mark vir Skatkiswissels in Suid-Afrika 1980–89, *South African journal of economics,* **61,** 3 (1993) 177–87

4838 **Seethal, C,** Transformation of the local state in South Africa (1979–1991): group areas, property super-taxation and civic organisations, *Urban geography,* **13,** 6 (1992) 534–56

4839 **Wilson, J S G,** The South African money markets, in his *Money markets: the international perspective* (London: Routledge, 1993), 363–86

Gender

See also: 4595, 4899, 4919, 5077, 5083, 5094

4840 **Amoateng, A Y,** Sociocultural organisation and fertility attitudes and behaviour of wives in Ezibeleni township, *South African journal of sociology,* **23,** 4 (1992) 118–24

4841 **Berger, I,** Gender and working-class history: South Africa in comparative perspective, in Johnson-Odim, C & Strobel, M (eds), *Expanding the boundaries of women's history* (Bloomington: Indiana University Press, 1992), 205–22

4842 **Bouwer, A,** Sie swart vrou se ervaring van haar man se steun vir haar universiteitstudies, *South African journal of sociology,* **24,** 2 (1993) 51–57

4843 **Cecillie, S,** *Servants and gentlewomen to the golden land.* Pietermaritzburg: University of Natal Press, 1993, 200pp

4844 **du Toit, B M,** *Aging and menopause among Indian South African women.* Albany: SUNY Press, 1990, 343pp

4845 **du Toit, D,** Die professionele oriëntasie en gesinslewe van die werkende getroude vrou, *South Africa journal of sociology,* **23,** 4 (1992) 124–32

4846 **Hassim, S,** Family, motherhood and Zulu nationalism: the politics of Inkatha Women's Brigade, *Feminist review,* 43 (1993) 1–25

4847 **Hassim, S, Walker, C,** Women's studies and the women's movement in South Africa: defining a relationship, *Women's studies international forum,* **16,** 5 (1993) 523–34

4848 **Hetherington, P,** Women in South Africa: the historiography in English, *International journal of African historical studies,* **26,** 2 (1993) 241–69

4849 **Hickson, J, Strous, M,** The plight of Black South African women domestics: providing the ultra-exploited with pyschologically empowering mental health services, *Journal of Black studies,* **24,** 1 (1993) 109–22

4850 **Khan, Q,** The health of domestic workers in South Africa, in Turshen, M (ed), *Women and health (Item 343)*, 79–88

4851 **Lazar, C,** *Women of South Africa.* Boston: Little, Brown, 1993, 134pp

4852 **Lewis, D,** Feminisms in South Africa, *Women's studies international forum,* **16,** 5 (1993) 535–42

4853 **Lubanga, N,** Nursing in South Africa: Black women workers organise, in Turshen, M (ed), *Women and health (Item 343)*, 51–78

4854 **Maconchie, M,** The allocation

of domestic tasks by white married couples, *South Africa journal of sociology,* **23,** 4 (1992) 112–18

4855 **Moodie, T D, Ndatshe, V,** Town women and country wives: migrant labour, family politics and housing preferences at Vaal Reefs mine, *Labour, capital and society,* **25,** 1 (1992) 116–32

4856 **Mosala, I J,** The implications of the text of Esther for African women's struggle for liberation in South Africa, *Semeia,* 59 (1992) 129–37

4857 **Myburgh, C O H, et al,** Identiteitsvestigingspatrone en opvoedingsverhoudings by adolessente van werkende moeders, *South African journal of sociology,* **24,** 2 (1993) 41–46

4858 **Redding, S,** Legal minors and social children: rural African women and taxation in the Transkei, South Africa, *African studies review,* **36,** 3 (1993) 49–74

4859 **Schreiner, B** (ed), *A snake with ice water: prison writings by South African women.* Fordsburg: COSAW, 1992, 277pp

4860 **Seidman, G W,** 'No freedom without the women': mobilisation and gender in South Africa 1970–1992, *Signs,* **18,** 2 (1993) 291–320

4861 **Seymour, E L,** A preliminary study of the role of women in the informal sector in Marabastad, *South African journal of ethnology,* **15,** 4 (1992) 126–133

4862 **Sibiya, E,** *Thoughts of an African woman: essays.* Braamfontein: Skotaville, 1990, 48pp

4863 **Todes, A, Walker, N,** Women and housing policy in South Africa: a discussion of Durban case-studies, *Urban forum,* **3,** 2 (1992) 115–38

4864 **Wells, J,** *We now demand! The history of women's resistance to Pass Laws in South Africa.* Johannesburg: Witwatersrand University Press, 1993, 184pp

Geography, human

See also: 2064

4865 **Payne, R, Stickler, P,** *The two South Africas: a people's geography.* Braamfontein: Human Rights Commission, 1992, 30pp

Health & welfare services

See also: 4849, 4850, 4853

4866 **Broomberg, J,** The role of private hospitals in South Africa. 2: towards a national policy in private hospitals, *South African medical journal,* **83,** 5 (1993) 324–29

4867 **de Villers, S,** Perceptions in anthropological context, with special reference to health care, *South African journal of ethnology,* **16,** 1 (1993) 9–16

4868 **London, L,** The Ray Alexander Workers' Clinic: a model for worker-based health services in South Africa?, *Social science and medicine,* **37,** 12 (1993) 1521–28

4869 **Marx, G L,** How healthy is South Africa? Medical schemes industry, *South African medical journal,* **83,** 11 (1993) 834–37

4870 **Mazibuka, R M,** Primary health care implementation: experiences from South Africa, *Community development journal,* **28,** 3 (1993) 266–79

4871 **Pretorius, A,** Alternative (complementary?) medicine in South Africa, *South African journal of sociology,* **24,** 1 (1993) 13–17

4872 **Reynolds, J, Swartz, L,** Professional construction of a 'lay' illness: 'nerves' in a rural 'coloured' community in South Africa, *Social science and medicine,* **36,** 5 (1993) 657–63

4873 **Susser, M,** A South African odyssey in community health: a memoir of the impact of the teachings of Sydney Kark, *American journal of public health,* **83,** 7 (1993) 1039–43

4874 **Volmink, J A, et al,** Attitudes of private general practitioners towards health care in South Africa, *South African medical journal,* **83,** 11 (1993) 827–33

4875 **Yach, D,** Development and health: the need for integrated approaches in South Africa, *Development southern Africa,* **9,** 1 (1992) 11–24

4876 **Yach, D, Tollman, S M,** Public health initiatives in South Africa in the 1940s and 1950s: lessons for a postapartheid era, *American journal of public health,* **83,** 7 (1993) 1043–50

History, general

See also: 4848, 5173

4877 **Burman, J,** *The unofficial history of the Cape.* Cape Town: Human and Rousseau, 1992, 164pp

4878 **Duminy, A,** Natal historical writing during the last two decades: a conspectus, in Edgecombe, D R, et al (eds), *Zulu origins (item 4895),* 12pp

4879 **Gebhard, W,** *Shades of reality: Black perceptions of South African history.* Essen: Blaue Eule, 1991, 229pp

4880 **Radebe, T,** *Natal and Zululand history.* Pietermaritzburg: University of Natal Library, 1992, 249pp

4881 **Ross, R,** *Beyond the pale: essays on the history of colonial South Africa.* Hanover: University Press of New England, 1993, 270pp

4882 **Shain, M,** Antisemitism and South African historiography, *Jewish journal of sociology,* **34,** 2 (1992) 111–20

4883 **Smith, I RR,** New lessons in South African history, *History today,* **43,** July (1993) 5–8

4884 **Van Jaarsveld, F A,** Recent Afrikaner historiography, *Itinerario,* **16,** 1 (1992) 93–106

4885 **van Onselen, C,** The reconstruction of rural life from oral testimony: critical notes on the methodology employed im the study of a Black South African sharecropper, *Journal of peasant studies,* **20,** 3 (1993) 494–514

4886 **Worden, B,** *The making of modern South Africa.* Oxford: Blackwell, 1993, 166pp

History, early

4887 **Grine, F E, Klein, R G,** Late Pleistocene human remains from the sea harvest site, Saldanha Bay, South Africa, *South African journal of science,* **89,** 3 (1993) 145–52

4888 **Hromnik, C A,** The Bow of Siva alias Heitsi Eibib in the rock art of the Cape Quena, *Journal of Asian and African studies,* **28,** 3/4 (1993) 243–52

4889 **Humphreys, A J B,** The significance of place names in archaeological research with particular reference to the northern Cape, *African studies,* **52,** 1 (1993) 43–53

4890 **Korsman, S A,** Archaeological evidence and ethnographic analogy: interpreting prehistoric social behaviour at Honingklip in the Eastern Transvaal, *South African journal of ethnology,* **15,** 4 (1992) 120–126

History, C18th

4891 **Boucher, M, Penn, N (eds),** *Britain at the Cape 1795 to 1803.* Houghton (South Africa): Brenthurst, 1992, 264pp

History, C19th

See also: 4843

4892 **Carlean, K,** Myths of the Mfecane and South African educational texts: a critique, in Edgecombe, D R, et al (eds), *Zulu origins (item 4895)*, 33pp

4893 **Cobbing, J,** Grasping the nettle: the slave trade and the early Zulu, in Edgecombe, D R, et al (eds), *Zulu origins (item 4895)*, 34pp

4894 **de Kock, L,** 'History', 'literature' and 'English': reading the Lovedale missionary record within South Africa's colonial history, *English Academy review,* **9,** (1992) 1–21

4895 **Edgecombe, D R, et al** (eds), *The debate on Zulu origins: a selection of papers on the Zulu kingdom and early colonial Natal.* Pietermaritzburg: Dept. of Historical Studies, University of Natal, 1991, var pp

4896 **Fast, H H,** 'In at one ear and out at the other': African response to the Wesleyan mission in Xhosaland, 1825–1835, *Journal of religion in Africa,* **23,** 2 (1993) 147–74

4897 **Girvin, S D,** The establishment of the Supreme Court of the Cape of Good Hope and its history under the chief justiceship of Sir John Wylde, *South African law journal,* **109,** 2 & 4 (1992) 291–306, 652–65

4898 **Hallencreutz, C F,** Thomas Mofolo and Nelson Mandela on King Shaka and Dingane, in Granqvist, R (ed), *Culture in Africa (item 10)*, 185–93

4899 **Krebs, P,** 'The last of the gentleman's wars': women in the Boer War concentration camp controvery, *History Workshop journal,* 33 (1992) 38–56

4900 **Kuper, A,** The 'house' and Zulu political structures in the nineteenth century, *Journal of African history,* **34,** 3 (1993) 469–87

4901 **Omer-Cooper, J,** Has the Mfecane a future? A reply to the Cobbing critique, *Journal of southern African studies,* **19,** 2 (1993) 273–94

4902 **Peires, J B,** Paradigm deleted: the materialist interpretation of the Mfecane, *Journal of southern African studies,* **19,** 2 (1993) 295–313

4903 **Stapleton, T J,** The memory of Maqoma: an assessment of Jingqi oral tradition in Ciskei and Transkei, *History in Africa,* **20,** (1993) 321–35

4904 **Stapleton, T J,** Reluctant slaughter: rethinking Maqoma's role in the Xhosa cattle-killing (1853–1857), *International journal of African historical studies,* **26,** 2 (1993) 345–69

4905 **van Aswegen, H J,** Grensverhoudinge in die noordwestlike Transgariep: die lotgevalle van die Kora tot 1858, *Contree,* 33 (1993) 19–26

4906 **Wright, J,** A T Bryant and the 'wars of Shaka', in Edgecombe, D R, et al (eds), *Zulu origins (item 4895)*, 17pp

4907 **Wylie, D,** Utilizing Isaacs: one thread in the development of the Shaka myth, in Edgecombe, D R, et al (eds), *Zulu origins (item 4895)*, 19pp

History, C20th

See also: 4604, 4864, 5213

4908 **Berridge, G R,** *South Africa: the colonial powers and 'African defence': the rise and fall of the white entente.* Basingstoke: Macmillan, 1992, 234pp

4909 **Borstelmann, T,** *Apartheid's reluctant uncle: the United States and southern Africa in the early Cold War.* New York: OUP, 1993, 298pp

4910 **Broodryk, M,** Die totstandkoming van die Afrikanerpartey en sy rol in die algemene verkiesing van 1943, *Journal of contemporary history,* **17,** 1 (1992) 89–111

4911 **Coetser, P W,** Die Afrikanerparty en die 1948-verkiesing, *Journal of contemporary history,* **17,** 1 (1992) 112–34

4912 **Delius, P,** Sebatkgomo and Zoutpansberg Balemi Association: the ANC, the Communist Party and rural organisation, 1939–55, *Journal of African history,* **34,** 2 (1993) 293–313

4913 **Gilbey, E,** *The lady: the life and times of Winnie Mandela.* London: Cape, 1993, 328pp

4914 **Goodhew, D,** The people's police force: communal policing initiatives in the Western Areas of Johannesburg, circa 1930–62, *Journal of southern African studies,* **19,** 3 (1993) 447–70

4915 **Grobler, H,** The Marasbastad riot, 1942, *Contree,* 32 (1992) 24–32

4916 **Grundlingh, L,** Aspects of the impact of the Second World War on the lives of Black South African and British colonial soldiers, *Transafrican journal of history,* 21 (1992) 19–35

4917 **Gunner, L,** Testimonies of dispossession and repossession: writing about the South African prophet Isaiah Shembe, *Bulletin of the John Rylands University Library of Manchester,* **73,** 3 (1991) 93–103

4918 **Harris, K L,** Samuel Alfred Long: martyr or murderer?, *Journal of contemporary history,* **17,** 2 (1992) 60–72

4919 **Hyslop, J,** *The representation of white working class women in the construction of a reactionary populist movement: "purified" Afrikaner Nationalist agitation for legislation against "mixed" marriages 1934–1939.* Johannesburg: University of the Witwatersrand, African Studies Institute, 1993, 29pp

4920 **La Hausse, P,** So who was Elias Kuzwayo? Nationalism, collaboration and the picaresque in Natal, *Cahiers d'études africains,* **32,** 127 (1992) 469–507

4921 **L'Ange, G,** *Urgent imperial service: South African forces in German South West Africa 1914–1915.* Rivonia: Ashanti, 1991, 352pp

4922 **Lewsen, P** (ed), *Helen Suzman's solo years.* Johannesburg: Ball, 1991, 276pp

4923 **Lodge, T,** Lionel Forman's trumpet: national communism in South Africa, 1953–59, *Africa,* **63,** 4 (1993) 601–610 (review article)

4924 **Lowry, D,** A fellowship of disaffection: Irish-South African relations from the Anglo-Boer War to the Pretoriastroika, 1902–1991, *Etudes irlandaises,* 17 (1992) 105–21

4925 **Miller, R B,** Science and society in the early career of H F Verwoerd, *Journal of southern African studies,* **19,** 3 (1993) 634–61

4926 **Mouton, F A,** Die teësinnige leier: Margaret Ballinger en die Liberale Party van Suid-Afrika, *Journal of contemporary history,* **17,** 1 (1992) 552–68

4927 **Mshengu, T, et al,** *Asinamali! The life of Msizi Dube.* Pietermaritzburg: University of Natal Press, 1992, 76pp

4928 **Nemutanzhela, T J,** Cultural forms and literacy as resources for political mobilisation: A M Malivha and the Zoutpansberg Balemi Association 1939–1944, *African studies,* **52,** 1 (1993) 89–102

4929 **Niehaus, I A,** Witch-hunting and political legitimacy: continuity and change in Green Valley,

Lebowa, 1930–91, *Africa,* **63,** 4 (1993) 498–530

4930 **Parnell, S,** Creating racial privilege: the origins of South African public health and town planning legislation, *Journal of southern African studies,* **19,** 3 (1993) 471–88

4931 **Pillay, G J,** *Albert Luthuli.* Pretoria: HSRC, 1993, 167pp

4932 **Rassool, C, Witz, L,** The 1952 Jan van Riebeeck Tercentary Festival: reconstructing and contesting public national history in South Africa, *Journal of African history,* **34,** 3 (1993) 447–68

4933 **Schoeman, K,** *Only an anguish to live here: Olive Schreiner and the Anglo-Boer war.* Cape Town: Human and Rousseau, 1992, 240pp

4934 **Seegers, A,** Towards an understanding of the Afrikanerisation of the South African state, *Africa,* **63,** 4 (1993) 477–97

4935 **White, W B,** The United Party and the 1948 General Election, *Journal of contemporary history,* **17,** 2 (1992) 73–97

4936 **Wood, G,** 'The horsemen are coming': rethinking the Pondoland rebellion, *Contree,* 33 (1993) 27–34

Industry & trade

See also: 4861, 5016

4937 **Bell, R T,** *The prospects for industrialisation in the new South Africa.* Grahamstown: Rhodes University, 1990, 39pp

4938 **Bernasek, A, Porter, R C,** *Private pressure for social change in South Africa: the impact of the Sullivan Principles.* East Lansing: University of Michigan Centre for Research on Economic Development, 1990, 59pp

4939 **Crush, J,** Bibliography of works on the South African gold-mining industry (post–1980), *Labour, capital and society,* **25,** 1 (1992) 151–65

4940 **Duncan, D, Payne, B,** Just-in-time South Africa: Japanese production systems in the South African motor industry, *Capital and class,* 50 (1993) 11–23

4941 **Fine, B,** *Total factor productivity versus realism: the case of the South African coal mining industry.* London: SOAS, Dept. of Economics, 1992, 26pp

4942 **Fourie, F C,** Economic concentration: a survey and evaluation of policy options, *South African journal of economics,* **61,** 3 (1993) 134–52

4943 **Fourie, F C, Smith, A,** Concentration, tariff protection and industrial performance in South Africa, *South African journal of economics,* **61,** 3 (1993) 116–33

4944 **Horn, G S, et al,** The informal sector in Mamelodi and Kwazakhele, *Africa insight,* **23,** 3 (1993) 168–75

4945 **Kantor, B,** Savings and investment: ownership and control in South Africa, *South Africa international,* **23,** 2 (1992/1993) 82–90

4946 **Koch, B R,** *The informal sector: small clothing manufacturers in Mitchells Plain.* Cape Town: SALDRU, 1991, 42pp

4947 **McCarthy, C,** Industrial development and distribution, in Schrire, R (ed), *Wealth or poverty? (Item 4779)*, 446–63

4948 **Oberhauser, A M,** Semiperipheral industrialisation in the global economy: transition in the South African automobile industry, *Geoforum,* **24,** 2 (1993) 99–114

4949 **Roux, A,** Nationalisation: an evaluation, in Schrire, R (ed), *Wealth or poverty? (Item 4779)*, 294–313

4950 **Smith, A,** Income

redistribution and competition policy, in Schrire, R (ed), *Wealth or poverty? (Item 4779)*, 464–80

4951 **Standish, B,** Public works programmes and economic development, in Schrire, R (ed), *Wealth or poverty? (Item 4779)*, 260–73

4952 **Thomas, W,** Supporting job creation: small business and informal sector development, in Schrire, R (ed), *Wealth or poverty? (Item 4779)*, 481–94

4953 **Truu, M,** Nationalisation and privatisation, in Schrire, R (ed), *Wealth or poverty? (Item 4779)*, 274–93

4954 **van Walbeck, C P,** The consequences of export instability: South Africa 1971–1988, *South African journal of economics,* **61,** 3 (1993) 166–77

4955 **Visser, C,** AIDS and insurance law: a preliminary laundry list of issues, *South African journal of human rights,* **9,** 1 (1993) 130–42

International economic relations

See also: 4414, 4622, 4938, 4948, 4983, 5024

4956 **Adelman, S,** The politics of research on sanctions in South Africa, *Canadian journal of African studies,* **27,** 1 (1993) 89–94

4957 **Blumenfeld, J,** The international dimension, in Schrire, R (ed), *Wealth or poverty? (Item 4779)*, 59–76

4958 **Davies, R,** Economic growth in a post-apartheid South Africa: its significance for relations with other African countries, *Journal of contemporary African studies,* **11,** 1 (1992) 51–71

4959 **Davis, S P,** Economic pressure on South Africa: does it work?, in Shepherd, G W (ed), *Effective sanctions (Item 4977)*, 65–80

4960 **Devarajan, K M,** Prospects for trade and economic cooperation with South Africa, *Africa quarterly,* **33,** 1–4 (1992/93) 11–16

4961 **Goldin, I,** *External financial assistance and post-apartheid South Africa.* Bellville: University of the Western Cape, Economic Policy Research Project, 1992, 35pp

4962 **Hale, T D,** *United States sanctions and South Africa: a selected legal bibliography.* New York: Greenwood, 1993, 362pp

4963 **Holden, M,** Trade policy, income distribution and growth, in Schrire, R (ed), *Wealth or poverty? (Item 4779)*, 314–28

4964 **Khan, H A,** Multiplier and stuctural path analysis of trade sanctions, in Shepherd, G W (ed), *Effective sanctions (Item 4977)*, 25–54

4965 **Leistner, E,** Migration of high-level African manpower to South Africa, *Africa insight,* **23,** 4 (1993) 219–24

4966 **Micou, A M,** *The donor community in South Africa: a directory.* New York: UN, 1993, 81pp

4967 **Moore, N H, et al,** South African divestment decisions and shareholder wealth, *Economics letters,* **42,** 2 (1993) 223–28

4968 **Mozia, T U,** Chronology of arms embargoes against South Africa, in Shepherd, G W (ed), *Effective sanctions (Item 4977)*, 97–108

4969 **Mozia, T U,** Chronology of economic embargoes against South Africa, in Shepherd, G W (ed), *Effective sanctions (Item 4977)*, 109–25

4970 **Mozia, T U,** Sanctions busting strategies, in Shepherd, G W (ed), *Effective sanctions (Item 4977)*, 127–33

4971 **Mozia, T U,** Sanctions against South Africa: a bibliography, in

Shepherd, G W (ed), *Effective sanctions (Item 4977)*, 135–42

4972 Nanda, V P, Multilateral sanctions against South Africa: a legal framework for comprehensive implementation, in Shepherd, G W (ed), *Effective sanctions (Item 4977)*, 1–23

4973 Odén, B, *Sydafrika och den internationella ekonomin.* Uppsala: Scandinavian Institute of African Studies, 1993, 13pp

4974 Sethi, S P, Operational modes for multinational corporations in post-apartheid South Africa: a proposal for a code of affirmative ethics, *Journal of business ethics,* **12,** 1 (1992) 1–12

4975 Sethi, S P, Bhalla, B B, Strategic economic alliances: an approach to integrating the economy of post-apartheid South Africa in subsaharan Africa, *Development southern Africa,* **9,** 3 (1992) 331–45

4976 Shepherd, G W, The anti-apartheid movement and international sanctions, in Shepherd, G W (ed), *Effective sanctions (Item 4977)*, 81–96

4977 Shepherd, G W (ed), *Effective sanctions on South Africa.* New York: Praeger, 1991, 148pp

4978 Singh, D, Trade between India and post-apartheid South Africa: prospects and possible hurdles, *Africa quarterly,* **33,** 1–4 (1992/93) 17–30

4979 Stevens, C, et al, EC trade preferences and post-apartheid South Africa, *International affairs,* **69,** 1 (1993) 89–108

4980 Tarp, F, *Situations- og perspektivanalayse Sydafrika.* Copenhagen: DANIDA, 1993, 47pp

4981 Tarp, F, *South Africa: background and possibilities for Danish Transitional Assistance.* Copenhagen: DANIDA, 1993, 110pp

4982 Wright, S, South Africa's strategic mineral exports: an analysis of the feasibility of a US embargo, in Shepherd, G W (ed), *Effective sanctions (Item 4977)*, 55–63

International relations

See also: 4437, 4444, 4453, 4626, 4908, 4909, 5157

4983 Amin, S, South Africa in the global system, *Monthly review,* **45,** 2 (1993) 1–7

4984 Banerjee, D, The security and strategic dimensions, *Africa quarterly,* **33,** 1–4 (1992/93) 159–69

4985 Barratt, J, Current constraints on South Africa's foreign policy and diplomacy, in Johnston, A, et al (eds), *Constitution making (Item 5194)*, 154–68

4986 Baynham, S, South Africa and the world in the 1990s, *South Africa international,* **23,** 3 (1993) 108–117

4987 Coetzee, S, South Africa within Africa: towards a framework for mutually beneficial relations, *Africa insight,* **23,** 1 (1993) 2–5

4988 Davis, R, Republican and Loyalist links with South Africa, 1970–1990, *Eire-Ireland,* **27,** 4 (1992) 47–68

4989 Geldenhuys, D, The changing nature of foreign involvement in South Africa, *South Africa international,* **23,** 4 (1992/3) 147–55

4990 Hill, K A, The domestic sources of foreign policy-making: congressional voting and American mass attitudes toward South Africa, *International studies quarterly,* **37,** 2 (1993) 195–214

4991 Johnston, A, Shezi, S, The ANC's foreign policy, in Johnston, A, et al (eds), *Constitution making (Item 5194)*, 169–80

4992 Kline, B, The United States and South Africa during the Bush administration, *Journal of Asian and African affairs,* **4,** 2 (1993) 68–83

4993 Mandela, N, South Africa: future foreign policy, *Foreign affairs,* **72,** 5 (1993) 86–97

4994 Murphy, C J, et al, Managing the new world order: lessons from the South African experience, *Urban League review,* **15,** 2 (1992) 75–89

4995 Nel, P, *Perceptions, images and stereotypes in Soviet-South African relations: a cognitive interpretative approach.* Stellenbosch: Dept of Political Science, 1992, 79pp

4996 Ojo, B A, Nigerian and French perspectives on the South African question, in Jacob, H J & Omar, M (eds), *France and Nigeria (Item 3395),* 79–91

4997 O'Meara, P, South Africa's contradictory regional goals, in Hunt Davis, R (ed), *Apartheid unravels (Item 4677),* 213–27

4998 Payne, R J, *The Third World and South Africa: post-apartheid challenges.* New York: Greenwood, 1992, 208pp

4999 Ramamurthi, T G, India's South African policy, *Africa quarterly,* **33,** 1–4 (1992/93) 1–10

5000 Sawant, A B, Some reflections on India's policy towards South Africa, *African currents,* 12 (1990) 1–20

5001 Schoeman, E, *South Africa's foreign relations in transition 1985–1992: a chronology.* Pretoria: SAIIA, 1993, 666pp

5002 Spence, J E, A post-apartheid South Africa and the international community, *Journal of Commonwealth and comparative politics,* **31,** 1 (1993) 84–95

5003 Subramanian, R R, South Africa's strategic significance in the Indian Ocean, *Africa quarterly,* **33,** 1–4 (1992/93) 171–77

5004 Sunter, C, *The new century: the world and South Africa.* Cape Town: Human and Rousseau, 1992, 187pp

5005 Vale, P, Confusion, conflit et compromis: la politique africaine de l'Afrique du Sud, *Année africaine 1992/93,* 375–91

5006 Vale, P, Foreign policy of a post-apartheid South Africa, in Johnston, A, et al (eds), *Constitution making (Item 5194),* 181–98

5007 Van Wyk K, Radloff, S, Symmetry and reciprocity in South African foreign policy, *Journal of conflict resolution,* **37,** 2 (1993) 382–96

5008 Wenzel, C, *Die Sudafrikapolitik der USA in der Ara Reagan: konstruktives oder destruktives Engagement.* Hamburg: Institut für Afrika-Kunde, 1990, 171pp

Labour & manpower

See also: 4542, 4683, 4757, 4789, 4794, 4810, 4850, 4855, 4857, 5235, 5335, 5341, 5345, 5355

5009 Anstey, M (ed), *Worker participation: South African options and experiences.* Kenwyn: Juta, 1990, 313pp

5010 Archer, S, Strategic choices in the labour market, in Schrire, R (ed), *Wealth or poverty? (Item 4779),* 211–36

5011 Barchiesi, F, Oreintamenti metodologici e bibliografici per lo studio del sindacalismo indipendente sudafricano, *Africa (Rome),* **48,** 1 (1993) 70–91

5012 Crush, J, Inflexible migrancy: new forms of migrant labour on the South African gold mines, *Labour, capital and society,* **25,** 1 (1992) 46–71

5013 Crush, J, 'The long-averted clash': farm labour competition in the South African countryside, *Canadian journal of African studies,* **27,** 3 (1993) 404–23

5014 Crush, J, et al, Introduction,

Labour, capital and society, **25,** 1 (1992) 7–13

5015 **Douwes Dekker, L,** *Industrial relations for a changing South Africa.* Johannesburg: Lex Patria, 1990, 380pp

5016 **du Toit, A,** The micropolitics of paternalism: the discourses of management and resistance on South African fruit and wine farms, *Journal of southern African studies,* **19,** 2 (1993) 314–36

5017 **Fact-Finding and Conciliation Commission,** *Prelude to change: industrial relations reform in South Africa.* Geneva: ILO, 1992, 250pp

5018 **Goedeche, E J, Ortmann, G F,** Transaction costs and labour contracting in the South African forestry industry, *South African journal of economics,* **61,** 1 (1993) 67–83

5019 **Hofmeyr, K, Templer, A,** Black management development and advancement, in Schrire, R (ed), *Wealth or poverty? (Item 4779),* 193–210

5020 **Jenkins, C,** *The effect of sanctions on formal sector employment in South Africa.* Brighton: University of Sussex, IDS, 1993, 28pp

5021 **Kraak, G,** *Breaking the chains: labour in South Africa in the 1970s and 1980s.* London: Pluto, 1993, 308pp

5022 **Maiden, P M** (ed), *Employee assistance programmes in South Africa.* New York: Haworth, 1992, 125pp

5023 **Maree, T,** The economic case for worker participation: codetermination, in Schrire, R (ed), *Wealth or poverty? (Item 4779),* 237–59

5024 **Marsh, P A,** Decolonisation in southern Africa and the labour crisis in South Africa: modernising migrant labour policies, in Hunt Davis, R (ed), *Apartheid unravels (Item 4677),* 142–64

5025 **Mohamed, S,** *Electrical and Allied Workers Trade Union of South Africa: a history.* Cape Town: SALDRU, 1991, 93pp

5026 **Moll, P G,** Black South African unions: relative wage effects in international perspective, *Industrial and labor relations review,* **46,** 2 (1993) 245–61

5027 **Moll, P G,** Industry wage differentials and efficiency wages: a dissenting view with South African evidence, *Journal of development economics,* **41,** 2 (1993) 213–46

5028 **Nürnberger, K,** *The scourge of unemployment in South Africa.* Pietermartitzburg: Encounter, 1990, 54pp

5029 **Phillips, S,** Employment creation, poverty alleviation and the provision of infrastructure: lessons from the labour-based construction of municipal services in Ilinge, *Urban forum,* **3,** 2 (1992) 81–113

5030 **Shanafelt, R,** Worker solidarity, differentiation, and manipulation of ethnicity: conflict at Vaal Reefs 1984–86, in Hunt Davis, R (ed), *Apartheid unravels (Item 4677),* 119–41

5031 **Zita, L,** Moving beyond the social contract, *African communist,* 133 (1993) 20–28

Language

5032 **Kashoki, M E,** Some thoughts on future language policy for South Africa with reference to the Language Plan of Action for Africa, *African studies,* **52,** 2 (1993) 141–56

5033 **Stultz, N M,** Contextual influences in language politics in Canada and South Africa, *Journal of Commonwealth and comparative politics,* **31,** 3 (1993) 67–91

Law

See also: 4935, 5214, 5215, 5233, 5322

5034 **Adams, C,** *Affirmative action in a democratic South Africa.* Cape Town: Juta, 1993, 166pp

5035 **Asmal, K,** Victims, survivors and citizens: human rights, reparations and reconciliation, *South African journal on human rights,* **8,** 4 (1992) 491–511

5036 **Asmal, K,** Victims, survivors and citizens: human rights, reparations and reconciliation in the South African context, *East African journal of peace and human rights,* **1,** 1 (1993) 1–22

5037 **Beatty, D,** The rule (and role) of law in a new South Africa, *South African law journal,* **109,** 3 (1992) 408–27

5038 **Bennett, T W, Roos, J W,** The 1991 Land Reform Acts and the future of South African customary law, *South African law journal,* **109,** 3 (1992) 447–71

5039 **Breitenbach, A,** The justification for judicial review, *South African journal on human rights,* **8,** 4 (1992) 512–32

5040 **Budlender, G,** The right to equitable access to land, *South African journal on human rights,* **8,** 3 (1992) 295–304

5041 **Cross, C,** An alternate legality: the property rights question in relation to South African land reform, *South African journal on human rights,* **8,** 3 (1992) 305–331

5042 **Davis, D M,** The case against the inclusion of socio-economic demands in a bill of rights except as directive principles, *South African journal on human rights,* **8,** 4 (1992) 475–90

5043 **Devine, D L,** Transition to a new South Africa: marine law issues to be resolved, *Marine policy,* **17,** 4 (1993) 303–308

5044 **Dlamini, C RM,** The law teacher, the law student and legal education in South Africa, *South African law journal,* **109,** 4 (1992) 595–610

5045 **Dyzenhaus, D,** *Hard cases in wicked legal systems: South African law in the perspective of legal philosophy.* New York: OUP, 1991, 289pp

5046 **Goldstone, R,** *Do judges speak out?* Johannesburg: SAIRR, 1993, 33pp

5047 **Haysom, N,** Constitutionalism, majoritarian democracy and socioeconomic rights, *South African journal on human rights,* **8,** 4 (1992) 451–63

5048 **Higginbotham, A L,** Seeking pluralism in judicial systems: the American experience and the South African challenge, *Duke law journal,* **42,** 5 (1993) 1028–68

5049 **Huebner, M S,** Who decides?: restucturing criminal justice for a democratic South Africa, *Yale law journal,* **102,** 4 (1993) 961–90

5050 **Jagwanth, S,** Policing of the conflict in the greater Pietermaritzburg area: a perception study, *South African journal on human rights,* **8,** 4 (1992) 536–55

5051 **Lewis, C,** The right to private property in a new political dispensation in South Africa, *South African journal on human rights,* **8,** 3 (1992) 389–430

5052 **Lowenberg, A D,** A post-apartheid constitution for South Africa: lessons from public choice, *Cato journal,* **12,** 2 (1992) 297–319

5053 **Lyster, R,** The protection of envionmental rights, *South African law journal,* **109,** 3 (1992) 518–28

5054 **Marais, D,** *South Africa: constitutional development, a multi-disciplinary approach.* Halfway House: Southern Book Publishers, 1993 (rev. edn.), 304pp

5055 **Marasinghe, L,** Constitutional reform in South Africa, *International and comparative law quarterly,* **42,** 4 (1993) 927–54

5056 **Mureinik, E,** Beyond a charter of luxuries: economic rights in the constitution, *South African journal on human rights,* **8,** 4 (1992) 464–74

5057 **Pavlich, G,** People's courts, postmodern difference, and socialist justice in South Africa, *Social justice,* **18,** 3 (1992) 29–45

5058 **Robinson, K,** False right or a realisable right?: the implementation of the right to shelter under the ANC proposed bill of rights for South Africa, *Harvard civil rights-civil liberties law review,* **28,** 2 (1993) 505–32

5059 **Sachs, A,** Towards a Bill of Rights for a democratic South Africa, *Journal of African law,* **35,** 1/2 (1991) 21–43

5060 **Swanson, E,** A land claims court for South Africa: report on work in progress, *South African journal on human rights,* **8,** 3 (1992) 332–343

5061 **van der Ropp, K F,** The new South African constitution taking shape, *Aussenpolitik,* **44,** 4 (1993) 383–92

Library - documentation

5062 **Hooper, T,** The case against the South African book boycott, *Logos,* **1,** 3 (1990) 6–13

5063 **Saratovskaya, I,** South African literature in Russia, *African research and documentation,* 58 (1992) 11–15

5064 **September, P E,** Public libraries and community information needs in a changing South Africa, *Journal of librarianship and information science,* **25,** 2 (1993) 71–78

5065 **Steynberg, S, Rossouw, S F,** The availability of research journals in South African academic libraries, *South African medical journal,* **83,** 11 (1993) 837–39

Literature

See also: 4933, 5176

5066 **Andon-Milligan, L H,** South Africa - a quality of light, *Critique: studies in contemporary fiction,* **34,** 1 (1992) 19–32

5067 **Attwell, D,** *J M Coetzee: South Africa and the politics of writing.* Cape Town: Philip, 1993, 147pp

5068 **Barnett, U,** South African literature of the 1980s, *Matatu,* 10 (1993) 139–53

5069 **Brink, A,** A precarious freedom: the writer in South Africa facing the future, *Logos,* **4,** 4 (1993) 174–80

5070 **Campbell, J M,** Beyond duality: a Bhuddist reading of Bessie Head's A question of power, *Journal of Commonwealth literature,* **28,** 1 (1993) 64–81

5071 **Carusi, A,** Post, post and post - or, where is South African literature in all this?, in Adam, I & Tiffin, H (eds), *Past the last post: theorizing postcolonialism and postmodernism* (New York: Harvester Wheatsheaf, 1991), 95–108

5072 **Chandramohan, B,** *A study in trans-ethnicity in modern South Africa: the writings of Alex La Guma.* Lewiston: Mellen Research University Press, 1992, 280pp

5073 **Chapman, M, et al** (eds), *Perspectives on South Africa English literature.* Parklands: Donker, 1992, 551pp

5074 **Chrisman, L,** Colonialism and feminism in Olive Schreiner's 1890s fiction, *English in Africa,* **20,** 1 (1993) 25–38

5075 **Davison, A, Filatova, I,** Olive Schreiner: a century in Russia, *English in Africa,* **20,** 1 (1993) 39–48

5076 **Eilersen, G S,** Historical roots and rural African culture as part of Bessie Head's frame of reference, in Granqvist, R (ed), *Culture in Africa (item 10)*, 173–83

5077 **Flockemann, M,** Tradition and transformation: 'one never knows', *Tulsa studies on women's literature,* **11,** 1 (1992) 113–23

5078 **Gorak, I E,** Colonial allegory: The story of an African farm, *Ariel,* **23,** 4 (1992) 53–72

5079 **Hon, P,** A radical rethinking of the art of poetry in apartheid society, *Journal of Commonwealth literature,* **28,** 1 (1993) 97–113

5080 **Hunter, E, MacKenzie, C** (eds), *Between the lines II: interviews with Nadine Gordimer, Menan du Plessis, Zoe Wicomb, Lauretta Ngcobo.* Grahamstown: NELM, 1993, 122pp

5081 **Johnson, D,** Starting positions: the social function of literature in the Cape, *Journal of southern African studies,* **19,** 3 (1993) 615–33

5082 **Knipp, T,** Going all the way: *eros* and *polis* in the novels of Nadine Gordimer, *Research in African literatures,* **24,** 1 (1993) 37–50

5083 **Lockett, C,** South African women's poetry: a gynocritical perspective, *Tulsa studies on women's literature,* **11,** 1 (1992) 51–61

5084 **Maake, N P,** C M Doke and the development of Bantu literature, *African studies,* **52,** 2 (1993) 77–88

5085 **Maake, N P,** A survey of trends in the development of African language literatures in South Africa: with specific reference to written Southern Sotho literature c.1900–1970s, *African languages and cultures,* **5,** 2 (1992) 157–88

5086 **MacKenzie, C,** Literary research in South Africa: the case of the National English Literary Museum, *Research in African literatures,* **24,** 3 (1993) 105–112

5087 **Made, P, Abrahams, B,** *Study guide to* In the fog of the season's end. Harare: Baobab, 1993, 42pp

5088 **Monsman, G,** *Olive Schreiner's fiction: landscape and power.* New Brunswick: Rutgers University Press, 1991, 201pp

5089 **Nuttall, S,** Reading J M Coetzee politically, *Journal of southern African studies,* **19,** 3 (1993) 731–35 (review article)

5090 **O'Brien, A,** Literature in another South Africa: Njabulo Ndebele's theory of emergent culture, *Diacritics,* **22,** 1 (1992) 67–85

5091 **Petterson, R,** Nadine Gordimer and 'the South African dilemma': the case of Liz van den Sandt in The late bourgeois world, in Granqvist, R (ed), *Culture in Africa (item 10)*, 195–202

5092 **Raju, J, Dubbeld, C,** *Richard Rive: a select bibliography.* Durban: Natal University Library, 1990, 23pp

5093 **Reckwitz, E,** I'm not myself anymore: problems of identity in writing by white South Africans, *English In Africa,* **20,** 1 (1993) 1–23

5094 **Ryan, P,** Black women do not have time to dream: the politics of time and space, *Tulsa studies on women's literature,* **11,** 1 (1992) 95–102

5095 **Serote, W, Wade, J P,** Stoking the Third World express: Wally Serote interviewed by Jean-Philippe Wade, *English in Africa,* **20,** 1 (1993) 49–63

5096 **Uledi-Kamanga, B J,** The irony of apartheid: a study in technique and theme in the fiction of Nadine Gordimer, *Journal of humanities,* 5 (1991) 1–15

5097 **Viola, A,** Children of Soweto:

Lindiwe Mabuza's short story 'Wake', *Commonwealth: essays and studies,* **15,** 1 (1992) 39–44

5098 Von Lucius, R, Athol Fugard: South African playwright of international repute, *South Africa international,* **23,** 2 (1992/1993) 78–81

Media

See also: 5102

5099 Abramson, G, Mightier than the sword: Jewish cartoons and cartoonists in South Africa, *Humor,* **4,** 2 (1991) 149–64

5100 Anon, Who killed Hani?, *African communist,* 132 (1993) 5–11

5101 Burton, S, Gultig, J, Media in the 'new' South Africa: 'the more it changes, the more it stays the same', *Africa quarterly,* **33,** 1–4 (1992/93) 115–25

5102 Charney, C, *Black power, white press: literacy, newspapers, and the transformation of township political culture.* Johannesburg: University of the Witwatersrand, African Studies Institute, 1993, 31pp

5103 Haron, M, The *Muslim News* (1960–1986): the expression of Islamic identity in South Africa, in Brenner, L (ed), *Muslim identity (item 963)*, 210–25

5104 Jackson, G S, *Breaking story: the South African press.* Boulder: Westview, 1993, 308pp

5105 Moss, G, Publishing in post-apartheid South Africa, *Logos,* **4,** 3 (1993) 140–46

5106 Philip, D, Oppositional publishing in South Africa from 1945 to 2000, *Logos,* **2,** 1 (1991) 41–48

Medical

See also: 753, 4723, 4753, 5310, 5316

5107 Dubow, S, Wulf Sachs' *Black Hamlet*: a case of 'psychic vivisection'?, *African affairs,* **92,** 369 (1993) 519–56

5108 Duckitt, J, Education and authoritarianism among English-speaking and Afrikaans-speaking white South Africans, *Journal of social psychology,* **132,** 6 (1992) 701–708

5109 Duckitt, J, Right-wing authoritarianism among white South African students, its measurement and correlates, *Journal of social psychology,* **133,** 4 (1993) 553–63

5110 Jameson, C P, Glover, P H, AIDS education in schools: awareness, attitudes and opinions among educators, theology students and health professionals, *South African medical journal,* **83,** 9 (1993) 675–79

5111 Karim, Q A, et al, Seroprevalence of HIV infection in rural South Africa, *AIDS,* **6,** 12 (1992) 1535–39

5112 Pretorius, T B, Willingness to use social support: use of the Network Orientation Scale with Black South African students, *Psychological reports,* **73,** 3 (1993) 1011–1017

5113 Russell, C, The AIDS crisis: a mining industry perspective, *Mining survey,* 2 (1991) 20–31

5114 Southall, H, South African trends and projections of HIV infection, in Cross, S & Whiteside, A (eds), *Facing up to AIDS (item 4753)*, 61–86

5115 Stones, C R, et al, The perception of political events in South Africa and personality correlates, *Journal of social psychology,* **133,** 1 (1993) 115–118

5116 Swartz, L, On the edge: ward rounds in a South African psychiatric emergency department, *Social science and medicine,* **35,** 9 (1992) 1115–22

5117 Tshibangiu, N N, HIV

infection in Bophuthatswana - epidemiologic surveillance 1987–1989, *South African medical journal,* **83,** 1 (1993) 36–39

5118 **Westaway, M S, Wolmarans, L,** Depression and self-esteem: rapid screening for depression in Black, low literacy hospitalised tuberculosis patients, *Social science and medicine,* **35,** 10 (1992) 1311–1315

5119 **Wilson, D, Lavelle, S,** AIDS prevention in South Africa: a perspective from other African countries, *South African medical journal,* **83,** 9 (1993) 668–74

Natural resources

See also: 4829

5120 **Braune, E,** The applicability of the concept of sustainable development in South Africa with reference to soil and water resource utilisation, *Africanus,* **22,** 1/2 (1992) 78–93

Planning

5121 **Fourie, A, Vawda, A,** The importance of a thorough geotechnical site investigation at the planning stage of urban development, *Urban forum,* **3,** 1 (1992) 57–72

Politics

See also: 819, 4460, 4770, 4792, 4838, 4846, 4859, 4860, 4913, 5021, 5030, 5100, 5109, 5115, 5270, 5317, 5354, 5357

5122 **Abdullah, F,** A response to Moluba's letter of resignation, *African communist,* 135 (1993) 21–25

5123 **Adam, H, Moodley, K,** Comparing South Africa: non-racial vs ethnonationalist revival, *Third world quarterly,* **14,** 2 (1993) 339–50

5124 **Adam, H, Moodley, K,** Forecasting scenarios for South Africa, *Futures,* **25,** 4 (1993) 404–413

5125 **Adam, H, Moodley, K,** *The opening of the South African mind: options for the new South Africa.* Berkeley: University of California Press, 1993, 277pp

5126 **Adam, H, Moodley, K,** South Africa: the opening of the apartheid mind, in McGarry, J & O'Leary, B (eds), *The politics of ethnic conflict regulation* (London: Routledge, 1993), 226–50

5127 **Adam, H, Moodley, K,** South Africa: revived nationalism vs non-racialism, *South Africa international,* **23,** 4 (1992/93) 140–46

5128 **Africa Watch,** *South Africa half-hearted reform: the official response to the rising tide of violence.* New York: Africa Watch, 1993, 73pp

5129 **Akinboye, S O,** Apartheid and democratisation process in South Africa, *Review of African political affairs,* **5,** 1/2 (1991) 64–74

5130 **Albright, D, Hibbs, M,** South Africa, the ANC and the atom bomb, *Bulletin of the atomic scientists,* **49,** 3 (1993) 32–37

5131 **Anon,** *Electoral proceedures for South Africa.* Pretoria: Human Sciences Research Council, Centre for Constitutional Analysis, 1993, 6pp

5132 **Aronson, R,** *Stay out of politics: a philosopher views South Africa.* Chicago: University of Chicago Press, 1990, 164pp

5133 **Atkinson, D,** Local negotiations: corporatism and political symbolism, in Johnston, A, et al (eds), *Constitution making (Item 5194)*, 67–86

5134 **Battersby, J, et al,** Running with the PAC, *Work in progress,* 92 (1993) 12–20

5135 **Bauer, C, Wessels, D P,** Bophuthatswana: its creation and quest for international recognition, *Journal of contemporary history,* **17,** 1 (1992) 19–35

5136 **Beck, K S,** Democratising the United Democratic Front: the muddy slope, in Hunt Davis, R (ed), *Apartheid unravels (Item 4677)*, 100–118

5137 **Bekker, J C,** The role of chiefs in a future South African constitutional dispensation, *Africa insight,* **23,** 4 (1993) 200–204

5138 **Bell, M E, et al,** Financing the post-apartheid city in South Africa, *Urban studies,* **30,** 3 (1993) 581–92

5139 **Bennun, M E,** Biopatong and after: reflections on the politics of violence in South Africa, *International journal of the sociology of law,* **21,** 1 (1993) 49–71

5140 **Bernstein, H,** Discovering exiles, *Southern African review of books,* **5,** 4 (1993) 10–12

5141 **Botha, T,** Federalism v. unitarism: which way forward?, *African communist,* 132 (1993) 40–46

5142 **Bouillon, A,** Pensées transitoires sur une Afrique du Sud dite 'intermédiare', *Année africaine 1992/93,* 161–88

5143 **Boyd, J B,** Review essay: persectives on South Africa's future, *African studies review,* **35,** 3 (1992) 105–113

5144 **Bradshaw, G,** Constitutional negotiation: the role of mediator in South Africa, in Johnston, A, et al (eds), *Constitution making (Item 5194)*, 54–66

5145 **Bundy, C, et al,** What's left for the left?, *Work in progress,* 89 (1993) 10–22

5146 **Calitz, J M** (ed), *Regional distribution of potential voters in South Africa, 1992.* Halfway House: Centre for Information Analysis, Development Bank of Southern Africa, 1992, 25pp

5147 **Cameron, R,** Regional Service Councils in South Africa: past, present and future, *Public administration,* **71,** 3 (1993) 417–39

5148 **Carrim, Y,** The ANC as a mass political organisation, in Johnston, A, et al (eds), *Constitution making (Item 5194)*, 89–114

5149 **Carrim, Y,** Indian South Africans in the transition to a post-apartheid South Africa, *Africa quarterly,* **33,** 1–4 (1992/93) 47–64

5150 **Chhabra, H S,** Democratic South Africa: prospects, *Africa quarterly,* **33,** 1–4 (1992/93) 81–90

5151 **Cilliers, J K, Mertz, P B,** *Focus on military and democracy: concept and role of armed forces and political control of defence in a democratic South Africa.* Halfway House: Institute for Defence Policy, 1993, 47pp

5152 **Cloete, F,** Between Scylla and Charybdis: policy choices and the development of democracy in South Africa, in Vanhanen, T (ed), *Strategies of democratisation* (New York: Crane Russak, 1992), 143–56

5153 **Coetsee, L,** A practical model for the management of resistance to change: an analysis of political resistance in South Africa, *International journal of public administration,* **16,** 11 (1993) 1815–37

5154 **Commonwealth Observer Mission to South Africa,** *Violence in South Africa: Phase 1.* London: Commonwealth Secretariat, 1993, 61pp

5155 **Corder, C K,** Scenario 2000: a perspective on a future South Africa, *International journal of public opinion research,* **5,** 2 (1993) 185–992

5156 **Darbon, D,** In hac lacrimarum valle: les enjeux précontraints d'une démocratisation cogérée en Afrique du Sud, *Année africaine 1992/93,* 189–214

5157 **Davies, J,** International pressure and the transition in South Africa, *New Zealand international review,* **18,** 3 (1993) 9–13

5158 **Davies-Webb, W,** *Umkhonto we Sizwe and the South African Communist Party: searching for a mission in the 1990s.* Bryanston: International Freedom Foundation (Southern Africa), 1991, 36pp

5159 **De Klerk, W,** The political process in South Africa, *South Africa international,* **23,** 2 (1992/1993) 65–70

5160 **de Kock, C, et al,** *The prospects for a free, democratic election.* Pretoria: HSRC, 1993, var pp

5161 **de Villiers, B,** An electoral system for the new South Africa, in Johnston, A, et al (eds), *Constitution making (Item 5194),* 28–53

5162 **de Villiers, J W, et al,** Why South Africa gave up the bomb, *Foreign affairs,* **72,** 5 (1993) 98–109

5163 **Decraene, P,** Sur la 'nouvelle Afrique du Sud' de MM de Klerk et Mandela, *Mondes et cultures,* **50,** 2–4 (1990) 575–80 (and see 581–86)

5164 **Driver, C J,** Between the hammer and the anvil: the quandary of liberalism in South Africa, in Hunt Davis, R (ed), *Apartheid unravels (Item 4677),* 58–76

5165 **Du Toit, B,** *Understanding South African political violence: a new problematic?* Geneva: UNRISD, 1993, 30pp

5166 **du Toit, J, Gagiano, J,** Strongmen on the Cape Flats, *Africa insight,* **23,** 2 (1993) 102–111

5167 **du Toit, P,** *Power plays; bargaining tactics for transforming South Africa.* Halfway House: Southern Book Publishers, 1991, 150pp

5168 **Dugard, J, et al,** *The last years of apartheid: civil liberties in South Africa.* New York: Ford Foundation & Foreign Policy Association, 1992, 254pp

5169 **Duvenhage, A,** Rewolusionêre of ewolusionêre verandering in 'n diepverdeelde samelewing - 'n perspektief vanuit Algerië vir Suid-Afrika, *Journal of contemporary history,* **17,** 1 (1992) 135–86

5170 **Everatt, D,** Death squads, *Southern African review of books,* **5,** 1 (1993) 1–6

5171 **Fischer, D,** Reversing nuclear proliferation: South Africa, *Security dialogue,* **24,** 3 (1993) 273–86

5172 **Ford, C A,** Political ideology and conceptual change: the rise and decline of apartheid racial theory in South Africa, *Archiv orientalni,* **60,** 4 (1992) 370–88

5173 **Forsyth, P,** Manipulating the past: the political use of history by Chief A N M G Buthelezi, in Edgecombe, D R, et al (eds), *Zulu origins (item 4895),* 17pp

5174 **Friedman, S** (ed), *The long journey: South Africa's quest for a negotiated settlement.* Johannesburg: Ravan, 1993, 206pp

5175 **Gocking, R,** Afrocentricity: implications for South Africa?, *Africa insight,* **23,** 1 (1993) 42–46

5176 **Gready, P,** Autobiography and the power of writing': political prison writing in the apartheid era, *Journal of southern African studies,* **19,** 3 (1993) 489–523

5177 **Grundy, K W,** South Africa: tortuous transition, *Current history,* **92,** 574 (1993) 229–33

5178 **Grundy, K W,** White politics in transition: multidimensional uncertainty, in Hunt Davis, R (ed), *Apartheid unravels (Item 4677),* 33–57

5179 **Gupta, V,** Violence and regionalism delay democratisation, *Africa quarterly,* **33,** 1–4 (1992/93) 107–114

5180 **Halisi, C R D,** Racial proletarianisation and some contemporary dimensions of Black Consciousness thought, in Hunt Davis, R (ed), *Apartheid unravels (Item 4677)*, 77–99

5181 **Hani, C,** La longue marche vers la démocratie, *Cahiers du communisme,* **69,** 1 (1993) 97–101

5182 **Harshe, R,** Understanding transition towards post-apartheid South Africa, *Economic and political weekly,* **28,** 38 (1993) 1980–83

5183 **Heitman, H R, et al,** *Restructuring the armed forces.* Halfway House: Institute for Defence Policy, 1993, 48pp

5184 **Herholt, A N J, Dombo, R J,** The political development of Venda: a study of a society in microcosm, *Journal of contemporary history,* **17,** 1 (1992) 69–88

5185 **Heymans, C,** Towards people's development: civic associations and development in South Africa, *Urban forum,* **4,** 1 (1993) 1–20

5186 **Howlett, D, Simpson, J,** Nuclearisation and denuclearisation in South Africa, *Survival,* **35,** 3 (1993) 154–73

5187 **Human Rights Commission,** *Political imprisonment in South Africa.* Braamfontein: the Commission, 1991, 67pp

5188 **Irvine, D,** Federalism and the new constitution, in Johnston, A, et al (eds), *Constitution making (Item 5194)*, 13–27

5189 **Jaster, R S, Jaster, S K,** *South Africa's other whites: voices for change.* Basingstoke: Macmillan, 1993, 151pp

5190 **Jeffrey, A J,** *Conflict at the crossroads in Bophuthatswana.* Johannesburg: SAIRR, 1992, 358pp

5191 **Jeffrey, A J,** *Spotlight on disinformation about violence in South Africa.* Braamfontein: SAIRR, 1992, 57pp

5192 **Johnston, A,** Introduction: South Africa since February 1990, in Johnston, A, et al (eds), *Constitution making (Item 5194)*, 1–9

5193 **Johnston, A,** Partition, asccomodation and assimilation: minorities and national constitutions, in Johnston, A, et al (eds), *Constitution making (Item 5194)*, 201–33

5194 **Johnston, A, et al** (eds), *Constitution making in the new South Africa.* London: Leicester University Press, 1993, 272pp

5195 **Kane-Berman, J,** *Political violence in South Africa.* Johannesburg: SAIRR, 1993, 104pp

5196 **Kapoor, S,** Towards a post-apartheid South Africa: an introductory bibliography, *Africa quarterly,* **33,** 1–4 (1992/93) 189–223

5197 **Kunert, D,** *Glasnost, new thinking and the ANC-SACP alliance: a parting of ways - socialism and oriental despotism.* Bryanston: International Freedom Foundation (Southern Africa), 1991, 206pp

5198 **Lange, K** (ed), *Perspektiven für Südafrika: Beiträge zur II. deusch-sowjetischen Tagung über Probleme des südlichen Afrika.* Munich: Kyrill & Method, 1991, 69pp

5199 **Lubisi, C,** Buthelezi and the 'Zulu kingdom', *African communist,* 134 (1993) 65–72

5200 **Lyon, P,** South Africa's political future, *Round table,* **82,** 327 (1993) 243–46

5201 **Maasdorp, G,** Drawing the lines: the economic implications of regional restructuring in South Africa, *Optima,* **39,** 1 (1993) 25–29

5202 **MacDonald, M, James, W,** The hand on the tiller: the politics of state and class in South Africa, *Journal of modern African studies,* **31,** 3 (1993) 387–405

5203 **Mackay, S,** *Towards*

deracialising local government. Braamfontein: SAIRR, 1993, 56pp

5204 **Mallaby, S,** *After apartheid.* London: Faber, 1993, 216pp

5205 **Mansfield, P,** *The Indaba's constitutional proposals revisited.* Pretoria: HSRC, 1991, 22pp

5206 **Maphai, V,** Prospects for a democratic South Africa, *International affairs,* **69,** 2 (1993) 223–38

5207 **Marais, D, et al** (eds), *South African civil service in the new South Africa: quo vadis?* Pretoria: University of South Africa, Dept. of Public Administration, 1991, 88pp

5208 **Marais, H, et al,** Can the ANC win?, *Work in progress,* 88 (1993) 6–20

5209 **Marais, H, et al,** Digging for the truth, *Work in progress,* 91 (1993) 10–22

5210 **Marais, H, et al,** Focus on youth, *Work in progress,* 90 (1993) 8–22

5211 **Mare, G,** *Brothers born of warrior blood: ethnicity and politics in South Africa.* Johannesburg: Ravan, 1993, 121pp

5212 **Maré, G,** *Ethnicity and politics in South Africa.* London: Zed, 1993, 125pp

5213 **Marx, A W,** Contested images and implications of South African nationhood, in Warren, K B (ed), *The violence within: cultural and political opposition in divided nations* (Boulder: Westview, 1993), 157–79

5214 **Mathews, A S,** Rounding up the usual suspects, *Cambridge law journal,* **51,** 2 (1992) 349–72

5215 **Mathews, A S,** South African security law and the growth of local and regional violence, in Hunt Davis, R (ed), *Apartheid unravels (Item 4677),* 18–32

5216 **Mayekiso, M,** 'Institutions that themselves need to be watched over': a review of recent writings on the civic movement, *Urban forum,* **4,** 1 (1993) 21–54

5217 **Mayekiso, M,** The legacy of 'ungovernability', *Southern African review of books,* **5,** 6 (1993) 24–27

5218 **Mbeki, T,** The end of the begining, *Africa forum,* **1,** 2 (1991) 41–45

5219 **McHenry, D E,** Review essay: the South African debate over the democratic transition, *African studies review,* **36,** 2 (1993) 95–101

5220 **Merrett, C E,** *The emergency of the state: a source guide to South African political issues, 1985–1990.* Durban: University of Natal Library, 1993, 66pp

5221 **Mills, G,** Armed forces in post-apartheid South Africa, *Survival,* **35,** 3 (1993) 78–96

5222 **Minty, A S,** South Africa: from apartheid to democracy, *Security dialogue,* **24,** 1 (1993) 69–84

5223 **Mohammed, J C,** Collective rights, transformation and democracy: some thoughts on a new constitutional dispensation in South Africa, *Africa development,* **17,** 1 (1992) 5–35

5224 **Moluba, T,** Letter of resignation, *African communist,* 135 (1993) 16–20

5225 **Nelson, C,** Die lewensvatbaarheid van 'n demokfrasie in Suid-Afrika, *Journal of contemporary history,* **17,** 2 (1992) 98–118

5226 **Nieuwmeijir, L, Cloete, F** (eds), *The dynamics of negotiation in South Africa.* Pretoria: HSRC, 1991, 138pp

5227 **O'Malley, K,** Liberalism in the new South Africa, *South Africa international,* **23,** 3 (1993) 100–107

5228 **Ottaway, D,** *Chained together: Mandela, de Klerk and the struggle to remake South Africa.* New York: Times Books, 1993, 291pp

5229 **Ottaway, M,** Direct and indirect internationalisation: the case of South Africa, in Midlarsky, M I (ed), *The internationalisation of communal strife* (London: Routledge, 1992), 233–51

5230 **Owen, K,** *These times: a decade of South African politics.* Parklands: Ball, 1992, 314pp

5231 **Ozinsky, M, Rasool, E,** Developing a strategic perspective for the Coloured Areas in the Western Cape, *African communist,* 133 (1993) 39–47

5232 **Periera, P,** *Coercion, boycott and stayaways.* Braamfontein: SAIRR, 1992, 24pp

5233 **Porteilla, R,** La réintégration des TBVC en Afrique du Sud: implications politiques et constitutionelles, *Année africaine 1992/93,* 215–42

5234 **Preston, J C, et al,** Endemic violence in South Africa: an odd solution applied to two educational settings, *International journal of public administration,* **16,** 11 (1993) 1767–91

5235 **Ramaphosa, C,** The role of trade unions in the transition, *African communist,* 133 (1993) 32–38

5236 **Rantete, J,** *Liberation and negotiation: the Pan Africanist Congress in the South African transition.* Johannesburg: University of the Witwatersrand, Centre for Policy Studies, 1992, 17pp

5237 **Sarakinsky, I,** The impulse to reform: the South African state from Vorster to Botha, *Journal of contemporary history,* **17,** 1 (1992) 1–18

5238 **Saxena, S C,** Nation-building in South Africa: agenda for the future, *Africa quarterly,* **33,** 1–4 (1992/93) 91–106

5239 **Saxena, S C,** Reforms in South Africa: right-wing reaction, *Ind-Africana,* **4,** 2 (1991) 36–51

5240 **Saxena, S C,** *South Africa: walking the last mile.* Delhi: Kalinga, 1992, 508pp

5241 **Schlemmer, L,** Violence: what is to be done?, *South Africa international,* **23,** 2 (1992/1993) 60–64

5242 **Shapiro, I,** Democratic innovation: South Africa in comparative context, *World politics,* **46,** 1 (1993) 121–50

5243 **Shubane, K,** The Soweto Accord: an evaluation of a precedent, in Johnston, A, et al (eds), *Constitution making (Item 5194),* 115–27

5244 **Sisk, T D,** The violence-negotiation nexus: South Africa in transition and the politics of uncertainty, *Negotiation journal,* **9,** 1 (1993) 53–71

5245 **Slovo, J,** The negotiations victory: a political overview, *African communist,* 135 (1993) 6–13

5246 **Sono, T,** *Reflections on the origins of Black Consciousness in South Africa.* Pretoria: HSRC, 1993, 154pp

5247 **Srinivasan, P,** 'Framing of a future' for South Africa, *African currents,* 11 (1990) 24–47

5248 **Strauss, A,** The 1992 referendum in South Africa, *Journal of modern African studies,* **31,** 2 (1993) 339–60

5249 **Strauss, A C P,** Die implikasies van die 1992-referendum in Suid Afrika, *Journal of contemporary history,* **17,** 2 (1992) 159–80

5250 **Stumpf, W E,** South Africa: nuclear technology and nonproliferation, *Security dialogue,* **24,** 4 (1993) 455–58

5251 **Thornton, R,** *Ethnicity and the geometry of power: one moment in the imagination of the polity.* Johannesburg: Witwatersrand University, African Studies Institute, 1993, 13pp

5252 **Till, G, et al,** *Focus on the South African navy.* Halfway House: Institute for Defence Policy, 1993, 47pp

5253 **Tjnneland, E N,** Negotiating democracy and human rights: the case of South Africa, in Andreassen, B A & Swinehart, T (eds), *Human rights in developing countries yearbook 1993* (Bergen: Chr Michelsen Institute, and others, 1993), 51–84

5254 **Truluck, A,** *'No blood on our hands': political violence in the Natal Midlands 1987-mid 1992, and the role of the state, 'white' political parties and business.* Pietermaritzburg: Black Sash (Natal Midlands Region), 1992, 255pp

5255 **Tucker, B, Scott, B,** *South Africa: prospects for a successful transition.* Cape Town: Juta, 1993, 314pp

5256 **van der Vyver, J D, et al,** *Democracy in South Africa.* Potchefstroom: Institute for Reformational Studies, 1993, 68pp

5257 **van Dyk, H,** *Conflict management at community level: a case study of the Ngotsche Cooperation Agreement.* Pretoria: HSRC, 1990, 34pp

5258 **van Kessel, I,** 'From confusion to Lusaka': the youth revolt in Sekhukhuneland, *Journal of southern African studies,* **19,** 3 (1993) 593–614

5259 **van Kessel, I,** Zuid-Afrika en de 'Leipzig optie': tussen de straat en de onderhandelingstafel, *Internationale spectator,* **46,** 10 (1992) 590–594

5260 **Van Ryneveld, P,** *The economics of good government in greater Cape Town.* Bellville: University of the Western Cape, Economic Policy Research Project, 1992, 15pp

5261 **van Wyk, M J,** Civil society and democracy in South Africa, *Africa insight,* **23,** 3 (1993) 136–40

5262 **Van Zyl Slabbert, F,** Prospects for democracy, *Africa forum,* **1,** 2 (1991) 46–49

5263 **Various authors,** *Towards violence-free elections in South Africa: a multinational panel report.* Pretoria: HSRC, 1993, 56pp

5264 **von der Ropp, K F,** The new South African constitution taking shape, *Southern Africa political and economic monthly,* **7,** 2 (1993) 60–63

5265 **Vorster, W S** (ed), *Building a new nation: the quest for a new South Africa.* Pretoria: University of South Africa, 1991, 203pp

5266 **Walters, S,** Non-governmental organisations and the South Africa state: present and future relations, *Community development journal,* **28,** 1 (1993) 1–10

5267 **Webster, E,** Moral decay and social reconstruction: Richard Turner and radical reform, *Theoria,* 81/2 (1993) 1–13

5268 **Wessels, D P,** Die herwormingsinisiatief en transformasieproses in Suid-Afrika, *Journal of contemporary history,* **17,** 1 (1992) 187–212

5269 **Ziota, L,** Unity of the left, *African communist,* 134 (1993) 30–38

Religion, philosophy

See also: 986, 4917, 5103, 5246

5270 **Borer, T,** Challenging the state: churches as political actors in South Africa, *Church and state,* **35,** 2 (1993) 299–334

5271 **Campbell, J,** *The social origins of African Methodism in the Orange Free State.* Johannesburg: Witwatersrand University, African Studies Institute, 1993, 25pp

5272 **Diesel, A, Mazwell, P,** *Hinduism in Natal.* Pietermartitzburg: University of Natal Press, 1993, 119pp

5273 **Gunner, E,** The dead child returned to Life: the sermon as oral narrative in Isaiah Shembe's Nazareth Baptist Church, in Görög-Karady, V (ed), *D'un conte ... à l'autre (item 38)*, 191–201

5274 **Hayes, S,** *Black charismatic Anglicans: the Iviyo loFakazi bakaKristu and its relations with other renewal movements.* Pretoria: University of South Africa, 1990, 227pp

5275 **Kilian, J,** *Religious freedom in South Africa.* Pretoria: University of South Africa, 1993, 166pp

5276 **Kritzinger, J J,** The numbers game: independent churches, *Africa insight,* **23,** 4 (1993) 246–49

5277 **Louw, T J G,** Philosophy of actuality: the work and thought of an individualist South African philosopher, *Man and world,* **26,** 2 (1993) 181–97

5278 **Mahlke, R,** 'The ancestors have a hold on us': an interview with a Zulu Zionist Church leader, *Africa Marburgensia,* **24,** 1 (1991) 61–71

5279 **Poqwe, K,** Theologies of Black South Africans and the rhetoric of peace versus violence, *Canadian journal of African studies,* **27,** 1 (1993) 43–65

5280 **Ramchandani, R R,** Towards understanding Gandhian relevance in non-racial South Africa, *Africa quarterly,* **33,** (1993) 1–23

5281 **Ramphal, R,** Changes in the religious views and practices of a minority group in South Africa, *South African journal of sociology,* **24,** 2 (1993) 58–61

5282 **Saayman, W,** *Christian mission in South Africa, political and ecumenical.* Pretoria: University of South Africa, 1991, 128pp

5283 **Saks, D,** 'The German *shul*': the contribution of Adath Jeshurun to orthodox Judaism in South Africa, *Africana notes and news,* **30,** 4 (1992) 133–40

Rural economy

See also: 1038, 1044, 4824, 5554

5284 **Auerbach, R M B, Lea, J D,** Some maize production parameters for KwaZulu, *Development southern Africa,* **9,** 1 (1992) 25–45

5285 **Binswanger, H P, Deiniger, H,** South African land policy: the legacy of history and current options, *World development,* **21,** 9 (1993) 1451–75

5286 **Brand, S, et al,** Agriculture and redistribution: growth with equity, in Schrire, R (ed), *Wealth or poverty? (Item 4779)*, 353–75

5287 **Christiansen, R E, et al,** Editors' introduction: experiences with agricultural policy - some lessons for South Africa, *World development,* **21,** 9 (1993) 1447–50

5288 **Cooper, D,** Re-forming the land question, in Schrire, R (ed), *Wealth or poverty? (Item 4779)*, 406–19

5289 **Crush, J, Jeeves, A,** Transitions in the South African countryside, *Canadian journal of African studies,* **27,** 3 (1993) 351–60

5290 **de Klerk, M,** Addressing land hunger, in Schrire, R (ed), *Wealth or poverty? (Item 4779)*, 376–405

5291 **de Klerk, M,** The financial crisis in South African agriculture and post-apartheid agrarian transformation, *Canadian journal of African studies,* **27,** 3 (1993) 361–79

5292 **de Wet, C,** A spatial analysis of involuntary community relocation: a South African case study, in Cernea, M M & Guggenheim, S E (eds), *Anthropological approaches to resettlement (item 1112)*, 321–50

5293 **Francis, E, Williams, G,** The land question, *Canadian journal of African studies,* **27,** 3 (1993) 380–403

5294 **Kassler, E, Groenewald, J,** Agriculture: an overview, in

Schrire, R (ed), *Wealth or poverty? (Item 4779)*, 330–52

5295 Kotze, J H, Basson, F, Land reform in South Africa: an overview, *Africa insight,* **23,** 4 (1993) 190–97

5296 Levin, R, Weiner, D, The agrarian question and politics in the 'new' South Africa, *Review of African political economy,* 57 (1993) 29–45

5297 Lipton, M, Lipton, M, Creating rural livelihoods: some lessons for South Africa from experience elsewhere, *World development,* **21,** 9 (1993) 1515–48

5298 Shackleton, C M, Are the communal grazing lands in need of saving?, *Development southern Africa,* **10,** 1 (1993) 65–78

5299 van Zyl, J, Vink, N, The mini farmer approach: a case study of the South African tea industry, *Development southern Africa,* **9,** 3 (1992) 365–81

5300 Vaughan, A, Options for rural restructuring, in Schrire, R (ed), *Wealth or poverty? (Item 4779)*, 420–45

5301 Vaughan, A, Macintosh, A, State and capital in the regeneration of a South African peasantry, *Canadian journal of African studies,* **27,** 3 (1993) 439–61

5302 Weiner, D, The land question in South Africa, in Prostermann, R L, et al (eds), *Agrarian reform and grassroots development* (Boulder: Lynne Reinner, 1990), 293–307

5303 Welz, D, *Mayibuye, Wiederkehr des Verdrängten: Berichte aus Südafrika.* Essen: Blaue Eule, 1992, 162pp

Science & technology

See also: 4807

5304 International Development Research Centre, *Towards a science and technology policy for a democratic South Africa: a report to the ANC, COSATU and SANCO.* Ottowa: IDRC, 1992, 80pp

5305 Morris, M L, Stavrou, S E, Telecommunication needs and provision to underdeveloped Black areas in South Africa, *Telecommunication policy,* **17,** 7 (1993) 529–39

Sociology

See also: 4840, 5112, 5283

5306 Borman, E, Mynhardt, J C, Ethnic attitudes and factors associated with social comparison and relative deprivation, *South African journal of sociology,* **24,** 2 (1993) 35–40

5307 Breytenbach, W J, *Whites in Africa: where, why, what now?* Stellenbosch: Stellenbosch University, Institute for Futures Research, 1990, 61pp

5308 Cravinho, J G, Portugueses na Africa do Sol: retrato politico de uma communidade emigrante, *Année africaine 1992/93,* 411–30

5309 Dharampal, Indians in post apartheid South Africa, *Ind-Africana,* **4,** 2 (1991) 15–35

5310 Doyle, P, et al, *AIDS in South Africa: the demographic and economic implications.* Johannesburg: Witwatersrand University, Centre for Health Policy, 1991, 74pp

5311 Fine, G A, Rumours of apartheid: the ecotypification of contemporary legends in the new South Africa, *Journal of folklore research,* **29,** 1 (1992) 53–71

5312 Hanks, D E, Liprie, M L, South African migration and the effects on the family, *Marriage and family review,* **19,** 1–2 (1993) 175–92

5313 Hiremath, J R, Indian South Africans - a contemporary portrait, *Africa quarterly,* **33,** 1–4 (1992/93) 31–45

5314 **Human Rights Commission,** *Children and repression 1987–1989.* Braamfontein: the Commission, 1990, 57pp
5315 **Kotzé, H J,** Overlapping values of the South African elite: applying an adapted Wilson-Patterson C-scale, *South African journal of sociology,* **24,** 1 (1993) 1–8
5316 **Magwaza, A S, et al,** The effects of chronic violence on preschool children living in South African townships, *Child abuse and neglect,* **17,** 8 (1993) 795–308
5317 **Marais, H, et al,** The new South Africa identity crisis, *Work in progress,* 93 (1993) 10–21
5318 **Minaar, A** (ed), *Communities in isolation: perspectives on hostels in South Africa.* Pretoria: HSRC, 1993, 271pp
5319 **Muller, M,** Easy demons: the children of '76, *Optima,* **39,** 2 (1993) 2–8
5320 **Saks, D Y,** South Africa's Italian community, *Africana notes and news,* **30,** 5 (1993) 178–85
5321 **Sharp, J, McAllister, P,** Ethnicity, identity and nationalism: international insights and the South African debate, *Anthropology today,* **9,** 4 (1993) 18–20
5322 **Sinclair, J,** South Africa - protecting children: poverty, abuse, divorce and political turmoil, *University of Louisville journal of family law,* **31,** 2 (1993) 461–76
5323 **Song, A,** The South African Chinese family, *Journal of comparative family studies,* **24,** 3 (1993) 353–65
5324 **Steyn, A,** Stedelike gesinstrukture in Republik van Suid-Afrika, *South African journal of sociology,* **24,** 1 (1993) 17–26
5325 **Thompson, L M,** The South African Indians: trapped in the middle, *Africa quarterly,* **33,** 1–4 (1992/93) 65–72
5326 **van Blerk, A,** No safe refuge, *Comparative and international law journal of southern Africa,* **25,** 3 (1992) 312–31

Social welfare

5327 **Donaldson, A,** Restructuring social services, in Schrire, R (ed), *Wealth or poverty? (Item 4779),* 143–60
5328 **Drower, S,** The contribution of group work in changing South Africa, *Social work with groups,* **16,** 3 (1993) 5–22
5329 **Hunter, P,** Housing, hostels and migrancy: a case study of accomodation practices at JCI's gold mines, *Labour, capital and society,* **25,** 1 (1992) 88–103
5330 **James, W,** Capital, African labour and housing at South Africa's gold mines, *Labour, capital and society,* **25,** 1 (1992) 72–86
5331 **Labourn-Peart, K,** Transforming mine housing in South Africa: the Anglo-Amalgamated home ownership scheme, *Labour, capital and society,* **25,** 1 (1992) 104–114
5332 **Patel, L,** *Restructuring social welfare: options for South Africa.* Johannesburg: Ravan, 1992, 178pp
5333 **Robbins, D,** Towards the golden West (sic), *Optima,* **39,** 2 (1993) 11–17
5334 **van den Berg, S,** Social reform and the reallocation of social expenditure, in Schrire, R (ed), *Wealth or poverty? (Item 4779),* 121–42

Urban studies

See also: 1148, 2064, 4730, 4863, 5–29, 5058, 5166, 5318

5335 **Adler, T,** Migrant labour, housing and trade unions in South Africa, *Urban forum,* **3,** 1 (1992) 1–11
5336 **Bolnick, J,** The People's

Dialogue on Land and Shelter: community driven networking in South African informal settlements, *Environment and urbanisation,* **5,** 1 (1993) 91–110

5337 **Bond, P,** Re-using the spaces of confinement: from urban apartheid to post-apartheid without postmodernism, *Urban forum,* **3,** 1 (1992) 39–55

5338 **Bond, P, Swilling, M,** World Bank financing for urban development: issues and options for South Africa, *Urban forum,* **3,** 2 (1992) 1–38

5339 **Cosser, E** (ed), *Homes for all: the challenge of homelessness.* Marshalltown: Christian Research, Education and Information for Democracy, (1990), 119pp

5340 **Crankshaw, O,** Squatting, apartheid and urbanisation on the southern Witwatersrand, *African affairs,* **92,** 366 (1993) 31–51

5341 **Crush, J,** The compound in post-apartheid South Africa, *Geographical review,* **82,** 4 (1992) 388–400

5342 **de Beer, F,** Housing policy in South Africa: a view from below, *Africa insight,* **23,** 2 (1993) 112–120

5343 **Hendler, P,** Living in apartheid's shadow: residential planning for Africans in the PWV region 1970–1980, *Urban forum,* **3,** 2 (1992) 39–80

5344 **Lamont, T M** (ed), *Housing in the new South Africa: National Housing Workshop, Bloemfontein, 1990.* Randbrug: Institute for Housing of Southern Africa, n.d., var pp

5345 **Levin, M,** Urban planning and employment creation, *Africa insight,* **23,** 4 (1993) 232–37

5346 **Lucas, G H G,** *Urbanisation of the RSA's population, 1985.* Pretoria: University of South Africa, Bureau of Market Research, 1990, 154pp

5347 **Lupton, M,** Collective consumption and urban segregation in South Africa: the case of two Coloured suburbs in the Johannesburg region, *Antipode,* **25,** 1 (1993) 32–50

5348 **Nathan, C D, Spindler, Z A,** Squatting as rent seeking and pressure-group competition: a South African case study, *Urban studies,* **30,** 3 (1993) 477–94

5349 **Ownhouse, S J, Nel, E L,** The 'greying' of Central: a case-study of racial residential desegregation in Port Elizabeth, *Urban forum,* **4,** 1 (1993) 81–92

5350 **Redding, S,** South African Blacks in a small town setting: the ironies of control in Umtata, 1878–1955, *Canadian journal of African studies,* **26,** 1 (1992) 70–90

5351 **Rogerson, C M,** Urban agriculture in South Africa: policy issues from the international experience, *Development southern Africa,* **10,** 1 (1993) 33–44

5352 **Rule, S P,** Propinquitous social diversity in Diepkloof, Soweto, *South African journal of sociology,* **24,** 1 (1993) 9–13

5353 **Saayman, G, et al,** *Urbanisation research in South Africa: priorities for the 1990s.* Pretoria: HSRC, 1991, 40pp

5354 **Seekings, J,** *South Africa's townships 1980–1991: an annotated bibliography.* Stellenbosch: Stellenbosch University, Research Unit for Sociology of Development, 1992, 236pp

5355 **Seekings, J, et al,** *Survey of residential and migration histories of residents of the shack areas of Khayelitsha.* Stellenbosch: Stellenbosch University, Research Unit for Sociology of Development, 1990, 66pp

5356 **Simkins, C, et al,** Designing a market-driven state-aided housing programme for South Africa: an application of the Urban Foundation's Housing Affordability Model, *Urban forum,* **3,** 1 (1992) 13–38

5357 **Swilling, M, Vawda, A,** Enabling institutions for development during the transition in South Africa, *Urban forum,* **3,** 1 (1992) 86–91

5358 **Tomlinson, R,** Competing urban agendas in South Africa, *Urban forum,* **3,** 1 (1992) 92–105

5359 **van Heerden, J H P,** Die behuisingsprobleem in Suid-Afrika: wettige plakkery is die enigste finansieël haalbare oplossing, *South African journal of sociology,* **24,** 2 (1993) 46–51

5360 **Wilson, G D H, Hattingh, P S,** Environmental preferences for recreation within deprived areas: the case of Black townships in South Africa, *Geoforum,* **23,** 4 (1992) 477–86

SWAZILAND

General

5361 **de Coqueréaumont-Gruget, A,** *Le royaume de Swaziland: un état dans l'Afrique du Sud.* Paris: Harmattan, 1992, 286pp

Agriculture, scientific

5362 **Osunade, M A A,** Land resource appraisal by small farmers of Swaziland, *UNISWA research journal,* **6,** 1 (1992) 93–104

5363 **Osunade, M A A,** Soils and the small farmers of Swaziland, *UNISWA research journal,* **6,** 1 (1992) 71–82

Anthropology

See also: 5374

5364 **Andermann, L,** 'To render visible': making sense among the Ndembu, in Howes, D (ed), *The varieties of sensory experience* (Toronto: University of Toronto Press, 1991), 203–209

5365 **Evans, J,** 'Where can we get a beast without hair?': medicine murders in Swaziland from 1970 to 1988, *African studies,* **52,** 1 (1993) 27–42

5366 **Russell, M,** Are households universal? On misunderstanding of domestic groups in Swaziland, *Development and change,* **24,** 4 (1993) 755–85

Economy - Development

5367 **Harris, B J,** *The political economy of the southern African periphery: cottage industries, factories and female wage labour in Swaziland compared.* Basingstoke: Macmillan, 1993, 296pp

Education

5368 **Rwomire, A,** Education and development in Swaziland: aims, strategies and challenges, in Siddiqui, R A (ed), *Subsaharan Africa (item 15)*, 149–66

Environment

5369 **Hackel, J D,** Rural change and nature conservation in Africa: a case study from Swaziland, *Human ecology,* **21,** 3 (1993) 295–312

5370 **Mushala, H M,** Legislation and soil conservation in Swaziland, *UNISWA research journal,* **6,** 1 (1992) 10–114

Gender

No entry. *See also:* 5367, 5395

History, C19th

5371 **Jones, H,** *Biographical register of*

Swaziland to 1902. Pietermaritzburg: University of Natal Press, 1993, 727pp

History, C20th

5372 **Simelane, H S,** Labour mobilisation for the war effort in Swaziland, 1940–1942, *International journal of African historical studies,* **26,** 3 (1993) 541–74

International relations

5373 **Bischoff, P H,** *Swaziland's international relations and foreign policy.* Bern: Lang, 1990, 555pp

Labour & manpower

No entry. *See also:* 5383

Law

5374 **Nhlapo, T,** *Marriage and divorce in Swazi law and custom.* Mbabane: Websters, 1992, 113pp

Media

No entry. *See also:* 5380

Medical

5375 **Lovell,** D M, et al, Bereavement reactions of female Scots and Swazis: a preliminary comparison, *British journal of medical psychology,* **66,** Sept. (1993) 259–74

Politics

5376 **Baloro, J,** The human right to free association and assembly and multiparty democracy: a study of the law and practice in Swaziland, *Africa insight,* **22,** 3 (1992) 206–11

5377 **Radipati, B D D,** Swaziland today: law and politics under King Mswati III, *Année africaine 1992/93,* 243–67

Rural economy

See also: 5384

5378 **Bowen, P N,** *A longing for land: tradition and change in rural Swaziland.* Aldershot: Avebury, 1993, 248pp

5379 **Dlamini, M P,** Managing rural development: the case of the Rural Development Areas Programme (RDAP) in Swaziland, *African administrative studies,* 39 (1992) 79–97

5380 **Nwosu, P O, Megwa, E,** Communications and rural development in Swaziland, *Africa media review,* **7,** 1 (1993) 1–17

5381 **Shields, M L, et al,** A londitudinal analysis of factors influencing increased technology adoption in Swaziland 1985–1991, *Journal of developing areas,* **27,** 4 (1993) 469–84

Sociology

See also: 5378

5382 **Gule, G,** Socio-cultural constraints to family planning in Swaziland, *Africa insight,* **23,** 4 (1993) 240–45

5383 **Leliveld, A,** *The impact of migrant labour on the Swazi homestead as a solidarity group.* Amsterdam: Free University, Faculty of Economics, 1992, 37pp

5384 **Simelane, H S,** The post-colonial state, class and the land question in Swaziland, *Journal of contemporary African studies,* **11,** 1 (1992) 22–50

ZIMBABWE

General

5385 **Baynham, S (ed),** *Zimbabwe in transition.* Stockholm: Almqvist & Wiksell, for Africa Institute (Pretoria), 1992, 280pp

5386 **Potts, D,** *Zimbabwe.* Oxford: Clio (rev. ed'n), 1993, 402pp

Agriculture, scientific

5387 **Hawkes, R K,** *Thatching grass: sources, adequacy and potential for local management in the Bulalimamangwe NRMP area.* Harare: CASS, University of Zimbabwe, 1992, 17pp

5388 **Katerere, M, Giga, D,** *Grain storage losses in Zimbabwe.* Dakar: ENDA, 1990, 97pp

Anthropology

See also: 5457

5389 **Jacobson-Widding, A,** Individual identity in African story telling, *Nordic journal of African studies,* **2,** 1 (1993) 5–33

5390 **Meekers, D,** The noble custom of *roora*; the marriage practices of the Shona of Zimbabwe, *Ethnology,* **32,** 1 (1993) 35–54

5391 **Parfitt, T,** *Journey to the vanished city: the search for a lost tribe of Israel.* London: Hodder & Staughton, 1992, 278pp

Arts

5392 **Axelsson, O,** Christian poetry and music drama: Black cultural expression in Zimbabwe, in Granqvist, R (ed), *Culture in Africa (item 10),* 15–44

5393 **Gecau, K, et al,** *Community based theatre in Zimbabwe.* Harare: Zimbabwe Foundation for Eduction with Production, 1991, 58pp

5394 **Jones, C,** *Making music: musical instruments of Zimbabwe past and present.* Harare: Academic Books, 1992, 183pp

Demography

5396 **Tumwine, J K, MacKenzie, S,** Child survival in a rural area in Zimbabwe, are we winning?, *Central African journal of medicine,* **38,** 1 (1992) 30–36

5397 **Zanamwe, L,** Age and sex characteristics of the population of Zimbabwe, an analysis based on the 1982 census, *Geographical journal of Zimbabwe,* 22 (1991) 15–32

Economic and social history

See also: 5442

5398 **Bessant, L, Muringai, E,** Peasants, businessmen, and moral economy in the Chiwesha Reserve, colonial Zimbabwe, 1930–1968, *Journal of southern African studies,* **19,** 3 (1993) 551–92

5399 **Bond, P,** Economic origins of Black townships in Zimbabwe: contradictions of industrial and financial capital in the 1950s and 1960s, *Economic geography,* **69,** 1 (1993) 72–89

5400 **Döpcke, W,** *Das koloniale Zimbabwe in der Krise: eine Wirtschafts- unnd Sozialgeschichte 1929–1939.* Hamburg: Lit, 1992, 449pp

5401 **Lander, R P,** The British South Africa Company: an essay on its commercial history, *Heritage of Zimbabwe,* 11 (1992) 1–40

5402 **Phimister, I,** Rethinking the reserves: Southern Rhodesia's Land Husbandry Act reviewed, *Journal of southern African studies,* **19,** 2 (1993) 225–39

5403 **West, M O,** Panafricanism, capitalism and racial uplift: the rhetoric of African business formation in colonial Zimbabwe, *African affairs,* **92,** 367 (1993) 263–83

Economy - Development

See also: 196, 18050, 2152, 4784, 5491

5404 **Balleis, P,** *ESAP and theology.* Gweru: Mambo, 1992, 40pp

5405 **Balleis, P,** *A critical guide to ESAP.* Gweru: Mambo, 1993, 64pp

5406 **Bond, P,** *The rise and fall of the Rhodesian economy.* Johannesburg: African Studies Institute, Witswatersrand University, 1993, 30pp

5407 **Hawkins, T,** Light at the end of Africa's tunnel, *Optima,* **38,** 1 (1992) 25–29

5408 **Kadenge, P G, et al,** *Zimbabwe's structural adjustment programme: the first year experience.* Harare: Sapes books, 1992, 27pp

5409 **Macgarry, B,** *Growth? Without equity?* Gweru: Mambo, 1992, 36pp

5410 **Mwanza, A,** Zimbabwe's economic liberalisation programme: justification and expected impact, *Southern Africa political and economic monthly,* **4,** 6 (1991) 25–29

5411 **Rushmere, M,** Zimbabwe returns to reality, *Executive,* Nov. 1992, 23–38

Education

See also: 213, 5462, 5518

5412 **Bennell, P W,** The cost effectiveness of alternative training modes: engineering artisans in Zimbabwe, *Comparative education review,* **37,** 4 (1993) 434–53

5413 **Bennell, P, Malaba, J,** Updating of rates of return to education: Zimbabwe in the late 1980s, *International journal of educational development,* **13,** 3 (1993) 277–87

5414 **Bennell, P, Ncube, M,** Education and training outcomes: university graduates in Zimbabwe during the 1980s, *Zimbabwe journal of educational research,* **5,** 2 (1993) 107–23

5415 **Bhunhu, N D,** Primary school agriculture education in Zimbabwe, in Mades, G G (ed), *Primary school agriculture (item 222),* 117–28

5416 **Chivore, B R S,** *Contributions of the teacher towards development in Zimbabwe.* Harare: Books for Africa, 1992, 74pp

5417 **Colclough, C, et al,** *Education in Zimbabwe: issues of quantity and quality.* Uppsala: Scandinavian Institute of African Studies, 1990, 166pp

5418 **Dehne, K L, Hubley, J,** Health education services in developing countries: the case of Zimbabwe, *Health education research,* **8,** 4 (1993) 525–36

5419 **Edwards, G, Tisdell, C,** The internal efficiency of the primary and secondary education systems in Zimbabwe, *Eastern African economic review,* **8,** 1 (1992) 12–25

5420 **Jambwa, P,** An investigation into the nature and extent of agriculture productive activities in primary schools in Harare Region, Zimbabwe, in Mades, G G (ed), *Primary school agriculture (item 222),* 9–15

5421 **Mungazi, D A,** *The fall of the mantle: the educational policy of the Rhodesian Front government and conflict in Zimbabwe.* New York: Lang, 1993, 260pp

5422 **Nyagura, L M,** Quantitative developments, quality and equity concerns in Zimbabwean primary and secondary education sectors,

Zimbabwe journal of educational research, **5,** 1 (1993) 21–40

5423 **Pattman, R, Shumba, T,** Schooling and the drought in Zimbabwe: the views and reactions of primary school senior teachers, *Zimbabwe journal of educational research,* **5,** 2 (1993) 190–205

5424 **Shumba, O,** Attitudes toward science: an exploratory survey of pupils presenting for national examinations, *Zimbabwe journal of educational research,* **5,** 1 (1993) 62–89

5425 **Shumba, O,** Nature of science (NOS) in science education: possibilities and constraints in a developing country, Zimbabwe, *Zimbabwe journal of educational research,* **5,** 2 (1993) 154–89

5426 **Zimbabwe Foundation for Education with Production,** *Schools in the struggle.* Harare: ZFEP, 1991, 88pp

Environment

See also: 5526, 5571

5427 **Bagg, W K,** River pollution in Harare, *Geographical education magazine,* **15,** 1 (1992) 7–15

5428 **Elwell, H A,** Soil degradation and management with particular reference to Zimbabwe, *Geographical education magazine,* **15,** 1 (1992) 16–23

5429 **Kavolo, S, Nehantz, G,** Soil and water conservation in Zimbabwe, in Hudson, N & Cheatle, R J (eds), *Working with farmers (Item 245)*, 41–45

5430 **Murombedzi, J C,** *Wetlands conservation under common property management regimes in Zimbabwe.* Harare: CASS, University of Zimbabwe, 1991, 20pp

5431 **Mvudulu, S,** Forestry commission links with NGOs in rural afforestation, in Wellard, K & Copestake, J C (eds), *NGOs and the state (Item 1096)*, 38–49

5432 **Nyamudeza, P, et al,** Farmer managment adoption of improved water management on vertisols in semi-arid southeastern Zimbabwe, in Hudson, N & Cheatle, R J (eds), *Working with farmers (Item 245)*, 197–202

5433 **Whitlow, R,** Gullying within wetlands in Zimbabwe: an examination of conservation history and spatial patterns, *South African geographical journal,* **74,** 2 (1992) 54–62

Food

See also: 5423, 5476, 5569, 5585

5434 **Amin, N,** *Peasant differentiation and food security in Zimbabwe.* New York: Social Science Research Council, Project on African Agriculture, 1990 (?), 34pp

5435 **Ascough, W J,** Action programmes and the future of food production: Zimbabwe, a case study, in Chole, E (ed), *Food crisis (Item 275)*, 245–52

5436 **Benhura, M A N, Chitsikum I C,** Food consumption patterns of the people of Dangamvura in Mutare, *Central African journal of medicine,* **37,** 11 (1991) 346–52

5437 **Benhura, M A N, Chitsikum I C,** Seasonal variations in the food consumption patterns of the people of Dangamvura in Mutare, *Central African journal of medicine,* **38,** 1 (1992) 8–13

5438 **Breslin, N,** *USAID, the state, and food insecurity in rural Zimbabwe: the case of Gokwe.* Johannesburg: African Studies Institute, Witswatersrand University, 1993, 31pp

5439 **Christensen, G, Thomas, D,** *Policy analysis for household food insecurity: case study, rural Zimbabwe.* Oxford: International Development Centre, 1993, 19pp

5440 **Lowenson, R,** Health in large-scale farming areas of Zimbabwe: a response, *Health policy and planning,* **7,** 2 (1992) 186–90

5441 **Nyoni, S,** The effects of and response to the 1992 drought in Zimbabwe, in Rimmer, D (ed), *Action in Africa (Item 525)*, 161–64

5442 **Page, S L J, Page, H E,** *Western hegemony over African agriculture in Southern Rhodesia and its continuing threat to food security in independent Zimbabwe.* New York: Social Science Research Council, Project on African Agriculture, 1992, 19pp

5443 **Thomas, D,** Testing for sectoral differences in child anthropometric status in Zimbabwe: a comment, *Health policy and planning,* **7,** 2 (1992) 181–85

Gender

See also: 5461, 5468, 5508, 5562, 5592

5444 **Brand, V, et al,** Women informal sector workers and structural adjustment in Zimbabwe, in Gibbon, P (ed), *Social change and economic reform (item 1880)*, 270–306

5445 **Fortmann, L, Nabane, N,** *The fruits of their labours: gender, property and trees in Mhondoro District.* Harare: CASS, University of Zimbabwe, 1992, 52pp

5446 **Hellum, A,** Gender and legal change in Zimbabwe: childless women and divorce from a socio-cultural and historical perspective, in Adelman, S & Paliwala, A (eds), *Law and crisis in the Third World* (London: Zell, 1993), 243–69

5447 **Jacobs, S,** Gender and land reform: Zimbabwe and some comparisons, *International sociology,* **7,** 1 (1992) 5–34

5448 **Kanji, N, Jazdowska, N,** Structural adjustment and the implications for low-income urban women in Zimbabwe, *Review of African political economy,* 56 (1993) 11–26

5449 **Loewenson, R,** Harvests of disease: women at work on Zimbabwean plantations, in Turshen, M (ed), *Women and health (Item 343)*, 35–50

5450 **Mahomed, K, Chawapiwa, A,** Socio-demographic characteristics of women presenting with abortion, a hospital based study, *Central African journal of medicine,* **38,** 6 (1992) 233–37

5451 **Stewart, S,** Working the system: sensitizing the police to the plight of women in Zimbabwe, in Schuler, M (ed), *Freedom from violence: women's strategies from around the world* (New York: UN Development Fund for Women, 1992), 157–71

5452 **Taylor, J, Stewart, S,** *Sexual and domestic violence: help, recovery and action in Zimbabwe.* Harare: Women and Law in Southern Africa Trust, 1992, 312pp

5453 **Zimbabwe Foundation for Education with Production,** *Ndangarira: Zimbabwean women in the liberation struggle.* Harare: ZFEP, 1991, 88pp

Geography, human

See also: 5458

5454 **Kimberley, M J,** Swynnerton of Gungunyana, a pioneer Zimbabwean natural historian, *Heritage of Zimbabwe,* 9 (1990) 47–61

Geography, physical

5455 **Nyamapfene, K, A** geographical overview of the soils of Zimbabwe and their agricultural potential, *Geographical education magazine,* **15,** 1 (1992) 63–73

5456 Williams, H, The drought, the facts and the future, *Zimbabwe science news,* **26,** 1/3 (1992) 15–18

Health & welfare services

See also: 5418, 5449

5457 Cavender, A P, Traditional medicine and an inclusive model of health seeking behaviour in Zimbabwe, *Central African journal of medicine,* **37,** 11 (1991) 362–69

5458 Chimhowu, A O, Tevera, D S, Intraprovincial inequalities in the provision of health care in the Midlands Province of Zimbabwe, *Geographical journal of Zimbabwe,* 22 (1991) 33–45

5459 Chinemana, F, Sanders, D, Health and structural adjustment in Zimbabwe, in Gibbon, P (ed), *Social change and economic reform (item 1880)*, 307–59

5460 Hecht, R, et al, Improving the implementation of cost recovery for health: lessons from Zimbabwe, *Health policy,* **25,** 3 (1993) 213–42

5461 Mbizvo, M T, et al, Maternal mortality in rural and urban Zimbabwe: social and reproductive factors in an incident case-referent study, *Social science and medicine,* **36,** 9 (1993) 1197–1205

5462 Mubvami, T, Olthof, W, Planning and maintenance of social services: health and education in Mhondoro, *Review of rural and urban planning in southern and eastern Africa,* 1 (1992) 49–92

5463 Pitts, M, Jackson, H, No joking matter: formal and informal sources of information about AIDS in Zimbabwe, *AIDS education and prevention,* **5,** 3 (1993) 212–219

5464 Renfrew, A, *ESAP and health.* Gweru: Mambo, 1992, 32pp

5465 Verkuyl, D A A, Family planning in Zimbabwe in the nineties, *Central African journal of medicine,* **37,** 10 (1991) 308–316

History, C18th

5466 Collett, D P, et al, The chronology of the Valley Enclosures: implications for the interpretation of Great Zimbabwe, *African archaeological review,* **10,** (1992) 139–61

History, C20th

See also: 5487, 5589

5467 Burrett, R, The Eyre brothers, Arthur and Herbert, *Heritage of Zimbabwe,* 9 (1990) 37–46

5468 Jeater, D, *Marriage, perversion and power: the construction of moral discourse in Southern Rhodesia, 1894–1930.* Oxford: Clarendon, 1993, 281pp

5469 Rowland, J R, The law reports as history: Southern Rhodesian Law Reports 1899–1920, *Legal forum,* **4,** 2 (1992) 46–54

5470 West, M O, Equal rights for all civilised men: elite Africans and the quest for European liquor in colonial Zimbabwe, 1924–1961, *International review of social history,* **37,** 3 (1993) 376–97

Industry & trade

See also: 5444, 5484, 5588

5471 Bennell, P, Market power and mark-ups: manufacturing industry in Zimbabwe, *Eastern African economic review,* **8,** 2 (1992) 135–41

5472 Chachage, C S L, et al, *Mining and structural adjustment: studies on Zimbabwe and Tanzania.* Uppsala: Scandinavian Institute of African Studies, 1993, 107pp

5473 Chimanikire, D, The introduction of liberalisation in Zimbabwe, *Southern Africa political*

& economic monthly, **4,** 7 (1991) 12–17

5474 **Durevall, D,** Trade liberalisation: the Zimbabwe way, in Blomström, M & Lundahl, M (eds), *Economic crisis (Item 119)*, 101–117

5475 **Jayne, T S,** Maize market reform in Zimbabwe, *Food policy,* **18,** 4 (1993) 308–315

5476 **Jayne, T S, Rubey, L,** Maize milling, market reform and urban food security: the case of Zimbabwe, *World development,* **21,** 6 (1993) 975–88

5477 **Kunaka, C,** The railways and the Zimbabwe coal crisis of the late 1980s, *Geographical journal of Zimbabwe,* 22 (1991) 1–14

5478 **Mupindi, S, Masuku, L,** *Price control as a means of consumer protection in Zimbabwe: a review of the price formation system.* Harare: ZIDS, 1991, 35pp

5479 **Pedersen, P O,** *Clothing rural Zimbabwe: sectoral strategies and local development.* Copenhagen: Centre for Development Research, 1993, 24pp

5480 **Posthuma, A C,** Organisational innovation in Zimbabwe: the viability of sustainable change, *IDS bulletin,* **24,** 2 (1993) 10–18

5481 **Takavarasha, T,** Trade, price and market reform in Zimbabwe: current status and constraints, *Food policy,* **18,** 4 (1993) 286–93

5482 **Turton, B J,** The role of the road motor services in the rural road transport sector in Zimbabwe, *Geographical journal of Zimbabwe,* 22 (1991) 46–61

5483 **Whiteside, A,** The impact of AIDS on industry in Zimbabwe, in Cross, S & Whiteside, A (eds), *Facing up to AIDS (item 4753)*, 217–40

International economic relations

See also: 4322

5484 **Kaliyati, J W G,** *The iron and steel industry in Zimbabwe and regional cooperation in the SADCC context.* Harare: Zimbabwe IDS, 1991, 42pp

International relations

See also: 4452

5485 **Klotz, A,** Race and nationalism in Zimbabwe's foreign policy, *Round table,* **82,** 327 (1993) 255–80

5486 **Nkiwane, S N,** Development of Zimbabwe's foreign relations 1980–1990, *Round table,* **82,** 326 (1993) 199–216

5487 **Reed, W C,** International politics and national liberation: ZANU and the politics of contested sovereignity in Zimbabwe, *African studies review,* **36,** 2 (1993) 31–59

Labour & manpower

5488 **Fulton, P R, Lucas, R E B,** Job security regulations and the dynamic demand for industrial labour in India and Zimbabwe, *Journal of development economics,* **40,** (1993) 241–75

5489 **Pape, J,** Still serving the tea: domestic workers in Zimbabwe, 1980–1990, *Journal of southern African studies,* **19,** 3 (1993) 387–406

5490 **Sachikonye, L,** The labour regime under SAP in Zimbabwe, *Southern Africa political and economic monthly,* **5,** 7 (1992) 41–44

5491 **Sachikonye, L M,** Structural adjustment, state and organised labour in Zimbabwe, in Gibbon, P (ed), *Social change and economic reform (item 1880)*, 244–69

5492 **Zimunya, V** (ed), *Skilled manpower needs of NGOs in*

Zimbabwe. Harare: University of Zimbabwe, School of Social Work, 1992, 27pp

Language

5493 **Pongweni, A J C,** The orature of a culture in transition: subversion and legitimation, *Journal of Asian and African studies (Tokyo),* 43 (1992) 149–168

Law

See also: 4322, 5542

5494 **Catholic Commission for Justice and Peace,** Country report on Zimbabwe (presented at the Commonwealth Africa Human Rights Conference, Harare, 11–14 October 1991), *Legal forum,* **4,** 1 (1992) 34–39

5495 **Coltart, D,** The Legal Resources Foundation, Zimbabwe, in Sandbrook, R & Halfani, M (eds), *Empowering people (Item 930),* 45–51

5496 **Hatchard, J,** The constitution of Zimbabwe: towards a model for Africa?, *Journal of African law,* **35,** 1/2 (1991) 79–101

5497 **Hatchard, J,** The rise and fall of the cane in Zimbabwe, *Journal of African law,* **35,** 1/2 (1991) 198–204

5498 **Kaseke, E,** Juvenile justice in Zimbabwe: the need for reform, *Journal of social development in Africa,* **8,** 1 (1993) 11–17

5499 **Mhlaba, L,** Whither parliamentary democracy: a look at recent constitutional changes in Zimbabwe, *Zimbabwe law review,* 7/8 (1989/90) 1–8

5500 **Naldi, G J,** Land reform in Zimbabwe: some legal aspects, *Journal of modern African studies,* **31,** 4 (1993) 585–600

Literature

See also: 5389

5501 **Abrahams, B, Humphrey, L,** *Study guide to* Harvest of thorns. Harare: Baobab, 1992, 108pp

5502 **Kahari, G P,** *The rise of the Shona novel: a study in development.* Gweru: Mambo, 1990, 407pp

5503 **Viet-Wild, F,** The elusive truth: literary development in Zimbabwe since 1980, *Matatu,* 10 (1993) 107–20

5504 **Viet-Wild, F,** 'Dances with bones': Hove's romanticized Africa, *Research in African literatures,* **24,** 3 (1993) 5–12

5505 **Viet-Wild, F,** *Survey of Zimbabwean writers: educational and literary careers.* Bayreuth: Bayreuth University, 1992, 172pp

Media

5506 **Arntsen, H, Lundby, K,** The 'electronic church' in a Zimbabwean communication environment, in Granqvist, R (ed), *Culture in Africa (item 10),* 45–67

5507 **Bond-Stewart, K,** The community publishing process in Zimbabwe, *African book publishing record,* **19,** 2 (1993) 93–96

5508 **George, N,** Using radio for community mobilisation: experiences in Zimbabwe and Kenya, *Africa media review,* **7,** 2 (1993) 52–68

5509 **Mbanga, E** (ed), *Press freedom in Zimbabwe.* Harare: Willie Musarurwa Trust, 1993, 98pp

5510 **Mbanga, T, Ling, M,** An aspiring Frankfurt emerges in Africa, *Logos,* **4,** 4 (1993) 209–214

5511 **Pitts, M, Jackson, H,** Press coverage of AIDS in Zimbabwe: a five year review, *AIDS care,* **5,** 2 (1993) 223–30

5512 **Denhe, H, et al,** Pattern of HIV infection in Hurungwe

District, Mashonaland West, Zimbabwe, *Central African journal of medicine,* **38,** 4 (1992) 139–43

5513 **Hore, R,** The medical costs of AIDS in Zimbabwe, in Cross, S & Whiteside, A (eds), *Facing up to AIDS (item 4753)*, 241–60

5514 **Jackson, H,** *AIDS: action now. Information, prevention and support in Zimbabwe.* Harare: AIDS Counselling Trust, 1992, 334pp

5515 **Kasule, J, et al,** Evaluation of a combined oral contraceptive pill in black Zimbabwean women, *Central African journal of medicine,* **37,** 12 (1991) 403–409

5516 **Mahomed, K, et al,** Seroprevalence of HIV infection amongst antenatal women in greater Harare, Zimbabwe, *Central African journal of medicine,* **37,** 10 (1991) 322–325

5517 **Moy, R J D, et al,** Early growth faltering in rural Zimbabwean children, *Central African journal of medicine,* **37,** 9 (1991) 275–282

5518 **Munodawafa, D,** Attitudes of teachers towards implementing AIDS prevention education programmes in secondary schools of Zimbawe, *Central African journal of medicine,* **37,** 12 (1991) 390–93

5519 **Nyachuru-Sihlangu, R H, Ndlovu, J,** Factual knowledge about AIDS and dating practices among high school students from selected schools, *Central African journal of medicine,* **38,** 6 (1992) 225–33

5520 **Reeler, A P,** Pathways to pyschiatric care in Harare, Zimbabwe, *Central African journal of medicine,* **38,** 1 (1992) 1–7

5521 **Zimunya, V** (ed), *AIDS home care: a baseline survey in Zimbabwe.* Harare: University of Zimbabwe, School of Social Work, 1992, 48pp

Natural resources

5522 **Fortmann, L, Nabane, N,** *Poverty and tree resources in Mhondoro District.* Harare: CASS, University of Zimbabwe, 1992, 16pp

5523 **Fortmann, L, Nabane, N,** *The use of indigenous trees in Mhondoro District.* Harare: CASS, University of Zimbabwe, 1992, 114pp

5524 **Fortman, L, Nihra, C,** *Local management of trees and woodland resources in Zimbabwe: a terminal risks approach.* Oxford: Forestry Institute, 1992, 47pp

5525 **Hasler, R P,** *Political and socioeconomic dynamics of natural resource management: the Communal Areas Management Programme for Indigenous Resources (CAMPFIRE) in Chapoto Ward 1989–1990.* Harare: CASS, University of Zimbabwe, 1992, 16pp

5526 **Marshall, B E,** The influence of man on the physical environments of the Zambezi River, *Geographical education magazine,* **15,** 2 (1992) 53–59

5527 **Matowanyika, J Z Z,** Energy planning and national development in Zimbabwe, *Canadian journal of African studies,* **26,** 1 (1992) 132–37 (review article)

5528 **Murombedzi, J C,** *Communal land tenure and common property resource management: an evaluation of the potential for sustainable common property resource management in Zimbawe's communal areas.* Harare: CASS, University of Zimbabwe, 1990, 29pp

5529 **Murombedzi, J C,** *Decentralising common property resources management: a case study of the Nyaminyami District Council of Zimbawe's wildlife management programme.* Harare: CASS, University of Zimbabwe, 1991, 26pp

5530 **Murombedzi, J C,** *Decentralisation or recentralisation? Implementing CAMPFIRE in the the Omay communal lands of Nyaminyami District.* Harare: CASS, University of Zimbabwe, 1992, 84pp

5531 **Murombedzi, J C,** *Need for appropopriate local level common property resource management institutions in communal tenure regimes.* Harare: CASS, University of Zimbabwe, 1990, 14pp

5532 **Murphree, M W,** *Decentralising the proprietorship of wildlife resources in Zimbabwe's communal lands: an outline of central issues.* Harare: CASS, University of Zimbabwe, 1990, 25pp

5533 **Murphree, M W,** *Wildlife management in Kanyati and Gatshe: institutional issues and guidelines.* Harare: CASS, University of Zimbabwe, 1992, 118pp

5534 **Nhira, C, Fortmann, L P,** *Local control and management of forest and environmental resources in Zimbabwe: institutional capacity.* Harare: CASS, University of Zimbabwe, 1991, 88pp

Planning

5535 **Mbiba, B,** Urban and regional planning informatics in the context of Zimbabwe: caution to the protagonists, *Review of rural and urban planning in southern and eastern Africa,* 1 (1992) 109–116

Politics

See also: 2152, 5453, 5494

5536 **Agere, S,** The promotion of good ethical standards and behaviour in public services in Africa: the case for Zimbabwe, *Africanus,* **22,** 1/2 (1992) 39–52

5537 **Agere, S T,** The size of the public service in Zimbabwe: implications for development, *African management development forum,* **2,** 1 (1991) 24–27

5538 **Auret, D,** *Reaching for justice: the Catholic Commission for Justice and Peace looks back at the past twenty years 1972–1992.* Gweru: Mambo, 1992, 277pp

5539 **Couzens, T** (ed), *Zimbabwe: the search for common ground since 1890: from the pages of DRUM magazine.* Lanseria: Bailey's African Photo Archives, 1992, 323pp

5540 **Darbon, D,** Zimbabwe: construire la maison en pierre, in Médard, J F (ed), *Etats d'Afrique noire (Item 896),* 305–22

5541 **Gustafsson, L, et al,** *Central authority blocks local autonomy: an evaluation of SIDA support to local government development in Zimbabwe 1983–1989.* Stockholm: SIDA, 1990, 65pp

5542 **Hatchard, J,** *Individual freedoms and state security in the African context: the case of Zimbabwe.* London: Currey, 1993, 209pp

5543 **Johnson, V D,** The structural causes of anticolonial revolution in Africa, *Alternatives,* **18,** 2 (1993) 201–27

5544 **Kriger, N,** Review essay: Zimbabwe - common terrain, *African studies review,* **36,** 3 (1993) 95–108

5545 **Kriger, N, Saunders, R,** Through a glass faintly, *Southern African review of books,* **5,** 2 (1993) 20–22

5546 **Mandaza, I, Prendergast, K,** Reflections on the period since the Lancaster House Agreement (interview), *Southern Africa political and economic monthly,* **5,** 7 (1992) 14–19

5547 **Maxwell, D J,** Local politics and the war of liberation in northeast Zimbabwe, *Journal of southern African studies,* **19,** 3 (1993) 361–86

5548 **Sithole, M,** Is Zimbabwe poised on a liberal path?: the state and prospects of the parties, *Issue,* **21,** 1/2 (1993) 35–43

Religion, philosophy

See also: 1017, 5392, 5404, 5506

5549 **Ludwig, F,** Elijah II: radicalisation and consolidation of the Garrick Briade movement 1915–1918, *Journal of religion in Africa,* **23,** 4 (1993) 296–317

5550 **Ranger, T,** Thompson Samkange: Tambaram and beyond, *Journal of religion in Africa,* **23,** 4 (1993) 318–46

Rural economy

See also: 5415, 5445, 5447, 5500, 5522, 5544

5551 **Barrett, J C,** *The economic role of cattle in communal farming systems in Zimbabwe.* London: Overseas Development Institute, 1992, 37pp

5552 **Bratton, M,** Ten years after: land redistribution in Zimbabwe, 1980–1990, in Prostermann, R L, et al (eds), *Agrarian reform and grassroots development* (Boulder: Lynne Reinner, 1990), 265–91

5553 **Chaguma, A, Gumba, D,** ENDA-Zimbabwe and community research, in Wellard, K & Copestake, J C (eds), *NGOs and the state (Item 1096)*, 67–76

5554 **Christiansen, R E,** Implementing strategies for the rural economy: lessons from Zimbabwe, options for South Africa, *World development,* **21,** 9 (1993) 1549–66

5555 **Copestake, J C,** Zimbabwe: country overview, in Wellard, K & Copestake, J C (eds), *NGOs and the state (Item 1096)*, 15–25

5556 **Cousins, B, Jackson, C** (eds), *Socioeconomic dimensions of livestock production in the communal lands of Zimbabwe.* Harare: CASS, University of Zimbabwe, 1992, 38pp

5557 **Cousins, B, Weiner, D,** *Dynamics of social differentiation in the communal lands of Zimbabwe.* Harare: CASS, University of Zimbabwe, 1992, 44pp

5558 **Cutshall, C R,** *Angwa/Chisunga Ward: a socioeconomic baseline survey of community households.* Harare: CASS, University of Zimbabwe, 1991, 107pp

5559 **Cutshall, C R,** *Kanyemba/Chapoto Ward: a socioeconomic baseline survey of community households.* Harare: CASS, University of Zimbabwe, 1990, 71pp

5560 **Drinkwater, M,** Cows eat grass don't they? Evaluating conflict over pastoral management in Zimbabwe, in Croll, E & Parkin, D (eds), *Bush base: forest farm (Item 1040)*, 169–86

5561 **Feltoe, E,** The land question in Zimbabwe, *Southern Africa political and economic monthly,* **5,** 7 (1992) 9–12

5562 **Fortmann, L, Bruce, J,** *You've got to know who controls the land and trees people use!: gender, tenure and environment.* Harare: CASS, University of Zimbabwe, 1991, 14pp

5563 **Fortmann, L, Nabane, N,** *Creating common property management: government projects and land use policy in the mid-Zambezi Valley.* Harare: CASS, University of Zimbabwe, 1991, 21pp

5564 **Hawkes, R K, Madzudzo, E,** *Crop and livestock losses to wild animals in the Bulalimamangwe NRMP area.* Harare: CASS, University of Zimbabwe, 1992, 16pp

5565 **Jayne, T S, Rukuni, M,** Distributional effects of maize self-sufficiency in Zimbabwe: implications for pricing and trade policy, *Food policy,* **18,** 4 (1993) 334–41

5566 **Jiriyengwa, S J,** Grain market liberalisation and social goals: the Grain Marketing Board in Zimbabwe, *Food policy,* **18,** 4 (1993) 316–24

5567 **MacGarry, B,** Siveira House: promoting the use of hybrid seed (1968–1983), in Wellard, K & Copestake, J C (eds), *NGOs and the state (Item 1096)*, 50–66

5568 **Makamure, K,** The land debate in Zimbabwe, laying the parameters, *Southern Africa political and economic monthly,* **5,** 7 (1992) 3–9

5569 **Masters, W A, Nuppenan, E A,** Panterritorial versus regional policy for maize in Zimbabwe, *World development,* **21,** 10 (1993) 1647–58

5570 **Mhone, G,** Communal agriculture in atrophy, *Southern Africa political and economic monthly,* **5,** 12 (1992) 20–23

5571 **Moore, D S,** Contesting terrain in Zimbabwe's eastern highlands: political ecology, ethnography and peasant resource struggles, *Economic geography,* **69,** 4 (1993) 380–401

5572 **Mungate, D,** Government experience of collaboration with NGOs in agricultural research and extension, in Wellard, K & Copestake, J C (eds), *NGOs and the state (Item 1096)*, 26–37

5573 **Murphree, M W, Cumming, D H M,** *Savanna land use: policy and practice in Zimbabwe.* Harare: CASS, University of Zimbabwe, 1991, 33pp

5574 **Mushita, A,** Zimbabwean farmers as the starting point, in Cooper, D et al (ed), *Growing diversity: genetic resources and local food security* (London: Intermediate Technology Publications, 1992), 69–77

5575 **Ndiweni, M,** The Organisation of Rural Associations for Progress and grassroots development, in Wellard, K & Copestake, J C (eds), *NGOs and the state (Item 1096)*, 77–84

5576 **Nhira, C,** *Kanyati/Gatshe Gatshe Land Use Project, Vol. 2.* Harare: CASS, University of Zimbabwe, 1992, 60pp

5577 **ORAP,** Towards the empowerment of rural people: the case of ORAP in Zimbabwe, in Sandbrook, R & Halfani, M (eds), *Empowering people (Item 930)*, 132–39

5578 **Peterson, J H,** *CAMPFIRE: a Zimbawean approach to sustainable development and community empowerment through wildlife utilisation.* Harare: CASS, University of Zimbabwe, 1991, 148pp

5579 **Scoones, I,** Coping with drought: responses of herders and livestock in contrasting savanna environments in southern Zimbabwe, *Human ecology,* **20,** 3 (1992) 293–314

5580 **Syme, A** (ed), *Commercial agriculture in Zimbabwe, 1990–91.* Harare: Modern Farming Publications, 1991, 182pp

5581 **Thirtle, C, et al,** Agricultural productivity in Zimbabwe, 1970–90, *Economic journal,* **103,** 417 (1993) 474–80

5582 **Wiebert, M, et al,** *Discrimination against agriculture in developing countries?* Tubingen: Mohr, 1992, 221pp

Science & technology

See also: 5412, 5424, 5425

5583 **Fayez, M B E,** Zimbabwe, in Patel, S J (ed), *Technological transformation in the Third World. Vol. 2* (Aldershot: Avebury, 1993), 143–326

Sociology

See also: 5519

5584 Bourdillon, M F C, *Poor, harassed, but very much alive: an account of street people and their organisation.* Gweru: Mambo, 1991, 107pp

5585 Cosminsky, S, et al, Child feeding practices in a rural area of Zimbabwe, *Social science and medicine,* **36,** 7 (1993) 937–47

5586 Kaarsholm, P, Le développement de la culture et les contractions de la modernisation dans le Tiers Monde: le cas du Zimbabwe, in Rist, G (ed), *La culture, otage du développement?* (Paris, Harmattan, 1993), 119–47

5587 Lockhart, D G, et al, The quality of life in Zimbabwe, *Geographical education magazine,* **15,** 2 (1992) 46–52

5588 Mahomed, K, Masona, D, Adolescent pregnancy: a prospective survey of contraceptive knowledge and reproductive behaviour, *Central African journal of medicine,* **37,** 10 (1991) 316–321

5589 Mhloyi, M M, Perceptions on communication and sexuality in marriage in Zimbabwe, in Rothblum, E D & Cole, E (eds), *Women's mental health (item 338),* 61–73

5590 Muchini, B, Unaccompanied Mozambican children in Zimbabwe: the interface with street children, *Journal of social development in Africa,* **8,** 2 (1993) 49–60

5591 Piotrow, P T, et al, Changing men's attitudes and behaviour: the Zimbabwe male motivation project, *Studies in family planning,* **23,** 6 (1993) 365–75

5592 Runganga, A, et al, The use of herbal and other agents to enhance sexual experience, *Social science and medicine,* **35,** 8 (1992) 1037–42

Social welfare

5593 Higgins, C M, Mazula, A, Community development: a national strategy in Zimbabwe, *Community development journal,* **28,** 1 (1993) 19–30

Urban studies

See also: 5399, 5584

5594 Gervais-Lambony, P, Mutamenti fondiari e condizione cittadina ad Harare, *Storia urbana,* **17,** 63 (1993) 177–201

5595 Musandu-Nyamayaro, O, Municipal water development and management practice in Zimbabwe: some critical comments with special reference to the impact of drought on urban development, *Review of rural and urban planning in southern and eastern Africa,* 1 (1992) 21–47

5596 Nel, E L, Berry, B B, Bulawayo's water crisis: an update, *Development southern Africa,* **10,** 1 (1993) 79–83

5597 Zinyama, L M, et al (eds), *Harare: the growth and problems of a city.* Harare: University of Zimbabwe, 1993, 193pp

ISLANDS

CAPE VERDE

Economic and social history

No entry. *See also:* 2983

Economy - Development

5598 **Borowczak, W,** Entwicklungsprobleme Kap Verdes: zur Rolle von Funktionseliten und strategischen Gruppen für die Entwicklungsprozess, in Meyns, P (ed), *Demokratie und Strukturreformen (Item 1174)*, 259–72

5599 **Meyns, P,** Die Suche nach einer geo-ökonomischen Nische - Kap Verde swischen verwalteter Anhängigkeit und einer Politik der Weltmarktintegration, in Meyns, P (ed), *Demokratie und Strukturreformen (Item 1174)*, 237–58

Education

5600 **Marques da Silva, E,** Die entwicklungspolitische Stellenwert der Erziehungsreform in Kap Verde, in Meyns, P (ed), *Demokratie und Strukturreformen (Item 1174)*, 273–85

Environment

5601 **Haagsma, B, Reij, C,** *Frentes de trabalho*: potentials and limitations of large scale labour employment for soil and water conservation in Cape Verde, *Land degradation and rehabilitation,* **4,** 2 (1993) 73–85

History, general

5602 **Rocha, A,** *Subsidios para a historia da Ilha da Santo Antão.* Praia: Imprensa nacional, 1990, 131pp

History, C20th

5603 **da Graca, J L,** *Fragmentos de um puzzle politico.* Praia: Arranjo Grafico, 1993, 13pp

Literature

5604 **Moser, G M,** Changing Africa: the first literary generation of independent Cape Verde, *Transactions of the American Philosophical Society,* **82,** P4 (1992) 1–102

Natural resources

5605 **Crowley, E L,** Evora, G, *Decentralisation, democratisation, public service provision and governance and management of renewable natural resources in Cape Verde.* Burlington: Associates in Rural Development, 1992, 251pp

Politics

See also: 5631, 5632

5606 **Lima, A,** Grundzüge des politischen Reformprozesses in Kap Verde, in Meyns, P (ed), *Demokratie und Strukturreformen (Item 1174)*, 286–303

Urban studies

No entry. *See also:* 1148

COMORES & MAYOTTE

General

5607 **Gohin, O, Maurice, P (eds),** *Mayotte. Actes du Colloque universitaire tenu à Mamoudzo, les 23 et 24 avril 1991.* Mamoudzo: Université de la Réunion, Faculté de droit et des sciences économiques, 1992, 369pp

Anthropology

5608 **Allaouni, M C,** Le vêtement es ses fonctions dans la société traditionelle Comorienne, *Ya Mkobe,* 4 (1990) 59–65

5609 **Allibert, C,** Le *muguru*: rôle et origines, *Annuaire de l'Océan indien,* **12,** (1990/91) 211–20

5610 **Blanchy, S,** Famille et parenté dans l'archipel des Comores, *Journal des Africanistes,* **62,** 1 (1992) 7–53

5611 **Mahamoud, S,** Cinq enquêtes sur le vêtement aux Comores, *Ya Mkobe,* 4 (1990) 70–75

Economic and social history

5612 **Ainouddine, S,** L'affair du domaine Wilson, 1871–1921, *Ya Mkobe,* 4 (1990) 23–29

5613 **Hébert, J C,** Le problème des aborigènes de Mayotte: les Shi-Bushi, *Annuaire de l'Océan indien,* **12,** (1990/91) 61–84

Economy - Development

5614 **Rochoux, J Y,** L'économie mahoraise: une tentative de schématisation de développement, *Annuaire de l'Océan indien,* **12,** (1990/91) 221–33

Education

5615 **Bacar, F S,** Literacy work in the Comoro Islands, *Journal of the African Association for Literacy and Adult Education,* **6,** 1 (1992) 37–41

5616 **Eyrard, J P,** L'enseignement à Mayotte, *Annuaire de l'Océan indien,* **12,** (1990/91) 185–96

Environment

5617 **Coudray, J,** Le lagon de Mayotte et sa protection, *Annuaire de l'Océan indien,* **12,** (1990/91) 169–83

History, early

5618 **Allibert, C,** Peuplement et population de Mayotte à travers les ages, *Annuaire de l'Océan indien,* **12,** (1990/91) 49–60

History, C19th

5619 **Martin, J,** Mayotte avant 1841, *Annuaire de l'Océan indien,* **12,** (1990/91) 85–90

History, C20th

5620 **Ali, D B,** Approche historique des structures administratives des Comores, *Ya Mkobe,* 4 (1990) 14–22

5621 **Flori, J B,** L'organisation judiciare à Mayotte: aperçu historique, *Annuaire de l'Océan indien,* **12,** (1990/91) 303–14

5622 **Maestri, E,** Mayotte, Madagascar, la Réunion et la France depuis 1841, *Annuaire de l'Océan indien,* **12,** (1990/91) 91–114

5623 Marchetti, P, Mayotte devant le processus de la décolonisation, *Annuaire de l'Océan indien,* **12,** (1990/91) 355–466

International economic relations

5624 Maurice, P, Mayotte et la CEE, *Annuaire de l'Océan indien,* **12,** (1990/91) 247–63

5625 Pilandon, L, Les relations économiques extérieurs de Mayotte, *Annuaire de l'Océan indien,* **12,** (1990/91) 235–46

International relations

See also: 5633

5626 Gohin, O, Mayotte française: aspects internationaux, constitutionnels et militaires, *Annuaire de l'Océan indien,* **12,** (1990/91) 115–38

Labour & manpower

5627 Cheyssial, E D, La décennie du double jeu, *Jana na leo,* 25 (1991) 14–28

Law

See also: 5621

5628 Brossier, P, L'état civile à Mayotte, *Annuaire de l'Océan indien,* **12,** (1990/91) 327–53

5629 Cregut, P, Le Conseil des contentieux administratif de Mayotte, *Annuaire de l'Océan indien,* **12,** (1990/91) 279–91

Literature

5630 Allaouai, M C, Brève réflexion sur les genres de la littérature Comorienne, *Ya Mkobe,* 4 (1990) 38–49

Politics

5631 Chacourou, A, Le régime administratif et financier de Mayotte, *Annuaire de l'Océan indien,* **12,** (1990/91) 265–78

5632 Gille, B, Le contrôle financier de la collectivé territoriale de Mayotte, *Annuaire de l'Océan indien,* **12,** (1990/91) 293–301

5633 Miclo, F, Le statut de Mayotte dans la République Francaise, *Annuaire de l'Océan indien,* **12,** (1990/91) 139–46

5634 Vérin, P, Les Comores indépendantes sous Ahmed Abdallah, 1978–89, *Mondes et cultures,* **50,** 2–4 (1990) 217–33

MADAGASCAR

General

5635 Bradt, H, Brown, M, *Madagascar.* Oxford: Clio, 1993, 138pp

Anthropology

See also: 5648, 5650

5636 Andrianavalona, N, La tradition initiatique à Madagascar, *Revue Madagascar, océan Indien,* 6 (1991) 47–57

5637 Faublée, J, Note dur un clan du sudest à Madagascar, *Journal des Africanistes,* **62,** 2 (1992) 155–60

5638 Wilson, P J, *Freedom by a hair's breadth: Tsimihety in Madagascar.* Ann Arbor: University of Michigan Press, 1992, 179pp

Arts

5639 Haring, L, *Verbal arts in Madagascar: performance in historical perspective.* Philadelphia: University of Pennsylvania Press, 1992, 242pp

Economic and social history

See also: 1265

5640 **Jarosz, L,** Defining and explaining tropical deforestation: shifting cultivation and population growth in colonial Madagasacar (1896–1944), *Economic geography,* **69,** 4 (1993) 366–79

5641 **Koerner, F,** Statistiques des concessions domaniales accordées à Madagascar aux Français, Malgaches et étrangers asiatiques (1899–1960), *Revue française d'histoire d'Outre-Mer,* **79,** 297 (1992) 557–578

5642 **Prou, M,** *Malagasy: ingérence ou invasion de Madagascar, 1895. Tome II.* Paris: Harmattan, 1993, 421pp

Economy - Development

5643 **Brasseul, J, Ramiaramanana, J,** The limitations of adjustment policies: the case of Madagascar, *African environment,* **7,** 25–28 (1990) 135–51

Environment

See also: 5656

5644 **Brasseul, J,** Relations entre écologie et économie à Madagascar, *Revue Madagascar, océan Indien,* 6 (1991) 24–31

5645 **Bretaudeau, H,** Le plan d'action environnement, *Revue Madagascar, océan Indien,* 6 (1991) 12–23

5646 **Schmid, S,** Sauvegards des forêts naturelles et développement rural à Madagascar: un premier bilan des actions en cours, *Cahiers d'outre-mer,* **46,** 181 (1993) 35–60

Finance

5647 **le Houerou, P, Sierra, H,** *Estimating quasi-fiscal deficits in a consistency framework: the case of Madagascar.* Washington: World Bank, 1993, 26pp

Gender

5648 **Astuti, A,** Food for pregnancy: procreation, marriage and images of gender among the Vezo of western Madagascar, *Social anthropology,* **1,** 3 (1993) 277–90

5649 **Ramamonjisoa, S,** Empowerment of women and democracy in Madagascar, *Review of African political economy,* 58 (1993) 118–23

5650 **Ravololomanga, B,** *Etre femme et mère à Madagascar (Tanala d'Ifanadiana).* Paris: Harmattan, 1993, 237pp

History, early

5651 **Dewar, R E, Wright, H T,** The culture history of Madagascar, *Journal of world prehistory,* **7,** 4 (1993) 417–66

History, C19th

5652 **Campbell, G,** Crisis of faith and colonial conquest. The impact of famine and disease in late nineteenth-century Madagascar, *Cahiers d'études africains,* **32,** 127 (1992) 409–453

5653 **Mosca, L,** Il Madagascar in una corrispondenza consolare statunitense (1987–1881), *Africa (Rome),* **48,** 2 (1993) 216–47

History, C20th

5654 **Mosca, L,** Une fonte per la storia di Antananarivo nella seconda decade del XX secolo: le carte Linton, *Africa (Rome),* **48,** 1 (1993) 93–109

5655 **Tiersonnier, J,** *Au coeur de l'Ile Rouge: 50 ans de vie à Madagascar:*

mémoires. Paris: Beauchesne; Antananarivo: Ambozontany, 1991, 151pp

Industry & trade

5656 **Maille, P,** Mendelsohn, R, Valuing ecotourism in Madagascar, *Journal of environmental management,* **38,** 3 (1993) 213–218

International relations

5657 **Verdier, I,** Le rôle clef de Madagascar dans l'océan Indien, *Revue Madagascar, océan Indien,* 7/8 (1991) 105–119

Medical

5658 **Boiteau, P, Allorge-Boiteau, L,** *Plantes médicinales au Madagascar.* Paris: Karthala, 1993, 135pp

Politics

See also: 5649
5659 **Chaigneau, P,** Madagascar, vers une réorientation politique, *Mondes et cultures,* **50,** 2–4 (1990) 230–37 (and see 238–43)
5660 **Rabemananjara, R W,** La révolution malgache de 1991, *Revue Madagascar, océan Indien,* 7/8 (1991) 139–52
5661 **Ravaloson, J,** Madagascar: la révolution tranquille, *Afrique 2000,* 15 (1993) 139–54

Religion, philosophy

5662 **Hubsch, B (ed),** *Madagascar et le christianisme.* Paris: Karthala, 1993, 520pp

Rural economy

5663 **Gallon, T P,** *Die Revitalisierung der 'Fokonolona'-Dorfräte im Rahmen der Landentwicklungspolitik der Demokratischen Republik Madagaskar.* Saarbrucken: Breitenbach, 1992, 333pp

Sociology

5664 **Fauroux, E,** Les migrations mahafales dans le processus de ruralisation de la ville de Toliara (Madagacascar), *Cahiers des sciences humaines,* **29,** 2/3 (1993) 547–64

MAURITIUS

General

5665 **Fanchette, R, Argo, P,** *Maurice à l'aube de l'an 2000.* Rose Hill: ed de l'Océan indien, 1992, 196pp

Anthropology

5666 **Haring, L,** Buried treasure, *Journal of Mauritian studies,* **4,** 1 (1992) 22–35

Demography

5667 **Jones, H,** The small island factor in modern fertility decline: findings from Mauritius, in Lockhart, D G, et al (eds), *The development process in small island states* (London: Routledge, 1993), 161–78
5668 **Kalla, A C,** The inequalities of morbidity and mortality in Mauritius: its ethnic and geographic dimensions, *Social science and medicine,* **36,** 10 (1993) 1273–83
5669 **Rallu, J L,** Tendenance récente de la fécondité à l'île Maurice, *Population,* **48,** 1 (1993) 184–89

Economic and social history

5670 **Barker, A J,** Distorting the record of slavery and abolition: the British anti-slavery movement and Mauritius, 1826–37, *Slavery and abolition,* **14,** 3 (1993) 185–207

5671 **Carter, M,** The family under indenture: a Mauritian case study, *Journal of Mauritian studies,* **4,** 1 (1992) 1–21

5672 **Grove, R,** Conserving Eden: the East India Companies and their environmental policies on St Helena, Mauritius and in Western India, *Comparative studies in society and history,* **35,** 2 (1993) 318–51

5673 **North-Coombes, A,** *A history of sugar production in Mauritius.* Rose Hill: Ed. de l'Océan Indien, 1993 (rev. ed'n), 174pp

Economy - Development

5674 **Minogue, M,** Mauritius: economic miracle or developmental illusion?, *Journal of international development,* **4,** 6 (1992) 643–47 (review article)

5675 **World Bank,** *Mauritius: expanding horizons.* Washington: World Bank, 1992, 156pp

Education

5676 **Rai, J,** Perspectives in medical education and research in Mauritius, *PROSI,* 284 (1992) 38–46

History, C18th

5677 **Chan Low, L J,** T'Eylandt Mauritius: la précolonisation, 1598–1968, *Journal of Mauritian studies,* **4,** 1 (1992) 36–66

History, C20th

5678 **Heerah, A C, Edun, E H (eds),** *And forward moved the caravan: selected writings and speeches of A W Foondun.* Moka: Mahatma Ghandi Institute, 1992, 197pp

5679 **Koenig, J A,** *Jules Koenig: une vie pour la justice.* Rose Hill: ed de l'Océan Indien, 1992, 105pp

Industry & trade

5680 **Bagnant, J,** The case of Mauritius, in Bhagavan, M R & Karekezi, S (eds), *Energy managment (Item 788),* 127–76

5681 **Ollivier, L,** Les pêches artisales mauriciennes: mutations recents d'une activité seculaire, *Cahiers d'outre-mer,* **46,** 183 (1993) 325–48

Labour & manpower

5682 Mauritius Sugar Producers' Association, Les relations industrielles dans l'industrie sucrière, *PROSI,* 279 (1992) 18–20, 23–24

Medical

5683 **Sussman, L K,** The use of herbal and biomedical pharmaceuticals on Mauritius, in van der Geest, S J & Whyte, S R (eds), *The context of medicines in developing countries* (Amsterdam: Spinhuis, 1991), 199–215

Politics

5684 **Eriksen,** T H, A future-oriented, non-ethnic nationalism? Mauritius as an examplary case, *Ethnos,* **58,** 3–4 (1993) 197–221

5685 **Eriksen, T H,** *Us and them in*

modern societies: ethnicity and nationalism in Mauritius, Trinidad and beyond. Oslo: Scandinavian University Press, 1992, 208pp

Rural economy

5686 Govinden, N, et al, Le mais à l'ile Rodrigues, *Revue agricole et sucrière de l'ile Mauritius,* **70,** 1/2 (1991) 59–67

Urban studies

5687 De, J, The process of urbanisation in Mauritius, *Geographical review of India,* **52,** 3 (1990) 50–59

REUNION

Demography

5688 Colliez, J P, Au rythme de croissance actuel: 100,000 Réunionnais de plus dans neuf ans, *Economie de la Réunion,* 57 (1992) 2–9

Economic and social history

5689 Fuma, S, *L'esclavagisme à la Réunion, 1797–1848.* Paris: Harmattan, 1993, 185pp

Education

No entry. *See also:* 5698

History, C20th

5690 Vergès, P, *D'une île au monde.* Paris: Harmattan, 1993, 319pp

Industry & trade

5691 Cimbaro, P, Progression spectaculaire de l'equipement des ménages: quand consommation ne rime pas avec modération, *Economie de la Réunion,* 56 (1991) 27–32

Labour & manpower

5692 Chevillon, M, Huit mois après la sortie de l'école: premier contact avec le marché du travail, *Economie de la Réunion,* 56 (1991) 8–12

5693 Cimbaro, P, Fonction publique territoriale: beaucoup d'emplois, peu de qualification, *Economie de la Réunion,* 59 (1992) 2–6

5694 Cimbaro, P, Un pied à l'étrier avec les Contrats Emploi Solidarité, *Economie de la Reunion,* 62 (1992) 14–17

5695 Colliez, J P, Projections de la population active: les jeunes et les femmes a l'assaut de l'emploi, *Economie de la Réunion,* 57 (1992) 10–18

5696 Hautcoeur, J C, Concentration des salaires du privé autour du SMIC, *Economie de la Réunion,* 58 (1992) 11–14

5697 Martin, L, Suivie d'un panel de jeunes chômeurs: après quatre ans l'emploi fait jeu égal avec le chômage, *Economie de la Réunion,* 58 (1992) 15–18

5698 Parain, C, La gageure de l'apprentissage: amener à l'emploi des jeunes sans formation de base, *Economie de la Réunion,* 56 (1991) 13–19

5699 Rochoux, J Y, Même si elle se poursuit, la performance économique ne réduira pas le chômage, *Economie de la Réunion,* 57 (1992) 19–27

Law

5700 Cimbaro, P, Malgré une aggravation certaine, la délinquance reste peu fréquente, *Economie de la Réunion,* 58 (1992) 2–10

Politics

No entry. *See also:* 5693

Sociology

5701 **Chane-Kune, S,** *Aux origines de l'identité réunionnaise.* Paris: Harmattan, 1993, 203pp
5702 **Hautcoeur, J C,** Un emploi pour les hommes, le mariage pour les femmes, *Economie de la Reunion,* 62 (1992) 2–5

Social welfare

5703 **Caillière, A,** Malgré le RMI et l'aide départmentale, les cotisations restent la base du système de protection sociale, *Economie de la Réunion,* 59 (1992) 9–13

Urban studies

5704 **Clamard, P, Herbet, J B,** Saint-Denis découpés en vingt quartiers bien typés, *Economie de la Reunion,* 61 (1992) 10–15
5705 **Herbet, J B,** Vivre en DSQ, *Economie de la Reunion,* 61 (1992) 6–9
5706 **Pavagan, C,** Une croissance urbaine plutôt modérée, *Economie de la Reunion,* 61 (1992) 2–5
5707 **Pavageau, C,** Les besoins augmentent, la construction sauvage aussi, *Economie de la Réunion,* 60 (1992) 2–7
5708 **Pavageau, C,** Quand ils ont réussi à s'installer, les jeunes sont les plus mal logés, *Economie de la Réunion,* 56 (1991) 20–25

SAO TOME

Economic and social history

5709 **Clarence-Smith, G,** Struggle over labour conditions in the plantations of São Tomé and Principe, *Slavery and abolition,* **14,** 1 (1993) 149–67

Economy - Development

5710 **Martin, S,** L'évolution économique de São Tomé et Principé, *Afrique contemporaine,* 166 (1993) 45–51
5711 **Siebert, G,** Strukturanpassung in São Tome und Principé - Programme und Probleme, in Meyns, P (ed), *Demokratie und Strukturreformen (Item 1174),* 189–207

Politics

5712 **Schümer, M,** Demokratisierung in São Tome und Principé, in Meyns, P (ed), *Demokratie und Strukturreformen (Item 1174),* 208–34

SEYCHELLES

Current affairs

5713 Commonwealth Secretariat, Observer Group, *Referendum on the draft constitution in Seychelles: 12–15 November 1992.* London: The Secretariat, 1992, 38pp

Language

5714 **Bollee, A,** Language policy in the Seychelles and its consequences, *International journal of the sociology of language,* 102 (1993) 85–99

Politics

5715 **Hatchard, J,** Re-establishing a multi-party state: some constitutional lessons from the Seychelles, *Journal of modern African studies,* **31,** 4 (1993) 601–612

AUTHOR INDEX

SUBJECT INDEX